CORPUS VITREARUM MEDII AEVI

GREAT BRITAIN ✦ VOLUME I

THE COUNTY OF OXFORD

CORPUS VITREARUM MEDII AEVI

PUBLISHED UNDER THE AUSPICES OF
THE COMITÉ INTERNATIONAL D'HISTOIRE DE L'ART
AND
THE UNION ACADÉMIQUE INTERNATIONALE

GREAT BRITAIN

VOLUME I

THE COUNTY OF OXFORD

WOODSTOCK. Now in Oxford, Bodleian Library. St. Thomas Becket received by Louis VII

THE COUNTY OF OXFORD

A CATALOGUE OF
MEDIEVAL STAINED GLASS

BY

PETER A. NEWTON

WITH THE ASSISTANCE OF

JILL KERR

LONDON
PUBLISHED FOR THE BRITISH ACADEMY
BY OXFORD UNIVERSITY PRESS
1979

Oxford University Press, Walton Street, Oxford OX2 6DP

OXFORD LONDON GLASGOW
NEW YORK TORONTO MELBOURNE WELLINGTON
KUALA LUMPUR SINGAPORE HONG KONG TOKYO
DELHI BOMBAY CALCUTTA MADRAS KARACHI
NAIROBI DAR ES SALAAM CAPE TOWN

ISBN 0 19 725970 7

© *The British Academy, 1979*

Printed in Great Britain
at the University Press, Oxford
by Eric Buckley
Printer to the University

FOR

FRANCIS† AND HONORIA WORMALD

FOREWORD

THIS is the first of the county surveys to be published in the *Corpus Vitrearum* series for England. It excludes the outstandingly important glass in Oxford City, which will be published in a further volume. The two surveys, of the county and the City, will form a coherent whole, the one complementing the other. Sincere gratitude is due to Dr. Peter Newton whose knowledge and scholarship together with the invaluable help of Miss Jill Kerr ensure that the task is well begun.

This Foreword provides the occasion too to record the service given to the *Corpus* by the late Derek Allen who was tireless in his concern for the project and devoted much of his energy and thought to it. In recent years he had taken the chair at the annual meeting for the *Corpus* at the Union Académique Internationale. Sad indeed it is that he did not live to see this Oxfordshire volume in print. The *Corpus* Committee remembers him with affectionate admiration. My predecessor as Chairman, Professor Francis Wormald, is also remembered with gratitude for implementing the *Corpus* project in this country and for placing it upon firm foundations of common sense and scholarship. Much of the impetus for beginning the English *Corpus* with Oxfordshire is due to the pioneering work of the Reverend Christopher Woodforde, Fellow and Chaplain of New College, Oxford, 1948–59, and Dean of Wells from 1959 until his death three years later. In those early days of the project Dr. Peter Newton's research was largely funded by the Pilgrim Trust, whose generous support is acknowledged here.

Thanks are due to the British Academy for financing this work and to the late Dr. Neville Williams, Secretary of the Academy until his death in January 1977, for his unfailing interest and support. On behalf of the Committee and Dr. Newton, I would also like to thank the incumbents and churchwardens in Oxfordshire who have allowed the survey of the glass in their churches without let or hindrance, often at some inconvenience to themselves.

The Oxfordshire volume will demonstrate very clearly to our foreign colleagues the strengths and weaknesses of the English heritage of ancient glass. Over the centuries destruction and wastage have been very great and only comparatively little of the large extent of glazing once installed has survived; and that which has is, with a few exceptions, fragmentary. The survivals do however reveal, first, the sensitive and highly accomplished brushwork of the English medieval glass painters. In this the linearity is distinct from the more mosaic treatment of Continental glass. Secondly, they are sufficient to demonstrate the exceptional interest of the iconographic schemes chosen for display and didactic purposes in our parish churches.

A. R. DUFTY

1978

PREFACE

WORK on a catalogue such as this necessarily entails requests for help from many people. It would be impossible to name them all here but I wish to thank them most sincerely. They include Mr. John Hopkins at the Society of Antiquaries, Dr. Richard Hunt, Dr. Albinia De La Mare, Dr. Jonathan Alexander, and the late Mr. Peter Spokes at the Bodleian Library; the late Miss Dorothy Miner at the Walters Art Gallery and Museum, Baltimore, U.S.A., and Dr. John Plummer at the Pierpont Morgan Library, New York; Mr. Bernard Barr at York Minster Library, and the staff of York City Reference Library. I am particularly grateful to the late Tom Tremlett, the late Hugh Stanford London, and Sir Anthony Wagner, Garter King of Arms, for permission to use the cards and notes for the new edition of Papworth.

Many academic colleagues and friends have been forthcoming with help and advice: Sir Roger Mynors, Mr. Christopher Hohler, Professor George Zarnecki, Mr. Richard Dufty, Mr. John Harvey, Mr. Christopher Johnson, Mr. David O'Connor, Dr. Richard Marks, Mr. Ben Johnson, Dr. Madeline Caviness, Mr. Julian Mumby, Dr. Alan Borg, Dr. Charles Kightly, Mr. Jeremy Haselock, and Mr. Richard Baumann.

I have had much help and guidance from the glaziers' workshops. At Norwich, Mr. Michael King, Mr. Paul Jefferies, and Mr. Geoffrey Carrick have been very helpful, as have Mr. Peter Gibson, Mr. Ian Addy, Mr. Ian Tomlinson, Mr. Keith Barley, Mr. Keith Hilton, and Mr. Christopher Wardale at York.

My colleagues in Europe have shown much interest, particularly the late M. Jean Lafond, the late Professor Hans Hahnloser, the late Professor Hans Wentzel, Dr. Eva Frodl-Kraft, and Professor Louis Grodecki.

I particularly wish to express my gratitude and thanks to the British Academy and the *Corpus Vitrearum* Committee for Great Britain past and present for their interest and financial support. For assistance in photography I have to thank the National Monuments Record, the Courtauld Institute, Mr. Christopher Wilson, Mr. Peter Spokes, and particularly Mr. Dennis King.

The final recension of the text, definition of quarry types, drawing of diagrams, and the index were achieved in collaboration with Miss Jill Kerr. I owe much to her enthusiasm, organization, and sense of humour. Her skills allied with those of Miss Lindsay Duguid have transformed my manuscript for publication. My thanks are also due to Miss Virginia Freeman who typed the manuscript.

Finally, two debts which I can never repay. Mr. Dennis King has taught me all that I know about techniques and restoration. I thank him most especially. The late Professor Francis Wormald, my former tutor, was a stringent but helpful critic. His interest, help, advice, and sound common sense were a great inspiration and it was a privilege to be his pupil. My final text was not seen by him. I hope that he would have approved it, I know that his criticisms would have improved it.

PETER A. NEWTON

York, 1978

CONTENTS

LIST OF PLATES

The illustrations follow the sequence of the text, but not all entries are illustrated. Unless otherwise stated, prints and complete photographic coverage of all the medieval glass in the county are available at the National Monuments Record (N.M.R.), Fortress House, London, which holds the Royal Commission on Historical Monuments, England (R.C.H.M.) archive, and at the Conway Library of the Courtauld Institute of Art, London (C.I.). Photographs are not to scale, but measurements are given in the text.

COLOUR

BLACK AND WHITE

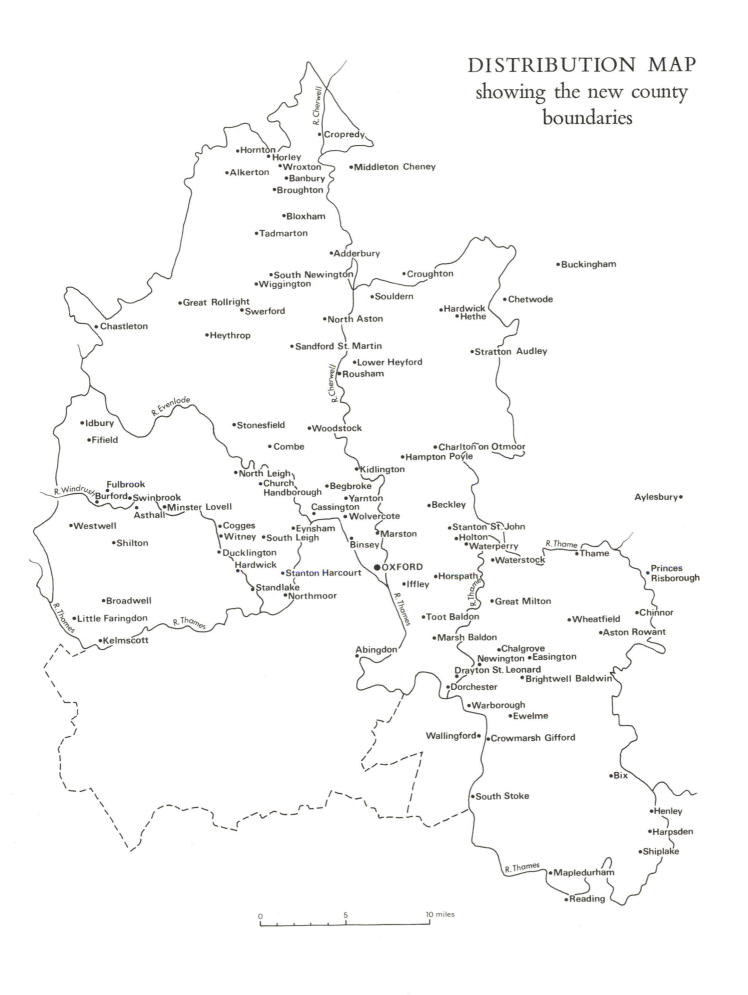

DISTRIBUTION MAP
showing the new county
boundaries

•Cropredy

•Hornton
•Horley
•Wroxton
•Alkerton •Banbury
•Broughton

•Middleton Cheney

•Bloxham

•Tadmarton

•Adderbury
                                          •Buckingham
•South Newington
•Wiggington   •Croughton

•Great Rollright   •Souldern   •Chetwode
•Swerford   •Hardwick
•Chastleton   •North Aston   •Hethe

•Heythrop   •Sandford St. Martin
                                          •Stratton Audley
R. Evenlode   •Lower Heyford
                         •Rousham

•Idbury   •Stonesfield   •Woodstock
•Fifield   •Combe
                                   •Charlton on Otmoor
                                 •Hampton Poyle
                 •North Leigh   •Kidlington
R. Windrush   Church
Fulbrook   Handborough •Begbroke
Burford •Swinbrook   •Yarnton   •Beckley   Aylesbury•
   •Minster Lovell   Cassington
Asthall   •Wolvercote
•Westwell •Cogges   •Eynsham   •Marston   •Stanton St. John
           •Witney South Leigh   •Holton
•Shilton   •Ducklington Binsey   •Waterperry   R. Thame
                 Hardwick   •Waterstock •Thame
                        •Stanton Harcourt •OXFORD   Princes
•Broadwell   •Standlake   •Iffley •Horspath   Risborough
•Little Faringdon   •Northmoor   •Great Milton
R. Thames   R. Thames   •Toot Baldon   •Wheatfield •Chinnor
•Kelmscott   •Aston Rowant
                                     •Marsh Baldon
                                Abingdon •Chalgrove
                                    Newington •Easington
                                   Drayton St. Leonard
                                    •Brightwell Baldwin
                                  •Dorchester
                                  •Warborough
                                    •Ewelme
                        Wallingford• •Crowmarsh Gifford
                                                    •Bix
                          •South Stoke
                                                    •Henley
                                                    •Harpsden
                                                    •Shiplake
                          R. Thames •Mapledurham
                                      •Reading

0   5   10 miles

GROUND PLAN (Burford) showing window numbering system

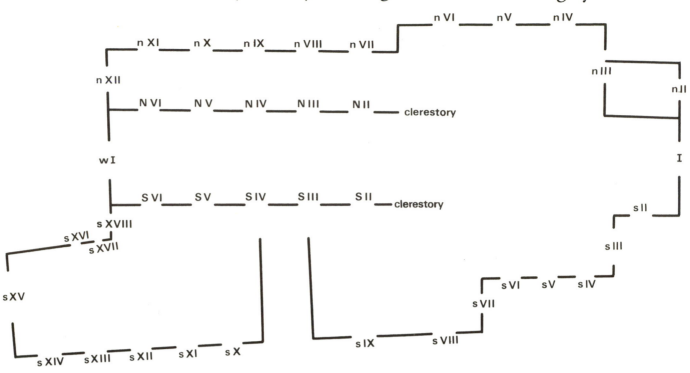

WINDOW PLAN
and panel numbering system

GLOSSARY OF TERMS

ABRADE: to scrape or grind away flashing to expose the base glass.

BACK PAINTING: painting on the exterior face of the glass.

CARTOON: a full-size design for a window.

CORROSION: deterioration of the surface of the glass; this normally results in pitting or crusting and may occur on either face.

FLASHING: application of a thin coat of coloured glass on a base glass. Flashed ruby is most commonly found.

GRISAILLE: geometric or leaf patterns of regular design painted on or leaded into white glass (usually with little or no pot-metal).

GROZING: the method of shaping glass by means of a metal tool with a hooked end which makes a characteristic 'bitten' edge.

MURREY: a colour ranging from purple to pink and reddish brown.

PAINT: a mixture of finely ground glass, iron or copper oxide, and a flux, applied to the glass and fired.

PLATING: protecting old glass by fitting modern glass to the exterior face, and sometimes both faces.

PICK or SCRATCH OUT: to remove paint with a stick or needle point before firing.

POT METAL: glass coloured throughout when molten with one or more metallic oxides.

QUARRY: a small pane of glass, usually diamond-shaped.

RESURFACING: conservation technique whereby the corroded surface of the glass is removed and the newly exposed surface polished.

SMEAR SHADING: an application of thin paint on the glass.

STIPPLING: a method of shading by dabbing paint.

YELLOW STAIN: a stain ranging from pale lemon to orange produced by applying a solution of a silver compound to the surface of the glass which, when fired, turns yellow. It is nearly always found on the exterior face of the glass.

Detail from the background to n. III Brightwell Baldwin showing the characteristic 'seaweed' foliage design.

Detail from window n. V, 2a at Waterperry shows the various techniques used in glass painting. STIPPLING is used to delineate the contours of the eyes, the edge of the face, the chin, neck, collar, and the outer edges of the head-dress. WASHES are used on the lower edge of the head-dress, under the eyes, and on the upper lip. The head-dress also shows the use of BACK PAINTING on the top half of the diamond-shaped coif, with the pattern PICKED OUT of a matt black wash on the headband and out of yellow stain on the lower half of the coif and neckband. The outer edge of the head-dress and the fleurs-de-lis of the coif are SCRATCHED OUT. PITTING appears as black dots on the face, neck, head-dress, and background.

QUARRY TYPES

11 22 33 44 55
10 21 32 43 54
9 20 31 42 53
8 19 30 41 52
7 18 29 40 51
6 17 28 39 50
5 16 27 38 49
4 15 26 37 48
3 14 25 36 47
2 13 24 35 46
1 12 23 34 45

BIBLIOGRAPHY

Birch, W. De Grey. *Catalogue of Seals in the Department of Manuscripts in the British Museum* (1887–1900, 6 vols.).

Bouchier, E. S. *Notes on the Stained Glass of the Oxford District* (1918).

—— 'Old Stained Glass in Oxfordshire', *Journal of the British Society of Master Glass Painters* (1931–2).

Cokayne, G. E. *The Complete Peerage* (1910–59, 12 vols.).

Ditchfield, P. M. *Memorials of Old Oxfordshire* (1903).

The Golden Legend or Lives of the Saints. As Englished by William Caxton (Dent & Co., 1900–9, 7 vols.).

Greening Lamborn, E. A. *The Armorial Glass of the Oxford Diocese 1250–1850* (1949).

Hutchinson, F. E. *Medieval Glass at All Souls College* (1949).

Lexikon der Christlichen Ikonographie (Herder, 1968–76, 8 vols.).

Nelson, P. *Ancient Painted Glass in Britain 1170–1500* (1913).

Newton, P. A. 'Schools of Glass Painting in the Midlands 1275–1430' (unpublished Ph.D. thesis, University of London, 1961).

Parker, J. H. *A Guide to Architectural Antiquities in the Neighbourhood of Oxford* (1846).

'The Parochial Collections made by Anthony à Wood and Richard Rawlinson', ed. F. N. Davies, *Oxfordshire Record Society* (1920–2, vols. II, IV, XI paginated in one).

Pevsner, N., and Sherwood, J. *The Buildings of England. Oxfordshire* (1974).

Royal Commission on Historical Monuments in the City of Oxford (1939).

Rushforth, G. M. *Medieval Christian Imagery* (1936).

Spokes, P. 'A Catalogue of the Glass in the Bodleian Library, Oxford' (unpublished typescript, Bodleian Library, Oxford, 1973).

The Victoria History of the Counties of England. A History of Oxfordshire (vols. I, 1939; II, 1907; III, 1954; V, 1957; VI, 1959; VII, 1962; VIII, 1964; IX, 1969; X, 1972).

'The Visitations of Oxfordshire, 1566, 1574 and 1634', ed. W. H. Turner, *Harleian Society* v (1871).

Winston, C. *Memoirs Illustrative of the Art of Glass Painting* (1865).

Woodforde, C. *The Stained Glass of New College, Oxford* (1951).

LIST OF ABBREVIATIONS

B.L.	London, British Library.
Bodl. Lib.	Oxford, Bodleian Library.
Cal. Inq.	*Calendar of Inquisitions.*
C.I.	London, Courtauld Institute.
E.E.T.S.	*Early English Text Society*
G.E.C.	See Cokayne, above.
Herder	See *Lexikon*, above.
J.B.S.M.G.P.	*Journal of the British Society of Master Glass Painters.*
N.M.R.	London, National Monuments Record.
N.O.A.S.	*North Oxfordshire Archaeological Society.*
O.A.H.S.	*Oxford Architectural and Historical Society.*
O.H.S.	*Oxford Historical Society.*
O.R.S.	*Oxford Record Society.*
P.C.	See 'The Parochial Collections' above.
R.C.H.M.	Royal Commission on Historical Monuments.
R.S.	*Rolls Series.*
V.C.H.	See *The Victoria History*, above.
Visitations	See 'The Visitations of Oxfordshire', above.

INTRODUCTION

A DETAILED survey and catalogue of the surviving medieval glass in England presents a number of problems. Not only has the glass suffered much but it also represents only a small proportion of the glazing which existed at the time of the Reformation.

The Royal Articles of Edward VI, 1547, were intended to bring about the total destruction of the art and artefacts of the Catholic religion and Article 28 reads:

Also, that they shall take away, utterly extinct and destroy all shrines, covering of shrines, all tables, candlesticks, or rolls of wax, pictures, paintings, and all other monuments of feigned miracles, pilgramages, idolatry, and superstition: so that there remain no memory of the same in walls, glass windows, or elsewhere within their churches and houses.[1]

The destruction of shrines, altars, and portable liturgical objects was easy to implement but the indiscriminate breaking of windows would have presented practical difficulties, destroying the fabric of the church and causing physical discomfort to the priest and congregation. That the authorities realized this is shown by Article 23 of the Royal Articles of 1559 which is almost identical to Article 28 of the 1547 Injunctions but which has after the words 'within their churches and houses' the 'preserving nevertheless or repairing both the walls and glass windows'.[2] Indiscriminate destruction was forbidden by Royal Proclamation 'against breaking or defacing of Monuments of Antiquites being set up in Churches, or other publick places, for memory, and not for superstition'. It was a punishable offence to 'breake downe or deface any image in glasse-windowes in any Church, without consent of the Ordinary'.[3]

For about one hundred years destruction was uneven and spasmodic[4] excepting the almost total loss of glass from the monasteries after the Dissolution in the years 1536–40. An indication of what had survived at this date is given in the survey made for the antiquary, Sir Christopher Hatton:

The sayd Mr Dugdale, receiving encouragement from Sir Christopher Hatton before mentioned, then a member of the House of Commons, who timely foresaw the neere approaching storme, in the Summer of 1641 taking with him one Mr William Sedgwick, a skylfull Armes-paynter repaired first to the Cathedral of St Pauls in the City of London and next to the Abbey-Church of Westminster, and there making exact draughs of all the monuments in each of them, copied the Epitaphs, according to the very Letter, as also the Armes in the Windows or cut in stone. And having done so rode to Peterborow in North[amp]tonshire, Ely, Norwiche, Lincolne, Newarke upon Trent, Beverley, S[o]uthwell, Kingston upon Hull, Yorke, Selby, Chester, Lichfield, Tamworth, Warwick: and did the like in all those Cathedrall, Collegiate, Conventuall and divers other Parochiall Churches, wherein any Tombes or Monuments were to be found; to the end that the memory of them, in case of that ruine then imminent might be preserved for future and better times.[5]

The result of William Dugdale and William Sedgwick's tour is a volume, now in the possession of the Earl of Winchelsea and Nottingham, with small-scale coloured sketches of windows and

[1] W. H. Frere, 'Visitation Articles and Injunctions of the Period of the Reformation', *Alcuin Club Collections* 15, ii (1910), 126.

[2] Ibid. 16, iii (1910), 16.

[3] Quoted in Cox and Ford, *The Parish Churches of England* (1935), 18.

[4] C. Woodforde, *The Norwich School of Glass Painting in the Fifteenth Century* (1950), 203–6.

[5] *The Life, Diary and Correspondence of Sir William Dugdale*, ed. W. Hamper (1827), 14.

monuments. It is an invaluable record and, although the emphasis is on heraldic windows, shields of arms, and donor figures, there is much of iconographical interest. For example at St. George's, Stamford (Lincs.), Sedgwick not only sketched the figures of the Founder Knights of the Order of the Garter and their wives, but also the twenty-one scenes from the life and martyrdom of St. George, patron of the Order, which were in the upper parts of the windows.[1]

The 'ruine then imminent' was the introduction in 1640 of a Bill in the House of Commons,

to proceed summarily in the matter by way of sending commissions into all the counties for the defacing, demolishing and quite taking away of all the images, altars or tables turned altarwise, crucifixes, superstitious pictures, ornaments and relics of idolatory out of all churches and chapels.[2]

This was finally passed on 28 August 1643. One of the Parliamentary Visitors who implemented it was the notorious William Dowsing who kept a journal of his activities in Suffolk between 6 January 1643 and 1 October 1644.[3] He and his deputies visited about 150 parishes and destroyed nearly 7,000 'superstitious pictures'.[4] There are no other such records of the destruction carried out in other parts of the country but the losses must have been enormous. In addition to this official iconoclasm the battles of the Civil War involved the destruction of both fabric and windows in parts of the country. The soldiers of the Parliamentary army used their cannon to blast out the windows of Peterborough Cathedral,[5] and in 1646 the Royalist forces were besieged in Lichfield Cathedral, the bombardment, under the direction of Sir William Brereton, resulting in the destruction of the spire.[6]

Although some glass survived civil war and religious strife, the story of loss and destruction continued. Medieval glass had little appeal in the eighteenth century, and at New College, Oxford, three waves of enthusiastic generosity swept out much of the fourteenth-century glass. The chapel now contains some of the most important examples of eighteenth-century glass painting in the country but reglazing programmes have entailed the loss of much original glass.[7] Later in the eighteenth century during the restoration of Salisbury Cathedral by James Wyatt,

whole cartloads of glass lead and other rubbish were removed from the nave and transepts, and shot into the town-ditch; whilst a good deal of similar rubbish was used to level the ground near the Chapter House.[8]

In other places extensive losses occurred when the releading of windows was entrusted to untrained jobbing glaziers. At Battlefield (Salop) an important series of mid-fifteenth-century windows[9] was taken down in 1790 and the restoration entrusted to a local farmer;[10] only a few fragments survived. Excessive corrosion of medieval glass, making it opaque or semi-opaque, also caused problems. At Winchester College (Hants) all the fourteenth-century glass was replaced with copies of the original made by the Shrewsbury firm of Betton and Evans which were installed between 1821 and 1825–9.[11] The reason for this could be easily understood when some of the original glass was recently returned to the college.[12]

[1] The Book of Draughts, ff. 151ᵛ–162.

[2] W. A. Shaw, *A History of the Church of England during the Civil Wars and under the Commonwealth, 1640–60* i (1900), 104.

[3] *The Journal of William Dowsing*, ed. C. H. Evelyn White (1885), 6–7.

[4] Ibid. 15–33. Woodforde, op. cit. 206–9.

[5] T. Gunton, *History of the Church of Peterborough* (1686), 333–8.

[6] Birmingham Reference Library. Sir W. Brereton's MS. Letter Book, pp. 250–1. Information from Dr. C. Kightly.

[7] Woodforde (1951), 16.

[8] C. Winston, *Memoirs Illustrative of the Art of Glass Painting* (1865), 106.

[9] B.L. Add. MS. 21236, ff. 339–50. Water-colour drawings copied by the Revd. Williams, early 19th c.

[10] W. G. D. Fletcher, *Battlefield Church* (1899). The surviving fragments are now at Prees (Salop).

[11] J. D. Le Couteur, *Ancient Glass in Winchester* (1928), 162–3.

[12] For the restoration of this glass see J. H. Harvey and D. King, 'Winchester College Stained Glass', *Archaeologia* ciii (1971), 166–74.

In the nineteenth century the term 'restoration' often meant nothing more than the gathering together of the surviving remains of medieval glass and leading it up for insertion in one or two windows. These composite windows generally showed little respect for the glass, which has been put back upside down, inside out, or both. Inscriptions were broken up and reset out of context and parts of different figures have been brought together with a total disregard for their original date, style, and design. An example of this process can be seen in the two chancel windows in North Leigh.

In some places the glass does not belong to the church and is a miscellaneous collection of different pieces presented by one benefactor. An example is Alderman Fletcher's collection presented to Yarnton between 1813 and 1816 and the pieces collected by the Revd. T. Ford about 1800 at Melton Mowbray (Leics).[1]

Medieval glass was also imported from the Continent in the eighteenth and nineneenth centuries.[2] Examples in Oxfordshire include the interesting remains of fifteenth and sixteenth-century glass from the ruined abbey church of St. Bertin at St.-Omer (Pas-de-Calais), and fifteenth and sixteenth-century roundels at Begbroke, Cassington, and Yarnton.

Documentation

There are no contracts for the provision of windows for any of the churches in Oxfordshire. There are records of payment to glaziers for work done at Adderbury church between 1397 and 1418 but only a few pieces of glass survive. In a number of places the glass can be associated with major rebuilding programmes which are documented, as at Dorchester Abbey (1293–1320 and later), Chinnor (chancel dedicated 1326), the Wilcote chapel at North Leigh (established 1438), and the rebuilding of the church at Ewelme as a mortuary chapel for the de la Pole family (1437–8).

In the absence of contemporary documents the sixteenth and seventeenth-century notes on heraldic glass often provide valuable information. The Oxford antiquarian scholar Anthony Wood (1632–95) was one of a small group of scholars led by Sir William Dugdale, Garter King of Arms, and his anti-quarian collections record much lost material and valuable secondary evidence for dating. Wood's autograph manuscripts and his collections of earlier secondary sources, for example the church notes of the 1574 Visitation, have been extensively used throughout this catalogue.

There has been no major survey of the medieval glass in the county. The accounts in Bouchier's two publications and Nelson's county Lists are short notes with neither critical assessment nor any attempt to substantiate dates or identify subjects. E. A. Greening Lamborn's book, *The Armorial Glass of the Oxfordshire Diocese* (1949), is a masterly work with detailed expositions on the heraldry and genealogies.

Heraldic Glass

The most extensive series of fourteenth-century shields in the county is to be found at Dorchester. It has been conjectured that these represent benefactors of the Abbey, but they may have merely a general significance akin to a local Roll of Arms. Other fourteenth-century examples are to be found at Asthall, Stratton Audley, South Newington, Broughton Castle, and Kidlington. The reasons for

[1] Newton ii (1961), 202–10.
[2] J. Lafond, 'Le commerce des vitraux anciens en Angleterre au XVIII et au XIX siècles', *Revue des Sociétés Savants de Haute-Normandie Histoire de l'Art*, no. 20 (1960), 5. 15.

the association of different shields of arms at this period is often difficult to determine. In some cases the shields represent families connected with the manor, but this is not always so, and it is worth noting that blood or feudal ties were not the only prerequisites for heraldic display; a bond of friendship was sufficient, as at Waterstock. In the fifteenth and sixteenth centuries more emphasis is placed on the display of family descents and alliances. This is well demonstrated at Stanton Harcourt, Ewelme, Mapledurham, Waterperry, and Waterstock. It is noticeable that the heraldic glass of the later fifteenth to sixteenth centuries demonstrates great technical expertise. The heraldry in the county has been extensively investigated by Greening Lamborn (see p. 3).

Inscriptions

   The majority of the inscriptions in the county are the names and styles accompanying figures of saints or donors in Latin using either Lombardic or black-letter script, and call for no particular comment. They range in date from the St. James at Stanton Harcourt of the third quarter of the thirteenth century to the donor inscription at Westwell 1522–3. Some notable inscriptions in the glass are given here and detailed transcriptions are made in the catalogue. The quotations from the Genealogy of Christ (Matthew 1: 1–16) that accompany the tree of Jesse window at Dorchester (fourteenth century) are extremely eccentric in the name forms and omission of abbreviation signs. Appropriate quotations from the Old Testament accompany the figures of Isaac and Daniel at Minster Lovell (fifteenth century). There are mis-spellings and misquotations at Dorchester (fourteenth century), and Horley (fifteenth century). A rarely represented scene, formerly at Ewelme, and now lost, of St. John being questioned by the Pharisees was accompanied by an abbreviated version of the gospel text (fifteenth century). The only other bible quotations are the standard angelic salutation to the Blessed Virgin at the Annunciation, for example Dorchester (fourteenth century) and Chastleton (fifteenth century). The varieties of abbreviations follow the usual forms. The text of the Creed was represented with figures of the apostles at Combe but only St. James Major survives accompanied by his appropriate verse (fifteenth century). Fragments of Creed scrolls occur at Marston. An unusual quotation from the final verse of the hymn *Cultor Dei Memento*, sung at compline on Easter Sunday accompanies the donor figures of Barworth and Salter at Newington (fifteenth century).

   An Anglo-French bidding inscription survives at Asthall (fourteenth century). Vernacular English inscriptions occur at Burford with a scene of the Sacrament of Marriage (late fifteenth century), and lost donor inscriptions are found in the Iwardby window at Mapledurham (fifteenth century) and in the Curson window at Waterperry (sixteenth century). The bird quarries holding scrolls of vernacular texts at Yarnton (fifteenth/sixteenth century) are probably the most extensive collection of this type of design to survive in England.

Monograms and Letters

   The first six letters of the alphabet incorporated into tracery designs in the two north windows at North Leigh are an unusual feature (fifteenth century). Other types of design incorporating initials and monograms can be found in several places (all fifteenth century), notably Waterperry, Beckley, and Warborough. These are either variations on the letter M, monogram MAR or IHC. Individual initials, for example the T's on roundels at Ewelme (fifteenth century), could relate to either a donor or the subject of a window. The initials N and M occur at Aston Rowant (fourteenth century). Inscriptions are transcribed as they are in the glass, with vertical lines for lead breaks, square brackets for modern insertions, round brackets for the expansion of abbreviations, and a dash to indicate omissions. Where letters are upside down or inside out, this is stated below.

Condition

Detailed comments on the physical condition of each panel of glass are given in the catalogue. The general condition of the glass is briefly outlined below, but it is misleading to isolate specific features as being applicable throughout.

The glass has suffered much from both iconoclasm and neglect; it has in a number of cases, been subjected to insensitive releading with glass being put back not only inside out and upside down (examples of this can be seen at Minster Lovell), but also replaced so that existing tie bars obscure important parts of the composition (the worst example is in the Brightwell Baldwin Crucifixion panel where the faces are completely hidden at two levels). Very little of the material can be shown to be *in situ*. There are no examples of glass in its original leads in the county: at some time or other all the glass has been releaded. Since no records survive describing pre-nineteenth-century restoration the original context of much of the glass and the point at which it was releaded remain matters for speculation.

Probably the most difficult glass to catalogue is in places where all the remaining fragments have been assembled, with little or no regard for style or date, into one or more windows as a series of medley panels. Typical examples can be seen at Binsey, Ewelme, Burford, Kidlington, and Marsh Baldon. This type of rearrangement which was very popular in the nineteenth century is not generally prac- tised today. Another common method was to place fragments as decorative splashes of colour in a surround of plain white quarry glazing as, for example, in the Dorchester Jesse, and at Ducklington, where the few fragments that remain are all that survived the recorded stone-throwing activities of schoolboys in the early nineteenth century. There are at least three examples of glass, removed from the windows in nineteenth-century 'restoration', being displayed as hanging panels against plain glazing without proper ties. This was the case until recently at Eynsham, Cassington, and Cropredy but all these have now been properly leaded into permanent glazing.

There is evidence of repair work being done *in situ*, for instance at Hampton Poyle, where the evangelists' symbols have the unusual characteristic of being set directly into the masonry without the use of leads. The leads currently in these panels are strap repair work of a later date executed without the removal of the glass.

All the glass exhibits some form of corrosion in varying degrees of intensity. The only consistent pattern to emerge is the poor condition of the thirteenth and fourteenth-century pot-metal glass as demonstrated at South Stoke and Chinnor, which is frequently so opaque as to make the original colour difficult to determine and the style of paint line almost indistinguishable. There is also consider- able paint loss in some of the fifteenth-century paint lines, for example, at Ewelme and Beckley.

The glass at Beckley was restored (after 1846) by Mr. Skidmore of Coventry. This is an extremely clever restoration with artificial ageing of the glass and it is very difficult to determine just how much is genuine without examining the cut lines out of the leads.

Recent restorations have been undertaken by Mr. D. King of Norwich, and Mr. M. C. Farrar-Bell of Clayton & Bell, Haddenham, Bucks. Mr. King has worked at Dorchester, Cassington, Yarnton, Newington, Kelmscott, Little Faringdon, and Cropredy. Mr. Farrar-Bell has worked at Aston Rowant, Begbroke, Charlton-on-Otmoor, Cogges, Eynsham, Great Milton, Iffley, North Leigh, Stanton Harcourt, Waterperry, and Wheatfield.

Colour and Technique

It is impossible to make general statements about the colour and technique of the glass in the county. The fragmentary nature of the glass—not one single main light survives—and the lack of a sequence of dated windows make it difficult to pinpoint the introduction of new techniques. Physical inspection of the glass is hampered by the almost universal practise of placing wire guards on the exterior of the window making it difficult to discern any back painting, particularly as much of the glass is not only corroded but also very dirty and obscured by lichen.

Thirteenth Century. Of the surviving thirteenth-century examples there are only five figured compositions extant (Kidlington, Stanton Harcourt, and Dorchester). The colours employed are a limited range of pot-metal ochre, ruby, green, murrey, and pale blue. Backgrounds are all plain coloured glass with no decorative patterned diapers. At Stanton Harcourt the figured composition of St. James is placed against a background of geometric grisaille painted on white glass with restricted use of colour on the bosses. A similar example of geometric grisaille is found at Stanton St. John where the colour bosses are green, murrey, pale blue, and blue. The painted ornament of the grisaille and the trace lines are very simple foliage trails in outline, with no modelling, against a cross-hatched background. Figure drawing makes limited use of wash, and modelling is achieved by brush strokes of different thicknesses. Inscriptions and borders are picked out of matt black wash.

Fourteenth Century. A considerable amount of glass of this period has survived. The colour range is more varied using red, blues, green, pot ochre, murrey, pink, and white glass, examples of which can be seen at Chinnor, Marsh Baldon, and Waterperry. Colour is used in an increasing number of combinations and colours of costumes are more varied (see, for instance, Chinnor and Waterperry). More range of tone is demonstrated within a group; the blues at Waterperry vary from turquoise to deep blue, and plain streaky ruby crown glass is used with great effect in the Virgin and St. Anne panel at Marsh Baldon. There is an increasing use of yellow stain and although it is impossible to fix a point for the introduction of this technique into the county, as the chronology of the glass cannot be precisely determined, the technique seems to have been established by the end of the first quarter of the century. Further developments in technique occur in figure modelling and canopies where smear shading is coupled with more varied brush strokes. Stipple shading is not found until the end of the century when it appears on the Adderbury knight. In the geometric grisaille with foliage painted on white glass, the cross-hatched background is abandoned as the trails become less rigidly symmetrical and the geometric grisaille gives way to the trellis of quarries. The coloured backgrounds to figured compositions become more varied in technique with the use of foliage diapers, or patterns picked out of a matt wash (as, for example, at Dorchester, Asthall, and Great Milton). Inscriptions and border designs are also picked out of matt black washes. The developments in colour and technique in Oxfordshire during the fourteenth century seem to be standard and consistent with those observable elsewhere in England.

Fifteenth Century. A notable feature throughout the fifteenth century is the predominance of white glass and yellow stain and the comparative absence of pot-metal coloured glass. Extensive use of white glass can be seen at Ewelme, North Leigh, and Minster Lovell. In the earlier part of the century coloured glass is all blue and red and is largely restricted to backgrounds and to figures below canopies. The predominance of blue and red glass can be seen in the Assumption of the Virgin and the Trinity at Newington, where the mantle of the Virgin is ruby, and the mantle covering the Three Persons of the Trinity is blue. In both cases this is the only coloured glass in the panel. This is a general tendency in fifteenth-century English glass painting but it seems exceptionally pronounced in Oxfordshire. The rich use of coloured glass in this period is found only in expensive designs such as the Beauchamp Chapel (Warwick) and the glass in Brown's Bedehouse at Stamford (Lincs.). Glass in the county that can compare with this luxury class of design are the two panels from Woodstock, now in the Bodleian Library, Oxford, which also have the only example in the county of non-armorial coloured inserts. Green and purple are rare extensions of the colour range, but they are found at Yarnton in the St. Christopher panel, and in the robe of Margaret Fitz Ellis at Waterperry.

The use of yellow stain becomes ubiquitous in the fifteenth century. It ranges from the drapery of large-scale figures down to the smallest decorative details of ornament, and minor architectural embellishments on canopies. The tone varies in intensity from a light lemon to a deep orange as found at Hampton Poyle and Kidlington.

Modelling is achieved by a combination of techniques, usually stipple shading and line. The high-lights are picked out of a matt wash, and the stipple shading on the draperies is reinforced with cross-hatched line. The diapered seaweed backgrounds are replaced by simple repeated patterns, often contiguous rosettes, either painted in outline, or picked out of a matt wash, the edges sometimes being defined with painted lines. The first discernible use of back painting in the county occurs at Ewelme, and can be seen again in several places such as Newington and Waterperry, and the technique varies considerably from the outstandingly competent Woodstock panels to the crude delineation of forms at Minster Lovell.

Late Fifteenth and Early Sixteenth Centuries. There is no particular change in the colour range in this period. The techniques established throughout the fifteenth century become more refined, for instance the use of needlepoints for scratching out highlights on draperies and faces. A fine example of this can be seen in the precision work on the faces and draperies in the Curson window at Waterperry. One major development is the increasing use of abrading small charges out of the field in heraldic glass, and the incidence of leaded inserts becomes more frequent. The earliest extant examples of abrading can be seen at Ewelme, and excellent examples survive at Iffley and Waterperry.

Iconography

This brief summary of the iconography of the glass in the county is intended to draw attention to the range of subjects represented.

Old Testament scenes and figures are rare. There are the remains of Adam digging and Eve spinning in two tracery lights at South Leigh (fifteenth century). The prophets Daniel and Ezechiel with their names and text scrolls at Minster Lovell are all that survive of a series of figures, and at Burford a name scroll for Ezechiel has also survived (all fifteenth century). A fragment of Jonah in the belly of the whale was probably part of a large composition at Dorchester (fourteenth century). There are the remains of two Trees of Jesse: a panel at Kidlington, which shows a king seated between two prophets (thirteenth century), and at Dorchester a few sad fragments (fourteenth century). The scrolls which accompanied the figures at Dorchester, now incomplete, included quotations from St. Matthew's Genealogy of Christ, a feature which has not been observed elsewhere in England.

There are a number of scenes from the lives of the Virgin and Christ. The incomplete nature of the glass makes it difficult to determine whether these are independent devotional images or parts of narrative sequences. St. Anne teaching the Virgin to read is represented at Marsh Baldon (fourteenth century) and at Beckley (fifteenth century), where the size indicates that they are main light glazing and not part of a narrative sequence. A third example at Kidlington is a restorer's composite (fifteenth century). Nine examples of the Annunciation to the Virgin survive in varying degrees of completeness. The best preserved is the panel in the east window of Dorchester Abbey (fourteenth century). There are the remains of three examples at Brightwell Baldwin: a Virgin Annunciate (fourteenth century), a Virgin Annunciate in a main light design, and a small Annunciation scene (both fifteenth century)· Other survivals are less complete: the head of Gabriel and a scroll of the Salutation at Burford, the Virgin, scroll and dove at Chastleton, and the head and shoulders of the Virgin and dove at Newington (all fifteenth century). A lily pot survives as a tracery light design, probably *in situ*, at Alkerton (late fifteenth century), and an incomplete figure of about the same date at Yarnton may represent the Virgin Annunciate.

Four representations of the Virgin seated holding the Christ Child call for no particular comment: Charlton-on-Otmoor, Dorchester, and South Stoke (fourteenth century), and Waterperry (sixteenth century). A fifteenth-century panel at Yarnton depicts the Virgin suckling the Christ Child.

The scenes from the iconography of the Virgin which survive all concern the events after her death. An incomplete panel of the Funeral of the Virgin at Stanton St. John (fourteenth century) must have been part of a narrative series. The Assumption is represented twice at Beckley, where the scene of St. Thomas receiving the Virgin's girdle is also incorporated (fourteenth century). At Newington the Assumption is pendent to the Trinity (1482–1511), the Coronation of the Virgin by Christ is represented at Beckley (fourteenth century) and the associated scene of the Virgin and Christ in Majesty, often confused with the Coronation of the Virgin, survives at Combe (fifteenth century). There are three figures of Christ; one at Dorchester and one at Aston Rowant (both fourteenth century), and a figure also at Aston Rowant (fifteenth century) may have been part of such a composition.

There are no narrative scenes of the life of Christ surviving, although there are ten representations of the Crucifixion, all incomplete: Horspath (late thirteenth, early fourteenth century), Kidlington, Asthall, and Brightwell Baldwin (all fourteenth century), Brightwell Baldwin (fifteenth century), Marsh Baldon, Horspath, and Hardwick (all fifteenth century), Heythrop (1522), and Westwell (1522–3). Christ in Majesty is represented at Ducklington and Sandford St. Martin (both fourteenth century). A distinction has been made between the type of frontal seated Christ and the seated Christ displaying the Wounds of the Passion. The latter is probably Christ in Judgement, although in the remaining examples there are no indications of the Resurrection of Souls. Examples of Christ displaying his wounds are found at Chinnor and Lower Heyford (both fourteenth century), Hardwick (fifteenth century), and Crowmarsh Gifford (sixteenth century). The Trinity is represented at Kidlington (fifteenth century) and at Newington (1482–1511) where it is pendent to the Assumption of the Virgin. There is an unusual Trinity emblem at Dorchester (fourteenth century). There are four certain and two probable examples of the frontal head of Christ as a tracery light design: Cassington, Lower Heyford, Tadmarton, Toot Baldon (all fourteenth century), and Yarnton (fifteenth century). One example of the Arma Christi, the Instruments of the Passion on a shield, is found at Horspath (late fifteenth century).

The four Evangelists with their symbols occur in two incomplete sets: St. Mark with his lion at Ewelme (fifteenth century) and the almost complete set at Heythrop (1522). The only complete example of the symbols of the four Evangelists is at Hampton Poyle (fifteenth century) and incomplete sets are found at South Newington (fourteenth century), Burford, North Aston, Great Rollright, and Stonesfield (fifteenth century). There are no surviving series of the twelve apostles but the St. James Major at Beckley (fourteenth century), the heads of St. James Major, St. Jude at Yarnton, and St. Thomas at Eynsham (all fifteenth century) are small-scale designs and may come from such a series designed for tracery lights. The figures of St. Peter and St. Paul at Mapledurham (fourteenth century) may be part of a series, but the design suggests that they could be an independent pair. The same observation can be made of the St. James at Stanton Harcourt (thirteenth century) and the St. Thomas at Yarnton (fifteenth century). A full-length figure of St. James Major holding a scroll with his verse of the Creed at Combe probably comes from a series of the Apostles and the Creed, as it is unlikely that an isolated single figure would be represented. There is also a head of St. James Major from a full-length standing figure at Burford (fifteenth century). The other survivals are slight: heads of St. Peter and St. Paul at Ewelme, which are the same as a tracery design at Bloxham (all fourteenth century), a name inscription for St. Andrew at Cogges (fourteenth century), the same saint in a canopy shafting at Ewelme (fifteenth century), and finally a small-scale figure of St. Thomas at Yarnton (sixteenth century).

The remaining single figures of saints represent a small fraction of the original amount of material. It is interesting to note that the surviving saints divide into reasonably balanced groups of the Universal saints of the Church and English saints. The latter category includes saints with a local interest. St. John Baptist is represented in the tracery light glazing of three places: Hardwick (early fourteenth century), Yarnton, and Burford (both fifteenth century). There is also an Agnus Dei roundel at Dorchester (fourteenth century). The remaining saints are mostly single examples and are given in tabulated form.

Universal Saints

St. Agnes. Minster Lovell (16th c.)
St. Barbara. Burford and Mapledurham (15th c.)
St. Christopher. Beckley (14th c.), Burford and Yarnton (15th c.), Heythrop (1522)
St. Cosmas or Damian. Minster Lovell (15th c.)
St. Dominic or another Dominican saint. Minster Lovell (15th c.)
St. Giles. Ewelme (15th c.), and a lost figure at Standlake (1502)
St. Ignatius of Antioch. Lost figure at Waterstock (c. 1480)
St. Lawrence. Dorchester and Chinnor (14th c.)
St. Leonard. Drayton St. Leonard (14th c.)
St. Lucy. Minster Lovell (15th c.)
St. Margaret. Burford (15th c.)

St. Mary Magdalen. Burford (15th c.)
St. Michael. Dorchester (14th c.), possibly Brightwell Baldwin (14th c.)
St. Nicholas. Yarnton (15th c.)
St. Peter Martyr. Minster Lovell (15th c.)
St. Sitha (Zita) of Lucca. Mapledurham (15th c.)
St. Stephen. Mapledurham (15th c.)

English Saints

St. Alban. Chinnor (14th c.)
St. Chad. Yarnton (16th c.)
St. Edmund, King and Martyr. Dorchester (14th c.) and a lost figure at Minster Lovell (15th c.)
St. Edward the Confessor. Shield at Burford (15th–16th c.), lost figure and shield at Minster Lovell
St. George. Adderbury (14th c.), Burford and Kelmscott (15th c.)
St. Osmund, Bishop of Salisbury. Lost figure at Standlake (1502)
St. Oswald. Lost figure and shield at Minster Lovell
St. Thomas Becket. Yarnton (15th c.)

Narrative scenes from the lives of saints are rare. Dorchester has two panels of scenes from the life of St. Birinus (one thirteenth century, the other fourteenth). A miracle of St. Frideswide is probably represented in an incomplete panel at Kidlington (fifteenth century). At Ewelme a lost window showed St. John Baptist being questioned by the Pharisees (fifteenth century), and there are two rare scenes from the life of St. Thomas Becket from Woodstock (fifteenth century).

Two scenes illustrating the Parable of Lazarus at Great Milton (fourteenth century) may have been part of a more extensive series, as was probably the case with the Sacrament of Marriage panel from Great Rollright (fifteenth century), which may have been part of a series of the Seven Sacraments. An inscription from another example of the same scene survives at Burford although the panel itself is now lost. Two of the Seven Works of Mercy which survive at Chinnor (fourteenth century) are the earliest examples of this subject that have been found in English glass painting. A Mass scene at Dorchester (fourteenth century) has defied further identification.

There are a number of saints and other fragments of figures that cannot be identified since most are incomplete, and all lack attributes or inscriptions.

Thirteenth Century. Stanton Harcourt. A bishop and a king
Fourteenth Century. Binsey. A female saint
                     Cassington. Two deacon saints
                     Chinnor. An archbishop and a bishop, probably saints
                     Dorchester. St. Peter as Pope (?), a bishop and a monastic saint
Fifteenth Century. Binsey. A female saint
                     Burford. An apostle, a crowned female saint, a bishop saint and a female saint
                     Combe. Two male saints
                     Cropredy. A crowned female saint
                     Ewelme. A female saint and an apostle
                     Horspath. A female saint and a crowned female saint
                     Shiplake. Two female saints
                     Yarnton. Two female saints and a youthful saint
Sixteenth Century. Brightwell Baldwin. Bishop saint

Style, Design, and Date

The aim of this section is to point out the most important examples of the stylistic developments of each period rather than to summarize general movements by isolating particular features. The developments which took place in Oxford City during this period which are referred to throughout the Catalogue are a better guide to the chronology of stylistic developments within the county. The glass in the city will be covered in the second volume of this series. Here the analysis of style and design has been restricted to the glass itself and detailed comparison with painting in any other media is considered inappropriate because of the differences in scale and technical demands. This study also covers very incomplete and fragmentary material which has been so much disturbed and subjected to the whims of restorers that it is dangerous to be dogmatic. As more material is brought to light by the publication of further county volumes in this series many of the assumptions and suggestions made here will be questioned and may need to be revised.

Thirteenth century. There is very little glass of this date surviving in the county, and it is mostly geometric grisaille glazing. The simplest, and possibly the earliest, examples are found in three small lancet windows in the chancel of Waterperry. There are three designs, two are a repeated design of either four leaves or sprays of vine foliage radiating from a coloured boss at the centre of the light, the third is a leaded design of contiguous ovals enclosing a painted design of vertical sprays of vine foliage, with horizontal sprays of vine springing from the coloured bosses linking the ovals. The vine foliage and grapes are extremely stylized and the background is painted with cross-hatched lines. At Holton are two fragments of the oval design enclosing a vertical stem with symmetrical vine leaves identical with that found at Waterperry; the borders are also the same.

A more elaborate example on a much larger scale is in the south lancet windows of the chancel at Stanton Harcourt. Again the grisaille has a repeated design, but here ovals are set within a geometric pattern. There is also a large circular design which includes two elements found at Waterperry in the one complete design. The coloured glass is used only in the bosses of geometric grisaille and for the border designs. Grisaille is painted on white glass against a background of cross-hatched lines.

At Stanton Harcourt the simple design of geometric grisaille incorporates a figure against a plain coloured background. There is no reason to suppose that this arrangement is not original and the painting of the figure's face and drapery folds suggests the third quarter of the thirteenth century. The two lancet windows containing geometric grisaille at Stanton St. John are possibly slightly later, (the foliage of the grisaille pattern in n. V is less stylized). The leaves are of a maple leaf type rather than the formal trails of vine foliage. However, it should be pointed out that the vine form is employed in the adjacent window, n. IV, so that small differences in style are not necessarily indicative of differences in date. The window design here incorporates shields of arms, but the glass is mostly modern or restorer's composite. It is possible that the arrangement is original and there is a comparable design in the Norbury (Derby.) chancel windows.

As has been noted there is little use of colour in the design of the above examples. A large roundel at Little Faringdon shows a symmetrical design of vine foliage and grapes set against a plain ruby background, the effect of which is very striking. This roundel was probably once part of a larger design. (It is said to have been brought from Salisbury Cathedral, but there is no evidence for this.)

The east window of Kidlington contains an important panel from a Tree of Jesse and this is the only evidence remaining of a large-scale thirteenth-century figured design in the county. Although the English origin of this panel has been queried, there is a close similarity between the figure of the king from the Tree of Jesse and the two seated figures of a bishop and a king in pointed vesicas at Stanton Harcourt. These two figures with their rigid hieratic poses and formal staring faces are difficult to interpret as a composition, particularly as their original context within an over-all design of a window is not known. A similar problem is encountered at Dorchester, in the panel of St. Birinus receiving a cross staff, which probably formed part of a series of narrative scenes of the life of the saint. There is a general similarity in the drawing of the heads, and the wide staring eyes, which suggests that, despite the archaic elements of the Birinus panel, it is probably about the same date as the Stanton Harcourt and Kidlington figures.

A window at Marston contains a reset geometric grisaille design of white glass and coloured bosses, and it is remarkable in that it has no painted ornament. Although the panel has been restored, and is made up with modern plain white glass, the extensive remains of the plain original glass and bosses are so unusual that the surviving design must be accepted. (It is extremely unlikely that any nineteenth-century restorer would devise and lead up such a complicated design.)

Fourteenth century, first quarter. There are eighteen churches containing glass that can be attributed to this period, and the material varies from a few fragments, as at Aston Rowant, to the extensive series of windows at Dorchester. The variety of styles exhibited within this series of related windows shows the difficulties of placing different styles within a larger context. Despite a general similarity, the variety in detail of the glass of this period suggests the work of highly individual, inventive glass painters, rather than stereotyped workshop production. It is perhaps more useful to consider the general points of design in order to see this glass against the background of the period.

It is important to begin with a dated example. The Crucifixion window at Asthall is probably to be associated with the chantry foundation of the Cornwall family of 1322-4. Although the glass has been much restored, there is enough of the original to establish the general design of the figures, backgrounds and canopies. The work is of extremely high quality. Apparently closely related in style are the two panels of scenes from the life of Lazarus at Great Milton; the Christ in Majesty at Aston Rowant; the east window Crucifixion panel at Kidlington; and the head of Christ at Tadmarton. (These are referred to as the Asthall group.) Within this group the head types are consistent having hair carefully arranged in modelled clumps, wide almond-shaped eyes, and lugubrious expressions with the mouth turned down at the corners. At Asthall the figures are set against a patterned foliage diaper background of plant trails with broad leaves. The close similarities between the Asthall group and the chancel windows of Merton College Chapel, Oxford, in both general design and particular points of style suggest that they are by the same workshop. The style of the Merton College windows can be related to the 'Court' style of painting of the late thirteenth, early fourteenth century and there are a number of other examples in Midlands glass that can be related to the Merton/Asthall group of windows. Further research should define the relationship more closely. This workshop was probably responsible for the surviving glass at Sandford St. Martin, and possibly the Evangelist symbols in the chancel windows at South Newington, and the Christ and St. John Baptist at Hardwick. The extensive remains of a series of windows at Dorchester can also be related to the Merton/Asthall group. There are similarities both in canopies and background diapers, but the detailed painting is generally much broader without the precision which is the hallmark of the Merton/Asthall group. The similarities vary. The St. Michael at

Dorchester, which has the elongated face, the arrangement of hair in clumps, the almond-shaped eyes and the long articulate fingers, is very close, whereas the spectators in the panel of St. Birinus preaching have hair which is simplified, and the painting of the features is done with thicker brush strokes. The Virgin at South Stoke, although much decayed, is very close to the Virgin and Child at Dorchester, and to the two deacon saints at Cassington.

Fourteenth century, second quarter and mid century. The chancel of the rebuilt church at Chinnor was dedicated in 1326 and the two side windows there are associated with this rebuilding. Each window contains two full-length figures of saints standing beneath canopies. There is a continuity in general stylistic terms from the earlier glass of the first quarter of the century, but there are changes in emphasis. This is particularly evident in the size of the figures in relation to the canopies. There are variations in foliage, decorative diapers and border designs. The leaves become much smaller, and are set in closer arabesque patterns. Heraldic charges are also used as background diapers behind the canopies, and small grotesque beasts are introduced in the serpentine foliage trails of the borders. A comparison with the Crucifixion window at Asthall shows marked differences although there are only two years between the dates of their execution. But it should be noticed that the canopies in both cases are rigidly horizontal to the picture plane, and no interest is shown in any perspective design. An innovation in design in the second quarter of the century is the introduction of perspective in the canopies. This can be seen in the incomplete canopies above the figures of SS. Peter and Paul at Brightwell Baldwin. Behind the main arch and gable are two small buildings with diagonally recessed side walls. As a feature of glass design the use of perspective has yet to be studied in detail. At York it is first observable in the great west window of 1338/9, and important examples are found in the north windows of the Latin Chapel at Christ Church, Oxford, of *c.* 1340.

This new interest in perspective is allied to a more plastic style of drapery painting. The figure of St. Peter at Brightwell Baldwin has a mantle pulled tightly against the body, with deeply recessed folds in contrast to the figure of St. Alban at Chinnor (*c.* 1326), where the mantle has long straight folds.

This more modelled style of drapery painting can also be seen in the Coronation of the Virgin and the other tracery lights at Beckley and the Virgin Annunciate at Brightwell Baldwin, which is set against a background of very broad serrated leaves. A comparable use of bold foliage design is found in the tracery lights of the chancel chapel at Cogges, which is a remarkable and striking design unique in the county.

As in the earlier part of the century there are a number of small fragments of glass which are evidence of flourishing workshop activity. The east window at Beckley contains a fragment of the Martyrdom of St. Thomas Becket, and the large head of a female saint, and at Lower Heyford a head of Christ from a tracery light has survived. All these fragments can be associated stylistically with the Latin Chapel windows of Christ Church, Oxford.

In the past little consideration has been given to the variations that are the result of the costs of different types of design. The St. Anne teaching the Virgin to read at Marsh Baldon and the donor figures at Waterperry are of the same period, but the St. Anne and the Virgin are large figures against a coloured background beneath a canopy whereas the Waterperry figures are tiny by comparison and set directly against a background of white quarries. The Waterperry figures are a more thrifty type of design, and there is a meticulous attention to painted detail. The more economical class of design is also found at Bloxham and in the north-aisle windows at South Newington where the painting of the heads, border pieces, and grisaille foliage in the tracery lights is highly simplified with little attention to detail.

Fourteenth century, second half. In comparison to the extensive survivals of the first half of the fourteenth century, there is little that can be attributed to the second half and it is a matter of speculation how much glass of this period has been lost. However, an important survival of painted glass design of this period is the series of windows produced by the glazier Thomas of Oxford for William of Wykeham's foundation at New College, Oxford (*c.* 1380–6). The glass in the county that can be compared with the products of this workshop is found in only three churches, the figure of a knight from Adderbury (now in the Bodleian Library), an incomplete figure of St. Paul at Cassington, and the figure of St. James Major at Beckley. It is known that Thomas of Oxford was working at Adderbury between 1397 and 1398 and the drawing of the knight's face is very close to that in the New College glass despite the differences in scale. The St. James figure is curious. It has similarities in drapery painting with the style of the mid century, but the resemblance of the drawing of the eyes, nose, and mouth to the Adderbury knight, and the design of cut-away pedestal on which the figure stands, are probably indicative of a later date.

Fifteenth century. There is a considerable amount of glass of this period surviving in the county but the divisions into stylistic categories are extremely complex, because of variations in scale. Although there is a general similarity in style in the fifteenth-century glass, details of design are extremely varied and suggest that the glass was produced by a number of separate workshops working within the context of the same style.

The style of the glass of the early part of the century is deeply indebted to the second style of the Thomas of Oxford workshop as established in the Jesse window from New College, Oxford (now in York Minster) and the windows of Wykeham's other foundation at Winchester College (Hants). This new style is characterized by a change in the proportion in figures and head types. The figures become shorter, the heads rounder with much more modelling; a combination of line and stipple shading, with particular emphasis being given to the eyes and the highlights of cheeks and nose picked out of a matt wash. The variety of decorative background patterns and foliage are almost universally replaced by the seaweed foliage diaper and there is a wider use of white glass and yellow stain, coloured glass being restricted to the backgrounds of figures and canopies. The influence of the second style of the Thomas of Oxford workshop had tremendous consequences for the development of glass painting in the first quarter of the fifteenth century throughout the Midlands. This can be seen in Oxfordshire, for example, in the figures of St. Paul and of the Virgin Annunciate at Brightwell Baldwin where the painting is closely related to the later Thomas of Oxford style, although lacking the quality of execution and design. The canopies are somewhat compressed, but the representation of the vaulted underside of the niches, crocketed gables, and finials do show an awareness of the Winchester College designs.

The figure of St. James Major at Combe is much closer in design to the Thomas of Oxford workshop. The drawing is powerful, and the draperies modelled with much more fluency. This figure and its canopy stand half-way between the later work of Thomas of Oxford and the development in canopy and figure design shown in the windows of the Ante-chapel to All Souls College, Oxford (*c.* 1441–7). Both the Combe cherubim and the New College Orders of Angels show the use of identical cartoons and decorative leaf patterns.

There are tantalizing fragments of incomplete figures belonging to this first stylistic group; the head of St. James Major at Burford, the head of St. Frideswide at Begbroke, and the two large heads of angels at Chalgrove. Although the remaining glass is incomplete, and nothing is known about its context in a design, the details in the drawing of the eyes, nose, and mouth, and the highlights picked out of delicate washes are of a consistently high quality.

The details of design characteristic of the glass of this period can be seen at Horley in the two figures of ecclesiastical donors, Henry Rumworth (rector 1416–20) and his successor, Robert Gilbert. Although the glass is more or less contemporary, the Rumworth figure is very carefully painted with the soft modelling characteristic of the Thomas of Oxford school and a background of seaweed foliage diapers picked out of a light matt wash, and although the Gilbert figure is less complete, it is quite close in the drawing of the features, but the painting and design are not as competent. A flat matt wash is used for the pileus; the hand is over large in proportion to the head, and the seaweed foliage diaper background is painted with a deeper tone wash and the foliage forms are much broader.

Similar in scale are the figures of two Cistercian monks, SS. Nicholas and Thomas Becket, in the traceries at Yarnton. There are similarities in the head types and seaweed foliage backgrounds, but at Yarnton the drapery painting is more linear. The modelling is a fine balance between painted lines of varying thickness and slight stipple shading and this is extremely sophisticated work both in concept and execution.

A comparably fine balance of varied line and stipple shading is achieved in the symbols of the four Evangelists at Hampton Poyle which are also tracery light designs *in situ*. The design is particularly successful in the deployment of the figures to fill the whole height and width of the trefoil-headed lights. The restricted blue seaweed diaper background and the elimination of any border successfully concentrates the design on the actual figures.

A related example of this 'soft' style of painting is found in the figures of St. Christopher and the Virgin and Child at Yarnton. Here the modelling is more dependent on extremely delicate stipple shading although the design is less competent, and exhibits some clumsy features. The head of the Christ Child with the Virgin is forced into an awkward profile, and the St. Christopher is a curious composition with the saint striding through a river which has no banks, set in juxtaposition to an architectural base inscribed with the saint's name. It seems possible that the artist has adapted two different cartoons without realizing the incongruity of the final design.

A similar incongruity of design within this group can be observed in the remains of a small Crucifixion at Brightwell Baldwin. The figures of Christ, the Virgin and St. John Evangelist survive with a fragment of seaweed foliage diaper, but the over-all composition is lost. There are inconsistencies within the surviving figures; the proportions of the hands are unrelated and the size of the nimbus in relation to the head is disproportionately large.

The over-large nimbus is a characteristic of a series of figures which can probably be dated to the second and third quarters of the fifteenth century. These are: God the Father at Begbroke, which is very close to the Brightwell Baldwin Crucifixion in the softness of the style, the St. Thomas Apostle at Yarnton, the Virgin and St. John from a Crucifixion at Marsh Baldon, the Virgin and Child with St. Anne at Beckley, the fragment of a female saint at Ewelme, and the head of a female saint at Cropredy. All these figures lack their original backgrounds, and it cannot even be established whether they were associated with canopy designs, but the large nimbs and hardening of the painted lines are similar to those in the Ante-chapel windows at All Souls College, Oxford (c. 1441–7).

The glass of the second half of the fifteenth century is characterized by an increasing economy of design with a restricted use of coloured glass. This is unusual in that two of the most extensive collections of glass were made for the chantry foundations of two important families, and are in contrast to the richness of the architecture and the monuments. This is first evident in the Wilcote Chapel at North Leigh (1438). The east window contained figures set below canopies, and the side windows had shields and crests set against a background of white-patterned quarries with no figured glazing. There is extensive repetition in the tracery lights, which all have decorative designs in white glass and yellow stain.

The glass associated with the de la Pole rebuilding of the church at Ewelme in 1437–8 is incomplete, but all the remaining glass is white with yellow stain, the only coloured glass being in the shields of the arms of the de la Pole family and its alliances. A feature of the glass at both Ewelme and North Leigh is a series of roundels painted with various animals and birds. Those of the former have precise references to heraldic badges, and those of the latter are probably also based on heraldry, although identifications have not been established. The backgrounds of the North Leigh roundels are diapered with contiguous rosettes picked out of a matt wash, and the style of painting is less precise than that of the glass at Ewelme. These features, combined with an unevenness of quality, are characteristic of the later part of the fifteenth century.

The decorative designs in the tracery lights at North Leigh are a mixture of the seaweed foliage diaper and an elaborate vine-leaf design. From this date (c. 1440) the use of the seaweed diaper is discontinued, and is replaced by variations on the contiguous rosette design. This decorative feature is a small-scale version of the large rosette and flower backgrounds that first appear in the windows of the Ante-chapel of All Souls College, Oxford (c. 1441–7).

Comparison between some examples dated in the second half of the fifteenth century demonstrates the lack of pronounced differences in style and design throughout this period of glass painting. The variations occur in the quality of execution, from sophisticated painting to extremely crude delineation of forms. For example, the Fitz Ellis window at Waterperry (1461–9) and the Barworth and Salter window at Newington (post 1482–pre 1511) are similar in their basic design of donor figures set against a repeated quarry pattern. Technically both these windows are extremely competent, with back painting and a nice use of yellow stain. The figures, however, are somewhat lifeless and stereotyped, and there are eccentricities in drawing and scale, for example in the large sword hilt of Robert Fitz Ellis and the awkward placing of his daughter or granddaughter. The angels in the Newington window are also stereotyped, with little or no individual variations of expression on their faces. At Newington the design of scrolls linking the lower and upper panels of the lights is an unusual feature for which no parallel has been found.

The tracery lights at Burford, probably of the third quarter of the fifteenth century, are particularly interesting in that they are a small-scale version based on a series of cartoons for main light glazing. This is suggested by the decorative details and the over-all design of the figures beneath tent canopies. There is considerable variety in decorative designs throughout this related series. The poses are varied, the expressions more animated, and it is an extremely sophisticated example of both painting and design.

Similar work of high quality is found at Mapledurham in the figures of SS. Stephen, Sitha, and Barbara which are probably from the centre of canopy designs. The figures are set against damask back-grounds, a new departure stylistically within the county, although the style of the figures is similar to that at Burford. Some of the windows at Mapledurham can be dated 1470–6, but the remains are so minimal that the place of these figures in the chronology of glazing within the county is difficult to determine.

The tracery lights in the chancel windows at Minster Lovell contain two different series of female saints which are probably contemporary, although the discrepancies in scale and design between the two series are quite marked. In one the figures are broad and well proportioned, in the other small and thin and rendered quite insignificant by the overpowering canopies. These variations in quality and sense of design can also be seen in the surviving fragments of canopies at Stanton Harcourt (c. 1480) which incorporate lifeless figures of angels. The figure of St. George at Kelmscott is spirited in design, but close examination shows that the artist has failed to produce a proportioned and articulate human figure. The legs of the saint are disproportionately long in relation to his torso.

Two different groups of glass can be attributed to the third quarter of the fifteenth century. The first group consists of: the Virgin Annunciate fragment at Newington, John Baptist at Yarnton, and the Sacrament of Marriage scene from Great Rollright, now in the Bodleian Library. The unifying feature is the rather sketchy painting of the broad heads, with very light matt washes for the hair. The second group consists of three panels only: the two Becket panels from Woodstock now in the Bodleian Library, and a Miracle of St. Frideswide at Kidlington. These are the best examples of glass painting of this date in the county. There is an extraordinary inventiveness of design and high technical com-petence in the panel of Becket being received by King Louis. The two main figures occupy the fore-ground, their attendants behind them and there is a sense of animation, almost of movement. The background is a luxurious green landscape studded with trees and individually coloured flowers against green herbage and this demonstrates an extraordinary versatility of technique and sense of design. The Penance of Henry II panel is an equally powerful composition. The monks' habits are painted with stippling of varying intensity, which creates an almost tactile quality. The most important feature of this panel, which has no parallel elsewhere in the county, is the study of the semi-naked body of the king, and the detail suggests that the artist may have been working from life.

This high quality of design can be contrasted with the figures of John Brown and his father, Thomas, at Waterstock (c. 1480). The drapery painting is competent, the heads are differentiated, but the effect is static and lifeless, with cursory design in the prayer desk and stiff flat hands. These two figures are similar to the St. Peter Martyr and either St. Cosmas or St. Damian at Minster Lovell. Although incomplete, the proportions are erratic, and the background diapers are sketched with scant attention to detail.

A distinct decline in style and design can be observed in the tracery lights of the south window at Iffley where the figures of cherubim and angels are roughly painted on white glass with no decorative diapers, and no relation to the position they occupy. This is in contrast to the Evangelist symbols at Hampton Poyle of the early part of the century.

Sixteenth century. The few surviving fragments of sixteenth-century glass demonstrate a considerable variety of quality within the space of a few years. At Heythrop, the remains of the windows made for John Ashfield and his family (1522) show notable variation in expertise of painting and design. These

donor figures, and the Virgin and St. John from a Crucifixion contrast with the figures of the Evangelists in the tracery lights of the east window, which seem stilted and ill proportioned, with lifeless
expressions and almost caricatured faces. This glass can be compared with the Crucifixion and donor
figures at Westwell (1522–3). The drawing is heavy and clumsy, and the perspective view of the
nimbus of St. John is incongruous. The difference in quality between the Westwell and Heythrop glass
suggests that the latter is a cheaper class of design, and may reflect the social status of the donors.

The Curson window at Waterperry (post 1527) is interesting in that the donor figures are over-
shadowed by the prominence given to their shields of arms. The painting is competent but there is
some repetition in the head types of the sons and daughters. It seems as if the artist of this window was
more interested in the display of technical expertise revealed in the shields where there is much detailed
work, including extremely clever abrading and staining in the charges.

Glass painting in England in the first half of the sixteenth century is dominated by the work of
glaziers from the Low Countries, the finest examples of which are to be found at King's College,
Cambridge. This style appears to have had little effect on the glass in Oxfordshire. Something of the
decline in the ability of native glaziers can be seen in the way a design by a Flemish glazier becomes
debased in repetition. The shields of Henry VIII and Edward Prince of Wales, formerly at Wroxton
Abbey (now in the Philadelphia Art Gallery, U.S.A.), have been attributed to Galyon Hone. The
shields are encircled by an elaborate wreath with clasps. One of these clasp designs is a bearded man's
head thrust through an oculus. Copies of this design occur at Yarnton and Holton and in the window
at Iffley Vicarage. The painting becomes coarser and the drawing less controlled, so that the Iffley
example is almost a parody of its prototype.

CATALOGUE

The Catalogue covers all the medieval stained glass in the churches of Oxfordshire, numbering the windows and panels according to the plan on page xx. A short bibliography for each church is given and a brief introduction to the main features of the glass is followed by a detailed survey of the condition, colour and technique, iconography, style and design of the stained glass. The ordnance survey number for the church is given for each place catalogued, and churches which are not in this volume but which are mentioned in the text are given with their county, e.g. Fairford (Glos.).

ADDERBURY

ST. MARY THE VIRGIN

O.S. SP 472 354.

MS. SOURCES

Oxford. Bodleian Library, MS. Top. Oxon. e. 286, ff. 104ᵛ–106.
London. British Library:
    MS. Harl. 6365, ff. 108ʳ–110ʳ. 17th c. Church Notes.
    Add. MS. 35211 Winston, vol. iii, N1–AA11, 53 and 54.
    Drawings 19th c.

PRINTED

Winston (1865), 311, 356, nos. 646 and 647.
P.C. (1920), 2–4.
Hobson, T. F. (ed.), 'Adderbury Rectoria', O.R.S. viii (1926).
Vyvyan, J. P., *The Story of Adderbury Parish Church* (1965).
V.C.H. ix (1969), 34–6.
Pevsner (1974), 413–15.

Adderbury was one of the churches appropriated by William of Wykeham, Bishop of Winchester, to his Oxford foundation, New College.[1] Papal licence was obtained for this in 1379, but the actual appropriation did not take place until 1381 when the living became vacant.[2] By the end of the century the existing windows of the church were in need of repair, and some new ones were provided. In 1397–8 Thomas of Oxford, glazier, was paid for making three windows in the vestry, and one over the altar, together with repairs to the windows of the chancel.[3] This glazier has been identified as the Thomas of Oxford who provided the windows for Wykeham's foundations at New College, Oxford, and Winchester College.[4]

In the early fifteenth century a major rebuilding of the chancel of the church took place. The preparations for this work began in 1408, and it was completed in 1419.[5] Payments to the glaziers are recorded from 1415 to 1418, the cost of the glazing amounted to £29. 6s. 4d., about one-third of the total costs of the rebuilding.[6]

Little is known about the glazing programmes for the windows of the church. The heraldic glass recorded in the seventeenth-century antiquarian notes has not survived.[7] Some losses took place in the nineteenth century. A detailed drawing by Charles Winston[8] proves that an incomplete figure of a military saint, possibly St. George, now in a window of the Bodleian Library, Oxford,[9] was removed from Adderbury. The church now retains only a few scraps of quarry glazing, probably coeval with the rebuilding of the chancel, 1415–18.[10]

n. III (East window of the vestry)

A5. Quarries.

Each quarry: h. 0·14 m. w. 0·11 m.

Three complete quarries and fragments of three others. Painted on white glass with yellow stain ornament. Identical design, quarry type 13.

    The glass is extremely corroded on both surfaces, and some of it is set inside out.

Date. 15th c., probably coeval with the building of the chancel, 1415–18.

A6. Quarries.

Each quarry. h. 0·14 m. w. 0·11 m.

One complete and two fragmentary quarries, design as A5. All are set inside out and very corroded. A fragment of large foliage design: a circular torse of two plaits with off-springing leaves, white and yellow stain, also set inside out.

Date. As A5.

---

[1] Hobson, op. cit. 72.
[2] Hobson, op. cit. 78.
[3] Hobson, op. cit. 74.
[4] Woodforde (1951), 3–7.
[5] Hobson, op. cit. viii–xx, 16–17.
[6] Hobson, op. cit. 20.

[7] P.C. (1920), 2–4.
[8] Winston (1865), 311.
[9] Spokes (1973), 17, serial no. 174. Given to the Bodleian Library 1962 by Dr. W. N. Wellacott. Spokes (1973), section 15 notes.
[10] V.C.H. ix (1969), 36, incorrectly states that there is 'now no stained glass of earlier date than the 19th c.'.

Glass removed from Adderbury

**Oxford. Bodleian Library. Duke Humfrey.
N. XXXVIII.**

(Duke Humfrey Library. North side. Second window from the east.)

2b. St. George (?)   PLATE 13

h. 0·14 m. w. 0·14 m.

A half-length figure, nimbed, facing three-quarters left, in armour, holding a spear and a shield.

Condition. Incomplete. The upper half of the figure only remains in a modern surround of plain white glass. The original glass is well preserved, with only slight pitting of the surface and minor paint loss.

Colour and Technique. Painted on white glass with stipple shading and yellow stain. The jupon is patterned with a delicate arabesque of foliage.

Iconography. The saint's right hand is raised in a gesture of greeting. The shield is plain and the jupon has only an embroidered pattern, so there is no heraldry to identify the figure. A possible identification is St. George. The church is dedicated to the Blessed Virgin Mary, and St. George was a particular champion of the Virgin.[1] In addition, William of Wykeham, who appropriated Adderbury to New College, was also, as Bishop of Winchester, Prelate of the Order of the Garter. St. George is one of the four patrons of the Order, and the chapel at Windsor is dedicated to him.[2]

Style and Design. The saint is shown wearing a mixture of mail and plate armour, a pointed bascinet with mail aventail overlapping a tight-fitting jupon with a heavy baldric around his waist. His arms are protected by plate vambraces and plate gauntlets with jointed fingers. All these features have parallels in monumental brass design *c.* 1360–1410.[3] An unusual feature is the shield with a cavity bouche for a lance cut in the dexter chief corner.[4]

The small size of the figure makes precise stylistic comparisons rather difficult. The delineation of the features, particularly the eyes with heavy lids, broad nose, and firm mouth, has a strong affinity with the early style of Thomas of Oxford's workshop. Compare, for example, the head of William of Wykeham at New College, Oxford, of *c.* 1380–6.[5]

Date. Late 14th c.

ALKERTON

ST. MICHAEL

O.S. SP 377 429.

MS. SOURCES

Oxford. Bodleian Library, MS. Top. Oxon. b. 75, ff. 46ᵛ and 48.
   Wyatt Papers 18th–19th c.

PRINTED

Pevsner (1974), 420–1.

A single piece of fifteenth-century glass remains: a two-handled pot containing a lily stem with five flowers. Although incomplete, it looks like a tracery light rather than part of a large composition and it may originally have been set between the angel and the Virgin Annunciate.[6] This fragment is probably that described in the report of the architects, Bodley and Garnet, *c.* 1878, as 'a very pretty quarry in glass in the north-west window'.[7]

---

[1] The Life of St. Julian relates how the Virgin resurrected the martyr Mercurius and sent him to slay Julian the Apostate, *Golden Legend* iii. 15–16. In England from the 13th c. onwards, St. George replaces Mercurius in illustrations of this legend, Newton i (1961), 253.

[2] E. Ashmole, *The History of the Most Noble Order of the Garter* (1715), 189, 129–30.

[3] H. Druitt, *A Manual of Costume as Illustrated by Monumental Brasses* (1906, fasc. edn. 1970), 156–64.

[4] Druitt, op. cit. 177 n. 2, gives only two examples on brasses, *c.* 1475 and 1476, and notes that such representations are rare.

[5] Woodforde (1951), pl. x.

[6] As, for example, the Lily Crucifix in a tracery light of window n. V. of the parish church of St. Michael, at the North Gate, Oxford. R.C.H.M. (1939), 142.

[7] Wyatt Papers, op. cit., f. 48.

n. III

Condition. Incomplete and cracked.

Colour and Technique. Painted in brown on white glass, the stem of the lily in yellow stain.

A1. A Lily Pot

h. 0·15 m. w. 0·10 m.

Date. 15th c.

ASTHALL

ST. NICHOLAS

O.S. SP 287 114.

PRINTED SOURCES

N.O.A.S. Report (1870), 18–19.

Ward, The Revd., 'Excursion to Astall Church', *Transactions of the Bristol and Gloucestershire Archaeological Society* xx (1895–7), 368–9.

Nelson (1913), 161.

P.C. (1920), 9.

Price, E. R., 'Two Effigies in the Churches of Asthall and Cogges', *Oxoniensia* iii (1938), 103.

Greening Lamborn (1949), 104.

Pevsner (1974), 424–5.

The glass remaining in the windows of the north transept chapel can be associated with the Cornwall family, tenants of the manor.

The tracery lights of the north window (n. IV) contain three shields of arms *in situ*. At the apex (B2) is an incomplete shield, originally[1] *argent on a fess sable three bezants or*, for Sir Richard de Cornwall,[2] who died in 1300.[3] He was an illegitimate son of Richard, Earl of Cornwall, tenant in chief of the manor.[4] The two lower tracery lights contain the arms of the two sons of Sir Richard (A2, A3): Sir Edmund de Cornwall,[5] the elder son and heir (d. 1354),[6] and Sir Geoffrey de Cornwall[7] (d. 1335).[8]

The main lights of this window contain a single row of figures, beneath canopies, set against a background of white quarries. The bezants of the Cornwall arms are repeated as a border motif throughout the window. The figure panels represent the Crucifixion: Christ on the cross between the Virgin Mary and St. John Evangelist. The centre panel has a bidding scroll: *Jesu eyet merci de moy*: which originally related to a donor figure of a woman which was placed in the lower part of the window and is now lost.[9] It is impossible to determine if the scroll is *in situ* or belonged originally in the lost panel.

The evidence of the heraldic glass, together with some documentary evidence, suggests that the donor figure represented Joan, widow of Sir Richard de Cornwall. In 1320 she had licence for the alienation in mortmain of messuages and lands, in Asthall and Asthall Langley, to the Prior and Hospital of St. John at Burford to find a chaplain to celebrate divine service daily in the church of St. Nicholas at Asthall.[10] The gift was completed in 1322, the priest to celebrate daily in the chapel of St. Mary and St. Catherine for the soul of Sir Richard and for the souls of Joan and her children after their deaths.[11]

[1] P.C. (1920), 9, records the complete shield, but incorrectly blazons the bezants as mullets.

[2] Charles Roll, no. 254, *c.* 1285 (The Society of Antiquaries MS. 517), ed. C. Perceval, 'Two Rolls of Arms of the Reign of King Edward I', *Archaeologia* xxxix (1864), 409.

[3] *Cal. Inq. Post Mortem* iii, 604, 488. A. Gibbon, *Early Lincoln Wills* (1888), 1.

[4] C. Moor, 'Knights of Edward I', *Harleian Soc.* lxxx (1929), 239.

[5] The Great Parliamentary Roll, *c.* 1312 (B.L. Cotton MS. Caligula A. xvii). *A Roll of Arms of the reign of Edward II*, ed. N. H. Nicholas (1829), 29.

[6] *Cal. Inq. Post Mortem* x, 158. Moor, op. cit. 239. G. W. Marshall 'The Barons of Burford', *The Genealogist* iii (1879), 225–30.

[7] The Boroughbridge Roll, 1322 (B.L. Egerton MS. 2850), ed. F. T. Palgrave, in *Parliamentary Writs* ii, part 11 (1830), 196.

[8] *Cal. Close Rolls, 1333–1337*, 449.

[9] P.C. (1920), 9.

[10] *Cal. Patent Rolls. Edward II. 1317–21*, 495. R. H. Gretton, *The Burford Records* (1920), 587–9.

[11] *V.C.H.* ii (1907), 154, citing Lincoln Episcopal Registers, Burghersh Institutions f. 261.

The heraldry and the appearance of a single female donor figure suggest that the window was made for Joan de Cornwall after the death of her husband. The establishment of the chantry chapel, 1320–2, would be an appropriate time for the undertaking of this work although the window could be somewhat earlier in date. This hypothesis is suggested by the siting of the canopied tomb, also attributed to Joan de Cornwall,[1] below the window. In type and style the tomb can hardly be later than c. 1320–5 and is probably contemporary with the chantry foundation.[2] The large crocketed gable of the tomb obscures the centre light of the window so that it is impossible to see the Crucifixion panel and it is difficult to believe that this eccentric arrangement would have resulted if the window and tomb were of the same date. The masonry joins of the wall and tomb appear to be a single build, suggesting that they are contemporary. It is perhaps worth while recalling other examples in this period where sculpture is not integrated into the architectural frame.[3] A probable dating of c. 1320–2 is suggested for the window.

The general design of n. IV, a single band of figures beneath canopies, set against a white ground, is a common type in English glass painting from the late thirteenth to the mid fourteenth century. Within the standard design distinctive developments and variations in detail are found. In the earlier examples the white background tends to have a geometric pattern, interlocking quatrefoils and diamonds etc., painted with symmetrical trails of foliage, as at Merton College, Oxford, c. 1289–96. The regular trellis of diamond-shaped quarries, painted with less obviously symmetrical trails of foliage, as at Asthall, developed from this and is more common in the later part of the period (for example in the windows of the Latin Chapel of Christ Church, Oxford, c. 1340), although the two types overlap. The coloured backgrounds to the Asthall figure panels are diapered with trails of large maple leaves, crossed by a horizontal patterned band, very similar to the earlier glass at Merton College Chapel (c. 1289–96).[4] By the mid fourteenth century the leaves tend to get much smaller in proportion and tighter, as, for example, at Christ Church, Oxford, c. 1340 and the west window of York Minster of 1338.[5]

The canopies above the figures at Asthall are extremely simple in design. A trefoil arch with large crockets and finial, set before a brick wall surmounted by a parapet and roof. Here again the basic features of the design show greater affinity with the earlier glass at Merton College[6] as opposed to the more advanced canopies, with an interest in perspective, as in the windows of the Latin Chapel at Christ Church, Oxford.[7] Yellow stain is not employed in the north window at Asthall, but is found on the quarries of the north-east window. All these features are consistent with the proposed dating of c. 1320–2.

It seems possible that this glass might have been produced by the workshop responsible for the earlier windows at Merton College.

n. III

1a–1c. Geometric Grisaille

Each panel: h. 0·46 m. w. 0·36 m.

Trellis of white quarries painted with a continuous trail of ivy leaves. Border: a serpentine stem with off-springing oak leaves.

Condition. Three quarries in 1a are modern copies; the original glass has pronounced exterior pitting.

Colour and Technique. Quarries painted in brown on white glass; border foliage, white glass touched with yellow stain set against plain ruby pot-metal glass.

Date. c. 1320–2.

1b. Geometric Grisaille

Panel: h. 0·46 m. w. 0·36 m.

Quarries: as 1a except that the foliage trail is of oak leaves. Border: vertical stem with off-springing crockets, yellow stain against plain ruby.

---

[1] Ward, op. cit. 369, attributed the tomb to Elizabeth, widow of Sir Edmund de Cornwall and lady of the manor in 1354.

[2] E. R. Price, op. cit.

[3] L. Stone, Sculpture in Britain. The Middle Ages (1955), 158.

[4] R.C.H.M. (1939), pl. 148.

[5] For a fuller discussion of the changes in design see General Introduction.

[6] R.C.H.M. (1939), pls. 145 and 148.

[7] Ibid., pl. 99.

Condition. Two complete and two half-quarries are modern copies, original glass has pronounced exterior pitting.

Date. As 1a.

A1, A4. Foliage Design

Vertical stem with two off-springing oak leaves and an acorn. Painted in brown on white glass, pronounced external pitting. *In situ*.

Date. As above.

A2, A3. Foliage Design

h. 0·26 m. w. 0·26 m.

White glass painted with sprays of oak leaves springing from a vertical stem, at the centre of each light a roundel with a foliage design of oak and maple leaves radiating from the centre. Painted in brown on white glass, very pronounced exterior corrosion. *In situ*.

Date. As above.

n. IV

1a, 1b, 1c. Geometric Grisaille

Each panel: h. 0·51 m. w. 0·35 m.

Trellis of white quarries painted with a vertical stem with off-springing trails of maple leaves. Border: continuous band of gold bezants.

Condition. Incomplete, quarries made up with modern copies, the original glass has a pronounced exterior pitting.

Colour and Technique. Quarries as n. III, 1a. Border: pot-metal ochre glass.

Iconography. The border design of bezants refers to the arms of the Cornwall family (see below).

2a. The Virgin Mary

h. 0·40 cm. w. 0·35 m.

Condition. The whole panel is modern, late 19th c.

2b. Christ on the Cross   PLATE 14 (a), (b)

h. 0·40 m. w. 0·35 m.

The dead Christ hanging on the cross.

Inscription. Scroll, Lombardic lettering:
| *JESU EYET* | *MERCI : DE MOY* |

Condition. Complete except for three small pieces of background diaper. The glass is very corroded on both surfaces.

Colour and Technique. Christ: white flesh, ochre nimbus and loin cloth, green cross. Blue background diapered with trails of maple leaves, at the centre a horizontal band of ruby glass diapered with a trail of trefoil leaves. Colours are all pot-metal glass painted in brown, very slight smear shading on the figure.

Iconography. The bidding scroll was originally associated with a donor figure, now lost.

The figure of the crucified Christ is the standard late medieval type: represented dead and nailed to the cross with three nails. Around his brow is a plain band. This is a not uncommon feature in 14th-c. glass painting. However, the hypothesis that the band is the crown of thorns is perhaps questionable.[1] Representations of the crown of thorns vary considerably and an attempt to clarify them made by Dom Ethelbert Horne appears to over-simplify the subject.[2] After the acquisition of the actual relic of the crown of thorns by St. Louis of France in 1239, the representations mostly conform to one or other of two types: either a series of thin straight cords bound with a spiral tie, or a twisted cable of two equal cords.[3] The former is a closer approximation to the actual relic which is a ring of rushes bound together by twisting ties.[4] After 1300 the complete crown of thorns with long protruding points is more usual.[5] It is possible that the plain band is a simplification made by the artist to represent the crown of thorns. However, much earlier examples of a plain band are not unknown,[6] sometimes with a jewel at the centre,[7] denoting it as a regal diadem, not the crown of thorns. It is not impossible that the artist's model derived from an 11th-c. prototype.

Date. c. 1320-2.

---

[1] E. Horne, 'A Crucifixion Panel in Wells Cathedral', *J.B.S.M.G.P.* iii (1929-30), 12.

[2] E. Horne, 'The Crown of Thorns in Art', *Downside Review* liii (1935), 48-51.

[3] Horne, ibid., views these as progressive rather than contemporary types.

[4] Ibid. 49, with illustrations.

[5] Horne's suggestion that this form did not appear until after 1300 is incorrect, see for example the fragment of an ivory crucifix, possibly English, of c. 1180-90, now in the Kunstindustrimuseet, Oslo: J. Beckwith, *Ivory Carvings in Early Medieval England* (1972), cat. no. 105. The drawing of the relic by Matthew Paris, c. 1253,

shows the points and he describes it as '*de iunccis marinis habentibus eminentissimos aculeos, ex IIII^or plectis contorta*' (Corpus Christi College, Cambridge MS. 16, f. 139b). M. R. James, 'The Drawings of Matthew Paris', *Walpole Society* xiv (1925-6), pl. xlv.

[6] B.L. Arundel MS. 60. f. 12^v. Psalter from New Minster, Winchester c. 1060. F. Wormald, *English Drawings of the Tenth and Eleventh Centuries* (1952), pl. 33.

[7] Vatican Library MS. Reg. 12. Bury St. Edmunds Psalter. Second quarter 11th c.; B.L. Cotton MS. Titus D., XXVII. f. 65. New Minster Church Offices, c. 1023-5. E. G. Millar, *English Illuminated Manuscripts from the Xth to the XIIIth Centuries* (1926), pls. 12 and 24.

2c. St. John Evangelist   PLATE 14(*c*)

h. 0·40 m. w. 0·35 m.

Standing facing three-quarters left and holding a book.

Condition. Incomplete, the cusped head of the diapered foliage background is a modern restoration. The medieval glass is very corroded on both surfaces.

Colour and Technique. St. John, white flesh and tunic, ruby mantle, stands on a green hillock. Blue background diapered with trails of maple leaves; at the centre a horizontal band of ochre glass diapered with a trail of trefoil leaves. Slight smear shading on the figure.

Iconography. Standard type, holding a book and resting his bowed head on his raised right hand.

Date. c. 1320–2.

3a, 3b, 3c. Canopy

h. 0·26 m. w. 0·35 m.

The figures each stand beneath an arch, a cusped trefoil springing from the vertical side shafts flanking each figure. The arch is surmounted by a crocketed gable and finial set in front of a brick wall pierced on each side of the finial by an oculus cusped quatrefoil. The wall has an embattlement and gabled roof topped with a cresting of trefoils.

Condition. Incomplete and restored. 3a and 3c are modern restoration, except for the side shafts of 3c.

Colour and Technique. The side shafts of the canopies are white patterned with a vertical diamond-shaped trellis, each diamond quatrefoil, pattern picked out of matt wash. The capitals, main trefoil arch, gable, and finial are all in deep ochre glass. White wall, bricks, and oculi picked out of a matt wash. Ochre roof and cresting. The colours are all pot-metal.

Date. c. 1320–2.

4a, 4b, 4c. Geometric Grisaille

h. 0·31 m. w. 0·35 m.

Quarries and borders as 1a–1c above.

A1, A4, B1, B3

Pieces of white oak foliage diaper *in situ*, very corroded.

A2. Shield of Cornwall

h. 0·40 m. w. 0·35 m. Shield: h. 0·23 m. w. 0·20 m.

Argent a lion rampant gules crowned or, over all on a bend sable three bezants or CORNWALL OF ASTHALL AND KINLET.

Condition. Complete but extensive corrosion, particularly on the coloured glass.

Colour and Technique. The argent field of the shield diapered with a trail of maple leaves, now very faint. The bend is a strip of pot-metal ochre, blacked out with paint to leave the charges showing. Lion is pot-metal ruby, the ochre crown separately leaded. Shield is set on a white background diapered with trails of oak leaves and acorns.

Date. c. 1320–2.

A3. Shield of Cornwall

h. 0·40 m. w. 0·35 m. Shield: h. 0·23 m. w. 0·20 m.

Argent a lion rampant gules, crowned or, over all on a bend sable three mullets or CORNWALL OF BURFORD.

Condition. Complete, but extensive corrosion, particularly on the coloured glass.

Colour and Technique. As A2.

Date. c. 1320–2.

B2. Shield of Cornwall

h. 0·40 m. w. 0·35 m. Shield h. 0·23 m. w. 0·20 m.

Argent on a fess sable three bezants or CORNWALL OF ASTHALL.

Condition. Incomplete, the field of the shield made up with alien pieces of foliage diaper and patterned strip. Glass very corroded.

Colour and Technique. Original background to shield of oak leaves and acorns as A2.

Date. c. 1320–2.

ASTON ROWANT

ST. PETER AND ST. PAUL

OS. SP 726 991

PRINTED SOURCES

N.O.A.S. Report (1886), 9–14.

Nelson (1913), 161.
Bouchier (1918), 63.
V.C.H. viii (1964), 38–9.
Pevsner (1974), 426–7.

There are only slight remains of fourteenth- and fifteenth-century glass in two windows, n. IV and n. IX. The present arrangement of the glass was probably made during the extensive restoration work begun in 1874, when the north wall of the nave was demolished, or during the general restoration by E. G. Bruton of 1884.[1] It was described in its present position in the short description published in 1886.[2] There has been some recent damage to the glass and small portions have been broken out deliberately.

The extant fourteenth-century glass is now all to be found in the tracery lights of two windows. Only one large figure remains, and is incomplete. This is a figure of Christ, probably from a representation of the Virgin and Christ in Majesty. Apart from this there is no evidence concerning the iconography of this series of windows.

The fifteenth-century glass is less fragmentary, and included a representation in the tracery lights of Christ and the Virgin seated in Majesty, flanked on either side by figures of angel musicians. Two lights survive, but not in their original order. A comparable arrangement in tracery lights of Christ and the Virgin in Majesty flanked by figures of angels (cherubim and censing angels) can be found in the east window of the chancel at Combe.

There is no surviving evidence or record of the subjects in the main lights of the windows.

It has been stated that 'the coats of Arms in the windows of the north chapel recorded by Rawlinson have disappeared'.[3] This is a mistake. Neither the published Parochial Collections[4] nor the Rawlinson MS. there cited contain a note of this.

Mr. M. C. Farrar Bell has recently releaded all the old glass.

n. IV

A2. Panel of Fragments

h. 0·50 m. w. 0·42 m.

Composite panel of fragments of different dates. All the pieces are corroded on both surfaces.

The principal pieces are: the heads of two females, painted on white glass, early 14th c.; fragments of white geometric grisaille, painted with a trail of oak leaves and acorns; a large border piece, a crowned 'M' of white glass and yellow stain; a similar border piece of a crowned 'M'; pieces of border design of white oak leaves, early 14th c.; border design of crowned initials, an 'M', an 'N' set inside out, and remains of one other, possibly a 'J', second half 14th c. Similar initials are used in the background diapers of the figures in New College, Oxford,[5] but the examples here are definitely border pieces as they are slightly curved to fit the cusping of a light.

A3. Panel of Fragments

h. 0·50 m. w. 0·42 m.

Pieces of white border grisaille, similar to the above, and oak border pieces, as above. A large fragment of background foliage diaper of vine leaf design. All fragments are corroded on both sides.

B2. Christ in Majesty

h. 0·50 m. w. 0·42 m.

Christ seated, crowned and holding an orb.

Condition. The panel is a restorer's composite of early and late 14th-c. glass. The figure of Christ is incomplete. The

[1] V.C.H. viii (1964), 38.
[2] N.O.A.S. (1886), 9–14.
[3] V.C.H. viii (1964), 39.

[4] P.C. (1920), 13.
[5] Woodforde (1951), pl. 12.

right hand and arm are missing, and missing portions of the drapery have been patched with plain white glass. The glass is corroded on both surfaces.

Colour and Technique. The nimbus is ruby, the crown pot yellow, and the face is painted on white glass with matt and smear shading. The cloak is white over a pot yellow tunic, with strong smear shading on the drapery.

Iconography. Christ seated holding an orb. The three-quarter turning pose suggests that this figure was originally part of a larger composition, not necessarily in a tracery light, which may have been a Coronation of the Virgin, or a Virgin and Christ seated in Majesty.

Style and Design. The style is similar to that of Merton College Chapel, Oxford (*c.* 1289–96),[1] particularly in the arched eyebrows and the slightly lugubrious cast of the mouth, but the painting style of the Aston Rowant figure is more modelled, with strong shading on the draperies.

Date. First quarter 14th c.

n. IX

PLATE 14 (*d*), (*e*), (*f*), (*g*)

A2. Fragments. 14th and 15th c.

h. 0·56 m. w. 0·18 m.

A panel of fragments. Canopy design showing an interest in perspective, painted in white and yellow stain against pieces of plain green, mid 14th c. Fragment of diaper flooring, white and yellow stain, 15th c. Two fragments of white quarries, one type 11, the other type 36. White and yellow stain, 15th c. All the glass is corroded.

A3. Fragments

h. 0·56 m. w. 0·18 m.

A panel of fragments, comprising a torso of a kneeling figure in prayer, pot yellow ochre mantle, blue tunic with strong smear shading, hands in white glass all set inside out. Early 14th c., probably the same date as the Christ in Majesty, n. IV, B2. Fragment of bold ivy-leaf diaper painted on white glass, possibly part of a tracery design, 14th c. Fragment of foliage design in white and yellow stain of a leaf and bordering, probably from an eyelet tracery. Two fragments of quarries types 27, 28 white and yellow stain, 15th c. Very little corrosion on the 15th-c. glass.

A4. Angel playing a Harp

h. 0·56 m. w. 0·18 m.

An angel full length facing three-quarter right, playing a harp, on a tiled floor set against a foliage background with a repeated border pattern.

Condition. The panel was complete but has been damaged since September 1963, and a portion of the glass at the apex of the light is now missing.

Colour and Technique. The whole panel is painted on white glass with extensive use of yellow stain for the angel's hair, harp, and wings, the veins of the background foliage diaper, and the repeated pattern of the border. Very fine stipple on the draperies. Parts of the foliage diaper are painted on the same piece of glass as the angel's wings and tunic. There is a slight use of stipple shading.

Style and Design. The workmanship is competent, but the style is rather crude and clumsy, particularly in the extreme elongation of the figure, the awkwardness of the hands and the static quality of the over-all design.

Iconography. Perhaps originally placed in A2, pendent to the Virgin and Christ in Majesty in lights A3 and A4.

Date. Second half 15th c.

A5. Christ in Majesty

h. 0·56 m. w. 0·18 m.

Christ seated holding an orb.

Condition. Incomplete. Christ's right hand, arm, and part of his face are missing, and the figure is set inside out. As with A4, there is a fragment missing in the apex of the tracery light subsequent to September 1963. Much of the original foliage diaper background is missing, and has been replaced with alien fragments of 14th- and 15th-c. glass.

Colour and Technique. The whole panel is painted on white glass with the cross of Christ's nimbus, his hair, beard, and tunic, and the repeated border pattern in yellow stain. There was originally a foliage-design diaper background identical to that of A4, of which only the apex area remains.

Iconography. Christ seated in benediction holding the orb. This was probably part of a composition of the Virgin and Christ in Majesty occupying the tracery lights A3 and A4 of this window, flanked by angel musicians. This panel has been described as 'Christ seated at a table',[2] and was interpreted by Bouchier as 'The institution of Our Lord's Supper'.[3] There is no evidence of a table, and Bouchier's suggestion can be disregarded.

Style and Design. The background diaper is identical to that of the angel in A4, and there is particular affinity in the drawing of Christ's hair, eyes, and nose. The drapery painting here is more fluid, and has more volume than the figure of the angel. The drawing of the hand is more articulate, and these slight differences suggest that this is probably the work of a more competent painter of the same workshop.

Date. Second half 15th c.

---

[1] R.C.H.M. (1939), pl. 145 (16).   [2] *V.C.H.* viii (1964), 39.   [3] Bouchier (1918), 63.

B2. Foliage Design *in situ*

h. 0·20 m. w. 0·18 m.

At the centre a large white rose set against a white foliage design with a repeated border pattern.

Condition. Incomplete. The right hand and lower lobes are missing and have been replaced with alien 15th-c. glass. One quarry, type 46.

Colour and Technique. Painted on white glass, the veins of the leaf and border pattern are in yellow stain.

Date. Second half 15th c.

BECKLEY

ASSUMPTION OF ST. MARY THE VIRGIN

OS. SP 563 113.

MS. SOURCES

Oxford. Bodleian Libary:
  MS. Top. Oxon. b. 75, ff. 58–9. The Wyatt Papers, 18th–19th c.
  MS. Top. Oxon. b. 220, f. 52. Church notes, *c.* 1804–40, attributed in part to J. E. Robinson.
  MS. Don. c. 90, f. 125. Notes dated 1804.
  MS. Don. c. 140, f. 82. Hinton's church notes, dated 1806.

PRINTED

Parker (1846), 205–8.
P.C. (1920), 34–5.
Nelson (1913), 127.
Bouchier (1932), 127.
Pevsner (1974), 447–8.

There are slight remains of what must have been a most interesting series of windows of the fourteenth and fifteenth centuries. The nineteenth-century church notes do not describe the glass in detail but an anonymous note of 1804 records 'several fragments of stained glass very antient, in the west window Christ with the reed in his hand'.[1] The latter figure is also noted by Hinton in 1806, but he specified the fragments as being 'several fragments of figures in glass very ancient'.[2] The figure of Christ has either not survived, or this is a misinterpretation of one of the remaining figures.

There is some more detailed information in D. P. Powell's notes of the 9 November 1803: 'There's only a scrap or two of painted glass left, representing St. Christopher wading over a river and the fish swimming about his feet and O(ur) S(aviour) on his shoulders directing him and St. James the Greater with his staff and script—these are of the more modern sort of glass. The windows and E(ast) window of the chancel in the ——[3] style with bits of glass such as I have generally found in those sort [*sic*] of windows.'[4]

Parker's published account of 1846 notes in the east window of the chancel and two side windows, 'in the heads of these windows are some beautiful remains of painted glass of the fourteenth century'.[5] It is known that some restoration of the glass took place after 1846. A note in the Wyatt papers states, 'When the Architectural Guide[6] was written the chancel contained some good remains of fourteenth-century glass. A case of this glass was sent to Mr. Skidmore[7] of Coventry and most unfortunately lost on the railway.'[8] It is not known if this glass was ever recovered; however, the three chancel windows mentioned in the Architectural Guide still contain fourteenth-century glass, much restored. It is probable that this restoration took place *c.* 1895 when the Victorian glass was inserted in the chancel windows. The restoration work is extremely clever and very difficult to detect. The techniques employed are close to those used by the Canterbury restorers Caldwell & Son.

The fourteenth-century glass appears to be of three different dates. First the Assumption of the Virgin

---

[1] Bodl. Lib. MS. Don. c. 90, f. 125. See also Robinson's Church Notes, f. 52, where the figure is not identified.
[2] Hinton's Church Notes, f. 82.
[3] The style is unspecified in the text.
[4] Wyatt Papers, f. 59.

[5] Parker (1846), 205.
[6] i.e. Parker (1846).
[7] The name is loosely scrawled in the script (reading confirmed by D. E. O'Connor).
[8] Wyatt Papers, f. 58.

(s. II), early fourteenth century. Second, the Assumption and Coronation of the Virgin (window I), and the St. Edmund (n. II), second quarter of the fourteenth century. Third, the St. James Major and St. Christopher (n. V), probably of the third quarter of the fourteenth century. There is no documentary evidence to substantiate the suggested datings and the divisions are based on differences in style and technique.

The first Assumption of the Virgin (s. II) appears to be the earliest in date. The painting has a somewhat archaic character but the use of yellow stain precludes a dating before c. 1310. The second group (windows I and n. II) is in a different style, with a linear emphasis in the painting of the faces, but with plastic modelling in the draperies. Although no other examples of this workshop are to be found in the county, it does have some similarity with glass elsewhere in the Midlands. A date in the second quarter of the century seems likely. The St. James Major and the St. Christopher (n. V) are quite distinct in style and design; no coloured glass is used, only white glass and yellow stain. Again there is nothing else in the county that can be attributed to the same workshop. They probably date from the third quarter of the fourteenth century.

The fifteenth-century glass depicts St. Anne teaching the Virgin to read (n. IV) and some quarries (s. V). The figures of St. Anne and the Virgin are extremely close in style and design to the figure of St. Bartholomew at Yarnton. This association, together with a general affinity with the Ante-chapel windows of All Souls College, Oxford, of 1441–7, suggests a date in the second quarter of the century.

The surviving glass shows a particular devotion to the cult of the Virgin Mary, containing scenes of her education by her mother St. Anne, her Assumption (represented twice), and her Coronation by Christ. This devotion was doubtless influenced by the dedication of the church to the Assumption of the Virgin Mary. In addition, the presence of the Benedictine nuns of Stukely Priory within the parish[1] may have had some influence on the choice of subjects.[2] However, there is no evidence as to the identity of the donors of the windows except for an incomplete inscription of the fifteenth century now lost.

I

1a, 1b, 1c. Canopies and Border Design

h. 0·28 m. w. 0·46 m.

Condition. Extremely restored, only small scraps are original: the traceried window behind the main arch in 1b; the apex crocketed gable in 1c; and part of the foliage diaper ground.

Colour and Technique. White glass and yellow stain, foliage diaper in pot-metal.

Style and Design. The canopies are too fragmentary to justify comment. The thin arabesque leaf trails of the foliage ground are a common characteristic of the second quarter of the 14th c.

Date. Second quarter 14th c.

A1. The Coronation of the Virgin

PLATES 1(*a*), 15(*a*), (*b*)

h. 0·56 m. w. 0·46 m.

The Virgin crowned by Christ.

Condition. The glass has been very skilfully restored. The original pieces have corrosion on both sides but there is no excessive pitting of the glass.

Colour and Technique. Pot-metal coloured glass. The Virgin has an ochre mantle over a green tunic, white flesh, hair and crown in yellow stain. Christ has a white mantle over a light-green tunic, white flesh, green throne. Strong smear shading with matt wash. Plain ruby ground with sprays of white vine leaves and grapes, individually leaded.

Iconography. Neither figure has a nimbus. Christ places the crown on the Virgin's head, a type established by the mid 12th c.[3] The earliest extant examples in English glass painting are at Canterbury Cathedral, c. 1200,[4] and Aldermaston (Berks.), 13th c.[5]

Style and Design. The quality of the design is uneven, the bodies of the figures are the same size, but their heads are disproportionate to each other. The figures are in three-quarter view, facing each other, their legs overlapping. This rather compressed design is probably the result of adapting the composition to fit a quatrefoil tracery light. The border

[1] *V.C.H.* ii (1907), 77–8.

[2] The 12th-c. seal of the Priory has a representation of the Annunciation. *V.C.H.* ii (1907), 78.

[3] G. Zarnecki, 'The Coronation of the Virgin on a Capital from Reading Abbey', *Journal of the Warburg and Courtauld Institutes* xiii (1950), 1–12.

[4] B. Rackham, *The Ancient Glass of Canterbury Cathedral* (1949), 51.

[5] Nelson (1913), pl. ix.

design is a repeated pattern of quatrefoils, white glass and matt paint, mostly restoration.

Date. Second quarter 14th c.

A2. The Assumption of the Virgin, and St. Thomas receiving her girdle   PLATES 1(*b*), 16(*a*), (*b*)

h. 0·56 m. w. 0·46 m.

The Virgin, carried by angels, hands her girdle to St. Thomas.

Condition. As A1. Slight exterior corrosion of the original glass, no deep pitting.

Colour and Technique. Pot-metal coloured glass. The Virgin has a puce tunic, white flesh, hair in yellow stain, ochre shroud. The girdle is green. St. Thomas has a green tunic, white flesh. The angels have white albs, wings in yellow stain. The tomb is white. Strong smear shading with matt wash. Plain ruby background.

Iconography. The episode of St. Thomas receiving the girdle is a late addition to the apocryphal legend of the Assumption.[1] It probably originated in Italy after the acquisition of the relic of the girdle by Prato in the 12th c.[2] The story was repeated in the *Golden Legend* as being apocryphal,[3] and was also discredited by later writers such as St. Antoninus, Bishop of Florence (1389–1459)[4] and Petrus de Natalibus, Bishop of Equilio (d. 1400).[5] The subject was probably first illustrated in Italian art.[6] Extant representations in British art are not common, except for the period *c.* 1290–1340,[7] and in the later 15th c.[8] The earliest example in English glass painting is probably the panel in the east window of the Stapleton Chantry at North Moreton (Berks), *c.* 1299.[9] The acquisition by Westminster Abbey of a relic of the girdle may have been the cause of the apparent popularity of the subject *c.* 1290–1340, although in the later Middle Ages the relic was thought to have been given by St. Edward the Confessor (d. 1066).[10] The Beckley panel is unusual in the reclining position of the Virgin, as she is carried upwards by the angels, and she herself hands down the girdle to St. Thomas, instead of standing upright with the girdle falling from her. The Virgin does not have a nimbus as in panel A1

above. Although much restored, the unusual composition is more likely to be original rather than an invention of the nineteenth-century restorer.

Style and Design. Executed by the same hand as panel A1. The smaller proportions of the figures, although partly dictated by the narrative, suggest that the two panels are not in their original relationship to each other. The Coronation was probably in the apex tracery light, now filled with modern glass. Another narrative panel, either the Death or Funeral of the Virgin, probably occupied panel A1 pendent to the Assumption. The border design is the same as A1, all restored.

Date. As above.

n. II   PLATES 1(*c*), 15(*c*), (*d*)

A1. St. Edmund

h. 0·56 m. w. 0·46 m.

St. Edmund, crowned and nimbed, holding two arrows.

Condition. Much restored. Only the white background, the hand holding the arrows, the shafts of the arrows, and part of the border are genuine.

Colour and Technique. The saint has an ochre mantle and shoes, green tunic, and white flesh. He stands on a green hillock. Painted in brown with strong smear and matt shading. White background painted with trails of leaves in outline. This arrangement is original; the saint's left hand and the adjacent foliage are painted on the same piece of glass. Border: repeated squared rosette pattern in yellow stain.

Iconography. A royal saint, crowned and nimbed, holding two arrows, no identifying inscription. The attributes suggest that the figure is St. Edmund, last King of the East Angles, born *c.* 840, and martyred by the Danes in 870.[11] Although he was finally decapitated, he is almost invariably represented holding arrows,[12] symbolizing the penultimate torture of his martyrdom. The centre of his cult was at

---

[1] 'The Assumption: Narrative by Joseph of Arimathea' in M. R. James, *The Apocryphal New Testament* (1960 edn.), 216–18.

[2] G. Bianchini, *Notizie istoriche intorno alla sacratissima cintola di Maria Vergine, che si conserva nella cita di Prato in Toscana* (1722). G. C. Trombelli, *Maria Sanctissimae vita ac gesta cultusque* (1761–5), sec. iii, cap. i, ii.   [3] *Golden Legend* iv, 241.

[4] Antoninus of Florence, *Chronicon partibus tribus distincta ab initio mundi ad MCCCLIX* (Venice, 1474–9), 3, tit. 8, c. 4, para. 2.

[5] Petrus de Natalibus, *Catalogus Sanctorum* (1369–72) (Lyons, 1508), lib. VII, cap. LXV, f. 193.

[6] Fresco at Spoleto, 12th c. G. Kaftal, *The Iconography of the Saints in Central and Southern Italian Painting* (1965), 1080–2, fig. 1261.

[7] Wall-paintings at Chalgrove (Oxon.), Broughton (Oxon.), and Croughton (Northants.), see A. Caiger-Smith, *English Medieval Mural Paintings* (1963), 161, 165, with full bibliography. Opus Anglicanum: The Syon Cope, 1300–20, and the Pienza Cope, 1315–35, see A. G. I. Christie, *English Medieval Embroidery* (1938), nos. 75 and 95. MS.

painting: The De Lisle Hours of the Virgin, *c.* 1320–30. Glazier MS., f. 161ᵛ, New York, Pierpont Morgan Library (Sotheby's Sale Catalogue, May 19th, 1958, 23 illus.). See plate 17 (*a*).

[8] Illustrated Catalogue of the Exhibition of English Medieval Alabaster Work. *The Society of Antiquaries* (1913), nos. 53, 54, 58, 59.

[9] Chantry founded 1299. *V.C.H. Berkshire* iii (1923), 496–7. M. D. Anderson, *Drama and Imagery in English Medieval Churches* (1963), 153, wrongly dates this panel as 15th c.

[10] John Flete, *History of Westminster Abbey*, ed. J. Armitage-Robinson, (1909), 70.

[11] The various Lives of St. Edmund are collected in 'Memorials of St. Edmund's Abbey', ed. T. Arnold, *Rolls Series* xcvi, i, ii, iii (1890, 1892, and 1896).

[12] A rare exception, where he is shown holding a scimitar, is found in the Pembroke Hours, *c.* 1460, Philadelphia Museum of Art, MS. Collins, 46, 65, 2, f. 43.

Bury St. Edmunds, Suffolk, where his body was enshrined.[1] The iconography of his life was established by the 12th c.[2] Single figures of the saint holding one, two, or three arrows are very common in the later Middle Ages, and the earliest extant examples are of the thirteenth century.[3] The popularity of his cult may reflect the veneration accorded to him by various kings of England from Edward the Confessor onwards.[4]

This panel is perhaps identical with the one, formerly in the west window, which was described as 'an ancient portrait with a Reed in one of the hands', and also as 'Christ with the reed in his hands'.

Style and Design. The drawing and modelling, if copied from the lost original, are so close to A1 and A2 in window I, as to justify an attribution to the same hand.

Date. Second quarter 14th c.

s. II

A1. The Assumption of the Virgin   PLATES 1(d), 16(c), (d)

h. 0·56 m. w. 0·46 m.

The Virgin in a mandorla carried by angels.

Condition. Complete, except for slight 19th-c. restorations.[5] The coloured glass is extensively corroded, particularly the pale pink (?) used for heads and hands which now appears brown.

Colour and Technique. The Virgin has a white robe. Angels: upper left, yellow stain tunic, ruby wings, pot yellow censer; centre, yellow stain mantle, ruby tunic, blue wings; lower, ruby mantle, yellow stain tunic, blue wings; upper right, pink (?, now brown) tunic, green wings, pot yellow censer; lower, ochre mantle, ruby tunic, green wings. Mandorla, plain border in yellow stain, enclosing a ruby field diapered with a foliage design. White background diapered with a foliage design, some pieces painted on the same glass as the adjacent plain border. Painted in brown with slight smear and matt shading.

Iconography. The Virgin carried up in a mandorla by four angels, with two censing angels above, commonly found in the 13th and 14th c.[6]

Style and Design. There is a general similarity, particularly in the drawing of the Virgin's head and the foliage background diaper, with the glass of Merton College Chapel,

Oxford (1289–96). However, the glass is of a much smaller scale, and detailed comparisons should not be made.

Date. Early 14th c.

n. III

1a, 1b. Roundels

d. 0·10 m.

Six roundels, one incomplete, inserted in the cusped heads of the two main lights. Probably intended for the centre of tracery lights in a foliage surround.

Colour and Technique. All white glass and yellow stain with stippled and matt shading.

Style and Design. Two types of design:
   (a) Three complete roundels and one fragmentary roundel of a foliage design of four identical trefoil leaves pointing inwards from the cusped outer border.
   (b) Two complete roundels of two interlocking triangles, with a rosette at their centre, on a foliage background.

Date. 15th c.

A1. Foliage Design

h. 0·32 m. w. 0·40 m.

Condition. In situ, incomplete, lower lobe missing.

Design. At the centre a large ruby rosette, very decayed, set on white glass, upper lobe painted with a single serrated leaf, side lobes plain. The border is a repeated pattern of contiguous rosettes and diamonds, in white and yellow stain, scratched out of matt wash.

Date. 15th c.

n. IV

1a. St. Anne and the Virgin

h. 0·66 m. w. 0·28 cm.

St. Anne left, the Virgin facing her and holding an open book.

Condition. The figures are complete, but there is a pronounced corrosion on both surfaces, and the paint is much worn. The original background is missing. Now set on modern quarries with imitation 15th-c. pattern.

[1] M. R. James, 'On the Abbey of St. Edmund at Bury', *Cambridge Antiquarian Society Publications* xxviii (1895).
[2] The earliest extant illustrated Life is a 12th-c. copy of Abbo of Fleury's *Passio Sancti Eadmundi* (original text written *c.* 985), New York, Pierpont Morgan Library, MS. 736.
[3] Secretum seal of Hugh of Northwold, Abbot of St. Edmondsbury and Bishop of Ely, example dated 1235. C. H. Hunter Blair, 'Durham Seals', in *Archaeologia Aeliana*, 3rd series, xiv (1917), 270–1. Glass roundel at Saxlingham Nethergate (Norfolk). See

C. Woodforde, *B.S.M.G.P.J.* v (1933–4), 163–4. The Cuerdon Psalter (Canterbury?, post 1262), New York, Pierpont Morgan Library, MS. 756, f. 9.
[4] Newton i (1961), 248–9.
[5] Bouchier (1932), 127, wrongly states that this panel is 'very restored'.
[6] For the iconography of the Assumption see T. S. R. Boase, *The York Psalter* (1962), 8–14. See also p. 30 n. 1 above.

Colour and Technique. White glass, except for the light-blue tunic of St. Anne and the Virgin's light-blue cote-hardi. Painted in brown with stippled matt shading, drapery patterns picked out in yellow stain.

Iconography. There is no known literary source for this subject of St. Anne teaching the Virgin to read. In the Apocryphal Gospels[1] and the later texts of St. Anne's life,[2] the instruction of the Virgin begins in the Temple after she had left her parents. Rushforth suggested that the subject was invented by an English artist in the late 13th c.[3] Perhaps the earliest extant representation is the wall-painting at Croughton, Northants., of the late 13th, early 14th c.[4] There appears to be no earlier example known on the Continent.[5]

The importance of England in the development of the cult of the Virgin is well known.[6] Although the festival of St. Anne was not universally observed in England until the Edict of Pope Urban VI, issued in November 1378,[7] there is evidence that her cult was established here by the 12th c. Her feast was kept with an octave at Worcester in the time of Bishop Simon, 1125–50,[8] and later at Shrewsbury.[9] Reading Abbey acquired a relic before the end of the century.[10]

Style and Design. There is a very close affinity in design with the figure of St. Thomas Apostle at Yarnton, I, 2b. The drapery pattern of groups of three small rosettes, the drawing of the hands, and the large nimbus in relation to the size of the heads are very similar. They were probably produced by the same workshop.

Date. Second quarter 15th c.

2a. Roundel
d. 0·90 m.

Monogram 'MAR' for Maria. White glass and yellow stain, background in matt wash 15th c.

n. V

1a. St. James Major and St. Christopher   PLATE 17 (*b*)
Figures: h. 0·38 m. w. 0·18 m.

St. James, left, vested as a pilgrim, facing St. Christopher who bears the Christ Child.

Condition. Well preserved, some slight exterior corrosion. The original surrounds are missing, now set on modern white quarries. The upper part of St. Christopher is modern.

Colour and Technique. Painted in brown on white glass with strong smear and matt shading and yellow stain. St. James has a blue hat. The fish in the water at the feet of St. Christopher are painted on the reverse of the glass.

Iconography. St. James wears a pilgrim's hat and holds a staff, attached to which is a wallet, with a scallop shell on its flap. The idea of distinguishing St. James by the pilgrim's wallet and staff originated in Spain in the 12th c.[11] The hat appears to have been introduced in the late 13th c. as a piece of deliberate realism. Different variations of the basic type have been distinguished and are common throughout Europe, except for Germany and Italy.[12]

Style and Design. St. James stands on a curious pedestal, his feet are painted on the same glass as this, so the arrangement is original. The small size suggests that the figures were originally set in tracery lights. They are identical in style and technique, presumably by the same artist whose work is not found elsewhere in the county.

Date. 14th c. (? third quarter).

s. V

2a, 2b, 2c. Quarries
Each quarry: h. 0·15 m. w. 0·11 m.

Thirteen complete quarries, the others fragmentary. Identical design, type 40, a fructed rose branch. All very corroded. Painted in brown on white glass, with stippled matt shading and slight yellow stain.

Late 15th c.

Lost Glass

Rawlinson records an inscription in the east window of the south aisle of the nave: 'orate pro animabus Thome Fowler armig(eri)'.[13] This Thomas Fowler of Buckingham was esquire of the body and gentleman of the chamber, to Edward IV and Richard III.[14] In April 1484 he was granted

---

[1] M. R. James, *The Apocryphal New Testament* (1960), 42 and 73.

[2] R. E. Parker, 'The Middle English Stanzaic Versions of the Life of St. Anne', *E.E.T.S.*, original series (1928), 174.

[3] Rushforth (1936), Bodl. Lib. MS. Douce 231, f. 3. This MS. however is probably to be dated post 1322.

[4] E. W. Tristram and M. R. James, 'Wall Paintings in Croughton Church', in *Archaeologia* lxxvi (1927), 79.

[5] J. Lafontine-Dosogue, 'Iconographie de l'enfance de la Vierge dans l'Empire Byzantin et en Occident', *Académie Royale de Belgique, Memoires*, tome xi, fasc. 3 et derniers (1965–6), ii. 107–9.

[6] R. W. Southern, 'The English Origin of the Miracles of the Virgin', *Medieval and Renaissance Studies* iv (1958), 177–216. See also G. Zarnecki, op. cit. 11–12.

[7] D. Wilkins, *Concilia Magnae Britanniae* iii (1737), 178–9.

[8] E. Bishop, 'On the Origin of the Feast of the Conception', *Liturgica Historica* (1928), 248.

[9] Bodl. Lib., MS. Rawlinson D. 1225, f. 83. Martirologium of St. Chad, Shrewsbury. *Natale sanctissime Anne gloriose genetricis semper virginis marie*, added in late 12th-c. hand to the Calendar.

[10] B.L. Egerton MS. 3031, f. 7ʳ. List of Relics: *De sancta anna matre sancte marie. Item de sepulchro eius.*

[11] E. Mâle, *L'Art religieux du XII siècle en France* (1928), 294 seq., and E. Mâle, *L'Art religieux du XIII siècle en France* (1910). Mâle's remarks should be compared with the detailed study by C. Hohler, 'The Badge of St. James', *The Scallop*, ed. Cox (1957), 51–69.

[12] Ibid. 65.

[13] P.C. (1920), 35.

[14] A. H. Lloyd, 'Two Monumental Brasses in the Chapel of Christ's College', *Cambridge Antiquarian Society Proceedings* xxxiii (1931–2), 61–82.

the office of Parker of the park of Beckley. Although, as a Yorkist, he received a general pardon in October 1485, he was removed from this office in the following year, when it was granted to Ralph Verney.[1] Fowler died before

March 1511. Although the inscription requested prayers for the souls of Fowler and, presumably, his wife, the window was doubtless made during his tenure as Parker, 1484–6.

BEGBROKE
ST. MICHAEL

O.S. SP 468 139.

PRINTED SOURCES

Willement, T., *A Concise Account of the Principal Works in Stained Glass* (1840), 16.

Parker (1846), 111.
Pevsner (1974), 449–50.

A miscellaneous collection of English and Continental glass ranging in date from the fifteenth century to the nineteenth century. Much of the glass was given by Mr. Thomas Robinson,[2] the son-in-law of Alderman W. Fletcher, a notable collector of medieval glass.[3] The glass was arranged and leaded into the windows by Thomas Willement, the stained-glass artist and antiquarian, in 1827.[4]

s. II

1a. St. Frideswide (?)   PLATE 17 (c)
h. 0·18 m. w. 0·13 m.

The nimbed head of a crowned nun, wearing a black habit, facing three-quarters right.

Condition. Incomplete, only the head remains, probably from a full-length standing figure.

Colour and Technique. Painted on a single piece of white glass, the crown and cusped border of the nimbus in yellow stain. The black habit is painted on both sides of the glass. The features are modelled with very delicate stippled shading.

Iconography. The figure who wears a black habit and is crowned is possibly St. Frideswide, the patron saint of Oxford, whose body was enshrined at Christ Church, Oxford.[5] Representations of her are extremely rare.[6]

Style and Design. The head type, with linear drawing of the eyes and bulbous tip of the nose, is standard early 15th-c.

Date. First quarter 15th c.

3a. God the Father   PLATE 17 (d)
h. 0·19 m. w. 0·13 m.

God the Father, half-length, facing three-quarters right, his hands raised before his chest.

Condition. Incomplete, possibly part of a larger composition depicting the Trinity. Slight pitting on the exterior.

Colour and Technique. Painted on white glass, the hair, beard and patterned hem of the tunic in yellow stain. Drapery folds modelled with stippled shading and cross hatching.

Iconography. The cross nimbus and elderly head with a long flowing beard suggest God the Father.

Style and Design. The large cross nimbus, large in proportion to the size of the head, has parallels in the windows of the Ante-chapel of All Soul's College, Oxford, *c.* 1441–7.[7] The careful painting and head type suggest an early 15th-c. style.

Date. 15th c., *c.* 1400–30.

n. III

3b. Roundel. Joseph being thrust into the well
d. 0·25 m.

In the centre foreground Joseph is thrust into the well by his brothers. On the extreme right the slaughtering of the

[1] Lloyd, op. cit., 69.   [2] Willement, op. cit.   [3] See Yarnton.
[4] The date of Willement's own glass made for the church.
[5] *Acta Sanctorum October* viii (1853), 568–89, *Nova Legenda Angliae*, ed. C. Horstmann (1901), 457–61. 'The Lives of Women Saints of our

Own Countrie of England', ed. C. Horstmann, *E.E.T.S.*, o.s. lxxx (1886), 80–1.
[6] *Herder* vi (1974), 331. See also Binsey and Kidlington.
[7] Hutchinson (1949), pls. i, ii, vi.

sheep; in the upper left background Joseph seeking his brothers; on the right Joseph taken out of the well and sold to the Ishmaelites.

Condition. Complete, painted on a single piece of glass. Slight pitting on the exterior. The glass has two old cracks, mended and backplated by Mr. M. C. Farrar Bell in 1976.

Colour and Technique. Painted on white glass, details picked out in yellow stain, stippled shading.

Iconography. The three scenes depict part of the story of Joseph (Genesis 37: 13–31).

Style and Design. The composition is probably a close copy of a lost design by the Master of the Story of Tobit, an anonymous follower of Hugo van der Goes, working *c.* 1470.[1] Related copies are found in a circular panel painting at Berlin[2] and a drawing by Jan Swart van Groningen, working *c.* 1522–33.[3]

Date. Early 16th c., Flemish. The costumes have been brought up to date.

n. IV

3a. Roundel. Tobit drawing the Fish out of the Water. 16th c.

d. 0·24 m.

Condition. Complete, painted on a single piece of glass. Slight exterior pitting, the paint is rather worn.

Colour and Technique. Painted on white glass, details picked out in yellow stain, stippled shading.

Iconography. The scene illustrated is part of the story of Tobit (Tobit 6: 1–4).

Style and Design. A close copy of the drawing by an associate of the Master of the Story of Tobit, working *c.* 1470.[4] Other copies of the same design are noted by A. E. Popham.[5] Another example is now in the Cloisters Museum, New York.[6]

Date. Early 16th c., Flemish.

s. IV

1a. Roundel. Coronation of the Virgin by the Trinity
d. 0·23 m.

God the Father seated left and God the Son seated right holding a crown above the head of the Virgin who sits before them. Above them the Holy Spirit in the form of a dove. Angels stand behind the throne. In the border are attendant figures of forty-six saints and the symbols of the four evangelists.

Condition. Complete, painted on a single piece of glass. Slight exterior pitting, the paint has worn thin in places.

Colour and Technique. Painted on white glass, details picked out with yellow stain, stippled and matt shading.

Iconography. The combination of the Coronation of the Virgin with a commemoration of All Saints and the symbols of the Evangelists is uncommon. Some of the saints can be identified by their attributes: at the top SS. Paul, Peter, John Baptist, John Evangelist, and Andrew; centre right SS. Anthony Abbot, Giles, and Anthony of Padua; lower centre SS. Cecilia, Agnes, Barbara, and Margaret; centre left SS. Cornelius Pope, Stephen, Lawrence, Denis, and Christopher.

Style and Design. The composition is probably derived from a mid 15th-c. design. It can be compared with the panel painting dated 1457 by the French artist, the Master I.M., now in the Kunstsammlung at Basle.[7] The drawing and painting are rather sketchy.

Date. Second quarter 16th c., Flemish.

3a. Roundel. Jael and Sisera

d. 0·21 m.

Jael is shown in the centre left foreground hammering a tent peg into the head of the sleeping Sisera. Landscape background with a battle in progress.

Condition. Complete, painted on a single piece of glass.

Colour and Technique. Painted on white glass, extensive use of yellow stain, stippled and matt shading.

Iconography. The scene depicts the death of Sisera (Judges 4: 1–24, particularly 17–21, and Judges 5: 24–6). The roundel does not conform to the Bible text. The scene takes place in a landscape instead of Jael's tent. This subject was popular in the late Middle Ages when Jael's triumph over Sisera was regarded as a prefiguration of the Virgin Mary's victory over the devil.[8]

Style and Design. The figures of Jael and Sisera are possibly loosely based on a design by the Master of Flemalle, known

[1] A. E. Popham, 'Notes on Flemish Domestic Glass Painting', *Apollo* viii (1928), 175–9.
[2] A. E. Popham, 'Die Josefslegende', *Berliner Museum Jahrgang* (1931), 73–6.
[3] A. E. Popham, *Catalogue of Drawings by Dutch and Flemish Artists in the British Museum* v (1932), 45–7.

[4] A. E. Popham, *Apollo*, op. cit. 177, fig. 1.
[5] Ibid.
[6] Accession no. 34.24.22.
[7] Inventory no. 473.
[8] The comparison is made in J. Lutz and P. Perdrizet, *Speculum Humanae Salvationis* i (1907), 63.

from a pen-and-ink copy now in the Landesmuseum, Brunswick.[1] The subject was popular in German and Flemish art of the 16th c. and the representations are varied.[2]

Date. First quarter 16th c., Flemish.

s. V

2b. Roundel. Joseph meeting his Father Jacob
                                                    PLATE 17 (*e*)
d. 0·22 m.

In the centre foreground Joseph, left, embraces his father Jacob. Jacob's wives and children emerge from a rocky landscape on the left, on the right two men doffing their caps. More of the retinue, four men and a camel, are shown at the top behind rocks.

Condition. Complete, painted on a single piece of glass. Extensive but not deep pitting on both surfaces.

Colour and Technique. Painted on white glass with extensive use of yellow stain. The paint is light brown in colour. Extremely delicate stippled and matt shading.

Iconography. The roundel has not previously been identified. The scene probably depicts Joseph meeting his father Jacob, 'At the first sight of him, he threw his arms about his neck and embraced him in tears' (Genesis 40: 29–30).

Style and Design. The composition is probably a close copy of a lost design by the Master of the Story of Tobit.[3] No comparable example of this composition has been found. However, the style, particularly the modelling of the drapery and details of costume, is very close to the three drawings of the story of Joseph, now in the Ashmolean Museum, Oxford, which are associated with the Master of the Story of Tobit.[4] The quality of the Begbroke roundel is first class and is without doubt the most important piece of Flemish glass painting to be found in the county.

Date. 15th c., *c.* 1470–80, Flemish.

BINSEY

ST. MARGARET

OS. SP 486 081

MS. SOURCES

Oxford. Bodleian Library:
  MS. Don. c. 90, f. 170ᵛ. Drawing dated 1801.
  MS. Top. Oxon. c. 313, f. 164ᵛ. Drawing by W. Hurst, dated 1908.

PRINTED

Parker, J., 'An Account of Binsey Church' *O.A.H.S.* N.S. ii (1864–7), 191–4.

Wood, A., 'A Survey of the Antiquaries of the City of Oxford Composed in 1661–6', ed. A. Clark, *O.H.S.* xvii (1890), 41–3.
Nelson (1913), 161.
Bouchier (1932), 127.
R.C.H.M. (1939), 148–9.
Greening Lamborn (1949), 110.
Pevsner (1974), 457.

The few remaining fragments of medieval glass are collected in the east window of the church. The arrangement was probably made in 1833 when the east wall of the chancel was rebuilt.[5]

Binsey was closely associated with the eighth-century St. Frideswide of Oxford, who, according to legend, built the original chapel and dedicated it to St. Margaret.[6] It was dependent upon her other foundation at Oxford, later the Augustinian Priory of St. Frideswide (now Christ Church Cathedral).[7] This historical connection is important as the two remaining fragments of fourteenth-century glass (2a, 2b) are undoubtedly by the workshops responsible for the Latin Chapel windows at Christ Church. One of these fragments (2b) originally came from a large panel of the martyrdom of St. Thomas Becket. Although the

---

[1] E. Panofsky, *Early English Netherlandish Painting* i (1953), 175, ii, pl. 104, fig. 225.
[2] F. Holstein, *German Engravings, Etchings and Woodcuts* (1949–74), 202. M. J. Friedländer and J. Rosenberg, 'Die Gemälde von Lucas Cranach', *Jahresgabe der Deutschen Vereins für Kunstwissenschaft* (1932), fig. 193. A. Pigler, *Barokthemen* (1956), 110. Herder ii (1970), 360–2.
[3] See p. 34 n. 1 above.
[4] K. T. Parker, *Catalogue of Drawings in the Ashmolean Museum,*

Oxford i (1938), nos. 8, 9, 10.
[5] Parker, op. cit., 193.
[6] See the Latin Life in *Legenda Anglie*, ed. C. Horstman, i (1901), 457–61. Also the English version in Bodl. Lib., Ashmole MS. 43, f. 153ʳ.
[7] 'The Cartulary of St. Frideswide', ed. S. R. Wigram, *O.H.S.* xxviii (1895), I, 10–11.

veneration of Becket was so widespread that this choice of subject does not require a particular explanation, it is interesting to note that Robert of Cricklade, prior of St. Frideswide's *c.* 1141–75, composed a book on the miracles of Becket.[1]

Anthony Wood, in his survey of 1661–6, recorded 'in one window part of St. Frideswide's picture'.[2] No proof of the identification is given. This figure has either disappeared since that date, or Wood's interpretation is of one of two remaining figures (2a, 2b).

The description of the extant glass given in the Royal Commission inventory[3] is very misleading. The figure of Edward Grim from the Becket panel (2b) is described as 'a man in civil costume', and the composite fifteenth-century figure (2c) as 'a female saint or angel with a book'.

I

1a, 1b, 1c. Quarries

Each quarry: h. 0·15 m. w. 0·11 m.

1a. Seven quarries, six type 17, one type 24.

A fragment. Head of a grotesque (? monkey) possibly part of a border piece. Yellow stain. *c.* 1350.

1b. Six quarries. All type 41.

1c. Eight quarries. Six type 17, one type 24, and one type 7.

Condition. All the quarries have pronounced exterior corrosion.

Colour and Technique. White glass, the design painted in line with stippled matt shading and yellow stain. The latter varies considerably in intensity, from pale lemon to deep orange.

Date. Late 15th c.

2a. Roundel. Female Head

d. 0·23 m.

Condition. Incomplete, a fragment of a jewelled hem (15th c.) has been inserted as a crown on the head. The face is cracked, and part of the flashed ruby ground has flaked off. Pronounced corrosion and lichen growth on both surfaces.

Colour and Technique. White face, hair in yellow stain, green neckband with blue clasp. Ruby ground diapered with trail of foliage, circular leaves. Painted in brown with smear and matt shading.

Iconography. Roundels of this size are very rare, compare Dorchester I, 5b, 5e. The plain outer border to the ruby

ground suggests that the present format is original. No nimbus. Identity of the figure unknown.

Style and Design. Extremely close to the female saints in the Latin Chapel at Christ Church, Oxford.[4]

Date. c. 1340.

2b. Martyrdom of St. Thomas Becket

h. 0·35 m. w. 0·23 m.

Condition. Incomplete, the upper part of the figure of Edward Grim and the legs of two of the four knights only remain. There is considerable corrosion on the exterior.

Colour and Technique. Painted in brown on white glass, with smear and matt shading, details of armour and hair in yellow stain.

Iconography. This fragment had not been identified. The identification of the subject is suggested by the figure holding a cross-staff with blood running from a wound in his forearm. The *Vita Sancti Thomae auctore Edwardo Grim* relates how the author was struck on the arm by the same sword blow which mortally wounded the saint in the head.[5] Becket was murdered in 1170, and canonized in 1173. The iconography of the martyrdom seems to have been established by *c.* 1200.[6] The wounded Grim is almost invariably shown holding a cross-staff,[7] and, although the later texts[8] state that he was a monk and the archbishop's cross-bearer, it is known that he was a secular clerk and that his presence at the martyrdom was fortuitous.[9]

Style and Design. Closely related to the female head (2a, above), and the Latin Chapel glass at Christ Church, Oxford.

Date. c. 1340.

---

[1] 'Thomas Saga Erikibyskups', ed. E. Magnusson, *Rolls Series* lxv. 2 (1883), xcii.

[2] Wood, op. cit. 43.

[3] R.C.H.M. (1939), 149.

[4] R.C.H.M. (1939), pl. 99.

[5] 'Materials for the History of Thomas Becket', ed. J. C. Robertson, *Rolls Series* lxvii. 2 (1876), 437.

[6] T. Borenius, *St. Thomas Becket in Art* (1932), ch. iv. T. S. R. Boase, *English Art, 1100–1216* (1953), 204, 288–9.

[7] The earliest datable example occurs on the counterseal of Hubert Walter, Archbishop of Canterbury 1193–1205. Borenius, op. cit. 74.

[8] *Golden Legend* ii. 195.

[9] Robertson, op. cit. xlv. 'Vita Sancti Thomae auctore Herberto de Boseham', *Rolls Series* lxvii (1877), 3, 498.

2c. Composite Figure

h. 0·45 m. w. 0·24 m.

Condition. The head of a female saint, associated with an incomplete torso of another figure holding a book. The head is extensively cracked, plated on the reverse, and all the glass is very badly corroded, with lichen growth on both surfaces. A drawing of 1801 shows the glass in much the same condition as now.[1]

Colours and Technique. White glass painted in brown with stipple shading, details picked out in yellow stain.

Iconography. The saint is probably St. Margaret, the patron saint of this church. Nimbed, she wears a chaplet of rosettes. The head of a cross-staff is painted on the same glass. A cross-staff, with which she subjected a dragon, is the common emblem of St. Margaret.[2]

Style and Design. The delicate drawing of the head is similar to one in All Souls College Chapel, Oxford, for example the St. Mary Magdalen of *c.* 1441–7.[3]

Date. Second quarter 15th c.

3a, 3b, 3c. Fragments

Fragments: mostly post medieval, but some small pieces of foliage diapers, 14th c., and two heraldic fragments, a *cross-crosslet sable*, and a *fleur-de-lis sable*, 14th c.

1b. A Shield

Argent three piles gules.

Identified by Greening Lamborn as 'probably fifteenth century'.[4] The glass is plain, unpainted, and the texture appears distinctly post medieval.

BIX

ST. JAMES

O.S. SU 728 853

Pevsner (1974), 457.

PRINTED SOURCES

Greening Lamborn, E. A., 'The Churches of Bix', *Oxoniensia* i (1936), 129–39.

Two panels of French early sixteenth-century glass are set in two north windows of the nave. They were brought here from the desecrated former parish church abandoned in 1875.[5] Their original provenance is not known. It has been conjectured that the panels were acquired when the Revd. John Cooper was the incumbent from 1785 to 1802.[6]

n. IV   PLATE 18 (a)

2a. Joseph meeting his Father Jacob (?)

h. 0·63 m. w. 0·47 m.

A young man stands left embracing an elderly man who genuflects before him, two kneeling women on the right observe the meeting, set in a landscape with two soldiers in the top background.

Condition. Incomplete. The missing portions of the landscape have been made up with modern white glass. General condition is good, slight pitting on the white glass, ruby glass is very corroded. Old breaks repaired with thick leads.

Colour and Technique. Left-hand figure has a ruby mantle over a light-blue robe, the centre figure has a white mantle and robe, the shoulder piece of the mantle, clasp, and cuffs, hem and hat decoration picked out in yellow stain. The woman on the extreme right has a murrey dress with ochre sleeve of an undertunic, ornaments of her head-dress in yellow stain. Landscape in white glass with accidental splashes of yellow stain. The draperies are finely drawn with stipple shading and cross hatching.

Iconography. The panel has been identified as 'a Merchant and his wife'.[7] This is unsatisfactory. The composition with the elderly man half-kneeling before the younger man, who leans forward to embrace him, and the fact that none of the figures are nimbed suggest an Old Testament scene, possibly Joseph meeting his father, Jacob (Genesis 40: 29–30).

Style and Design. The panel has been described as French[8] and also as Flemish, late 15th c.[9] A French origin is more likely.

[1] Bodl. Lib. MS. Don. c. 90, f. 170 v.
[2] *Golden Legend* iv. 66–72.   [3] Hutchinson (1949), pl. xv.
[4] Greening Lamborn (1949), 110.

[5] Greening Lamborn, op. cit. 129.
[6] Ibid., 134.   [7] Ibid., 134.
[8] Ibid., 134.   [9] Pevsner (1974), 457.

Date. First half 16th c.

1a. Modern inscription at the base of the light. 'This window was reset in memory of Hugh Edward Hoare Churchwarden who died July 1929.'

n. V

2a. The Miracle at Cana   PLATE 18 (*b*)
h. 0·63 m. w. 0·48 m.

Christ stands left, his hand raised in blessing. The Virgin Mary and an apostle stand behind. On the right, seven stone jars being filled with water. The heads of the bridal pair at the top centre.

Condition. Incomplete. A large section is missing and is made up with modern, plain, white glass; the heads of the bridal pair have been shattered at some time and have been repaired with thick lead work. Much of the drapery painting is in poor condition.

Colour and Technique. The Virgin has a white wimple and white mantle patterned with a repeated flower design in yellow stain, purple tunic. Christ has a murrey robe, patterned hem, and cuffs in yellow stain; apostle and bridal pair in white glass; ruby curtains. The pots in white with yellow stain bands. Architecture painted on white glass with marbling and splashes of yellow stain.

Iconography. The miracle at the marriage feast at Cana when Christ changed the water into wine (St. John 2: 1–12).

Style and Design. Like the other panel, this also has been described as French, and as Flemish, late 15th c.[1] A French origin seems more likely. The use of perspective is quite developed.

Date. 16th c.

1a. Modern inscription at the base of the light: 'This window was reset in memory of Robert Riches who died March 1923 also of Elizabeth Emily Riches.'

BLOXHAM
ST. MARY

O.S. SP 431 356.

PRINTED SOURCES
Nelson (1913), 161.

Oscar Moreton, C., 'The Story of Bloxham Parish Church', *Parish Guide*, n.d., 12.
Pevsner (1974), 477–80.

The remaining glass is now collected together in one window and has been described by Nelson as 'a few fragments of decorated glass'. It consists of a number of fairly complete panels of similar design which probably came from three windows all of the same date. The panels of geometric grisaille in the heads of the main lights are painted with trails of oak leaves and acorns (2a, 2b, and 2c); those in the quatrefoil tracery lights have trails of ivy leaves (A2, A3). The borders of each also differ. The smaller traceries also have ivy-leaf trails, but here the borders of the quarries are in yellow stain, (A1, A4, B1, B3). It is these differences in detail which suggest that the glass comes from three windows of similar design.

Each of the three large quatrefoil tracery lights has a human head at the centre. The head of Christ is modern (B2); the other two are probably to be identified as St. Peter and St. Paul respectively (A2, A3). They have no attributes, the identification is suggested by the traditional tonsure of St. Peter and the bald head of St. Paul. The arrangement of nimbed heads set simply against a background of quarries could be original. There are irregularities: the nimbus of St. Peter forms a regular surround to the head, whereas that of St. Paul does not. An examination of the cut edge of the adjacent quarries would be the only way to establish whether this arrangement is medieval.

The glass is so very decayed that it is difficult to be precise about its date. If it is coeval with the architecture, a dating in the second quarter of the fourteenth century is most probable.

[1] See p. 37 n. 7 and 8 above.

n. VI

Condition. All the glass is very corroded and the details are indistinct.

2a, 2b, 2c. Geometric Grisaille and Borders
h. o. 40 m. w. 0·60 m.

Colour and Technique. A trellis of white quarries of rather irregular shape, at the centre of each light a vertical stem with off-springing asymmetrical trails of oak leaves and acorns. Border of pot-metal glass; ochre cups, white fleurs-de-lis, and ochre castles alternating with pieces of plain ruby. Inserted border piece: a bird displayed, colour indistinct.

A1, A4, B1, B3. Geometric Grisaille
h. 0·40 m. w. 0·20 m.

Trellis of white quarries painted with sprays of maple leaves, borders of the quarries in yellow stain.

A2. Head of St. Peter, Geometric Grisaille, and Borders
h. 0·60 m. w. 0·60 m.

Colour and Technique. Border design of fleurs-de-lis altern-ately ochre and white, alternating with pieces of plain ruby. Quarries as 2a above, except that here the foliage is ivy. Head of St. Peter painted on white glass, hair in yellow stain, plain ruby nimbus.
Inserted border piece: a grotesque dragon, white and yellow stain.

A3. Head of St. Paul and Borders
h. 0·60 m. w. 0·60 m.

Colour and Technique. Borders and quarries as A2. Head of St. Paul painted on white glass, hair in yellow stain, plain ruby nimbus.

B2. Head of Christ, Quarries, and Borders
h. 0·60 m. w. 0·60 m.

Colour and Technique. Borders and quarries as A2 above. The head of Christ is modern, except the ruby glass in the nimbus. Inserted border pieces: an owl, a heron, a grotesque (indistinct), also the head of a large grotesque dragon, all white and yellow stain.

Date. All the glass is 14th c., probably the second quarter.

BRIGHTWELL BALDWIN
ST. BARTHOLOMEW

O.S. SP 653 950.

MS. SOURCES
Oxford. Bodleian Library, MS. Top. Oxon. d. 88, f. 12–12ᵛ. Oxfordshire Collection. Collections of T. Delafield, dated 1747.

PRINTED
Visitations (1871), 83–4.

Nelson (1913), 161.
Bouchier (1918), 66–7.
P.C. (1920), 52–5.
Bouchier (1932), 127.
Coxe, H., *St. Bartholomew's Brightwell Baldwin* (1934).
Greening Lamborn (1949), 111–13.
Pevsner (1974), 484–5.

The extensive remains of fourteenth- and fifteenth-century glass constitute one of the most important collections in the county. Although there has been a certain amount of restoration *c.* 1895, the work was well done and complements the original glass.

The fourteenth-century glass consists of two figures of SS. Peter and Paul set beneath canopies, unfortunately the latter have been cut down to fit their present position (n. IV, 2a and 2b). As both figures are facing right, it seems possible that they are part of a series of figures of the Twelve Apostles rather than a pendent pair. Also of the fourteenth century is the Virgin Annunciate (s. VII, A2). This figure may have been at the centre of a large canopy design, probably from either the east window of the south aisle or the east window of the chancel, as these are the only windows big enough to accommodate such a design.

The fifteenth-century glass has interesting examples of different scales and classes of design. The St. Paul and Virgin Annunciate (n. III, 2a and 2b) are large figures against coloured backgrounds with canopies above. The small Crucifixion (n. II, 2b) has no pot-metal-coloured glass, the only colour is yellow stain. The Annunciation (s. V, 3a and 3b) is probably an even cheaper class of design, figures set against quarries, although this arrangement may be a restorer's composite.

n. II

2b. The Crucifixion

h. 0·71 m. w. 0·34 m.

Christ: h. 0·42 m. w. 0·23 m.
Virgin: h. 0·30 m. w. 0·11 m.
St. John: h. 0·33 m. w. 0·12 m.

Christ on the Cross, between the Virgin Mary and St. John Evangelist.

Condition. The figures survive intact together with a small portion of the original background, the remainder replaced by plain white quarries. The original glass has extensive light corrosion; the details of the design are clear.

Colour and Technique. No coloured glass, painted in dark-brown paint on white glass with stippled and line cross-hatched modelling. Extensive use of yellow stain for details of hair, nimbs, patterned drapery, hems, and the underside of the cross.

Iconography. The Virgin and St. John stand either side of Christ, who is represented dead on the cross. Standard late medieval type.

Style and Design. Originally the figures were set against a background diaper of a seaweed foliage design. The small portion that remains is adjacent to, and painted on the same pieces of glass as, the body of Christ and transverse beam of the Cross. An unusual feature for a design of this small scale is that the figures of the Virgin and St. John each have a very large nimbus. There is some affinity between the figure of Christ and the one now in the east window of Merton College, Oxford, I. 3b.[1] The heads are similar with long strands of hair framing the face and falling down on to the chest. The Brightwell Baldwin artist, however, has a less fluid and more broken style of line painting.

Date. Second quarter 15th c.

n. III

1a, 1b. Quarries

Panel: h. 0·48 m. w. 0·46 m. Quarries: h. 0·14 m. w. 0·10 m. Quarries: type 46, six complete, eight fragmentary, and three modern copies in panel 1a: six complete, eleven fragmentary, and three modern copies in 1b. All 14th c.

Quarries: 1a, one type 22, two type 18. 1b, two type 18.

Condition. The present arrangement is a restorer's composite, the border pieces have been cut down. All the quarries are corroded, the 15th-c. ones in particular, the paint very worn.

Colour and Technique. All white glass with yellow stain.

Borders. Repeated pattern of a trellis design enclosing fleurs-de-lis, yellow stain on a matt black background. 15th c.

Date. 15th c.

2a. St. Paul Apostle

PLATE 19 (*a*), (*b*)

h. 0·86 m. w. 0·51 m.

St. Paul, full length, facing three-quarters left, an open book in his left hand, a sheathed sword, point downwards, in his right.

Condition. The panel has been carefully restored, the modern pieces are splashed with dark paint to imitate corrosion. The original white glass is well preserved, but the coloured glass is very corroded, almost opaque in parts. In addition there is lichen on both surfaces, particularly strong on the reverse of the coloured glass.

Colour and Technique. The saint's head, hands, attributes, and mantle are painted on white glass; brown paint with very light stipple and line shading; details of hair, borders of the nimbus, mantle, and sword belt in yellow stain. Pot-metal ruby tunic. Blue background diapered with a seaweed foliage design. Canopy sideshafts in white glass and yellow stain.

Iconography. Bouchier identified this figure as 'either St. Paul or the patron St. Bartholomew'.[2] Both saints were beheaded.[3] However, from the early 13th c. onwards, St. Paul is generally represented holding a sword[4] whereas St. Bartholomew's usual attribute is a knife, symbolizing the penultimate torment of his martyrdom when he was flayed alive.[5] No example of St. Bartholomew holding a sword has been found. In addition the Brightwell Baldwin figure has a bald head and a long flowing beard, consistent features in medieval representations of St. Paul. It would

---

[1] R.C.H.M. (1939), pl. 147.
[2] Bouchier (1918), 67.
[3] The early texts differ in their accounts of the martyrdom of St. Bartholomew. See *Acta Sanctorum, Augusti* (1761), v. 34, 38, 40, and 44. Also the *Golden Legend* v. 37 and 41.

[4] E. Mâle, *L'Art religieux du XIII siècle en France* (1931), 365. Braun, J. *Tracht und Attribute der Heiligen in der Deutschen Kunst* (1943), 590. G. Kaftal, *Iconography of the Saints in Central and South Italian Painting* (1965), 852–3.
[5] Mâle, op. cit. 365. Braun, op. cit. 120. Kaftal, op. cit. 153.

therefore appear that Bouchier's alternative identification is not acceptable, and that the Brightwell Baldwin figure is a St. Paul.

Style and Design. The style is very linear, the modelling of the drapery folds is extremely delicate, with slight contrasts of tone. There is some affinity in drawing with the figures of Apostles in the Ante-chapel of All Souls College, Oxford, of *c.* 1441–7,[1] but there the drapery modelling is much stronger. See also panels 3a and 3b below.

Date. Second quarter 15th c.

2b. The Virgin Annunciate PLATE 19 (*a*), (*b*)

h. 0·86 m. w. 0·51 m.

The Virgin Mary, full length turning to the left. The Holy Dove flying down beside her face, a large pot of lilies by her feet.

Condition. Extensively restored in the same manner as the St. Paul, 2a, above. The original glass is very corroded, particularly the coloured glass. The nimbus is completely opaque. Lichen on both surfaces as panel 2a above.

Colour and Technique. White glass except for the Virgin's blue tunic and ruby background. Extensive use of yellow stain for the Virgin's hair, the repeated rose-design pattern and hem of her mantle, the lily pot, and details of the canopy side shafts. Brown paint with very light stippled and line shading, very slight back painting on the mantle. Ruby background diapered with a seaweed foliage design.

Iconography. The Holy Dove and pot of lilies establish that this is the Annunciation scene, but the panel is too incomplete for detailed comment. It is possible that in the original glazing scheme there was a pendent panel of the Archangel Gabriel.

Style and Design. Certain points of design suggest that this panel is the work of the same hand as the St. Paul, panel 2a. The drawing of the eyes and ears is identical, and there is the same very thin modelling of the drapery. The repeated large rosette pattern on the mantle is similar in type to the patterned draperies of the female saints in the Ante-chapel of All Souls College, Oxford,[2] but the precise pattern is not duplicated there.

Date. Second quarter 15th c.

3a. Canopy

h. 0·43 m. w. 0·51 m.

Condition. Almost complete, one inserted piece, set inside out, from an identical canopy design, restoration at the apex of the light. Corrosion on both surfaces but the design is clear.

Colour and Technique. The canopy is painted on white glass; brown paint with delicate stipple and line shading. Details of cusps, crockets, and ornament picked out in yellow stain. Set against a ruby background, diapered with a seaweed foliage design.

Style and Design. 3b below is identical in design. There is a general affinity with one of the canopy designs in the Ante-chapel windows of All Souls College, Oxford, of *c.* 1441–7. For example, compare the canopy in the St. Matthias panel.[3] There are similarities in the projecting broad vaulted niche, with pendant bosses at the centre flanked by two smaller vaulted niches, each with a crocketed gable above. The proportions are different, the All Souls canopies are more elongated and the small details of decoration are not the same.

Date. As above.

3b. Canopy

h. 0·43 m. w. 0·51 m.

The design is identical with 3a above, except that here the background seaweed foliage diaper is blue. Two pieces of the canopy and part of the background diaper are restoration. Corrosion on both surfaces but the design is clear.

A1. Shield of Stody

h. 0·23 m. w. 0·20 m. Shield: h. 0·13 m. w. 0·13 m.

Ermine on a saltire engrailed sable a leopard's head or STODY.[4]

Condition. Recorded in this window by Wood in 1658.[5] However, the shield and its surround appear to have been cut down slightly at the top to fit their present position. Slight corrosion, old leaded repairs.

Colour and Technique. White glass, dark brown paint. The leopard's head and foliage diaper background to the shield in yellow stain, plain white border with a small rosette design in the top foil of the light.

Style and Date. Greening Lamborn assigned the shield to John Stody who was Lord Mayor of London in 1357.[6] He was a Vintner and a benefactor of the Company.[7] He died in 1376.[8] William Stody, Vintner, who died in 1378 may have

---

[1] Hutchinson (1949), 17.
[2] Ibid., pls. xiv–xviii.
[3] Ibid., pl. xii.
[4] College of Arms MS. B. 22. Collingborne's Book, no. 373, *c.* 1490.
[5] P.C. (1920) 52–5, Wood's notes are dated 15 Apr. 1658, Oxford, Bodl. Lib., Wood MS. B. 15, f. 49. The 1574 Visitation does not give

the shield's location and tricks the leopard's face as *a bezant or.* Visitations (1871), 83–4.
[6] *Calendar of Letter Books . . . (etc.) of the Corporation of London,* ed. R. R. Sharpe (1904), Letter Book F. 78, 241, 268, 286.
[7] J. Stow, *A Survey of London,* Introduction and notes by C. L. Kingsford i (1971 edn.), 106, 240.
[8] *Letter Books,* op. cit. Letter Book H. (1907), 41.

been his son.[1] A 14th-c. dating for the shield is not in accordance with the sketchy painting of the foliage diaper, painted on the same glass as the shield. The style suggests a later 15th-c. date. The Stody family had no known connection with the manor of Brightwell Baldwin. Greening Lamborn suggested a possible connection with the Barentine family[2] whose shield of arms is in the adjacent light, A2, below.

Date. 15th c.

A2. Shield of Barentine

Panel: h. 0·23 m. w. 0·20 m. Shield: h. 0·12 m. w. 0·10 m. *Sable three eagles displayed argent beaked and legged or* BAREN-TINE.

Condition. Complete, old leaded repair, possibly *in situ* but now set inside out. Slight corrosion, the paint is very worn.

Colour and Technique. White glass, dark brown paint, back painting on the eagles, their beaks and legs in yellow stain. The shield is set against a patterned background diaper of contiguous circles picked out of a matt brown wash on yellow stain. Plain white border with a rosette design in the top foil of the light.

Style and Design. Rather unsophisticated work; little attention to detail in the drawing of the eagles. This and the shield of Bereford in the adjacent light, A3 below, appear to be the work of the same glass painter.

Date. 15th c. The Barentines of Chalgrove were overlords of a manor in Brightwell Baldwin.[3] Drew Barentine was a member and benefactor of the Goldsmiths' Company, London,[4] Lord Mayor of London 1398–9 and again in 1408.[5] He died in 1416–17.[6] This London connection may explain the display of the Stody arms, A1 above.[7] The shield was recorded in this window by Wood in 1658.[8]

A3. Shield of Bereford

Panel: h. 0·23 m. w. 0·20 m. Shield: h. 0·12 m. w. 0·10 m. *Argent crusily fitchy and three fleurs-de-lis sable* BEREFORD.

Condition. Complete, old leaded repair, slight corrosion.

Colour and Technique. Painted on white glass, the patterned

background, border, and rosette in the top foil are identical with A2 above.

Style and Design. See A2 above.

Date. Greening Lamborn[9] attributed this shield to John Bereford, Mayor of Oxford, and a contemporary of John Stody (see A1 above). John Bereford has no known connection with the family at Brightwell Baldwin. Lee noted a shield of Bereford with an inscription *Baldwin Bereford militis*;[10] Wood's notes confirm that a Bereford shield was in this window.[11] This shield may have been additional to the one in the tracery light; the latter is complete, and there is no room for an inscription; unless, of course, the extant shield is a modern copy omitting the inscription. The glass appears to be genuine. Baldwin Bereford, noted in the lost inscription, succeeded his brother John to his lands in the manor of Brightwell Baldwin, and died without issue by March 1406.[12]

A4. Shield of Waters

Panel: h. 0·23 m. w. 0·20 m. Shield: h. 0·12 m. w. 0·10 m. *Sable on a chief argent three chaplets or* WATERS.

Date. Modern version of a shield blazoned by Lee as *sable on a chief argent three chaplets gules bossed or.*[13] Lee gives two examples of this shield, one with the inscription *Henry Waters and Julian his wife.* Wood did not note them in 1658, so they had disappeared by then. The display of these arms has not been accounted for.

n. IV

1a. Quarries and the Weighing of a Soul   PLATE 2 (*a*)

Panel: h. 0·48 m. w. 0·45 m. Quarries: h. 0·14 m. w. 0·10 m.

Condition. A composite panel, much restored, the modern portions splashed with paint in imitation of corrosion. Quarries: two type 2, 15th c., very corroded, one other with the Stafford knot badge, 15th c., very corroded, the paint completely perished. All the other quarries are modern imitations.

The Weighing of a Soul: a hand holding a balance, in the left pan a half-length naked soul in prayer, a book in the

---

[1] *Letter Books*, op. cit. 103, 141. His heir appears to have been his daughter Agnes; his widow Isabella married Philip Derneford, also a Vintner.

[2] Greening Lamborn (1949), 113.

[3] Ibid. Pedigrees in *Notes and Queries* clxxxi (1941), 156, and clxxxiii (1942), 190, 350.

[4] Stow, op. cit. i. 305. Greening Lamborn (1949), 113.

[5] *Letter Books*, op. cit. Letter Book H, 445. Letter Book I, 69–70. *Notes and Queries* clxxxiii, op. cit. 350.
Greening Lamborn (1949), 113.

[8] See p. 41 n. 5 above.

[9] Greening Lamborn (1949), 113.

[10] Visitations (1871), 83.

[11] P.C. (1920), 55. The transcript is defective in parts. See Wood's MS. Bodl. Lib. Wood MS. B. 15, f. 49.

[12] G. Baker, *The History and Antiquities of the County of Northampton* ii (1823–30), 682. *Cal. of Patent Rolls*, Henry IV, 1401–5, 402–3, 405. Ibid. 1405–8, 162. *V.C.H. Berks* iii (1923), 547. Greening Lamborn (1949), 111.

[13] Bodl. Lib. Wood MS. D. 14, f. 90ᵛ. The chaplet is also given in trick. The published transcript is incomplete and inaccurate. Visitations (1871), 84.

left pan, a winged devil attempts to pull down the pan with a pronged fork.

Condition. Incomplete, part of a larger composition, the hand and balance are modern restorations. The original glass well preserved.

Colour and Technique. Painted on white glass with slight touches of yellow stain, stippled and matt shading.

Iconography. St. Michael weighing souls is sometimes combined with a miracle of the Virgin saving a soul, 'the Blessed Virgin Mary came in to his help and laid her hand upon the balance wherein were but few good deeds. And the devil enforced him to draw on that other side.'[1] There are a number of representations of the scene in English mural paintings, a particularly fine example of the late 14th c. is at Swacliffe (Oxon.).[2]

Style and Design. The remains are so slight that detailed comment is difficult, particularly as there are no comparable examples in the county. The strong stippled modelling and perspective view of the scales suggest a mid 14th-c. date.

Date. 14th c., *c.* 1350–70.

Border Design. A serpentine trail of vine leaves and grapes. Painted on white glass, grapes in yellow stain against a matt black background. 14th c. Four pieces are genuine, the rest are modern imitation.

1b. Quarries

Panel: h. 0·48 m. w. 0·45 m. Quarries: h. 0·14 m. w. 0·10 m.

Condition. A composite panel, much restored as 1a above. Five complete and nine fragmentary, quarries type 46, painted on white glass, centre rose and borders in yellow stain. 14th c.

Border. As 1a above, 14th c. Six pieces are modern imitation.

2a. St. Peter Apostle   PLATE 2 (*b*)

h. 0·86 m. w. 0·51 m.

Full length facing three-quarters right, his head turned three-quarters left, two large keys in his raised left hand.

Condition. Incomplete, much of the lower part of the figure and adjacent background is modern restoration. The original portions are very corroded and covered with lichen on the exterior.

Colour and Technique. Ochre pot-metal nimbus, head and right hand on pink glass, pot-metal ochre mantle over a white tunic, patterned hem in yellow stain. The left hand holding the keys is painted on the same glass as the adjacent background, keys in yellow stain. Background of white glass diapered with a delicate foliage design picked out of a matt black wash.

Iconography. He holds two keys, his standard attribute based on Christ saying to him, 'And I will give unto thee the keys of the kingdom of heaven' (Matthew 16: 19). Perhaps the earliest example is the 5th-c. mosaic in San Paolo Fuori le Mura, Rome.[3]

Style and Design. See 2b.

Date. 14th c. (second quarter).

2b. St. Paul Apostle   PLATE 2 (*c*)

h. 0·86 m. w. 0·57 m.

Full length facing three-quarters right, looking upwards. In his right hand he holds a sword by its point, its hilt resting against his shoulder.

Condition. Incomplete, the lower part of the figure and much of the adjacent background are modern restorations. Original portions as 2a above.

Colour and Technique. Pot-metal ochre nimbus, head and hands painted on pink glass, pot-metal ochre mantle over a ruby tunic. Background of white glass diapered with a delicate trail of vine foliage and grapes picked out of a matt black wash.

Iconography. He holds a sword, the symbol of his martyrdom. From the 13th c. onwards he is generally represented holding an unsheathed sword by its hilt, the point either downwards, resting on the ground, or upwards. At Brightwell Baldwin he holds a sheathed sword, the hilt upwards. This manner of holding the sword appears to have originated in France in the 13th c., although in the French examples he holds the sword with both hands.[4] Other English examples of this type occur in the glass at Stanford-on-Avon (Northants.), *c.* 1315–26,[5] in the 14th-c. copes at Toledo[6] and St. Bertrand de Comminges,[7] and in the 15th-c. glass at Great Malvern (Worcs.).[8]

Style and Design. The figures of St. Peter, 2a, and St. Paul are evidently companion figures, possibly part of a series

[1] *Golden Legend* iv, 252.

[2] This and other examples are noted in A. Caiger-Smith, *English Medieval Mural Painting* (1963), 61, pl. xxi.

[3] E. Mâle, *L'Art religieux du XII siècle en France* (1928), 252 n. 1. Damaged by fire in 1832. G. Kaftal, *Iconography of the Saints in Central and Southern Italian Painting* (1965), 867, cites the 8th-c. mosaic in the apse of S. Salvatore alla Scala Santa (Triclinio Leaniano), Rome, as the earliest example.

[4] E. Mâle, *L'Art religieux du XIII siècle en France* (1931 edn.),

365. Y. Delaporte and E. Houvet, *Les Vitraux de la cathédrale de Chartres* i (1926), 456, Window CXI, pl. ccxx.

[5] Newton i (1961), 223–4.

[6] A. Christie, *English Medieval Embroidery* (1938), 156–8, pl. cix, Panel 8, S(an)c(tu)s Paulus.

[7] Ibid. 129, pl. lxx, panel 13 (no label).

[8] Rushforth (1936), 102–3. Incomplete tracery light of the east window.

of the Twelve Apostles. The drawing of the features is extremely close even though the head types are, by tradition, quite different. The drapery folds with the mantle drawn around the right thigh then hanging in falling folds from the left arm are virtually identical. The drapery painting is very linear, there is no pronounced modelling. It is a very individual style, and the monochrome foliage diaper backgrounds are unusual. In head types, drapery painting, foliage diapers, and canopy design with perspective views, these figures appear to stand half-way between the earlier Merton College Chapel, Oxford, windows of *c.* 1289–96 and the Latin Chapel windows of Christ Church Cathedral, Oxford, of *c.* 1340.

Date. 14th c. (second quarter).

3a, 3b. Canopies

h. 0·43 m. w. 0·51 m.

Two identical canopy designs.

Condition. Incomplete, cut down to fit their present position. Slight corrosion but the design is clear.

Colour and Technique. Painted on white glass, slight smear shading, details picked out in yellow stain.

Style and Design. Two traceried side shafts, each terminating in a crocketed gable, flank the two figures, 2a and 2b. Over the head of each figure is an arch cusped cinquefoil surmounted by a crocketed gable and finial (the latter 15th c.). Within the gable is a roundel with a frontal lion's face between three trefoils; on either side of the gable is a small house structure with diagonally recessed side walls and a tiled roof; the latter is incomplete.

Date. First quarter 14th c.

A1. Shield

Panel: h. 0·23 m. w. 0·20 m. Shield: h. 0·15 m. w. 0·10 m.

Gules a chevron ermine between three quatrefoils voided with a crosslet on each UNIDENTIFIED.

Date. Modern, blazon probably copied from Lee's record of these arms.[1]

A2. Shield of Conyers for Norton (?)

Panel: h. 0·23 m. w. 0·20 m. Shield: h. 0·15 m. w. 0·10 m.

Azure a maunche ermine, in chief a martlet argent CONYERS for NORTON (?).[2]

Date. Modern. The 16th-c.[3] and 17th-c.[4] church notes do not record such a shield in the church.

A3. Badge   PLATE 20 (*a*)

h. 0·23 m. w. 0·20 m.

A hart couchant, in profile facing right.

Condition. Complete. Slight decay, the paint is flaking.

Colour and Technique. Painted on white glass, slight stipple shading, background in yellow stain patterned with line cross hatching, plain white border with a rosette in the top foil.

Style and Design. See A4.

Date. 15th c.

A4. Badge   PLATE 20 (*b*)

h. 0·23 m. w. 0·20 m.

A lion statant regardant.

Condition. Complete, slight corrosion.

Colour and Technique. As A3 above.

Style and Design. Both the hart and the lion could be proper heraldic badges; they could equally be heraldic motifs adapted as decorative designs.

Date. 15th c.

s. II, s. III, s. IV

Small scraps of 14th-c. glass are in the tracery lights of these windows. Not catalogued.

s. V

1a. Shield of Bereford

Panel: h. 0·27 m. w. 0·40 m. Shield and frame: d. 0·25 m.

Argent crusily fitchy and three fleurs-de-lis sable BEREFORD.

Circular frame inscribed in black-letter script:

| +*Insignia* | *Edmundi· de·* | *Bereford·militis·* | *Domini* | *huius* | *manerii·* |

Date. 19th c. Either a copy of a lost original[5] or a reconstruction based on Wood's notes.[6]

---

[1] Visitations (1871), 83.
[2] Identification suggested by Greening Lamborn (1949), 113.
[3] Visitations (1871), 83.   [4] P.C. (1920), 52–3.
[5] Lee, 1574, noted a shield of Bereford then in the east window of the chancel. Visitations (1871), 83. Wood noted the same arms in a chancel window. P.C. (1920), 54.

[6] Greening Lamborn (1949), 111, states that the present inscription 'restores one noted by Wood'. Wood, however, simply blazoned the shield and added 'by the name of Bereford, sometime Lord of this place'. Neither Lee nor Wood records the Christian name Edmund.

Sir Edmund de Bereford who died in 1354 held a manor in Brightwell Baldwin.[1] His lands there passed in succession to his two illegitimate sons, John[2] and Baldwin.[3] The latter died without issue c. 1404–6.[4]

The shield is set against fragments of medieval glass, including three border pieces, or parts of a canopy shafting patterned with a repeated design of lozenges, each enclosing an eagle displayed. The corner pieces have a cusped trefoil design, white and yellow stain. 14th c.

1b. Shield of Park

Panel: h. 0·27 m. w. 0·40 m. Shield and frame: d. 0·25 m.

Azure three stags' faces or PARK.

Circular frame inscribed in black-letter script

| +*Insignia·* | *Joh(ann)is· K*|*irby· Arm(igeri)·* | *Patroni* | *istius· eccl(es)iae* |

Date. 19th c., either a copy of a lost original or a reconstruction. The inscription is a misinterpretation of Wood's transcript: 'underneath writt, but imperfect ... *Joh kirby ... patroni istius .....*'.[5] Wood's reading of the surname is unsatisfactory. Lee's Visitation notes (1574) trick two shields of these arms with the name Park written above them.[6] In 1747 Delafield noted the same arms, then in the east window, together with an incomplete inscription that he read as: *An(im)a Joh(ann)is Park Patroni ist*—[7] The family of Park held lands in the manor of Brightwell Baldwin.[8] The John Park commemorated in the inscription is probably John Park of Brightwell who, with his wife Isabel, conveyed the lands in Bishopstone (Bucks.) to Richard Gurney in 1394.[9]

The shield is set against fragments of medieval glass, including four identical border pieces, each a lozenge enclosing a rose with a traceried design; the corner pieces each contain a trefoil flower, white and yellow stain. 14th c.

2a. Composite Panel

h. 0·27 m. w. 0·40 m.

Two 17th-c. shields set against fragments of medieval glass, pieces of crocketed pinnacles from canopy designs and two incomplete border pieces, each a white fleur-de-lis. 14th c.

2b. Composite Panel

h. 0·27 m. w. 0·40 m.

A 17th-c. shield is set against fragments of medieval glass:
Four border pieces as 1a above.
Pieces of border design, a serpentine stem, with off-springing leaves, a bird perched beneath each leaf, white and yellow stain. 14th c.
Border piece: a grotesque beast, its tongue terminating in two trefoil leaves, a shawl around its neck, white and yellow stain. 14th c.
An incomplete small female head, white and yellow stain. 14th c.

3a, 3b. The Annunciation

Panels: h. 0·74 m. w. 0·40 m. Figures: h. 0·34 m.

3a. The Archangel Gabriel   PLATE 19 (c)

Represented facing three-quarters right, holding a scroll, inscribed in black-letter script: | *Ave·* | *gracia· plena·d(omin)us·* |

3b. The Virgin Annunciate

Represented standing, a book in her left hand, her right hand held across her breast. A lily pot stands beside her feet.

Condition. The archangel is virtually complete except for the wings, only the lower tips remain. The Virgin and lily pot are complete, but are now set inside out. All the glass is extremely corroded on both surfaces.

Colour and Technique. No coloured glass, painted on white glass, light brown paint with very delicate stippled and line modelling. The archangel's hair, feathered legs and wings, and the Virgin's hair and body are in yellow stain.

Iconography. The scroll bears the opening phrase of the archangel's salutation to the Virgin (Luke 1: 28.) The literary origin of the motif of the Virgin's book is obscure.[10] The first known pictorial representation of it occurs on a 9th-c. ivory of the Metz school, where it is shown lying open on a prayer desk.[11] This formula was taken over in Anglo-Saxon art of the 10th c.[12] It is a common feature of later medieval art.[13]

The earliest known representation of a pot of flowers in the Annunciation scene is found in a 10th-c. Coptic Syn-

[1] *Cal. Inq. Post Mortem* x, Edward III, 249, 29 Edward III.
[2] Ibid., no. 321, 30 Edward III.
[3] *V.C.H. Berks* iii (1923), 547. Greening Lamborn (1949), 111.
[4] See p. 42 n. 12 above.
[5] P.C. (1920), 54, where the surname is read as *Kirb*—. Greening Lamborn (1949), 111, read it as '*Joh: pirb*—. Wood was probably misled by the script of the original. In black-letter script the capitals K and P are very similar in form.
[6] Visitations (1871), 83.
[7] Bodl. Lib. MS. Top. Oxon. d. 88, f. 12, op. cit.
[8] *Feudal Aids,* 1284–1431 iv. 172, 176. *Cal. Inq. Post Mortem* x, Edward III, no. 321, 31 Edward III.
[9] Greening Lamborn (1949), 111, pl. 44, citing a charter in the possession of Mr. E. G. Gurney of Eggington.
[10] The problems are fully discussed by Professor Pächt in O. Pächt, C. R. Dodwell and F. Wormald, *The St. Albans Psalter* (1960), 63–7.
[11] Pächt, op. cit. 67, pl. 117 *c.*
[12] Ibid. 66. The Benedictional of St. Ethelwold, B.L. Add. MS. 49598, f. 5ᵛ, and the Gospel Book of Boulogne, Bibliothèque Municipale, MS. 11, f. 11ʳ.
[13] For the later iconography of the Annunciation see G. F. Millet, *Recherches sur l'Iconographie de l'Évangile* (1916), 69–72, and D. M. Robb, 'The Iconography of the Annunciation in the Fourteenth and Fifteenth Centuries', *The Art Bulletin* xviii (1936), 480–525.

axary.[1] The motif is not found in Western Europe until the 13th c. In these early examples, the flowers are of generalized form, not yet a lily, and have been interpreted as a symbol of Spring, the time when the Annunciation took place.[2] In later examples the lily is commonly represented and symbolizes the Immaculate Conception[3] and also the body of Christ.[4]

Style and Design. The figures are set against a background of quarries. This is probably a restorer's composite. The figures are small-scale, and can hardly have been designed for their present position. The figure painting is of high quality. The style is curious; the elaborate cascade of drapery folds from the archangel's shoulder suggests that the artist may have been dependent on a 14th-c. model.

Date. Mid 15th c.

3a, 3b. Quarries

Each quarry: h. 0·15 m. w. 0·10 m.

The two panels contain thirty complete quarries and fragments of others, all very corroded, those in panel 3b are mostly set inside out.

Identical design, quarry type 1. Painted on white glass, the quatrefoil flower at the centre in yellow stain. 15th c.

A1. Fragment

h. 0·34 m. w. 0·10 m.

The centre portion of a large canopy, white and yellow stain, 14th c.

A2. Archbishop Saint

h. 0·34 m. w. 0·10 m.

Condition. Restored, all the centre portion is 19th c., the whole panel is now set inside out, corroded on both surfaces.
Colour and Technique. Painted on white glass, light-brown paint, background of white foliage against a line hatching on yellow stain.
Iconography. The nimbus, mitre, and head of a cross-staff indicate an archbishop saint, and are all painted on the same piece of glass. The 19th-c. portion is possibly a free invention as the crosses are not represented on the pall.

Date. Probably late 15th c.–early 16th c.

A3. Archbishop Saint

h. 0·34 m. w. 0·10 m.

19th-c. work, copying the original portions of A2.

A4. Fragments

h. 0·34 m. w. 0·10 m.

The centre portion of a shield of arms: *argent crusily fitchy and three fleurs-de-lis sable* BEREFORD. 14th c. For the family of Bereford see 1a above.

s. VI

2a. Composite Panel

h. 0·46 m. w. 0·50 m.

Condition. A composite panel of unrelated pieces. It is difficult to determine if any piece is *in situ*; however, the patterned background and rose design may belong here. Pieces include a white lion seated on green herbage. The lion is completely corroded and opaque. Much of the original paint is intact but only visible on close inspection. 14th c.

Background diaper: pattern of contiguous circles, each enclosing a crosslet, white glass, pattern scratched out of a matt wash of black paint. Some pieces have a plain border, curved to fit the head of a main light or tracery light. 14th c.

Border design: a line of diamond-shaped frames, each cusped quatrefoil, linked one to the other by an oculus cusped quatrefoil, yellow stain on a matt black background. The pieces are curved to fit into a cusped head or tracery light. 14th c.

A white rose: yellow central floret. 14th c. This could belong with the background diaper, but if this were so the absence of an enclosing border has to be accounted for.

2b. Composite Panel

h. 0·34 m. w. 0·50 m.

Condition. Composite panel as 2a above.

Contents include: background diaper, rose and traceried border as 2a; two other roses adjacent to the lower cusps, both incomplete; quarries: one complete and two half-quarries, type 10, painted on white glass, centre motif and borders in yellow stain. 14th c.

2c. Composite Panel

h. 0·46 m. w. 0·50 m.

Condition. Composite panel as 2a above.

Contents include: background diaper, roses and traceried border as 1a and 2a above; a large seated monkey (?) very corroded like the lion in 2a. 14th c.

---

[1] Mâle, *L'Art religieux du XIII siècle en France* (1925, 6th edn.), 245–6.
[2] Ibid., citing the teaching of St. Bernard, quoted in the *Golden Legend*: 'Nazareth interpretatur flos unde dicit Bernardus, quod flos nasci voluit de flore, in flore, et floris tempore.' (Not found in Caxton's English translation.)

[3] Rushforth (1936), 85, cites the text of St. Zeno of Verona, 4th c., where three lily blossoms on a stem symbolize the Conception. Text in P. L. Migne, *Patrologia Latina* xi (1845), 415. Later texts are numerous.
[4] E. W. Tristram, *English Wall Painting of the Fourteenth Century* (1955), 22, citing 14th-c. vernacular poetry and sermons.

A1, A2. Composite Panels

h. 0·38 m. w. 0·34 m.

Small fragments of background diapers, canopy, and border pieces. 14th c. An incomplete figure of a censing angel, chain and censer in A1, head and arm in A2. White glass very corroded, early 14th c.

B1. Composite Panel

h. 0·54 m. w. 0·34 m.

Small fragments of canopy designs, foliage diapers, border pieces as 2a above, and drapery. Border piece, a fleur-de-lis in a lozenge frame. A large pot containing flowers, the latter incomplete, painted on white glass, the lily pot probably from an Annunciation. 14th c.

B2. Composite Panel

h. 0·54 m. w. 0·34 m.

Small fragments, three fragments of quarries as 2b above, traceried border as 2a above, two fleur-de-lis border fragments as B1. A small nimbed head of a female saint wearing a wimple, white glass, early 14th c. Fragment of a male head, bearded, three-quarters left, white glass, hair in yellow stain, early 15th c.

C1, C3. Traceries

h. 0·25 m. w. 0·16 m.

Condition. *In situ* (?) but incomplete. Slight decay.

Colour and Technique. Painted on white glass with a matt black background, patterned border in yellow stain separated from the stonework by a strip of plain white glass.

Style and Design. The patterned border encloses a triangular frame cusped trefoil. Not identical, the patterned borders are different designs.

Date. 14th c.

C2. The Blessed Virgin Mary (?)

h. 0·50 m. w. 0·36 m.

She stands facing three-quarters left, head looking down, hand in benediction below the head.

Condition. The figure is composite, the green and pot-yellow draperies are reused pieces, coeval in date with the head.

Iconography. Possibly the Virgin, the raised hand being that of the Christ Child.

Date. Early 14th c.

---

¹ Visitations (1871), 83–4.
² T. Banks, *Baronia Anglica Concentrata* ii (1843), 46–7.

s. VII

A2. The Virgin Annunciate   PLATE 19 (*d*)

Light: h. 0·79 m. w. 0·16 m. Virgin: h. 0·41 m. w. 0·28 m.

Condition. The panel is composite, the figure and its background almost complete, the rest made up with fragments of architecture, background diaper as s. VI. 2a–2c, traceried border pieces, possibly *in situ*, design as s. VI. 2a–2c, all 14th c.

Virgin Annunciate: full length facing three-quarters left, a book in her veiled left hand, her right hand on her breast.

Condition. The lower part of the Virgin's tunic, feet, and a small part of the foliage background are missing. Well preserved, slight pitting.

Colour and Technique. Painted on white glass, Virgin's hair and mantle in yellow stain, delicate smear and matt shading on the drapery. Background diaper, arabesque of broad kidney-shaped leaves, white against a matt black background.

Iconography. The inclined head, gesture of the right hand, and book are consistent with the proposed identification. The lily pot now inserted in s. VI. B1 possibly belongs with this composition.

Style and Design. A piece of extremely high-quality design and painting, especially the drawing of the right hand with the slightly bent little finger, the fluid modelling of the drapery, and the natural pattern created by the simple hem line of the mantle. The facial features are extremely close to the three north windows of the Latin Chapel of Christ Church Cathedral, Oxford, *c.* 1350, for example, the Virgin and Child. The background foliage diaper is alike in type, although at Brightwell Baldwin the leaves are larger and broader. The semicircular head of the panel and vertical sides have a thin outer border, suggesting that the panel was enclosed by an architectural frame, possibly forming the centre part of a canopy design.

Date. Mid 14th c.

Lost Glass

In addition to the extant shields the 1574 Visitation also records the arms of Blount, then in the east window, and the arms of Argentine, the latter coupled with the unidentified shield now n. IV, A1.¹ The Argentine arms probably commemorated Reginald de Argentine (d. 1326), first husband of Agnes, daughter of Sir William de Bereford.² Two other shields recorded in the 1574 Visitation appear to be mistaken tricks of the arms of Stody and Bereford, and a third, untinctured, may have been the arms of St. George.³

---

³ Visitations (1871), 83–4.

BROADWELL

ST. PETER AND ST. PAUL

O.S. SP 253 043

MS. SOURCES

Oxford. Bodleian Library, MS. Top. Oxon. b. 75, f. 63. Wyatt Papers, MS. of D. T. Powell, c. 1805.

PRINTED

Visitations (1871), 29.
P.C. (1920), 52.
Fisher, A. S. T., *The History of Broadwell, Oxfordshire, with Filkins, Kelmscott and Holwell* (1968).
Pevsner (1974), 488–90.

There are slight remains of fourteenth- and fifteenth-century glass in the tracery lights of two windows on the south side of the chancel, s. II and s. III. A lost window contained representations of three knights, each holding up his shield of arms. It is possible that they were Knights of the Order of St. John of Jerusalem in England. A figure described c. 1805 as representing 'a Lady kneeling praying to a saint with inscription in the Norman character' is no longer extant.[1]

s. II

A1. Roundel

d. 0·14 m.

A Tudor rose design.

Condition. A complete roundel, corroded on both surfaces, set against imitation 15th-c. quarries of 19th-c. date.

Colour and Technique. White glass, light-brown paint with stippled shading, the inner rose in yellow stain, the outer in white.

Date. Second half 15th c.

s. III

A2. Foliage Design

h. 0·35 m. w. 0·18 m.

A frontal lion's face, encircled by oak foliage, with patterned borders.

Condition. Possibly *in situ* and complete. The lion's face is very corroded and virtually opaque. The white glass has corrosion of varying intensity but the design is clear.

Colour and Technique. The lion's face is in deep ochre pot-metal glass. The foliage is broadly painted on white glass. Border design of contiguous circles in yellow stain on a matt background.

Style and Design. The panel appears to be of one piece. Although the outer border is a repeated design the sections adjacent to each other are not all in line, particularly the lower right-hand lobe, but it is possible that this is poor workmanship rather than a restorer's composite.

Date. 14th c.

A1 and A3. Small scraps of medieval glass. Not catalogued.

Lost Glass

Richard Lee's Visitation notes record some lost heraldic glass. The published versions of these notes[2] and Wood's copy[3] both contain errors and omissions and the arms are not identified.

'In a wyndowe'[4]

A shield, in trick: *argent a fess gules, in dexter chief a mullet gules* ODDINGESELES.

The family of Oddingeseles had a moiety of the manor of Broadwell.[5] Their arms are carved on the corbels of the chantry chapel on the north side of the chancel. Three shields in trick: *azure three arrows in pale points downwards or* ARCHER. Quarterly, 1,4 *or two pales embattled and counter embattled azure.* 2,3 *azure two bars or*[6] UNIDENTIFIED. *Ermine on a fess gules three cinquefoils or*[7] ARDEN. 'Thes 3 ware in a wyndowe with iii knights holdyng them up with whit crosses on ther shoulders in this fashion.' Two crosses in trick; left, *a cross patonce*; right, *a cross moline.*

---

[1] Powell MS., op. cit., f. 63.
[2] Visitations (1871), 29.
[3] P.C. (1920), 52.
[4] P.C. (1920), 52, gives it as 'In one of the chancell windows'.
[5] *Feudal Aids, 1284–1431* iv. 162, 182, 194. *Cal. Inq. Post Mortem,* iv. 318; viii. 10; x. 57; xv. 330–3. Fisher, op. cit. 15–17, 20–6.
[6] Visitations (1871), 29, reverses the tinctures of quarters 1 and 4.
[7] Ibid. The cinquefoils are incorrectly blazoned as fleurs-de-lis. Fisher, op. cit. 32, repeats this. The three shields are omitted in P.C. (1920), 52.

The date of this window and the identities of the three knights commemorated have not been established. There is some relevant historical evidence. The advowson of the church of Broadwell was held by the Knights Templars until the Order was abolished in 1311.[1] It was afterwards granted to the Order of St. John of Jerusalem in England[2] and remained in the possession of the Order until the Dissolution.[3] It is possible that the white crosses, worn by the three knights on their shoulders, indicated that they were Knights Hospitallers. The early examples of the Hospitallers cross, when used as a badge, show some variety of form.[4]

The inclusion of the arms of Archer possibly supports this interpretation. This Warwickshire family[5] bore *azure three arrows points downwards or*.[6] Thomas le Archer was Prior of the Order of St. John of Jerusalem in England from 1321 to 1327.[7] His seal, as Prior, bears his personal arms on the reverse: *three arrows in pale, points downwards*.[8] Two other knights of the same surname, and probably of the same family, were Knights Hospitallers. In 1338 John Larcher, senior, was preceptor of Dalby (Leics.) and John Larcher, junior, was preceptor of Fryer Mayne (Dorset).[9]

The identification of the Arden arms is problematic. The relationships between the different branches of the family are by no means certain. One member of the family known to have a connection with the Hospitallers was Thomas Arden who, in 1286, granted to the Order all his rights in the manor of Ryton upon Dunsmoor (Warwicks.).[10] His arms were *checky or and azure, a chevron gules*.[11] The Ardens of Drayton[12] bore *ermine a fess checky or and azure*.[13] The coat at Broadwell, *ermine on a fess gules three cinquefoils or*, is given for Arden in later rolls of arms,[14] but without any individual being specified.

The third shield of arms at Broadwell has not been traced.

BROUGHTON CASTLE
CHAPEL

O.S. SP 418 383

PRINTED SOURCES
Greening Lamborn (1949), 116.

V.C.H. (1969), ix. 89.
Pevsner (1974), 495–6.

The three shields now in the apex tracery lights of the east window of the chapel are probably not *in situ*. They represent prominent local landowners but have no known connection with either the Manor of Broughton, or John de Broughton, the builder of the castle. It is unlikely, as Greening Lamborn pointed out, that they would have originally occupied the head of the east window to the exclusion of the builder's own shield. The display of arms could have been motivated by personal relationships between families, possibly linked by tenure connections. All the shields date from the first quarter of the fourteenth century.

[1] *Liber Antiquus de Ordinationibus Vicariarum tempore Hugonis Wells Lincolniensis Episcopi, 1209–35*, ed. A. Gibbons (1888), 3. Rotuli Hugonis de Welles, i, ed. W. P. W. Phillimore, *Lincoln Record Society*, iii (1912), 183. *Calendar of Patent Rolls 1307–13*, 460, 462, 488. Fisher, op. cit. 7, 17.

[2] *Cal. Inq. Miscellaneous, 1307–49*, 303. Fisher, op. cit. 17.

[3] Publications of the Record Commissioners, *Valor Ecclesiasticus tempore Henrici VIII* ii (1814), 178. Fisher, op. cit. 17.

[4] J. A. Goodall, 'The Arms and Badge of the Order of St. John of Jerusalem', *Revue de l'Ordre Souverain Militaire de Malte*, 8th year, N.S. 2 (1959), 62–71, 65–6, fig. 3. 'Rolls of Arms Henry III', ed. T. D. Tremlett and H. Stanford, London, *Aspilogia* ii (1967), 25–6, citing E. J. King, *The Seals of the Order of St. John of Jerusalem* (1932), pl. III, fig. 2.

[5] W. Dugdale, *The Antiquities of Warwickshire* (2nd edn. 1730), 780–1.

[6] The marshalling of the charges varies, either *in pale*, or *two and one*.

[7] Report of the Prior Philip de Thame for 1338. 'The Knights Hospitallers in England', ed. L. B. Larking with a historical introduction by J. M. Kemble, *The Camden Society* lxv (1857), lvii–lx, lxxi–lxxii. E. J. King, *The Grand Priory of St. John of Jerusalem in England* (1924), 28–9.

[8] *Third Report of the Royal Commission on Historical Manuscripts* (1872), 45. MSS. of the Duke of Devonshire at Hardwick Hall (Derbys.). Another seal is recorded where the arrows are marshalled two and one. W. Burton's *Book of Seals*, 17th c. Bowditch Collection U.S.A. (location unknown), f. xxxv, seal 10. King, op. cit. 99, records only one seal, in the Public Record Office, where the arms are illegible.

[9] King, op. cit. ii, 65.

[10] Dugdale, op. cit. 926; *The Knights Hospitallers in England*, op. cit. 125, 234. *Calendar of Patent Rolls 1281–1292*, 225.

[11] Dugdale, op. cit. 297; Birch ii (1892), 6903. 'Sir Christopher Hatton's Book of Seals', ed. L. C. Loyd and D. M. Stenton, *Northamptonshire Record Society* xv (1949), 49.

[12] *V.C.H.* ix (1969), 104–5.

[13] *A Roll of Arms of the Reign of Edward II*, ed. N. H. Nicolas (1829), 73. Birch ii (1892), 6901.

[14] e.g. Starkey's Roll, c. 1460, copy C, Oxford, Queen's College, MS. 158, 257, shield 7.

I

B1, B3. Border Fragments

h. 0·23 m. w. 0·23 m.

Fragments of border designs. B1 three fleur-de-lis, pot yellow and matt black paint, two swans and one stork, white glass, picked out of matt black wash. B3 two fleurs-de-lis, fragments of four more, one inserted piece of modern ruby. One grotesque wyvern, white glass and matt black paint. All slightly corroded. Cut down and releaded into squares. All 14th c.

B2. Shield of Sutton

d. 0·32 m.

Or a lion rampant queue fourchée SUTTON.

Condition. Incomplete, the sinister side of the shield has been patched with two pieces of alien white glass. Field of shield very decayed. One piece of modern blue glass inserted into field at base of lion's tail.

Colour and Technique. Pot metal glass. Field of shield diapered with pattern of squared trellis with each fret containing a repeated eight-pointed star design picked out of a background of matt black paint. Shield set on a ruby, roundel diapered with trails of foliage picked out of a background of matt black paint.

C1. Shield of Mohun

d. 0·32 m.

Or a cross engrailed sable MOHUN.

Condition. Shield originally painted on a single piece of glass, two old leaded breaks. Fragments of alien blue glass inserted into top right border.

Colour and Technique. The field of the shield is diapered with a repeated pattern design as B2, ruby circular surround diapered with trails of small trefoil leaves picked out of a matt black background of paint.

C2. Shield of Arden

d. 0·32 m.

Ermine a fess checky or and azure ARDEN.

Condition. Incomplete, the field above the fess is missing and is patched with a piece of modern ruby glass. The circular surround has a small hole upper left.

Colour and Technique. Coloured glass is pot metal, ermine field painted on a piece of plain white glass, ruby circular surround diapered with trails of small trefoil leaves picked out of a background of matt black paint.

Date. B2, C1, C2 all early 14th c.

BURFORD
ST. JOHN BAPTIST

O.S. SP 254 124

MS. SOURCES

London. British Library:
  Harleian MS. 965, f. 28ᵛ. Church Notes of R. Simmonds dated 1644.
  Harleian MS. 4170, p. 41. Church Notes dated 1660.

PRINTED

Visitations (1871), 3–4.

Nelson (1919), 161.
P.C. (1920), 65–74.
Gretton, R. H., *The Burford Records* (1920).
Greening Lamborn (1949), 117.
The Church of St. John Baptist, Burford, ed. F. S. Tucker (5th rev. edn., 1960).
Pevsner (1974), 502–8.

In 1826 all the surviving pieces of medieval glass were collected together and glazed into the heads of the main lights and traceries of the east window of the chancel and the west window of the nave.[1] A head of St. James Major was removed from the west window in 1874, when the main lights were filled, and inserted in the north window of the north transept.[2] The arms of St. Edward the Confessor and the fragments in the tracery lights of this window were presented to the church in 1911.[3]

Although a considerable amount of glass, mostly fifteenth century, has been preserved, it is unfortunately

---

[1] Gretton, op. cit. 108.　　[2] Ibid.　　[3] Ibid. Tucker, op. cit. 30.

very fragmentary. Most of the glass is of small-scale design for tracery lights. It is possible to reconstruct in part some of the original iconographic programmes:

a. The Twelve Apostles, early fifteenth century. Only one figure remains, possibly St. Peter (I, A8).

b. Male saints, third quarter of fifteenth century. St. George (w. I, A5) and a St. Christopher bearing the Christ Child (I, A7) may belong together. The two saints are often associated.[1]

c. Angels, third quarter of fifteenth century. The remains of two or three different series. Two identical figures wear ermine tippets, and may be part of a series of the Nine Orders of Angels (w. I, A2 and A9). Another pair, identical in design, may have been supporters for shields of arms (w. I, A3 and A8). Four cherubim, each standing on a wheel (w. I, A2, A3 and A9), are virtually identical, with only small differences of decorative detail on the centres of the wheels.[2]

d. Female saints, third quarter of fifteenth century. This is the most extensive series of figures. The saints depicted are a royal saint or the Virgin Mary (w. I, D3), an unidentified saint (w. I, D4), St. Barbara (w. I, D5), St. Margaret (w. I, D6), and St. Mary Magdalen (w. I, A6). There is no doubt that these figures are related. The dress is much the same: tunics with high waistbands, voluminous mantles with large jewelled hems and clasps at the neck. Their heads are all alike in style and design.

These figures are not necessarily from a single series of lights as the same cartoon was used for another figure of St. Barbara (I, A5), the only difference being the rayed pattern on the nimbus. The striking tent canopy designs (w. I, D3, D4 and D6) may belong with these saints and are related to the work of the important London glazier, John Prudde, the king's glazier.[3] The impression of these figures and canopies is that they are a small-scale version of an important lost series of designs for main light glazing.

e. St. John Baptist, third quarter of fifteenth century (I, A4). No companion figures remain.

f. Symbols of the Evangelists, third quarter of fifteenth century. The bull of St. Luke (w. I, D2). Rushforth associated this roundel with the angel in I, A3, and identified the latter as the symbol of St. Matthew.[4] The angel is very decayed and set inside out. It is larger in scale than the bull of St. Luke.

I

2b, 2c. Canopies

h. 0·40 m. w. 0·60 m.

Each light contains the apex of a canopy design painted on white glass.

Condition. Slight corrosion, otherwise good.

Colour and Technique. Architectural details of crockets and flags in yellow stain set against coloured background, 2b red, 2c blue.

Style and Design. Although only the tops of the canopies remain, the central pier, flanked by a series of crocketed pinnacles with a flag either side, is the same design with slight variations as found in the Ante-chapel windows of All Souls College, Oxford, of *c.* 1441–7.[5]

Date. Second quarter 15th c.

Modern copies of the canopy design in 2a, 2d, and 2e. Some small pieces of medieval glass incorporated in 2a.

A2. Roundel

d. 0·12 m. Panel: h. 0·40 m. w. 0·25 m.

A roundel with an IHC monogram set against foliage design, *in situ*.

Condition. Complete except for the top foil, which is replaced by alien pattern design.

Colour and Technique. Roundel in white glass, IHC in yellow stain. Foliage, yellow stain against a matt black background, plain white border.

Style and Design. See A9.

Date. Late 15th c.

A3. Angel

h. 0·60 m. w. 0·25 m.

An angel, half-length facing three-quarters right emerging from clouds.

Condition. A fragment of a larger composition, the panel

---

[1] Newton i (1961), 254.

[2] Gretton, op. cit. 108, citing notes compiled by G. M. Rushforth, groups together all these figures as belonging 'to a series representing the Nine Orders'.

[3] See below, w. I, D3.

[4] Gretton, op. cit. 108.

[5] Hutchinson (1949), pls. ii, iv, viii, x.

made up with scraps of canopy and other designs. The angel is very decayed and set inside out.

Colour and Technique. Angel painted on white glass, details picked out in yellow stain.

Style and Design. The panel is too decayed and the details too indistinct for stylistic analysis.

Date. First quarter 15th c. (?).

A4. St. John Baptist

h. 0·75 m. w. 0·25 m.

Full length facing three-quarters left, holding a lamb on a book in his left hand, pointing to it with his right hand.

Condition. A small tracery light reset here with scraps of 15th-c. glass. The figure is incomplete, tunic modern restoration, ruby background is probably alien.

Colour and Technique. Figure and canopy painted on white glass, canopy in deep orange yellow stain. Vaults of canopy have strong pebbled dashes.

Iconography. Standard.[1]

Style, Design, and Date. The glass is much obscured by decay and leaded repair. If the figure and canopy are of a piece, probably mid 15th c.

A5. Composite Panel

h. 0·90 m. w. 0·25 m.

Condition. A medley of unrelated fragments including an incomplete figure of St. Barbara nimbed, facing three-quarters right holding a palm and a model tower in her left hand. Only the head and shoulders remain. Part of a wheel, possibly from a figure of St. Catherine.

Colour and Technique. Painted on white glass, details of hair, palm, and tower in yellow stain.

Style and Design. St. Barbara painted from the same cartoon as the figure in w. I, D5.

Date. Second quarter 15th c.

A6. Composite Panel

h. 0·90 m. w. 0·25 m.

Condition. Fragments of unrelated glass; a large female head facing three-quarters left and a fragment of an Annunciation; the head of the Archangel Gabriel facing three-

quarters right holding a sceptre and a scroll inscribed in black-letter script: | *a plena d(omi)n(u)s | tecu(m)* |, part of the salutation *Ave Maria.*[2]

Colour and Technique. Head, scroll, and sceptre originally painted on a single piece of glass, details of hair, amice, and sceptre in yellow stain.

Style and Design. A plain white border on the same glass suggests that this figure was originally part of a tracery design.

Date. Mid 15th c.

A7. Composite Panel

h. 0·75 m. w. 0·25 m.

Condition. A medley of unrelated fragments including an incomplete figure of St. Christopher bearing the Christ Child. St. Christopher originally full length, facing three-quarters right. Only the upper part of the figure remains, set inside out.

Colour and Technique. Painted on white glass, Christ's tunic and hair in yellow stain. St. Christopher has a white mantle, hem in yellow stain, and a blue tunic. Staff in yellow stain.

Iconography. St. Christopher carrying the Christ Child. Standard iconography. Here the staff is represented (as in German iconography) flowering into two oak leaves and an acorn.[3]

Style and Design. It is possible that this is a companion panel to St. George, w. I, A5.

Date. Mid 15th c. (?).

A8. Composite Panel

h. 0·60 m. w. 0·25 m.

Condition. Incomplete figure of an apostle (St. Peter?) facing three-quarters right holding a book. Lower part of figure missing, panel made up with fragments of 15th-c. glass.

Colour and Technique. Apostle painted on white glass, hair and beard in yellow stain, very delicate stipple shading.

Iconography, Style, and Design. The bearded head type is consistent with the early 15th-c. standard depiction of the saint in English glass painting, e.g. Christ's Entry into Jerusalem and the Last Supper at Great Malvern Priory (Worcs.)[4] and the west window of Tong (Salop).[5]

Date. Early 15th c.

---

[1] Compare the St. John Baptist at Yarnton, n. VI, 2b.
[2] See Brightwell Baldwin, s. V, 3b.
[3] See Yarnton, n. V, 2a.

[4] Rushforth (1936), figs. 12, 13.
[5] Newton iii (1961), 599–600.

A9. Roundel

d. 0·12 m. Panel: h. 0·40 m. w. 0·25 m.

A roundel with inscribed monogram: M(ARI)A

Condition. Top foil missing, otherwise complete and *in situ.* Pendent to A2 above.

Colour and Technique. White glass, monogram in yellow stain set against a foliage design on A2.

Style and Design. Common both on roundels and quarries.[1]

Date. 15th c.

n. VI

1b. Shield of St. Edward the Confessor

h. 0·26 m. w. 0·21 m.

Azure a cross paty or between five martlets or EDWARD THE CONFESSOR.

Condition. Complete, old leaded repair, some paint loss particularly at the base of the field. Provenance unknown, given to the church in recent years.[2]

Colour and Technique. Field in blue glass diapered with a feathery foliage design picked out of a wash of matt black paint, birds and cross in yellow stain, separately leaded.

Iconography. The cult of Edward the Confessor in the later Middle Ages was stimulated by the personal devotion of Richard II, who used the arms attributed to Edward the Confessor impaled with the royal arms *c.* 1395.[3] Representations of the arms of the Confessor are commonplace in rolls of arms and chronicles in the later Middle Ages.[4]

Style, Design, and Date. The foliage diaper and the scalloped outline of the shield are suggestive of a late 15th-c. date.

3b. Composite Panel

h. 0·42 m. w. 0·42 m.

Condition. Composite panel of fragments; the head of a woman facing three-quarters left, scroll inscribed in black-letter script: *Sancti dei.*

Colour and Technique. Female head painted on white glass with line and stipple shading, wearing a butterfly head-dress of the Edward IV period.[5]

Iconography. Secular dress, and therefore probably a donor figure. Compare Margaret Fitz Ellis of *c.* 1461–9 at Waterperry (n. V, 2a).

Style and Design. Glass painting of high quality. Nothing comparable in the county has been found.

Date. c. 1470–80 (?).

5b. Composite Panel

h. 0·58 m. w. 0·58 m.

Fragments of canopy design, 15th c. At the centre an inserted head of St. James Major.

Condition. Head and nimbus and the apex of the pilgrim staff painted on a single piece of glass. Probably from a full-length standing figure. Slight all-over corrosion.

Colour and Technique. Painted on white glass with black line and stipple shading. Nimbus and cockle shell in yellow stain with plain white border.

Iconography. Represented as a pilgrim, with a pilgrim's staff and hat with a cockle shell on the brim.[6]

Style, Design, and Date. The soft modelling combined with the linear emphasis on the eyes and the head type are indicative of an early 15th-c. date, and are related to the second style of Thomas of Oxford.

A1–A6, B1, B2, C1. Fragments

A1: h. 0·24 m. w. 0·14 m.
A2–A4: h. 0·62 m. w. 0·24 m.
A6: h. 0·24 m. w. 0·14 m.
B1–2: h. 0·20 m. w. 0·20 m.
C1: h. 0·26 m. w. 0·30 m.

Each light contains miscellaneous fragments of medieval and post-medieval glass, all said to have been given to the church some years ago.[7] The glass is too fragmentary for detailed comment. Important pieces are:

A2. Incomplete head of an angel (?) facing three-quarters right, painted on white glass, hair in yellow stain. 15th c. Remains of a quarry, type 50, 14th–15th c., white and yellow stain.

A5. A veiled female head facing three-quarters left, the Virgin Mary (?). White and yellow stain, early 16th c.

B1. Male head blowing a trumpet, facing three-quarters right. White glass and yellow stain. (?) an angel, early 16th c.

B2. Head of a man incomplete, nimbed (?). White glass and yellow stain, set upside down, 15th c.

C1. Bearded male head facing three-quarters left, white glass and yellow stain, late 15th, early 16th c.

[1] See Marston, I, 4a, 4b.
[2] Tucker (ed.), op. cit. 30.
[3] M. V. Clark, *Fourteenth Century Studies* (1937), 272–92. J. H. Harvey, 'The Wilton Diptych, A Re-examination', *Archaeologia* xcviii (1961), 5–6.
[4] e.g. Bodl. Lib. Laud MS. 73, f. 66ʳ. Treatise on Heraldry and the Brut Chronicle.
[5] Druitt (1970), pl. facing 273, Long Melford (Suffolk), Clopton brass *c.* 1480.
[6] For full discussion of the iconography of St. James Major see Beckley, n. V, 1a and Combe, s. IV, 3c.
[7] Tucker, op. cit. 30.

w. I   PLATE 20 (c)

2a, 2b, 2d, 2e. Canopy Designs

h. 0·42 m. w. 0·60 m.

Each panel contains fragments of canopy designs, all painted on white glass, details picked out in yellow stain. The fragments are too incomplete to permit a reconstruction of the over-all design. Particular details, for example the design of a niche with a pendant vault flanked by an arch and gable, and the pebble-dash painting of the interior of the architecture, 2d, and the central apex of the canopy in 2b are extremely close to the canopy designs of the Antechapel windows at All Souls College, c. 1441–7[1] (as are the remains in I, 2b and 2c).

A1. Composite Panel

h. 0·60 m. w. 0·24 m.

The upper part of the panel contains a flat serrated foliage design in a pattern border, painted on white glass, rib of the leaf and border in yellow stain. Possibly *in situ*. Lower part of the panel contains miscellaneous fragments. 15th c.

A2. Composite Panel

h. 1·00 m. w. 0·24 m.

Fragments of 15th-c. glass set against a modern coloured background, the principal portions being: a composite figure made up from the head and shoulders of an angel wearing an ermine tippet (probably one of the Orders of Angels), and the legs of a cherubim standing on a wheel, hands clasped before the chest, painted on white glass, details picked out in yellow stain, early 15th c.; fragment of a winged beast with a clawed foot (? part of a dragon), white and yellow stain, 15th c.

A3. Composite Panel

h. 1·00 m. w. 0·24 m.

Fragments of 15th-c. glass: composite figure, head and shoulders of an angel, frontal, possibly originally a supporter to a shield, now set on the incomplete legs of a small figure of a cherubim standing on a wheel, white glass, yellow stain, stippled and matt shading. Early 15th c.

A4. Composite Panel

h. 0·60 m. w. 0·24 m.

Small fragments of 14th- and 15th-c. glass. The only notable feature is part of a patterned cresting in white glass and yellow stain with a coloured jewel leaded into the white glass pattern design.

A5. Composite Panel

h. 0·87 m. w. 0·24 m.

In the upper half of the light is a figure of St. George spearing the dragon, probably from a tracery light, but not *in situ*. St. George in armour, full length facing three-quarters left, is trampling the dragon under his feet and thrusting a spear into its head.

Condition. Incomplete. Part of the dragon is missing.

Colour and Technique. Painted on white glass with stipple shading, details picked out in yellow stain. The figure is represented on a patterned floor against a plain white background painted on the same piece of glass as the figure.

Iconography. St. George, the patron saint of England, was extremely popular throughout the Middle Ages, and there are many representations of him.[2] The most popular devotional image seems to have been the equestrian figure of the saint.[3] The general design of St. George standing on the dragon may have been derived from the 14th-c. seal of St. George's Chapel, Windsor.[4] Other examples in glass painting are a lost 14th-c. window at Coleshill (Warwicks.),[5] the west window of Merton College Chapel, Oxford, early 15th c.,[6] and a recently discovered panel at Windsor Castle (Berks.) c. 1480.[7]

Above the St. George is a fragment of a tracery light design, not *in situ*; the design originally showed a roundel at the centre encircled by a double twist stem with offspringing leaves and flowers painted on white glass, flowers and foliage and one of the twisted stems in yellow stain against a plain white background with a plain yellow border in yellow stain. 15th c. At the base of the light is a hand and part of a figure holding a scroll inscribed in black-letter script: | *Ezechiel* |

A6. Composite Panel

h. 0·87 m. w. 0·24 m.

Fragments of 15th-c. glass. Composite figure: upper half St. Mary Magdalen facing three-quarters left holding an ointment pot in her right hand, painted on white glass, hair and pattern drapery in yellow stain. The pose of the figure with the ointment pot held up in the right hand can be compared with the large figure of the saint in the Antechapel to All Souls College, Oxford.[8] Adjacent to the figure is a patterned background with a plain border and a flat semicircular head. This belongs to the incomplete figure holding a long wand leaded below the St. Mary Magdalen. In the lower part of the light, small fragments of an archbishop figure with a cross pall and a fragment of a bishop holding a crozier, 15th c. In the upper part of the

---

[1] Hutchinson (1949), pls. 4, 5.
[2] Newton i (1961), 253–6. *Herder* vi (1974), 365–90.
[3] There is one representation at Kelmscott I, 2b.
[4] Cast at the Society of Antiquaries, London.
[5] The window depicted King Edward III kneeling before St.

George. B.L. Egerton MS. 3510, p. 18. Newton iii (1961), 862–3.
[6] R.C.H.M. (1939), pl. 147.
[7] Information and photograph from Mr. D. King of Norwich.
[8] Hutchinson (1949), pl. 15

light is a fragment of a foliage design from a tracery, a sea-weed design in yellow stain on white glass in a plain white and yellow stain border, 15th c.

A7. Composite Panel

h. 0·60 m. w. 0·24 m.

Very small fragments of 15th-c. glass. An incomplete nimbed head of a bishop saint holding a crozier. Fragments of drapery and wings, and a hand holding a staff, all painted on white glass with yellow stain. Mid 15th c.

A8. Composite Panel

h. 1·00 m. w. 0·24 m.

Bust-length figure of an angel, similar to the fragments in A2 and A3 above. The legs of a cherubim standing on a wheel, an incomplete roundel with the monogram IHC, all white glass and yellow stain, 15th c. Small scraps of foliage design and canopy work.

A9. Composite Panel

h. 1·00 m. w. 0·24 m.

Incomplete figure of an angel painted from the same cartoon as the one in A2, legs of a cherubim standing on a wheel as A2, A3, and A8, small fragments of canopy design and draperies, 15th c.

A10. Composite Panel

h. 0·60 m. w. 0·24 m.

In the centre a roundel, large white rose painted on white glass with a central floret in yellow stain. Small fragments of canopies and decorative designs. 15th c.

B1, B2. Composite Panel

h. 0·23 m. w. 0·10 m.

Inserted pieces of foliage designs from tracery lights painted on white glass, yellow stain. 15th c.

C1. Foliated Cross

h. 0·09 m. w. 0·09 m.

Foliated cross painted on white glass against a matt black background, the arms of the cross overlap the plain border. Complete and *in situ*. 15th c.

D1. Composite Panel

h. 0·28 m. w. 0·18 m.

Roundel, a sun in splendour, yellow stain against a plain matt background, badge of the House of York, conforming in type to the seals of Edward IV.[1] Set on scraps of foliage and canopy design. All 15th c.

D2. Composite Panel

h. 0·42 m. w. 0·18 m.

An incomplete roundel, the bull of St. Luke. Standing, facing right holding a scroll between its feet inscribed in black-letter script: | *lucas* |. Yellow stain on a white ground, patterned with contiguous rosettes painted in outline, set against fragments. All 15th c.

D3. Composite Panel

h. 0·87 m. w. 0·23 m.

An incomplete tracery light showing a royal female saint, crowned and nimbed, full length facing three-quarters right holding a rosary. Figure's feet and original background are missing. Painted on white glass, details picked out in yellow stain. Above the figure a small canopy from a tracery light. The design shows the top of an ornamented cresting, above it a triple ogee with a chevron design representing the inside of a tent canopy. This class of design appears to have originated in the workshop of John Prudde, mid 15th c. Very rich examples are found at Croughton (Warwicks.),[2] and also in the royal window at Great Malvern (Worcs.).[3] Set against small fragments of canopies, a bearded man's head set upside down, fragment of a hand holding something, small pieces of foliage design, all 15th c.

D4. Composite Panel

h. 0·87 m. w. 0·23 m.

An incomplete tracery light, a full length female saint holding a book, facing three-quarters right, painted on white glass, details picked out in yellow stain. The figure's feet and original background are missing. Above the figure, tent canopy identical to that in D3. Set against fragments of tiled flooring, canopy cresting, and foliage designs.

D5. Composite Panel

h. 0·87 m. w. 0·23 m.

An incomplete tracery light of St. Barbara holding a tower and a palm, full length facing three-quarters right, painted on white glass, details of hair and pattern tunic in yellow stain. Painted from the same cartoon as the incomplete figure in I, A5. Above the figure is a fragment of a central portion of a canopy painted in white glass, yellow stain, mid 15th c. Set against small fragments of canopy and foliage design. In the right border of the light is an inscription in black-letter script: | *How a ionge ma(n) weddeþ* |.[4] Possibly from a panel depicting the sacrament of marriage from a series of the Seven Sacraments. 15th c.

---

[1] See Stanton Harcourt, s. VII, 2a, 2b, 2c.
[2] CI photograph.
[3] Rushforth (1936), figs. 182–5.

[4] Rushforth (1936), 30, correctly interpreted the inscription, but misread it as: 'How a manne ma(y) wedde'.

D6. Composite Panel

h. 0·87 m. w. 0·23 m.

A large figure of St. Margaret from a tracery light, originally full length, facing three-quarters right holding in her left hand a cross-staff which she thrusts into the mouth of the dragon. Only the head, right arm, and adjacent drapery, cross–staff, and head of the dragon at her feet remain. The rest of the figure is made up of alien glass. Above the figure a tent canopy, identical with D3 and D4, set against fragments of canopies, foliage designs, and rosettes. 15th c.

D7. Composite Panel

h. 0·42 m. w. 0·18 m.

Roundel, a sun in splendour, identical with D1, and a fragment of another. Set against fragments of canopy and foliage designs. 15th c.

D8. Foliage Design

h. 0·28 m. w. 0·18 m.

A white serrated leaf in a pattern border, *in situ*, separated from the masonry by a strip of plain white glass. White leaf ribs picked out in yellow stain on a matt black background, white border patterned with contiguous circles in yellow stain. 15th c.

Lost Glass

The 1574 Visitation records two shields in the windows of the church:[1] one for Clare, Earls of Gloucester, Lords of the Manor and town of Burford; the other of Pynnok impaling Woodward (?). The latter, dated 1485, commemorated John Pynnok (d. 1486) who built the Trinity chapel on the south side of the church.[2] The heraldry and the media in which the arms were found are recorded inconsistently in the later antiquarian notes.[3]

CASSINGTON

ST. PETER

O.S. SP 455 106.

MS. SOURCES

London. British Library, Harleian MS. 6365, p. 116. 17th-c. Church Notes.
Oxford. Bodleian Library:
  Top. Oxon. e. 286, f. 109. Church Notes of N. Greenwood, dated 1659.
  Top. Oxon. b. 220, f. 27ᵛ. Robinson, *Church Notes 1810–1830*.

PRINTED

Nelson (1913), 161.
Bouchier (1918), 92.
Bouchier (1932), 127 (misspelt as Carrington).
Greening Lamborn (1949), 117.
Pevsner (1974), 522–3.

I

A2. Roundel. Arms of the See of York

d. 0·38

Gules two keys in saltire argent in chief a crown or SEE OF YORK. Surrounded by a green chaplet with ruby bands.

Condition. Complete, the ruby glass is decayed, and the painting on the chaplet is thin. Set against a modern foliage design imitating a 14th-c. one.

Colour and Technique. The charges are leaded in. Greening Lamborn noted this, and that 'there is no abrading of the red flash'.[4] Although the abrading technique was highly developed at this period, the size of the charges doubtless precluded the use of the method here.

Date, Style, and Design. The moulded column form with foliate decoration on the shaft of the key and the imperial form of the crown, with the open arches are indicative of an early 16th-c. design. The style corresponds with Cardinal Wolsey's glass in the west window of Christ Church Hall, Oxford.[5] Wolsey was Archbishop of York in 1515. The glass was probably brought here from Christ Church Hall, Oxford, as the Dean and Chapter were patrons of the living.[6]

n. II   PLATE 21 (*a*)

1c. Roundel. Joseph taking Leave of his Father, Jacob

d. 0·23 m.

In the foreground stands Jacob, facing three-quarters right

---

[1] Visitations (1871), 3–4.
[2] Gretton, op. cit., 88–9, 113, 120.
[3] Bodl. Lib. MSS. Rawl. B. 400, f. 219, Rawl. B. 400b, f. 21, Wood E. 1, ff. 13–17ᵛ; B.L. MSS. Harl. 965, f. 28ᵛ, Harl. 4170, f. 36, p. 41.

[4] Greening Lamborn (1949), 117.
[5] Ibid.
[6] The 17th-c. Church Notes do not refer to any such arms in the church.

addressing his son. Beside them stand five male attendants. In the left middle ground Joseph is seen asleep in a shed with his dreams represented on two small roundels above the shed; upper left background, Joseph being directed by a shepherd; upper right background, Joseph put into the pit by his brothers, the slaughter of a goat, and the staining of the coat by its blood.

Condition. Before 1972 the roundel was in four pieces with a leaded repair. During the recent restoration the pieces were stuck together and a backing plate of plain glass added. Slight pitting all over, and the paint is very thin in places.

Colour and Technique. Painted on white glass, details of figures and costumes picked out in yellow stain. Landscape, except for centre background, in yellow stain. Stipple shading.

Styles and Design. The composition is probably based on a lost original by the Master of the Story of Tobit, working *c.* 1470. (See Begbroke n. III, 3b, s. V, 2b.) A later version of the same composition in reverse and omitting the background scenes, on a rectangular panel, is in the Victoria and Albert Museum.[1] The foreground figures are more carefully painted than those in the background, which are more sketchily executed, perhaps by another hand of the same workshop.

Date. Flemish, early 16th c.

n. III

1b. Composite Panel, St. Paul   PLATE 21 (*c*)

h. 0·30 m. w. 0·14 m.

St. Paul full length facing three-quarters right holding a book in his right hand.

Condition. Complete. The white drapery is an alien patch, blue background and green grass by the feet are a composite of old and modern glass. Placed in present position in 1972. The panel was previously hanging loose the wrong way round in the south window of the chancel.

Colour and Technique. Head and hands painted on white glass, nimbus in yellow stain, tunic in deep green, blue book, white shoes.

Style and Design. High quality work, particularly the painting of the face and hands. Probably from the workshop of Thomas of Oxford, second style.

Date. Late 14th c.

s. III

1a. Roundel, Deacon Saint   PLATE 21 (*b*)

d. 0·15 m.

A deacon, half-length frontal holding a book.

Condition. The present arrangement is probably original rather than a fragment of a full-length figure. Background alien, slight corrosion on figure, nimbus and background very corroded.

Colour and Technique. Head, amice and hand holding book painted on white glass, ruby nimbus and blue dalmatic, pot-metal ochre background. Backpainting on hair. Plain green border.

Style and Design. See 2b below.

Date. Early 14th c.

1b. Roundel, A Deacon Saint

d. 0·15 m.

The head of a deacon saint wearing an amice, frontal.

Condition. Composite, made up with alien pieces of old glass.

Colour and Technique. Head and amice painted on white glass, ruby nimbus.

Style and Design. The two heads, 1a and 1b, are possibly painted from the same cartoon, pattern on the amice also identical. They may have been originally set at the centre of a grisaille pattern or a trail of geometric grisaille, as for example at Merton College Chapel, Oxford.

Date. As above.

2a. Roundel, Head of Christ   PLATE 21 (*b*)

d. 0·27 m.

Condition. Composite. A frontal head of Christ set against fragments of oak-leaf diaper and plain coloured glass.

Colour and Technique. Head painted on white glass with backpainting, ruby nimbus, cross in pot-metal ochre.

Iconography. Head has a plain, straight banded fillet around the brows, perhaps to indicate the crown of thorns. (See Asthall n. IV, 2b.)

Style and Design. Close to the two deacon saints in 1a and 1b, particularly the flattened nose and the protruding ears. If the adjacent white oak foliage is to be associated with the head it is possible that the glass was originally set in a tracery light, as for example at Tadmarton.

Date. 14th c.

---

[1] B. Rackham, *Guide to the Collection of Stained Glass in the Victoria and Albert Museum* (1936), pl. 48.

2b. Roundel, Foliage Designs

d. 0·27 m.

A composite panel of fragments of foliage designs, mostly single leaves. Before the recent restoration this glass was loose in the vestry.

Date. 12th and 13th c.

3b. Roundel, Foliage Design

d. 0·15 m.

Complete but very decayed. At the centre a small white rose with four pot yellow leaves radiating from it, set against a green square on a ruby ground. Probably the central ornament of a geometric grisaille pattern.

Date. Early 14th c.

Lost Glass

The antiquarian notes record two shields in the east window of the chancel, the arms of England and Montague.[1]

CHALGROVE
ST. MARY

O.S. SP 637 966.

n. V

1a, 1c. Heads of Two Angels   PLATE 21 (*d*)

h. 0·15 m. w. 0·15 m.

Two identical heads of angels have been inserted at the head of the outer main lights of this window, set in a surround of modern plain white glazing.

Condition. Original portions well preserved, with only slight corrosion.

Colour and Technique. Each angel is painted on a single piece of white glass, the hair and ornament of the amice in yellow stain. Very linear modelling, with light stippled matt washes for the features.

PRINTED SOURCES
Pevsner (1974), 525–6.

Iconography. The remains are not extensive enough to be evidence for the precise subject represented here. The heads are the conventional 15th-c. angel type. Their size suggests that they came from the main lights of a window.

Style and Design. A single cartoon was used for both these figures, identical in all respects. The painting is of first-class quality. The corkscrew disposition of the hair with the knot at the centre of the brow is commonly found in glass painting *c*. 1400 and later.[2] Compare, for example, the figures of angels as supporters of *c*. 1395–1415 and the head of God the Father at Kidlington, window I, 3a, 3b, 3c.

Date. Early 15th c.

CHARLTON-ON-OTMOOR
BLESSED VIRGIN MARY

O.S. SP 562 158.

PRINTED SOURCES
Prior, C. E., 'Notes on an Oxfordshire Benefice', *O.A.S. Report* (1910), 13–19.

Nelson (1913), 161.
Bouchier (1918), 67.
Bouchier (1932), 127.
Pevsner (1974), 529–30.

Seven windows in the chancel retain some fourteenth-century glass *in situ* in the tracery lights. A late thirteenth-century Virgin and Child has been inserted in a tracery light of the east window. The window

---

[1] B .L. Harl. MS. 6365 op. cit., Bodl. Lib. MS. Top. Oxon. e. 286 op. cit., P.C. (1920), 77.

[2] A general discussion of stylistic similarities in early 15th-c. glass can be found in Newton i (1961), 110–34.

was reglazed by Mr. M. C. Farrar Bell in 1965. The six side-windows of the chancel retain much of their original glass in the tracery lights. It appears that all the traceries contained foliage designs in white glass with a very restricted amount of coloured glass. There is considerable variety in the types of foliage. This is best seen in n. IV, B1, B2, where the general pattern is identical, but one uses a trefoil leaf form with clusters of fruit, the other an oak leaf with trefoil fruit forms. Comparison should be made with the similar foliage tracery designs also in white glass at Wiggington n. II, and n. III.

I

B2. Fragments

h. 0·45 m. w. 0·45 m.

A panel of extremely corroded fragments of unrelated designs including: a nimbed head of a female saint facing three-quarters right, probably 14th c., small pieces of green and ruby drapery, and small scraps of border.

B3. Virgin and Child

h. 0·45 m. w. 0·45 m.

Virgin seated in the frontal position, holding the Christ Child on her left arm.

Condition. The glass is extremely corroded and incomplete. The Virgin's head has been replaced by that of a king.

Colour and Technique. The coloured glass is all pot metal. The Virgin wears a green mantle over a ruby tunic. Christ Child apparently in white glass which has turned to a brownish tone with decay. White throne with an ochre cushion. The inserted head of a king is painted on white glass similarly decayed to a brownish tone, green crown and ruby nimbus set against pieces of plain blue glass patched with later fragments of canopy work.

Iconography. The Virgin is offering a round object, possibly an apple, to the Christ Child.

Style and Design. The details of the drapery painting are so extremely corroded that it is difficult to date this with precision. The reused head of a king is probably contemporary with the figure of the Virgin and Child; the crown has a simplified line pattern for its jewelled base.

Date. Second half 13th c., probably from the 13th-c. church, and reused in the 14th-c. rebuilding.

C2. Quarries

h. 0·45 m. w. 0·45 m.

Two quarries, 14th c. (?), extremely decayed, lower set inside out. Quarry type not discernible.

n. II

A1. Foliage Design

h. 0·15 m. w. 0·16 m.

Four sprays of foliage radiating from the centre of the light.

Condition. The glass is very decayed, the upper foil appears to be an alien patch. *In situ.*

Colour and Technique. Painted on white glass, foliage in yellow stain with plain white border.

Style and Design. See Introduction.

Date. Mid 14th c.

B1. Composite Panel

h. 0·15 m. w. 0·36 m.

A medley of unrelated fragments grouped around a modern plain orange boss at the centre. All the medieval glass is extremely corroded.

Date. Mid 14th c.

B2. Tracery Design

h. 0·15 m. w. 0·36 m.

Condition. Complete except for modern plain orange boss at the centre and two patches in the lower foil of the light. In 1963 the 14th-c. glass was set inside out.

Colour and Technique. White glass, border pattern, repeated design in yellow stain.

Style and Design. The original design is unusual in that it appears to have been plain white glass with a coloured boss at the centre and a patterned border. Parts of the border are painted on the same glass as the adjacent plain pieces. The simplicity of design is unusual. See C2 below.

Date. Mid 14th c.

C2. Tracery Design

h. 0·23 m. w. 0·23 m.

Condition. In situ. Incomplete, the plain ruby roundel at the centre is modern, and the upper foil of the light has been replaced by an incomplete white quarry, type 46, probably 15th c.

Colour and Technique. As B2.

Style and Design. As B2, the pattern border is identical. Although the glass appears to be *in situ*, it is worth noting that the design, evidently made for a tracery light, does not echo its architectural setting, and the plain white strip between the pattern border and the masonry of the light varies in width.

Date. 14th c.

n. III

A1. Foliage Design

h. 0·15 m. w. 0·16 m.

Four leaves radiating from a coloured boss at the centre.

Condition. The white glass is well preserved, the boss is so decayed that its colour is uncertain. *In situ.*

Colour and Technique. Foliage painted on white glass against a matt black background, patterned border in yellow stain separated from the masonry by a strip of plain white glass.

Style and Design. See n. IV, A1.

Date. Mid 14th c.

C2. Foliage Design

h. 0·23 m. w. 0·23 m.

Condition. Incomplete, the lower foil is missing. *In situ.*

Colour and Technique. As A1, except the boss at the centre of the light.

Style and Design. See n. IV, B2.

Date. Mid 14th c.

C1, C3. Trefoil Design

(Measurements unobtainable.)

Condition. Complete. *In situ.*

Colour and Technique. White glass, cusped border in yellow stain with a plain white border.

Style and Design. A simple cusped trefoil design.

Date. Mid 14th c.

n. IV

A1. Foliage Design

Identical with n. III, A1.

B1. Foliage Design

h. 0·15 m. w. 0·36 m.

An arabesque of tight foliage leaves radiating from a circular stem at the centre of the light.

Condition. Complete, except for the lower tip of the bottom foil. *In situ.*

Colour and Technique. Foliage painted on white glass on a matt background, patterned border in yellow stain.

Style and Design. See B2.

Date. Mid 14th c.

B2. Foliage Design

h. 0·15 m. w. 0·36 m.

An arabesque of foliage leaves radiating from a circular stem at the centre of the light.

Condition. Complete, except for the upper foil which is missing. *In situ.*

Colour and Technique. As B1.

Style and Design. The glass in the two companion lights (B1 and B2) appears to be *in situ*. The foliage designs are close but the leaf form differs. In B1 the central arabesque has broad trefoil leaves with small fruit clusters, in B2 the foliage is more of a type of oak leaf with trefoil fruit clusters. The border designs also differ. A1 has a serpentine running trail, B2 has an undulating line with a repeated dot pattern.

Date. Mid 14th c.

C2. Foliage Design

h. 0·23 m. w. 0·23 m.

At the centre a square patterned boss with four white leaves of foliage radiating from it.

Condition. Complete except for the lower foil, which has been replaced by an incomplete set of four quarries painted on a single piece of glass. Quarry type 31. *In situ.*

Colour and Technique. Central boss blue glass painted with a rosette design. Foliage painted on white glass against a plain matt black background, patterned border in yellow stain separated from the masonry by a strip of plain white glass.

Style and Design. The glass appears to be *in situ*, but here again the leaf type is slightly different to the foliage in the other lights in this window.

Date. Mid 14th c.

s. II

A1. Foliage Design

h. 0·15 m. w. 0·16 m.

Condition. Complete. *In situ.*

Colour and Technique, Style and Design. Identical with n. II, A1.

Date. Mid 14th c.

B2, B3. Composite Panels of unrelated fragments

h. 0·15 m. w. 0·16 m.

Mostly plain glass. 14th c.

C2. Tracery Design

Condition. Incomplete coloured boss at centre replaced with plain white glass. *In situ.*

Style and Design, Colour and Technique. The glass is a composite of two designs, one identical with n. II, C2, the other has a different pattern on the border.

Date. Mid 14th c.

s. III

A1. Foliage Design

h. 0·15 m. w. 0·16 m.

Condition. Incomplete, two foils are patched with alien fragments. *In situ.*

Colour and Technique, Style and Design. Identical with s. II, A1 and n. II, A1.

Date. Mid 14th c.

s. IV

A1. Foliage Design

h. 0·15 m. w. 0·16 m.

Condition. Complete. Very corroded. *In situ.*

Colour and Technique, Style and Design. Identical with s. II, A1, n. II, A1, and s. III, A1.

Date. Mid 14th c.

B2, B3, Composite Panels

n. 0·15 m. w. 0·16 m.

Composite of unrelated fragments, some set inside out and semi-opaque through decay.

C2. Tracery Design

h. 0·23 m. w. 0·23 m.

At the centre a white rosette set against plain white glass with a pattern border.

Condition. Incomplete. The upper and lower foils patched with alien glass. *In situ.*

Colour and Technique, Style and Design. Same as n. II, B2. Repeated border design identical.

Date. Mid 14th c.

CHASTLETON
ST. MARY THE VIRGIN

O.S. SP 248 292.

PRINTED SOURCES
Nelson (1913), 173.
Pevsner (1974), 531.

There are minor remains of glass in two windows, one in the vestry, the other in the south clerestory of the nave. A restoration scheme was proposed in 1971. When this is carried out all the glass will be set in one window.

n. II

1b. The Virgin Annunciate   PLATE 22 (*a*)

h. 0·23 m. w. 0·65 m.

The Virgin Mary kneeling at a prayer desk, the Holy Dove flying down adjacent to her face. To the left is a scroll, inscribed in black-letter script:

| *Ave gr(aci)a plena d(omi)n(u)s Tecu(m)* |

Condition. A fragment of a larger composition, cut down to a quarry shape. Cracked, with pronounced pitting on the inner surface.

Colour and Technique. Painted on white glass, very light brown paint, with stippled matt and line shading, the details picked out in yellow stain.

Iconography. The scroll bears the opening phrase of the Archangel's Salutation to the Virgin: '*Ave, gracia plena: Dominus tecum: Benedicta tu in mulieribus*' (St. Luke 1: 28). The scene takes place in an elaborate architectural setting, the Virgin kneeling at a prayer desk which has an open book on it. (The literary origin of the motif of the Virgin's book is obscure.)[1]

The earliest known representation of the Virgin kneeling at the Annunciation is Giotto's fresco in the Arena Chapel, Padua, of *c.* 1305.[2] Although such representations are common in Italian painting from this date onwards, they are not found in north-west Europe until the third quarter of the 14th c. The earliest known French example occurs in a Franciscan Missal, of *c.* 1350, illuminated by a follower of Jean Pucelle.[3] In England it is first found in the Carew-Poynz Hours, of *c.* 1350–60, a manuscript closely related

in style to contemporary work on the Continent.[4] It is often found from the late 14th c. onwards.[5]

The architectural setting at Chastleton is probably part of a large canopy; it should not, therefore, be interpreted as having a particular significance.[6]

Style and Design. Although cut down in size, the small scale suggests that originally this glass was the central part of a large architectural canopy, possibly pendent to another that contained the Archangel Gabriel. The simplified drawing of the architecture, with little ornamental detail, would be appropriate to such a position.

Date. Mid 15th c.

s. II

1a. Fragments

Condition. A medley panel of fragments, mostly set inside out. Roundel: a variegated rose, white and yellow stain. 15th c. Roundel: a white star, border design of two intertwined thorn branches, white and yellow stain. 15th c.

Fragments of an inscription, black-letter script set inside out: | *Orate* |.

CHINNOR
ST. ANDREW

O.S. SP 756 008.

MS. SOURCE

Francis Buttanshaw, 'An Account of the Church and Restoration, *c.* 1866', unpublished MS. in the possession of the Rector of Chinnor.

PRINTED

'St. Andrews' Parish Church and its Restoration', *N.O.A.S.* xii (1874), 4.
Visitations (1871), 112–3.
P.C. (1920), 88–9.
Bouchier (1918), 68–9.
Greening Lamborn (1949), 118.
V.C.H. viii (1964), 76–7.
Pevsner (1974), 534–6.

There are four windows containing medieval glass, all fourteenth century. The two windows in the chancel are the most complete and interesting, n. II and s. II. Each window contains the figure of a saint

---

[1] See Brightwell Baldwin, s. V. 3b.

[2] D. Robb, 'The Iconography of the Annunciation in the Fourteenth and Fifteenth centuries', *The Art Bulletin* xviii (1936), 480–525.

[3] Bodl. Lib. Douce MS. 313, f. 5ᵛ. M. Meiss, *French Painting in the time of Jean de Berry* (1967), 212, fig. 663.

[4] Cambridge Fitzwilliam Museum, MS. J. 48, f. 63ʳ. M. R. James, *A Descriptive Catalogue of the Manuscripts in the Fitzwilliam Museum* (1895), 111. M. Rickert, *Painting in Britain. The Middle Ages* (1965), 148.

[5] For example, B.L. Add. MSS. 29704–5, f. 99, 1391–8. M. Rickert, *The Reconstructed Carmelite Missal* (1952), 103, pl. 10. For the Herman Scheere group of MSS., 1405–15, see E. Panofsky, *Early Netherlandish Painting* (1953), 117–18, figs. 170, 174–6, 179.

[6] Robb, op. cit. 495, stresses that the ecclesiastical setting of the Annunciation is the outstanding characteristic of its French iconography in the late 14th and early 15th c. See also M. Meiss, *French Painting in the Time of Jean de Berry* (1968), 27–30.

standing beneath a canopy in each main light and one of the Works of Mercy in the centre tracery light. Two of the saints are anonymous, a bishop and an archbishop (n. II), facing SS. Lawrence and Alban in the opposite window (s. II). It is certain that the two windows are of the same date and the product of one workshop. There are many features in common: the grassy sward the figures stand upon is a repeated design, and the background foliage diapers in n. II, 2b and s. II, 2a are identical. The drapery painting is consistent, very slight modelling and repeated pleating tucks along the hems of garments. More conclusive is the fact that the four canopy designs are identical except for small variations in details of colour and crocket types. The white patterned backgrounds behind the tops of the canopies are of two types, both in each window. There are some variations, for example a difference in the detailed drawing of the eyebrows and eyes of the archbishop with long eyebrows and a double line, open at the end, for the upper and lower eyelids (n. II, 2b), compared with the shorter eyebrows and a single line for the eyelids, closed at the ends, for St. Alban (s. II, 2b). There is a similar variety in the grotesque border figures in s. II. The wyverns differ in pose and action, there is no repetition of a standard design.

All these factors suggest that this is the product of a sophisticated and inventive workshop. It has been stated that these two windows are fifteenth century.[1] This can hardly be correct. The canopies with their complete lack of any interest in perspective design, the broad leaves of the foliage diapers, border designs, drapery painting, and head types can only be accommodated in the first half of the fourteenth century. There is documentary evidence for a precise dating. The chancel was rebuilt in the early fourteenth century, and, with the high altar, was dedicated in 1326.[2] It is therefore suggested that the windows are the same date.

A Christ in Judgement (n. V, A2), and a shield of the Zouche family (n. X, A1), which had a holding in the manor of Chinnor, are possibly the products of the same workshop.

The windows were restored by Messrs. Clayton & Bell when the church was restored 1863–6. Their replacement pieces are very skilfully executed and difficult to detect.

n. II — PLATE 22 (b)

1a, 1b. Geometric Grisaille

h. 0·70 m. w. 0·54 m.

Imitation medieval design by Clayton & Bell.

2a. Bishop — PLATE 22 (c)

h. 0·70 m. w. 0·54 m.

A bishop in mass vestments, full length facing three-quarters right, in benediction holding a crozier.

Condition. The face, most of the chasuble, and parts of the background are Clayton & Bell restoration. The original glass is very corroded on both surfaces.

Colour and Technique. Mitre in yellow stain, amice ruby, pot-metal ochre chasuble with patterned white stole, green dalmatic, white alb with ruby apparel, pot-metal ochre sandals, white gloves and crozier. Green sward by feet set against a blue background diapered with trails of strawberry leaves picked out of a matt black wash.

Iconography. Although the figure has no nimbus it is probably a bishop saint. Originally there may have been an inscription with his name, see s. II, 2b.

Style and Design. See above.

Date. c. 1326.

2b. Archbishop — PLATE 22 (d)

h. 0·70 m. w. 0·54 m.

An archbishop in mass vestments, full length facing three-quarters left in benediction, holding a cross-staff.

Condition. The figure is complete, part of the background is Clayton & Bell restoration. The glass is very corroded on both surfaces.

Colour and Technique. White mitre, pink face, purple amice, green chasuble with plain white pall, pot-metal ochre maniple and dalmatic, white alb with ruby apparel and pot-metal ochre sandals, white gloves and cross-staff. Green sward by feet, blue background diapered with trails of oak leaves picked out of a matt black wash. The drapery modelling has a strong linear emphasis with slight smear shading. Very slight modelling of the facial features and hair.

Iconography. As 2a, but here an archbishop saint.

Style and Design. See introduction above.

Date. c. 1326.

[1] V.C.H. viii (1964), 77.   [2] Buttanshaw MS., op. cit. V.C.H. viii (1964), 77.

3a. Canopy Design

h. 1·05 m. w. 0·54 m.

The bishop stands below an arch with traceried side-shafts. The arch is cusped cinquefoil and has a crocketed gable and finial. Behind the main arch is a two-storied structure with blind tracery supporting a traceried window with an arch and crocketed spire, flanked by side-shafts and two pairs of flying buttresses. The outer buttresses are the heads of the side-shafts of the main arch beside the figure.

Condition. Complete. Slight restoration by Clayton & Bell.

Colour and Technique. The main arch and side-shafts are in white glass, crocketed arch and finial with ruby base in pot-metal ochre. The base of the structure behind the main arch is obscured by decay, possibly once green. Blind tracery, white glass with a blue and green cresting. Traceried window, white, arch and crocketed spire in pot-metal ochre, side-shafts also ochre with blue crocketed spires, spires of the inner pair of flying buttresses also blue, outer pair pot-metal ochre. The lower part of the canopy is set against a plain ruby ground. The spires of the apex of the canopy are set against patterned white glass which appears to be a combination of foliage motifs and heraldic charges. Just below the shoulders of the light are two square pieces each painted with a double-headed eagle displayed, picked out of a matt black background. Above the right-hand eagle is a lion statant, shaped to fit the shoulder of the light.

Style and Design. See introduction above.

Date. c. 1326.

3b. Canopy Design

h. 1·05 m. w. 0·54 m.

The design is the same as 3a with slight variations in colour and details of the crocket of the upper spires. The white background behind the apex of the canopy also differs; here the pattern appears to be a repeated design of twists of foliage with a lion statant below the right shoulder of the light.

Condition. Complete. Minor restoration by Clayton & Bell. It is difficult to know how much of the white patterned glass is the restorer's arrangement.

Date. c. 1326.

1a, 2a, 3a. Borders

w. 0·06 m.

A serpentine vine stem with bunches of grapes.

Condition. All restoration, except for those in the cusped head of the light.

Colour and Technique. Vine stem and grapes in white glass, leaves in deep green set against pieces of plain ruby.

Date. c. 1326.

1b, 2b, 3b. Borders

w. 0·06 m.

A serpentine trail of roses.

Condition. Some restoration.

Colour and Technique. Stem with offspringing trails of clusters of buds painted on green glass, roses in deep pot-metal ruby set against pieces of plain blue glass.

Date. c. 1326.

A1, A3. Censing Angel

h. 0·18 m. w. 0·06 m.

In the lower foil a foliage design. The upper foil a demi-figure of an angel swinging a censer.

Condition. Complete.

Colour and Technique. Painted on white glass.

Date. c. 1326? The glass is so small that without a close inspection it is impossible to judge if it is original or restoration.

A2. Works of Mercy. Giving Drink to the Thirsty

h. 0·70 m. w. 0·52 m.

All restoration by Clayton & Bell except for the left-hand side of the mantle worn by the old man. There is no evidence to show how much of the modern design is copied from a lost original, or how much is Clayton & Bell's own design to complement the scene in the window opposite, s. II, A2.

Date. c. 1326 and 1863–6.

n. V   PLATE 24 (*a*)

A1. Censing Angel

h. 0·18 m. w. 0·06 m.

In the lower foil a foliage design, above a demi-figure of an angel swinging a censer.

Condition. Complete and *in situ*. The paint is rather worn.

Colour and Technique. Painted on white glass, angel's alb in yellow stain.

Style and Design. The same design as n. II, A1 and A3.

Date. Second quarter 14th c.

A2. Christ in Judgement   PLATE 24 (*a*)

h. 0·70 m. w. 0·52 m.

Christ enthroned in benediction holding an orb in his left hand.

Condition. The figure is complete. The left-hand side of the throne and the plain blue background are probably restoration.

Colour and Technique. Flesh: pink glass. Deep ruby mantle over a green robe, pot-metal ochre throne, plain blue background. Strong smear modelling on the ruby mantle.

Iconography. The resurrected Christ. The marks of the nails shown on the feet, his hand raised in benediction. The original design may have had the Resurrection of Souls in the lower tracery lights.[1]

Style and Design. The drawing of the features, particularly the open end-lines of the eyes are similar to the heads in n. II and s. II.

Date. Second quarter 14th c.

n. X

A1. Shield of Zouche

h. 0·35 m. w. 0·35 m.

Gules bezanty or a chevron argent ZOUCHE.

Set against white glass painted with trails of oak leaves and acorns.

Condition. Apparently complete, the coloured glass of the shield is very corroded, the foliage trails less so. The chevron should probably be ermine.[2] The glass is medieval, and it may be assumed that the painted ermine spots have worn off as the shield was tricked as now at the 1574 Visitation.[3]

Colour and Technique. The coloured glass is all pot-metal. Foliage painted in outline on plain white glass, separated from the masonry by a strip of plain white glass.

Date. First half 14th c. A third share in the manor was inherited by Helen, daughter of Roger de Quincy, Earl of Winchester. She married Alan, Lord Zouche, who died in 1270.[4] In 1279 the tenant was Oliver la Zouche,[5] a younger son of Helen. His son John was living there in 1316, and was still living in 1359.[6] Greening Lamborn described the arms as Zouche of Dene.[7]

s. II   PLATE 23 (*a*)

1a, 1b. Geometric Grisaille

Imitation medieval design by Clayton & Bell, as n. II, 1a and 1b.

1a–3a, 1b–3b. Borders

w. 0·16 m.

A serpentine trail of foliage inhabited by grotesques and hybrids.

Condition. The foliage is all restoration, except for two pieces, as are the grotesques with the exception of the following:

East side, reading from the bottom upwards:
4. A wyvern in profile facing left, lower half modern.
6. A wyvern facing left, head in profile facing right.
10. A wyvern in profile facing left, very decayed.

West side of east light, reading from the bottom:
2. A wyvern, raised wings, in profile facing right, head in profile facing left.
11. A wyvern in profile facing right, head thrown right back.

The foliage below grotesques 6 and 8 is genuine.

East side of west light, reading from the bottom:
6. A two-legged beast with a bearded human head wearing a cowl, in profile facing left.
8. A similar beast with a beardless human head, sticking out his tongue and wearing a close-fitting cap.

West side of west light, reading from the bottom:
7. A wyvern in profile facing left.
8. A wyvern in profile facing right.

All the grotesque beasts are different in details, there is no repetition of one design.

Colour and Technique. Foliage in pot-metal ochre, grotesques in white glass set against pieces of plain blue.

Style and Design. This is the earliest datable example of this class of design extant in the county. Grotesque border designs are a particular feature of some of the aisle windows of the nave of York Minster.[8]

Date. c. 1326.

2a. St. Lawrence   PLATE 23 (*c*)

h. 0·70 m. w. 0·54 m.

St. Lawrence full length facing three-quarters right, he holds a book in his right hand and a gridiron in his left hand.

---

[1] e.g. The tracery lights of the east window of the north aisle at Stanford-on-Avon (Northants.). Newton ii (1961), 358–91.

[2] 'Sire Olyver la Souche, de goules, besaunte de or, a un cheveron de ermyne.' *A Roll of Arms of the Reign of Edward the Second*, ed. N. H. Nicholas (1829), 69.

[3] Visitations (1871), 113. 'In glas'.

[4] G.E.C. xii, part ii (1959), 934. *V.C.H.* vii (1964), 60.

[5] *V.C.H.* ibid. See also n. 2 above. G.E.C. op. cit. 934 n. 9.

[6] *V.C.H.* vii (1964), 60 n. 27.

[7] Greening Lamborn (1949), 118. *V.C.H.* ibid. notes that it is not clear why they are called Zouche of Dene.

[8] York Minster, north aisle of nave, particularly the second and third window from the east (n. XXIV and n. XXV). G. Benson, *The Ancient Painted Glass Windows in the Minster and Churches of the City of York* (1918), 32–6.

Condition. The figure is complete, part of the background is restoration by Clayton & Bell. The original glass is very corroded, the face and hands are almost opaque.

Colour and Technique. Pot-metal ochre nimbus, face and hands in pink glass, ruby amice, green fringed dalmatic over white tunical with ruby apparel, pot-metal ochre sandals. Green sward by feet, set against a blue background diapered with oak-leaf trails picked out of a matt black wash.

Iconography. He holds a gridiron, symbol of his martyrdom. St. Lawrence was a native of Spain, taken to Rome by St. Sixtus, who ordained him as his archdeacon. He was martyred during the Dacian persecution in A.D. 258, being submitted to various tortures before being roasted on a gridiron and then beheaded.[1] His cult was widespread throughout Europe during the Middle Ages. The earliest extant representation of the saint with the gridiron as symbol of his martyrdom is the 5th-c. mosaic in the Mausoleum of Galla Placida in Ravenna.[2] The first English representation is found on the embroidered maniple given by Queen Aelfflæd (d. before A.D. 916) to Frithestan, Bishop of Winchester 909–31, and later presented to the Shrine of St. Cuthbert. He is depicted in deacon's vestments, name inscription LAVRENTIVS DIACONVS, but has no attribute.[3] There are many representations of him in English art,[4] but the only narrative window that has survived in England is the east window of the parish church of St. Lawrence at Ludlow (Salop). It contains twenty-seven scenes, and was probably given by Thomas Spofford, Bishop of Hereford 1421–8.[5]

Style and Design. See above.

Date. c. 1326.

2b. St. Alban   PLATES 3 (*a*), 23 (*d*)

h. 0·70 m. w. 0·54 m.

St. Alban full length facing three-quarters left, secular dress, no nimbus,[6] he holds a long rod in his right hand. Inscription in black-letter script: | S(*anctus*) *alb*|*anu*(*s*) |

Condition. The figure and background are complete. The glass is very corroded on both sides.

Colour and Technique. Head and hands in pink glass, green cap with white turned-up brim, purple tunic split at the front to show white lining, with lappet sleeves and green undertunic, pot-metal ochre hose and shoes. Green sward by feet. Set against a blue background diapered with a squared trellis, alternating pattern of a lion rampant and an eagle displayed, picked out of a matt black wash. Inscription on pale yellow ochre glass, picked out of a matt black wash. The drapery modelling has a strong linear emphasis with slight smear shading. Very slight modelling of the facial features and hair.

Iconography. St. Alban, the proto-martyr of England, was martyred during the persecution of Diocletian, 303–12.[7] His cult was centred at the great Benedictine monastery of St. Albans, originally founded by King Offa of Mercia to enshrine the relics of the saint in 793.[8] The cult was established at a very early date. In 429 St. Germanus of Auxerre visited the tomb on a reforming mission to England and took away relics of the dust stained with the martyr's blood.[9]

The earliest extant English representations of the saint date from the 12th c.[10] An important 13th-c. illustrated Life by Matthew Paris, monk and chronicler of St. Alban's Abbey, is preserved at Trinity College, Dublin.[11] Single figures of St. Alban are rare. The earliest example is the 12th-c. seal of the Abbey.[12] The rod held by the figure at Chinnor may be intended to indicate his courtly status; in the later Middle Ages he was regarded as a prince.[13] His usual attribute is the cross that he carried at the time of his martyrdom.[14] He is also represented holding a sceptre or the

1 *Golden Legend* iv, 208–28.

2 *Herder* vi (1974), 374–80, particularly 375, fig. 1.

3 *The Relics of St. Cuthbert*, ed. C. F. Battiscombe (1956), 13–14, 375–401.

4 For examples in English glass painting see Newton i (1961), 264.

5 E. W. Ganderton and J. Lafond, *Ludlow Stained and Painted Glass* (1961), 14–17. The window was restored by David Evans of Shrewsbury 1828–32. Although much of the glass is modern, some drawings made before the restoration show that the restored portions are careful copies of the original. Birmingham, University Library, *Mytton MS.* Shropshire collections.

6 Another 14th-c. example of the omission of the nimbus occurs at Aldwincle (Northants.) in the figures of St. Christopher and St. George. Newton i (1961), 254; ii. 312–14.

7 Bede, *Historia Ecclesiastica Gentis Anglorum*, vii, in *Venerabilis Baedae Opera Historica*, ed. C. Plummer i (1896), 18–22. *Golden*

Legend iv, 236–53.

8 G. Levison, 'St. Alban and St. Albans', *Antiquity*, (1941), 337–8.

9 Plummer, op. cit. xviii, 36–7.

10 Miniature of his martyrdom in the St. Albans Psalter at Hildesheim, St. Godehard, p. 146, probably before 1123. C. R. Dodwell, O. Pächt, and F. Wormald, *The St. Albans Psalter* (1960), 7, pl. 99.

11 W. R. L. Lowe and E. F. Jacob, *Illustrations to the Life of St. Alban* (1924).

12 Birch i, 58, 3939, cast lxiv.

13 For example the early 15th-c. devotion, 'Prynce of knythode: throwoute the grete breteyne/Noble of blode: large of hospitalyte', B.L. Arundel MS. 249, f. 7ʳ.

14 For the usual form of the cross see Pächt et al., *The St. Albans Psalter* (1960), 8–9.

sword of his martyrdom.[1] His cult is also found in Germany at Cologne,[2] and in France at the Abbey of Bec.[3]

Style and Design. See above.

Date. c. 1326.

3a. Canopy Design

h. 1·05 m. w. 0·54 m.

Condition. Complete, slight restoration by Clayton & Bell.

Colour and Technique, Style and Design. The same as n. II, 3a and 3b, with only slight variation in detail. The white patterned background behind the apex of the canopy is extremely indistinct through decay; it appears to be a repeat of the double-headed eagle and lion design in n. II, 3a.

Date. c. 1326.

3b. Canopy Design

h. 1·05 m. w. 0·54 m.

Condition. Complete, except for slight restoration by Clayton & Bell.

Colour and Technique, Style and Design. Same as n. II, 3a, 3b, with only slight variation in detail. The white patterned background is extremely decayed and indistinct; it appears to repeat the foliage and lion statant design of n. II, 3b.

Date. c. 1326.

A1, A3. Censing Angels

h. 0·18 m. w. 0·16 m.

In the lower foil a demi-figure of an angel swinging a long censer, the censer and its chain occupy most of the two foils of the light.

Condition. Complete, except for a small patch at the top of A1.

Colour and Technique. Painted on white glass, details in yellow stain.

Date. 14th c., *c.* 1326? The glass is so small that without a close inspection it is impossible to judge whether it is original or restoration.

A2. Works of Mercy. Clothing the Naked PLATE 23 (*b*)

h. 0·70 m. w. 0·52 m.

An elderly man stands left before the open doors of a house, he hands a garment to a half-naked cripple who faces him wearing a pair of long drawers and leaning on a tau crutch.

Condition. Complete, only a small part is restoration. The glass is very decayed.

Colour and Technique. The flesh is painted on pink glass, the benefactor has a blue cap, ochre mantle with ochre and white chaperon, blue shoes. Cripple's drawers in white glass, ochre crutch, the gift garment is green. Ochre doors, brickwork in white, with a blue tiled roof. The figures stand on a green sward, sprinkled with plants. Blue background diapered with a foliage design, an arabesque of small trefoil leaves picked out of a matt black background wash of paint. In each side-foil is a miniature oak tree in pot-metal ochre. Smear shading on the drapery and heads, but very restricted in use.

Iconography. Six of the Seven Works of Mercy represent the deeds spoken of by Christ (Matthew 25: 31–46). The seventh and final work, burying the dead, was added from Tobit 1: 16–18. The earliest representations known are of the 12th c., and of Continental origin.[4] There are many English examples of the later 14th and 15th–16th c. in glass painting[5] and wall-painting.[6] The example at Chinnor is notable in that it appears to be the earliest extant example in English glass painting. There are six side-windows in the chancel. It seems probable that at the head of each window was one of the Works of Mercy, the seventh being excluded, as in the 15th-c. window at All Saints, North Street, York.[7]

Style and Design. By the same hand as the figures in the main lights 2a, 2b. The delineation of the facial features and the restricted use of modelling are exactly the same.

Date. c. 1326.

Lost Glass

Antiquarian sources record a shield and inscription for Sir Reynold de Malins (d. 1384) who held lands in the Manor, and his two wives.[8]

[1] East window of the Beauchamp Chapel, Warwick, 1447. C. Woodforde, *English Stained and Painted Glass* (1954), pl. 16. Kildare Hours, *c.* 1425. New York, Pierpont Morgan Library MS. M. 105, f. 58. Sarum Hours, mid 15th c., ibid. MS. M. 46, f. 35ᵛ. Anglo-Flemish Hours, *c.* 1490, Cambridge, Fitzwilliam Museum MS. J. 57, f. 21ᵛ.
[2] Cologne, Monastery of St. Pantaleon. The relics of a Roman martyr of the same name were given by the Empress Theophano in 984 and were mistakenly associated with the English saint. E. P. Baker, 'The Cult of St. Alban and Cologne', *Royal Archaeological Journal*, xciv (1937).
[3] Relics list of 1134. The relics were probably taken there by St. Anselm, Abbot of Bec 1078–93. *The Life of St. Anselm Archbishop of* *Canterbury by the monk Eadmer*, ed. R. W. Southern (1962), 56 n. 1.
[4] *Herder* i (1968), 245–51.
[5] C. Woodforde, *The Norwich School of Glass Painting in the Fifteenth Century* (1950), 193–6. G. M. Rushforth, 'An Account of Some Painted Glass from a House at Leicester', *Archaeological Journal*, 2nd ser. xxv (1918), 62–4.
[6] E. W. Tristram, *English Wall Painting of the Fourteenth Century* (1955), 99–101. A. Caiger-Smith, *English Medieval Mural Paintings* (1963), 53–5.
[7] E. A. Gee, 'The Painted Glass of All Saints Church, North Street, York', *Archaeologia* cii (1969), 163–4.
[8] Visitations (1871), 113. *V.C.H.* viii (1964), 61, 77.

CHURCH HANBOROUGH
ST. PETER AND ST. PAUL

O.S. SP 426 128.

PRINTED SOURCES
P.C. (1920), 161.
Pevsner (1974), 543-4.

There are only slight remains of fifteenth-century glass in a window of the south chantry chapel and a window of the south aisle. It is known from the seventeenth-century antiquarian sources that one of the windows of the chantry chapel then contained figures of three men and three women and an inscription stating that 'they repaired the window in 1453'.[1] It is probable that the remaining glass is also of this date.

s. IV

A1, A4. Fragments

h. 0·12 m. w. 0·10 m.

Small pieces of foliage design, as A2 and A3 below.

A2, A3. Foliage Design

h. 0·16 m. w. 0·30 m.

Two identical foliage designs, showing a large rose set against a background foliage diaper.

Condition. Complete and *in situ.* Old leaded repairs, little corrosion.

Colour and Technique. Painted on white glass. The white rose has a central floret in yellow stain. The formalized seaweed foliage diaper is in white, picked out of a matt black background, within a plain yellow stain border. The rose and the lower lobe of foliage are painted on a single piece of glass proving the authenticity of the arrangement.

Style and Design. The rosettes are quite common (see Burford, I, A10), but complete tracery designs of this type do not survive elsewhere in the county.

Date. 15th c., probably *c.* 1453.

s. V

2a, 2c. Foliage Design

h. 0·07 m. w. 0·07 m.

Condition. Top cusp of each light retains an identical foliage

which would have been repeated in the other cusps, now lost. The surviving glass is well preserved. *In situ.*

Colour and Technique. A spray of white foliage against a yellow stain background, patterned with a black-lined hatching, and a plain white border.

Date. 15th c.

A1-A6. Foliage Design

h. 0·14 m. w. 0·14 m.

A repeated foliage design taken from the one cartoon: two large white leaves springing from a rose in the right-angled corner.

Condition. Complete and *in situ,* except for one missing lobe in A1. Old leaded repairs. The glass is well preserved with little decay.

Colour and Technique. Painted on white glass, the leaves in yellow stain with a white central rib against a plain matt background and plain white border.

Style and Design. The leaf form is identical with the upper lobe foliage design in the window above (s. IV, A2, A3).

Date. Mid 15th c., *c.* 1453.

---

[1] P.C. (1920), 161. '*orate pro bono statu Ricardi snareston ceterorumque qui reparaverunt istam fenestram anno domini MCCCCLIII.*' The figures represented Richard Snareston and Margaret his wife, and William Bayley and Thomas Roch with their wives. The south window of the church contained the figure of John Sprot, date unknown. The identities of these people have not been established.

COGGES

ST. MARY

O.S. SP 361 096.

PRINTED SOURCES

P.C. (1920), 98–9.
O.A.H.S. N.S. ii (1870), 141–3.

Visitations (1871), 47.
Price, E. R., 'Tombs at Asthall and Cogges, Oxfordshire', *Oxoniensia*, iii (1938), 103.
V.C.H. ii (1907), 161–2.
Pevsner (1974), 550–5.

The tracery lights of the east window of the north transept chapel retain much of their original foliage designs *in situ*. At an earlier restoration panels of plain modern glass made up the considerable portions of missing glass. In 1965 the glass was releaded by Mr. Farrar Bell and the lost glass was made up with copies of the original surviving parts: a highly successful and accomplished piece of work.

The original design is an extremely striking one, and as a design has no real parallels elsewhere in the county. The bold leaf patterns are all in white glass and yellow stain against a matt black background. There is a restricted use of coloured glass applied only to the plain borders of some of the roundels set in the foliage. The yellow stain varies in intensity of tone from a light lemon to a deep orange. All medieval glass dates from the second quarter of the fourteenth century.

n. II   PLATES 24 (b), (c), 25 (a)

A1, A2. Foliage Design 1

h. 0·27 m. w. 0·27 m.

Two identical designs, at the centre a roundel painted with a rosette design in a plain border set against four serrated leaves.

B1 to B4. Foliage Design 2

h. 0·54 m. w. 0·24 m.

Four identical designs. From the lower point of each light springs a branch with offspringing circular leaves alternating with small trefoil offshoots that diverge to encircle the rosette roundel, identical with that in A1 and A2, at the centre of each light, reuniting to form a central leaf in the top foil of the light. The lead lines of the composition are assimilated into the pattern incorporated with a painted framework superimposed on the foliage design.

C1, C2. Foliage Design 3

h. 0·36 m. w. 0·27 m.

A central boss of a geometric tracery design of eight segments, each cusped trefoil, radiating from a circle in the centre and set against circular foliage springing from the base of the light. The top foils with the foliage set upside down are both modern restorations.

D1, D4. Foliage Design 4

h. 1·05 m. w. 0·36 m.

Similar arrangement to foliage design 2, but with fewer small leaves. The original over-all design was lost before the recent restoration, so the panels as they stand must be viewed as composite. At the centre of each light a roundel painted with a star, 15th-c., not *in situ*. In D1 an inserted inscription in Lombardic script: | A(N)DREAS |

D2, D3. Foliage Design 5

h. 90 m. w. 0·39 m.

From the lower point of the light springs a stem with off-springing trefoils and circular leaves which diverges to encircle three roundels set along the central axis of the light. The middle roundel of D2 is original, a spiral design of three serrated leaves, the others 15th-c. insertions; stars and a large crown. The upper roundel of D2 has a different leaf form, unlike any other in the window; the painting is inferior in quality and is possibly an insertion or restoration.

E1. Foliage Design 5

h. 0·21 m. w. 0·30 m.

At the centre a roundel painted with a quatrefoil flower set between two sprays of oak leaves springing from the base and apex of the light respectively.

Lost Glass

The 1574 Visitation records thirteen shields of arms in the windows of the church.[1] Only five of these survived the Civil War.[2] (The exact locations are not specified.)

Argent on a bend azure three mullets of six points or, a label of five points gules (MOREBY).

Gules a bucks face argent (DUSTON?).

Barry of eight or and gules (FITZALAN OF BEDALE).

Per fess dancetty gules and or, in chief a bar or (UNIDENTIFIED).[3]

Barry nebuly of six or and gules (LOVEL OF TITCHMARSH)

Argent three crosses crosslet fitchy sable, on a chief azure three mullets or (CLINTON, EARL OF HUNTINGDON).

Barry of eight argent and azure on a bend gules three martlets or (GREY OF COGGES).

Argent a fess gules (ODDINGESELES).

Barry of eight argent and azure, a bend gules (GREY OF ROTHERFIELD).

Or a fess between two chevrons gules (FITZWALTER OR GREY?).

Azure a chevron gules and a chief argent (HAMON?). 'Over it written *Will(el)mus hamon monke of (the) Ab(bey of) F(e)campe, prior of Cogges.*'

(GREY OF ROTHERFIELD).

(GREY OF COGGES). 'Underneath it is writt obscurly in Saxon character *le dame de grey*.'[4]

The manor of Cogges was held by the Greys of Rotherfield, and some of the shields refer to Sir John de Grey (d. 1311), and his son John, Lord Grey (1300–59).[5] The elder John married Margaret, daughter of William de Oddingeseles, sister and co-heiress of Edmund de Oddingeseles.[6] Margaret was apparently married again, in or before 1319, to Robert de Moreby of Moreby (Yorks.).[7] Her sister Ida married John de Clinton, Lord Clinton of Maxstoke (d. 1310)[8] and their younger son William (d. 1354) was created Earl of Huntingdon in 1337.[9] Sir John de Grey, Lord Grey of Rotherfield, married Catherine, younger daughter and co-heiress of Sir Brian Fitz Alan, Lord Fitz Alan.[10] The '*dame de grey*' referred to in the lost inscription and the differenced arms of Grey may represent Joan de Valoignes (d. 1312), wife of Robert de Grey (d. 1295).[11] William Hamon, the king's surgeon, was Prior of Cogges,[12] and either resigned or died before 1377 when Thomas Tynny was appointed Prior.[13] The alien priory of Cogges was attached to the Benedictine Abbey of Fécamp.[14]

COMBE

ST. LAWRENCE

O.S. SP 414 158.

PRINTED SOURCES

Parker (1846), 153–6.
Ditchfield (1903), 186.
Nelson (1913), 161.

Bouchier (1918), 93.
P.C. (1920), 101.
Bouchier (1932), 128.
Emden, C. S., *Combe Church and Village* (1951, reprinted 1970).
Pevsner (1974), 552.

The remaining glass is only a small portion of a series of at least six windows that appear to have been made at the same time by a single workshop. The evidence for this is the repetition of stock cartoons for the figures of cherubim and foliage designs in the tracery lights and canopies in the head of the main lights. There is no other example of so much repetition surviving in the county. Unfortunately, only one figure, St. James Major, survives from the main light glazing of these windows (s. IV, 3c). This is the only remaining figure from a series of the Twelve Apostles, each with his verse of the Creed inscribed on a scroll.

---

[1] Visitations (1871), 47.
[2] P.C. (1920), 98–9, the transcript of Bodl. Lib. Wood MS. B. 15. f. 56 is defective.
[3] Wood's trick suggests that the shield was incomplete, the blazon may therefore be incorrect.
[4] The 1574 Visitation translated the inscription into English.
[5] *Feudal Aids* iv. 156, 163, 178.
[6] G.E.C. vi. 144–5.
[7] Ibid.

[8] Ibid. iii. 312–13.
[9] Ibid. vi. 648–9.
[10] Ibid. vi. 145–6.
[11] C. Moor, 'Knights of Edward I', *Harleian Society*, lxxi (1929), 154. Price, *Oxoniensia*, op. cit.
[12] *V.C.H* ii (1907), 162.
[13] Ibid.
[14] Ibid.

There is a marked difference in quality of design and execution between the St. James Major and the cherubim in the tracery lights. A similar distinction has been observed in the great east window of Malvern Priory, glazed between 1423 and 1429.[1] It is possible that the less important work for the traceries was entrusted to a junior member of the workshop that supplied the glass.

PLATE 26 (a), (b)

2c. Roundel

d. 0·14 m.

A large rose, painted on white glass, lips of the petals in yellow stain, plain border in yellow stain. 15th c.

5a–5e. Canopies

h. 0·24 m. w. 0·39 m.

The apexes of five identical canopy designs set against plain coloured backgrounds, alternately ruby and blue. See s. IV. 4c for the original design.

Date. Second quarter 15th c.

A1–A10

Each eyelet contains a scrap of glass, not *in situ* and not catalogued.

B1. Censing Angel

h. 0·45 m. w. 0·17 m.

An angel kneeling facing three-quarters right swinging a censer.

Condition. Complete except for the lower left drapery and lower cusp. Slight all-over corrosion.

Colour and Technique. Angel, painted on white glass, hair and wings in yellow stain, set against a plain blue ground, slight stippled shading.

Iconography. One of the company attending Christ and the Virgin in the centre lights of the window.

Date. Second quarter 15th c.

B2, B3, B4. Cherubim

B2: h. 0·56 m. w. 0·17. B3: h. 0·66 m. w. 0·17 m. B4: h. 0·70 m. w. 0·17 m.

Each light contains a figure of a cherubim.

Condition. Some restoration, all the original glass has slight corrosion.

Colour and Technique. Painted on white glass, yellow stain on the wings around the torso, wheels in white and yellow stain, slight stippled shading. Set against plain coloured backgrounds, alternately red, blue, and ruby.

Iconography. Cherubim with six wings, standing on a wheel wearing a cross diadem around the brows, knotted scarf at the neck, and a jewelled belt around the waist (Ezekiel 10: 2, 9, 12–13, 19).

Style and Design. The three figures are painted from a single cartoon, the only variation being which way the head is turned.

Date. As above.

B5, B6. The Virgin Mary and Christ in Majesty

h. 0·73 m. w. 0·17 m.

The Virgin seated left, turning towards Christ who blesses her.

Condition. Very restored.

Colour and Technique. Original portions painted on white glass, repeated rosette pattern on Christ's tunic in yellow stain. Slight stippled shading.

Iconography. Standard, the Virgin is already crowned.

Style and Design. The painting of Christ's head and drapery is much finer in execution than the angels and cherubim. The figures are the most important of the series, the focal point of the whole tracery of the largest window in the church, and it is likely that they were painted by a senior member of the workshop.

Date. As above.

B7, B8, B9. Cherubim

B7: h. 0·70 m. w. 0·17 m. B8: h. 0·66 m. w. 0·17 m. B9: h. 0·56 m. w. 0·17 m.

Each light contains a cherubim, painted from the same cartoon as B2, B3, and B4.

All restored.

Date. As above.

[1] Rushforth (1936), 54 *et seq.*

B10. Censing Angel

h. 0·45 m. w. 0·17 m.

Identical composition to B1 reversed.

Date. As above.

n. III   PLATE 27 (*a*), (*b*)

1a. Fragments

A fragment of an inscription, in black-letter script: | *Ora* |, 15th c. An incomplete bird design, perhaps a tit, painted on white glass with yellow stain, 15th c. A piece of a quarry, an ivy-leaf trail, 14th c. All set against modern white glass.

1b. Fragments

Two quarries, white and yellow stain, a variant of type 4, 15th c. Set against modern white glass.

1c. Fragments

Two quarries, white and yellow stain, as 1b, 15th c. Bird design, incomplete surround, a bird standing on one leg, preening its feathers, white and yellow stain. 15th c.

3a, 3b, 3c. Canopies

h. 0·35 m. w. 0·48 m.

The tops of three identical canopy designs. Set against plain coloured backgrounds, alternately blue, ruby, and blue. See below, s. IV, 4c for the original design.

Date. Second quarter 15th c.

A1, A2. Foliage Design

h. 0·10 m. w. 0·10 m.

A flat quatrefoil leaf with serrated leaves, in white and yellow stain against a plain matt background, in a plain white border. Painted on a single piece of glass, no leading.

Condition. Complete, the paint of A2 is corroded. *In situ.*

Date. As above.

B1, B6. Foliage Design

h. 0·24 m. w. 0·08 m.

At the centre a small white rosette enclosed by two leaf-sprays with serrated edges, in white and yellow stain against a plain matt background in a plain white border.

Condition. Complete, painted on a single piece of glass, B1 repaired. *In situ.*

Date. As above.

B2, B3, B4, B5. Cherubim

h. 0·56 m. w. 0·18 m.

Each light contains the figure of a cherubim. Painted from the same cartoon as window I.

Condition. Restored, the original glass is slightly corroded.

Date. As above.

C1, C2. Foliage Design

h. 0·10 m. w. 0·10 m.

Identical design as A1 and A2 above. *In situ.*

Date. Second quarter 15th c.

D1. Modern roundel. | *Maria* | in monogram, set against plain pieces of medieval glass.

n. IV   PLATE 27 (*c*), (*d*)

The tracery lights A1–C2 inclusive are a repeat of the design in n. III.

Condition. Restored, see diagram.

D1. Modern roundel, *Ihesus* monogram set against plain pieces of medieval glass.

Date. Second quarter 15th c.

n. V   PLATE 27 (*e*), (*f*)

The tracery lights A1–D1 inclusive are a repeat of the design in window n. III.

Condition. Restored.

D1. Roundel, *Maria* in monogram, original.

Date. Second quarter 15th c.

s. IV

1b. Bird Quarry

h. 0·14 m. w. 0·11 m.

A partridge standing on one leg, the left leg raised. White and yellow stain with matt and stippled shading. Incomplete. 15th c. Set against modern white glass.

2a and 2b.

h. 0·14 m. w. 0·11 m.

Two quarries in each light, white and yellow stain, a variant of type 4. 15th c.

3a. Head of a Saint

h. 0·16 m. w. 0·18 m.

The frontal head of a male saint.

Condition. Incomplete, originally part of a full-length figure. Slight all-over pitting. One old leaded repair.

Colour and Technique. Painted on white glass with highlights picked out of a wash of matt light-brown paint, nimbus and background in yellow stain with a plain white border.

Iconography. Bearded elderly type of head, possibly an apostle, but a precise identification cannot be made.

Style and Design. The drawing and stipple shading are very close to the St. James Major in 3c. The scale is much smaller, and the figure must have been part of a different series.

Date. Second quarter 15th c.

3b. Quarry

h. 0·14 m. w. 0·11 m.

Single quarry, white and yellow stain as 2a. 15th c.

3c. St. James Major   PLATE 25 (b), (c)

h. 1·46 m. w. 0·48 m.

St. James Major, full length facing three-quarters left. The pedestal below his feet is inscribed in black-letter script:

| S(anctus) | Iacob(us) | m|aior |

Above his head and to the right of the figure is a long scroll inscribed in black-letter script:

| (Qui) | co(n)ceptus | (est) | [de Spiritu san]|cto | ·n|atus | ex | [Maria] | v|irgine |

Condition. Complete, only slight restoration. The glass is

corroded, and the paint has perished in parts, particularly on the right side of the face and parts of the scroll.

Colour and Technique. The figure, scroll, tiled floor, and pedestal are painted on white glass, pilgrim's hat, border of nimbus, and hairy tunic in yellow stain. Stippled and matt shading on the head and drapery. Set against a blue background diapered with a seaweed-foliage design picked out of a matt black background. Side-shafts to the canopy above are in white glass, details picked out in yellow stain.

Iconography. St. James dressed as a pilgrim with a hairy tunic and hat with a scallop-shell pilgrim's badge on its front, a wallet on his left hip, and holding a staff with a thin wand bound to it. The pilgrimage to the shrine of St. James at Santiago de Compostela in Spain was second in importance only to that of Rome.[1] By the 12th c. the scallop shell was the recognized badge of a pilgrim to Compostela.[2] The transfer of the pilgrim's badge, wallet, and long staff to St. James himself originated in Spain[3] and was absorbed into French art in a modified form in the early 13th c. at Rheims, Amiens, and Chartres.[4] The hat that the saint sometimes wears appears to have been introduced in the late 13th c. as a piece of deliberate realism.[5] The addition of the thin rod bound to the staff appears to be an English invention, possibly a token of pilgrimage. Rushforth linked the rods with two 12th-c. representations of St. James standing between two cypress trees from which the side-branches have been cut.[6] The trees are apparently a reference to the Transfiguration of Christ on Mount Sion.[7] The earliest known English representations of a pilgrim, not St. James, bearing a staff with a rod bound to it, are the early 14th-c. wall-paintings at Faversham (Kent),[8] and a later 14th-c. panel painting at Frampton Court (Glos.).[9] Both depict the scene from the life of St. Edward the Confessor when the saint gives his ring to St. John Evangelist disguised as a pilgrim.[10] These two paintings suggest that the rod and staff do not necessarily have a particular association with St. James. The source for the iconography may be the Book of Psalms (Psalm 23: 4). '*Nam et si ambulavero in medio umbrae mortis, non timebo mala: quoniam tu mecum es. Virga tua, et baculus tuus, ipsa me consolata sunt.*' An indulgence of Innocent VIII granted by Alexander VI for the rebuilding of the hospital and foundation of two chapels at St. James,

---

[1] E. Mâle, *L'Art religieux du XII siècle en France* (1922), 294 et seq., *L'Art religieux du XIII siècle en France* (1948), 310–11. Herder iv (1974), 23–9.

[2] C. Hohler, 'The Badge of St. James', *The Scallop*, ed. I. Cox, (1956), 56, citing the 12th-c. text *Liber Sancti Jacobi*.

[3] Ibid. 60, citing the jamb figure of the west door of the Abbey Church of Santa Maria de Teva (*c.* 1140–50?).

[4] Mâle, op. cit. Hohler, op. cit. 62–3. The French examples omit the staff; their combination of wallet, book, and sword of martyrdom seems to be peculiar to north France.

[5] Hohler, op. cit. 65–6.

[6] Rushforth (1936), 93–6.

[7] Ibid. 95, citing the 12th-c. text *Liber Sancti Jacobi*.

[8] T. Willement, *Archaeologia Cantiana* i (1853), 151–3. Willement's drawing shows the details more clearly than the published engraving; the rod has a serrated edge explaining his description of it as a 'palm branch'. London, Society of Antiquaries, Prints and Drawings; Kent, Red Portfolio, f. 16.

[9] E. W. Tristram, *English Wall-Painting of the Fourteenth Century* (1955), 173–4, pl. 25.

[10] M. Block, 'La Vie de S. Edouard le Confesseur par Osbert de Clare', *Analecta Bollandiana* xli (1923), 124–8. Ailred of Rievaulx, *Vita S. Edwardi Regis* in Migne, *Patrologia Latina* cxv. 769–70. *Golden Legend* vi, 26–8.

Compostela, was printed by Wynkyn de Worde at Westminster in 1498. It has a circular woodcut seal showing St. James, with the legend *VIRGA ET BACVLVS TVVS IPSA ME CONSOLATA SV(N)T.*[1] However, the seal shows the saint holding a plain staff. As this is a very late example it could be argued that de Worde made the association with the text of the Psalm. The earliest known example of St. James with a rod attached to his staff is in a tracery light of a window of the chapel at Haddon Hall (Derbys.) *c.* 1427.[2]

Above the head of St. James is a long scroll inscribed with the verse of the Creed attributed to him.[3] Fragments of other verses of the Creed and the figures of SS. Paul, Bartholomew, and Thomas were recorded in the 18th c. as part of the nave windows,[4] and it seems that the nave windows had a series of the Twelve Apostles, each with his verse of the Creed, possibly in the three windows of the north wall of the nave, each of four main lights.

Style and Design. The over-all design with a dominance of white glass and yellow stain, the only coloured glass being the blue seaweed diaper background, is a consistent feature of various workshops in the Midlands *c.* 1400–30.[5] There is also some affinity with the figures of apostles in the Ante-chapel windows of All Souls College, Oxford, of *c.* 1441–7. The St. James Major there is similar in stance, with his mantle pulled tight over the left thigh, and falling in long folds from the right hand. Both stand on a tiled floor with a diagonally recessed base.[6] Although the canopy designs are rather different, particularly in scale, there are similarities in detail (see 4c). At Combe the background diaper is the seaweed foliage, not the diagonal patterned bands which appear to be an innovation at All Souls.

Date. Second quarter 15th c.

4b. Canopy

h. 0·35 m. w. 0·48 m.

The top of a canopy set against a plain, pale-pink background. (See 4c for the original design.)

4c. Canopy

h. 0·35 m. w. 0·48 m.

The vertical side-shafts framing St. James Major (3c) support a three-sided vaulted niche springing from two capitals level with the saint's head. Each face of the niche has a rounded arch, cusped trefoil, surmounted by a crocketed gable and finial. Each gable has a repeated tracery design of

a circle between three foils. Between the centre and side-faces of the niche are two pendant bosses. At the centre above and behind the main niche is a diagonally turned spire, terminating in a large capital at the apex of the light, flanked by two gable ends, each pierced with a round-headed lancet window below a traceried design with crocketed gable and finial and side-shafts with crocketed spires.

Condition. Mostly complete, minor restoration.

Colour and Technique. Painted on white glass, stippled and matt shading, details picked out in yellow stain.

Style and Design. The general type of three-sided niche with pendant bosses and prominent vaulted inside of the niche probably originated as a stained glass design in the workshop of Thomas of Oxford in the 1390s.[7] Parallels with the Combe design can be made with the east window of Great Malvern Priory (Worcs.) *c.* 1423–39[8] and the Ante-chapel windows of All Souls College, Oxford, of *c.* 1441–7. In small points of detail, the round-headed arches each cusped trefoil, the diagonally turned side-shafts, the simple rounded crockets, central upper spire and capital are closest to All Souls.[9] There are differences, particularly in the proportions, as the All Souls canopies are much smaller in relation to the figures, and the design of the upper storey of the canopy is more simplified.

Date. Second quarter 15th c.

A1–D1. Tracery Lights

The tracery lights repeat the same design as n. III.

Condition. Incomplete and restored.

Date. 15th c.

s. V

1a. Fragments

Three fragments, very incomplete, possibly quarries with a rose motif. 15th c. Set against modern plain white quarries.

1b. Angel?

h. 0·15 m. w. 0·12 m.

Nimbed, head facing three-quarters left, painted on white glass, delicate stippled and matt shading. 15th c. Set against modern plain white quarries.

[1] E. Gordon Duff, *Fifteenth Century English Books* (1917), no. 213, pl. 15.
[2] Newton ii (1961), 54–5.
[3] For the iconography of the Apostles' Creed and a discussion of some of the English examples see M. Caviness, 'Fifteenth Century Stained Glass from the Palace of Hampton Court, Herefordshire', *The Walpole Society* xlii (1968–70), 35–60, particularly 57–60.
[4] See Lost Glass below.
[5] See the General Introduction, and Newton i (1961), ch. iv.
[6] Hutchinson (1949), pl. iii.
[7] J. D. Le Couteur, *Ancient Glass in Winchester* (1926). J. Harvey and D. King, 'Winchester College Stained Glass', *Archaeologia* ciii (1971), pl. xcii.
[8] Rushforth (1936), 93–6.
[9] Hutchinson (1949), pls. i–xii.

1c. Fragments

Two small fragments of 14th-c. quarries, very incomplete, a variant of type 4.

3b. Canopy

h. 0·35 m. 2. 0·48 m.

The top of a canopy, set against plain pale-pink background. See s. IV, 4c above for the original design.

A1–D1. Tracery Lights   PLATE 27 (g), (h)

The tracery lights are a repeat of the same design as n. III.

Condition. Incomplete and restored.

Date. 15th c.

Lost Glass

Rawlinson described the glass existing *c.* 1725 as follows: 'In the east window of the chancell are 10 figures, one of the Virgin, another of King David and six angels, underneath a woman kneeling and opposite a man, under them: *Orate........ animabus miat.........s et........ oris ville Oxonie et........ uxoris........ hanc fen .... Armes over Az(ure) a bend or between 3 leopards heads or, the same impaling Arg(ent) on a bend sinister gules 3 wings arg(ent).* In a north window: St. Paul........ *vivos et mortuos. St. Bartholomew sanctam ecclesiam catholicam et corporis resurrectionem.* In a south window: St. Thomas .... underneath Thomas *Anno Domini mill(esim)o ccc........ Jesus est amor meus de sepulta Le........ orate pro Agneta.*'[1]

The incomplete texts associated with the figures of the Apostles are parts of three verses of the Creed:

(7) '*Inde venturus est iudicare vivos et mortuos*'
(9) '*Sanctam ecclesiam catholicam sanctorum communionem*'
(11) '*Carnis resurrectionem*'.

It is noticeable that the surviving figure of St. James Major and his verse of the Creed are not included in this account. In addition the figure of St. Paul, if correctly identified, must have been part of another series of figures as he is not associated with the verses of the Creed.

It has been suggested that the two kneeling figures in the east window of the chancel represented William Dagvyle and his wife.[2] He was Mayor of Oxford from 1465 to 1467 and again in 1470, 1472, and 1475.[3] Benefactor of Lincoln College, Oxford, d. 1476,[4] he was buried in the church of All Saints, Oxford, beside his first wife Joan (d. 1473).[5] His widow Margaret survived until 1523.[6] This identification is quite possible but the recorded inscription is too incomplete for positive proof.

CROPREDY
ST. MARY

O.S. SP 469 466.

PRINTED SOURCES
Pevsner (1974), 559–60.

n. V

2b. Head of a Virgin Saint   PLATE 28 (a)

h. 0·15 m. w. 0·15 m.

The head of a crowned female saint, nimbed, facing three-quarters left.

Condition. In 1962 this head, painted on a single piece of glass, was hanging loose in a window of the north aisle. The glass was then cracked and in imminent danger of falling to pieces. It was repaired in 1963 by D. King of Norwich, the breaks leaded with fine string lead, cleaned, and subsequently leaded into its present position. One small piece of the nimbus was missing, and has been replaced by a piece of 15th-c. glass. There is extensive corrosion on both surfaces.

Colour and Technique. Painted on white glass, crown and hair, beaded border and nimbus in yellow stain with matt and fine stipple modelling.

Iconography. Possibly the Blessed Virgin Mary, but no conclusive identification can be made.

Style and Design. The painting of the features is quite delicate, but the crown, particularly its jewelled base, is rather clumsy in execution. The large size of the nimbus in relation to the head is similar to the female saints in the windows of the Ante-chapel of All Souls College, Oxford,[7] of 1441–2. Also related is the head of a crowned female saint in the north window of the chancel of Drayton Beauchamp (Bucks.).[8]

---

[1] P.C. (1920), 101.

[2] Emden, op. cit. 9.

[3] A. Wood, 'Survey of the Antiquities of the City of Oxford', ed. A. Clark, iii. O.H.S. xxxvii (1899), 24.

[4] A. Wood, *The History and Antiquities of the Colleges and Halls in the University of Oxford*, ed. J. Gutch (1786), 238–9.

[5] Wood, *City*, op. cit. 148.

[6] Wood, *Colleges*, op. cit. 239.

[7] Hutchinson (1949), pl. xvi.

[8] Post-restoration photograph, The York Glaziers Trust, neg. nos. 1/2, plate vol. 1, no. 6, 35 mm. vol. 4, no. 3.

CROWMARSH GIFFORD
MARY MAGDALENE

O.S. SU 615 839.

PRINTED SOURCES

Greening Lamborn (1949), 118–19.
Pevsner (1974), 561–2.

n. III

1a. God the Father. Composite Panel

h. 1·22 m. w. 0·40 m.

Condition. Composite panel of fragments incorporating an incomplete bust-length figure of God the Father, frontal in benediction, holding the orb and crowned. Fragment of an inscription: | *iacobus* |, black-letter script.

Colour and Technique. God the Father, face missing, arched imperial crown in yellow stain and white glass, ruby robes, hands and orb painted on white glass, details picked out in yellow stain. Angels above the crown painted in black on yellow stain with pale-blue clouds above.

Style, Design, and Date. Only the crown, drapery, hands, and orb of God the Father are acceptable as genuine 16th-c. glass, although the inscription also may be of this date. The remainder is very fragmented pieces of inscription, lobes of tracery lights and plain glass, all probably 18th or 19th c., composite in imitation of a window of medieval fragments.

Date. Original pieces, early 16th c.

n. IV

1a. Composite Panel of Fragments

h. 0·70 m. w. 0·90 m.

Fragments of architectural tracery designs, Tudor badge of a portcullis and crown, fragments of tracery painted with heraldic badges, pomegranate badge and the roots of a tree, head of a male saint. The glass has been described as:

'A jumble of fragments, mainly of the Tudor period'[1] with the exception of the 16th-c. shield of PAULETT impaling NORREYS OF RYCOTE at the base of the light;

all the remainder has the appearance of being imitation medieval design, late 18th–19thc.

n. V

1a. Composite Panel

h. 0·41 m. w. 0·40 m.

Fragments of 17th-c. glass mixed with imitation medieval fragments of 18th- and 19th.-c. date.

1b. Christ in Judgement

h. 0·81 m. w. 0·40 m.

Seated Christ in Judgement exhibiting the wounds of the Passion and surrounded by a ring of cherubs.

Condition. Incomplete. The drapery of Christ below the waist is a composite of different pieces of drapery, the rayed nimbus surrounding his proper nimbus is a restorer's conceit. The right-hand group of cherubs is probably modern.

Colour and Technique. Head and body of Christ painted on white glass, delicate stipple shading on the head. Nimbus, white (decayed to brown) cross in ruby, slate blue-grey drapery with stipple shading. Cherubs, right, in yellow stain, lower left cherub painted on ruby glass.

Iconography. Standard pose for a Christ in Judgement.

Style and Design. The glass is too fragmentary for precise stylistic analysis. The frontal head of Christ has an affinity with the Anglo-Flemish glass at King's College, Cambridge,[2] but is not close enough to be attributed to the hand of any of the glaziers working there.

Date. Early 16th c.

---

[1] Greening Lamborn (1949), 118.   [2] H. Wayment, *King's College, Cambridge*, C.V.M.A. (1972).

DORCHESTER

ABBEY OF SS. PETER AND PAUL

O.S. SP 597–943.

MS. SOURCES

London. British Library:
  Add. MS. 29943, f. 106. Carter drawing, 18th c.
  Add MS. 35211, vol. iii, n. 1–AA11, nos. 56, 57, 59. Winston,
    drawings.
Oxford. Bodleian Library:
  MS. Top. Oxon. e. 286, ff. 122–5, N. Greenwood, Notes 1660.
  MS. Top Eccles d. 6. p. 111. Stukeley drawing, 1736.
  Gough Maps 26, f. 42ᵛ. Notes dated 1736 and 1768.
  Gough Maps 227. Drawings of Dorchester by J. Carter, 1793.
    Drawings VII, XI, XII, XIII, XIV, XVI.

PRINTED

Camden, W., *Britannia*, 2nd edn., with additions by R. Gough, ii
  (1806), 27.
Addington, H., *Some Account of the Abbey Church of SS. Peter and
  Paul at Dorchester, Oxon.* (1847).
Visitations (1871), 106–10.
Macfarlane, W. C., 'Note on Dorchester Abbey', *Newbury and
  District Field Club Transactions* iii (1875–6).
Nelson (1913), 162–3.
Bouchier (1918), 70.
P.C. (1920), 114–23.
Bouchier (1932), 128.
V.C.H. vii (1962), 61.
Pevsner (1974), 576–83.

The Saxon episcopal see at Dorchester which had been in existence since the seventh century was removed to Lincoln in 1092. Bishop Alexander suppressed the secular canons in 1140 and gave their endowments to the Austin Canons. The abbey was established by 1142,[1] but little is known about its history until the thirteenth century. In 1224 a petition was sent to the Pope requesting permission to translate the bones of St. Birinus, the first Saxon bishop, to a more worthy place,[2] and after an inquisition the translation was authorized in the following year.[3]

A rebuilding campaign must have been envisaged at the end of the thirteenth century, for in January 1293 Oliver Sutton, Bishop of Lincoln, granted an indulgence of twenty days to facilitate the collection of alms for the fabric fund of the abbey. The indulgence was to last for five years,[4] and the provision of a new shrine for the remains of St. Birinus was included in this campaign. The first version of Ranulph Higden's Polychronicon (which ended in 1327) records the provision of the new shrine;[5] however, the author's final recension of the text, revised to 1340,[6] does not give a date for the shrine at Dorchester. Three later copies of the text record that the shrine was constructed *c.* 1320,[7] which seems to have been only one stage of the rebuilding programme; it has been suggested that the extension to the choir took place *c.* 1340.[8]

There is no documentary evidence for dating the glass. Nothing is known about it until the brief notes on the subject-matter made by Anthony Wood in the seventeenth century,[9] and the sketches and drawings made by Carter at the end of the eighteenth century.[10] Since then the glass has been much moved about, the major portion being moved to the east window in the earlier part of this century. The east window and the roundels in the heads of the sedilia were cleaned and releaded by D. King of Norwich in 1969.

[1] *V.C.H.* ii (1907). Addington, op. cit.
[2] Calendar of Papal Letters, i (1893), 95.
[3] Ibid. 103.
[4] 'The Rolls and Register of Bishop Oliver Sutton 1280–1290' ed. R. M. T. Hill, *Lincoln Record Society* lii (1958), iv, memoranda 56–7.
[5] 'Polychronicon Ranulphi Higden', ed. J. R. Lumby, *Rolls Series* vi (1876), 41.

[6] V. H. Galbraith, 'An Autograph Manuscript of Ranulph Higden's Chronicle', *Huntington Library Quarterly* xxiii (1959–60), 1–18.
[7] *Rolls Series*, op. cit. 4, n. 6, also Oxford, Trinity College MS. 10, f. 66ᵛ dated 1484.
[8] Pevsner (1974), 578–9.
[9] P.C. (1920), 117–18.
[10] Bodl. Lib. Gough Map 227, op. cit.

The earliest glass without doubt is the panel of St. Birinus receiving a cross-staff (n. III, 2b). It has here been assigned to the mid thirteenth century but it should be emphasized that the lack of comparative glass in the country makes this dating a very tentative one.

The remainder of the glass can be attributed to the late thirteenth or early fourteenth century. Although there is a general affinity, there are considerable variations in details that suggest it is the work of a number of glass painters, rather than one workshop working in a consistent style.

The two roundels of an archbishop and a pope in the heads of the sedilia can be attributed to one artist. This is small-scale work and there is meticulous attention to detail. Although the compositions of seated figures in benediction are virtually identical, and the backgrounds are alike, there is no mechanical repetition, the head types are quite distinct, particularly in the painting of the hair (Sedilia 1b, 1c).

This small-scale style presents a contrast with the much larger figured panels, now in window I. These panels present particular problems of interpretation on grounds of style and design, there is also the problem of composite restoration work. The donor figure of Radulphus de Tiwe (I, 3c) and St. Lawrence (I, 3d) can be associated: they both have plain backgrounds and the canopies are identical. However, the particular details are quite different. The Tiwe head is gaunt with strong stubble on his chin. The St. Lawrence is more carefully painted and the conventions for eyes, nose, and mouth are different from the Tiwe head. Also, the heads are not compatible in size. The conclusion is inevitable that some of the work must be a restorer's composite.

The head of Tiwe can be compared with the head of a saint, possibly St. Birinus (I, 4b). There is a similar angularity, sketchy painting of the ears, and depiction of stubble on the chin. The head of St. Lawrence, on the other hand, can be related to the Christ Child (I, 4c), with similar round faces, hair organized in careful clumps, identical drawing of eyes, noses, and mouth. While the Christ is a vigorous piece of design, the Virgin is quite different, a rigid frontal pose, with a long thin face, completely lacking animation.

The two outstanding panels in the east window are the St. Michael spearing the dragon (3b) and St. Birinus preaching (3e). The St. Michael is somewhat disturbed, but the design retains its vigour and the painting of the head and draperies is extremely competent. The Birinus panel is the only one of the large figure panels to have a foliage diaper background. It is an interesting composition; the saint is an elongated figure towering over the people listening to him, particularly King Cynegils, who is seated on the ground. Also noteworthy is the use of either pink or white glass to differentiate the faces.

The Tree of Jesse window (n. III) is now a series of heads clumsily attached to bodies made up of alien scraps; however, the heads do show a stylistic consistency of type. The prophets have long lugubrious faces, sharp-pointed eyebrows, and mouths turned down at the corners. The heads of youths are less severe but the conventions of drawing are the same, particularly the line of the nose continued down above the mouth, which is wide with a squared centre. These similarities suggest that the association of these heads is correct.

The east window contains a series of heads in roundels which can be grouped together (I, 3a, b, c, d, e, f). They are all painted on white glass, and there is the use of yellow stain. Originally they may have been set at the centres of white geometric grisaille or quarries.

The Mass scene at the head of the sedilia (1a) is somewhat isolated. Again it is small-scale precision work. The arabesque of background foliage design suggests that it is probably the latest in date of the remaining glass.

This rich diversity of detail makes it very difficult to propose a precise chronological sequence. A technical point, the absence of yellow stain, except for the roundels I, 3a–d and f, suggests that much of this glass is early fourteenth century. It is therefore suggested that the glass should be associated with the rebuilding campaign that began in 1293 and continued into the first two decades of the fourteenth century with the building of the new shrine c. 1320.

I

3a. The Annunciation   PLATE 28 *(b)*, *(c)*

h. 1·70 m. w. 0·81 m.

The Virgin stands right facing the archangel Gabriel who holds a scroll, inscribed in Lombardic script:

| AVE | M|ARIA | GRAC(IA) P|LENA |

A long lily in a pot stands on the floor between them.

Condition. Incomplete. Missing portions are made up with alien pieces of contemporary glass; the draperies in particular are composite. Corrosion of varying intensity; the paint on the archangel's head has perished completely.

Colour and Technique. Virgin: ruby nimbus white head and hands, slight smear shading on the hair, murrey drapery. Archangel: ruby nimbus, head and hands on white glass, composite blue mantle and tunic. White lily and pot, set against a plain green background.

Iconography. Standard.

Date. Early 14th c.

The remainder of the light is a composite of different pieces:

PLATE 29 *(c)*

Roundel: d. 0·27 m. Head of a king, facing three-quarters right, head, white hair and beard painted on a matt wash, crown in yellow stain, plain matt wash background, plain border, set within an ochre border patterned with quatre-foils picked out of a matt black wash.

Date. 14th c., *c.* 1320 ?

Roundel: d. 0·22 m. Foliage design, an ochre boss, painted with a cinquefoil design set in a surround of flat acanthus leaves, painted on white glass.

Date. Early 14th c.

Geometric grisaille: fragments of grisaille painted with either trails of roses or maple leaves. Early 14th c.

Borders: serpentine trail of white ivy leaves set against plain coloured pieces. Early 14th c.

3b. St. Michael   PLATE 3 *(c)*, 29 *(d)*, *(e)*

h. 1·70 m. w. 0·81 m.

St. Michael: full length facing three-quarters left, trampling on a dragon and spearing it with a cross-staff, beneath an arch and canopy.

Condition. Incomplete, partly composite as 3a above. Corro-sion of varying intensity.

Colour and Technique. Head, hands, and wings painted on white glass, ruby nimbus, green mantle over ochre tunic, ruby dragon, blue background diapered with trails of rounded trefoil leaves, picked out of a matt wash, very incomplete. The arch has green columns with ochre traceried side-shafts, crocketed arch and gable with finial in white; the tympanum has an elaborate window tracery design scratched out of matt wash. Behind the gable a square building with ochre wall, bricks painted in outline with a green course surmounted by an ochre parapet of contiguous quatrefoils, scratched out of a matt wash, and a blue roof, the latter cut off at the top, flanked by two traceried shafts with crocketed gables and finial.

Iconography. Standard. The cross-staff instead of a spear is not common.

Style and Design. The awkward elongation of the right arm is an old restoration.

Date. Early 14th c.

The remainder of the light is a composite of different pieces. Roundel: d. 0·17 m. Head of St. Edmund, king and martyr, crowned facing three-quarters left. Painted on white glass, hair painted on matt wash. Smear shading, background plain matt wash, plain border. On either side of the roundel is an inscription in Lombardic script:

| S(ANCTUS) IEADM| |UND(US) REX |.

Below is an arrow head, point downwards, possibly an allusion to his martyrdom.[1]

Date. 14th c. *c.* 1320.

Roundel: d. 0·22 m. Foliage design as 3a above.

Date. Early 14th c.

Geometric grisaille: white grisaille painted with trails of maple leaves. Early 14th c.

Border pieces: Thirteen pieces of a vertical stem with offspringing sprays of oak leaves and acorns set against plain coloured glass. A striking design.

Date. Early 14th c.

3c. The Monk Radulpus de Tiwe   PLATE 4 *(b)*

h. 1·70 m. w. 0·81 m.

Represented kneeling in prayer facing three-quarters right below an arch and canopy, looking upwards. Above his head an inscription in Lombardic script:

| +RADVLPVS DE TIWE |

Condition. The panel is basically complete, only slight corro-sion, some paint loss on the inscription.

---

[1] *Golden Legend* vi 243–7.

Colour and Technique. Head and hands painted on pink glass, smear shading on the face, blue habit with white lining, white tunic and shoes. Ground below painted with wavy lines, smear shading. Background plain ruby glass very streaky. Columns, the trefoil arch, and crocketed gable are white, traceried side-shafts end in a crocketed gable. Behind the main arch is a two-storied building, green brick walls pierced with lancet windows, a parapet above, and a blue domed roof flanked by ochre traceried shafts and crocketed gables and finial. The canopy is set against a patterned background, squared design alternately a quatrefoil and a plain square.

Iconography. He is tonsured and wears monastic habit, represented in prayer, a standard attitude in representations of donor figures. The cross before his name is probably pure decoration, a convention used for inscriptions on seals.

Date. Early 14th c. No documentary evidence relating to Tiwe has been found.

3c

The remainder of the light is a composite of different pieces:

Roundel: d. 0·24 m. Head of a man wearing a cap, facing three-quarters left, white face, hair and beard painted on matt wash, cap in yellow stain, plain matt background, plain border, set within a patterned border, repeated design of squared quatrefoils picked out of matt wash.

Date. 14th c., *c.* 1320.

Roundel: d. 0·22 m. Foliage design as 3a.

Geometric grisaille: white grisaille painted with either trails of maple leaves or roses. Early 14th c.

Borders: Serpentine trail of white maple leaves set against pieces of plain coloured glass. Early 14th c.

3d. St. Lawrence   PLATE 30 (d)
h. 1·70 m. w. 0·81 m.

Represented standing facing three-quarters right below an arch and canopy. He holds a book and a gridiron.

Condition. Incomplete, missing portions made up with alien medieval glass. Corrosion of varying intensity.

Colour and Technique. Blue nimbus, head and hands on white glass, ochre amice, green dalmatic, only the right arm is good, ochre maniple, and ochre shoes. Blue gridiron. Plain ruby background, very disturbed. Arch and canopy as 3c above.

Iconography. Standard, he holds the gridiron of his martyrdom.

Date. Early 14th c.

The remainder of the light is a composite of different pieces:

Roundel: d. 0·17 m. Head of a king. Virtually the same as 3a. Cartoon reversed.

Date. 14th c., *c.* 1320.

Roundel: foliage design as 3a above.

Geometric grisaille: white grisaille painted with trails of maple leaves. Early 14th c.

Borders: serpentine trail of white maple leaves set against pieces of plain coloured glass. Early 14th c.

3e. St. Birinus Preaching   PLATE 4 (a), 29 (a)
h. 1·70 m. w. 0·81 m.

St. Birinus stands right preaching to a small group of laymen and the seated King Cynegils, beneath an arch and canopy.

Condition. Substantially complete except for the canopy. Carter's drawing shows a lost figure behind the saint. Corrosion of varying intensity, paint loss on some of the heads.

Colour and Technique. St. Birinus: ochre mitre, pink face and amice, green chasuble, white alb with pink apparel, white gloves and ochre maniple, ochre crozier. King Cynegils: ochre crown, pink face and hands, ochre mantle over ruby tunic, white shoes, ochre sceptre beside him. Crowd: faces and hands are either pink or white, two foreground figures, one a murrey mantle and ruby tunic, the other a green mantle, strong smear shading. Background: blue foliage diaper of maple-like leaves picked out of a matt wash. Arch cusped a cinquefoil with crocketed gable and finial in deep ochre glass. Behind the gable is a blue brick wall, remainder of canopy missing.

Iconography. St. Birinus was sent by Pope Honorius to Britain to convert the Saxons. He landed in Wessex in 634. After the conversion to Christianity of King Cynegils in 635, the see of Dorchester was established with St. Birinus as the first bishop. He died in 650.[1] The scene probably represents the saint preaching before King Cynegils. No comparable examples have been found and scenes from the saint's life are extremely rare.[2]

Date. Early 14th c.

The remainder of the light is a composite of different pieces:

Roundel: w. 0·16 m. Mitred head of a bishop facing three-quarters right. Head white, hair painted on a matt wash, background a plain matt wash, plain border.

Date. 14th c., *c.* 1320.

---

[1] Venerabilis Baedae *Historiam Ecclesiasticam Gentis Anglorum*, ed. C. Plummer, i (1896), 139–40.   [2] *Herder* v (1973), 369.

Roundel: d. 0·22 m. Foliage design as 3a above.

Sixteen border pieces. Oak sprays as 3b above. Early 14th c.

Small scraps of geometric grisaille. Early 14th c.

3f. Bishop
PLATE 30 (*f*)

h. 1·70 m. w. 0·81 m.

A mitred bishop full length facing three-quarters left, holding a crozier, below an arch and canopy.

Condition. The figure is a composite of alien pieces of glass shaped to look like vestments. The canopy is also composite of canopy shaftings and finials. The over-all design made by a restorer.

Colour and Technique. Head painted on pink glass, matt wash on the hair. Plain ruby background.

Date. Early 14th c.

The remainder of the light is a composite of different pieces:

Roundel: d. 0·17 m. Head of a king, crowned facing three-quarters left, painted on white glass, hair, beard, and crown in yellow stain, background squared hatching picked out of a matt wash. Extremely corroded, considerable paint loss.

Date. 14th c., *c*. 1320.

Roundel: d. 0·22 m. Foliage design as 3a.

Geometric grisaille: white painted with trails of either roses or maple leaves. Early 14th c.

Border pieces: serpentine trails of white maple leaves set against pieces of plain coloured glass. Early 14th c.

4a. Fragments

h. 1·14 m. w. 0·33 m.

Condition. Small scraps of geometric grisaille, a quarry with the letters *C O*. 17th c.

4b. Roundels and Fragments
PLATE 30 (*e*)

h. 1·14 m. w. 0·81 m.

Condition. The panel is composite, individual pieces of glass well preserved, particularly the white glass.

Roundel: d. 0 20 m. Head of St. Birinus? Frontal, nimbed and tonsured, patterned amice. Green nimbus, head and amice on white glass, plain ruby background, plain border.

Date. Early 14th c.

Roundel: d. 0·16 m. Mitred head of a bishop, facing three-quarters left, white glass, hair painted on matt wash. Similar to 3e above.

Roundel is cut down, present surround is composite.

Date. Early 14th c.

Fragments of geometric grisaille, painted with trails of maple leaves. Early 14th c.

Border pieces: fifteen ochre fleur-de-lis border pieces set against pieces of plain ruby. Early 14th c.

4c. Virgin and Christ Child
PLATE 30 (*g*)

h. 1·14 m. w. 0·81 m.

Frontal Virgin, seated below an arch holding an apple, the Christ Child on her left knee holds a small bird and extends his right hand in blessing.

Condition. The figures are complete except for alien pieces on the Virgin's right shoulder and part of the throne. The arch is composite but the trefoil outline of the panel is probably genuine.

Colour and Technique. Virgin: ochre crown, head and hands on white glass, ochre mantle and ruby tunic. Christ: white nimbus, head and hands, tunic green, matt and smear shading on the draperies. Plain blue background.

Iconography. Standard. The Virgin's nimbus is not represented.

Style and Design. The rigid frontal pose of the Virgin and the raised arm of Christ are close to the very corroded panel at South Stoke, window s. III.

The remainder of the light is a composite of different pieces:

Geometric grisaille: white trails of maple leaves, a few fragments only, much of the grisaille in the centre and upper part of the light is modern. Early 14th c.

Border pieces: serpentine trail of white maple leaves set against pieces of plain coloured glass. Early 14th c.

4d. Fragments

h. 1·14 m. w. 0·33 m.

Small scraps of grisaille and foliage designs.

Border pieces: as above.

4e. Fragments

h. 1·14 m. w. 0·33 m.

Small scraps of geometric grisaille, maple-leaf trails, 14th c., one piece with stylized vine foliage, 13th c.

Border pieces: serpentine trail of maple leaves set against pieces of plain coloured glass.

4f. Christ in Majesty PLATE 30 (*i*)

h. 1·14 m. w. 0·81 m.

Christ seated, frontal, head three-quarters left, holding a book, his right hand raised in benediction.

Condition. Composite, the upper half of the figure is sound, lower half and feet from a much smaller figure. Background and framing also composite.

Colour and Technique. Cross of the nimbus is ochre, head and hands white, ruby mantle, and green tunic. Fragments of blue foliage diaper, picked out of a matt wash.

Iconography. Originally possibly the right half of a scene of the Virgin and Christ in Majesty.

Date. Early 14th c.

The remainder of the light is a composite of different pieces:

Geometric grisaille: white with maple trails, one piece oak foliage. Early 14th c.

Border pieces: serpentine trail of maple leaves, set against plain coloured pieces. Early 14th c.

4g. Emblem of the Trinity PLATE 30 (*b*)

d. 1·14 m. w. 0·81 m.

The names of the three persons of the Trinity and God, in Lombardic script:

| PATER | EST |: | FILI(US) : EST | SP(IRITU)S | S(AN)C(TU)S | EST | DEUS |

Above the name of God, two hands elevating a chalice.

Condition. The inscriptions, hand, and chalice are probably in their original positions, the setting on very broken pieces of plain ruby may be restoration work.

Colour and Technique. Inscriptions on ochre glass, letters picked out of matt black wash. White hands, plain ochre chalice. Plain ruby background.

Iconography. The emblem of the Trinity arranged as here, but without the chalice and hands, is first found in England as a heraldic shield in the *Chronica Maiora* of Matthew Paris (1245–59)[1] and also in his collection of miscellaneous historical pieces.[2] No other example incorporating an elevated chalice has been found however. At this date the representations are not standardized.

Date. Early 14th c.

The remainder of the panel is a composite of different pieces:

Roundel: d. 0·17, the *Agnus Dei*, standing in profile to left, head profile right holding a cross banner. Painted on white glass, smear shading, plain matt background and plain

border. Close in design to the *Agnus Dei* roundels in the Library windows of Merton College, Oxford.[3]

Date. Early 14th c.

Geometric grisaille: trails of either maple leaves or roses, early 14th c.

Border pieces: sixteen fleur-de-lis ochre border pieces, set against plain ruby, 14th c.

4h. Fragments

h. 1·14 m. w. 0·33 m.

A small shield. *Checky or and azure*, Warenne, the glass looks post-medieval. Small scrap of grisaille and foliage designs. 14th c.

5b. Roundel, Head of a Queen PLATE 30 (*a*)

Panel: h. 1·98 m. w. 0·81 m. Roundel: d. 0·38.

Crowned, facing three-quarters right.

Condition. The lead-line composition is probably original, the hair cauls are alien glass.

Colour and Technique. Head painted on white glass, smear shading, ochre crown with a blue cap inside the crown, plain ruby background.

Date. Early 14th c.

The remainder of the panel is a composite of different pieces: Small fragments of grisaille and foliage designs.

Border pieces: ochre fleur-de-lis set against pieces of plain blue, mostly modern, and ochre lions statant alternating with plain ruby pieces. 14th c. rather worn.

At the top of the light: PLATE 3 (*b*)

Tracery light: resurrection of a king, h. 0·51 m. w. 0·33 m. A king, crowned, facing right holding a sceptre climbing out of a tomb, its lid on the left. White head, crown in yellow stain, purple mantle over yellow tunic, tomb in ochre glass, blue front, green lid, blue background diapered with light arabesque of foliage. Strong smear shading. Mid 14th c. Provenance unknown. Presented by the Revd. Best.

5e. Roundel, Head of a Queen PLATE 30 (*c*)

Panel: h. 1·98 m. w. 0·81 m. Roundel: d. 0·38 m.

Crowned, facing three-quarters left.

Condition. Only the face is genuine. The remainder alien pieces, lead-line composition follows 5b above.

[1] T. D. Tremlett, and H. Stanford London, 'Rolls of Arms Henry III', *Aspilogia* ii (1967), 61.   [2] B.L. Cotton MS. Julius D. VII, f. 3.
[3] H. W. Garrod, *Ancient Painted Glass in Merton College, Oxford* (1931), 47–8.

Colour and Technique. Face painted on white glass. Smear shading. Same cartoon as 5b reversed.

Date. Early 14th c.

The remainder of the light is a composite of different pieces: Geometric grisaille, mostly modern.

Border pieces as 5b above.

Tracery light: resurrection of a bishop, h. 0·51 m. w. 0·33 m. A half-length bishop, hands raised in prayer, standing in a tomb, facing left. Head in white glass, mitre in yellow stain, pot-yellow chasuble, purple under sleeves, tomb as 5b. Background blue diaper of contiguous circles each enclosing a geometric design. Mid 14th c. Provenance as 5b.

n. II

Tree of Jesse

The window is of unusual form, a Tree of Jesse combining sculpture and painted glass. The centre vertical jamb forms the tree, springing from the loins of Jesse carved on the window-sill. The tree has five off-springing branches undulating across the main lights, with carved figures on the jambs and sides of the window. Unfortunately, the glass has suffered much, and it would be more accurate to describe it as a collection of sixteen heads, fragments of inscriptions, and miscellaneous scraps. An inscribed quarry records the last arrangement of the fragments 'Remade by Guildford Glass works 1926. F. E. Howard. Archit.'. Neither can be said to have shown much sensitivity towards the glass. As the remains are so slight, an abbreviated catalogue form is used here.

Condition. Fragments of figures, with the exception of 3d. The bodies are composite oblong shapes of miscellaneous fragments, set against plain diamond-shaped quarries. All the medieval glass is corroded.

The heads are all h. 0·13–0·15 m. w. 0·10 m.

The inscriptions are all in Lombardic capitals.

1a. Head of Youth

Beardless, facing three-quarters right, blue cap.

Fragments of inscriptions:

|SA| and |NDRE|

1b. Head of Youth   PLATE 29 (b)

Beardless, facing three-quarters right.

Fragments of inscriptions:

|IORA | YGHI'A| |C'|

1c. Head of Youth   PLATE 29 (b)

Beardless, facing three-quarters left. Also fragment of a bearded head and two large ochre birds.

Fragments of inscriptions:

|SROM|ITIVDAF'EI'|

1d. Head of Prophet

Bearded, facing three-quarters right, ruby cap. Fragments of ochre and ruby drapery, two hands, forefinger of right hand touching the third finger of the left hand in a gesture of exposition.

Fragments of inscriptions:

|ARAM|CHIM|

2a. Head of Youth

Beardless, facing three-quarters right, murrey nimbus, set inside out.

Fragment of an inscription:

|TGYSAA|

2b. Head of Youth

Facing three-quarters left, green and ochre cap.

2c. Head of Prophet

Bearded, facing three-quarters left.

Fragments of inscriptions:

|G'ABI|VI [second letter cut short] |I'OROB.|

Roundel. Two interlocked triangles, one plain the other of oak foliage. White on matt background 14th c.

2d. Head of Man

Bearded, facing three-quarters right.

Fragments of inscriptions:

|AMINAD|ABG'NASON| and in black-letter script
|thome|

3a. Head of Man

Tonsured and bearded, facing three-quarters right.

Fragments of inscriptions:

|LBE|FILIID| |MAS| first letter incomplete.

3b. Head of a Prophet

Bearded, facing three-quarters right.

Fragments of inscriptions:

|BRAA| ? The letter A appears as two As written together.
|HOSYAN|

3c. Head of Prophet

Bearded, facing three-quarters left.

Fragment of an inscription, set inside out:

|SG'MA|NLIVDG'EL| second fragment worn, reading
uncertain.

3d. Prophet

Full length facing three-quarters right, holding a scroll inscribed:

|IOATASC'|

Bearded, head and hands in white glass, purple mantle,
ochre tunic, bare white foot.

4b. Head of Prophet

Bearded, facing three-quarters right.

Fragments of inscriptions:

|SALOMONE|DAVREXG'|

4c. Head of Prophet

Bearded, facing three-quarters left.

Fragments of inscriptions:

|ICOM| Another fragment painted on a narrow strip of
glass |BAPTIZAT|CONVERSOS| AD FI|DEM|

Probably from a lost panel of St. Birinus baptizing.

5a. Head of Man

Beardless, facing three-quarters left, blue sleeve and white
hand.

Fragments of inscriptions:

|AMO'G'|NSI'AM|

5d. Head of Man

Beardless, facing three-quarters right, green cap, ochre sleeve.

Fragments of inscriptions:

|ROBO|ASG'|BI'AM|

Iconography. The inscriptions have been transcribed in the
original abbreviated forms as they are so fragmentary and
somewhat eccentric in form. However, it is clear that some
of the texts are based on the genealogy of Christ (St.
Matthew 1:1–17).

2d |AMINAD|ABG'NASON| v. 4. *Aram autem genuit
Aminadab. Aminadab autem genuit Naasson.*

4b |SALOMONE|DAV REX G'| v. 6. *David autem rex
genuit Salomonem.*

5d |ROBO| v. 7. *Salomon autem genuit Roboam.*

5a |AMO'G'| v. 10. *Amon autem genuit Josiam.*

3b |HOSYAN| possibly v. 8 *Joram autem genuit Oziam.*

2c |I'OROB| possibly v. 7. *Roboam.*

3c |NLIVDG'EL| possibly v. 15. *Eliud autem genuit Eleazar.*

Style and Design. The heads described as prophets are of
a consistent type, long thin faces, with flowing hair and
beards, and floppy caps. The youths have round faces but
the details of eyes, mouths, and the lower line of the noses
continued down to the lips are very similar.

Date. Early 14th c.

n. III

2b. St. Birinus receiving a Cross-staff PLATE 31 (*a*), (*b*)

Now leaded up as a roundel, d. 0·37 m.

St. Birinus stands centre facing left holding a crozier, with
his right hand he receives a cross-staff from an archbishop
seated left, a spectator with hands raised in prayer on the
extreme right. Inscription in Lombardic script:

|BERNIVS|

Condition. The panel was cut down to its present size before
1793 when it was sketched by J. Carter.[1] The glass is
corroded but the paint is in quite good condition. The
lower part of the archbishop figure is patched with contemporary but alien glass.

Colour and Technique. Archbishop: low white mitre with
lappets, white head and hands, ochre amice, ruby chasuble
with white cross pallium, green tunicle, ochre apparel to
the alb (missing). Throne: ochre base and top, green sides,
and blue front piece (much disturbed). Birinus: white low
mitre and crozier, white head and hands, ruby chasuble,
green dalmatic and ochre tunicle, both the latter patterned,
white alb and ends of stole, green shoes. White shaft to
cross-staff, cross in ochre. Spectator: head, hands, and
mantle, green tunic and yellow shoes. Plain blue background.

Iconography. St. Birinus holds a crozier, the proper insignia
of his rank as bishop, he receives a cross-staff which, being
reserved for archbishops, cannot be an insignia of rank. It
must therefore have some other meaning. It was the custom
in the early church to assemble around a cross when pro-
cessing.[2] It is possible that the scene represents St. Birinus
receiving the mandate of Pope Honorius to convert the
Saxons. St. Birinus was consecrated as bishop by Asterius,
Bishop of Genoa.[3] It is possible that the archbishop figure
is intended to represent either Pope Honorius or Bishop
Asterius. Either identification presents difficulties. If it is the
Pope, why a mitre instead of a papal tiara; if the bishop,
why does he have an archbishop's cross pallium? However,
such discrepancies do occur in representations of historical
events at this period, particularly if the artist did not have
earlier models to follow.

---

¹ Carter, Drawing XIV.   ² F. Cabrol and H. Leclercq, *Dictionnaire d'Archéologie chrétienne et de Liturgie* iii, part 2 (1914), 3102–3.
³ Bede, op. cit., see 81 n. 1.

Style and Design. The lack of early glass in the county makes this a difficult piece to place. The low form of mitre and simple crozier have 12th-c. parallels. However, the drapery is too related to the body for such an early date. The linear V-shaped folds indicate a dating in the mid 13th c.

Date. 13th c., *c.* 1250 ?

n. IX

1a. Shield of England PLATE 4 (c)
h. 0·34 m. w. 0·28 m.

Gules three lions passant gardant in pale or ENGLAND.

Condition. The glass is rather corroded but complete.

Colour and Technique. Pot-metal glass, no decorative diapers.

Date. Early 14th c.

1b. Shield of Cornwall
h. 0·26 m. w. 0·23 m.

Argent a lion rampant gules crowned or, a bordure sable bezanty or RICHARD, EARL OF CORNWALL.

Condition. Complete but rather corroded. The glass, particularly the lion and bezants, is semi-opaque.

Colour and Technique. Pot-metal glass, no decorative diapers.

Date. 13th–14th c. Richard, Earl of Cornwall died without legitimate issue in 1308.

1c. Shield of Lancaster
h. 0·34 m. w. 0·28 m.

Gules three lions passant gardant in pale or, a label of three points azure three fleurs-de-lis or to each point EARL OF LAN-CASTER.

Condition. Complete but rather decayed.

Colour and Technique. Pot-metal glass, no decorative diapers.

Date. Early 14th c. Either for Edmund, Earl of Lancaster, d. 1322, or his son Thomas, executed 1322.

2a. Fragments
h. 1·52 m. w. 0·64 m.

Condition. A composite panel of fragments as assembled at the 1969 restoration.

Geometric grisaille foliage: design of interlocked quatrefoils and diamonds, white glass painted with a vertical stem at the centre of the light with off-springing trails of maple leaves. Incomplete, early 14th c.

Roundel: quatrefoil leaf design, each foil a flat serrated leaf, alternately ochre and blue. Early 14th c.

Roundel: fragment only of a frontal head and shoulders of an ecclesiastic. As window I, 4b. Early 14th c.

Remains of canopy: pot-metal ochre arch with crockets and finial, human head label stops. 14th c.

Border pieces: serpentine trail of maple leaves set against pieces of plain ruby. Early 14th c.

s. II

Twenty-one shields of arms. They are set on a modern background of plain white quarries.
The shields are all the same size. h. 0·36 m. w. 0·29 m. All the glass is very corroded, some of it almost opaque.

1a. Shield of Marshal
Party per pale or and vert a lion rampant gules WILLIAM MARSHALL, EARL OF PEMBROKE.

All pot-metal glass, the gold field diapered with a foliage design picked out of a matt wash.

The arms were later borne by the Bigods, Marshals of England, who acquired the office and arms by the marriage of Hugh Bigod, Earl of Norfolk, with Maud, eldest daughter and coheiress of William Marshal.[1]

Date. 14th c.

1b. Fragments
Fragments leaded into a shield shape. A large fish with Jonah inside its body. Whale painted on white glass, Jonah has yellow stain tunic. Mid 14th c.

1c. Shield of Hussey
Barry wavy ermine and gules HUSSEY.
The topmost ermine bar is modern. The ermine diapered with a cross-hatched pattern.

The arms are given for Henry Hussey or Hose in Walford's Roll *c.* 1273.[2] Greening Lamborn ascribes them to Foliot? but does not cite any evidence for the ascription.[3]

1d. Shield of Tyes
Argent a chevron gules TYES.
The chevron is modern. Argent field pattern with a fretwork design with a cinquefoil in each fret.
Henry Lord Tyes held lands at Shirburn, Albury, Fretwell, Noke, and elsewhere at his death in 1308.[4]

---

[1] *Aspilogia* ii, op. cit., 18; G.E.C. ix. 589–90, x. 358–77.   [2] *Aspilogia* ii, 199.   [3] Greening Lamborn (1949), 124.   [4] Ibid.

2a. Shield of Segrave

Sable a lion rampant argent, over all a bend gules SEGRAVE.

The forelegs and right hind leg are modern. Lion and field painted on the same glass, the field a dense matt black wash.

Greening Lamborn assigned this shield to Sir Nicholas Segrave, d. 1318.[5]

2b. Shield of England. Heir Apparent

Gules three lions passant gardant in pale or, a label of five points azure ENGLAND, HEIR APPARENT.[2]

Probably for Edward of Caernarvon, created Prince of Wales in 1301 and succeeded as Edward II in 1307.

2c. Shield of Geneville

Azure three horse-brays open in pale or, on a chief ermine a demi-lion rampant gules GENEVILLE.

The ermine chief is modern, the lion old glass but alien.

Geoffrey, Lord Geneville, d. 1314, held Begbroke in the right of his wife Maud Lacy.[3] The barony became extinct on his death.[4]

2d. Shield of Cornwall

Argent a lion rampant gules crowned or, a bordure sable bezanty or CORNWALL.

The lion's head and forepaw are alien old glass. Richard, Earl of Cornwall, died without legitimate heirs in 1308.[5] The bastard line of the family continued to hold lands after this date in Oxfordshire, but bore a different coat of arms.[6]

3a. Shield of Castile and Leon

Quarterly 1, 4 argent a lion rampant sable LEON. *2, 3 Gules a castle or* CASTILE.

The first and fourth quarters are modern, the lion is also incorrect, it should be purpure.

The shield doubtless commemorates Eleanor of Castile, consort of Edward I, d. 1290.

3b. Shield of Grey

Barry argent and azure a bend gules GREY OF ROTHERFIELD.

The argent bars are modern.

The family held extensive lands not only in Oxfordshire but throughout the Midlands.[7]

3c. Shield of Fitzalan

Gules a lion rampant or FITZALAN, EARL OF ARUNDEL.

The ruby field is diapered with a foliage design picked out of a matt wash.

Probably commemorates Richard Fitz Alan, Earl of Arundel, d. 1302.[8]

3d. Shield of de Vere

Quarterly gules and or, a rowel argent in the first quarter and a bordure indented sable DE VERE.

The rowel is modern.

The differenced arms of de Vere for Sir Hugh de Vere, a younger brother of Robert de Vere, Earl of Oxford d. 1319.[9]

5b. Shield of Ferrers

Vairy or and gules FERRERS OF CHARTLEY.

The family and its various cadet lines had extensive holdings in the Midlands. The shield probably commemorates Sir John Ferrers of Chartley, d. 1312.[10]

5c. Shield of Bigod

Or on a cross gules five escallops argent BIGOD.

The gold field is modern. The escallops are painted on roundels.

Sir John le Bigod, d. 1305, a younger brother of Roger, Earl of Norfolk, bore this differenced coat of Bigod.[11]

5d. Shield of Fitz Walter

Or a fess between two chevrons gules FITZ WALTER.

The gold field is diapered with a squared fret, each fret encloses a rose design, picked out of matt wash. Set inside out.

Robert, Lord Fitz Walter, d. 1325, held considerable lands of the Earldom of Cornwall.[12]

6b. Shield of Tony

Argent a maunch gules TONY.

The field is modern.

The family's main holdings were in Berkshire.[13]

---

[1] Greening Lamborn (1949), 124.
[2] Glovers Roll. *Aspilogia* ii, op. cit., 115.
[3] Greening Lamborn (1949), 123.
[4] G.E.C. v. 628.
[5] Ibid. iii. 430.
[6] See Asthall.
[7] G.E.C. vi. 144.

[8] Greening Lamborn (1949), 123.
[9] Ibid.
[10] Ibid. 122. G.E.C. v. 307.
[11] Greening Lamborn (1949), 122.
[12] G.E.C. v. 472, Greening Lamborn (1949), 122.
[13] Greening Lamborn (1949), 122.

6c. Shield of Ferrers

Vair argent and azure FERRERS.

A differenced coat of Ferrers borne by Sir Hugh Ferrers, younger son of William de Ferrers, Earl of Derby, and his descendants.[1]

6d. Shield of Hastings

Or a maunch gules HASTINGS.

The field has a hatched diaper, the plain pieces are modern.
   The shield doubtless commemorates John, Lord Hastings of Abergavenny.[2]

7b. Shield of Wake

Or two bars gules, in chief three roundels gules WAKE.

Probably commemorates John, Lord Wake of Liddel, d.1300. The family seem to have had no Oxfordshire lands.[3]

7c. Shield of Latimer

Gules a cross paty or LATIMER.

The upper arm of the cross is modern.
   The family had lands in Oxfordshire. The shield probably commemorates William, Lord Latimer, d. 1304.[4]

7d. Shield of St. John

Argent on a chief gules two rowels or pierced vert. The field is mostly modern, original parts diapered with a pattern of squares and roundels enclosing flower designs picked out of a matt wash. John, Lord St. John of Basing, d. 1302, Lord of Stanton and other local lands, is probably commemorated by this shield.[5]

Date. The shields are generally assigned to the period *c.* 1300–7.[6] The families represented may have been benefactors of the abbey, but there is no documentary evidence for this suggestion.

Chancel Sedilia

The wall at the top of each of the four seats of the sedilia is pierced with a sexfoil light, a most unusual arrangement.

1a. Roundel. Mass Scene   PLATE 31 (c)

Roundel d. 0·28 m.

At the centre a seated priest holding a Mass book receives a wafer from a ciborium held by a deacon on the left, on the right a subdeacon holding the cruets of wine and water.

Condition. The roundel is substantially complete, the glass

is very corroded on the exterior, particularly the ochre glass. Some paint loss on the subdeacon's head.

Colour and Technique. Priest: head and hands, amice, chasuble, and maniple all white, ochre alb with white apparel. Deacon and subdeacon: white heads and hands, their vestments in ochre, drapery folds painted on the front of the glass and a repeated pattern painted on the reverse. Smear shading on the vestments. Blue background diapered with an arabesque of foliage trails picked out of a matt wash.

Iconography. The priest has no nimbus, and is therefore not a saint. The scene is probably the offertory, the preparation of the gifts, before the Canon Missal of the Mass. No comparable representations have been found. It is possible that it was part of a Seven Sacraments composition, replacing the usual Elevation of the Host.

Date. Second quarter 14th c.

The roundel is set against a composite background of fragments of geometric grisaille.

1b. Roundel. Archbishop   PLATE 31 (d)

Roundel d. 0·27 m.

A mitred archbishop, enthroned in benediction, holding a crozier.

Condition. Complete except for the left side of the chasuble and part of the background. Glass well preserved.

Colour and Technique. Ochre mitre, light-pink head and amice, ochre chasuble, ruby tunicle, white alb, white cross pallium and gloves, patterned shoes, pattern scratched out of matt wash, ochre crozier. Ruby throne with white base and seat. Plain green background, a plain ruby boss leaded in on either side of the figure, plain ruby border.

Iconography. No nimbus and no identifying attribute.

Style and Design. Companion figure to 1c.

Date. Early 14th c.

The roundel is set against a composite background of fragments of geometric grisaille, 13th and 14th c.; three foils of white foliage sprays on a plain ruby ground may be from tracery lights, 14th c.

1c. Roundel, A Pope   PLATE 30 (h)

d. 0·27 m.

A Pope with single crown tiara, enthroned in benediction holding a cross-staff.

Condition. Complete, the glass is well preserved, little corrosion.

[1] Ibid., *Aspilogia* ii, op. cit., 143.
[2] G.E.C. vi. 346. Greening Lamborn (1949), 122.
[3] Ibid. 121.
[4] Ibid. G.E.C. vii. 463.
[5] Greening Lamborn (1949), 121.
[6] Addington, op. cit. 41–9. Greening Lamborn (1949), 120–1.

Colour and Technique. Ochre tiara, light-pink face, ochre amice, green chasuble, ruby tunicle, white alb, white cross pallium, maniple, and gloves, smear shading on vestments, patterned shoes, pattern scratched out of matt wash. Ochre throne with a blue cushion and a white base. Plain ruby ground, the glass very streaky, with plain white boss either side of the figure. Plain green border.

Iconography. No nimbus. The papal tiara with a single circlet crown was in use during the 12th and 13th c. The second circlet or crown proper was added by Pope Boniface VIII, 1294–1303.[1] Although the figure has no nimbus St. Peter Apostle is sometimes represented in papal regalia. As he is one of the patron saints of the abbey this identification is possible.

Style and Design. Companion figure to 1b above, figures similar but varied in detail, the drapery of the alb over the feet and backgrounds are identical in design.

Date. Early 14th c.

Composite background of fragments as 1b.

1d. Fragments

Condition. A composite panel of fragments of grisaille and foliage designs placed here when the St. Birinus panel was moved to n. III.

Lost Glass

The drawings of Dorchester made by John Carter 1792–3 include a panel now lost then in a north window of the nave.[2] The drawing suggests that it was the same size as the panel of St. Birinus preaching, as the two are drawn on the same sheet but 'sketched small and very slight, owing to the great distance from the eye'.

The panel depicted a priest celebrating at an altar, before him is a chalice, in the left background a sailor in a boat. The scene doubtless had reference to the story that when St. Birinus was sailing to Britain he left behind a corporal given to him by Pope Honorius. The saint left the ship and walked on the sea to the shore to reclaim it.[3] No other representation of this scene has survived.

Antiquarian sources also include reference to fourteen shields of arms, no longer extant, which appear to be part of the series surviving in s. II and n. IX.[4]

DRAYTON ST. LEONARD

ST. LEONARD

O.S. SP 596 965.

MS. SOURCES

Oxford. Bodleian Library, MS. Top. Oxon. d. 93, f. 86. Notes by the Revd. F. H. Woods, 1882.

PRINTED

Parker (1842), 326.
Nelson (1913), 163.
Bouchier (1918), 72–3.
Bouchier (1932), 128.
Pevsner (1974), 587–8.

n. II

1a. St. Leonard   PLATE 32 (*a*)

h. 0·91 m. w. 0·27 m. Figure: h. 0·38 m.

Full-length figure facing three-quarters left holding a crozier and fetters.

Condition. The upper part of the figure and adjacent background are original; the remainder is the work of Messrs. Clayton & Bell, 1861.[5] While the original white glass is well preserved, the purple background is extremely corroded and almost opaque.

Colour and Technique. Figure painted in brown paint on white glass, strong smear shading, details picked out in yellow stain. Pot-metal purple background, diapered with a foliage design.

Iconography. Modern inscription *S. LEONARDUS.* No nimbus, represented as a mitred abbot in benediction, holding a crozier, a large chain fetter hangs from his right

---

[1] M. Didron, *Christian Iconography*, ed. M. Stokes (1886), ii. 74–5.

[2] Bodl. Lib. Gough Maps 227, pl. xvi, op. cit. See plate 31 (*e*).

[3] 'Liber Monasterii de Hyde A.D. 455–1023', ed. E. Edwards, *Rolls*

Series xlvi (1866), 12; *Nova Legenda Anglie*, ed. C. Horstman (1901), 118.

[4] *Visitations* (1871), 106–10.

[5] Bodl. Lib. MS. Top. Oxon. d. 93, op. cit.

wrist.[1] St. Leonard was the founder and first abbot of the monastery of Noblac, near Limoges, where he died *c.* 559.[2] His cult was international and he was popular in England where there were 177 known church dedications to him.[3] In English art he is commonly represented either in monastic habit, holding a crozier,[4] or as a deacon.[5] It is rare to find him represented as a mitred abbot[6] or archbishop.[7] Chains or fetters are almost invariably found as his attribute, referring to his patronage of prisoners.[8]

Style and Design. The style appears to be very individual, with fluid painting of the drapery and face, rather anguished eyes, and brusque cursory representation of the dark stubble of hair on the chin. No other work exactly like this is extant in the county.

Date. The figure has been described as being of the 15th c.[9]

and as perpendicular.[10] A 14th-c. dating, however, is more acceptable. The smear shading and the foliage patterns on the mitre and purple background are typical of the 14th c. A precise dating is difficult. The details of drawing of the eyebrows, nose, and mouth reflect the mid-century conventions, as found, for example, in the Latin Chapel windows at Christ Church, Oxford. The drawing of the eyes, however, has more affinity with the work of Thomas of Oxford, at New College, Oxford (mid 1380s). These factors suggest a dating in the third quarter of the 14th c.

n. I

A1, A3

Two scraps of 14th-c. white grisaille with a foliage trail of oak leaves.

DUCKLINGTON

ST. BARTHOLOMEW

O.S. SP 359 076.

MS. SOURCES

London. British Library, MS. Lansdown 874, f. 140ᵛ. Church Notes, 1595.
Oxford. Bodleian Library:
  MS. Top. Oxon. b. 75, f. 78. Wyatt Collections, 1805.

MS. Top. Oxon. b. 78, f. 165. Collections for the History of Ducklington by W. D. McRae, rector, 1872.

PRINTED

P.C. (1920), 128.
Pevsner (1974), 588–9.

Two nineteenth-century accounts reveal that in the early nineteenth century there was considerably more medieval glass than the few scraps that now survive:

'In the great East window which is very beautiful, sculptured in stone is the Virgin sitting, with her arms held up and praying to a figure of the Almighty sitting opposite her, both pointing to a representation of Our Saviour painted in glass in the upper quatrefoil compartment of the window. The upper tracery of this fine and very singular window is full of fine glass, tops of canopies as at Kidlington, borders etc. and some of them composed of birds.'[11]

The Revd. W. D. McRae's notes reveal the fate of some of this glass:

'The East window of the North aisle was formerly filled with stained glass (amongst which the old clerk, Fisher, remembers seeing as he tells me candlesticks and coats of arms) but boys used to stand by the cottage at the East end and pelt the window with stones till all was destroyed but the few coloured scraps that now remain at the top.'[12]

[1] Bouchier (1918), 72–3, incorrectly states that the chain was 'apparently added in the restoration'. Only the lower part is modern.

[2] *Acta Sanctorum, Novembris* iii (1910), 139–210. *Golden Legend* iv, 132–9.

[3] F. Bond, *Dedications of English Churches* (1914), 174.

[4] Many examples from the 13th c. onwards, e.g. the 13th-c. Cuerdon Psalter. New York, Pierpont Morgan Library, MS. 756, f. 9.

[5] e.g. the 13th-c. wall-painting at Frindsbury (Kent), see E. W. Tristram, *English Medieval Wall Painting II. The Thirteenth Century,* 2 vols. (1950), 546.

[6] There is a 15th-c. example in a window at Great Malvern (Worcs.), Rushforth (1936), 232, fig. 118.

[7] There is a 15th-c. example in a window at Thirsk (Yorks.), *Journal of the Royal Archaeological Institute* ii (1846), 78–9.

[8] He is said to have obtained from King Clovis the privilege of releasing all those prisoners whom he should visit. All the miracles related in the *Golden Legend* are concerned with prisoners, 133–8.

[9] Parker (1842), 326. Bouchier (1918), 72–3.

[10] Nelson (1913), 163.

[11] Bodl. Lib., MS. Top. Oxon. b. 75, f. 78.

[12] Ibid. b. 78, f. 165, Oct. 1872.

I

A1. Fragments of Grisaille Foliage

h. 0·46 m. w. 0·37 m. (approx.).

At the centre a roundel enclosed in a pattern border with offspringing sprays of ivy-leaf foliage.

    The central roundel of white and ruby glass is modern. The sprays of ivy foliage are painted on white glass, the same piece of glass as the yellow stain pattern border to the central medallion. The pieces of white foliage design have curved edges and appear to be *in situ*.

Date. Mid 14th c.

A2. Geometric Grisaille

As A1.

C3. Fragments.

h. 0·76 m. w. 0·38 m.

Two border pieces. Two crow-like birds in profile facing each other, painted on white glass. A small crocketed spire, white and yellow stain. A small lion's face, frontal pot-metal yellow. All fragments set against a background of plain white glass. Mid 14th c.

D1, D2. Fragments

h. 0·51 m. w. 0·26 m.

Six pieces of serrated leaf design, three in each light. Pot-metal yellow. Probably border pieces, perhaps associated with the birds in C3 above. Set against plain white modern glass. Mid 14th c.

C1. Fragments

Three leaf borders, as D1 and D2. Small frontal head of Christ, painted on pale pink or brown glass. Part of the complete figure described by Wyatt (see Introduction). Set in plain white glass.

Lost Glass

The armorial glass has been lost since 1595 when the most extensive notes were made.[1] These recorded three single shields, and four shields with an incomplete inscription.
Azure semy of fleurs-de-lis argent a lion rampant gardant argent (HOLLAND).
Barry nebuly or and gules (LOVEL).
Azure a daunce or between thirteen billets or (DEINCOURT).
Inscription; '*Henry . . . Et Emma sa Feme*' with the following shields:
Argent on a bend gules three martlets or (UNIDENTIFIED).
Gyronny of eight argent and gules (BASSINGBOURNE).
Sable semy of fleurs-de-lis or (LEHAM)
Or a fess sable (UNIDENTIFIED).
No evidence has been found to establish a date for this glass.

EASINGTON
ST. PETER

O.S. SP 663 972.

PRINTED SOURCES
Nelson (1913), 163.

Buckland, W. M., *A History of Easington* (pamphlet, n.d.).
Pevsner (1974), 591.

I

1a, 1b, 1c. Quarries

Each quarry h. 0·14 m. w. 0·11 m. (approx.).

Condition. Extremely corroded. All set inside out in a trellis quarry design of modern plain white quarries.

Colour and Technique. Painted on white glass, central rosette in yellow stain.

Style and Design. Quarry type 47.

Date. 14th c.

B1. Roundel

A ruby roundel patterned with a rosette design. Very corroded and set inside out. Details indistinct. 14th c.

---

[1] B.L. MS. Lansdown 874, f. 140ᵛ, P.C. (1920), 128, records five shields, one of which seems to have been damaged.

EWELME
BLESSED VIRGIN MARY

O.S. SP 647 914.

MS. SOURCES

Oxford. Bodleian Library, MS. Top. Oxon. b. 75, ff. 109ᵛ–110ᵛ. Wyatt's Collections, 18c–19c.

PRINTED

Hearne, T., *Duo rerum Anglicarum scriptores veteres* (1732), ii. 541–73.

Napier, H., *Historical Notices of Swyncombe and Ewelme* (1858).
Visitations (1871), 38–42, 83.
V.C.H. ii (1907), 156.
Nelson (1913), 163.
Bouchier (1918).
P.C. (1920), 128–9.
Greening Lamborn (1949), 125–6.
Pevsner (1974), 598.

The remaining fragments of glass have been collected together and set into two windows, the east window of the Chapel of St. John Baptist (s. II) and a window of the vestry (n. III). Nearly all the glass is fifteenth-century and its condition is extremely poor as much of the paint has almost entirely perished. This glass has been dated c. 1435.[1] Pevsner gives the date of the rebuilding of the church as c. 1432[2]. However, there is some documentary evidence to suggest a later date. In 1437 William de la Pole, Earl of Suffolk and lord of the manor of Ewelme, together with his wife Alice obtained a licence to establish an almshouse at Ewelme.[3] By 1442 the foundation was complete but the statutes drawn up by the founder are later, dating from 1448–50.[4] The first master was John Seynesbury 'late persone by long continuance of tyme of the said parysh of Ewelme . . . for his longe continuede service and attendaunce that he had in the bylding of the said chirche and howse also'.[5] It seems likely that the rebuilding of the church took place after 1437, and was completed some time before 1448–50 when the statutes were issued. It is probable that the fifteenth-century glass is of about the same date.

There are four remaining shields of arms commemorating the families of William de la Pole, his wife Alice Chaucer, and their alliances (s. II A3–6). Some differences in size suggest that they come from at least two different series of shields but of the same date. The seventeenth-century antiquarian notes record twelve shields in all, but it is evident that some losses occurred before that date.[6]

There are a number of roundels painted with various animals. The roundels are all the same size and are identical in technique and decorative details, suggesting they are a related series (s. II, 1a, 1d, 2a–d, and 5b). They appear to be more than a decorative menagerie, although of course such sets are known.[7] One beast with horns and tusks, spotted fur, collared and chained (1d, 2a, and 5b) is very close to the animal supporters found in the seals of William de la Pole, first Duke of Suffolk, d. 1450[8] and his son John, d. 1491.[9] The latter examples have been described as heraldic antelopes[10] but it seems that they should be more properly described as yales.[11] The other animals here all occur in heraldic contexts. There are two lions sejant and cowed (2c and 2d). Lions are used as supporters on the seal[12] of Sir Edmund de la Pole, d. 1419, brother of

[1] Nelson (1913), 163.

[2] Pevsner (1974), 598.

[3] W. Dugdale, *Monasticon Anglicanum*, ed. J. Caley, Sir H. Ellis, and B. Bandinel, vi, part II (1846), 716–17; *V.C.H.* ii (1907), 156.

[4] T. Hearne, op. cit. 541–73.

[5] Ibid. 544.

[6] P.C. (1920), 138, the shield there given as Roet or Chaucer quartering England was recorded by Wood as the dexter half of an impaled shield. Bodl. Lib. Wood MS. E I, f. 215.

[7] For example, three late 15th-c. roundels of an antelope, ass, and

marten with name scrolls in English at Greystoke church (Cumberland), s. III.

[8] Birch, iii (1894), 12764, A.D. 1430. Harl. Ch. 54.1.10. Reproduced in W. St. John Hope, *The Stall Plates of the Knights of the Order of the Garter* (1901), pl. l.

[9] Birch, iii (1894), 12753, A.D. 1467–87, cast. XXXV. 37.

[10] Ibid. St. John Hope, op. cit.

[11] See the remarks of H. Stanford London in *Royal Beasts* (1956), 35 n. 3.

[12] Birch, iii (1894), 12748, A.D. 1414, B. L. Cott. Ch. XXXVIII. 87.

William, first Duke of Suffolk.[1] However, as the lions are sejant and cowed the Yorkist badge of the white[2] lion of March may be intended.[3] The white hart (5b) and white hind (2b) are also Yorkist badges.[4] Finally the unicorn (1a) was a crest of Thomas Chaucer (d. 1413).[5] The Ewelme roundels have links with heraldic badges and supporters perhaps with a Yorkist element in their choice. The de la Pole family had particular association with the house of York. The two families were united by the marriage in 1460 of John de la Pole, second Duke of Suffolk, to Elizabeth daughter of Richard Plantagenet, Duke of York.[6] It is possible that this marriage may have prompted the choice of subject for the roundels. However, it should be emphasized that in fifteenth-century context such a display of badges and cognizances could be justified on a purely personal level without any particular blood relationship.

s. II

1a, 1d, 2a, 2b, 2c, 2d. Heraldic Roundels
Panels: 1a, 1d, h. 0·30 m. w. 0·52 m. 2a–2d. h. 0·20 m. w. 0·52 m.
Roundels: d. 0·18 m.

1a. Unicorn
Facing left, head turned to the right.

1d. Yale
Collared and chained, in profile facing left.

2a. Yale
As 1d.

2b. White Hind
Trotting to the left.

2c. Lion
Sejant and cowed, facing right.

2d. Lion
Sejant and cowed, facing left.

All the roundels are set against fragments and quarries type 19; in 1a and 1d are some incomplete square decorative designs, each a plant in circular frame.

Condition. The roundels are complete except for 1d and 2d, which have small losses. The glass is extremely corroded and the paint in all cases is very worn.

Colour and Technique. Painted on white glass, grassy banks in yellow stain, background diapers of contiguous rosettes with yellow stain centres, plain yellow stain borders. The lions are in yellow stain, the yales have white bodies spotted with clumps of fur in yellow stain.

Iconography. It is possible that all these beasts are heraldic badges, rather than purely decorative work.[7]

Style and Design. There can be no doubt that these roundels are part of a single series. They are identical in size, the grassy banks and rosette backgrounds are also identical. The two yales are identical and the two lions are painted from a single cartoon in reverse positions.

Date. 15th c.

1b. Fragments
h. 0·30 m. w. 0·52 m.

Condition. A half-length figure of St. Andrew holding a saltire cross, fragments of canopies and quarries type 19. All very corroded, the paint very worn, particularly on the quarries.

Colour and Technique. White glass and yellow stain, the yellow stain of St. Andrew's nimbus, cross, and hem of mantle is deep orange in tone.

Iconography. St. Andrew's saltire cross is his standard attribute.

Date. 15th c.

1c. Fragments
h. 0·30 m. w. 0·52 m.

Condition. Fragments of canopy designs including the figure of a prophet standing in a side-shafting, a large crown from a figure, and quarries type 19. Corrosion of varying intensity, the quarries very worn.

3a. Cherubim
Panel: h. 0·52 m. w. 0·52 m. Figure: h. 0·42 m. w. 0·15 m.

---

[1] Pedigree in Napier, op. cit., facing 322.
[2] The Ewelme lions are yellow. However, as all the roundels are in white and yellow stain, with no coloured glass, it is probable that the artist disregarded the proper heraldic tinctures.
[3] Stanford London, op. cit. 29–32.
[4] The badges were derived from Richard II and his mother. See J. R. Planche, 'On the Badges of the House of York', *British Archaeo-*

logical Journal xx (1864), 18–33; M. V. Clarke, *Fourteenth Century Studies* (1937), 272–92, and J. H. Harvey, 'The Wilton Diptych. A Re-examination', *Archaeologia* xcviii (1961), 6–8.
[5] Stanford London, op. cit. 49–50.
[6] Napier, op. cit. Pedigree facing 322. G.E.C. xii, part 1 (1953), 448–9.
[7] See Introduction.

A full-length cherubim standing on a wheel, set against fragments of canopy designs and quarries, type 19, as 1a above.

Condition. The figure is probably composite, the head may be an addition as the lead lines do not follow through from the body. Corrosion of varying intensity, the paint on both the figure and the quarries is very worn.

Colour and Technique. Painted on white glass, the hair, body, wings, and wheel in yellow stain.

Iconography. Wheels properly belong to the cherubim (Ezechiel 10: 2, 9, 12, 13, 19) but the iconography is inconsistent in the later Middle Ages.

Style and Design. The figure is extremely thin and tall. The tiled floor, painted on the same glass as the feet and wheels, suggests that originally the figure was set below a canopy. Fragments of similar figures are found in 3d and 4d below.

Date. 15th c.

3b. Head of the Virgin?

Panel: h. 0·35 m. w. 0·52 m. Head: h. 0·22 m. w. 0·22 m.

Nimbed and crowned female head, facing three-quarters right. Set against quarries type 19, as 1a above, and modern plain glass.

Condition. All of a piece, old leaded repair. The glass is extremely corroded, the paint almost completely gone.

Colour and Technique. Painted on white glass, the hair, crown, and cusped border of the nimbus in yellow stain.

Iconography. No particular attribute to verify identification.

Style and Design. The few visible details suggest some affinity with the Virgin's head at Cropredy.

Date. 15th c.

3c. Head of Female Saint

Panel: h. 0·35 m. w. 0·52 m. Head: h. 0·35 m. w. 0·22 m.

Condition. Probably a composite, head of a young saint wearing a jewelled circlet around her brow, leaded up with the nimbus of another figure, the head of a cross-staff painted on the same glass as the nimbus. Extremely corroded, the paint is almost completely gone.

Colour and Technique. Painted on white glass, the hair in yellow stain.

Style and Design. The few visible details suggest some affinity with the female saint at Binsey, window I, 2c.

Date. 15th c.

3d. Cherubim

h. 0·52 m. w. 0·52 m.

Condition. Figure of a cherubim almost identical to that in 3a above, the position of the feet differ, lower part of another as 3a above, and a fragment of a third much smaller in size. Set against fragments of canopy designs and quarries type 19 as 1a above. The glass has corrosion of varying intensity, the paint very worn, particularly on the quarries.

Date. 15th c.

4a. Angel

Panel: h. 0·52 m. w. 0·52 m. Figure: h. 0·34 m. w. 0·15 m.

A winged angel, genuflecting, facing three-quarters right. Set against fragments of canopy designs and quarries, type 19 as 1a above and small pieces of 14th-c. diaper.

Condition. The figure is complete, originally represented censing. Only a small piece of the censer remains, painted on the same glass as the raised wing and diapered background. Extremely well preserved, very little corrosion, and only minor paint loss.

Colour and Technique. Painted on white glass, edge of the nimbus in yellow stain. Smear shading on the drapery with back painting on the strong drapery lines and hair. Background diaper of quatrefoils picked out of a streaky wash of matt black paint.

Style and Design. Possibly from a large tracery light, there is part of a plain curved border painted on the same glass as the figure's right foot.

Date. 14th c.

4b. St. Mark Evangelist

h. 0·66 m. w. 0·52 m. Figure: h. 0·46 m. w. 0·23 m.

St. Mark seated facing three-quarters right, his lion at his feet. Set against fragments, quarries type 19, as 1b above. Small pieces of 14th-c. geometric grisaille painted with rose trails and an inscription, probably a motto, in black-letter script:

|Sur|toute|.

Condition. The figure and lion are complete but the paint is very worn. Original background almost entirely missing. Quarries also very worn.

Colour and Technique. Figure painted on white glass, nimbus and hem of mantle in yellow stain, white tunic powdered with yellow stain rosettes, line hatching and stippled shading, back painting on the beard and hair, lion in yellow stain. Background, by the lion, simple cross-hatching in outline.

Iconography. Standard, presumably originally there would have been a series of the four Evangelists with their emblems, the saint's head in 4c below may be one of them.

Style and Design. The drawing of the lion, and the rosette diaper are close to the roundels 2c and 2d, probably painted by the same artist.

Date. 15th c.

4c. Head of Evangelist

Panel: h. 0·66 m. w. 0·52 m.

Condition. The head of a saint, bearded, facing three-quarters left, set against small fragments of canopies, quarries type 19, as 1a above, made up with modern plain white glass. Corrosion is of varying intensity, the paint very worn, particularly on the head and quarries.

Colour and Technique. Head painted on white glass, nimbus in yellow stain, back painting on the hair and beard.

Iconography, Style, and Design. The head is close in painting style and size to the St. Mark, 4b above, the nimbs are identical. Probably one of the Evangelists, either St. Matthew or St. Luke as St. John is generally represented without a beard.

Date. 15th c.

4d. Heads of St. Paul and St. Peter   PLATE 32 (*d*)

Panel: h. 0·66 m. w. 0·62 m.

Condition. The heads are at the top of a panel of fragments, and the more substantial pieces are, reading upwards, the legs and feet of a cherubim standing on a wheel, similar to 3d above, 15th c.; and an angel standing in a canopy, white and yellow stain, extremely decayed. 15th c. Border pieces: crowns in white and yellow stain. 15th c. Border pieces: foliage design, white and yellow stain. 15th c.

Quarries: type 19, as 1a, the paint very worn.

Colour and Technique. Heads painted on pink glass, the St. Paul is a stronger colour than the St. Peter. Smear shading on the hair and beards.

Iconography. The identification is tentative, they conform to the standard types for these two saints, St. Paul with balding hair and St. Peter with a tonsure.

Style and Design. The two heads are close to each other in style, particularly the drawing of the eyes and ears and turned-down mouth. There is a general similarity to the earlier glass at Merton College Chapel, Oxford.

Date. First quarter 14th c.

5a. Fragments

h. 0·40 m. w. 0·52 m.

Two triangular-shaped pieces of glass painted with a flat

foliage design, yellow stain on a matt black background, plain border. 15th c. Probably from an eyelet tracery light. A foliage corner piece from the framing to a shield, white and yellow stain. 15th c.[1]

Two rosette bosses, one pot-metal ochre, the other purple, 14th c. Fragment of canopy, white and yellow stain, 14th c. Roundel, an eight-pointed star, pot-metal ochre. 15th c.

5b. Fragments

h. 0·40 m. w. 0·52 m.

Two triangular foliage designs as 5a.

Incomplete roundel: a hart lodged. Incomplete roundel, a yale. Both in colours and technique, style, and design are the same as the roundels 1a, 1d, 2a–d. 15th c.

Two roundels, each painted with the letter T, white glass, letter and border in yellow stain. Possibly a personal initial (for Thomas Chaucer ?).

5c. Fragments

h. 0·40 m. w. 0·52 m.

Two triangular foliage designs, as 5a.

Roundel, letter T as 5b.

Two elaborate patterned designs, white and yellow stain 15th c., possibly from a tracery light.

5d. Fragments

h. 0·40 m. w. 0·52 m.

Two triangular foliage designs as 5a.

Roundel: star design as 5a.

Two patterned designs as 5c.

A1. Monogram Ihc

h. 0·64 m. w. 0·22 m.

Condition. A complete tracery light reset in a larger tracery. Slight corrosion.

Colour and Technique. Painted on white glass, the *Ihc̄* and its surround in yellow stain, background diaper of contiguous rosettes, white and yellow stain plain border.

Date. 15th c.

Fragment of an inscription in Lombardic script:

|*ABD*|

A2. Fragments

h. 0·70 m. w. 0·22 m.

A mosaic of small 14th- and 15th-c. fragments.

---

[1] See Lost Glass below.

A3. Shield of de la Pole impaling Stafford

Panel: h. 0·70 m. w. 0·22 m. Shield: h. 0·28 m. w. 0·21 m.

Azure a fess or between three lions faces or DE LA POLE *impaling argent a chevron gules* STAFFORD.

Set against small fragments of canopy designs. Above the shield a fragment of a larger composition, a horned animal nuzzling a human hand, possibly St. Giles and the stag, white and yellow stain, 15th c. The head of a small lion seated in a niche of a canopy shafting, white and yellow stain.

Condition. The shield is complete except for the upper part of the fess of the de la Pole arms. The paint is very worn.

Colour and Technique. The charges are leaded in, the fields of both arms are diapered, a rough pebble pattern on the de la Pole arms and a fern-like foliage on the Stafford arms, both picked out of a light matt wash. The coloured glass is very light in tone.

Date. Michael de la Pole, second Earl of Suffolk, d. 1415, married Katherine, daughter of Hugh, second Earl of Stafford.[1] Their son William, Duke of Suffolk, was founder of the chantry and almshouses and rebuilder of the church.

A4. Shield of Lancaster impaling Neville

Panel: h. 0·70 m. w. 0·22 m. Shield: h. 0·24 m. w. 0·21 m.

Quarterly 1, 4 *azure three fleurs-de-lis or* FRANCE 2, 3 (*gules*) *three lions passant gardant in pale or* ENGLAND *a label of two points ermine* JOHN OF GAUNT, DUKE OF LANCASTER *impaling gules a cross saltire argent* NEVILLE. Set against fragments, above the shield a large incomplete head of a bearded saint, facing three-quarters left, white and yellow stain. 15th c.

Condition. The first quarter of the arms of Gaunt has been set upside down, the saltire cross of the Neville arms is a modern restoration. The paint is very worn. The ruby field of the Neville arms is corroded.

Colour and Technique. The blue fields of the arms of France are diapered with a rough pebble pattern picked out of a light matt wash. The lions of the arms of England are painted and stained, the ruby field is omitted.[2] The coloured glass is very light in tone.

Date. Ralph Neville, Earl of Westmorland, d. 1425, married Joan, daughter of John of Gaunt, Duke of Lancaster, by Catherine Roet, sister to Philippa, mother of Thomas Chaucer of Ewelme.[3] The Lancaster arms are here given precedence.

A5. Shield of Lancaster impaling Neville

Panel: h. 0·70 m. w. 0·22 m. Shield: h. 0·28 m. w. 0·21 m.

Shield as A4 above set against fragments.

Condition. Complete except for the top piece of the field and the lower part of the saltire cross of the Neville arms; these are restoration.

Colour and Technique. As A4, here the field of the Neville arms is patterned with contiguous circles painted in outline.

Date. 15th c.

A6. Shield of Roet for Chaucer impaling Burghersh of Ewelme

Panel: h. 0·70 m. w. 0·22 m. Shield: h. 0·21 m. w. 0·16 m.

Gules three catherine wheels or ROET FOR CHAUCER *impaling argent a chief* (*gules*) *over all a lion rampant queue fourchée or* BURGHERSH.

Shield set against fragments.

Condition. Complete except for a small part of the lower field of the Burghersh arms. The glass is very corroded and the paint worn.

Colour and Technique. The Chaucer arms are on a single piece of glass, the wheels abraded and stained yellow. The ruby chief of the Burghersh arms is painted in outline, the tincture omitted.[4] The coloured glass is very light in tone.

Date. Geoffrey Chaucer, d. 1400, married Philippa, daughter of Sir Paon Roet. Their son Thomas Chaucer, d. 1434, discarded his father's arms and adopted his mother's. He married Maud daughter and coheiress of Sir John Burghersh of Ewelme. Their daughter and heir Alice Chaucer brought the manor in marriage to William de la Pole, Duke of Suffolk.[5]

A7 and A8

Small fragments of 14th- and 15th-c. glass.

n. III

2a, 2b, A1, A2, and A3. Quarries

Quarry size h. 0·14 m. w. 0·11 m.

The quarries are all type 19, white and yellow stain. 15th c. In all cases the paint is very worn.

The three tracery lights each contain a modern roundel of plain white glass, the same in diameter as the heraldic roundels in s. II, so it is possible that some of the 15th-c. roundels were originally in this window.[6]

[1] Napier, op. cit. 322. G.E.C. xii, part 1 (1953).

[2] Greening Lamborn (1949), 125, thought the field 'must have been coated with red'. The use of the abrading technique is precluded by the small area of the quarter.

[3] G.E.C. op. cit.

[4] Greening Lamborn (1949), 126. 'the ruby of the chief all gone'. It is more likely that it was omitted. See above, n. 2.

[5] G.E.C. op. cit.

[6] It used to be a common practice for glaziers to retain the pattern of the leading as found, even if pieces were moved or discarded.

Lost Glass

The Wood–Rawlinson notes record a lost scene:[1] 'In a south window of the church are the pictures of two men talking: *Tu quis es? Christus es tu? non sum ego Christus.*' This is the episode in the life of St. John Baptist when the Jews sent priests and Levites from Jerusalem to ask him who he was '*Tu quis es? Et confessus est, et non negavit: et confessus est: Quia non sum ego Christus*' (St. John's Gospel 1:19–20). It is possible that this scene was one of a series illustrating the life of St. John Baptist. The south chapel and the Almshouse were both dedicated to St. John Baptist.[2]

The Wyatt Collections contain a large water-colour copy of a shield of de la Pole quartering Wingfield, set in foliated surround.[3] The shield has been lost, one piece of the surround is now leaded into s. II, 5a.

Antiquarian sources also include a shield, no longer extant, of Montacute and Monthermer quarterly impaling Burghersh for Thomas Montague, Earl of Salisbury (d. 1428) and his second wife, Alice Chaucer (d. 1475), who later married William de la Pole, Earl of Suffolk.[4]

EYNSHAM
ST. LEONARD

O.S. SP 433 092.

MS. SOURCES

Oxford. Bodleian Library:
 MS. Top. Oxon. e. 286, f. 113. Greenwood's Church Notes, dated 1659–60.
 MS. Top. Oxon. b. 75, f. 84ᵛ. Wyatt Collections, 19th c.

PRINTED

Parker (1846), 137.
Visitations (1871), 44.
Nelson (1913), 163.
Bouchier (1918), 95.
P.C. (1920), 143.
Pevsner (1974), 600–1.

The surviving medieval glass was rearranged and leaded into a window of the south aisle of the nave in 1965. This work was carried out by Mr. M. C. Farrar Bell.[5] Before the restoration the glass was in three separate panels which were displayed hanging from the tie bars in front of the plain white glazing of a south window.

It has been conjectured that the glass was brought here from the adjoining Benedictine Abbey of Eynsham.[6] There is no evidence for this hypothesis. The Wyatt Collections record glass in the tracery lights of the chancel, said to be of the time of Edward I.[7] There is no glass of this period now in the church. It is possible that this glass was identical with the remaining fragments, a mistake being made about their date.

s. IX

The restoration is recorded in an inscription at the base of the two main lights: 'These fragments of medieval glass were assembled in 1965 in loving memory of Eleanora Sutton by her children.'

2a. Composite Panel

h. 0·40 m. w. 0·37 m.

A medley of fragments. The most important piece is an incomplete figure of the Apostle St. Thomas.

St. Thomas   PLATE 32 (*b*)

h. 0·38 m. w. 0·15 m.

He stands facing three-quarters right holding a closed book and the spear of his martyrdom. Above his head is a scroll inscribed in black-letter script:

$$|S(an)c(tu)s\ t|(homas)|\ or(a)|$$

Condition. Only the upper half of the figure remains, slight corrosion on both surfaces. The name portion of the scroll, 'homas' was extremely corroded but intact when examined in 1963.[8] It was replaced by a plain piece of glass at the 1965 restoration.

Colour and Technique. Painted on white glass, light-brown paint with stippled shading, the book cover and cusped edge of the nimbus in very light-yellow stain.

---

[1] P.C. (1920), 138.
[2] *V.C.H.* ii (1907), 156. St. John Baptist is represented on the seal of the Almshouse.
[3] Bodl. Lib. MS. Top. Oxon. b. 75, ff. 109ᵛ–110ᵛ.
[4] G E.C. xi, 393–5. Visitations (1871), 83.

[5] Information from Mr. M. C. Farrar Bell.
[6] Bouchier (1918), 95. Nelson (1913), 163.
[7] Bodl. Lib., MS. Top. Oxon. b. 75, f. 84ᵛ. Parker (1846), 137, also refers to 'fragments of early Decorated glass in the heads of three windows on the south side of the chancel'.   [8] Photograph CI.

Iconography. The Apocryphal Acts of Thomas relate how the saint was speared to death.[1] The builder's rule, which is the earlier attribute of the saint,[2] seems to have been generally replaced by the spear in the later Middle Ages.[3] Even so, he is represented holding both attributes on the sculptured west front of Exeter Cathedral (Devon), *c.* 1400,[4] and the builder's rule alone in a 16th-c. panel at Yarnton (w. II, 2c). Figures of the saint holding a spear are common in the later Middle Ages.

The bidding scroll is curious, the inscription, *Sanctus Thomas ora*, is probably meant for *Sancte Thoma ora pro me*, or, *pro nobis*. This invocation suggests that originally the saint may have been represented with a donor figure or figures beside him.

Style and Design. The style is very linear, with restricted and light modelling. There is some similarity, particularly in the drawing of the features, to the Virgin Annunciate at Newington (s. VI, 2a) and the St. John Baptist at Yarnton, (n. VI, 2b).

Date. Mid 15th c.

2b. Composite Panel

h. 0·42 m. w. 0·35 m.

A medley of fragments.

Foliage designs: four fragments of two designs, each a flat serrated quatrefoil leaf with either a rosette or plain boss at the centre. Painted on white glass with yellow stain. 15th c. Probably tracery-light designs.

Canopies: various fragments of canopy design, all in white glass and yellow stain. 15th c. The pieces are too fragmentary to allow a reconstruction of the original designs.

4a. Tracery Light   PLATE 32 (*c*)

h. 0·28 m. w. 0·16 m.

A trefoil light, showing a crane, its wings raised, standing in profile facing right.

Condition. Complete, slight corrosion on both surfaces.

Colour and Technique. Painted on white glass, light-brown paint with stippled shading, yellow stain on the under side of the bird's front wing; background diaper of circles in yellow stain against matt paint, plain border.

Iconography. The earliest example of birds occupying tracery lights extant in the county is at South Newington, (n. IV, C1) of *c.* 1325–50. A much more sophisticated example of this design is found at Stanford-on-Avon (Northants.), *c.* 1325–30. The nave south aisle windows contain naturalistic birds, cranes, falcons, and cormorants, all *in situ.*[5] Although not common, examples continue until the late 15th c., as seen at Fulbrook (s. II, A1 and A2), at North Aston (s. II, A2 and A5), and at Barton-on-the-Heath (Warwicks.)[6] The Eynsham panel was incorrectly described by Bouchier as 'an eagle in yellow and white with a nimbus'.[7]

Style and Design. The style is very linear with restricted modelling, very akin to the St. Thomas, 2a.

Date. Mid 15th c.

4b. Roundel

d. 0·20 m.

At the centre a plain ruby boss with eight radiating leaves, alternately white and ochre.

Condition. Very corroded, particularly the ochre glass.

Colour and Technique. The coloured glass is all pot-metal, white leaves picked out of a matt black background.

Style and Design. Originally the roundel was probably the central feature of a trellis of quarries or geometric grisaille.

Date. 14th c.

Lost Glass

There are some inconsistencies between the antiquarian notes on the lost heraldic glass. The most detailed account is in the Harleian MS., which is followed here.[8]

'East window of the chancel'

Argent fretty gules on each joint a bezant (TRUSSELL).

(TRUSSELL)

'North windows of the chancel'

Gules a lion rampant or (FITZ ALAN, EARL OF ARUNDEL)

Gules three lions passant gardant in pale or (ENGLAND)

'South windows of the chancel'

Argent a cross gules (HERTECLAWE)

Checky or and azure (WARENNE, EARL OF SURREY)

[1] M. R. James, *The Apocryphal New Testament* (1924), 436–7. See also *Golden Legend* ii, 148.

[2] James, op. cit. 371–3. *Golden Legend*, ii, 138–48, for the legend of the saint commissioned to build a palace for King Gundaphorus of India.

[3] K. Künstle, *Ikonographie der Heiligen* (1926), 555. Rushforth (1936), 92, no. 3. J. Braun, *Tracht und Attribute der Heiligen in der Deutschen Kunst* (1943), 694–5. J. Lafond, *Les Vitraux de l'Église Saint Ouen de Rouen*, C.V.M.A. France IV, tome 2 (1970), 212 n. 3, attributes the first appearance of the spear to Italian painting of the 14th c. Earlier examples are found in Germany and Belgium, how-

ever, see Braun, op. cit.

[4] Rushforth (1936), 93 n. 1, correcting Prideaux, *Figure Sculpture of the West Front of Exeter Cathedral* (1912), pl. xx, C21, and 29, where the attributes are described as the saw and the club of St. Simon.

[5] Newton i (1961), 29–30; ii, 375–80.

[6] *V.C.H. Warwicks.* v (1949), 16. An unpublished photograph, C.I.

[7] Bouchier (1918), 95.

[8] P.C. (1920), 143. Also B.L. Harleian MS. 6365, ff. 121ᵛ–123, partly published in *The Topographer* iii (1791), 113. These notes are the same as Greenwood, Bodl. Lib. MS. Top. Oxon. e. 286, f. 113.

'In a south window of the Church a man praying, under him this, *Orate pro anima Hugonis Hulte[1]/Hulle[2] quondam rectoris de Haneborgh.*'

'In another south window'

Barry nebuly argent and gules (DE AMORY)

'In the great west window'

Argent a lion rampant gules (UNIDENTIFIED)

'In a south window'

Quarterly 1, 4 *azure two squirrels[3]/wolves[4] rampant combatant or* 2, 3 *argent on a chevron sable three spears heads or* (UNIDENTIFIED)

'Shield . . . *a lion rampant holding a ragged staff or*' (UNIDENTIFIED). Location unspecified.[5]

Also unlocated are the following:

Argent a lion rampant gules (crowned or) a bordure sable bezanty or (PLANTAGENET, EARL OF CORNWALL)

Three padlocks (SYDENHAM?)[6]

Or on a fess sable between three roundels quarterly ermine and gules, three plates triangular argent (UNIDENTIFIED)

It is difficult to assign a date and associations to such a diverse collection of shields. The old arms of England suggest a date before 1340 for the glass in the chancel. Hugo Hulle or Hulte has not been traced.

FIFIELD

ST. JOHN THE BAPTIST

O.S. SP 239 187.

MS. SOURCES

Oxford. Bodleian Library, MS. Top. Oxon b. 75, ff. 67–9. Wyatt Collections, 19th c.

PRINTED

Gardner, R., *Gazetteer and Directory of the County of Oxford* (1852), 844.

Greening Lamborn (1949), 126–8.

Pevsner (1949), 603.

There are only slight remains of medieval glass. A shield of the arms of Zouche of Haringworth and its grisaille foliage background were moved, after 1852,[7] from a tracery light of the east window of the chancel,[8] to their present position, window s. III, 1a. Greening Lamborn dated this shield as early fourteenth century.[9] The shield is of the early pointed form and this, combined with the absence of any decorative diapers, although not conclusive, might suggest a somewhat earlier date. The other two tracery lights of the east window doubtless contained other shields of arms, but no record of them has been found. The reasons for the commemoration of the Zouche family are not obvious. They had no direct connection with the manor of Fifield, which was part of the fee of Ferrers. The connections between the two families are possibly significant. In 1253 Eon la Zouche had been granted the marriage of Agatha, sixth daughter of William de Ferrers, Earl of Derby.[10] He transferred this, before July 1255, to Hugh Mortimer of Chelmarsh, whom Agatha married some time before 1258.[11] However, a later commemoration is possible as both Eon la Zouche and Agatha Ferrers were related by blood, they were grandchildren of Roger de Quincy, Earl of Winchester.[12]

The same window now contains a late fifteenth-century shield, window s. III, 1b. It is not recorded in Wyatt's Collections[13] and may have been imported from elsewhere at the restoration of the church, after 1852. This shield poses a series of problems. It shows the arms of Barton of Smethells and Holme quartering the quarterly arms of Radcliffe of Smethells. Greening Lamborn noted, 'Although the Barton shield usually bears a fess between three stags' faces, the quarterings here, and particularly their curious duplication, make it clear that this shield represents the marriage, 1486, of John Barton of Holme, Newark (*I.P.M.*,

[1] Greenwood, op. cit.
[2] Variant reading in P.C. (1920), 143.
[3] Harleian MS., op. cit.
[4] Bodl. Lib. Wood MS. E. 1, f. 43, omitted in P.C. (1920), 143, op. cit.
[5] 1574 Visitations (1871), 44, and P.C. (1920), 143.
[6] Tinctures not given; only the 1574 Visitation records this coat.
[7] Gardner, op. cit. 844.

[8] Shield and its surround sketched in Bodl. Lib. MS. Top. Oxon. b. 75, op. cit., f. 68.
[9] Greening Lamborn (1949), 126.
[10] G.E.C. xii. 11, 937. Greening Lamborn (1949), 126–8, wrongly states that she was the daughter of the last Earl Ferrers (Robert de Ferrers, honours forfeited 1266). [11] G.E.C., op. cit., ibid. ix, 280.
[12] Ibid. iv, 199; xii, part II, 395–7.
[13] Bodl. Lib. MS. Top. Oxon. b. 75, op. cit.

5 April 1517)[1] with his second cousin Cecilia, daughter and heir of Sir Ralph Radcliffe; and Cecilia was granddaughter of Edmund Radcliffe, brother of Sir Ralph, descended from Robert Radcliffe, who acquired Smethells with a coheir of Adam de Norley, heir of Walton.'[2]

Greening Lamborn's statement seems to imply that the glass painter made a mistake in representing the Barton arms as '*azure three stags faces or*'. This would not appear to be the case. The Domville Roll, *c*. 1470,[3] ascribes the arms '*azure a fess between three stags faces caboshed or*' to John Barton (d. 1491). However, carved on the porch of Holme church, rebuilt by this John Barton, this coat, in conjunction with his initials and rebus, appears with the addition of a *mullet on the fess*.[4] His great-grandson Andrew Barton (1499–1549) entered his arms at the Visitation of Lancashire in 1533 as '*azure on a fess between three stags heads or a mullet sable*'.[5] This evidence suggests that this is the proper coat of Barton. But the simpler coat for Barton, without the fess and mullet, and quartering the quarterly arms of Radcliffe, is also carved on the porch at Holme and occurs in the glass now set in the east window.[6] The simpler coat was probably borne for difference by the younger John Barton during the lifetime of his grandfather John and his father Ralph. The former died in 1491,[7] but the date of the latter's death is not known.

The main holdings of the Barton family were at Smethells (Lancs.), and Holme-by-Newark (Notts.); no direct connection between the family and Fifield is known. A John Barton held lands in the adjoining parish of Idbury in 1428.[8] A Thomas Barton, surveyor of Hampton, is mentioned in a sixteenth-century document relating to Burford Priory, which held lands in Fifield.[9] However, no precise relationship between these persons and the Bartons of Smethells and Holme has been established.

The shield is set against an incomplete ground of quarries, each bearing a spray of foliage, encircled by a gold crown. This design is possibly a crude version of the crown in the thornbush, in allusion to the victory of Henry VII at Bosworth Field in 1485, that is found as a quarry design.[10]

s. III

1a. Shield of Zouche

h. 1·22 m. w. 0·31 m. Shield: h. 0·30 m. w. 0·25 m.

Gules bezanty or a quarter (ermine) ZOUCHE OF HARINGWORTH.

Condition. Very corroded, the quarter is old plain white glass with no visible trace of painted ermine, this could be the result of weathering. Before its removal from the east window it was set inside out.[11] At the base and lower sides of the shield, part of its original background of oak leaves.[12]

Colour and Technique. Shield, field and bezants in plain pot-metal glass, no decorative diapers. Oak trail painted in simple trace lines on white glass.

Date. Late 13th–early 14th c.

Fragments of Geometric Grisaille

Set above and below the shield are fragments of a geometric pattern of interlocked quatrefoils, white glass painted with a vertical stem, with off-springing trails of leaves, two types, oak and maple. The original over-all design is uncertain. Probably part of the original glazing of the side windows of the chancel.[13]

1b. Shield of Barton quartering Radcliffe

h. 1·22 m. w. 0·31 m. Shield: h. 0·25 m. w. 0·20 m.

Quarterly 1, 4 *azure three stags' faces or* BARTON 2, 3 *quarterly of six*, i, iv *argent two bends engrailed sable* RADCLIFFE ii, v *gules a cross engrailed argent* NORLEY iii, vi *argent a mullet sable* WALTON.

Condition. Good, some slight corrosion of the glass and scaling of the paint.

[1] This is a mistake for 1528. See '*Cal. Inq. Post Mortem* relating to Nottinghamshire', *The Thoroton Society, Record Series* (1900), part iii, 178–80.   [2] Greening Lamborn (1949), 128.
[3] 31 v. Shield 1235; formerly collection of Sir S. C. Cockerell.
[4] N. Truman, 'Medieval Glass in Holme-by-Newark Church, (Notts.) part iv, *J.B.S.M.G.P.* viii (1939–42), 106.
[5] *Visitation Lancs. 1533*, ed. W. Langton, Chetham Society, cx (1882), 197–8.
[6] Truman, op. cit. He blazons the shield incorrectly.
[7] Will in *Miscellanea Genealogica et Heraldica*, ed. J. J. Howard, 2nd

ser. iv (1892), 218.
[8] Greening Lamborn (1949), 128, citing *Feudal Aids* iv. 188.
[9] Greening Lamborn (1949), 128, citing R. Gretton, *Burford Records* (1920), 639.
[10] B. Rackham, *A Guide to the Collections of Stained Glass* (Victoria and Albert Museum), 1936, 58, pl. 20.
[11] Tracing in Bodl. Lib. MS. Top. Oxon. b. 75, f. 69.
[12] Ibid., f. 68, very slight drawing of shield and surround when in the east window.
[13] Ibid., f. 68, a very minute sketch.

Colour and Technique. Pot-metal glass, no decorative diapers. The Radcliffe and Walton quarters are painted on a single piece of glass, the cross of the Norley arms is leaded as a plain cross, the engrailing done in paint.

Date. Late 15th c.

Ten quarries: identical design, a spray of foliage, encircled by a gold crown. White glass, design stippled matt paint and yellow stain. Late 15th c. Quarry type 53.

Roundel: a star design, yellow stain and matt paint on white glass, very decayed, 15th c. An identical roundel is found at Great Rollright, window s. V, A2.

n. V

Ia. Fragments

Two incomplete pieces of canopy work, crenellated battle-

ments, set upside down, white glass, stippled paint, and yellow stain, *c.* 1400 (?)

A1–4. Fragments

Identical foliage designs *in situ*

h. 0·15 m. w. 0·15 m.

Decorative spray of four serrated leaves, radiating from a rosette plaque at the centre.

Condition. Rather corroded, A3 and A4 are incomplete.

Colour and Technique. White glass, leaves trace lines in black paint with stippled shading, centre rosette in yellow stain.

Date. Mid 15th c.

FULBROOK

ST. JAMES

O.S. SP 258 131.

PRINTED SOURCES
Pevsner (1974), 609–10.

s. II

Tracery lights *in situ*, each h. 0·20 m. w. 0·16 m.

A1. Eagle

Facing right, wings displayed and beak open, above it three rosettes. 15th c.

A2. Peacock

In profile facing left, above it three rosettes. 15th c.

A3. Incomplete, two rosettes remain in the top cusps. 15th c.

A4. Incomplete, two rosettes, as A3.

Condition. A1 and A2 are possibly in their original leading. The latter is cracked. In 1963 there was only very slight corrosion on both surfaces of the glass. Since then there has been considerable deterioration of both surfaces of the glass, so much so, that in panel A1 the design is almost obliterated

completely by the excessive powdery white corrosion on both surfaces.

Colour and Technique. Painted in brown on white glass, with very light stippled matt shading, details picked out in yellow stain.

Iconography. The earliest extant example in the Midlands of birds occupying complete tracery lights is at Stanford-on-Avon (Northants.), *c.* 1325–30. The nave south aisle windows contain naturalistic birds, cranes, falcons, and cormorants, all *in situ*.[1] Although not commonly found, this class of design continues until the late 15th c., as is seen, for example, at North Aston, and Barton-on-the-Heath (Warwicks.).[2]

Style and Design. The design of a bird with three rosettes above is original, each bird is painted on the same piece of glass as the centre rosette. The birds are very precisely yet delicately painted. The work of this artist is not found elsewhere in the county.

Date. 15th c. (? third quarter).

[1] Newton i (1961), 29–39; ii, 375–80.

[2] Unpublished. Photograph CI.

GREAT MILTON

ST. MARY

O.S. SP 628 024.

PRINTED SOURCES

Ellis, T., *History of Great Milton* (1819).
E. E., 'Account of Great Milton', *The Gentleman's Magazine* (1820), xc. 9.
Parker (1846), 304–6.
The Itinerary of John Leyland in or about the years 1535–1543, ed. L. T. Smith (1907), i. 116.

Visitations (1871), 37–8.
Nelson (1913), 163.
Bouchier (1918), 73.
P.C. (1920), 214.
Bouchier (1932), 129.
Pevsner (1974), 622.

The two remaining tracery lights in the east window of the north aisle of the nave contain two early fourteenth-century panels of particular interest. The scenes represented are probably Lazarus begging and the death of Lazarus, from the parable of Dives and Lazarus. They may originally have been part of a more extensive series of scenes and it is also possible that the present arrangement may be a medieval composite, the figures being taken from an earlier series of scenes and given new backgrounds to fit them into their present position. This hypothesis would explain certain oddities of design and iconography but without a precise record of the condition of the panels before the last releading,[1] and an examination of the cut lines of the glass, this cannot be stated with any certainty.

n. V

A2. Death of Lazarus   PLATE 4 (*d*), 33 (*a*)

h. 0·52 m. w. 0·42 m.

The shrouded corpse of Lazarus lies, left to right, in the foreground, behind the corpse stand two angels.

Condition. Incomplete, part of the left-side angel, part of the corpse, and much of the lower foil are missing and have been made up with alien pieces of contemporary glass, pieces of canopy architectural design. The coloured glass is very corroded.

Colour and Technique. The shrouded corpse is painted on white glass. Left-hand angel: pink face and hands, blue nimbus, brown amice, white surplice at throat and green alb, green wings. Right-hand angel: pink face and hands, ruby nimbus, green amice, white surplice at throat, light-blue alb, blue wings. White background patterned with a diamond trellis, each trellis encloses a circle in outline, pattern scratched out of a matt wash of black paint, separated from the stonework by a strip of plain white glass. Slight smear modelling, back painting on the angel's hair.

Iconography. See A3 below.

Style and Design. See A3 below.

Date. Early 14th c.

A3. Lazarus Begging   PLATE 4 (*e*), 33 (*b*)

h. 0·52 m. w. 0·42 m.

Lazarus, full length facing three-quarters right, head in profile, he leans on a tau-shaped crutch and lifts his right arm and hand in supplication.

Condition. Incomplete, patched with alien pieces of white geometric grisaille glass.

Colour and Technique. Lazarus's head, arms, and legs painted on pink glass, pot-metal ochre loin cloth, blue tunic, green crutch with a ruby cross piece, he stands on a small green sward. Foliage painted on white glass. Set against a blue background patterned with circles in outline scratched out of a matt black wash. Separated from the stonework by a strip of plain white glass.

Iconography. The two panels probably depict two scenes from the Parable of Dives and Lazarus (Luke 16:19–31). The subject was very popular both in England and abroad, particularly in the 11th–13th c.[2] In England the subject was

---

[1] The glass of the main lights is dated 1915.
[2] *Herder* iii (1971), 21–4. Wall-painting at Hardham, Sussex, identification not certain, however. E. W. Tristram, *English Medieval Wall Painting. The Twelfth Century* (1944), 130. 13th-c. examples at Findon (Sussex), Ulcombe (Kent), and Winchfield (Hants). E. W. Tristram, *English Medieval Wall Painting. The Thirteenth Century* (1950), 546, 605, 622. A lost wall hanging, probably 13th c. from the Abbey of Bury St. Edmunds (Suffolk). M. R. James, 'On the Abbey of St. Edmund at Bury', *Cambridge Antiquarian Society* xxviii (1895), 130–43, 186–202.

particularly favoured by King Henry III, who ordered paintings of Dives and Lazarus for the castles at Guildford (Surrey), Northampton (Northants.), Ludgershall (Wilts.).[1]

The first scene represents two angels receiving the soul of Lazarus. In such death scenes the soul is generally depicted as a small naked human figure emerging from the mouth of the deceased.[2] This area is missing in the panel. An unusual feature is that the head of Lazarus is completely shrouded by the grave clothes; usually the face is displayed.[3] In the second scene where the half-naked Lazarus leans on a crutch and lifts his hand in supplication, the pose and costume can be paralleled in earlier representations of Lazarus begging.[4] Here, the gesture is meaningless, as there is no figure of Dives. However, Lazarus is looking directly upwards. The area above his head to the right is patched with alien glass and it is possible that originally Lazarus was gesturing towards the hand of God above him.

Although the two scenes can be related to the Lazarus story, only part of it is illustrated and, reading from left to right, in wrong chronological sequence. The panels could have been put in the present wrong order at some earlier restoration. It seems unlikely that the original iconographic programme would have completely omitted Dives and it is therefore possible that there was a series of tracery lights illustrating the parable.

Style and Design. This is painting and design of high quality. The origins of the style, the facial types, the treatment of the hair, the long pointed noses, lugubrious mouths, and the long gesticulating fingers, are to be found in the works of the late 13th–early 14th-c. style.[5] In this respect they have a close affinity with the windows of Merton College Chapel of *c.* 1296. Compare, for example, the head of the left-hand angel with the Archangel Gabriel from the east window tracery at Merton College (I, D1).

Date. Early 14th c.

s. V

A4. Foliage Design

A spray of foliage, small trefoil leaves, in yellow stain on a matt black background, plain white border. *In situ* 14th c.

Lost Glass

Parker noted in 1846 that an Early English window on the south side of the chancel then contained: 'a mutilated medallion of painted glass. A king crowned and a kneeling female, as if in supplication, crowned.'[6] The subject represented was possibly a Virgin and Christ in Majesty with the figure of the Virgin displaced from its original position beside Christ.

The antiquarian notes record four shields in the windows of the church:[7]

Barry nebuly argent and gules a bend azure (DAMORY)

Argent two bars gemelles gules on a canton gules a mullet of six points argent (WACE)

Gules on a chevron argent three lions rampant azure gouté or (COBHAM?)

Barry nebuly argent and gules (DAMORY).

The Damory arms probably commemorated Sir Richard Damory, Lord Damory (d. 1330), and his brother Sir Roger Damory, Lord Damory (d. 1321–2).[8] The family held lands in Oxfordshire, but no connection with Great Milton has been traced.[9] Sir Richard de Louches (d. before 1327) was Lord of a manor at Great Milton and married to Elena, daughter of William Wace.[10] The identification of the Cobham arms has not been verified.

---

[1] E. W. Tristram, *Thirteenth Century*, op. cit. 548, 578, 583. T. Borenius, 'Cycles of Images in the Palaces and Castles of Henry III', *Journal of the Warburg and Courtauld Institutes* (1943), vi. 40–1.

[2] e.g. the 12th-c. sculpture of the death of Lazarus on the west front of Lincoln Cathedral. F. Saxl, *English Sculptures of the Twelfth Century* (1954), pl. iii. The death of a sinner, probably Dives, 12th-c. sculpture in the Yorkshire Museum, York. T. S. R. Boase, *English Art 1100–1216* (1953), 236–7.

[3] As Lincoln, n. 2 above. Also the death of Lazarus in the early 14th-c. Arundel Psalter, B.L. Arundel MS. 83, f. 128. *Herder* iii (1971), 33, fig. 1.

[4] Prefatory leaf to a 12th-c. Psalter, English, New York, Pierpont Morgan Library MS. 521. M. R. James, 'Four Leaves of an English Psalter 12th c.', *The Walpole Society* (1937), xxv. 10, pl. v.

[5] F. Wormald, 'Paintings in Westminster Abbey and Contemporary Paintings', *Proceedings of the British Academy* xxxv (1949), 161–76.

[6] Parker (1846), 306.

[7] Visitations (1871), 37–8. P.C. (1920), 214.

[8] G.E.C. iv, 42–5, 46–7.

[9] *V.C.H.* v, 160–1, 286, vi, 58–9.

[10] Ibid.

GREAT ROLLRIGHT
ST. ANDREW

O.S. SP 327 315.

PRINTED SOURCES
P.C. (1920), 243.
Pevsner (1974), 623–4.

s. V

The 15th-c. glass in the tracery lights is all painted on white glass with stipple and matt shading and yellow stain against a plain matt black background. The glass is probably not *in situ*, two of the roundels have been cut down to fit their present position. Each is set against a modern background of white glass painted with imitation Tudor roses.

A1, A6. Roundel, a Star

d. 0·12 m.

Condition. Cut down to fit present position. Slight decay.

Style and Design. Possibly originally the centre of a large tracery light or from the cusped head of a main light, as at Stanton Harcourt, s. VII, 2a, 2c.

Date. Second half 15th c.

A2. Roundel, a Star

d. 0·12 m.

Condition. Complete, slight corrosion.

Colour and Technique. Painted on white glass with stipple and line shading. Rosette in yellow stain at centre against a matt black background with an irregular pattern scratched out of black paint.

Style and Design. Star of sixteen rays, alternately straight-sided and a mixture of straight and wavy edges. It would be incautious to regard this design as representing the Yorkist badge a sun in splendour. (See Stanton Harcourt s. VII, 2a, 2c.)

Date. Second half 15th c.

A5. Roundel, a Rose

d. 0·12 m.

A large white rose with a central floret in yellow. Painted on white glass, yellow stain. Originally set with a border

of a branch with thorns, now cut down. Possibly the Yorkist badge of a white rose, but see above, A2. Second half 15th c.

B1. Roundel, the Eagle of St. John

d. 0·13 m.

Nimbed eagle facing left holding a scroll inscribed in black-letter script:

$$|Ioh(ann)es.|$$

Condition. Incomplete, cut down to fit its present position. Slight corrosion.

Colour and Technique. Painted on white glass, stipple shading with accidental splashes of yellow stain.

Iconography. Probably part of a series of the symbols of the four Evangelists.

Style and Design. The drawing is careful, the style very linear with slight use of modelling washes.

Date. Second half 15th c.

Glass removed from Great Rollright

A panel depicting the Sacrament of Marriage 'formerly in a window of Rollright Church in Oxfordshire'[1] was acquired by Alderman William Fletcher before 1793[2] and presented by him in 1797 to the Bodleian Library, Oxford.[3]

Oxford. Bodleian Library

PLATES 5, 33 (c)

West window, Seldon End. LVIII. Spokes serial no. 241.

h. 0·26 m. w. 0·35 m.

At the centre a priest joining the hands of a nuptial couple before eight witnesses, two streams of Christ's blood descend on to the couple's hands.

Condition. Incomplete, restored in 1963–4 by D. King of Norwich, when some missing parts were made up with alien fragments of 15th-c. figures. An 18th-c. drawing shows four figures, two on either side of the main group, which have been lost. (See Plate 33 (d).)[4]

---

[1] MS. note by Gough in Bodl. Lib. MS. Top. Oxon. c. 16, f. 120. Spokes (1973), n. 21.
[2] Note by Gough with a coloured lithograph in Bodl. Lib. Gen. Top. a. 6, pl. lxxxv, p. 114. Spokes (1973), ibid.
[3] W. D. Macray, *Annals of the Bodleian Library, Oxford, 1598–1807* (1868), 38. [4] Bodl. Lib. Gough Maps 26, f. 72.

Colour and Technique. The heads and hands are all painted on white glass, the details of hair and head-dresses picked out in yellow stain. The priest has a white alb, patterned amice, and crossed stole in yellow stain. The bridegroom wears a gown with long scalloped sleeves and short fur collar, the bride has a green mantle over a white tunic patterned with rosettes in yellow stain. Witnesses, l. to r.: the first two are alien insertions, man in white tunic, buttons and elaborate belt in yellow stain, green hat, only the head of his companion is seen, hat in yellow stain. The two women have ruby mantles and simple white wimples. Background: blue, patterned with a repeated rosette design picked out of a matt wash. Blood of Christ in pot-metal ruby.

Iconography. Before the last restoration, the panel had a late 18th-c. inscription describing the scene as:

|The Marriage|of Henry VI with|Margaret of Anjou|

This theory was discredited by Macray.[1] The true identity of the scene was established by Rushforth, who recognized it as the Sacrament of Marriage from a series of the Seven Sacraments.[2] He distinguished two different types of composition for this series, based on the remains of ten windows. In the first the Sacraments are grouped around the figure of Christ and connected to him by channels of blood flowing from his wounds. In the second type the central figure of Christ is shown crucified on the cross. He suggested that the Great Rollright panel belonged to the first type, and was originally set beneath the feet of Christ.[3]

Style and Design. This is indifferent work both in design and execution. The figures are stereotyped and lifeless, the drapery painting is poor. For example, the roses on the bride's tunic are superimposed as a flat pattern, and are unrelated to the folds of the drapery, and the witness behind the bridegroom is a clumsy piece of drawing with the low-slung belt creating the impression of being around his thighs rather than his waist.

Date. Third quarter 15th c.

Lost Glass

Wood's notes give three shields in the windows of the church:[4]

Argent a lion rampant sable crowned or, a bordure azure (BURNELL)

Sable two bars argent in chief three roundels argent in fess point a mullet or (FITZJOHN?) *impaling* (BURNELL)

(FITZJOHN?)

The Burnell family held the manor and advowson of Great Rollright.[5] The identities of the individuals represented by the shields have not been established.

HAMPTON POYLE
ST. MARY VIRGIN

O.S. SP 498 155.

MS. SOURCES

London. British Library, Harleian MS. 4170 pl. (18th c.).
Oxford. Bodleian Library:
   MS. Top. Oxon. e. 286, f. 125ᵛ. Notes by N. Greenwood dated
    1660. (Copied in B.L. Harl. MS. 4170.)
   MS. Top. Oxon. b. 75, f. 96ʳ. Drawings, dated 1804.

n. II

Tracery lights, *in situ*, each h. 0·28 m. w. 0·20 m.

All inscriptions are in black-letter script.

PRINTED SOURCES

H. E., 'A Specimen of a History of Oxford', *The Gentleman's Magazine*, lxxvi (1806), 524, 809–11.
Parker (1846), 54–5.
Greenfield, B. W. 'The Descent of the Manor of Hampton Poyle', *The Herald and Genealogist*, i (1863), 208–24, 321–44.
Nelson (1913), 163.   V.C.H. vi (1959), 167.
P.C. (1920), 157.   Pevsner (1974), 630.

A1. Lion of St. Mark   PLATE 34 (*a*)
Scroll inscribed |Marcus|

A2. Angel of St. Matthew   PLATE 34 (*b*)
Scroll inscribed |Matheus|

---

[1] Macray, op. cit.

[2] G. M. Rushforth, 'Seven Sacraments Compositions in English Medieval Art', *Antiquaries Journal*, ix (1929), 83–100.

[3] Rushforth, op. cit., also discusses a number of isolated Sacrament scenes, or fragments of such, where the over-all design is unknown. His examples are all 15th-c., and he states that the first type of composition is not found in the north of England. It is possible that a lost window of St. Sampson's, York, was of this type, T. Gent, *A History of the Famous City of York* (1730), 187. See also E. P. Baker, 'The Sacraments and the Passion in Medieval Art', *The Burlington Magazine*, lxvi (1935), 81–9. F. Wormald, 'Some Popular Miniatures and their Rich Relations', *Miscellanea Pro Arte. Festschrift für Herman Schnitzler* (1965), 281–3, pls. clvi–clvii. *Herder* iv (1972), 5–11.

[4] Bodl. Lib. Wood MS. E. 1, f. 123. The published account in P.C. (1920), 243, omits the second and third shields.

[5] G.E.C. ii. 434–5. *Cal. Inq. Post Mortem* iii, 65, 194. *Feudal Aids*, iv, 160, 184.

A3. Bull of St. Luke PLATE 34 (c)
Scroll inscribed |*Lucas*|

A4. Eagle of St. John PLATE 34 (d)
Scroll inscribed |*Thoannes*|

Condition. Each panel is set directly into the masonry, white glass cracked, old repairs carried out *in situ* using strap leading. White glass, slight exterior corrosions, blue backgrounds very corroded.

Colour and Technique. The figures are each painted on a single piece of white glass; that of A1 and A3 has an unusually strong green tinge. Painted in brown with very delicate stippled shading, details picked out in yellow stain. The drapery modelling of A2 is stippled on the reverse of the glass. Blue backgrounds, diapered with a seaweed foliage design.

Iconography. The 'four living creatures' of St. John's vision of the Divine Majesty representing the Evangelists (St. John, Rev. 4: 6 seq.).[1] Standard form. The sequence Mark, Matthew, Luke, and John does not follow that of the Gospels. The inscription |*Thoannes*| is a mistake for *Iohannes.*

Style and Design. Painted by an individual artist whose work is not found elsewhere in the country. The painting style is predominantly linear. The stipple shading is very lightly applied and subordinated to the painted line. The symbols of St. Mark and St. Luke have a slightly archaic look, possibly reflecting a dependence on an earlier model book.[2]
Date. c. 1400–30.

Lost Glass

The 17th-c. antiquarian sources record a shield then existing in this window: *checky argent and sable* ELMRUGGE *impaling argent a saltire gules, a bordure sable bezanty or* POYLE. The marriage represented by this impalement has not been traced. The same coat, together with a single coat of Poyle, is carved on a late 14th–early 15th-c. tomb recess at the east end of the north aisle of the nave.[3] This suggests that the Poyle represented by the impalement was a daughter of either John de la Poyle (d. 1423) or his son Henry, who predeceased him.[4] This family acquired the manor by the marriage of Walter de la Poyle with Isabel daughter of Stephen de Hampton. It continued in their possession until 1422, when John de la Poyle assigned it to feoffees.[5]

A drawing of 1804 shows a quatrefoil tracery light with a shield of Elmrugge on a circular ruby ground set on a trellis of quarries. The same artist also recorded parts of two other quatrefoil tracery lights glazed with white quarries, each quarry painted with a single rosette, with a coloured boss at the centre of the light. The date of this glass was probably 14th c.[6]

HARDWICK
ST. MARY

O.S. SP 577 296.

MS. SOURCES
Oxford. Bodleian Library, MS. Top. Oxon. a. 67, f. 300. Buckler Drawing, 1825.

PRINTED
J. C. Blomfield, 'History of Cottisford, Hardwick and Tusmore', in *The History of the Present Deanery of Bicester* (1882), ii. 46–51.
P.C. (1920), 164–5.
V.C.H. vi (1959), 72–3.
Pevsner (1974), 632–3.

The glass that remained in 1660 was described thus:

'In the chancell in the Northe Windowe is a person of St George, with glory round the head with yellow haire, cloathed in Green and Purple, with a pastoral staffe killing a redd dragon.

'In the South window St Helena with a redd cross over the alter, a Presepe[7] in one part of the windowe,

[1] See the detailed account on the iconography of the Symbols in G. M. Rushforth (1936), 89–90.
[2] Similar observations have been made about MS. painting. R. W. Schiller, *A Survey of Medieval Model Books* (1963), 117.
[3] No tomb inscription of such is extant. *V.C.H.* vi (1959), 167
[4] Greenfield, op. cit. 337. The pedigree of Elmrugge is very incomplete. See G. Steinman-Steinman, 'Account of the Manor of Croham', *Collectanea Topographica et Genealogica* v (1838), 169–70.
[5] Greenfield, op. cit. 210–11. *V.C.H.* op. cit. 161. For the relationships between the families involved in the transaction see also G. Wrottesley, 'Pedigrees from Plea Rolls', *The Genealogist*, N.S. xviii (1902), 180.
[6] Oxford, Bodl. Lib. MS. Top. Oxon. b. 75, f. 96ʳ.
[7] Latin *praesepe*, a manger, i.e. a Nativity of Christ.

and the Resurrection in another, a person with a glory holding in his hand an Agnus Dei opposite a pilgrim, and another figure sitting radiated.

'In the North windowe of the Church a Bishop with a pastoral staffe above, and belowe two larger figures of a Bishop with a large cross staffe and a king person rob'd.

'N.B. This is admirable glass painting.'[1]

This account presents some problems due to either incomplete description or wrong identification. The north window St. George is suspect. A figure in green and purple garments, presumably not in armour, killing a dragon with a pastoral staff is more likely to have been a St. Catherine. The figures of St. John Baptist and Christ in Majesty, now in the east window (1, A 2 and B 2), are probably the south-window figures described as respectively holding an Agnus Dei and sitting radiated. These are fourteenth century. The west window now contains two late fifteenth-/early sixteenth-century panels of the Crucifixion and Christ in Judgement. Blomfield states that at the restoration of the church in 1878–9,

'The West window was restored to its original proportions the rich stained glass figure work of the old window being put in the centre'[2]

It should be noted, however, that neither panel is described in the account of 1660 so they may have been brought from elsewhere some time after that date.

I

A2. St. John Baptist

h. 0·50 m. w. 0·34 m.

Full length figure facing three-quarters left, in benediction and holding an Agnus Dei.

Condition. Very corroded, the details indistinct; the background, except for the left-hand lobe, is restoration.

Colour and Technique. The flesh and Agnus Dei probably painted on pink glass, tunic in yellow stain, grass in green pot-metal. White background patterned with contiguous circles painted in broad outlines.

Iconography. He holds a large Agnus Dei, set on a circular dish, in reference to his prophecy '*Ecce agnus dei qui tollis peccata mundi*' (St. John 1: 29).

Date. Early 14th c., restored 1878–9.

B2. Christ in Majesty

h. 0·50 m. w. 0·34 m.

Christ seated in benediction and holding an orb.

Condition. Very corroded. The ruby nimbus and orb are restoration.

Colour and Technique. Flesh probably painted on pink glass, mantle in yellow stain, pot-metal ruby tunic, white throne, and green cushion. Background as A2.

Iconography. Standard, in benediction.

Date. Early 14th c., restored 1878–9.

w. I

1b. The Crucifixion   PLATE 6 (*a*), (*b*), (*c*)

h. 0·56 m. w. 0·51 m.

Christ crucified between the Virgin and St. John Evangelist.

Condition. Complete except for one small insertion and very well preserved.

Colour and Technique. Painted in brown with stippled shading and either line or needlepoint hatching. Flesh in white glass. Christ's crown of thorns, loin cloth, and the cross in yellow stain. The Virgin has a white mantle over a ruby tunic patterned with large rosettes painted in outline. The figures stand on a green grass bank against a blue background patterned with conventional shell-like clouds painted in outline with stipple and line shading.

Iconography. Standard, particular emphasis on the blood flowing from Christ's wounds.

Style and Design. A competent but somewhat wooden style, the features frozen and the proportions slightly awkward, for example, the short arms of Christ.

---

[1] Blomfield, op. cit. 46–7, from an unidentified MS. in the Bodleian Library.
[2] Ibid. 51. The pre-restoration state of the window is recorded in

Buckler's drawing of the exterior of the church, Oxford Bodl. Lib. MS. Top. Oxon. a. 67, f. 300.

Date. Late 15th–early 16th c.

2b. Christ in Judgement

h. 0·42 m. w. 0·27 m.

Christ displaying the Wounds of the Passion, seated on a rainbow, a lily branch and sword in His mouth, orb at feet.

Condition. Virtually all modern, except for the body and limbs of Christ, the head repainted.

Iconography. The lily and sword refer to the division of the Blessed and Damned (Matthew 25: 34 and 41).[1]

Date. Late 15th–early 16th c., restored 1878–9.

Lost Glass

The antiquarian notes record seven shields in the windows of the church.[2]

'In the chancel windows':

Ermine a cross gules (NORWOOD)

Gules fretty of three pieces or (AUDLEY)

Barry nebuly sable and argent (ELLESFIELD)

Gules three bendlets argent (MAVESYN)

Quarterly 1 argent a chevron gules between three unicorns heads erased azure (HORNE) *2, 5 bendy or and azure a bordure gules* (MERBURY) *3, 4 argent a chevron sable between three eagles (ravens) heads erased sable* (NORREYS) *impaling*[3] *argent on a fess sable between three lions heads erased gules three anchors or* (FERMOR)

'In the church windows':

Argent a saltire gules a bordure sable bezanty or (POYLE)

Gules fretty of three pieces a bordure argent semy of fleurs-de-lis sable (AUDLEY OF ELLESFIELD).

The Audley family held the manor of Hardwick in the 14th c.[4] The quarterly arms of Horne impaling Fermor were probably 16th c., as William Somerton purchased a third part of Hardwick in 1514, and the Manor Farm House was built by Sir Richard Fermor c. 1580–1643.[5] The Horne–Fermor marriage has not been traced, and the display of the Poyle, Norwood, and Mavesyn arms has not been accounted for.

HARPSDEN
ST. MARGARET

O.S. SU 764 809.

MS. SOURCES

Oxford. Bodleian Library, MS. Top Oxon. b. 75. Wyatt Collections, notes dated 1803.

PRINTED

Greening Lamborn (1949), 130–1.
Pevsner (1974), 634–5.

The north window of the nave contains two fifteenth-century shields identified by Greening Lamborn as the arms of Forster and Forster impaling Stonor (?). However, as he points out, the charges differ from the proper arms of these families: 'The Stonor arms usually have *two dances and a chief*, and the Forster *chevron is engrailed*.'[6] The sixteenth-century glass in the Forster manor at Aldermaston (Berks.) included a shield *sable on a chevron engrailed argent, a crescent sable impaling azure two dances or, a chief argent*. Beneath it was inscribed 'Forster and Stonard'.[7] The Forsters inherited Harpsden in the mid fifteenth century by marriage with the heiress of the Harpsden family. Humphrey Forster married Alice daughter of Thomas Stonor.[8] He appears to have married twice as at his death in 1487 he left a widow, Sibyl.[9]

n. IV

3a. Shield of Forster impaling Stonard (?)

h. 0·19 m. w. 0·15 m.

Sable on a chevron argent between three arrows points downwards argent a crescent sable FORSTER *impaling azure three dances or* STONARD?

---

[1] The symbols and text rarely occur together, a notable exception is Roger Van der Weyden's Last Judgement altarpiece of 1443–51 at Beaune; E. Panofsky, *Early Netherlandish Painting* (1953), 188–9.

[2] P.C. (1920), 165–5.

[3] The impaled coat is incorrectly given as a quartering in P.C. (1920), 164–5.

[4] *V.C.H.* vi (1959), 169–70.

[5] Ibid.

[6] Greening Lamborn (1949), 130–1.

[7] Bodl. Lib. Ashmole MS. 850, pp. 20 et seq.

[8] Greening Lamborn (1949), 130–1. W. Harvey, 'Visitation of Berkshire, 1566', ed. W. H. Rylands, *Harleian Society*, lvi (1907), 29.

[9] *Cal. Inq. Post Mortem* Henry VII, i, no. 413.

Condition. Considerable corrosion, the paint flaking, incomplete, made up with modern glass.

Colour and Technique. The Forster arms painted on white glass, the charges picked out of a matt black wash.

Date. Second half 15th c.

3c. Shield of Forster

h. 0·19 m. w. 0·15 m.

Sable on a chevron argent between three arrows points downwards argent a crescent sable FORSTER.

Condition. Considerable corrosion, the paint flaking.

Colour and Technique. Painted on a single piece of white glass, the charges picked out of a matt black wash.

Date. Second half 15th c.

4b. Male Head

h. 0·10 m. w. 0·05 m.

Incomplete bearded head, white and yellow stain, inserted inside out.

Date. 15th c.

HETHE

ST. EDMUND AND ST. GEORGE

O.S. SP 594 295.

PRINTED SOURCES

Blomfield, J. C., *The History of the Present Deanery of Bicester* (1888–92), 19.

P.C. (1920), 173.
Greening Lamborn (1949), 131.
Pevsner (1974), 645–6.

The east window of the north aisle has a shield of Ferrers in a tracery light. The masonry of the window is mid fourteenth-century design. The glass is *in situ* but appears to be later in date. The diaper on the shield and the seaweed foliage background are indicative of a late fourteenth-century dating. Wood recorded another shield in this window, *argent a cross gules*,[1] probably for St. George as patron of the church.[2]

The manor of Hethe passed into the possession of Ferrers of Groby through the marriage of Henry, Lord Ferrers (d. 1343) with Isabel, daughter and co-heiress of Sir Theobald de Verdon.[3]

I

A1. Fragments

The original east window was reset as the east window of the north aisle of the nave in the 1859 restoration by G. E. Street.[4]

h. 0·15 m. w. 0·15 m.

Fragments of three different foliage designs, including a large white rose set on a serrated leaf. All white glass and yellow stain. Coarse work. 14th–15th c.

C2. Shield of Arms for Ferrers

h. 0·22 m. w. 0·21 m.

Argent seven voided lozenges for FERRERS. The proper arms of Ferrers were *gules seven voided lozenges or.*

Condition. Complete and *in situ*. Cracked in several places.

Colour and Technique. Shield, field diapered with contiguous circles, the charges painted in outline. Set against a background of seaweed foliage diaper of white foliage picked out of matt paint, with very light yellow stain. Plain white border. All painted on a single piece of glass.

Date. Late 14th c.

---

[1] P.C. (1920), 173.
[2] Blomfield, op. cit., incorrectly gives the two shields as a single coat for Heath of Shelswell.

[3] Blomfield, op. cit. 6–7. Greening Lamborn (1949), 131. G.E.C. v. 340. White Kennett, *Parochial Antiquities of Ambrosden, Burcester,* etc. (1695), 377, 505, 508, 520, 523.   [4] Pevsner (1974), 465.

HEYTHROP

OLD PARISH CHURCH OF ST. NICHOLAS

O.S. SP 352 278.

PRINTED SOURCES

Ditchfield (1903), 187.

P.C. (1920), 175–6.
Greening Lamborn (1949), 132–3.
Pevsner (1974), 646–7.

The glass suffered extensive damage and loss in 1941 when it was blown out by a bomb. The remaining pieces were collected together and stored in the cellar of the premises of Thomas & Sons, decorators, 52 Holywell Street, Oxford. Most of the glass was restored after the war by Miss Joan Howson, although some was mislaid and remained in the cellar in Holywell Street until it was transferred for safe keeping to the Bodleian Library and later, in 1965, to the Oxford City and County Museum at Woodstock.[1] These pieces are the heads of the four daughters of Eleanor Ashfield and a few other fragments originally in window s. II, panel 1c.

The glass is all in the same style and comes from a series of windows given by the Ashfield family, who held lands here. One window, s. II, dated 1522 by an inscription, was a memorial to John Ashfield, d. 1521, and his wife Eleanor, and is placed immediately above their tomb. Wood described this window in detail. It had full-length figures of St. John Baptist, the Virgin, and St. Christopher. Below these were representations of John Ashfield with four sons, and his wife Eleanor with four daughters. Between these two memorial groups, in the centre light, was an angel holding a shield of the arms of John Ashfield impaling the arms of Seymour of Evenswynden quartering Winslow (?) for his wife.[2] The St. Christopher, now set in the east window, and the Ashfield figures remain, all very incomplete (I, 1b, II, 1a and 1c). Before 1941 the figures of the Virgin and St. John Evangelist, now in the east window, were incorporated in this south window. It is possible that this insertion took place before 1674 when Wood made his notes; his description, therefore, might be misleading.[3]

The east window possibly had a representation of the Crucifixion, and the figures of the Virgin Mary and St. John the Evangelist as placed here by Miss Howson may now be back in their original position (I, 1a, and 1c). The tracery lights contain the figures of the four Evangelists, and two other figures both incomplete (A1–A6). The latter two both face left, suggesting that they are not part of the same series of tracery lights as the Evangelists. All these figures lack their original backgrounds, so it is impossible to know which, if any, are *in situ*. Wood recorded the arms of Ashfield impaling Winslow (?) in this window, suggesting that this too was commemorative of John and Eleanor Ashfield.[4] Another south window also had their arms and an inscription with the date 1523.[5]

I

h. 0·78 m. w. 0·39 m.

All the figures in this window are now set against a modern background of plain white quarries.

1a. The Virgin Mary

Nimbed, full length, facing three-quarters right.

Condition. Complete, except for her feet.

Colour and Technique. Head painted in brown on white glass, very pronounced stippled matt shading, nimbus in yellow stain, plain blue mantle.

Iconography. Her hands are crossed on her breast, a mantle

---

[1] Copy of a memorandum by P. S. Spokes, Bodl. Lib. File 85, 6 May 1965. Information kindly supplied by Mr. Spokes in a letter to the author dated 21 October 1969.

[2] P.C. (1920), 175–6.

[3] Greening Lamborn (1949), 132–3, wrongly states that the Virgin and St. John 'had been removed since Wood noted them to the east window'.

[4] P.C. (1920), 175–6.

[5] Ibid.

covers her head; probably from a Crucifixion and a companion figure to St. John Evangelist, 3a.

Style and Design. The drawing and modelling of the features are very close to the Ashfield figures, s. II.

Date. 1522.

2a. St. Christopher

h. 0·91 m. w. 0·39 m.

Full length, facing three-quarters left, the Christ Child on his shoulder.

Condition. The figure of the saint is incomplete, the original drapery much disturbed, missing parts made up with modern stippled glass. The Christ Child is all a modern invention, made up in leaded outline, except the orb with a cross banner which is original.

Colour and Technique. Flesh painted in brown on white glass, pronounced stippled matt shading, blue mantle, its green hem picked out in yellow stain on the blue glass, staff in pot-metal ochre glass.

Iconography. Standard.

Style and Design. Originally part of the Ashfield memorial window s. II.

Date. 1522.

3a. St. John Evangelist

h. 0·78 m. w. 0·39 m.

Nimbed, facing three-quarters left.

Condition. Incomplete, originally a full-length standing figure. The drapery below his knees and the right foot are alien additions, as is the ruby mantle.

Colour and Technique. Painted in brown on white glass, pronounced stippled matt shading, the hair in yellow stain, plain blue nimbus. Plain white mantle and tunic.

Iconography. Probably from a Crucifixion and a companion figure to the Virgin, 1a above.

Style and Design. As 1a above.

Date. c. 1522.

A1. St. Paul (?)

h. 0·21 m. w. 0·11 m.

Condition. The lower half of the figure only remains.

Colour and Technique. Painted in brown on white glass, with yellow stain.

Iconography. The figure holds a book and a sword, and possibly represents St. Paul.

Date. c. 1522.

A2. St. Matthew (?)

h. 0·35 m. w. 0·12 m.

Condition. Incomplete, the angel symbol at his feet is missing.

Colour and Technique. Painted in brown on white glass, nimbus in yellow stain.

Iconography. Standard, he holds a book.

Date. c. 1522.

A3. St. Mark   PLATE 35 (*a*)

h. 0·37 m. w. 0·17 m.

Condition. Figure is complete.

Colour and Technique. Ruby mantle, remainder white glass, hair in yellow stain.

Iconography. Standard, he holds a book, his lion at his feet.

Date. c. 1522.

A4. St. Luke   PLATE 35 (*b*)

h. 0·37 m. w. 0·17 m.

Condition. Figure is incomplete, slight loss of drapery.

Colour and Technique. Blue mantle, remainder white glass, his bull in white and yellow stain.

Iconography. Standard, he holds a pen (?) and closed scroll in his right hand, his bull at his feet.

Date. c. 1522.

A5. St. John Evangelist

h. 0·37 m. w. 0·14 m.

Condition. Figure is incomplete, mantle made up with modern stippled glass.

Colour and Technique. Ruby tunic, remainder in white glass, hair in yellow stain.

Iconography. Standard, he holds a book, his eagle at his feet.

Style and Design. These four figures A2–A5 are a single set, all painted by the same hand.

Date. c. 1522.

A6. Fragment

A small fragment of a human torso. White and yellow stain drapery.

Date. c. 1522.

s. II

Originally this window had a black-letter inscription across the bottom of the main lights which read:

| Orate pro animabus Johannis Ashfield et
| Elianore uxoris eius qui istam fenestram
| fieri fecerunt anno domini MCCCCCXXII de
| quibus animabus propitietur deus amen.[1]

1a. John Ashfield and Sons   PLATES 7 (a), 35 (c)

h. 0·60 m. w. 0·39 m.

Donor figures in prayer, beneath them part of the inscription, in black letter:

| Orate pro | animab(us) Johannis |
| fecerunt anno | domini MCCCCC |

Condition. Very incomplete and much damaged, losses made up with alien medieval and modern white glass.

Colour and Technique. The original pieces are painted in brown on white glass, with very pronounced stippled matt shading, varying in tone. The hair of the first son is in yellow stain. The arms *argent a trefoil slipped (gules) between three mullets (gules)* on Ashfield's tabard (now incomplete) and sleeve are painted in outline, the tinctures were either omitted or have perished. Greening Lamborn stated 'the ruby flash of the charges had gone' but there is no trace of the characteristic scratches adjacent to the charges which would be present if this technique had been used.

Style and Design. Although the details of the drawing of the eyes, noses, and mouths are exactly the same, the heads of the sons are painted less carefully than the head of Ashfield.

Date. 1522.

1c. Eleanor Ashfield and Daughters   PLATE 35 (d)

h. 0·60 m. w. 0·39 m.

Donor figures in prayer, beneath them part of the inscription:

| [ux]ori[s],...m....n |

Condition. Only the head and shoulders of Eleanor Ashfield

and part of the prayer desk remain, the daughters are in leaded outline and modern stippled white glass.

Colour and Technique. Head painted in brown on white glass, stippled matt shading; gable head-dress in dark black, white bodice, edge in yellow stain.

Date. 1522.

Originally Eleanor Ashfield had a heraldic mantle; *quarterly 1, 4 gules two pairs of wings in fess or* SEYMOUR OF EVENSWYNDEN. 2, 3 *or a lion rampant parted per fess gules and sable* WINSLOW (?).[2]

2b. Helm and Mantling

h. 0·33 m. w. 0·24 m.

A visored helm with elaborate mantling, now incomplete, white and yellow stain, *c.* 1522.

Glass removed from Heythrop

Oxford City and County Museum, Woodstock, Oxon.

Fragments of glass from Heythrop Old Parish Church.

Ref. s. II, 1c.

1c. The Daughters of Eleanor Ashfield

Four young women, facing three-quarters left.

Condition. Incomplete, only the heads remain, together with part of the blue dress of the extreme right-hand figure.

Colour and Technique. Heads painted in brown on white glass, pronounced stipple matt shading, details of hair, and head-dresses picked out in yellow stain. Background white glass.

Style and Design. Background is medieval and could be part of the original design of this panel.

Date. 1522.

Fragments

Small pieces of drapery and plain white glass, original location uncertain. Two small pieces of a lion rampant, possibly part of the heraldic mantle of Eleanor Ashfield (see above s. II, 1c).

---

[1] P.C. (1920), 175.   [2] Greening Lamborn (1949), 132–3, has a detailed note on the problematic identification of these two coats.

HOLTON

ST. BARTHOLOMEW

O.S. SP 605 064.

MS. SOURCES

London. British Library:
  Harleian MS. 4170, p. 5, 1660.
  Landsdown MS. 874, f. 137ᵛ. Collections of N. Charles. 17th c.
Oxford. Bodleian Library:
  MS. Top. Oxon. e. 286, ff. 127ᵛ–128. Notes by N. Greenwood, 1660.
  MS. Top. Oxon. b. 75, f. 90. Wyatt Collections, copy of notes of D. T. Powell, May 1804.

MS. Top. Oxon. d. 92, f. 212ᵛ. Notes by the Revd. F. H. Woods 1882.

PRINTED

Visitations (1871), 104 (L566 1574 and 1634).
Bouchier (1918), 78.
P.C. (1920), 178–9.
Bouchier (1932), 129.
Greening Lamborn (1949), 133.
V.C.H. v (1959), 175–6.
Pevsner (1974), 649–50.

The church now contains very little medieval glass. Two fragments of thirteenth-century geometric grisaille (s. III, 1a, 1b) are of interest in indicating the distribution of this class of design. A sixteenth-century shield of the arms of Brome quartering Baldington is now set in the west window of the tower (w. I, A1). Originally the shield was probably surrounded by a decorative chaplet, and four ornamental clasps from such a chaplet survive. The shield is probably the one recorded in the seventeenth century in a south window of the south aisle of the nave. The antiquarian notes record seven more shields surviving in the windows of the church. No trace of these has survived, nor have 'the fragments of the figure of a bishop or saint' noted in May 1804.[1] The glass was cleaned and releaded in 1972 by D. King of Norwich.

n. III

1a. Canopy Design

h. 0·20 m. w. 0·22 m.

Condition. Incomplete, very corroded, the details of the painted design are very worn.

Colour and Technique. Ochre arch, surmounted by a small green building with ochre roof, flanked by white buildings with ruby roofs. The coloured glass is all pot-metal.

Style and Design. The glass is so worn that interpretation is difficult. However, it appears to be of a piece. The diagonal placing of the side buildings, above the main arch, although more simplified, can be compared with the canopies now in the east window of Eaton Bishop (Herefords.). *c.* 1330.[2]

Date. 14th c. (? first half).

s. II

1a. Geometric Grisaille

h. 0·28 m. w. 0·36 m.

Condition. Extensive corrosion on both surfaces. The glass is mostly so opaque that it is impossible to see how much is part of an original design.

Date. Probably 13th c.

s. III

1a, 1b. Geometric Grisaille

h. 0·19 m. w. 0·18 m. 1b: w. 0·16 m.

Condition. Incomplete. The glass was mostly set inside out prior to restoration 1972. Corrosion on both surfaces.

Colour and Technique. Trace lines in brown paint on white glass, medallions at base in pot-metal blue.

Style and Design. Portions of a leaded geometric design, painted with vine foliage. An identical and much more complete example of this class of design is found at Waterperry (n. II, 2a). There three contiguous ovals are linked by coloured medallions; running up the middle of the ovals is a vertical stem with off-springing trails of vine leaves, painted in outline on a cross-hatched ground.

Date. 13th c. probably 1250–75.

---

[1] Bodl. Lib. MS. Top. Oxon. b. 75.

[2] R.C.H.M., *Herefordshire* i (1931), pl. 91.

w. I

A1. Shield of Brome quartering Baldington

h. 0·63 m. w. 0·56 m. Shield: h. 0·23 m. w. 0·16 m.

Quarterly 1, 4 *sable on a chevron argent three sprigs of broom or (for vert), a bordure argent* BROME 2, 3 *argent on a chevron sable between three roundels sable, three roses argent seeded or*[1] BALDINGTON.

Four decorative clasps remain from chaplet surround to shields.

Condition. The shield is almost complete, except for two small portions of the fourth quarter, made up with modern white glass. Old breaks in the first and third quarters and also the left-hand clasp. Extensive corrosion on both surfaces. Set against modern white glass.

Colour and Technique. The shield is painted on white glass, strong black paint with back painting, the broom sprigs and rose seeds in yellow stain. Clasps: brown paint on white glass, fine needle-point hatching and stippled shading, the hair and beards of the heads and ornamental details picked out in yellow stain.

Style and Design. The four decorative clasps, each showing a bearded male head thrust through an oculus in a decorative frame, are based on a single design, with slight variations in detail. The lower head is less well executed than the others and the painting is much less precise. Similar clasps are found at Yarnton (n. IV, 6a, 6c) and Trinity College, Oxford.[2] They can be compared with the clasps on two complete chaplets surrounding shields from Wroxton Abbey, Oxon.,

datable 1537–47, now in the Philadelphia Museum of Art, U.S.A. The latter, however, are much more sophisticated in execution.

Date. Mid 16th c. The shield is of the scalloped Tudor form, as for the royal arms of Henry VIII at Marsh Baldon (I, 1b). William Brome, second son of John Brome of Brome (Warwicks.), married Agnes, daughter and heir of Thomas Baldington of Albury and Holton. He died in 1461.[3] His descendants used the quarterly coat of Brome and Baldington. The 17th-c. notes record two shields of Brome quartering Baldington, but only one was then complete, in a window of the south aisle of the nave. They were each associated with a shield of Brome impaling Rous, for Sir John Brome (d. 1558) and his wife Margaret, sister and heir of Thomas Rous of Racley (Warwicks.)[4]

Provenance. Probably from a window of the south aisle of the nave. Present position first recorded c. 1882.[5]

Antiquarian Sources. The notes as printed in the Parochial Collections[6] are incomplete and misleading. The following transcript, relating to the extant glass, is given from Wood's MS.,[7] Greenwood's notes are identical.[8] 'In the east window of the chancell *France and England quarterly. Over all a crowne. Armes of Brome quartering first Argent on a Chevron sable between three pellets 3 quarterfoyles argent* (BALDINGTON). This scheild is broken in the middle so the 2 last coates[9] are wanting. *Party per fess Brome and the quarterfoyles impaling Sable two bars Engrailled argent* (ROUS). (South aisle monuments.) In a south window of the aforesaid Ile are the armes of Brome with quarterings before mentioned. Also the armes of Brome and Rouse impaled.'

HORLEY

ST. ETHELREDA

O.S. SP 417 439

PRINTED SOURCES

Nelson (1913), 163.
P.C. (1920), 181.
Keyser, C. E., 'A visit to the Churches of Croughton (Northants.),

and Hanwell, Horley and Hornton (Oxon.)', *British Archaeological Association Journal*, N.S. xxvii (1921), 130.
St. Edmund Hall Magazine iii (1931), 56–9.
Kirby, W. T. 'Clerical portraits in stained glass. Two famous Oxfordshire Rectors', *Antiquaries Journal* xlii (1962), 251–2. (Reprinted with additions in *J.B.S.M.G.P.* xiii (1959–63), 565–8.)
Pevsner (1974), 652–3.

The remaining glass, except for a few small fragments, is fifteenth-century and much of it remains *in situ* in the tracery lights of the windows of the north aisle of the nave. Its particular interest centres on two named

[1] Greening Lamborn (1949), 133, blazons the roses as '*three quatrefoils silver*'. [2] South window of the Old Library.
[3] F. Macnamara, *Memorials of the Danvers Family* (1895), 143. Greening Lamborn (1949), 133. *V.C.H.* v (1959), 171.
[4] *V.C.H.* v (1959), 171. Inscription on monument north wall of the chancel, recorded in Bodl. Lib. Wood MS. E. 1, f. 240. P.C.

(1920), 178.
[5] Bodl. Lib. MS. Top. Oxon. d. 92, op. cit., f. 212ᵛ.
[6] P.C. (1920), 178–9.
[7] Bodl. Lib. Wood MS. E. 1, f. 241ʳ.
[8] Bodl. Lib. MS. Top. Oxon. e. 286, op. cit.
[9] i.e. the third and fourth quarters.

donor figures, Henry Rumworth and Robert Gilbert, who as successive prebendaries of Sutton-cum-Buckingham in the cathedral church of Lincoln were also rectors of Horley.

Henry Rumworth (n. IV, B1) had a distinguished career at Oxford and in the church. He was principal of St. Edmund Hall, c. 1395–c. 1402, and a Fellow of Queen's College, 1402–6.[1] He was appointed prebendary of Sutton-cum-Buckingham in 1412.[2] The inscription in the window names him as Archdeacon of Canterbury. His appointment to this post was made in 1416.[3] He died in 1420 and, as he made no bequest in his will[4] to the church of Horley, it is probable that the window was given in his lifetime. Robert Gilbert (n. V, B1) succeeded him in the prebend of Sutton-cum-Buckingham.[5] His career was varied. He was a Fellow of Merton College, 1398–1402, and later Warden, 1417–21.[6] He held numerous ecclesiastical preferments, the most important being that of Dean of York from 1426[7] until his elevation to the Bishopric of London in 1436.[8] He died in 1448. The inscription in the window simply names him as Magister Roberus (sic) Gylbard.[9] This suggests that the glass was made after 1420 when he succeeded Rumworth and possibly before his appointment as Dean of York in 1426, certainly before 1436 when he became bishop.

Although these two windows are adjacent and virtually identical in architectural design, the styles of their painted glass are very different. The Rumworth figure is precisely, yet delicately, painted with fluid modelling and a very light seaweed foliage background diaper. The figure of Gilbert, by comparison, is much harder in its drawing: the proportions are less articulate and the raised left hand is over-large in proportion to the head. The background diaper of seaweed foliage is broader and painted much darker. The letters of the inscription are eccentric and the christian name misspelt. These differences suggest the work of two distinct glaziers. Although stylistic differences do not necessarily indicate a difference in date, these in conjunction with the historical evidence suggest that the glazing of the north aisle windows was started by Henry Rumworth during the period 1416–20 and subsequently completed by Robert Gilbert after 1420.

n. IV

A2. Foliage Design

h. 0·51 m. w. 0·10 m.

Complete and *in situ*. Painted in brown on white glass, the foliage in yellow stain. Date. 1416–20.

B1. Henry Rumworth   PLATE 7 (b)

h. 0·56 m. w. 0·36 m.

Tonsured, he wears a blue-sleeved mantle, with furred collar and cuffs, over a ruby robe, with a large white purse hanging from his belt.

Inscriptions. In black-letter script:

[miserere]|mei|.deus.|

below the figure

[magister]|henricus|[rumw]orthe archi|diaconus cantuarie.|

Condition. *In situ* but incomplete, background made up with alien fragments of 15th-c. glass. The coloured glass is very decayed, almost opaque.

Colour and Technique. All white glass except for the pot-metal ruby robe and blue mantle. Painted in brown with very delicate stipple and matt shading. The details of the purse tassels and floor diaper are in yellow stain. The white seaweed foliage diaper background is picked out of very light brown paint.

Border: a repeated pattern of a circle enclosing a quatrefoil. At the base, adjacent to the floor, are two strapwork and foliage plaques in white and yellow stain.

Iconography. Donor figures in the tracery lights of a window are not common. The earliest extant examples in the county are in the east window of St. Lucy's Chapel at Christ Church, Oxford. Early 14th c.[10]

Style and Design. Very close to the figures of clerics now in

[1] A. B. Emden, *An Oxford Hall in Medieval Times, being a history of St. Edmund Hall* (1927), 116–25, 162, 166 n., 222, 271. A. B. Emden, *A Biographical Dictionary of the University of Oxford to 1500*, iii (1959), 1607.
[2] J. Le Neve, *Fasti Ecclesiae Anglicanae 1300–1541*, compiled by H. P. F. King, i (1962), 114.
[3] Ibid., compiled by B. Jones, iv (1963), 8.
[4] Emden (1927), op. cit. 122–4, 282–4.
[5] Le Neve, op. cit. i. 114.

[6] Emden (1959), op. cit. ii (1958), 766–7.
[7] Le Neve, op. cit., vi (1963), 8.
[8] Ibid., compiled by J. M. Horn, v (1963), 3.
[9] He was a D.Th. by 1413 and is shown in the window wearing a doctor's pileus. However, doctor as a style and title is apparently uncommon at this date. The account of his induction as Dean refers to him as '*Magistrum Robertum Gilbert presbiterum sacre pagine professorem*' (York Minster Library, Dean and Chapter Muniments. L2(3)a, f. 156r).   [10] R.C.H.M. (1939), 42.

the west window of Merton College Chapel Oxford, and probably from the workshop of Thomas of Oxford.[1]

Date. 1416–20.

A5. Foliage Design

Complete and *in situ*. Identical to A2 above.

n. V

A1, A3

Fragments of quarries, type 15. 15th c.

A2

Fragments of three roundels, identical foliage design, very decayed. 15th c., not *in situ*.

B1. Robert Gilbert   PLATE 7 (*c*)

h. 0·56 m. w. 0·36 m.

He wears a ruby robe, a blue mantle trimmed with ermine, and a doctor's black pileus. Beside him a scroll, inscribed in black-letter script:

|*Magister Rob|erus Gy|lbard*|

Condition. In situ but incomplete, the drapery is made up with a piece of 15th-c. glass and a piece of modern glass.

Colour and Technique. Painted on white glass. The hair is in yellow stain, pot-metal ruby robe and blue mantle. White seaweed diaper, background picked out of dark paint.

Iconography. See n. IV, A3 above.

Style and Design. The style is uneven, the drawing hard and clumsy, particularly the large left hand. The epigraphy of the inscription is somewhat eccentric.

Date. 1420–36.

Insertions: border pieces, four complete, two fragmentary; a bold design of a foliage spray interlaced in a ring, white glass and yellow stain. 15th c.

A5. Foliage Design

h. 0·51 m. w. 0·10 m.

In situ, but incomplete. Seaweed foliage diaper, in a plain border, a large rose set at the centre. White and yellow stain.

n. VI

A2. Foliage Design

h. 0·51 m. w. 0·10 m.

In situ, but incomplete, identical to n. IV, A2 above.

B1. Fragments

h. 0·56 m. w. 0·36 m.

A quarry design, type 15, painted on a circular piece of glass, probably from a tracery light as the same design, in a cusped border, is at the apex of the light. The latter could be *in situ*, 15th c. Fragments of foliage diapers, 14th c., patterned borders 15th c. and a small cross-crosslet or, possibly from a shield of arms.

A5. Foliage Design

In situ, identical to A2 above, but very incomplete.

s. IV

2b. Fragments

Pieces of foliage designs and patterned borders, very incomplete and decayed. 14th and 15th c. One quarry, type 36.

The remains of two large fishes, one painted on white glass, the other on pink glass, are possibly from a panel of St. Christopher, 14th c. Three cross-crosslets or and pieces of ruby glass, 14th c.[2]

Lost Glass

Rawlinson described the Rumworth window as 'In one of the north lights is a Bishop holding a cross, a Virgin crowned and surrounded by rays of glory, in her hand a sword, over them all a man kneeling in a praying posture and *Henricus numeravit pec.* . . .'[3] This description is too general to attempt an identification of the figures.

---

[1] This glass is at present concealed behind a 'trompe l'œil' painting.
[2] Greening Lamborn (1949), 8, firmly identified these fragments as part of a shield of Beauchamp, Earl of Warwick, *gules a fess or*

between six cross-crosslets or. Traces of the same coat are painted on the wall of the tower. There are no antiquarian notes to prove this possible identification.   [3] P.C. (1920), 181.

HORNTON
ST. BARNABAS

O.S. SP 393 450.

PRINTED SOURCES
Greening Lamborn (1949), 134.
Pevsner (1974), 654.

A fragmentary shield here has been blazoned by Greening Lamborn as '*ermine a cross (azure?) fretty argent with fleurs-de-lis or in the frets*', for an unidentified member of the Verdun family, lords of Hornton, Hethe, and Bournton in the reign of Edward I. It is quite possible that the fleurs-de-lis are simply a decorative diaper and the blazon is, more simply, *ermine a cross or* (for a colour) *fretty argent*. The substitution of yellow stain for the proper colour of the cross enabled the glazier to eliminate intricate lead lines. This device is quite common in fourteenth and fifteenth-century glass painting. (See Hethe.)

2a. Shield of Verdun

h. 0·10 m. w. 0·10 m.

Ermine a cross or fretty argent VERDUN.

Condition. Incomplete, the lower half with part of a plain surround only remains.

Colour and Technique. Painted in brown on white glass, the cross in yellow stain.

Date. 14th c.

2b. Foliage Design

h. 0·10 m. w. 0·10 m.

Condition. Two fragmentary pieces leaded together to form

a pendent to the shield 2a.

Colour and Technique. Vine foliage, painted in outline on white glass, background of cross-hatched lines.

Date. 13th c.

A1. Quarry Design

h. 0·9 m. w. 0·6 m.

Quarry, type 3, painted on a shaped piece of glass, possibly from a cusped light, white and yellow stain. 15th c.

There are four very small fragments in the tracery of the chancel east window, not catalogued.

HORSPATH
ST. GILES

O.S. SP 572 049.

MS. SOURCES
Oxford Bodleian Library:
MS. Don. c. 90, f. 106. Collections by H. Hinton and J. Hunt, early 19th c.
MS. Top. Oxon. b. 220, f. 71. Collections by J. E. Robinson, c. 1804–40.
MS. Top. Oxon. d. 92, ff. 58–9. Notes by the Revd. F. H. Woods, dated 1882.
MS. Top. Oxon. c. 313, f. 164. Copy of a tracing of 1853 made by H. Hurst, c. 1908.

PRINTED
Parker (1846), 348–54.
Ditchfield (1903), 186.
Nelson (1913), 163–4.
Bouchier (1918), 78–9.
P.C. (1920), 183.
Bouchier (1932), 129
V.C.H. v (1957), 187–8.
Pevsner (1974), 655–6.
Bird, S. W. H., *A Guide to the Parish Church of St. Giles, Horspath* (n.d.), 15–18.

The windows contain a small collection of glass, very incomplete with much composite work, brought together in the nineteenth century. Not all the glass is indigenous to the church and there is one panel of fragments of Swiss glass (s. III, 2b). The Revd. F. H. Woods, writing in 1882, states: 'There are besides several pieces of ancient glass which have been collected from various sources and placed in the windows of the church.'[1] Three sixteenth-century shields of arms (n. III, 4a, s. III, 3a, 3b) are not included in the collections of Wood and Rawlinson[2] and were probably imported from elsewhere.

n. II

2a. The Temptation of Adam

h. 0·30 m. w. 0·46 m.

Eve, on the left, offers the apple to Adam. Between them is the serpent wound around the Tree of Knowledge.

Condition. Incomplete, made up with plain white glass. The paint has perished in parts.

Colour and Technique. White glass, light-brown paint with stipple shading, details picked out in yellow stain.

Style, Design, and Date. The Revd. F. H. Woods, writing in 1882, refers to this panel as modern.[3] Greening Lamborn, however, thought that it was 15th c.[4] The panel has some appearance of being antique, the paint was badly fired and has worn very thin in places. The drawing style, particularly the heads and the serpent, suggests that this is a late 18th–19th-c. antiquarian exercise in a medieval style.

2b. The Crucifixion

h. 0·30 m. w. 0·46 m.

Christ on the Cross, between the Virgin Mary left, and St. John Evangelist, right.

Condition. Incomplete, made up with modern white glass. In some parts the paint has completely perished, but faint indications of the design can be made out, e.g. Christ's feet, the base of the cross and the adjacent herbage. Although the glass is all of the same date, it is possible that the panel is composite as there is some discrepancy in scale between the figures of the Virgin and St. John, the former being bigger.

Colour and Technique. White glass, light-brown paint with fine stipple shading, details picked out in yellow stain.

Iconography. At first sight this appears to be a standard representation of the Crucifixion. However, two details call for comment and give support to the suggestion that the panel, as it is now, is composite. First, although the

paint is very worn, the base of the cross rests on a globe of the world. A comparable example in a narrative scene of the Crucifixion has not been found, but it is a common feature in representations of the Trinity as the Seat of Mercy.[5]

Secondly, the herbage to the right of the cross is painted on a single piece of glass which has no other painted decoration except for a plain diagonal line, between Christ's torso and St. John's waist. This line can hardly be interpreted as being part of a plain quarry background as the design is not carried through to the herbage below. It is explicable as one of the streams of blood, flowing from the body of the crucified Christ, as found in some representations of the Seven Sacraments.[6] A late 15th-c. wall painting at Kirton in Lindsay (Lincs.) also showed the base of the cross resting on a globe of the world.[7] However, this interpretation is suspect as there is no trace of similar streams of blood from the feet of Christ. The evidence is inconclusive, but it would seem that this panel contains some rather unusual features, not found in standard representations of the Crucifixion.

Style and Design. The probable composite nature of the panel and its poor condition preclude any detailed comment. The simplified drawing of the hands, patterned drapery hems, and the grain of the cross suggest that the work is all of one period.

Date. Second half 15th c.

Provenance: before the 1852 restoration this panel was in the west window of the tower[8] and was associated with a shield of the *Arma Christi*.[9]

n. III

1a, 1b. Quarries

h. 0·15 m. w. 0·12 m.

Two quarries, very corroded, identical design of a wheat-sheaf, type 43, yellow stain on white glass. 15th c.

2b. Virgin Saint   PLATE 36 (*b*)

h. 0·31 m. w. 0·23 m.

[1] MS. Top. Oxon. d. 92, op. cit., f. 59.

[2] P.C. (1920), 183.

[3] MS. Top. Oxon. d. 92, op. cit., f. 59.

[4] *V.C.H.* v (1957), 188, citing Greening Lamborn's annotated copy of Bouchier (1918). Bodl. Lib. 1373, e. 64, pp. 78–9.

[5] For example the panel, *c.* 1475, at Stamford (Lincs.). J. P. Hoskins, P. A. Newton, and D. King, *The Hospital of William Browne, Merchant, Stamford, Lincolnshire* (1971), 10, pl. 13, the monumental brass, *c.* 1507, of John Strangbou at Childney, (Berks.). C. M. Keyser,

'The Churches of Sparsholt and Childney', *Berks, Bucks and Oxon Archaeological Journal* xi (1905–6), 102–3.

[6] G. M. Rushforth, 'Seven Sacraments Compositions in English Medieval Art', *Antiquaries Journal* ix (1929), 83–100, particularly 91–4.

[7] Ibid. 93–4, pl. lx.

[8] Parker (1846), 348; Bodl. Lib. MS. Top. Oxon. d. 92, op. cit., f. 59.

[9] See w. I, 2b.

Crowned and nimbed, facing three-quarters right.

Condition. The head only remains, very corroded on both surfaces, multiple breaks, plated on both sides. Set against modern, plain green glass.

Colour and Technique. White glass, light-brown paint with stippled and line shading; hair and crown in yellow stain.

Iconography. Either the Virgin Mary or a royal saint.

Style and Design. The drawing of the features and the plain crown with jewels in outline and no modelling have some affinity with the windows of the Ante-chapel of All Souls College, Oxford, of *c.* 1441,[1] particularly the figure of the Virgin Mary.[2]

Date. Mid 15th c.

3b. Virgin Saint

h. 0·31 m. w. 0·23 m.

Nimbed, the head partially covered, looking upwards three-quarters right.

Condition. The head and shoulders only remain. Very corroded on both surfaces, the paint very worn. Set against modern plain ruby glass.

Colour and Technique. White glass, light-brown paint, very fine stippled shading, hair and nimbus in yellow stain.

Iconography. Possibly the Virgin Mary from a Crucifixion.

Style and Design. Although much worn this is an extremely high class of design, with very sophisticated drawing and execution, particularly the hair and soft drapery modelling.

Date. Second half 15th c.

4a. Shield of Gresley

h. 0·15 m. w. 0·10 m.

Vairy ermine and gules GRESLEY.

Condition. Incomplete, made up with modern white glass. Set against modern, plain blue glass.

Date. 16th c.

4b. Fragments

h. 0·15 m. w. 0·10 m.

Condition. Fragments of 16th-c. heraldic glass, leaded together to make a composite shield. Set against modern, plain ruby glass.

---

[1] Hutchinson (1949), 17–18.
[2] Ibid., frontispiece and pl. xiii.
[3] Bouchier (1918), 78.

n. VII

1a. Royal Saint?

h. 0·20 m. w. 0·16 m.

Condition. The upper half of the figure only remains. The head is incomplete. Corroded on both surfaces, the paint is very worn. Bearded male figure; although incomplete the cut-line suggests that the head was nimbed. Although the paint is very worn, the remains of a crown are just visible. He holds a gold wand in his right hand, possibly a sceptre. The head is missing.

Colour and Technique. White glass, light-brown paint, with very fine stippled shading, details picked out in yellow stain.

Iconography. He is probably a royal saint, and Bouchier's suggestion that the figure possibly represented St. Paul, holding a sword, is untenable.[3]

Style and Design. The glass is so worn that it precludes detailed comment.

Date. Second half 15th c.

n. II

2a. The Virgin Mary

h. 0·30 m. w. 0·20 m.

The Virgin Mary full length, facing three-quarters right.

Condition. The figure is complete, set against pieces of plain medieval ruby glass with extensive corrosion on both surfaces. The irregular outline of the ruby glass suggests that the arrangement of figure and background is not original, probably 19th-c. restoration work.[4]

Colour and Technique. Head and coverchief in white glass, with an ochre mantle over a green tunic. Pot-metal coloured glass, dark-brown paint, with smear and stippled shading.

Iconography. Represented looking upwards, her hands raised beside her face, gestures appropriate for the Virgin Mary at the Crucifixion.

Style and Design. As 2b below.

Date. Late 13th–early 14th c.

2b. St. John Evangelist

h. 0·31 m. w. 0·20 m.

St. John full length, facing three-quarters left.

---

[4] The copy of the tracing of 1853 gives notes on the colours of the figure, but no indication of any background. Bodl. Lib. MS. Top. Oxon. c. 313, op. cit., f. 154.

Condition. The figure, which is virtually complete with only the raised right hand missing, is in the same state as it was in 1853.[1] Plain ruby background as 2a with extensive corrosion on both surfaces.

Colour and Technique. Head, hand, and feet in white glass. He wears an ochre mantle over a murrey tunic. Pot-metal coloured glass and dark-brown paint with smear and stippled shading.

Iconography. The figure is beardless, and this and the gestures of the hands are appropriate for St. John Evangelist at the Crucifixion, forming a pendent to the Virgin Mary (2a). Although neither figure now has a nimbus this identification is probable. Before the 1840 restoration these two figures were associated with an incomplete Crucifixion in the east window of the chancel.[2]

Style and Design. The two figures are the same size. They show identical details of design, particularly in the drawing of the faces; large eyes, a continuous line for the eyebrow and nose, the turned-down corners of the mouth, and full rounded chin. The drapery style is quite simple. St. John's mantle is swathed across the upper part of his body, with falling vertical folds, framing the body on either side. All these features show general similarities to the choir windows of Merton College Chapel, Oxford, of 1289–96. The origins of both can be found in the works of the 'Court School' of *c.* 1270–1308,[3] although the Horspath figures lack the elegance and finesse of execution of the Merton figures.

Date. Late 13th–early 14th c.

Provenance: removed from the east window of the chancel in 1840. It is not known if they were part of the original glazing of that window, which before restoration also contained 15th-c. heraldic glass.[4]

Panels 2a and 2b are set against a leaded geometric background, of 19th-c. date, incorporating some medieval glass. The latter is fragmented and is not described.

s. III

2a. Composite Figure

h. 0·39 m. w. 0·38 m.

Condition. The figure consists of a large head of an angel, facing left, set on the small body of an archbishop, facing right. The latter is also composite, the ruby chasuble being made up with alien pieces of glass.

Colour and Technique. The angel's head is on white glass with brown paint and very slight stippled shading, hair and pattern on amice in yellow stain. The archbishop's vestments are in white glass with the border of the chasuble, fringes of the dalmatic and staff in yellow stain.

Iconography. The identification of the figures can only be made in general terms. The head is nimbed and the long flowing hair and amice are common for representations of angels.

Style and Design. The angel's head is painted in a simple and rather bold way, the face has a strong outline, the features rather simplified, particularly the drawing of the ear. It is not closely paralleled by any other work in the county.

Date. Second half 15th c.

2b. Composite Panel

h. 0·39 m. w. 0·38 m.

Condition. Panel of fragments, mostly Swiss, 16th–17th c.

3a. Shield of Stanhope

h. 0·15 m. w. 0·10 m.

Quarterly ermine and gules STANHOPE.

Condition. The shield is complete, set against modern plain ruby and blue glass.

Date. 16th c.

3b. Shield of Elton (?)

h. 0·15 m. w. 0·10 m.

Or two pale gules, on a bend argent three mullets or ELTON? The correct arms of Elton are *paly of six gules and or, on a bend sable three mullets or.*

Condition. Restored, the bend and the field above it are probably 19th c. Set against modern plain ruby and blue glass.

Date. 16th c.

s. IV

1a. Composite Figure

h. 1·20 m. w. 0·38 m.

Condition. The figure appears to be that of a mitred archbishop, holding a cross-staff and book. It is a restorer's

---

[1] Ibid.
[2] 'In the east window are the arms of William Waynfleet, Bishop of Winchester, on each side a saint, and over all part of a Crucifixion.' Bodl. Lib. MS. Top. Oxon. b. 220, op. cit., f. 71. Also Bodl. Lib.

MS. Don. c. 90, op. cit., f. 106. Parker (1846), 354, records the transfer to their present position.
[3] Newton i (1961), 5, 10.
[4] See n. 2 above.

composite, made up from a miscellany of 14th and 15th-c. glass.

Iconography. Noted by Bouchier[1] and Nelson[2] as 'an abbot, probably of Oseney', but the composite nature of the panel precludes any such precise identification. The most notable features of the panel are the incomplete head of a priest wearing an amice and the hand holding a closed book. These are compatible in scale and technique and probably belong together.

Colour and Technique. White glass, with strong brown paint, stippled shading, yellow stain on the amice.

Style and Design. The drawing of the features is quite distinctive, and is not closely paralleled by any other work in the county.

Date. Second half 14th c.

s. V

a1. Roundel

d. 0·10 m.

Roundel. A foliage design of eight flat serrated leaves, radiating from a central boss.

Condition. Complete, extensive corrosion on both surfaces.

Colour and Technique. Pot-metal glass, the central boss is plain murrey, ochre leaves, plain ruby background.

Style and Design. The roundel appears to be *in situ.* Although this type of roundel is common, particularly as part of a geometric grisaille decoration, it is rarely found as a complete tracery design as here.

Date. Second half 13th c.

w. 1

2b. Shield of the Arma Christi

Shield of the Instruments of the Passion flanking the cross and crown of thorns.

Condition. Very incomplete, the lower sinister half showing the spear, ladder, hammer, and part of the cross remains together with a misplaced portion with the head of the vinegar sop now leaded above it. The missing pieces have been made up with modern plain white glass.

Colour and Technique. Dark brown paint on white glass, the Instruments picked out in yellow stain.

Iconography. The Arma Christi, i.e. the Instruments of Christ's Passion displayed as heraldic charges on a shield first occur in the early 14th c. in various parts of Europe.[3] The earliest English example extant is found on the seal of the warden of the house of Grey Friars at Cambridge *c.* 1300.[4] In manuscript painting the earliest English example that has been found is in Walter de Milmete's copy of Aristotle's *De Secretis Secretorum* made for presentation to the Prince Edward *c.* 1326–7.[5] In the De Bois hours after 1328, a shield of the Arma Christi is painted in the margin of the Office of the Cross.[6] Examples in glass painting of about the same period cannot be precisely dated[7] but there are numerous examples, in other media, throughout the 15th–16th c.[8]

Style and Design. The drawing is simple, but precise.

Date. The scalloped outline of the shield suggests a late-15th–early-16th-c. date.

Lost Glass

Rawlinson's notes record, 'In a south light of the chancell has been a coat of armes, now lost, there only remaining po....a...., etc. 1499.'[9] This is no longer extant.

[1] Bouchier (1918), 79.

[2] Nelson (1913), 164.

[3] E. Male, *L'Art religieux de la fin du moyen âge en France* (1908), 104. R. Berliner, 'Arma Christi', *Münchner Jahrbuch der Bildenden Kunst* vi (1955), 35–152, particularly 48–54.

[4] A. B. Tonnochy, *Catalogue of British Seal Dies in the British Museum* (1952), 176, no. 836, pl. xviii.

[5] B.L. Add. MS. 47680, f. 14ʳ. Not noted by Berliner.

[6] New York. Pierpont Morgan Library MS. M. 700, f. 11. The manuscript can be dated after 1328 as the calendar has the Feast of the Conception of the Blessed Virgin Mary on 8 December, not adopted in Canterbury and London until that year.

[7] For example, Clifton Campville (Staffs.) and Austrey (Warwicks.).

Newton i (1961), 199–201; iii. 673, 841. Burrell Collection, Glasgow. Inv. No. 93. Reg. No. 45.12. *Stained and Painted Heraldic Glass Burrell Collection 1962*, Exhibition Catalogue, no. 35, as 15 c. but is actually early 14th c.

[8] Berliner, op. cit. 48–54. Mr. Cuming, 'On the Shield of the Passion', *British Archaeological Association Journal* xxxi (1875), 91–7. Rushforth (1936), 255–7, figs. 132–3. C. Woodforde, *Stained Glass in Somerset 1250–1830* (1946), 194–201. C. Carter, 'The Arma Christi in Scotland', *Proceedings of the Society of Antiquaries of Scotland*, xc (1956–7), 116–29. C. Dodgson, 'English Devotional Woodcuts of the Late Fifteenth Century', *The Walpole Society* xvii (1928–9), 95. Herder i (1958), 184–7.

[9] P.C. (1920), 183.

IDBURY

ST. NICHOLAS

O.S. SP 236 201.

PRINTED SOURCES
Nelson (1913), 173.
Pevsner (1974), 658.

n. IV

B3. Female Head

d. 0·11 m.

Condition. The glass is well preserved. If the glass is complete in itself it should be termed a roundel; however, it could equally be the nimbed head of a large figure of a saint.

Colour and Technique. Painted in brown on white glass, smear and matt shading, background or nimbus in yellow stain.

Style and Design. There is some similarity to the three north windows of the Latin Chapel in Christ Church, Oxford (n. VII–IX).

Date. Mid 14th c.

n. V

A3. Foliage Design

h. 0·10 m. w. 0·14 m.

Condition. Complete and *in situ*.

Colour and Technique. A white trefoil leaf, with a yellow stain centre, on a matt brown background in a plain white border.

B1, B2, B3, B4. Foliage Designs

h. 0·16 m. w. 0·14 m.

Condition. Originally each light had an identical foliage design but only B3 is complete though damaged. The remainder is fragmentary and made up with modern white glass.

Colour and Technique. At the centre a square white frame, enclosing a white quatrefoil leaf, with four offspringing serrated leaves, in yellow stain, matt brown background, and plain white border.

Style and Design. The painting is clumsy and lifeless.

Date. Second half 14th c.

Not Catalogued: Some very small scraps of foliage designs in a south clerestory window and west window of the nave.

IFFLEY

ST. MARY THE VIRGIN

O.S. SP 527 035.

MS. SOURCES

London. British Library:
  Harleian MS. 6365, f. 45ʳ
  Add. MS. 37035, f. 6. H. Ellis, Church Notes, 1790.
Oxford. Bodleian Library:
  Wood MS. B. 15, f. 99. A. Wood, Notes, 6 August, 1657.

Wood MS. E. 1, f. 185. A. Wood, Notes, 16 August, 1657.
MS. Top. Oxon. e. 286, f. 85ʳ. N. Greenwood, Notes, 1658.

PRINTED

Bouchier (1932), 129.
R.C.H.M. (1939), 154.
Greening Lamborn (1949), 134.
Pevsner (1974), 658–61.

n. V   PLATE 36 (a)

2b. Fragments

h. 0·29 m. w. 0·23 m.

Fragment of a shield: *a crescent argent on a field gules.* Part of a shield: *gules two chevrons argent in fess point a crescent argent for difference* FETTIPLACE. In the 17th c. this shield was in the west window.[1] The crescent is abraded out of the

---

[1] Bodl. Lib. Wood MS B. 15, f. 99, MS. Top. Oxon. e. 286, f. 85 .

ruby field. Set in a surround of miscellaneous fragments: two triangular designs, each cusped cinquefoil, white and yellow stain, probably eyelet tracery lights.

Date. 15th c.

A1. Foliage Design

h. 0·18 m. w. 0·13 m.

A single leaf springing from the top foil of the light is painted on white glass, ribs of the leaf in yellow stain, ground crossed with single-line hatching, plain white border. It is painted on a single piece of white glass, complete and *in situ*. 15th c.

A3. Kneeling Angel

h. 0·23 m. w. 0·13 m.

A kneeling angel in profile facing right, hands raised in prayer.

Condition. Complete and *in situ*. Slight corrosion.

Colour and Technique. Painted on white glass, hair and wings in yellow stain. Stippled shading, plain white background, no border.

Iconography, Style, and Design. See A7 below.

Date. Late 15th c.

A4. Archangel (?)

h. 0·30 m. w. 0·13 m.

Condition. Only the head and shoulders remain. The lower part of the panel has been shattered and patched from the outside with a plain piece of white glass.

Colour and Technique, Style, Design, and Iconography. See A6 below.

Date. Late 15th c.

A5. Fragments

h. 0·33 m. w. 0·13 m.

The upper part of the head of a male saint, facing three-quarters right. White glass and yellow stain, early 15th c. Lower part of the face and raised hands of a nimbed saint or angel in profile facing left. White glass and yellow stain, 15th c. Fragment of an inscription in black-letter script:

|SUO III|

A6. Archangel (?)

h. 0·30 m. w. 0·13 m.

Full length, facing three-quarters left, hands raised in prayer. *Condition.* Slight corrosion. An old leaded repair and breaks, probably *in situ*.

Colour and Technique. Painted on white glass, hair and wings, feathered body, and legs touched yellow stain of a very orange tone. Set against a plain white ground, no border.

Iconography. The feathered body and legs, together with the ermine tippet around the shoulders suggest one of the higher orders of angels.[1]

Style and Design. The figures A4 and A6 are companion pieces. Minor variations in design, in the pose of the head and position of the hands. The disposition of the figures against a plain background without a border is most unusual.

Date. Late 15th c.

A7. Kneeling Angel

h. 0·23 m. w. 0·13 m.

Drawn from the same cartoon as A3 in reverse.

Condition. Complete, one crack. Both A3 and A7 have a single lead line across the same point in the panel. This division is probably original.

Colour and Technique. As A3 above.

Iconography, Style, and Design. Both figures are painted on a plain white background. This suggests that they are pendent figures to the archangels A4 and A6. If so, they may perhaps be glazier's workshop stock cut to occupy their present positions.

Date. Late 15th c.

A8. Rose

h. 0·13 m. w. 0·13 m.

A large white rose with a yellow central floret is painted on white glass, yellow stain, and not *in situ*. This may be intended as the Tudor Rose badge, it may equally be a purely decorative design. Late 15th c.

A9. Foliage Design

h. 0·18 m. w. 0·13 m.

Identical design to A1. Reversed and incomplete, patched lower right, late 15th c.

s. V

1b. Shield of de la Pole impaling the House of York and Quarries

h. 1·07 m. w. 0·52 m. Shield: h. 0·28 m. w. 0·26 m.

---

[1] For variety of costume for the orders of angels in the 15th c. see P. B. Chatwin, 'Decoration of the Beauchamp Chapel, Warwick, with Special Reference to the Sculptures', *Archaeologia* lxxvii (1928), 313–14.

Quarterly 1, 4 azure a fess or between six lions' faces or DE LA POLE *2, 3 argent a chief gules over all a lion rampant queue fourchée or* BURGHERSH *impaling quarterly 1, 4 azure three fleurs-de-lis or* FRANCE *2, 3 lions passant gardant in pale or* ENGLAND *A label of three points argent with three roundels (gules) on each point* HOUSE OF YORK.

The de la Pole arms are incorrect, there should be three not six lions' faces this is probably an error by the glazier.

Condition. The third quarter of de la Pole quartering Burghersh which had a missing field, and the body of the lion and the lower lion missing from the third quarter of the York arms, was completed by Mr. M. C. Farrar Bell in 1975.

Colour and Technique. Quarters 1, 4 de la Pole; all pot-metal glass, traces of a foliage pattern on the fess. 2, 3 Burghersh; the body of the lion painted on the white glass of the field, and stained yellow, the lion's head abraded on the flashed ruby chief and stained yellow. Impaling quarterly 1, 4 France field pot-metal blue, in the first quarter the two upper fleurs-de-lis are in yellow stain, painted on the same piece of glass as the adjacent label, the lower fleur-de-lis and those in the fourth quarter are in pot-metal ochre. 2, 3 England; field in pot-metal ruby, lions in pot-metal yellow-ochre glass, except the upper one in the second quarter which is painted on the same white glass as the label and stained yellow, the roundels on the label in yellow stain. The use of yellow stain as a substitute for small coloured charges to avoid intricate leading is quite common.

Quarries. Types 24, 18, and 19, yellow stain.

Date. Late 15th c., post 1452–3 when John de la Pole, Duke of Suffolk, 1422–91, married Elizabeth (d. 1500), daughter of Richard, Duke of York, sister of Edward IV and Richard III.[1]

A4. Bird Quarry PLATE 36 (c)

h. 0·12 m. w. 0·13 m.

A hexagonal piece of glass containing a bird in profile facing right, pecking at the ground within a circular frame.

Condition. Slight decay, cracked in eight places.

Colour and Technique. Painted on white glass, stipple shading, bird's feathers and plain border picked out in yellow stain.

Style and Design. See A5.

Date. Late 15th to early 16th c.

The hexagonal shape of the glass is without parallel in the county and may be domestic glazing imported into the church.

A5. Bird Quarry PLATE 36 (c)

h. 0·33 m. w. 0·13 m. Quarry: h. 0·11 m. w. 0·13 m.

A partridge perched on a branch, in profile looking upwards holding a worm in its beak.

Condition. Incomplete, the quarry has been cut down at four corners and the lower corner broken and repaired with a cement patch.

Colour and Technique. Painted on white glass, stipple shading, the bird's wing and tail feathers, bands on the body and head in yellow stain, as is the foliage.

Style and Design. Medieval glazing quarries painted with birds are a common feature of English 15th and 16th-c. glass design. (See Yarnton.)

Iffley Rectory
Tudor Rose Badge.

Panel: h. 0·58 m. w. 0·32 m. Badge: h. 0·42 m. w. 0·32 m. Tudor rose proper encircled by an elaborate chaplet with a crown above.

Condition. Incomplete, the right hand and lower clasps of the chaplet are alien. The surround to the rose is made up of alien pieces of glass, as is the crown above.

Colour and Technique. Apex clasp: ram's skull between foliage painted on white glass, deep-yellow stain background, green chaplet with maroon bands. Composite, lower clasp is missing replaced by plain blue glass; side clasps differ, left man thrusting his head through an oculus, right rose set in foliage. Foliage: ruby flash abraded and stained white. Crown: composite of alien pieces, the outline is based on a standard design but the whole may be a restorer's composite.

Style and Design. A crude piece of work, the profile head of a man thrust through an oculus is a late version of a design attributed to Galyon Hone. (See Wroxton Abbey.)

Date. Early 16th c.

[1] J. W. Clay, *Extinct and Dormant Peerages of the Northern Counties of England,* (1913), 52. G.E.C. xii, pt. 1 (1953), 449–50.

KELMSCOTT
ST. GEORGE

O.S. SP 249 994.

MS. SOURCES

Oxford. Bodl. Lib., MS. Top. Oxon. b. 75, f. 103. Wyatt Collections 18th–19th c. (probably copied from Powell's church notes c. 1805.)

PRINTED

Nelson (1913), 164.
P.C. (1920), 186.
Greening Lamborn (1949), 135.

The east window contains an equestrian figure of St. George killing the dragon. There is no documentary evidence for the date of the glass. The antiquarian sources reveal that in the mid eighteenth century the east window also contained a figure of the Virgin Mary with the infant Christ.[1]

The glass was in an extremely poor condition when examined in 1964, it was cracked and had a pronounced growth of lichen on the exterior. It was cleaned and releaded in 1975 by D. King of Norwich and a new piece was painted for the missing right foot of the figure and incomplete head of the dragon.

I

2b. St. George
PLATE 36 (d)

h. 0·59 m. w. 0·34 m.

Equestrian St. George riding to the right, spearing the dragon below the horse's hooves.

Condition. Incomplete, the panel is made up with modern white glass. The glass has corrosion on both surfaces.

Colour and Technique. Painted in brown on white glass, very delicate stipple shading, details picked out in yellow stain.

Iconography. See Burford w. I, A5.

Style and Design. Simple class of design, originally set against a background of plain white quarries, part of which remains. The drawing is spirited and carefully executed but not outstanding.

Date. Greening Lamborn suggested *c.* 1500, as St. George is 'in armour of the late fifteenth century'.[2] St. George wears a globose breastplate painted with his cross. For the rest the armour is entirely of plate: sallet with tail protecting the neck, taces protecting the thighs, and leg and arm defences and cuffed gauntlets. These features are typical of the period *c.* 1420–30 (shortly afterwards the besagews protecting the armpits went out of fashion in England). A later dating is not

precluded, as the design could be a deliberate antiquarian exercise. Mid 15th c.

s. III

3a. Quarry and Borders

Quarry: h. 0·14 m. w. 0·14 m.

Condition. The quarry is complete, the two border pieces are fragmentary, slight corrosion on both surfaces.

Colour and Technique. Painted on white glass, the crowns in yellow stain.

Style and Design. The quarry is painted with a large stylized pomegranate design, possibly derived from the pomegranate badge of Aragon.[3] See quarry type 54.

Date. Late 15th–16th c.

s. V

A1. Foliage Design

h. 0·07 m. w. 0·88 m.

A flat trefoil leaf design in white against a matt black background in a cusped yellow stain border. Complete and *in situ.*

Date. Late 15th c.

---

[1] P.C. (1920), 186.   [2] Greening Lamborn (1949), 135.
[3] The designs vary in type from the open type here and on a quarry at Queens' College, Cambridge, to the more 'naturalistic' representations found on a quarry at Brandeston (Suffolk). A. W. Franks, *A Book of Ornamental Glazing Quarries* (1849), 62, 102. So

far as is known the badge is not represented in English art until after the marriage of Arthur, Prince of Wales, with Katherine of Aragon in 1501. It is carved on the frieze of his tomb at Worcester. F. Sandford, *A Genealogical History of the Kings of England* (1677), 445. See also T. Willement, *Regal Heraldry* (1821), 67–8.

B1, B2, B3, B4. Foliage Designs

h. 0·14 m. w. 0·14 m.

Condition. Incomplete, coloured glass very decayed.

Style and Design. Originally probably four identical designs of a plain-coloured boss encircled by a cable-twist stem with offspringing leaves.

B1. Nothing remains.
B2. Ruby boss and fragment of foliage.
B3. Green boss.
B4. Ruby boss and foliage in lower lobe.

Date. Late 15th c.

Fragments of quarries, type 18, 15th c., have been inserted in B1 and B4.

KIDLINGTON
ST. MARY THE VIRGIN

O.S. SP 497 148.

MS. SOURCES

Oxford. Bodleian Library:
MS. Dugdale II, f. 150ᵛ. Notes by Sir William Dugdale, dated 1644.
MS. Top. Oxon. e. 286, ff. 87ᵛ–88ʳ. Notes by N. Greenwood, dated 1659.
MS. Top. Oxon. b. 75, ff. 107, 109–10. Wyatt Collections 18th–19th c.
London. British Library:
Harleian MS. 6363, f. 83ᵛ, 17th c.
Add. MS. 3705, f. 3, dated 1796.

PRINTED

Parker (1846), 59–60.
Visitations (1871), 33–5.
Stapleton, B., 'Three Oxfordshire Parishes', *O.H.S.* xxiv (1893), 1–198.
Nelson (1913), 164.
Bouchier (1918), 80.
P.C. (1920), 188–94.
Bouchier (1932), 80–1.
Freeborn, H., *The Parish Church of St. Mary, Kidlington* (n.d. c. 1945).
Greening Lamborn (1949), 135–9.
Woodforde, C., *English Stained and Painted Glass* (1954), 4.
Pevsner (1974), 671–2.

The surviving glass dates from the thirteenth, fourteenth, and fifteenth centuries and is very fragmentary. It represents only a small fraction of the original glazing scheme, and two panels at least are not indigenous to the church. The Visitation notes of 1574 record fifty-four shields of arms and crests then existing in various windows of the church.[1] Dudgale's notes of 1644 record twenty-two shields, but as he omits two of the surviving shields his notes may have been selective;[2] and the same observations must be made of Greenwood's notes of 1659 which list fourteen shields.[3] Wood's notes incorporate the 1574 Visitation and are not to be regarded as a record of the glass then extant.[4] Seven shields only survive and two of these probably came from Exeter College, Oxford.

The Churchwardens' Accounts for repairs and repaving in 1789 state that 'the labourers have much demolished the remnants of antiquity'.[5] A restoration of the church was undertaken in 1829 when Robertson, the architect employed, instructed Russell of St. Clements to gather together the glass in the clerestory windows and the windows of the north aisle of the chancel, and to set it in the chancel: 'the best of the whole is to be applied to the east window and the residue to the south window of the chancel.'[6] The south window of the chancel was cleaned and releaded in 1924[7] and the east window was restored in 1951 by Miss Joan Howson, who rearranged and reconstructed some of the panels.[8] No detailed account or photographic record was made in this latter rearrangement.[9]

The south window of the chancel (s. II) now contains two shields of identical size with the same foliage

[1] Visitations (1871), 35–6.
[2] Bodl. Lib. Dugdale MS. II, f. 150ᵛ, op. cit.
[3] Bodl. Lib. MS. Top. Oxon. e. 286, ff. 87ᵛ–8, op. cit.
[4] P.C. (1920), 188–94.   [5] Freeborn, op. cit., p. 8.
[6] Mrs. H. E. Freeborn (Howard), '*Twixt Cherwell and Glyme*'

(1927), 357, quoted in Greening Lamborn (1949), 135–6.
[7] Freeborn, op. cit. 12.
[8] A photograph of the whole window prior to this restoration exists, N.M.R. Unfortunately much of the fine detail is not clear.
[9] Correspondence from Miss Howson, 1960.

diaper on the fields. One is the arms of Plescy (1a), the other of Fiennes (1b). It is known from the anti-quarian sources that they were part of a series of eight shields recorded in the east window of the chapel on the south side of the chancel:[1]

In the east window

1. *Argent six annulets gules* PLESCY.
2. *Gules a fess or between six cross crosslets or* BEAUCHAMP.
3. PLESCY.
4. *Or two bars gules* MAUDIT.[2]
5. PLESCY.
6. *Azure three lions rampant or* FIENNES.
7. *Gules six bezants or* ZOUCHE OF ASHBY.
8. PLESCY.[3]

The reasons for this particular display of heraldry have not been fully established. They appear, in part at least, to have been retrospective and dynastic. Shields 1, 3, 5, and 8 represent the de Plescy family, lords of the manor of Kidlington.[4] Sir John de Plescy married Margaret, daughter and coheiress of Henry de Newburgh, Earl of Warwick (d. 1229) by Margery daughter and heiress of Henry d'Oilly (d. 1196).[5] This Sir John de Plescy became Earl of Warwick by the right of his wife but, having no issue by her, the earl-dom passed on his death in 1262–3 to her nephew William de Maudit, who in turn died without issue in 1268.[6] The earldom then passed to his nephew William de Beauchamp (d. 1298).[7] The common link between these families is the tenure of the earldom of Warwick and this is possibly the reason for com-memorating the arms of Maudit (shield 4) and Beauchamp (shield 2) alongside those of de Plescy. The inclusion of the arms of Fiennes (shield 6) and Zouche of Ashby (shield 7) cannot be accounted for on genealogical and dynastic grounds. There is no direct connection known between the families of de Plescy and Zouche, and the latter has only an indirect connection with the earldom of Warwick. Ela Longespee (d. 1276), daughter of William Longespee, Earl of Salisbury (d. 1225–6), married Thomas de Newburgh, Earl of Warwick (d. 1242),[8] and her niece Ela Longespee married Roger de la Zouche of Ashby (d. 1285).[9] The Fiennes family were also allied to the Longespee family as Isolt, granddaughter of Sir William Fiennes (d. 1301), married, c. 1288, Hugh Audley of Stratton Audley (d. 1325–6), whose mother Ela (d. 1299) was the daughter of William Longespee, Earl of Salisbury (d. 1255).[10] These connections are so distant and varied that they can hardly be cited as contributory reasons for the display of the arms of Fiennes and Zouche in this window. A resolution of the problems is hampered by the incomplete knowledge of the Plescy pedigree. Hugh, Lord Plescy (d. 1301), married one Margaret; their son also Hugh (d. 1337) married one Millicent, but their family names are not known.[11]

The genealogical evidence is of little help in establishing the date of the shields, but their general shape, decorative diapers, and absence of yellow stain are consistent with an early fourteenth-century dating.

This window also contains two other shields, both probably of the later fourteenth century. The arms of Elmerugge (3a) are probably to be dated c. 1349–79. Hugh, Lord Plescy, died in 1349 and his widow Elizabeth remarried Sir Roger de Elmerugge, who died in 1376. Elizabeth died in 1379, leaving no issue by either marriage.[12] The second shield, rather worn and probably made up in part, shows the arms of le Strange of Knockyn (3b). Hugh, Lord Plescy (d. 1301), gave lands in Berkshire to his daughter Margaret, wife of William de Bereford.[13] Their son Edmund died in 1354 leaving his three sisters as coheiresses, one

[1] The 1574 Visitation, Dugdale, and Wood are all consistent on this, Greenwood omits shield 4. The Fiennes shield was noted in this window in 1796. B.L. Add. MS. 3705, f. 3, op. cit.
[2] Stapleton, op. cit. 55, incorrectly transcribes the trick as '*or two bars gules, with an annulet in chief*'.
[3] The antiquarian sources do not identify the eight shields.
[4] Stapleton, op. cit. 12–19. G.E.C. x. 545–51.

[5] Stapleton, op. cit. 11–12. G.E.C. x. 546–7. Ibid. xii, part ii, 366–7.   [6] Ibid. 367–8.   [7] Ibid. 368–70.
[8] Ibid. 365.   [9] Ibid. 394–5.   [10] Ibid. i. 347.
[11] Ibid. x. 550.
[12] Ibid. 551. The pedigree given in Stapleton, op. cit. 23, is incorrect.
[13] *V.C.H. Berkshire* iv (1924), 387.

of whom was Margaret, wife of Sir James Audley,[1] whose son William held the d'Oilly fee in Kidlington in 1366.[2] His contemporary, of a collateral branch of the family, James, Lord Audley (1312–86), married, c. 1351, as his second wife, Isabel, said to be a daughter of Roger, Lord le Strange of Knockyn.[3]

There are two panels bearing the arms of Stapledon and Stafford, Bishops of Exeter, with angel supporters (I, 3a and 3c). They are not mentioned in any of the antiquarian sources and were probably brought here from Exeter College, Oxford, at some date before 1829, when they were incorporated in the east window. The college was refounded in 1564 and its Rectors from this date until 1887 were also Vicars of Kidlington.[4]

Walter de Stapledon, Bishop of Exeter 1307–26, in conjunction with his brother Sir Richard de Stapledon founded Stapledon Hall, later known as Exeter College, Oxford. He had licence in mortmain in 1312 and the founder's statutes were published in 1316.[5] Edmund de Stafford, Bishop of Exeter 1395–1419, was a generous benefactor of the college, he 'gave the said college books for divine service in its chapel and a chalice, and books for the library and built a chamber twenty-four feet long under the library, which he lengthened, heightened and covered with lead, and rebuilt the porch of the chapel and covered it with lead and built a small new chamber under the porch and half covered the Hall and built the new west gate, all which cost him over 200 marks in money not including the books.'[6]

The two panels are identical in size, technique, and style and were probably made for a window of Stafford's rebuilding. Shields of their arms are recorded by Wood as being in the Hall and Old Library.[7]

The identification of one shield is problematic (I, 5b). It has been blazoned *argent a knot of saltire form, the four ends radiating from the letters TO in monogram, all sable*. The arms have been tentatively attributed to Thomas of Hooknorton, Abbot of Oseney 1430–52.[8] No seal or record of his arms has been found but the abbey held the advowson of Kidlington church.[9] The shield is the same size as two others; the arms of de la Pole quartering Burghersh for Chaucer (also I, 5b) and the arms of the township of Kidlington (s. II, 5a). They all appear to be late fifteenth-century or early sixteenth-century. Wood records a group of seventeen shields under the heading 'in other windowes of the church, some of which have been in the isles and as I thinke in the chancel'.[10] Shields 10 and 11 of this list are the quarterly arms of de la Pole, one with a label, and Shield 12 the arms of the township. Below shields 10 and 11 Woods notes 'Under which two quartered coates is this written in an old English character Thomas Mawnfield'. Shields 14, 15, and 16 of Wood's list are respectively the arms of the township, the de la Pole arms, and the shield that has been ascribed to Thomas of Hooknorton.[11] Wood notes 'under which the coat here drawne (i.e. 15 and 16) was this written Thome Mawnfeld et Johanna uxor eius'. Another set of Wood's notes record a de la Pole shield and an inscription 'Orate pro animabus Tho(me) Manifil et Johanne uxoris eius' as being in a clerestory window of the nave.[12] A fragment of a Mawnfeld inscription is inserted in I, 1c. The association of the shield attributed to Thomas of Hooknorton with an inscription to Thomas Mawnfeld suggests that the shield might refer to the latter. Mrs. Stapleton noted that 'we know nothing of Thomas Mawnfeld' but suggested that he was possibly an agent to the de la Poles, lords of the manor and to Oseney Abbey.[13] The Mawnfeld alias Manfield family held lands in Oxfordshire and Berkshire and were merchants of the Staple at Calais.[14] In 1480 John Manfelde granted to trustees a messuage in the parish of Mary Magdalene, Oxford.[15] The Thomas Mawnfeld recorded in the inscriptions at Kidlington may be identical with Thomas Manfield, born before 1480, son and heir of Robert Manfield.[16]

[1] Ibid. *Cal. Inq, Post Mortem*, x. 249.
[2] Stapleton, op. cit. 21.   [3] G.E.C. i. 339–40.
[4] Stapleton, op. cit. 44–5. Freeborn, op. cit. 35–6. Greening Lamborn (1949), 136–8.
[5] C. W. Boase, 'Registrum Collegii Exoniensis', *O.H.S.* xxvii (1894), iii–xiii.   [6] Ibid. liii–liv.
[7] A. Wood, 'Survey of the Antiquities in the City of Oxford, 1661–6', ed. A. Clark, iii. 112, *O.H.S.* xxxvii (1899).
[8] Stapleton, op. cit. 59. Greening Lamborn (1949), 316.
[9] Stapleton, op. cit. 1–2.
[10] P.C. (1920), 191–3. Bodl. Lib. MS. Wood E. 1, ff. 95ᵛ–96ʳ.

Wood's list is identical with that in the 1574 Visitation, where the medium is not specified, Visitations (1871), 35. Bodl. Lib. MS. Wood D. 14, f. 34ᵛ. The editors of both MSS. transcribe these lists incorrectly.
[11] Visitations (1871), 35, and P.C. (1920), 192, both omit shield 16.
[12] Bodl. Lib. Wood MS. B. 15, f. 65.
[13] Stapleton, op. cit. 57.
[14] H. S. Salter, 'The Cartulary of Oseney Abbey', ii. 274, *O.H.S.* xc (1929). *Cal. Patent Rolls*, 1441–6, 33. Ibid. 1446–52, 479–80. Ibid. 1452–61, 403, 406, 569.   [15] Salter, op. cit. 274.
[16] *Cal. Inq. Post Mortem* Henry VIII, ii. 485.

There is some indirect evidence to support the attribution of the shield to Thomas Mawnfeld alias Manfield. The same features are repeated on the late fifteenth–early sixteenth-century panelling of the choir stalls at Kidlington. Another panel has a rebus of Kidlington set above a wool sack upon which is a knot of saltire form, the four arms radiating from the letter T. The incorporation of the wool sack and the fact that the Mawnfelds were merchants of the Staple at Calais suggests that these are devices of Thomas Mawnfeld.[1] If this identification is correct the shield might be more correctly blazoned, *argent a knot of saltire form, the four ends radiating from the letter T set within a circle.* Merchants' marks incorporating an initial and a circle are not uncommon.[2]

There is a substantially complete, but very decayed, panel from a Tree of Jesse, dated 1250–80 (I, 2b). There are no other examples of this date in the county. A reconstructed panel of the fifteenth century has been tentatively identified as a miracle of St. Frideswide of Oxford (I, 1c). Wood records that about 1630 the canons of Christ Church, Oxford, 'took down all the old windows (except four in the Divinity Chapel) which were set up anciently by the canons of St. Frideswyde's Priory containing several parts of that saint's life, besides the arms of many noblemen that had been benefactors to that monastery'.[3] It is not impossible that the Kidlington panel may have been imported from Christ Church, for at the time the windows were taken down Dr. J. Prideaux, Rector of Exeter College and Vicar of Kidlington, was also a canon of Christ Church.[4]

I   PLATE 37

1a. Composite Panel

h. 0·50 m. w. 0·61 m.

Condition. Fragments assembled in 1951. A head of Christ, very worn, the nimbus alien; pieces of patterned and foliage diapers, white ivy and trefoil leaves. All *c.* 1290–1340.

Inscriptions. Two fragments, in black-letter script, both 15 thc.

|p(ro) a(n)i(m)a| |non|

The end of a word, painted on part of a canopy fragment.

1b. Composite Panel: Archbishop

h. 0·61 m. w. 0·56 m.

Condition. The figure is composite with the vestments, hands, and feet made up from alien pieces of 14th-c. glass. The figure's head is very worn and the mitre does not belong to it.

Iconography. Identified by Freeborn as 'probably St. Thomas à Becket'.[5] There is no evidence to support this identification. Bouchier's suggestion that the figure is a 'portrait of Thomas of Kidlington, abbot of Oseney' (1330–73) is equally unsubstantiated.[6]

Date. All the fragments *c.* 1290–1340, except for fragments of grisaille vine leaves, *c.* 1250 (?).

1c. Miracle of St. Frideswide (?)   PLATE 8

h. 0·53 m. w. 0·53 m.

A young female saint, crowned and nimbed, stands on the left. Three other royal figures, two ladies and an elderly man, are all crowned. All the figures, except for the saint and a man blowing a trumpet, look down at a man who kneels before them. Only his head remains, but it is painted on the same piece of glass as the adjacent hand, proving its lower position in the original composition. He wears a close-fitting cap, tied under the chin, distinguishing him from the courtly figures.

Condition. An incomplete panel; eleven related heads and parts of their bodies remain, but much of the original composition has been lost and made up with alien fragments of different dates. Before the 1951 reconstruction the incomplete figures were incorporated in two panels.

Colour and Technique. Painted in brown on white glass, with light washes of matt and stipple shading, the details of hair, crowns, and drapery pattern picked out in yellow stain.

Iconography. The surviving fragments have been identified as representing the Purification of the Virgin Mary,[7] but this is incorrect. A tentative reading of the scene is that it represents St. Frideswide of Oxford restoring the sight of one of the messengers of Prince Algar, who had been struck blind attempting to seize her.[8] This panel was probably one of a series of scenes illustrating the life of St. Frideswide.

---

[1] The obverse of the seal of the office of the Mayoralty of the Wool Staple at Calais shows the *Agnus Dei* between three wool sacks. Birch, v (1898), no. 19012, matrix, 14th c.

[2] E. M. Elmhirst, 'Merchants' Marks', ed. L. Dow, *Harleian Society* cviii (1959).

[3] A. Wood, *The History and Antiquities of the College and Halls in the University of Oxford*, ed. J. Gutch (1786–90), 462.

[4] Freeborn, op. cit. 35. *Dictionary of National Biography* xvi, 354.

[5] Freeborn, op. cit. 19.

[6] Bouchier (1932), 129.

[7] Freeborn, op. cit. 19. Prior to the last restoration the fragments incorporated the basket and doves, now in 2a.

[8] See the Latin life in John Capgrave, *Nova Legenda Angliae*, ed. C. Horstmann (1901), 458–9.

Wood records such a series at Christ Church, Oxford, taken down *c.* 1630.[1]

Style and Design. The design and painting of the heads are very close to the two Becket panels from Woodstock Chapel now in the Bodleian Library and were probably produced by the same workshop.

Date. c. 1450(?).

Alien insertions: parts of a canopy design; two banners, each charged with a sun-burst badge. A fragment of a scene: a small lion beside a human foot. All white glass and yellow stain, 15th c.

Inscriptions. Fragments of two different inscriptions, both in black-letter script, 15th c.:

|Orate p(ro)|a(n)i(m)ab(us)|;|Thome|(M)anfyl(d)|

2a. Composite Panel. The Virgin and Child

h. 0·94 m. w. 0·61 m.

Condition. Fragments assembled in 1951.

An incomplete Virgin and Child, the head and shoulders of the Virgin, with the hand of the Child on her breast. White glass and yellow stain, late 15th c.

The other fragments include: a hand holding a basket containing two doves from a presentation of Jesus in the Temple (Luke 2: 23–4); a part of a chasuble; pieces of canopies and patterned draperies. All 15th c. Very incomplete and disordered.

2b. Panel from a Tree of Jesse

h. 0·64 m. w. 0·51 m.

Centre, a seated frontal king, grasping the branches of the vine, a small prophet figure stands on either side.

Condition. The panel is substantially complete, minor losses in the vine and background; the head of the right-hand prophet replaced by an alien 14th-c. head. The glass is very corroded on both surfaces.

Colour and Technique. The flesh parts are brownish-pink glass. The king has a gold crown, purple mantle, green robe, and ruby shoes. Left-hand prophet: ruby nimbus and mantle, white robe and shoes. Right-hand prophet: ruby nimbus, ochre mantle, green robe, and white shoes. The

vine stem and leaves white, the grapes either white or ruby, set against a plain blue ground. Painted in dark brown on pot-metal glass, the colours deep in tone.

Iconography. The basic design of a king seated frontal against the vertical stem of the tree, with a prophet standing on either side in the branches of the tree, was established in the 12th c.[2] The earliest examples extant in glass are French, at S. Denis, *c.* 1142–4,[3] and at Chartres, *c.* 1150–5.[4]

A panel at Canterbury[5] and another at York,[6] both *c.* 1180–1200, are close in style and design to S. Denis but are very incomplete.

There are the remains of similar 13th-c. Jesse Trees at Salisbury Cathedral (Wilts.),[7] Westwell (Kent),[8] and Nackington (Kent).[9] A distinguishing feature of these later trees is that the tree becomes a vine, replacing the formalized foliage of the earlier examples.

Style and Design. Woodforde doubted the English origin of this panel, but offered no alternative.[10] There are similarities between English and French work of the 13th c., but the similarities in the stylized drawing of the vine here and at Salisbury and Westwell perhaps favour an English origin. The drapery painting is too decayed for detailed comparison.

Date. c. 1250–80 (?).

2c. St. Anne teaching the Virgin to Read

h. 0·92 m. w. 0·61 m.

Condition. The panel is composite, assembled in 1951. The head and shoulders and right hand of St. Anne, part of the Virgin's bodice, and the book held before her are original; the remainder is made up with modern stippled glass and alien pieces of medieval coloured glass.

Colour and Technique. Painted in brown on white glass, stipple shading, details of hair and hems picked out in yellow stain.

Iconography. See Beckley (n. IV, 1a). The writing on the book is shown as a scribble.

Style and Design. The hard cursory drawing and painting of the Virgin's bodice and book contrast with the more detailed painting of St. Anne's head.

Date. Later 15th c.

---

[1] Wood, op. cit. 462.

[2] A. Watson, *The Early Iconography of the Tree of Jesse* (1934).

[3] Ibid. 112–20, 166–7. See also the chapter by L. Grodecki in M. Aubert *et al.*, *Le Vitrail français* (1958), particularly 106–7.

[4] Watson, op. cit. 120–5. Grodecki, op. cit. 106.

[5] Two panels remain, north window of the Corona, returned to the Cathedral after 1949. B. Rackham, *The Ancient Glass of Canterbury Cathedral* (1949), 116–17, pl. 13b, on the evidence of a copy thought the original to be early 13th c. J. Baker, *English Stained Glass* (1960), 62–3, pl. 11, wrongly describes the panel as 'dubious 13th c.'. The authenticity of these panels has been established by

M. H. Caviness, 'The Canterbury Jesse Window. The Year 1200: A Symposium', *The Metropolitan Museum of Art, New York* (1975), 373–93. Dr. Caviness suggests a dating 1190–1207, ibid. 381.

[6] J. Knowles, *The York School of Glass-Painting* (1936), 7–8.

[7] J. Carter, *The Ancient Architecture of England* (1795–1837), pl. 79, fig. Winston, (1865), 108–10.

[8] C. Winston, *Hints on Glass Painting* (1867), pl. 10, fig. 2. N. Westlake, *History of Design in Painted Glass* i (1879–84), 77.

[9] Rackham, op. cit. 116–17. K. H. J. in *Archaeologia Cantiana* l (1939), 161.

[10] Woodforde, op. cit. 4.

3a. Shield of Stapledon, Angel Supporters

h. 0·53 m. w. 0·30 m.

Argent two bends wavy sable, a bordure sable semy of pairs of keys or WALTER DE STAPLEDON, BISHOP OF EXETER, 1307–26.

Inscription. In black-letter capitals:

|[G|U]|A|L|[T]|E|[R]|U|S| |[S]|T|A|P|L|E|D|O|[N]|

Condition. The remaining glass is substantially complete and well preserved; originally surmounted by a canopy, now lost except for two pendant bosses, painted on the same glass as the adjacent wings of the upper angel.

Colour and Technique. The angels have white albs, hair and wings in yellow stain, painted in brown with stipple shading. The bends on the shield are in darker paint, the border leaded separately stained yellow and blacked out to show the keys. Blue ground patterned with rosettes.

Iconography. Single figures of angels, each holding a shield are quite common in 15th-c. tomb sculpture and glass painting.[1] Three angels as supporters are rare. Near-contemporary examples are found on the north porch of Westminster Hall (*c.* 1398),[2] and in the east window of Haddon Hall chapel (Derbys.), dated 1427.[3]

Style and Design. See 3c.

Date. c. 1395–1415; from Exeter College, Oxford (?).

3b. The Trinity

h. 0·84 m. w. 0·69 m.

Condition. A composite panel assembled in 1951. The figure of God is made up from two different figures; the head, with the hair in plain matt paint from one; the chest, with the hair over the shoulders, in yellow stain from another. The small Christ crucified is a modern reconstruction, except for his left hand and the cross adjacent to it. The draperies are made up of alien pieces of 15th-c. glass.

Colour and Technique. Original portions painted in brown on white glass with stippled matt shading and yellow stain. The blue ground, patterned with contiguous circles, is incomplete and possibly alien to the figures.

Iconography. Standard Seat of Mercy type.

Date. c. 1425–50.

Border pieces: *lions passant gardant or,* set against plain

ruby pieces; *fleurs-de-lis or,* set against plain blue pieces, all pot-metal glass. 14th c.

3c. Shield of Stafford, Angel Supporters

h. 0·53 m. w. 0·30 m.

Or a chevron gules, a bordure azure semy of mitres or EDMUND DE STAFFORD, BISHOP OF EXETER, 1395–1419.[4]

Inscription. In black-letter capitals:

|[E]|D|M|U|N|[D]|U|S| [S|T]|A|F|F|O|R|D|

Condition. Before 1951 the panel was set inside out, slight corrosion on both surfaces. Shield: the sinister half of the chevron and the field below are old restorations. One mitre in the bordure, the torso of the upper angel, and the head of the angel lower right are modern, 1951. Ruby background very opaque.

Colour and Technique. The field is yellow stain, with patterned diaper, now very faint. The mitres are in yellow stain, leaded into the bordure. Angels as 3a. Ruby background, diapered with rosettes.

Iconography. See 3a.

Style and Design. This and 3a are companion pieces. They are identical in size and the angels are drawn from the same cartoon.

Date. c. 1395–1419; from Exeter College, Oxford (?).

4a. Composite Panel

h. 0·84 m. w. 0·61 m.

Condition. Fragments assembled in 1951.

A tracery light: a seraphim, standing on a wheel, background diaper of contiguous circles, each enclosing a rosette. White glass stipple shading and yellow stain. Very incomplete, the figure's torso and wheel are restored and the head is alien but contemporary, probably that of an archangel. *c.* 1425–50. Remains of quarries, types 45 and 46.

4b. The Crucifixion

h. 0·61 m. w. 0·69 m.

Christ crucified between the Virgin and St. John Evangelist.

Provenance. Recorded in 1796 in the east window of the chapel on the south side of the chancel.[5] Removed to the present window in 1828.

---

[1] The earliest example has been thought to be the tomb at Elford (Staffs.) attributed to Sir Thomas Arderne (d. 1391). E. S. Prior and A. Gardner, *An Account of Medieval Figure-sculpture in England* (1912), 444, fig. 515. Rushforth (1936), 26 n. 1. However, A. Gardner, *Alabaster Tombs* (1940), 52–3, attributes the tomb to Sir John Ardenne (d. 1408). Rushforth states that 'angels holding armorial shields appear first on the sides of alabaster tombs'. Earlier examples, however, occur in MS. painting, e.g. B.L. Add. MS. 21926, f. 2, added drawing pre-1369.

[2] J. H. Harvey, 'The Wilton Diptych—A Re-examination', *Archaeologia* xcviii (1961), pl. x, fig. c.

[3] F. H. Cheetham, *Haddon Hall* (1904), 78–83. Detailed description in Newton ii (1961), 36–7.

[4] His episcopal seal has a shield of the arms of the see of Exeter only, Birch, i (1887), no. 1565.

[5] B.L. Add. MS. 3705, f. 3, op. cit. Bodl. Lib. MS. Top. Oxon. b. 79, f. 107.

Condition. Incomplete, the Virgin's head and Christ's hands are missing. The earlier restorations of these pieces were removed by Miss Howson, who rearranged the panel, incorporating alien fragments of 14th-c. glass.[1] The plain blue background is probably alien to the figures.

Iconography. The Virgin and St. John stand either side of the crucified Christ, standard type. The crown of thorns is represented as a plain banded fillet (see Asthall, n. IV, 2b).

Style and Design. Very close to the side windows of the chancel of Merton College Chapel, Oxford. The head of St. John should be compared with the head of St. Stephen (s. III, 2a).

Date. c. 1300.

Border pieces, as 3b.

4c. Composite Panel

h. 0·84 m. w. 0·61 m.

Fragments assembled in 1951. An incomplete tracery light of a seraphim, a companion to those in 4a and 5b, with the original head replaced by that of an archangel (?). Background diaper of contiguous rosettes. *c.* 1425–50.

Quarries as 4a.

5a. Composite Panel

h. 0·53 m. w. 0·61 m.

Fragments assembled in 1951. Pieces of canopies, all very fragmentary, the over-all designs missing. 15th c.

5b. Composite Panel

h. 0·56 m. w. 0·69 m.

Fragments reassembled in 1951: an incomplete tracery light of a seraphim, which is a companion to 4a and 4c, though the legs, wheel, and adjacent background are missing. *c.* 1425–50.

A shield: quarterly 1, 4 *azure a fess between three lions' faces or* DE LA POLE 2, 3 *argent a lion rampant queue fourchée or* BURGHERSH FOR CHAUCER.

Condition. Before 1951 the first and fourth quarters had been disarranged and the second quarter was inside out.

Colour and Technique. The lions' faces of the first and fourth quarters are painted in outline and stained yellow on the same glass as the field. The field of the second and third quarters is patterned with contiguous circles in outline, the lion in yellow stain.

The correct arms of Burghersh of Ewelme were *argent a chief gules, over all a lion rampant queue fourchée or.*[2] The small size of the shield might explain the omission of the chief to simplify the leading design, but it may have been indicated in outline and subsequently worn off.

Date. After 1430–2 when Alice, daughter and heiress of Thomas Chaucer by his wife Maud, daughter and coheiress of John de Burghersh, Lord Kerdeston, married William de la Pole, Earl of Suffolk.[3] The manor of Kidlington was inherited by them on the death of Thomas Chaucer in 1436.[4] William de la Pole died in 1450, Alice in 1475.[5] The shield probably commemorates their son John de la Pole, Duke of Suffolk, who died in 1491–2.[6]

A fragment of a canopy with a shield, painted on the same glass:

Shield: *argent a knot of saltire form, the four ends radiating from a letter T set within a circle all sable* THOMAS MAWN-FELD (?).

Condition. The paint has worn thin in parts.

Colour and Technique. Painted in brown on white glass, the field of the shield diapered with a foliage design.

Previously attributed to Thomas of Hooknorton, Abbot of Osney. The attribution to Thomas Mawnfeld is discussed above, p. 127.

Date and Provenance. This shield is the same size as the quarterly coat of de la Pole above and the arms of the township of Kidlington (s. II, 5a). They probably belong to a window given by Thomas Mawnfeld, late 15th–early 16th c.

Fragments of canopies, including two banners, each charged with a cross form flying from pinnacles; white and yellow stain on a black ground speckled white, 15th c. These pieces are curved to fit the cusped shoulders of a light.

5c. Composite Panel

h. 0·53 m. w. 0·61 m.

Condition. Fragments assembled in 1951.

---

[1] The restorations may have been of 1828 or earlier, see the photograph before restoration. N.M.R. (see p. 125 n. 8 above).

[2] The arms are similar to those borne by the baronial family of this name, but their connection has not been established, see G.E.C. vii. 194.

[3] Ibid. viii, 199. Ibid. xii, part i. 447.

[4] Napier, *Historical Notices of Swyncombe and Ewelme* (1858), 28–30. Stapleton, op. cit. 26–30.

[5] G.E.C. xii, part i, 147. The quarterly coat of de la Pole and

Burghersh for Chaucer is represented on the tombs of Alice and her father Thomas Chaucer at Ewelme (Oxon.). See E. A. Greening Lamborn, 'The arms on the Chaucer Tomb at Ewelme', *Oxoniensia*, v (1940), 78–92.

[6] The same arms appear on his Garter Stall plate. W. H. St. John Hope, *Garter Stall Plates* (1901), pl. lxxix. His signet seal bears the Burghersh lion only. Birch iii (1895), no. 12751. Add. 26309. Date, 1488.

Very fragmentary pieces of canopy work. the over-all designs missing. 15th c.

B1. Sun

d. 0·04 m.

The sun, wavy rays radiating from the centre. Pot yellow. Companion piece to B6.

B2. Composite Panel

h. 0·84 m. w. 0·27 m.

Fragments assembled in 1951.

Modern inscription 'The glass in this window was repaired by Russell in 1828'.

B3. Composite Panel

h. 0·84 m. w. 0·27 m.

Fragments assembled in 1951.

Headless figure, made up of alien pieces of 15th-c. glass.

B4. Composite Panel

h. 0·84 m. w. 0·27 m.

Fragments assembled in 1951.

Small head of an angel or priest, wearing an amice; white and yellow stain. Close in style to the heads in 1c, 1425–50. Fragments of quarries type 39.

B5. Composite Panel

h. 0·84 m. w. 0·27 m.

Fragments assembled in 1951.

Modern inscription 'This glass was releaded and rearranged by Joan Howson in 1951'.

B6. Moon

The moon with human features. Pot yellow, probably from a panel of the Crucifixion. Set on modern white quarries. Companion piece to B1. See also s. II, 8a, 8b. 14th c.

C1. Fragment of quarry type 25.

D1. The Holy Dove

h. 0·08 m. w. 0·12 m.

Incomplete and set upside down. White and yellow stain, 15th c. Probably from a Trinity.

s. II

1a. Tracery Light and Shield of Plescy

Tracery light: h. 0·30 m. w. 0·75 m.

Not *in situ*. Serrated leaf design, white and yellow stain on a matt ground. Late 15th–16th c.

Shield: h. 0·30 m. w. 0·29 m.

Argent six roundels gules PLESCY.

Condition. Good, a small portion of the field is restoration.

Colour and Technique. The white field has a foliage diaper, rounded quatrefoil leaves, picked out of a matt wash. The ruby is pot-metal glass.

Provenance: from the east window of the chapel, south side of the chancel (see above, pp. 125–6).

Date. Early 14th c.

Borders: assorted fragments. Two quarries type 45, an initial m, roundels.

1b. Tracery Light and Shield of Fiennes

Tracery light: h. 0·30 m. w. 0·75 m.

Not *in situ*. Leaf design, technique as 1a. Late 15th–16th c.

Shield: h. 0·30 m. w. 0·29 m.

Azure three lions rampant or FIENNES.

Condition. Good, but some exterior pitting. The upper dexter lion is a replacement by Russell, 1828. Before this restoration the shield was set in a yellow roundel, diapered with trails of foliage, all apparently within by a foliage border.[1]

Colour and Technique. The blue field has a foliage diaper, identical with 2a. The lions are in pot-metal glass.

Provenance: as 1a.

Date. Early 14th c.

Stapleton suggested that these were the arms of Sandford.[2] Sir John de Plescy (d. 1263) married first Christian (d. pre-1243), daughter and coheiress of Sir Hugh de Sandford of North Moreton (Berks.).[3] There is no evidence to justify this suggestion.

Borders: fragments of quarries and roundels. One each of quarries type 25, 26, 36, 37, 47, two of type 45.

2a. Quarries

Each quarry h. 0·14 m. w. 0·10 m.

Two type 39, two type 49, the latter very corroded. 15th c.

Borders: fragments of architecture, foliage designs, border pieces, a lion statant regardant, and one quarry type 42.

---

[1] Bodl. Lib. MS. Top. Oxon. e. 75, f. 107ʳ. The border design is lightly sketched in pencil. The details are indistinct.
[2] Stapleton, op. cit. 55.   [3] G.E.C. x. 545.

2b. Quarries

Each quarry h. 0·14 m. w. 0·10 m.

Two type 39, two type 51.

3a. Shield of Elmrugge

h. 0·25 m. w. 0·20 m.

Checky argent and sable ELMRUGGE.

Condition. The lower half of the shield is modern. The paint of the original part is very worn and flaking.

Colour and Technique. Originally painted on a single piece of glass, the argent chequers are each patterned with a quatrefoil design picked out of a light matt wash.

Provenance: Wood records two examples of this coat, one in the east window of the chancel, the other in the north window of the north aisle.[1]

Date. After 1349 and probably before 1379.

Borders: fragment of an inscription, Lombardic script *ET* and fragments of architecture.

3b. Shield of le Strange

h. 0·23 m. w. 0·18 m.

Gules two lions passant in pale or LE STRANGE.

Condition. Poor, the painting of the lions is very worn, the plain ruby field is very fragmented, possibly alien.

Colour and Technique. All pot-metal glass.

Provenance: formerly in a window of the north aisle.[2]

Date. Mid 14th c.

Borders: fragments of architecture and one quarry type 46.

4a. Quarries

Two type 39, one type 49, two type 51.

Borders: miscellaneous fragments including a shield *argent barry nebuly sable.* 14th c.

4b. Quarries

Two type 39, two type 51.

5a. Two Heads and Shield of Township of Kidlington

Heads: h. 0·10 m.

Condition. Poor, pink glass with pronounced corrosion on both surfaces, the paint is flaking.

Iconography. Both heads nimbed, possibly angels, but this arrangement may not be original.

Date. First half 14th c.

Shield h. 0·20 m. w. 0·15 m.

Party per fess argent and sable, in chief a pike embowed, in base a ram statant argent TOWNSHIP OF KIDLINGTON

Condition. Good, slightly corroded. Greening Lamborn wrongly states that the upper part is new glass.[3]

Technique. The fish is painted in outline, the tinctures omitted, the argent field is patterned with contiguous circles painted in outline.

Provenance: original location not known but probably from a window given by Thomas Mawnfeld. The de la Pole and Mawnfeld shields (I, 5b) are companion pieces.

This coat and a similar carving on the choir stalls have been interpreted by Stapleton: 'the Pike represents the fisheries of Gosford; the Ram the sheep of Campsfield, the principal industries of the place. . . . The whole would stand as the arms of the Township.'[4]

Date. Late 15th c.

Borders: architectural fragments.

5b. Fragments

Borders: assorted architectural fragments. Post-medieval shield.

6a. Quarries

Two type 34, two type 51.

Borders: assorted fragments.

6b. Quarries

Quarries and borders as 6a.

7a. Roundel

d. 0 35 m.

Foliage design, pot yellow and green. 14th c.

Borders: fragments of architecture, a large five-petalled rose, and foliage design.

7b. Roundel

Foliage design as 7a.

Borders: fragments of architecture, two large five-petalled roses, and foliage designs.

8a, 8b. Fragments

Three moons, with human features, yellow pot-metal 14th c., six fragments of foliage designs.

A1. Composite Panel

Two incomplete grotesques, each of a winged dragon, yellow stain and stippled matt. 15th c.

---

[1] Wood MS. E. 1, f. 96. P.C. (1920), 190. [2] Ibid. 191.
[3] Greening Lamborn (1949), 138. [4] Stapleton, op. cit. 59.

Lost Glass

The antiquarian notes record forty shields of arms and eighteen heraldic crests in the windows, which present problems of interpretation as some of the shields were moved from their original positions by the mid 17th c. The following account is based on the 1574 Visitation notes[1] and those of Wood.[2]

'In the chapel or south aisle joyning to the Chancell were these armes in the windows.

In the east window':

1. PLESCY

2. BEAUCHAMP

3. PLESCY

4. MAUDIT

5. PLESCY

6. FIENNES

7. ZOUCHE OF ASHBY

8. PLESCY

(These shields are considered in the introduction, 125–8.)

'In a south window of the said chapel':

9. *Argent a chief azure over all a lion rampant queue fourchée or* (BURGHERSH) impaling *azure a fess or between three lions faces or* (DE LA POLE).

The proper order of the impalements is reversed, and the recorded shield was probably a composite of two different shields. The de la Pole connections are discussed above, 125–8.

10. *Argent a saltire engrailed sable* (BOUTETORT?).[3]

'In the east window of the chancel':

11. *Checky argent and sable* (ELMRUGGE) 'This is also in the north window of the north isle'.

12. *Gules fretty of three pieces or a bordure argent charged with eight fleurs-de-lis or* (AUDLEY OF ELLESFIELD).

13. *Or two bends azure* (D'OILLY).

One shield of Elmrugge remains in s. II, 3a, 1349–79. William Audley held the d'Oilly fee in Kidlington in 1366 (see introduction, 125–8).

'In the windowes of the north isle':

14. *Gules two lions passant in pale sable* (LE STRANGE). This shield survives in s. II, 3b.

15. *Vairy gules and argent on a canton gules a garb argent* (DE LA BECHE) 'This coat . . . seems imperfect.' Elizabeth Elmrugge (d. 1379), whose arms are in s. II, 3a, was daughter of William de la Beche of Missenden and Kidlington.[4]

16. *Argent a chevron sable between three buckles sable* (CROXFORD)

17. (CROXFORD) *impaling barry of six azure and argent* (GREY?)

'Underneath written *Robertis Croxford et Johana uxor eius*'.

18. *Gules three catherine wheels or* (ROET FOR CHAUCER)

19. *Quarterly* 1, 4 (DE LA POLE) 2, 3 *argent on a bend gules three pairs of wings argent* (WINGFIELD) *impaling* (ROET FOR CHAUCER)

20. (DE LA POLE)

21. (WINGFIELD)

'At the bottom of the window where these coates are, is written: *Orate pro animabus Hugonis Holkot* . . .'

The identities of Robert Croxford and Hugh Holkot have not been established, and the display with the Wingfield and Chaucer arms has not been accounted for.

'In the west window of the church'

22. *Quarterly* 1, 4 (DE LA POLE) 2, 3 (WINGFIELD) *impaling . . . a lion rampant . . .* (sic).

'In other windowes of the church, some of which have been in the isles and as I thinke in the chancell':

23. *Sable a lion rampant argent crowned or* (SEGRAVE)

24. (PLESCY)

Sir John de Segrave (d. 1325) married Christian, daughter of Sir Hugh de Plescy.[5]

25. *Or fretty of three pieces gules on a chief sable three bezants* (VERDON?)

26. *Or a lion rampant sable* (MAREYS? CLIVEDOVER?)

27. *Or a bend sable cotised sable between six martlets sable* (BEAUCHAMP?)

[1] Visitations (1871), 33–5.

[2] Bodl. Lib. MS. Wood E. 1, f. 93ʳ–97ʳ. Wood's original manuscript has been used rather than the published versions in P.C. (1920), 188–94, and Stapleton, op. cit. 55–8.

[3] The editor of the 1574 Visitation (Visitations (1871) 33–5),

included this shield with those in the east window of the chapel, Wood's location is supported by Dugdale's notes, Bodl. Lib. MS. Dugdale II, f. 150ᵛ.

[4] Stapleton, op. cit. 55–8. G.E.C. x. 550–1.

[5] Stapleton, op. cit. 16. G.E.C. xi. 607–8.

28. *Argent semy of cross-crosslets fitchy sable three fleurs-de-lis sable* (BEREFORD)

Sir William de Bereford (d. 1326–7) married Margaret, daughter of Sir Hugh de Plescy.[1]

29. *Argent a bend lozengy sable* (GLASTINGBURS? BRADDENE?)

30. *Argent two bars nebuly sable* (BASSET)

The Basset family had a holding in the manor in the 12th c. and 13th c.[2] Sir Hugh de Plescy (d. 1292) married Isabel, daughter and coheiress of John Biset by Alice Basset.[3]

31. *Argent a lion rampant sable* (STAPLETON)

Sir Nicholas de Stapleton (d. after 1209) married Margery, daughter and heiress of Miles Basset of Haddlesley.[4] The relationships between the different branches of the Basset family are not clear.

32. *Quarterly 1, 4* (DE LA POLE) *2, 3* (BURGHERSH)

33. *Quarterly 1, 4* (DE LA POLE) *2, 3* (BURGHERSH) *over all a label of three points argent*

'Under which two quartered coates is this written in Old English character: *Thomas Mawnfelde*.'

34. (TOWNSHIP OF KIDLINGTON)

35. *Sable a lion rampant argent crowned or on its shoulder a fleur-de-lis* (SEGRAVE)

The arms of Sir Stephen de Segrave (d. 1325) as heir to his father, Sir John de Segrave (d. 1325) shield 23 above.[5]

36. (TOWNSHIP OF KIDLINGTON)

37. *Quarterly 1, 4* (DE LA POLE) *2, 3* (BURGHERSH)

38. (MAWNFELD *alias* MANFIELD)

'Under which (last two shields) was written: *Thome Mawnfeld et Johanna uxor eius*' The arms of de la Pole, The Township of Kidlington and Mawnfeld survive, all 15th-c., in I, 5b, s. II, 5a and I, 5b respectively.

39. *Gules three fleurs-de-lis or* (CANTELUPE)

William de Cantelupe (d. 1250) married Matilda, widow of Henry d'Oilly.[6]

40. *Argent on a bend sable three plates argent* (TRILLOCK)

'Under which last is written Lawrence Trieloc and Anne his wyffe. An(no) 140 . . .' The identities of these donors have not been established.

The eighteen heraldic crests in the windows have been blazoned from the tricks in the 1574 Visitation[7] and Wood's notes.[8] They are not assigned to specific shields of arms and the problems of identification are outside the scope of this study.

---

[1] *Cal. Inq. Post Mortem* vi. 748; T. Banks, *Baronia Anglica Concentrata* ii (1843), 46–7.

[2] Stapleton, op. cit. 8–10.

[3] G.E.C. x. 548–9. Alice Basset was daughter and coheiress of Thomas Basset of Headington, ibid x. 548 n. 4.

[4] Ibid. xii, part 1, 262.

[5] Ibid. xi. 608–9.

[6] Stapleton, op. cit. 6–7.

[7] Visitations (1871), 33–5.

[8] P.C. (1920), 188–94.

LITTLE FARINGDON
DEDICATION UNKNOWN

O.S. SP 226 014.

s. IV

1b. Canopy Fragments

h. 0·46 m. w. 0·28 m.

Before restoration by D. King of Norwich in 1968, these fragments were hanging loose in two south clerestory windows.

Condition. Five large and four small pieces of canopy fragments, original over-all design not known. Part of the surviving pieces are probably from the centre of the canopy, a bust-length angel standing below a vaulted niche. Quite well preserved with only slight decay on both surfaces.

Colour and Technique. White glass, yellow stain, stipple and matt shading.

Style and Design. Similar quatrefoil patterns on the parapet are found at Yarnton I, 3a, 3c, 4b.

Date. c. 1400–30.

2b. Roundel, Vine Foliage   PLATE 38 (b)

d. 0·41 m.

A spray of white vine leaves and grapes against a plain ruby ground, now leaded as a circular medallion.

PRINTED SOURCES
Pevsner (1974), 685.

Condition. White glass has some surface corrosion, but is basically sound. The ruby glass was extremely decayed and was abraded and resurfaced on the exterior during the 1968 restoration.

Style and Design. There is a local tradition that this piece of glass came from Salisbury Cathedral (Wilts.). An identical composition (Plate 38 (c)) is found in the Metropolitan Museum, New York (Accession No. 13.64.10.), which is also thought to have come from the same source, although there is no evidence for either provenance. The drawing of the vine foliage is close to that of the Salisbury Jesse.

Date. Mid 13th c.

3b. Male Torso

h. 0·23 m. w. 0·10 m.

Bust length, facing three-quarters right. Added fragment of 17th-c. inscription:

|MAGISTRA|

The head is slightly decayed on both sides, the plain blue of the shoulder is alien. Painted on white glass, hair and beard yellow stain. Strong matt washes on the hair and beard, stipple shading, very linear drawing of eyes. Second half 14th c.

LOWER HEYFORD
ST. MARY

O.S. SP 485 248.

MS. SOURCES

Oxford. Bodleian Library, MS. Top. Oxon. c. 51, f. 32. Church Notes by W. H. Turner, 1867.

PRINTED

Visitations (1871), 36.
Blomfield, J. C., *The History of the Present Deanery of Bicester, Oxfordshire* vi (1882–94), 41.
Greening Lamborn (1949), 131.
V.C.H. vi (1959), 182–94.
Pevsner (1974), 693.

The surviving pieces of fourteenth and fifteenth-century glass are now inserted in the west window of the south aisle of the nave. The most important piece of the earlier glass is a tracery light with a frontal bust of Christ. Its original location is unknown but it could date from *c.* 1338 when renovations to the chancel fabric were ordered.[1] The frontal bust-length pose may be related to the Veronica image of Christ, established in the thirteenth century.[2]

Two fifteenth-century shields survive, one the arms of Achard, the other Achard quartering de la Mare. The de la Mare family held the manor and the advowson from the twelfth century until 1493.[3] Peter de la Mare (d. 1349) married Joan, the heiress of Peter Achard (d. 1361) of Aldermaston, (Berks.).[4] Their descendants used the quarterly coat of Achard and de la Mare. This practice may have originated with Thomas de la Mare (d. 1404) to distinguish himself from his elder brother, Robert (d. 1382).[5] Lee in 1574 recorded above the second shield at Lower Heyford an inscription, since lost: '*Will bocher rectoris Will Manypenne*'.[6] William Bucher was presented to the living by Sir Thomas de la Mare in 1474 and died in 1490.[7] The shields and the quarries probably date from this period.

w. I

1a. Christ in Judgement

h. 0·18 m. w. 0·15 m.

Condition. Incomplete, only the lower part of the legs and feet resting on the orb remain. Very corroded.

Colour and Technique. Painted in brown on white glass, the drapery in yellow stain.

Iconography. The bleeding wounds on the feet are shown. The orb is divided into the three elements, for earth, water, and air. The iconography is derived from Isaiah 66: 1 'Thus saith the Lord, Heaven is my throne, earth the footstool under my feet'. It is a common feature of representations of the Last Judgement.

Date. Mid 14th c.

1b. Scroll

h. 0·15 m. w. 0·13 m.

Condition. Incomplete, inscribed in black-letter script:

|Nate · penta dabo · q(ue)vis|

Painted on a single piece of glass, a fragment of a large composition, subject unknown.

Date. 15th–16th c.

2a. Bust of Christ

h. 0·25 m. w. 0·30 m.

Condition. Slight exterior corrosion; incomplete, small lobes made up with modern white glass.

Colour and Technique. Painted in brown on white glass, hair and border pattern in yellow stain, matt and slight smear modelling. Background pattern of diamond trellis, each diamond cusped quatrefoil, picked out of matt brown paint.

Iconography. Bust length frontal pose, like a Veronica.

Style and Design. Stylized, very linear with flat matt washes.

Date. Mid 14th c., original location not known, but obviously the apex tracery light of a window. Other examples in tracery lights are found at Tadmarton and Toot Baldon.

3a. Shield of Achard

h. 0·20 m. w. 0·18 m.

Or a bend lozengy sable ACHARD.

Condition. Incomplete, old breaks repaired.

Colour and Technique. Yellow stain on white glass, the bend painted in black, the field patterned with contiguous circles in a very light brown paint.

Date. 15th c. possibly 1471–90.

3b. Shield of Achard quartering de la Mare

h. 0·20 m. w. 0·18 m.

Quarterly 1, 4 or a bend lozengy sable ACHARD *2, 3 gules two lions passant gardant in pale argent* DE LA MARE.

Condition. Incomplete, slightly cut down.

Colour and Technique. The Achard quarterings as 3a, the lions are separately leaded, the ruby field plain pot-metal.

Date. 15th c., possibly 1471–90 when William Bucher was rector. In 1867 these two shields were noted as being in the east window of the chapel in the south aisle of the nave.[8]

[1] Blomfield, op. cit. 40. *V.C.H.* vi (1959), 193.
[2] The earliest English examples, mid 13th c., are found in the work of Matthew Paris. M. R. James, 'The Drawings of Matthew Paris', *The Walpole Society* xiv (1925–6), 25–6, pl. xxix.
[3] *V.C.H.* vi (1959), 183.
[4] Ibid. and *V.C.H. Berkshire* iii (1923), 338–9.
[5] Late 14th-c. glass at Aldermaston (Berks.). Greening Lamborn (1949), 13. See also Bodl. Lib. Ashmole MS. 850, f. 19.
[6] Visitations (1871), 36, 52.
[7] Blomfield, op. cit. 41, 52. Greening Lamborn (1949), 131. The medieval presentations are listed in Bodl. Lib. MS. Top. Oxon. d. 460, p. 93.   [8] Bodl. Lib. MS. Top. Oxon. c. 51, f. 32, op. cit.

Fragments: Five border pieces, each a lion statant or, alternating with pieces of plain ruby. 14th c.

Foliage designs: white glass painted with trails of foliage, oak, hawthorn, and kidney-shaped leaves, probably from geometric grisaille designs. 14th c. White herbage, the base of a green shaft from a Crucifixion(?), 14th c.; a human ankle beside foliage, subject unknown, 14th c. Quarries: two complete, eleven fragmentary, type 23, 15th c.

MAPLEDURHAM

ST. MARGARET

O.S. SU 670 767.

MS. SOURCES

London. Guildhall Library, City of London, MS. 439/3. J. Dunkin, *History of Oxfordshire. Langtree Hundred 1823–1825.*

PRINTED

The Topographer i (1789), 409–14.

Manning, P., *Oxford Journal of Monumental Brasses* i (1899), 287–95.

Nelson (1913), 164.

Cooke, A. H., 'The Early History of Mapledurham', *O.R.S.* vii (1925).

Greening Lamborn (1949), 140–1.

Pevsner (1974), 694.

The windows of the church were recorded in the seventeenth century by Richard St. George[1] and Richard Symmonds.[2] Their accounts make it possible to establish the date and original position of some of the surviving glass.

The Bardolf aisle on the south side of the church was built by Sir Robert Bardolf before his death in 1395.[3] Its east window contained the figures of Sir Robert and his wife Amice together with shields of their arms.[4] They also provided one of the windows of the chancel.[5] All that remains of their benefactions is a single shield of the Bardolf arms now in the east window of the chancel (I, A1).

In the mid fifteenth century two windows were made for members of the Iwardby family, tenants of the manor.[6] One of these was above the tomb of John Iwardby senior (d. 1470). Its particular interest is the use of English for its lengthy inscriptions.[7] The only remnant of this window is a restored shield of Neville impaling Beauchamp now in I, A4. The other Iwardby window was probably made for Jane Iwardby (d. 1476), as it included figures of angels holding shields of arms of her father, her two husbands, and her second husband's mother.[8] Two of the shields and supporters are now in I, A2 and A3. The three figures of saints each from the centre of a canopy design now in I, 2a, 2b, and 2c may have been incorporated in one of the two Iwardby windows.

I

2a. St. Stephen   PLATE 38 (*d*)

h. 0·23 m. w. 0·50 m. Figure: h. 0·18 m. w. 0·14 m. St. Stephen facing three-quarters right, nimbed, he wears a deacon's dalmatic, holds a book in his left hand, in his right hand the stones of his martyrdom.

Condition. Incomplete, originally a full-length figure as 2b below. The canopy surround is all modern.

Colour and Technique. Painted on white glass, details picked out in yellow stain. Behind the saint a white hanging patterned with stylized birds and foliage in yellow stain. Very delicate stippled modelling.

Iconography. Standard late medieval form, vested as a deacon and holding the stones of his martyrdom.

Style and Design. See 2c.

Date. Mid 15th c.

[1] Bodl. Lib. Rawlinson MS. B103. Cooke, op. cit. 123–9.
[2] B.L. Harleian MS. 965. Cooke, op. cit. 123–9.
[3] Cooke, op. cit. 32. 'Some Oxfordshire Wills', ed. J. Weaver and A. Beardwood, *O.R.S.* xxxix (1958), 8–9.
[4] Cooke, op. cit. 124–5.
[5] Ibid. 125–6.
[6] Ibid. 44–52.
[7] Ibid. 126–7. See also Lost Glass.
[8] Cooke, op. cit. 128. See also Lost Glass.

2b. St. Sitha (Zita of Lucca) PLATE 38 (e)

Figure: h. 0·28 m. w. 0·14 m.

St. Sitha, full length facing three-quarters left, nimbed, she holds a book in her right hand and two keys hang on a cord in her left hand.

Condition. The figure and surround are complete, painted on a single piece of glass, very slight corrosion. The canopy surround and its background are all modern.

Colour and Technique. Painted on white glass, saint's hair and border of nimbus in yellow stain; she stands on a black and white chequered floor. Behind her a white hanging with a repeated foliage design in yellow stain. Very delicate stipple shading.

Iconography. There are a number of English 15th-c. representations of a female saint named 'Sitha' or 'Citha', for example: stained glass at Mells (Somerset),[1] the rood screen at Barton Turf (Norfolk),[2] and the Kildare Book of Hours of c. 1425.[3] Two examples show quite conclusively that the name is an anglicized form of Zita; an English 15th-c. chasuble at Stonyhurst College made for the Bonvici family of Lucca resident in London,[4] and a 15th-c. English copy of her life by Fatinello dei Fatinelli.[5]

St. Zita was a serving woman in the household of the Fatinelli family of Lucca. She died in 1272.[6] Her cult became very widespread in the 15th c. but she was not canonized until 1696.[7] Her cult in England merits more detailed investigation, she has been confused by some writers with St. Osyth of Chich.[8]

Style and Design. See 2c.

Date. As above.

2c. St. Barbara

h. 0·23 m. w. 0·50 m. Figure: h. 0·18 m. w. 0·14 m.

St. Barbara, nimbed facing three-quarters left, holding a miniature tower in her right hand and a palm branch in her left hand.

Condition. Incomplete, originally a full-length figure as 2b

above, slight corrosion, old leaded repair. The canopy surround below the tie-bar is all modern.

Colour and Technique. Painted on white glass, the saint's hair, palm, and border of nimbus in yellow stain, behind the saint a white tapestry hanging patterned with stylized foliage in yellow stain. Very delicate stippled modelling.

Iconography. Standard form, holding a miniature tower,[9] symbolizing her imprisonment by her father, and a martyr's palm.[10]

Style and Design. The three figures are closely related to each other. The device of setting the figure against a figured hanging is common to all three, the details of the pattern differ, however. The SS. Sitha and Barbara are drawn from a standard cartoon, the heads and drapery with the mantle hanging over the right arm and a bunch of folds against the body by the left hand, are identical. The painting is competent but the figures are somewhat stereotyped and lifeless. The size and shape of the panels with a semicircular head suggests that they were each designed for the centre of a canopy design. This class of design is not common, but it is found from the second quarter of the 14th c.[11]

Date. As above.

3a. Canopy

h. 0·32 m. w. 0·50 m.

Condition. Very restored, only the pinnacles and towers in the top cusps are genuine.

Colour and Technique. Painted on white glass, strong yellow stain and stippled modelling. Set against a plain blue background.

Style and Design. The over-all design is a 19th-c. restorer's very sympathetic reconstruction, it is impossible to say to what extent it might copy a lost design.

Date. Mid 15th c.

3c. Canopy

h. 0·32 m. w. 0·50 m.

---

[1] Emblems: three loaves and two keys, named 'Sca Sitha'. C. Woodforde, *Stained Glass in Somerset* (1946), 181. F. Bond and B. Camm, *Roodscreens and Lofts* (1909), 226–7.

[2] Emblems; rosary, bunch of keys, and a bag. J. Gunn, *Illustrations of the Rood Screen at Barton Turf* (1869), pl. 1.

[3] Emblems: book, rosary, bunch of keys, and loaf of bread. *Memoria sancte sitha virginis.* New York. Pierpont Morgan Library, MS. M105, f. 83.

[4] Emblems: book rosary, and two keys 'Sca Sitha'. *The Stonyhurst Magazine* iii (1888), ii (1909), 226.

[5] Sotheby's Sale, 30 November 1971. Bibliotheca Phillippica, Part VI, Lot 509, Catalogue 66–8. Phillipps MS. 8831, f. 48. Text of Life, f. 148b, miniature of St. Zita holding a book and household keys.

[6] *Acta Sanctorum*, iii April (Antwerp 1675), 499–527.

[7] E. W. Kemp, *Canonisation and Authority in the Western Church* (1948), 124. A. Saint-Clair, *Vie de Sainte Zite* (1920). L. Schlegel, *Die Heilige Zita, Diensmago in Lucca* (1936). P. Puccinelli, *S. Zita, Vergine Lucchese* (1949).

[8] An article in *The Times* newspaper, Tuesday, 24 May 1927, has added to the confusion.

[9] The tower is very plain and at first sight looks more like an ointment-pot, suggesting a St. Mary Magdalen, my mistaken identification in Pevsner (1974), 694. However, by comparison with the two related figures of SS. Mary Magdalen and Barbara at Burford, where the same design is used for both the ointment-pot and tower, the identification seems justified.

[10] *Golden Legend* vi. 198–205.

[11] For example in York Minster, windows n. XXVI, n. XXVII, n. XXX and s. XXXVI, canopy figures.

Condition. Very restored, the few genuine pieces are the same design as 3a above.

Date. As above.

A1. Shield of Bardolph

h. 0·20 m. w. 0·20 m.

Gules three cinquefoils argent BARDOLPH.

Condition. Restored, the lower cinquefoil, the lower right of the field of the shield, and all the surround are modern. The ruby glass is very corroded.

Colour and Technique. Pot-metal ruby, too corroded to see if it has any pattern diaper on it. The cinquefoils are simply drawn.

Date. Possibly from a window of the Bardolph aisle completed before 1395. However, a Bardolph shield was noted in a chancel window in the 17th c. See Lost Glass below.

A2. Shield of Missenden, Angel Supporter

h. 0·35 m. w. 0·20 m.

Or a cross engrailed gules (in dexter chief a martlet sable) MIS-SENDEN.

Condition. The head and shoulders of the angel above the shield are a modern copy of that in A3 below. The shield is very corroded. It is impossible to see if the recorded martlet charge survives. Fragments of an inscription, in black-letter script:

|S|CUDE| ?

set inside out.

Colour and Technique. Shield in pot-metal ruby and ochre glass, the engrailing of the cross painted on the cross, now very faint. Angel: white glass, details of feathers and alb in yellow stain.

Date. Greening Lamborn read the shield as *or a cross gules* for Burgh, Earl of Ulster, and associated it with the Bardolph family.[1] It seems more likely that it is the Missenden arms recorded in a north window of the church in the 17th c. (See A3.) Mid 15th c., after *c.* 1440 and before 1476.

A3. Shield of Annesley, Angel Supporter

h. 0·35 m. w. 0·20 m.

Paly or and azure on a bend gules a mullet argent ANNESLEY.

Inscriptions. In black-letter script:

|d(omin)us tecu(m)| |Iwar|[dby]|

Condition. The shield and the upper part of the angel above it are set inside out. Slight corrosion, the angel disfigured by old leaded repair. The '*dominus tecum*' is an insertion of old glass.

Colour and Technique. The shield is in plain coloured glass no decorative diaper on the field or charge. The mullet is abraded out of the ruby glass of the bend. Angel: white glass, hair, apparel of alb and feathers picked out in yellow stain, stippled shading.

Iconography. The inserted inscription is part of the archangel's salutation to the Virgin Mary at the Annunciation *Ave Maria gracia plena dominus tecum*. No other vestige of an Annunciation scene remains. For shields with angel supporters see Kidlington (1, 3a, 3c).

Date. The shield was originally in a north window of the church and was set above an inscription 'Jane Iwardeby'[2] for Jane, daughter of Sir Hugh Annesley, who married John Iwardby 1440.[3] She died in 1476.[4] The two shields A2 and A3 were part of a series of four commemorating Jane Iwardby and her two husbands. Mid 15th c. after *c.* 1440 and before 1476.

A4. Shield of Neville impaling Beauchamp

h. 0·20 m. w. 0·20 m.

Gules on a saltire argent a rose gules NEVILLE *impaling quarterly 1, 4 gules on a fess between six crosses crosslets or a crescent sable* BEAUCHAMP *2, 3 checky or and azure* WARENNE Edward Neville, Lord Abergavenney and his wife Elizabeth Beauchamp.

Condition. The shield is set inside out and is much restored. The field of the Neville arms and the lower half of the saltire are modern, as are the third and fourth quarters of the Beauchamp arms. The shield has been cut down to fit its present position.

Colour and Technique. Pot-metal coloured glass, the crosslets of the Beauchamp arms are abraded out of the ruby field and stained yellow.

Date. Originally in a window commemorating the Iwardby family and their alliances. After 1461 and probably before 1476.[5]

s. III[6]

2a. Composite Panel (condition and arrangement in 1963)

A half-length frontal angel holding a crown. Painted on white glass, the hair and crown in yellow stain, stippled modelling. Set inside out. 16th c.

5a–5f. Canopies (condition and arrangement in 1963)

Composite panels of fragments of canopies, white and yellow stain.

[1] Greening Lamborn (1949), 140–1.
[2] See Lost Glass.
[3] Cooke, op. cit. 47–8.   [4] Ibid. 53–4.
[5] See Lost Glass.
[6] The Bardolph aisle is private property and can be viewed by arrangement. The glass was rearranged in 1975 by Mr. Laurence Lee.

w. 1

2b. Canopy Finial (condition and arrangement in 1963)

h. 0·07 m. w. 0·11 m.

The apex of a shaft, white and yellow stain. Mid 15th c.

A3, A4. Foliage Designs *in situ* (condition and arrangement in 1963)

h. 0·15 m. w. 0·15 m.

At the centre a rosette with two offspringing leaves, white and yellow stain. Mid 15th c.

Lost Glass

The windows were recorded by Richard St. George in 1615 and by Richard Symmonds in 1644.[1] In using these notes priority has been given to Richard St. George as the glass was more complete when he recorded it. The following is a collation of both texts.

Bardolph Aisle

(Drawing of the monumental brass to Sir Robert Bardolph, d. 1395.)

'In the Chappel window where the said Robert lieth buried: *Orate pro Roberto Bardolph milite et Amica uxore eius qui istam Capellam Construxerunt.*'

Kneeling figure of Sir Robert Bardolph, above him a shield: *gules three cinquefoils argent* (BARDOLPH).

Kneeling figure of his wife, Amice, daughter of Sir Alan Buxhull, K.G. Above her a shield: *argent a lion rampant azure fretty argent* (BUXHULL).

Sit Robert Bardolph's will of 1395 suggests that the south aisle chapel was built during his lifetime, as he leaves: '*corpus meum ad sepeliendum in quadam aela ecclesie parochialis de Maplederham Gurney*'; he also provided for the repair of the aisle.[2] His wife's will of 1412 is somewhat more precise: '*Item lego ad reperacionem et sustentacionem nove capelle in parte australi dicte ecclesie de Mapledreham modo constructe x marcas*'.[3]

St. George and Symmonds concur in their accounts of the windows of this aisle. Symmonds also records a Bardolph figure and shield in the east window of the chancel.[4]

'A north window of the church.'

Four shields, 'not so old as the former', held by angels.

Sable a pelican in her piety argent (LYNDE). Written under on a scroll: ——*Lyn*——*de*——.

Argent on a saltire engrailed sable a cinquefoil argent, on a chief sable two pierced mullets argent (IWARDBY). Written under on a scroll: *Iwardeby.*

Paly of six argent and azure, on a bend gules a mullet argent (ANNESLEY). Written under on a scroll: *Jane Iwardeby.*

Or a cross engrailed gules in the first quarter a martlet (MISSENDEN). Written under on a scroll: *Missenden.*

The third and fourth shields remain, now set in I, A2 and A3. The shields commemorate Jane, daughter of Sir Hugh Annesley,[5] and her two husbands William Lynde (d. 1438)[6] and John Iwardby (d. 1470).[7] The Missenden arms commemorate her second husband's mother, Katherine, who was daughter and heiress of Sir Bernard Missenden[8] (Jane Iwardby, d. 1476).[9] The heraldic evidence therefore suggests a dating of after 1440, the date of her second marriage, and before her death in 1476.

The other shields of Iwardby recorded in the 17th c. notes do not have the cinquefoil on the saltire; however, this coat was certainly borne by John Iwardby, junior, son of John and Jane Iwardby.[10]

'North window of the chancel.'

First light: kneeling figures of John Iwardby and his wife Jane. Scrolls: *Almighti Jesu my maker bring me to Bliss John Iwardby thelder.*

Mary moder I you pray help me Jane Daughter of Hugh Ansly knight.

Shield: *argent a saltire engrailed sable on a chief sable two pierced mullets argent* (IWARDBY) impaling *paly argent and azure on a bend gules a mullet (argent)* (ANNESLEY).[11]

Second light: kneeling figures of John Iwardby and his wife Katherine and their deceased son. Scrolls: *God have mercy on me John the son of John and Jane Iwarbye.*

Help Mary mother gracious Lady me Katerin daughter of Edward Neville Lord Abergavenney.

God have mercy on me John the son of John the son of John.

Inscription below the figures: *John Iwarby and Katherine his wife specialy you pray to say as oft as ye this window see ii deprofundis for them Edward Elizabeth John and Jane there fathers and mothers or on(e) pater noster and on(e) Ave and for the soule of John wich here by the walle lieth sonne of the said John and Katherine of whome almighti Ihesu have mercy.*

Below the figures and inscriptions are four shields: *quarterly 1, 4 FRANCE MODERN 2, 3 ENGLAND impaling*

---

[1] See p. 134 n. 2, 3.

[2] Cooke, op. cit. 32.

[3] Ibid. 41, 133.

[4] Ibid. 124–6.

[5] Ibid. 43–4.

[6] Ibid. 44.

[7] Ibid. 47–8, 52.

[8] Ibid. 47–8.

[9] Ibid. 53.

[10] Iwardby Hours, Bodl. Lib. MS. Gough Liturg. 19, ff. 15ᵛ–16ʳ.

[11] St. George and Symmonds differ in their accounts of this shield. It seems probable that it had been broken and repaired when Symmonds noted it.

(*gules*) *a saltire* (*argent*) NEVILLE. Cecily Neville, wife of Richard Duke of York, mother of Edward IV.

Quarterly of argent with gules a fret or, over all a bend sable DESPENSER *impaling quarterly* 1, 4 *quarterly* i, iv FRANCE ii, iii ENGLAND *a label of three points*, 2, 3 *quarterly* i, iv CASTILE ii, iii LEON. Thomas Despenser Earl of Gloucester and his wife Constance.

Gules on a saltire argent a rose gules NEVILLE OF ABERGAVENNY *impaling quarterly* 1, *gules on a fess between six martlets or* (*recte cross-crosslets or*) *a crescent sable* BEAUCHAMP OF ABERGAVENNY 2, *checky or and azure* WARENNE 3, *quarterly of argent with gules a fret or, over all a bend sable* DESPENSER 4, *or three chevrons gules* CLARE. Arms of Edward Neville Lord Abergavenny and his wife Elizabeth. *Argent a saltire engrailed sable, on a chief sable two pierced mullets argent* IWARDBY *impaling quarterly* 1, NEVILLE OF ABERGAVENNY 2, BEAUCHAMP OF ABERGA-

VENNY 3, WARENNE 4, CLARE 5, DESPENSER. Arms of John Iwardby and his wife Katherine.

Date. The window was a double commemoration of John Iwardby senior, his wife Jane, their son John junior, and his wife Katherine. The shields of arms had particular reference to Katherine, the daughter of Edward Neville, Lord Abergavenny, and the distinguished connections of her family. A tentative terminal date is suggested by the undifferenced arms of France and England quarterly impaling Neville which were used by Cecily, Duchess of York, after her son succeeded to the throne as Edward IV in 1461.[1] The window was above the tomb of John Iwardby senior (d. 1470) so it is possible that the window was about the same date.

Although the 17th-c. notes are only concerned with the donor figures and heraldry; the bidding scrolls suggest that the donor figures were associated with figures of Christ and the Virgin Mary.

MARSH BALDON
ST. PETER

O.S. SP 563 992.

MS. SOURCES

Oxford. Bodleian Library, MS. Top. Oxon. b. 75, ff. 53–5. Wyatt Papers 18th–19th c. Copy of Powell's notes dated 1805.

PRINTED

Parker (1846), 386–8.

Nelson (1913), 164.
Bouchier (1918), 82.
P.C. (1920), 15.
Bouchier (1932), 129–30.
Greening Lamborn (1949), 105–8.
Woodforde, C., *English Stained and Painted Glass* (1954), 14.
V.C.H. v (1957), 46.
Baker, A., *English Stained Glass* (1960), 110, pls. 23, 24.
Pevsner (1974), 699.

The surviving glass is a varied collection, dating from the late thirteenth to the sixteenth century. It is now distributed over two windows in the chancel. There are only two pieces which are probably *in situ*, the two censing angels in the tracery of the fifteenth-century east window, (I, A2 and A5). The glass has been moved about quite considerably. The two fourteenth-century shields (I, 3a and 3c) had been moved to the east window before 1660.[2] The present arrangement of the glass was probably made in the second half of the eighteenth century. The glass in the east window was all removed to a window in the north aisle in 1806[3] and returned to the east window in 1890.[4]

There are a few fragments of thirteenth-century vine foliage and a small roundel of the head and shoulders of a bishop which is probably late thirteenth-century (I, A4). Unfortunately these are so excessively decayed that any dating must be tentative.

There are two fourteenth-century shields of the arms of Giffard and de la Mare (I, 3a and 3c). They are

---

[1] Birch iii (1894), 12093. Add. Chart. 15478, dated 1477.
[2] P.C. (1920), 15.

[3] *V.C.H.* v (1957), 46.
[4] Ibid., citing Bodl. Lib. MS. Top. Oxon. c. 105, ff. 108–14.

identical in size and shape, correspond in technique, and presumably belong together, although their original location is not known. The vigorous drawing and absence of diaper patterns suggests an early fourteenth-century dating. The de la Mare family held the manor of Marsh Baldon from before 1166 until the death of Robert de la Mare in 1382.[1] The Giffard shield probably refers to either Sir John Giffard of Brimpsfield (d. 1299) or his son John, Lord Giffard, executed 1322, leaving no issue.[2] Although they held no lands in Marsh Baldon they held the important township of Burford.[3] Greening Lamborn explained the display here of the Giffard arms by relating it to their inheritance of lands held in the manor in the thirteenth century by the Morteyn family.[4] However, the inheritance by marriage was late in the fourteenth century and can hardly be relevant to the shield. Furthermore this is a different branch of the family, namely the Giffards of Twyford (Bucks.).[5] They originally bore the Giffard arms differenced with a blue label,[6] which they subsequently dropped, but this cannot have been until after the death of John, Lord Giffard, in 1322. If the glass is later than 1322 it doubtless commemorates John Giffard of Twyford (1301–69). He inherited the lands of his maternal grandfather in Fringford and Somerton in 1328.[7] The latter manor adjoins Upper Heyford, which was held by the de la Mares.[8]

The other fourteenth-century glass is of very high quality, but unfortunately little remains. All that survive are an incomplete St. Anne instructing the Virgin and a male head from a figure of similar size (I, 2b and 1b). Woodforde attributed this glass to the workshop responsible for the three northern windows of the Latin Chapel in Christ Church, Oxford.[9] The resemblances are very close, particularly the drawing of the heads and the expressive hands, with long articulate fingers. Woodforde dated the Christ Church windows c. 1365. There is some historical evidence to suggest a dating of some twenty years earlier.[10]

The fifteenth-century glass, although more extensive and complete, is badly obscured by extensive corrosion. Two large figures remain of the Virgin Mary and St. John Evangelist (I, 2a, 2c). These came from a Crucifixion window; there is no trace remaining of the crucifix, possibly a victim of the seventeenth-century iconoclasm.[11] Although it is impossible to be certain, there is some slight evidence in the cut-line of the glass, to suggest that the present arrangement of these figures against a background of square white quarries is original. It is also possible that the large and very striking fleurs-de-lis and foliage border pieces, which now form the borders of the main lights, also came from this Crucifixion window. Their date is probably mid fifteenth century. Two incomplete figures of censing angels in the tracery of the east window are probably in situ (A2 and A5). An incomplete figure of a cleric (A3) is painted in exactly the same style and belongs with them. These are to be dated in the second quarter of the fifteenth century.

A shield of the arms of Burton (s. II, 3b) has been dated by Greening Lamborn as sixteenth-century.[12] The absence of decorative diapers makes a confident dating difficult. However, the drawing of the charges favours a fifteenth-century date. The shield is not recorded in the antiquarian notes and its presence here has not been accounted for.

The sixteenth-century glass, except for one fragment, is all heraldic and consists of shields of arms, each encircled by an elaborate wreath of foliage. There are three shields of the royal arms, two of these very incomplete (I, 1b and s. II, 3a), and four shields of the Pollard family and their alliances (I, 1a, 1c, 3b, and s. II, 1a, 1b). The wreaths for the royal arms are embellished with pomegranates and the initials H. R. indicating a date in the reign of Henry VIII (1509–47). It seems probable that this glass came from the Pollard house at Nuneham, brought here when the house was pulled down in 1764. The evidence for this and the heraldry of the Pollard shields are fully considered by Greening Lamborn and are not repeated here.[13]

[1] V.C.H. v (1957), 33.
[2] G.E.C. v, 639.
[3] Cal. Inq. Post Mortem iii, no. 544, ibid.
[4] Greening Lamborn (1949), 105.
[5] See the pedigree by G. Moriarty in The Genealogist, N.S. xxxviii (1922), 202–3.
[6] See N. H. Nicolas, A Roll of Arms of the Reign of Edward the Second (1829), 3, 29.

[7] V.C.H. v (1957), 46; vi (1959), 128, 292.
[8] Ibid. 183.
[9] Woodforde, op. cit. 14.
[10] This evidence will be discussed in the Oxford City volume of this series.
[11] Woodforde, op. cit. 45, gives some examples.
[12] Greening Lamborn (1949), 108.
[13] Greening Lamborn (1949), 106–8.

I

1a. Composite Panel

h. 0·54 m. w. 0·46 m.

Shield of Pollard quartering Davye.

h. 0·20 m. w. 0·15 m. with surround h. 0·48 m. w. 0·30 m.

Quarterly 1, 4, *argent a chevron azure between three escallops gules* POLLARD 2, 3 *argent a chevron sable between three mullets gules pierced argent* DAVYE.

Encircled by a wreath of green foliage, with purple bands, a pomegranate flower at the top, ornamental side plaques, and a cartouche at the bottom.

Condition. Complete, the paint has worn very thin.

Colour and Technique. Shield, coloured charges are in pot-metal glass leaded in, the mullets abraded, the fields diapered with a foliage design. Wreath and bands pot-metal glass, the other accessories white glass and yellow stain.

Date. Early 16th c.

Quarries: two complete and two half-complete, type 9, white and yellow stain, very decayed. 15th c.

Border pieces: six complete, each a fleur-de-lis encircled by foliage, white and yellow stain, picked out of matt black ground. Three others, each a quatrefoil leaf in a diamond-shape frame with offspringing trefoil leaves, white and yellow stain. Three quarries type 12, fragment of quarry type 9. All 15th c.

1b. Composite Panel

h. 0·54 m. w. 0·46 m.

Shield of England.

h. 0·21 m. w. 0·18 m. with surround h. 0·43 m. w. 0·30 m.

Quarterly 1, 4 *azure three fleurs-de-lis or* FRANCE 2, 3 *gules three lions passant gardant in pale or* ENGLAND. Encircled by a green wreath with purple bands, the side plaques inscribed H and R, the lower cartouche *DIEV ET MON DROIT*.

Condition. Complete, but the paint has worn very thin.

Colour and Technique. Shield: fleurs-de-lis separately leaded in yellow stain, field pot-metal blue diapered with a foliage design, the England quarters were each a single piece of flashed ruby, the lions abraded and stained yellow. Wreaths and bands, pot-metal, the accessories white and yellow stain.

Date. Early 16th c.

Quarry: one incomplete, type 9. Border pieces: as 1a both types, also four quarries type 12. 15th c. Man's head: painted in brown on white glass, hair and beard in yellow stain, very corroded, style as 2b below. One fragment of quarry type 4. Date: second quarter to mid 14th c.

1c. Composite Panel

h. 0·54 m. w. 0·46 m.

Shield of Pollard.

h. 0·20 m. w. 0·15 m. with surround h. 0·48 m. w. 0·30 m.

Quarterly of five: 1, *argent a chevron azure between three escallops gules* POLLARD 2, *argent a chevron sable between three roundels (?) gules pierced argent* DAVYE 3, *argent a chevron sable between three hearts sable* BARON 4, *argent a chevron sable between three hunters horns sable* CORNU 5, *argent three eagles displayed gules* DODESCOMBE.

Encircled by a wreath, identical to 1a above.

Condition. Complete, the paint worn very thin, in parts completely gone; this prevents a precise reading of the charges in the second quarter but they look like roses.

Colour and Technique. Shield: coloured charges in pot-metal glass, the roundels 2 and the eagles 5 are abraded. The sable charges painted in brown on white glass. Wreath light-purple foliage, dark-blue bands, accessories as 1a.

Date. Early 16th c.

Quarries: several type 9, three painted on square pieces of glass, see 2a below. Border pieces as 1a.

2a. The Virgin Mary

h. 0·75 m. w. 0·46 m.

Nimbed, full length, facing three-quarters right, tiled plinth at feet, quarry background.

Condition. Incomplete, patched with fragments of 15th-c. glass. The figure is very corroded, with lichen on both surfaces. Intrusion of quarry type 12 into drapery.

Colour and Technique. Painted in brown on white glass, stipple shading, slight use of yellow stain, hair, drapery hem, and patterned floor. Figure set on a groundwork of square white quarries, type 9. This arrangement could be original, see 2c.

Border: fleurs-de-lis as 1a.

Iconography, Style, and Design. See 2c.

Date. Mid 15th c.

2b. St. Anne and The Virgin   PLATE 38 (*a*)

h. 0·75 m. w. 0·46 m.

The infant Virgin standing on the left holding an open book from which St. Anne teaches. Canopy above.

Condition. Incomplete, the upper half of St. Anne and the Virgin's head and arms survive, patched with alien pieces of 14th-c. glass, all corroded.

Colour and Technique. St. Anne's nimbus, head with veil and wimple all painted on a large single piece of white glass, nimbus and hair cauls in yellow stain. Her mantle is deep-green pot-metal glass with a ruby clasp, over a deep-ochre pot-metal tunic. The Virgin's head and nimbus in white glass, hair in yellow stain, tunic in pot-metal ruby. Plain background, very streaky ruby. The figures stand beneath a trefoil arch surmounted by a small canopy, incomplete at the top, all in white and yellow stain.

Iconography. St. Anne instructing the Virgin to read, see Beckley n. IV.

Style and Design. Attributed by Woodforde[1] to the workshop responsible for the Latin Chapel windows, Christ Church, Oxford.

Date. Second quarter to mid 14th c.

Border pieces: Leaf in diamond-shaped frame, as 1a, 15th c.

2c. St. John Evangelist

h. 0·75 m. w. 0·46 m.

Nimbed, full length, facing three-quarters left, tiled plinth at feet, quarry background.

Condition. Incomplete, made up with alien fragments of 15h-c. glass. The figure is very corroded, with lichen on both surfaces.

Colour and Technique. Painted in brown on white glass, stippled shading, details of nimbus, hair, drapery hem, and pattern of roses on mantle and pattern floor in yellow stain. Set against a groundwork of square white quarries, type 9. The shaped pieces adjacent to the left foot and right elbow, each of two quarries with the lead line between them painted on the glass, suggests this arrangement is original. Border: fleurs-de-lis as 1a.

Iconography. St. John and the Virgin, 2a, from a Crucifixion; they stand in the traditional postures of grief, the Virgin with her hand on her breast and covered head, St. John resting his head on his raised right hand.

Style and Design. Simple arrangement of figure standing on tiled plinth, quarry background, no coloured glass. The quality of the drawing is obscured by the excessive decay.

Date. Mid 15th c.

3a. Composite Panel

h. 0·51 m. w. 0·46 m.
Shield of Giffard.
h. 0·33 m. w. 0·28 m.
Gules three lions passant in pale or GIFFARD.

Condition. The head of the middle lion is missing, very repaired and corroded. Between 1806 and 1890 this was set inside out.[2]

Colour and Technique. Painted in brown on plain coloured pot-metal glass.

Date. Early 14th c.

Quarries: as 2a, 2c. Border pieces: fleurs-de-lis as 1a.

3b. Composite Panel

h. 0·51 m. w. 0·46 m.
Shield of Pollard quartering Davye.
h. 0·20 m. w. 0·15 m. with surround h. 0·33 m. w. 0·30 m.
Quarterly coat identical to 1a, but here in a circular green wreath with red and blue bands and similar plaques and cartouches.

Condition. All very worn.

Colour and Technique. As 1a.

Date. Early 16th c.

Border pieces: fleurs-de-lis as 1a.

3c. Composite Panel

h. 0·51 m. w. 0·46 m.
Shield of de la Mare.
h. 0·33 m. w. 0·28 m.
Gules two lions passant gardant in pale or DE LA MARE.

Condition. Corroded and repaired.

Colour and Technique. as 3a.

Date. Early 14th c.

Quarries: as 2a, 2c, Border pieces: fleurs-de-lis as 1a.

A1. Composite Panel

Shield of England.
h. 0·21 m. w. 0·18 m.

Condition. Shield complete, enclosed by incomplete wreath. Heraldry, technique, and colour identical with 1b, except wreath, which is blue with red bands.

Date. Early 16th c.

A2. Censing Angel

h. 0·35 m. w. 0·18 m.

Condition. In situ but incomplete, made up with alien fragments.

Colour and Technique. Painted in brown on white glass, details of costume and herbage in yellow stain; background:

---

[1] Woodforde, op. cit. 14.

[2] Recorded by Parker (1846), 386-8.

yellow stain, patterned with contiguous circles, broadly painted.

Iconography. This and its companion figure, A5, were pendent to two figures, at A3 and A4, perhaps Christ and the Virgin.

Style and Design. Although very different in scale the drapery painting and head type are very like the Virgin and St. John Evangelist (2a and 2c), and are probably by the same glass painter.

Date. Mid 15th c.

A3. Composite Panel

h. 0·35 m. w. 0·18 m.

Donor figure: a priest, tonsured and in prayer, wearing a blue habit, incomplete, lower half missing. The work of the same painter as A2. This figure was probably originally in A6.

Date. Mid 15th c. The remainder of this light is small scraps, including the centre portion of the pedestal to St. John Evangelist. Fragment of quarry type 12.

A4. Composite Panel

h. 0·35 m. w. 0·18 m.

Condition. Excessive exterior corrosion, the glass virtually opaque.

Roundel: frontal head of a bishop, perhaps late 13th c., but all the details indistinct.

Fragments of 13th-c. white vine foliage, painted in outline, background of hatched lines.

A5. Censing Angel

h. 0·35 m. w. 0·18 m.

Condition. In situ, incomplete, head and shoulders missing. Painted from the same cartoon as A2, but reversed. Fragment of quarry type 5.

Date. Mid 15th c.

A6. Composite Panel

h. 0·35 m. w. 0·18 m.

Small fragments of foliage designs and the torso of a figure. Fragment of quarry type 12.

s. II

1a. Shield of Pollard quartering Davye

h. 0·20 m. w. 0·15 m. with surround h. 0·46 m. w. 0·28 m.

POLLARD *quartering* DAVYE, identical with I, 1a except that here the wreath is blue with green bands.

Condition. Complete, except for the pomegranate at the top of the wreath. The paint has worn very thin.

Date. Early 16th c.

1b. Shield of Pollard

h. 0·20 m. w. 0·15 m. with surround h. 0·46 m. w. 0·28 m.

Quarterly coat of five, identical with I, 1c, except that here the eagles of the fifth quarter are arranged one and two.

Condition. The encircling wreath is composite; all very worn.

Date. Early 16th c.

3a. Composite Panel

Shield of England.

h. 0·20 m. w. 0·15 m. with surround h. 0·46 m. w. 0·28 m.

FRANCE *quartering* ENGLAND; quarters 1 and 2 only remain, incomplete and very decayed. Fragmentary wreath, side plaques each inscribed HR with a Tudor rose between the letters.

Date. Early 16th c.

3b. Shield of Burton

h. 0·17 m. w. 0·17 m.

Sable a chevron or between three owls argent BURTON.

Condition. Complete, very well preserved.

Colour and Technique. Painted on a single piece of white glass, the field matt black paint, the chevron in yellow stain.

Date. 15th c. (?)

A1–3. Fragments

Very broken, mostly 16th c., many set inside out.

Head of a Sibyl (?)

h. 0·20 m. w. 0·13 m.

A woman wearing an elaborate head-dress.

Condition. A fragment from a large figure.

Colour and Technique. Painted on white glass, stippled shading and needle-point hatching, turban in yellow stain.

Iconography. Uncertain, possibly a Sibyl.

Date. Early 16th c.

MARSTON

ST. NICHOLAS

O.S. SP 528 089.

MS. SOURCE

Oxford. Bodleian Library, MS. Top. Oxon. d. 92, ff. 87–8. Church Notes by F. H. Woods, 1882.

PRINTED

Parker (1846), 185–8.
Nelson (1913), 164.
Bouchier (1918), 82.
Pevsner (1974), 700.

I

The main lights contain modern glass figures on a groundwork of quarries which are copied from the original surviving quarries at the heads of each light and the bases of the first and second lights. All 15th c.

Each quarry h. 0·15 m. w. 0·10 m.

1a. Quarries types 20 and 21. 15th c.

2a. Quarries types 20 and 21. 15th c.

3a. The plain end of a white scroll, originally set on a groundwork of quarries types 20 and 21. Part of an incomplete quarry painted on the same piece of glass.

2b. Inscribed Scroll

w. 0·07 m.

Part of a scroll inscribed in black-letter script:

|[adoramus deum]|creatorem|nostrum|

The first part of the scroll is modern, the second part is painted on the same glass as the adjacent quarries, type 20. The scroll was more complete in 1882 but even then was partly illegible. Woods transcribed it as:

'nostrum....creatorum caeli.'[1]

The scroll probably refers to St. Peter's verse of the Creed:
'Credo in Deum patrem omnipotentem creatorem celi et terre.'[2]
(See n. II, 1b.)

4a, 4b, 4c. Quarries and Roundels

The cusps retain part of their original quarry glazing with three roundels in the cusps of each light. All the glass is corroded, and the roundels have been cut down to accommodate the insertion of the modern figures. Quarries as 1a.

4a. Three roundels

l. to r.   M (for Maria)
Ihc̄. (Jesus)
Rose

All are painted on white glass with yellow stain. Four quarries, type 20, one is painted on the same piece of glass as the roundel with the 'M' initial. Fragment of an inscription in black-letter script:

|.RO.|

4b. Three Roundels

l. to r.   M (for Maria)
Ihc̄. (Jesus)
M(ER)CI

Four quarries, type 20, two are painted on the same piece of glass as the adjacent roundels. All white glass and yellow stain.

4c. Two Roundels

l. to r.   M(ER)CI
Ihc̄. (Jesus)

Three quarries, type 20, one painted on the same glass as adjacent roundel. White glass and yellow stain.

A3. Fragments

Lower part of drapery of figure facing three-quarters right, white glass and yellow stain; yellow-stain foliage pattern. Fragment of St. Peter, a hand holding two keys, one white, the other yellow stain. 15th c.

B2. Monogram

Christus monogram: x̄p̄c̄. White glass painted in a black background, a pattern of repeated circles painted in line. In situ, cemented into the tracery. 15th c.

n. II

Each quarry h. 0·15 m. w. 0·10 m. All 15th c.

1a. Quarries

Thirteen quarries leaded up with modern white quarries in a trellis pattern. Twelve quarries type 24, painted on

---

[1] Bodl. Lib., Woods MS. Top. Oxon. d. 92, op. cit.

[2] W. Maskell, The Ancient Liturgy of the Church of England (1882), 72.

white glass. Rosette and foliage in yellow stain. Paint very thin and corroded.

One quarry a musician playing a lute, type 55. Full length, facing three-quarters right, painted on white glass, the lute and musician's hat in yellow stain. Extremely decayed and almost impossible to decipher.

1b. Quarries

Six quarries: three fragments leaded up in a trellis of modern white quarries. Three type 20, the other three type 24. All extremely decayed. Fragment of a Creed scroll:

$$|s.unicum|$$

the line of a quarry painted on the same glass below the scroll. Text, St. Andrew's verse of the Creed:

'*Et in Ihesum Christum filium eius unicum dominum nostrum.*'

n. III

1b. Geometric Grisaille   PLATE 38 (*f*)

A trellis design of interlocking diamond and square shapes with circular bosses.

Condition. Incomplete, made up with modern plain white glass, original glass very corroded.

Colour and Technique. All white glass except for the bosses running up the centre of the light, which are in ruby.

Style and Design. An extremely complicated pattern design, no painted decoration on the white glass, it is therefore extremely difficult to date. No other example is found in the county.

Date. Probably 13th c.

n. IV

2a. Quarries and Roundels

Three quarries type 20. Two roundels in the cusps, the centre roundel is lost:

l. to r.   Rose
                (lost)
                M(ER)CI

All very decayed, particularly the latter. 15th c.

2c. Roundels

Two roundels in cusps.

l. to r.   M(ER)CI
                (lost)
                Ihc̄ (*Jesus*)

All very decayed. 15th c.

3a. One roundel, centre cusp *Ihc̄* (?). Extremely decayed. 15th c.

n. V

2a, 2b.

Very small fragments of quarries, type 21, small fragment of *Ihc̄* roundel very decayed. 15th c.

n. VI

2b. Roundel

Incomplete, a star painted on white glass, yellow stain. Similar to, but not identical with, Stanton Harcourt s. VI, 4a, 4c, and also Great Rollright s. V1, A1, A6. Fragments of two other roundels are too decayed to be deciphered. 15th c.

s. II

2b. Four quarries type 20, a fragment of a roundel painted with a monogram, possibly *Ihc̄*, very incomplete, inserted into modern plain quarry glazing. All 15th c.

s. III

1a. Modern quarry glazing incorporating six complete quarries, type 24. One quarry type 43, ornamented with a wheatsheaf in yellow stain, very decayed. Possibly the heraldic badge of the Kemp family. 15th c.

2a. Two quarries, type 20, two fragments of geometric grisaille, both painted with stylized leaf design on a cross-hatched ground. 15th c.

s. IV

1b. Roundel, a star design as n. VI, 2b. 15th c.

2b. Monogram, *Mar(ia)*, very compressed, within a circle set against a background of rays. White and yellow stain with plain white border. 15th c.

w. I

A2. Small fragments; fragment of a woman's head with an elaborate head-dress, early 15th-c. White and yellow stain, stipple shading, set inside out.

A6. Quarry, type 20. Very decayed.

MINSTER LOVELL
ST. KENELM

O.S. SP 325 114.

MS. SOURCES

London. British Library, Harleian MS. 4170, p. 42. Church notes
dated 16 June 1660.
Oxford. Bodleian Library, MS. Top. Oxon. b. 75, f. 116. Wyatt
Collections 18th–19th c.

PRINTED

'The Diary of Richard Symmonds', edited D. Long. *The Camden
Society* lxxiv (1859), 15–16.
Visitations (1871), 4–5.
Nelson (1913), 164.
Bouchier (1918), 94–5.
Bouchier (1932), 130.
Pevsner (1974), 707.

The glass has been neglected in the past and has suffered much from unskilled repair, some of it being placed inside out and upside down. Much of the remaining glass was made for the tracery lights of the windows but only two panels have survived intact: the figures of the Patriarch Isaac and the Prophet Daniel (I, A3 and A8). Very little is known about the glazing of the main lights of the windows. In the seventeenth century Symmonds recorded the remnants of figures of St. Edward Confessor and St. Oswald with their coats of arms, in the west window and Wyatt later recorded two large but incomplete figures of St. Peter the Apostle.[1]

There were two glazing campaigns at different dates in the fifteenth century and the glazing of the chancel can be divided into two groups, probably contemporary with one another. The first group includes the figures of Isaac and Daniel, (I, A3 and A8) and the three women saints (n. II, A4, n. III, A3, and s. III, A3). The painting is competent but the style is rather mechanical and repetitive. This is best seen in the figures of Isaac and Daniel which are virtually a mirror image of each other, and they touch rather than hold their scrolls. The profile pose and the disposition of the scrolls is formal and lifeless, more reminiscent of heraldic supporters than real figures. The second group consists of the figures of St. Agnes and St. Lucy (n. III, A4 and s. III, A4). This has much similarity with the first group in particular points of detail: in background diapers and architectural ornament. However, the proportions of the figures are much smaller and are almost lost under their canopies. The St. Lucy is the more complete, and the panel appears to be all of a piece and not a restorer's composite. The nave group consists of the figures of a Dominican saint and St. Peter Martyr (n. VI, A2, A3), St. Cosmas or Damian (s. V, A3), and the remains of an Order of Angels (w. I, A2 and A8). The style is consistent, particularly the broad heavy faces and similar background diapers. A lack of documentation makes the dating of the glass extremely difficult but it is probably to be assigned to the third quarter of the fifteenth century. The nave figures with the rougher background diapers are probably the latest of the series.

I

A3. Isaac
PLATE 38 (g)

h. 0·50 m. w. 0·20 m.

Represented standing in profile facing right below a canopy. He holds a scroll inscribed: |In|ysaac vocabitur tibi semen|. Below his feet a label inscribed |Ysaac|. Both inscriptions are in black-letter script.

Condition. Complete and *in situ*. All-over corrosion of varying intensity, the centre part of the panel is now cracked and has a small hole.

Colour and Technique. The whole panel is painted on white glass, with the figure's tunic and floppy hat in yellow stain. Background of cross-hatched lines. By his feet contiguous rosette diaper in yellow stain. Details of the canopy picked out in yellow stain. Very slight stipple shading.

---

[1] See Lost Glass below, p. 152.

Iconography. The text is from Genesis 21:12: '*Cui dixit Deus: Non tibi videatur asperum super puero, et super ancilla tua: omnia quae dixerit tibi Sara, audi vocem ejus; quia in Isaac vocabitur tibi semen.*'

Style and Design. See A8 below.

Date. Third quarter 15th c.

A8. The Prophet Daniel   PLATE 38 (*h*)

h. 0·50 m. w. 0·20 m.

Represented standing in profile facing left below a canopy. He holds a scroll inscribed |*Post ebdondas XLIIas octidetur christus*|. Below his feet a label is inscribed |*Daniel*|. Both inscriptions are in black-letter script.

Condition. Complete and *in situ*. All-over corrosion of varying intensity.

Colour and Technique. The whole panel is painted on white glass. The figure's hair, beard, hat, and hose are in yellow stain. Background to figure is a rough pebble-pattern diaper in line and matt wash. Details of the canopy picked out in yellow stain. Very slight stipple shading.

Iconography. The text is from Daniel 9: 26: '*Et post hebdomades sexaginta duas occidetur Christus: et non erit ejus populus qui eum negaturus est.*' The glass painter has made mistakes in spelling and numbering, XLII for LXII. The text is found in representations of Prophets flanking figures of the Apostles, each of the latter with the verse of the Creed associated with him.[1] But the inclusion of the Patriarch Isaac precludes such a series here.

Style and Design. The two figures are almost a mirror image of each other with only slight differences in decorative detail. The canopy designs are identical.

Date. Third quarter 15th c.

n. II

A3. Fragments

h. 0·50 m. w. 0·20 m.

Condition. A composite panel of ten different fragments leaded up with modern plain white glass. The most complete pieces are:

Head of a Male Saint

Beardless youth nimbed facing three-quarters right, he wears a pointed hat with a shallow brim. Adjacent to the head and painted on the same glass are crocketed spires. Painted on white glass, details of patterned nimbus and crockets in yellow stain. Probably from a tracery light. 15th c.

Cherubim

A fragment, only the raised right hand and part of a wing remain, white glass, wing in yellow stain. 15th c.

One of the Orders of Angels.

A fragment, only the body remains, represented holding two staffs, both incomplete. From a tracery light, side shafts of a canopy, painted on the same glass as the figure same design as window I, A3 and A8 above.

Date. Third quarter 15th c.

A4. Fragments

h. 1·50 m. w. 0·20 m.

Condition. A composite panel of thirteen fragments leaded up with modern plain white glass. The more complete pieces are:

Royal Figure

Represented standing facing left. The head and arms are missing. He wears a mantle with ermine trim and tippet. From a tracery light, the side shaft of a canopy painted on the same glass as the figure. White and yellow stain. 15th c. Possibly the St. Edmund noted by Wyatt.[2]

King

Elderly bearded figure, crowned, holding a sceptre, facing three-quarters left, right hand raised. Background foliage diaper, cusped frame on the left, and architectural feature above all painted on the same piece of glass, white and yellow stain. Third quarter 15th c..

St. Helena

Represented standing, facing three-quarters left, crowned and nimbed, holding the True Cross in her right hand. From a tracery light, the side shaft of a canopy painted on the same glass as the figure. White and yellow stain. Iconography standard but only a small portion of the figure remains set sideways on and the subject is not immediately apparent. Third quarter 15th c.

Fragment of an inscription. Black-letter script |*xpia*| from a lost figure of St. Christopher.

n. III

2b. Fragments

h. 0·24 m. w. 0·34 m.

Condition. Small fragments of canopies and side shaftings. A small incomplete figure of a youth, facing three-quarters left and standing in a canopy shafting. White and yellow stain. 15th c.

---

[1] M. R. James, *A Peterborough Psalter and Bestiary of the Fourteenth Century* (Roxburghe Club, 1921), 13, 15.
[2] See Lost Glass below, p. 153.

A3. Female Saint

h. 0·50 m. w. 0·20 m.

Originally full length, facing three-quarters left, below a canopy. Nimbed, she holds a book in her right hand.

Condition. Incomplete, the upper part of the figure is patched with modern plain white glass and the lower part of the legs and feet are missing. The figure is now set inside out.

Colour and Technique. Painted on white glass, the figure's hair, hem of mantle, and rib-vaults of the canopy are in yellow stain. Slight stipple shading.

Iconography. No attribute to identify the figure.

Style and Design. A tracery light, possibly a companion figure to the St. Helena n. II, A4 above and the female saint s. III, A3 below.

Fragment: Small piece of figure, facing three-quarters right; in his raised left hand he holds the end of a scroll inscribed in black-letter script |*geba(n)t*|.

Date. Third quarter 15th c.

A4. Female Saint. St. Agnes?

h. 0·50 m. w. 0·20 m.

A female saint originally full length facing left below a canopy; fragments of other canopies, an inscription in black-letter script: |*S(an)c(t)a: agnes:*|.

Condition. The female saint and the canopy fragments, except that at the apex of the light, are all inside out. The saint is incomplete and the paint has almost completely perished. The inscription may come from another figure.

Style and Design. The glass is too decayed for much comment but this is possibly a companion figure to the St. Lucy s. III, A4.

Date. Third quarter 15th c.

s. III

2b. Fragments

h. 0·24 m. w. 0·34 m.

Condition. Fifteen fragments of canopies and side shaftings. A small incomplete figure of a youth, facing three-quarters right, standing in a canopy shafting; same cartoon, reversed, as n. III, 2b above with a slight change in pattern detail of the tunic. White and yellow stain. 15th c.

A3. Female Saint

h. 0·50 m. w. 0·20 m.

Originally full length, facing three-quarters right, below

a canopy, holding a book (?) in one hand and a rosary in the other. Incomplete scroll in black-letter script |*Se*|.

Condition. Incomplete, the upper half of the figure, feet, and much of the canopy are missing. Remaining portion of the figure is set upside down and inside out.

Colour and Technique. Painted on white glass, the figure's hem of mantle and rosary in yellow stain. Slight stipple shading.

Iconography. No particular attribute to identify the figure.

Style and Design. A tracery light, possibly a companion figure to St. Helena n. II, A4 and female saint n. III, A3 above, with affinities in size, drapery painting, and side shafts of canopy.

Date. Third quarter 15th c.

A4. Female Saint. St. Lucy?

h. 0·50 m. w. 0·20 m.

Represented standing, facing three-quarters right, below a canopy. Nimbed, she holds a book, inscription in black-letter script: |*S/(an)c(t)a Luca*|.

Condition. The panel is substantially complete except for three portions made up with modern white glass. All-over corrosion slight in this case, the paint in the middle part of the panel has worn very thin. The inscription may come from another figure, as it is too large in scale.

Colour and Technique. Painted on white glass, hair, border of nimbus, and hem of mantle in yellow stain. Background: rough pebble pattern painted in black on yellow stain. Details of canopy in yellow stain. Slight stippled shading.

Iconography. St. Lucy has a variety of emblems relating to her life and martyrdom, none of which is represented here.[1] In an early 14th-c. panel in the nave clerestory at York she is represented with a sword piercing her throat,[2] and in the early 16th-c. glass at Winchester she holds a sword.[3]

Style and Design. Possibly a companion figure to the saint in n. III, A4—same scale of design.

Date. Third quarter 15th c.

n. V

A3. St. Lucy

h. 0·50 m. w. 0·20 m.

Originally represented standing facing three-quarters left, below a canopy. Nimbed, she holds a book. Inscription in black-letter script: |*S(an)c(t)a|Lucia*|.

Condition. The figure and canopy are set inside out, the paint is now very faint and there is extensive corrosion.

[1] *Herder* vii (1974), 415–20.
[2] G. Benson, *Ancient Painted Glass Windows in the Minster and Churches of the City of York* (1914), 47.
[3] J. W. Le Couteur, *Ancient Glass in Winchester* (2nd edn., 1928), 41.

Colour and Technique. Painted on white glass, with her hair and tunic in yellow stain, the details are indistinct owing to corrosion.

Iconography. See s. III, A4 above.

Style and Design. Possibly a companion figure to the female saints n. II, A4, n. III, A3, and s. III, A3 but the details too indistinct to be certain.

Date. Third quarter 15th c.

A4. Fragments

h. 0·50 m. w. 0·20 m.

Condition. Eleven fragments of canopies and a geometric design. All white glass and yellow stain. 15th c.

n. VI

A2. Dominican Saint

h. 0·50 m. w. 0·20 m.

A Dominican friar, nimbed, facing three-quarters left.

Condition. Incomplete, leaded up with modern pieces of plain glass. The coloured glass is very decayed and the paint on the background diaper is very thin.

Colour and Technique. Head painted on white glass, hair and nimbus in yellow stain, plain blue habit. Background patterned diaper of contiguous rosettes, painted in outline with yellow stain centres. Slight stipple shading.

Iconography. A companion figure to St. Peter Martyr A3, possibly St. Dominic the founder of the order. The present arrangement of the pieces is suspect and the open book, now to the left of the saint's head, was probably held against his chest.

Style and Design. As A3 below.

Date. Third quarter 15th c.

A3. St. Peter Martyr

h. 0·50 m. w. 0·20 m.

St. Peter Martyr represented standing facing three-quarters left, nimbed; his head is pierced by a short sword and he wears Dominican habit.

Condition. Incomplete, much of the figure is missing, leaded up with plain modern glass and fragments of canopies.

Colour and Technique. Saint's head painted on white glass, hair, edge of nimbus, and details of sword picked out in yellow stain. Habit in dark blue glass, white tunic. Background patterned diaper of contiguous circles painted in outline, centres in yellow stain. The hilt and pommel of the sword and part of the nimbus are painted on the same piece of glass as the adjacent patterned diaper.

Iconography. The figure has been identified as St. Thomas Becket.[1] This is unlikely, there are no archiepiscopal vestments or insignia that are usually found in representations of Becket. The dark blue, for black, habit, white tunic, and tonsured head pierced by a sword suggest St. Peter Martyr, Dominican friar of Verona who was martyred in 1252 and canonized by Pope Innocent IV in 1253.[2] The earliest known English representation is found in the Grandison Psalter of after 1262 and probably before 1276.[3] In the English province the devotion paid to the saint seems to have approached that paid to St. Dominic, the founder of the Order.[4] Other English representations are found on the 14th-c. Thornham Parva retable (Suffolk),[5] in the Taymouth Hours also 14th-c.,[6] a 15th-c. manuscript Lives of the Saints, in English, in the Bodleian Library, Oxford,[7] and a York Hours,[8] and in stained glass at Stamford (Lincs.),[9] New Buckenham (Norfolk),[10] and Long Melford (Suffolk).[11]

Style and Design. A companion figure to the unidentified saint in A2 above, the drawing is very close and the rather crude background diapers are similar. Probably *in situ*, border shaped to shoulder of the light.

Date. Third quarter 15th c.

s. V

2b. Fragments

h. 0·26 m. w. 0·36 m.

Twelve fragments of canopy designs, white and yellow stain, 15th c., very incomplete.

A2. Fragments

h. 0·50 m. w. 0·20 m.

Thirteen fragments of canopy designs, white and yellow stain, 15th c., very incomplete.

[1] T. Borenius, *St. Thomas in Art* (1932), 32.

[2] T. De Leontino, 'Vita Sancti Petri Marturis', *Acta Sanctorum Aprilis*, iii (1886), 686–727. G. Kaftal, *Iconography of the Saints in Tuscan Painting* (1952). 309–20. V. Aluce, *Iconografia di S Pietro da Verona, martire Domenicano* (1955). L. Réau, *Iconographie de l'art chrétien*, iii, part 3 (1959), 1107.

[3] B.L. Add. MS. 21926, f. 14. W. Hinnebush, *The Early English Friars Preachers* (1951), 154.   [4] Ibid.

[5] Ibid. W. W. Lillie, 'A Medieval Retable at Thornham Parva', *Burlington Magazine* lxiii (1933), 99.

[6] B.L. Yates Thompson MS. 13, f. 191ᵛ. M. R. James, *A Descriptive Catalogue of the Second Series of Fifty Manuscripts (Nos. 51–100) in the Collection of Henry Yates Thompson* (1902), no. 57.

[7] Bodl. Lib. Tanner MS. 17, f. 93ᵛ.

[8] Dean and Chapter Library, York Minster MS. Add. 2, f. 105, made before 1445.

[9] Church of St. John Baptist. North aisle of nave, second window from the east, *c.* 1450.

[10] C. Woodforde, *The Norwich School of Glass Painting in the Fifteenth Century* (1950), 110 and 171.   [11] Ibid. 118.

A3. St. Cosmas or St. Damian PLATE 38 (*i*)

h. 0·50 m. w. 0·20 m.

Represented standing, facing three-quarters left, nimbed, wearing academic robes, with a doctor's black cap, a urine flask in his raised right hand, and a long surgeon's knife in his left.

Condition. The panel is virtually complete except at the bottom, where the saint's feet are missing. Slight all-over corrosion.

Colour and Technique. Head, hands, flask, and knife painted on white glass, nimbus in yellow stain. Ruby robes with white fur trim and collar, black cap. Background, patterned diaper of contiguous rosettes painted in outline, centres in yellow stain.

Iconography. The twin brothers SS. Cosmas and Damian who practised medicine and were martyred in the reign of the Emperor Diocletian *c.* 287.[1] Their cult was extremely popular and widespread throughout Europe in the Middle Ages.[2] They are commonly represented in doctor's robes holding medical objects such as the urine flask.[3] The surviving English examples are rare,[4] for example in the early 14th-c. Queen Mary Psalter[5] and the Book of Hours of John Lacy of 1420.[6]

Style and Design. Close to the two saints in n. VI, A2 and A3 above, particularly in the drawing of the head and rough background diaper.

Date. Third quarter 15th c.

w. I

A2. Fragments

h. 0·84 m. w. 0·24 m.

Small fragments of canopies, white and yellow stain. 15th c. At the base of the light an inscription in black-letter script |*Vi*(*r*)*tutes*| probably *in situ*. A lost figure of Virtues from a series of the Nine Orders of Angels. See A8 below.

Date. 15th c.

A8. Powers

h. 0·84 m. w. 0·24 m.

In armour, full length facing three-quarters left, thrusting a spear into a devil's head trampled below the feet. At the base of the light an inscription in black-letter script: |*Potestates*|.

Condition. The figure is virtually complete, part of the left arm and wings are missing and much of the original black-ground has been replaced by plain white glass, canopy at apex incomplete and patched with alien pieces. All-over corrosion of varying intensity on the white glass, the ruby glass very corroded and nearly opaque.

Colour and Technique. Painted on white glass with extensive use of yellow stain for the feathered body and wings, stippled shading. Devil in pot-metal ruby.

Iconography. Figure of Powers from a series of the Nine Orders of Angels. If the series was originally in the tracery lights of this window, which has only eight main traceries and two small ones, the series would either have been condensed in some way or extended into the main lights of the window. The church had two different series of the Nine Orders as the two fragments in n. II, A3 are smaller in size and scale.

The subject of the Nine Orders in medieval thought and art is vast and complex.[7] There are many examples in English glass painting of the 14th c. and 15th c. Important examples are found at New College, Oxford, where nearly all the tracery lights of the chapel were filled with them, *c.* 1380–1386,[8] two 15th-c. series at Great Malvern Priory,[9] and examples in Norfolk and Suffolk.[10] The great variety in representation and detail compared with the only slight remains at Minster Lovell do not justify a more detailed investigation.

Style and Design. The drawing of the head is very like the St. Cosmas or St. Damian, s. V, A3.

Date. Third quarter 15th c.

Lost Glass

The heraldic glass relating to the Lovel family and their alliances was already incomplete when it was recorded in the 17th c. and none of it now survives.[11] There was a shield of Lovel quartering Holland, either for John, Lord Lovel (d. 1414) or his son William Lovel, Lord Lovel and Holland (d. 1455).[12] Only Symmonds records two shields then extant in the west window: 'under these coates thus written the remnants of the Saints are still (there) *azure*

---

[1] *Golden Legend* v, 172–7.

[2] The material is extensively studied in M.-L. David-Danel, *Iconographie des saints médecins Côme et Damien* (1958).

[3] Ibid., ch. iii.

[4] Ibid. 225 notes only two medieval examples for England.

[5] G. F. Warner, *The Queen Mary's Psalter* (1912), 49, pl. 267, figs. c and d.

[6] Oxford, St. John's College MS. 94, f. 6ᵛ.

[7] A recent account is in *Herder* i (1968), 626–42, particularly 639–40. For the textual background see C. A. Patrides, 'Renaissance

Thought on the Celestial Hierarchy: The Decline of a Tradition', *Journal of the History of Ideas* xx, no. 2 (1959), 155–66.

[8] C. Woodforde, *The Stained Glass of New College, Oxford* (1951), ch. III.

[9] Rushforth (1936), 209–16, figs. 98–104, 250–3, figs. 129, 130.

[10] Woodforde (1950), op. cit. 129–37.

[11] The Manor House also contained seven shields of arms showing the descent of the Lovel family and their alliances which are no longer extant. Visitations (1871), 4.

[12] Visitations (1871), 4. G.E.C. viii. 221–2.

a cross flory between four martlets or SANCTUS EDWAR-
DUS CONFESSOR. *Gules a cross flory or* SANCTUS OS-
WALDUS'.[1] It is not known if other English royal saints
were also represented, but the shield of the Confessor's
arms at Burford is of unknown provenance and may have
been acquired from here. The attributed arms of St. Oswald
vary in their blazon. The arms generally assigned to him
are *azure a cross or between four lions rampant argent*.[2]

The Wyatt Collections record some of the extant inscrip-

tions and others now lost. 'In the small Gothic compart-
ments of the chancel windows these pictures in brilliant
glass, Daniel, St. Edmund, Sancta Helena, Sancta Agnes,
Sancta Luca, Sancta Ceelia and some other, there appears
to have been a large one of St. Peter in the north window
the triple crown mitre and part of the cross exceeding rich
remain. In the transept Sancta Lucia, Sancta Appolinia, St.
Petre with the church and on his head a rich mitre with
3 ducal coronets around it.'[3]

NEWINGTON
ST. GILES

O.S. SP 608 956.

MS. SOURCES

Oxford. Bodleian Library, MS. Top. Oxon. d. 93, ff. 30–4. Restoration Notes, late 19th c.

PRINTED

Parker (1842), 323.

Scott, J. O., 'A Stained Glass Window in Newington Church', *The
Reliquary and Illustrated Archaeologist*, n.s. iv (1898), 116–17.
Ditchfield, P. M., *Memorials of Old Oxfordshire* (1903), 186.
Nelson (1913), 164.
Bouchier (1932), 131.
Greening Lamborn, E. A., 'The Painted Window at Newington',
O.A.S. Report (1938), 59–62, pl. 3.
Pevsner (1974), 715–16.

The north window of the chancel retains a substantial amount of its original glazing *in situ*. It is a two–light
window with a kneeling figure of a priest at the base of each light (n. II, 1a and 1b). Above these are representations of the Assumption of the Virgin Mary and the Trinity (n. II, 2a and 2b). There are no inscriptions, or any record of such to identify the donor figures. However, there are particular points of evidence
that enable their identity to be tentatively established. Greening Lamborn pointed out that both were
members of the higher clergy as they wear grey furred almuces, and were also doctors. The more complete figure, (n. II, 1b), wears a doctor's black pileus, and there is a large pileus, surrounded by the end
of a bidding scroll, at the head of each light (n. II, 3a and 3b). On the basis of this internal evidence Greening Lamborn suggested that one figure represented Dr. Richard Salter, who was collated to the living of
Newington in 1482, and that the other was probably his predecessor in the living, Dr. Stephen Barworth,
who was rector from 1478 to 1482. Greening Lamborn also suggested that the window was either commissioned by both men or by Salter, who also wished to commemorate his predecessor.[4] Either hypothesis
is equally possible, particularly as the living of Newington was not the only connection between Salter and
Barworth. They were both Fellows of All Souls College, Oxford, during the period 1459–63,[5] and later
Canons of Salisbury Cathedral, 1485–1508.[6] Barworth died in 1511 and Salter in 1518.[7] It is not known if
Salter vacated the living of Newington before his death. This evidence suggests a probable dating between
1482 and 1519, or between 1482 and 1511 if the window was a joint donation. Richard Salter also gave
a window to Standlake church, where he was rector from 1473 to 1508.

The window is quite simple in design. The two lights are each divided into three horizontal bands:
donor and quarries; narrative scene; quarries and ornament. The colours are predominately white and

[1] *The Diary of Richard Symmonds*, op. cit.
[2] For example Bodl. Lib. MS. Laud 733, f. 52ᵛ, mid 15th c. See also
Newton ii (1961), 249 n. 112.
[3] Wyatt Collections, op. cit., f. 116.
[4] Greening Lamborn, op. cit.
[5] Richard Salter, fellow, adm. 1459, still in 1465, probably in

1467. Stephen Barworth, fellow, adm. 1450, still in 1463. A. B.
Emden, *A Biographical Register of the University of Oxford to 1500*
(1959), 1633 and 125 respectively.
[6] Emden, op. cit. Salter was Canon in 1483, vac. by October 1508;
Barworth Canon in 1485, vac. 1507.
[7] Ibid.

yellow (yellow stain on white glass) with a very restricted use of ruby and blue glass in the narrative panels. A most unusual and highly distinctive feature of the design is a bidding scroll, running from the donor panel at the base through to the top of the light, where it surrounds a large black pileus. No other comparable examples in glass painting appear to have survived and the idea may be somewhat indebted to monumental brass design.[1]

The drawing and modelling of the figures are very delicate and precise. They would appear to be the work of a competent artist. Although there is no other work in the county that can be attributed to the same artist, there is some affinity, despite the great difference in scale, to the three late fifteenth-century roundels in the Chapter House of Christ Church Cathedral, Oxford.[2]

In 1963 the window was found to be in a rather dilapidated condition, both the interior and exterior surfaces were covered with a strong growth of green lichen, and the leading was in need of attention. It was restored in 1971 by D. King of Norwich. The glass was treated to inhibit further lichen growth, cleaned, and releaded. Some slight rearrangement of alien glass, intruded at an earlier restoration, took place.

n. II PLATE 39 (a)

1a. Donor

h. 0·61 m. w. 0·43 m.

An incomplete figure of a priest (the torso only survives) kneeling, wearing a grey furred almuce.

Original background missing, replaced by modern white glass incorporating some medieval pieces, all incomplete, set here in 1971: head of a man facing left, white and yellow stain, mid 14th c., four quarries type 48, 14th c., two quarries type 49, 14th c., pieces of border, canopy, and foliage designs, 14th–15th c.

1b. Donor PLATE 39 (d)

h. 0·61 m. w. 0·43 m.

A priest, kneeling, wearing a grey furred almuce and a doctor's black pileus. Above his head a scroll which continues up into the panels 2b and 3b. Scroll inscribed in black-letter script:

|Gloria|eterno patri|et christo|vero|Regi|paraclito que|
sancto et|nunc et|imperpetuum amen.|

At the base of the panel is a fragment of an inscription in black-letter script:

|soris.|

Condition. The original glass has extensive corrosion on both surfaces. The scroll is complete, the middle part of the inscription is very worn, and could only be read by using a strong surface light during the last restoration. Lower part of panel missing, replaced by modern plain white quarries.

Colour and Technique. The only coloured glass is the donor's flashed ruby robe. Remainder, white glass, light brown paint with stippled matt shading, some with cross hatching, details picked out in yellow stain. Matt back painting on robes and face.

Iconography. The donor was probably represented at a prayer desk venerating the Trinity in the above panel, 2b. The inscription on the scroll, invoking the Trinity, is the final verse of the hymn

*Cultor Dei memento
te fontis et lavacri
rorem subisse*[3]

sung at Compline on Easter Sunday in the use of Sarum.[4]

Style and Design. The disposition of the figure against a background of quarries is original, the beginning of the scroll is painted on the same piece of glass as the adjacent quarry. The remainder of the design is somewhat conjectural. The donor was probably represented at a prayer desk with a tiled floor below. The outline of part of the prayer desk is indicated at the right-hand side of the figure where the glass has its original grozed edge. The lower edge of the ruby robe and the adjacent tiled floor have original grozed edges and fit together. For the style, see Introduction above.

Identical quarries, type 19, are found at Ewelme s. II.

Date. Late 15th c., after 1482, before 1519.

2a. Assumption of the Virgin PLATE 39 (b)

h. 0·61 m. w. 0·43 m.

The Virgin crowned and in royal robes, against a background of rays, supported by angels.

[1] Greening Lamborn, op. cit., cites Wood's description of the brass at New College, Oxford, of Dr. Thomas Gascoyne, d. 1457: 'the picture of a doctor in his gown . . . two hands issuing out of the clouds, holding over his head a doctoral cap', A. Wood, *The History and Antiquities of the Colleges and Halls in the University of Oxford*, ed. J. Gutch (1786–90), 207.

[2] Staircase window south of Chapter House.

[3] U. Chevalier, *Repertorium Hymnologicum*, i (1892), no. 4053.

[4] *Breviarium ad usum insignis ecclesiae Sarum*, fasc. 1, ed. F. Procter and C. Wordsworth (1882), dccxv.

Condition. Incomplete. Before the 1971 restoration the missing portions were made up with obtrusive large white quarries, and the Virgin's robe was patched with a large border piece.[1] The quarries have been replaced by modern stippled antique glass, and the border pieces moved to a less incongruous position. The original glass has extensive corrosion on both surfaces. The Virgin's ruby mantle, which was opaque, was abraded and the back of the glass resurfaced.

A scroll, originally continuous from panels 1a to 3a, as in the adjacent light, is now incomplete. The small portions of inscription that remain are in black-letter script, the paint is extremely worn. They appear to read:

|........|: m|......|: *delicia* :|....|pand|...|

Colour and Technique. The only coloured glass is the flashed ruby mantle of the Virgin. Remainder painted on white glass as 1b above. The yellow stain varies in intensity from light lemon to deep orange. Slight matt back painting on all the figures.

Iconography. The rays replace the mandorla found in 13th- and 14th-c. representations.[2] In the Newington panel the Virgin is borne up by two of the Nine Orders of Angels: cherubim and angels. The Golden Legend, quoting the story as told by Dennis, the disciple of Paul (the Pseudo Dionysius) states 'all the Hierarchies lifted her up'.[3]

Date. Late 15th c., after 1482, before 1519.

Insertions. A border piece, a crowned M, white and yellow stain, incomplete, 15th c. A fragment of a square quarry (?) painted with a design of a bird holding a seed in its beak in a cusped border, 15th c.[4]

2b. The Trinity PLATE 39 (c)
h. 0·61 m. w. 0·43 m.

The Trinity is represented by three human figures, enthroned, their feet resting on a rainbow; behind them are five cherubim. The Son, displaying the Wounds of the Passion, is distinguished from the other two Persons, who, although not identical with each other, are very alike.

Condition. Slightly incomplete. The panel had been patched

with the fragments of quarries, borders, and the male head. These were moved in the 1971 restoration to 1a. The original glass has extensive corrosion on both surfaces. The blue glass was opaque, and was abraded and resurfaced in 1971. Some old lead repairs were removed, the breaks joined with Araldite, and the glass backed with exterior plating, in particular the head of the right-hand Person of the Trinity and the two cherubim above. The missing portions were made up with modern stippled antique glass.

Colour and Technique. The only coloured glass is the blue mantle common to the Three Persons of the Trinity. The remainder is painted on white glass, as 1a above. Extensive use of yellow stain, variety of intensity as 2a. Back painting on all figures, particularly pronounced on the blue mantle.

Iconography. Anthropomorphic representations are less common than those in which the Holy Spirit takes the form of a dove above or between the two other Persons.[5] The earliest known English example of the anthropomorphic type is found in the Sherborne Pontifical of the 10th c.[6] but it was not until the 15th c. that it became a regular feature.[7] The later examples tend to represent the Son seated on the right hand of the Father, in accordance with Psalm 110:1.[8] The Newington panel is unusual in two aspects: the Son, wearing the Crown of Thorns, is seated at the centre, and an angel holds a crown over his head. In the over-all scheme of the window, the panels of the Assumption of the Virgin in 2a and the Trinity complement each other. The tendency to associate the Virgin with the Trinity was characteristic of the late 14th and early 15th c.[9]

Date. Late 15th c., after 1482, before 1519.

3a. Quarries and Scroll
h. 0·51 m. w. 0·43 m.

A doctor's black pileus surrounded by the end of a scroll continued from 2a. Background of quarries, type 19 as panel 1b.

Condition. Paint on quarries very worn. The pileus is disfigured by 16th-c. graffiti: 'Christopher Hovenden. W. B. 1586 A.D. W. B. C.'[10]

[1] This arrangement is shown quite clearly in the photograph published in 1898; the window was then said to have been partly releaded recently. Oldridge-Scott, op. cit. 116–17. No details are given in the notes on the restoration of the church. MS. Top. Oxon. d. 93, op. cit.

[2] Compare Beckley, s. II, A1. For the earlier iconography of the Assumption see T. S. R. Boase, *The York Psalter* (1962), 8–14.

[3] *Golden Legend*, iv (1909), 237. A late 15th-c. wall-painting at Exeter Cathedral shows the Assumption combined with the Coronation of the Virgin in the presence of the Trinity, attended by the Nine Orders of Angels. G. M. Rushforth, 'Late Medieval Paintings in Exeter Cathedral', *Devon and Cornwall Notes and Queries*, xvii (1932–3), 99–104.

[4] Square quarries are rare; even so the earliest examples are of the

14th c., e.g. Whitwell (Rutland), Newton iii (1961), 512–14.

[5] M. Didron, *Iconographie chrétienne: Histoire de Dieu* (1843), 523–607. A. Hackle, *Die Trinität in der Kunst* (1931).

[6] Paris, Bibl. Nat., Latin MS. 943. F. Wormald, *English Drawings of the Xth and XIth Centuries* (1952), 78 n. 54, pls. 4a, b, 5a. See also E. Panofsky, *Tomb Sculpture* (1964), 44.

[7] Rushforth (1936), 405 n. 2, lists examples in English 15th-c. glass.

[8] The order of representation was by no means invariable, see Didron, op. cit.

[9] Hackle, op. cit. 2. See also n. 3 above.

[10] Christopher Hoveden, Fellow of All Souls College, Oxford, 1575, d. 1610, brother of Robert Hoveden, Warden of All Souls College and rector of Newington 1572–1614. J. Foster, *Alumni Oxonienses 1500–1714* (1891), 752.

Style and Design. The disposition of scroll and quarries is original, the end of the scroll is painted on the same glass as the quarries below.

Date. Late 15th c., after 1482, before 1519.

3b. Quarries and Scroll

h. 0·51 m. w. 0·43 m.
Same design as 3a.

Condition. Paint on quarries very worn. 16th-c. graffiti scratched on the pileus: 'William B...e.t Curatt, 1586 April iii'[1]

s. II

A1. Fragments

(Measurements unobtainable.)
An incomplete head of a female saint, nimbed, wearing a fur-trimmed bonnet and wimple, white and yellow stain, early 15th c.

Fragments of black-letter inscriptions, 15th c.:

|: primo : paupere|mensa : de|·pensa·|

s. III

A1. Foliage Design

(Measurements unobtainable.)

At the centre a coloured roundel of four radiating leaves, alternately ruby and green, patterned border set on white glass painted with trails of ivy leaves. Incomplete, probably *in situ.* 14th c.

s. VI   PLATE 39 (*e*)

2a. The Annunciation

h. 0·45 m. w. 0·36 m. Figure: h. 0·15 m. w. 0·15 m.

Condition. Incomplete. The head and shoulders of the Virgin with the Dove flying down beside her face, background of quarries. Two complete quarries and nine fragments, all type 8. Slight corrosion.

Colour and Technique. Light brown paint on white glass, stippled matt shading, details picked out in yellow stain.

Iconography. The extant portion is the normal iconography, with the Virgin on the right.

Style and Design. The disposition of figures and quarries is original, part of one quarry is painted on the same glass as the figure. The quarries have a bold foliage design, type 8. The style of figure drawing appears to be close to the St. John the Baptist at Yarnton, n. VI, 2b.

Date. Mid 15th c.

NORTH ASTON
ST. MARY THE VIRGIN

O.S. SP 482 288.

MS. SOURCES
Oxford. Bodleian Library MS. Top. Oxon. b. 75, f. 136. Wyatt Collections 18th–19th-c., copy of D. T. Powell's notes of *c.* 1805.

PRINTED
Parker (1846), 85.
Visitations (1871), 59.
Bouchier (1918), 84.
P.C. (1920), 130.
Bouchier (1932), 130.
Greening Lamborn (1949), 104–5
Pevsner (1974), 718.

The surviving medieval glass is in two windows of the chapel on the south side of the chancel. There is a fragment of an inscription with an incomplete date which indicates that some of the glass, if not all, could be of the period 1480–90. There is a fragment of a shield of the arms of Anne impaling Giffard and the same arms and those of Ashton impaling Giffard were repeated on an alabaster tomb on the north side of this chapel, which had an inscription, now lost, recorded as *Johns Ann et Alicia uxor eius ob. MCCCCXVI.*[2] The date must be a mistranscription of *MCCCCCVI* as an early fifteenth-century dating is incompatible with the style and design of the tomb. Greening Lamborn dated the tomb *c.* 1490 and assigned it to John Anne and his wife Isabel, daughter of Thomas Ashton and Elizabeth, his wife, daughter of Roger Giffard.[3]

[1] The surname is not legible.   [2] Visitations (1871), 59.   Giffard Isabel. See G. A. Moriarty, 'The Streatley Family', *Records of*
[3] Greening Lamborn (1949), 104–5. He incorrectly calls Elizabeth   *Buckinghamshire* xiii (1934–40), 396.

This identification conflicts with the recorded inscription which gives the wife's name as Alice, not Isabel. In addition, this pedigree does not account for the impaled coat of Anne and Giffard. A window of the manor house formerly contained a shield of Anne quartering Ashton and impaling Giffard.[1] This in conjunction with the heraldry of the tomb suggests that John Anne, d. c. 1506, was a son of the Anne–Ashton marriage and that he married Alice Giffard.

s. II

Traceries *in situ*
h. 0·36 m. w. 0·12 m.

A2. Eagle

Facing left, the wings displayed and the head facing right, a coronet about its neck.

A5. Eagle

As A2 but faces right.

Condition. The top foil of each light contains inserted fragments: A2 a piece of drapery, A5 a hand holding a palm leaf. External corrosion, more pronounced on A2.

Colour and Technique. The eagles are painted on a single piece of glass, with stippled matt shading and details in yellow stain.

Iconography. The eagles may have a heraldic significance. For figures of birds in tracery lights see Eynsham s. IX 4a.

Style and Design. The eagles are drawn from the same cartoon, one in reverse. The representation is odd in that they have peacocks' tails.

Date. Late 15th c.

s. III

A1, A2, A3. Three Roundels

d. 0·15 m.

Each shows an eagle, A1 faces right, the others left.

Condition. All complete, old breaks leaded, slight exterior corrosion.

Colour and Technique. Painted on white glass with stippled matt shading.

Iconography. Probably no heraldic significance.

Style and Design. Drawn from a single cartoon, in reverse.

Date. Late 15th c.

Insertion. A2, a fragment of an inscription in black-letter script:

|hton.|
|ccc⁰|

The two parts painted on one piece of glass. Rawlinson recorded an incomplete inscription: '*dominus noster Ashton et uxor eius MCCCC octogesimo*'.[2]

B1. Roundel, Bull of St. Luke

d. 0·27 m.

Condition. Very incomplete, only the head, wings, and tail remain. The area of the body patched with an incomplete roundel: an eagle as A1.

Iconography. Part of a series of the symbols of the four Evangelists.

Style and Design. See B2.

Date. Late 15th c.

B2. Roundel, Eagle of St. John (?)

d. 0·27 m.

Condition. Complete, old breaks leaded, slight corrosion.

Colour and Technique. As A1.

Iconography. Possibly part of a series of the symbols of the Evangelists, but the eagle has no nimbus.

Style and Design. Possibly a companion to B1, being the same size, but with different patterned borders.

Date. Late 15th c.

C1. Fragments

Heraldic fragments: *two lions passant in pale argent*; *three martlets argent*.

These come from a shield recorded c. 1805[3] as: *argent on a bend sable three martlets argent, a crescent for difference* ANNE *impaling gules three lions passant in pale argent* GIFFARD.

Date. Late 15th c.

---

[1] Visitations (1871), 59. The prominence given to the Ashton arms on the tomb and in the windows reflects the fact that John Anne was kinsman and co-heir of William Ashton, d. 1504. *Cal. Inq. Post Mortem* Henry VII iii, no. 173.

[2] P.C. (1920), 10, where the name is transcribed as 'Antlon'

In Rawlinson's MS. the word has been corrected and is difficult to read, but certainly appears to be Ashton, Bodl. Lib. Rawlinson MS. B.400 c, f. 194.

[3] Parker (1846), 85. Bodl. Lib. MS. Top. Oxon. b. 75, f. 136. It was then in the east window of the chapel.

NORTH LEIGH
ST. MARY

O.S. SP 387 137.

PRINTED

Nelson (1913), 164.
Bouchier (1918), 95.
P.C. (1920), 231–2.
Bouchier (1932), 130.
Greening Lamborn (1949), 143–4.
Pevsner (1974), 721.

MS. SOURCES

London. British Library, Harleian MS. 4170, pp. 50–1. Church notes dated 1660.

The remaining glass is in three windows of the chantry chapel of the Wilcotes family (n. II, n. III, and n. IV). The chapel was built by Lady Elizabeth Wilcotes, daughter and heiress of Sir John Trillowe and widow of Sir William Wilcotes, d. 1410. A licence to found the chantry was obtained in 1438 and it has been suggested that by that date the chapel would have been completed and the glass in position.[1] This is by no means certain and a dating of *c.* 1438–1440 is probably more correct. The glass is all of one date, but of two different classes of design. The east window main lights had figures below canopies, but only the latter survive (n. II, 2a–2d) while the lowest range of tracery lights is now filled with fragments. One small fragment of a saint's head and part of an emblem may be part of the original scheme for these lights but this cannot be proved (n. II, B2 and B4). The smaller traceries contain two repeated foliage designs (n. II, C1–D2). The same designs are repeated in the traceries of the two side windows (n. III, C1–D2 and n. IV, C1–D2). These traceries also contain the beginning of an alphabet, the letters A to H, each letter painted on a roundel (n. III, B1, B3, B5, and B7, same lights in n. IV). It is possible that a didactic purpose was intended,[2] but in the Middle Ages the alphabet was put to various different uses both in the liturgy[3] and private devotions[4] and it is impossible to be precise as to why it is represented here. The main lights of these two windows were different in design from the east window, with shields and crests set against a background of quarries, but unfortunately only a few fragments remain (n. IV, 2b–2d and one shield of Wilcotes (now set in n. II, E2). There are also roundels which are painted with animal figures and birds (n. III, 2a–2d). It is possible that these also have a heraldic significance, but no precise parallels in heraldic crests and badges have been found. With the exception of the blue backgrounds of the canopies and shield in n. II no coloured glass remains. This more economical class of design is in contrast to the lavish architecture of the chapel, particularly its spectacular fan vaulting.

n. II

2a–2d. Canopies   PLATE 40 (*b*)

h. 0·60 m. w. 0·34 m.

The heads of four identical canopy designs.

Condition. Virtually complete with very limited restoration. The glass is exceptionally well preserved.

Colour and Technique. Canopies painted on white glass, details of ribbed vaults and traceried windows picked out in yellow stain. The backgrounds are alternately blue and ruby, diapered with a seaweed foliage design picked out of a matt black wash.

Style and Design. A cusped arch with crocketed gable and finial, above it a two-storied structure, the lower storey having two traceried window designs each surmounted by a crocketed gable and finial, their tops flanking a vaulted niche with crocketed gable and finial in the second storey. The canopy occupies the full width of the light, without a border design. Although the over-all design is different,

---

[1] Greening Lamborn (1949), 143.

[2] For tiles patterned with alphabets see Loyd Haberly, *Medieval English Paving Tiles* (1937), 22–6.

[3] For example, in the consecration of a church or chapel. W. Maskell, *Monumenta Ritualia Ecclesiae Anglicanae*, i (1846), 173.

[4] 'ABC of Devotion, English Register of Godstow Nunnery near Oxford', ed. A. Clark, *E. E.T.S.* o.s. cxxix (1905), 4. 'ABC Poem on the Passion', H. A. Person, *Cambridge Middle English Lyrics* (2nd edn., 1962), 5–6.

the small details show similarities to the canopies in the Ante-chapel windows of All Souls College, Oxford, of *c.* 1441–7, in the prominence of rib vaulting of the canopy arch and niches, the diagonally turned capitals and side shafts, and quatrefoil window tracery with a boss at the centre of the light.[1]

Date. c. 1440.

B1. Fragments

h. 0·50 m. w. 0·14 m.

Small fragments of a patterned floor design and side shafts painted on the same piece of glass, fragment of white drapery. *c.* 1440.

B2. Fragments

h. 0·50 m. w. 0·14 m.

Profile head of a saint, patterned border painted on the same glass, from a tracery light; the foot of a figure of similar size. Fragments of canopy and ruby seaweed diaper. *c.* 1440.

B3. Fragments

h. 0·50 m. w. 0·14 m.

Pieces of canopies, decorative diapers, part of an inscription in black-letter script: |*ARIS*|. *c.* 1440.

B4. Fragments

h. 0·50 m. w. 0·14 m.

Fragment of a heraldic crest; an oak tree and acorns in white and yellow stain. The base point of a scimitar probably comes from a figure of an Apostle. Fragments of canopies. *c.* 1440. An incomplete inscription, in Lombardic script:

$$|OP(ER)IS|$$

B5. Fragments

h. 0·50 m. w. 0·14 m.

Border pieces with crowns and foliage designs in white and yellow stain. Fragments of canopies. *c.* 1440.

B6. Fragments

h. 0·50 m. w. 0·14 m.

Border pieces as B5 and fragments of canopies. *c.* 1440.

B7. Fragments

h. 0·50 m. w. 0·14 m.

The head of a six-headed beast, probably part of a dragon from a figure of St. Michael, in white and yellow stain. Fragments of drapery and canopies. *c.* 1440.

B8. Fragments

Fragments of a heraldic crest, *an eagle displayed argent* WIL-COTES, is painted on the same glass as part of a quarry design. Quarry type 16. The crest was originally above the shield of Wilcotes in the apex tracery light, E2.[2] Crown border piece as B5. Fragments of canopies. *c.* 1440.

C1–C4. Foliage Designs *in situ*

h. 0·30 m. w. 0·28 m.

Identical design repeated of a frontal lion's face jessant sprays of foliage.

Condition. Complete except for the top foils on C2 and C4, which are modern copies. The glass is very well preserved with only slight corrosion.

Colour and Technique. Lions' faces in yellow stain, white foliage picked out of a matt black wash, plain border yellow stain band separated from the stonework by plain white glass.

Style and Design. The design is derived from the charge in heraldry of a *lion's face jessant de lis*, the arms of the Cauntelo family.[3]

Date. c. 1440.

D1 and D2. Foliage Designs

h. 0·30 m. w. 0·28 m.

Condition. Incomplete, the centre and foliage in the lower foil of each light is modern restoration. The design is original. See n. III, D2 below.

E2. Shield of Wilcotes

h. 0·42 m. w. 0·42 m.

Azure an eagle displayed argent armed and legged or WIL-COTES.

Condition. The shield is complete but not *in situ* as it is too wide for its position. It is set against modern white glass with a fragment of a tracery design above the shield.

Colour and Technique. The field of the shield is in very light blue glass diapered with contiguous rosettes picked out of a light matt wash, white eagle, beak and legs in yellow stain, stippled shading.

Date. c. 1440.

[1] Hutchinson (1949), pls. i–xviii.
[2] Pre-restoration photographs at the N.M.R.

[3] For the arms see 'Rolls of Arms Henry III', ed. T. D. Tremlett and H. Stanford London, *Aspilogia* ii (1967), 119–20.

n. III

2a. Roundel, Quarries, and Borders PLATE 40 (a)

h. 0·60 m. w. 0·34 m. Roundel: d. 0·14 m. Quarries: h. 0·14 m. w. 0·11 m.

Roundel: a stag standing facing right on a grassy bank, a tree behind left.

Condition. Old leaded repair, the borders disarranged; the glass is well preserved with only slight corrosion.

Colour and Technique. Roundel painted on a single piece of white glass. Stag white with matt wash and cross-hatched line modelling, horns in yellow stain. Tree and bank are matt wash, the grass painted, the foliage scratched out of the wash. Background diaper of contiguous rosettes, sketchily painted. The plain border and coloured surround are modern.

Quarries: type 16, white and yellow stain.

Borders: crowns and foliage plaques in white and yellow stain.

Style and Design. The arrangement of roundel, quarries, and borders is probably original and the quarries at the apex of the light are all painted on a single piece of glass set directly into the stonework of the cusps. The painting is eccentric and the borders and quarries are painted with more precision than the roundel.

Date. c. 1440.

2b. Roundel, Quarries, and Borders

h. 0·60 m. w. 0·34 m.

Roundel: an eagle standing on and pecking at the branch of a tree.

Condition, Style and Design. As 2a; the background diaper of the roundel is identical.

2c. Roundel, Quarries, and Borders

h. 0·60 m. w. 0·34 m.

Roundel: a double-headed eagle displayed or, holding a gimel ring in its beaks. Left-hand portion is restoration.

Condition, Style and Design. As 2a above, the background diaper of the roundel is identical, the eagle in yellow stain.

2d. Roundel, Quarries, and Borders

h. 0·60 m. w. 0·34 m.

Condition, Style and Design. As 2a above, except that here the roundel is a copy of 2a omitting the tree, the left part of it is restoration.

B1, B3, B5, and B7. Roundels and Foliage Designs

h. 0·50 m. w. 0·14 m.

Identical foliage designs. At the centre of each is a roundel with a letter of the alphabet, in sequence left to right: *E. F. G. H.*

Condition. Complete and *in situ*; the glass is very well preserved with only slight corrosion. In B7 the foliage is restoration.

Colour and Technique. The letters are in yellow stain against a background of cross-hatched painted lines and a plain yellow stain border. The seaweed foliage is picked out of a matt black wash, patterned beaded border in yellow stain picked out of a matt black wash, within a plain white border.

Style and Design. The design is all of one piece and the border of each roundel is painted on the same glass as the adjacent foliage.

Date. c. 1440.

B2, B4, B6, and B8. Vine Foliage

h. 0·50 m. w. 0·14 m.

Identical design repeated, at the centre an ornamental foliage design with two thick sprays of vine leaves and grapes springing from its border.

Condition. Incomplete, carefully restored with good modern copies for the missing portions. B2 and B6 centre foliage is modern. B4 centre and bottom foliage modern. B8 mostly modern. *In situ.*

Colour and Technique. Foliage design picked out of a matt wash, vine stem, grapes, and veins of the leaves in yellow stain. Background of cross-hatched painted lines, plain white border.

Style and Design. The design is all of one piece, the border is painted on the same glass as the vine foliage.

Date. c. 1440.

C1–C4. Foliage Designs

Identical design repeated of a frontal lion's face jessant in foliage.

Condition. The glass is well preserved with only slight corrosion. *In situ.*

Colour and Technique, Style and Design. Identical to n. II, C1–C4 above.

Date. c. 1440.

D1 and D2. Foliage Designs

h. 0·30 m. w. 0·28 m.

Identical design repeated of a large rose set on four serrated leaves.

Condition. Restored, the rose and foliage below in both are modern. The design is original, see n. IV, D2 below.

Date. c. 1440.

E2. Monogram and Foliage

h. 0·42 m. d. 0·42 m.

Condition. A large *M* for *Maria* of 16th-c. date inserted at the centre. The foliage in the lower foil is disturbed, the remainder *in situ.*

Colour and Technique. Foliage picked out of matt wash, plain white border.

Date. c. 1440.

n. IV   PLATE 40 (*d*)

2a–2d. Quarries and Crests

h. 0·30 m. w. 0·34 m.

Condition. The heads of the lights retain quarries *in situ,* identical with n. III, 2a–2d above. At the lower edges of 2b–2d and painted on the same glass as the adjacent quarries are the tops of three heraldic crests.

2b. Head of an eagle with raised wings, WILCOTES.
2c. A white helm with gold ornament and ermine mantle.
2d. Indistinct, possibly a plume of feathers.[1]

At 2a is a small fragment of a roundel, a bear collared and chained to two ragged staves. Background diaper as n. III, 2a above.

Colour and Technique. All white glass and yellow stain.

Style and Design. Although the remains are very slight they suggest that the shield of arms and crests recorded in the windows in the 17th–18th c. were set in the main lights against a background of quarries.[2]

Date. c. 1440.

B1, B3, B5, and B7. Roundels and Foliage Designs

h. 0·50 m. w. 0·14 m.

Designs identical with n. III, B1, B3, B5, and B7 above except that here the letters in sequence left to right are: *A. B. C. D.*

Condition. The glass is very well preserved, only slight corrosion. *In situ.* B7 is entirely modern.

Colour and Technique, Style and Design. As n. III, B1, etc. above.

Date. c. 1440.

B2, B4, B6, and B8. Vine Foliage Designs

h. 0·50 m. w. 0·14 m.

Designs are identical with n. III, B2, B4, B6, and B8 above.

Condition. The glass is well preserved, with only slight corrosion. *In situ.* B8 is entirely modern.

Colour and Technique, Style and Design. As n. III, B1, etc. above.

Date. c. 1440.

C1–C4. Foliage Designs

h. 0·30 m. w. 0·28 m.

Designs identical with n. III, C1–4 above.

Condition. The glass is well preserved with only slight corrosion. The lion's face in C2 is probably restoration. *In situ.*

D1 and D2. Foliage Designs

h. 0·30 m. w. 0·28 m.

Identical design as n. III, D1 and D2 above.

Condition. The glass is well preserved with only slight corrosion. The rose and foliage below in D1 are restored and those in D2 slightly incomplete. *In situ.*

Colour and Technique. Rose in yellow stain, leaves white and yellow stain picked out of a matt black wash, plain white border.

Style and Design. The design is of one piece. The rose and the foliage below are painted on the same piece of glass.

Date. c. 1440.

E2. Foliage Design

h. 0·42 m. w. 0·42 m.

Condition. Incomplete, at the centre an inserted fragment, two keys *in saltire.* 16th c.

Style and Design. The foliage is probably *in situ* but the lower foil is different from the others.

Date. c. 1440.

Lost Glass

Rawlinson's notes on the armorial glass have been published.[2] Wood's notes, however, are more complete and detailed:[3]

'Armes in severall windowes of North-Leigh church'

Argent three bars azure on a canton argent a demi-lion rampant gules (GREY?)

Argent a saltire between four escallops sable. Crest an oak tree proper acorned or BURIDGE.

---

[1] See Lost Glass.   [2] P.C. (1920), 231–2.   [3] Bodl. Lib. Wood MS. E. 1, f. 54.

Argent on a chevron sable between three pellets sable three roses argent. Crest a plume of feathers issuing out of a wreath argent shadowed sable (UNIDENTIFIED).

Ermine on a canton gules an owl argent, winged and beaked or. Crest an owl argent with a coronet about its neck or, white mantling with ermine spots (BARTON).

Argent on a bend azure three roses or crest a chapeau gules with an upturned brim ermine, set on a twisted torse argent studded with three roses or COKESAY.

Azure an eagle displayed argent, legged and beaked or, on its dexter wing an escallop (?) sable. Crest an eagle's head with wing argent out of a wreath (WILCOTES).

Azure an eagle displayed argent legged and beaked or, around its neck a coronet gules. Crest an eagle's head with wings out of a coronet gules (WILCOTES OF GREAT TEW).

Azure an eagle displayed argent, legged and beaked or. Crest an eagle's head out of a wreath.

Argent a chevron sable between three roses gules (incomplete) (NEW COLLEGE, OXFORD).

Bendy, a quarter ermine (BISHOPDEN).

Barry dancetty of six argent and gules (BALUN) in the east window of the chancel.

NORTHMOOR
ST. DENIS

O.S. SP 422 029.

s. V

2a, 2b. Roundel and Geometric Grisaille

Quarries: h. 0·14 m. w. 0·13 m.

Roundel (2a): d. 0·16 m.

Condition. The roundel is excessively decayed but the fragments of grisaille glass have only very slight traces of decay.

Colour and Technique. Roundel: six-petal rose with a green centre in a plain brown border. Any paint has perished. Geometric grisaille: painted on white glass, no yellow stain.

PRINTED SOURCES
P.C. (1920), 233.
Pevsner (1974), 722.

Style and Design. The geometric grisaille retains little of the original over-all pattern, but it was of the type springing from a vertical stem at the centre of the light, a piece of which remains adjacent to the roundel.

Date. First quarter (?) 14th c.

Lost Glass

The shield recorded by Wood and Rawlinson,[1] 'or a fess fuzille sable' is no longer extant. It was probably the shield (or) *a fess dancetty* (sable) VAVASOUR as found on the 14th-c. de la Mare tomb in the north transept of the church.

ROUSHAM
ST. JAMES

O.S. SP 470 243.

MS. SOURCES
Oxford. Bodleian Library, MS. Top. Oxon. e. 286, f. 95ʳ. Church Notes of N. Greenwood 1658–9.

PRINTED
Nelson (1913), 173.
P.C. (1920), 248.
Pevsner (1974), 739.
Parish Church Pamphlet (n.d.).

The fourteenth-century fragments of medieval glass in the west window of the south aisle have been leaded

[1] P.C. (1920), 233.

together with later glass relating to the Cottrell and Dormer families. This glass is said to have come from the Dormer manor house at Barton (Oxon.).[1]

s. V

Roundel and Geometric Grisaille

Quarries: h. 0·14 m. w. 0·13 m.

Roundel: d. 0·20 m.

The roundel and pieces of later glass are set against a background of white geometric grisaille painted with trails of maple leaves springing from a central vertical stem overlaid by a regular diamond-shaped trellis. Only three pieces of the grisaille are genuine, the remainder is a 19th-c. restoration artificially aged. Early 14th c.

Roundel: A quatrefoil design of four white serrated leaves radiating from a blue rosette at the centre superimposed upon a square with an ochre leaf at each corner. Enclosed by a plain green background and set within two plain borders, the inner is pot yellow, the outer pot ruby. The coloured glass is all pot-metal and very corroded on both surfaces. The plain outer borders are probably restored and composite. Early 14th c.

Lost Glass

The antiquarian notes record six shields in the windows of the church.[2]

In the east window of the chancel:

Azure a cross argent (AYLESBURY)

Azure a saltire engrailed gules (TIPTOFT)

Argent two bars and a canton gules (DE BOIS)

Argent a lion rampant gules (crowned or) a bordure sable bezanty or (PLANTAGENET, EARL OF CORNWALL).

In a north window:

(AYLESBURY).

In a north window of the church:

Quarterly 1, 4 azure two chevrons or (CHAWORTH) *2, 3 argent an escutcheon within an orle of cinquefoils (sable)* (CALTOFTE), *impaling quarterly 1, 4 azure a cross argent* (AYLESBURY) *2, 3 or three piles argent (for gules) a bordure sable bezanty* (BASSET OF WELDON).[3]

The single shields were probably of 14th-c. date. Edmund, Earl of Cornwall, granted a messuage at Rousham to Walter de Aylesbury in 1296[4] and the family continued to hold lands there throughout the 14th c.[5] The presence of the Tiptoft and De Bois arms has not been accounted for. The quarterly coat of Chaworth and Caltofte impaling Aylesbury quartering Basset represents Sir Thomas Chaworth (d. 1458), who married Isabella, daughter of Sir Thomas de Aylesbury.[6]

SANDFORD ST. MARTIN
ST. MARTIN

O.S. SP 421 266.

MS. SOURCES

Oxford. Bodleian Library, MS. Top. Oxon. d. 91, f. 66ᵛ. Notes by the Revd. F. H. Woods 1882.

s. III

C1. Head of Christ

h. 0·17 m. w. 0·20 m.

Frontal head of Christ. Ruby nimbus with green cross.

The head is extremely decayed, and the details obscured.

PRINTED

Marshall, E., *An Account of the Parish of Sandford* (1886).
Nelson (1913), 170.
Bouchier (1932), 95–6.
Pevsner (1974), 750–1.

It is apparently intact, with old leaded repair work. 14th c. set against modern plain glass.

s. IV

A2. Christ in Majesty   PLATE 40 (c)

h. 0·36 m. w. 0·33 m.

[1] Church Pamphlet.
[2] Greenwood MS., op. cit., P.C. (1920), 248.
[3] The blazon printed in P.C. (1920), 248 is incorrect.
[4] C. Moor, 'Knights of Edward I', *Harleian Society* lxxx (1929), 29.

[5] *Cal. Inq. Post Mortem* iii, 604, *Feudal Aids*, iv, 164, 178, 196.
[6] Monument at Launde Abbey (Leics.) W. Burton, *Description of Leicestershire* (1627), 159.

Figure: h. 0·30 m. w. 0·21 m.

Christ is seated in benediction holding an orb in his right hand.

Condition. The pot-metal glass is corroded, the white glass less so. The whole figure is set against a plain white modern surround. The head now has a large unrepaired hole in it.

Colour and Technique. The head, hands, and feet are painted on white glass with smear shading. The ruby nimbus has a cross of pot yellow ochre, and the figure wears a brown cloak with a blue tunic. The tracery of the throne is in green pot metal.

Iconography. This is the figure of the resurrected Christ wearing a crown of thorns, but the other wounds in the hands and feet are not indicated. It is probably a single devotional image and not part of a larger composition.

Style and Design. Probably related to the early glass at Merton College, Oxford, but the damage and decay prevent close stylistic analysis.

Date. Early 14th c.

s. V

2a. Roundel. (Apex of left main light)

d. 0·15 m.

Four white ivy leaves radiating from a plain red circle at the centre. Extremely decayed. 14th c.

SHILTON
HOLY ROOD

O.S. SP 267 083.

n. II

Quarries

Each quarry: h. 0·14 m. w. 0·11 m.

A collection of forty-three quarries leaded up with modern plain glass in a trellis design filling the entire lancet window.

Condition. The quarries are very decayed. The corrosion varies in intensity, but the design is legible.

Colour and Technique. Painted on white glass. The leaf designs painted in outline with very little shading.

PRINTED SOURCES
Pevsner (1974), 754–5.

Style and Design. Thirty-two quarries type 32. The basic design of each is the same, a single leaf on a vertical stem springing from the base of the quarry. There are slight variations of leaf form.

Four quarries type 34. An eight-point star formed by a central four-point star with subsidiary points in the angles.

The other quarries are either plain old glass, or obscured by decay.

Date. 14th c.

SHIPLAKE
ST. PETER AND ST. PAUL

O.S. SU 767 783.

PRINTED SOURCES

Willement, T., *A Concise Account of the Principal Works in Stained Glass* (1840), 21.
Climenson, C. J., *A History of Shiplake, Oxon.* (1894).

De Givenchy, M. C., Communication. Société des Antiquaires de la Morine, *Bulletin Historique* x (1897–1901), 192–5.
Bouchier (1932), 130–1.
Greening Lamborn (1949), 154–5.
Pevsner (1974), 755–6.

Five windows contain French glass of the late fifteenth–early sixteenth century (I, s. II, s. IV, s. V, and w. I) from the abbey church of St. Bertin at St.-Omer. Much of the glass was bought at St.-Omer by the Revd. J. B. Boteler and given to the church by him in 1828. The east and west windows of the south aisle were acquired from the same source in 1830[1] and presented to the church by the Revd. A. E. Howman.[2] The glass was rearranged by the glass painter and antiquarian scholar Thomas Willement.[3]

Nothing is known about the original position of this glass at St.-Omer. A rebuilding of the abbey church was begun by the abbot Gilbert 1246–64. The scheme was too grandiose for his successors, the choir was demolished and a more modest scheme was started by the abbot Henri de Condesaire in 1330. It was a protracted process; Abbot Guillaume Filatre 1447–73 appears to have played an important role but it was not completed until 1520.[4] The abbey was devastated at the time of the French Revolution, the church sold in 1799, and the surviving fabric demolished in 1830.[5] A detailed study of the style and design of this glass is not entered into here. However, it is hoped that the material will be incorporated into the relevant French volume of the C.V.M.A.

I   PLATE 41 (a)

1a. St. Anthony Abbot   PLATE 41 (b)
h. 0·50 m. w. 0·48 m.

Condition. Probably a complete panel, only slight corrosion.

Colour and Technique. Purple cap, white habit with blue tau cross, separately leaded on right shoulder, holds purple-covered book, leaf edges in yellow stain, and a bell also in yellow stain. Set against a green foliated background enclosed by a frame of pale pink clouds with a demi-figure of an angel in each corner, white albs, hair, apparel, and wings in yellow stain.

Iconography. Standard attributes of tau cross and bell.

Style and Design. See 5b.

Date. Late 15th c.

1b. The Blessed Peter of Luxembourg
d. 0·58 m.

Condition. A large roundel; the glass is incomplete and extremely corroded. The figure's head may be an alien insertion.

Colour and Technique. Head painted on white glass, hair and nimbus in yellow stain, cardinal's robes in pot-metal ruby, white fur trim at neck. Shield to left, *argent a lion rampant queue fourchée sable* (for *gules*), *armed langued and crowned or,* above the shield an incomplete cardinal's hat painted on white glass, knots of the tassels in yellow stain. Prayer desk and vision of crucifix painted on white glass, ornament and

rays behind crucifix in yellow stain, the details very obscure through decay.

Iconography. Greening Lamborn[6] mistakenly took Climenson's reference to Adolphus, son of Baldwin II 'Le Chauve', Count of Flanders[7] as referring to this panel. Greening Lamborn in turn suggested that the subject represented is the Mass of St. Gregory.[8] This is incorrect. The subject is the vision of Christ Crucified experienced by Peter of Luxembourg, who was born at Ligny in 1369, was created Bishop of Metz in 1384, and became Cardinal of San Giorgio in Velabro in 1386. He died at Villeneuve-les-Avignon in 1387.[9] The *processus* for his canonization began in 1390[10] but he was not beatified until 1527.[11] He was venerated as a saint throughout the 15th c.[12]

He experienced his vision of Christ Crucified at Avignon while walking to the Church of St. Pierre.[13] The identification of the panel can be verified on two counts. The arms of Luxembourg, although not given in their proper tinctures, are ensigned with a cardinal's hat and can be compared with the shield of arms in his personal prayer-book.[14] Secondly, the composition of the panel is very close to the illustration of his vision which prefaces the prayer composed by him found in a Parisian Book of Hours of *c.* 1410.[15] No other example of this scene has been found in painted glass.

Date. 15th c.

1c. St. John Evangelist
h. 0·50 m. w. 0·48 m.

Condition. The panel is probably complete, only slight corrosion.

[1] Climenson, op. cit. 370.
[2] Willement, op. cit. 21.
[3] Ibid.
[4] 'Essai sur la Mosaïque de St. Bertin', *Société des Antiquaires de la Morine, Mémoires,* i (1833). E. Wallet, *Description de l'ancienne abbaye de St. Bertin* (1834).
[5] Wallet, op. cit. 29, and engravings showing the ruined state, 1814–21.
[6] Greening Lamborn (1949), 154. De Givenchy, op. cit. 195.
[7] Climenson, op. cit. 398.
[8] Greening Lamborn (1949), 154.
[9] 'Vita auctore anonymo', *Acta Sanctorum* July, i (1867), 509–16; 'Vita altera auctore Henrico Albio S. J.', ibid. 516–25.
[10] Ibid. 525.
[11] H. Albi, *La Vie de B. Pierre, Cardinal de Luxembourg* (Avignon, 2nd edn., 1651), 125–32.
[12] For examples, see *Herder* viii (1976), 185.
[13] 'Vita . . . Henrico Albio', op. cit. 520, cap. III.
[14] Avignon. Musée Calvet MS. 207, f. 8ʳ and 16ᵛ. Paris, Bibl. Nat., *Les Manuscrits à peintures en France du XIIIᵉ au XVIᵉ siècle* (1955), Cat. no. 136.
[15] U.S.A. Baltimore, Walters Art Gallery. MS. W. 232, f. 93.

Colour and Technique. Figure painted on white glass, except for pot-metal blue tunic, hair and poisoned cup in yellow stain. Blue foliated background, cloud frame and corner angels as 1a above.

Iconography. Standard, the saint blesses the poisoned cup and the poison emerges in the form of a dragon.

Style and Design. See 5b.

Date. Late 15th c.

2a. St. Barbara

h. 0·50 m. w. 0·48 m.

Condition. The panel is probably complete, only slight corrosion.

Colour and Technique. Ruby nimbus, head painted on white glass, hair in yellow stain, purple tunic, tower in white glass, green foliated background, cloud frame in blue glass. Corner angels as 1a above.

Iconography. Standard, holding a model of the tower where she was confined by her father (see Mapledurham 1, 2c).

Style and Design. See 5b.

Date. Late 15th c.

2b. St. Peter Apostle

h. 0·50 m. w. 0·58 m.

Condition. The panel is probably complete, only slight corrosion.

Colour and Technique. Modern purple nimbus, head and mantle painted on white glass; he holds a book with a purple cover and a large key in yellow stain. Ochre foliated background, cloud frame in blue glass, corner angels as 1a above.

Iconography. Standard, two keys are more common, derived from Matthew 16:19.

Style and Design. See 5b.

Date. Late 15th c.

2c. St. Catherine

h. 0·50 m. w. 0·48 m.

Condition. The panel is probably complete, only slight corrosion.

Colour and Technique. Painted on white glass except for the pot-metal ruby tunic. Brown hair, wheel and sword in yellow stain. Green foliated background, cloud frame in blue glass, corner angels as 1a above.

Iconography. Standard, the wheel and sword symbolize her torments and execution.

Style and Design. See 5b.

Date. Late 15th c.

3a, 3c. Coronation of the Virgin
3a. The Virgin Mary

h. 0·50 m. w. 0·48 m.

Condition. Incomplete fragment, the upper half of a large composition. Corrosion of varying intensity, the white glass is better preserved. Ruby tunic is composite.

Colour and Technique. Ruby nimbus, head and hands in white glass, hair and crown in yellow stain, blue mantle, ruby tunic, throne in pot-metal ochre. Angels in white, hair and wings in yellow stain. Background of blue clouds studded with ochre rosettes, separately leaded.

Iconography. Standard, crowned by two angels.

Style and Design. See 3c.

Date. Late 15th c.

3b. St. Omer

h. 0·50 m. w. 0·58 m.

Condition. The panel is incomplete and disturbed, only slight corrosion.

Colour and Technique. Painted on white glass, ornaments of mitre and cope in yellow stain. Shield: *gules a double traverse cross argent* ST. OMER.[1] Purple foliated background, cloud frame in green glass, corner angels as 1a above.

Iconography. St. Omer, i.e. Audomar, Bishop of Thérouanne 637, d. 669.

Style and Design. See 5b.

Date. Late 15th c.

3c. God the Father

h. 0·50 m. w. 0·48 m.

Companion figure to the Virgin Mary, 3a.

Condition. As 3a.

Colour and Technique. Purple nimbus, face, hands, and mantle painted on white glass, crown and cross orb yellow stain, purple tunic, pot-metal ochre throne, background diaper and angels as 3a.

---

[1] M. Coolen, 'Les armoires de St. Omer', Société des Antiquaires de la Morine, *Bulletin Historique* xvii (1946–52), 394–7.

Iconography. Companion figure to 3a above. God the Father, elderly head type, is depicted rather than Christ, which is unusual.

Style and Design. Identical thrones and background diapers in 3a and 3b, angels drawn from the same cartoon reversed.

Date. Late 15th c.

4a. Seraphim

h. 0·55 m. w. 0·48 m.

Condition. Figure incomplete, background at top restored.

Colour and Technique. Face and flesh of seraphim painted on ruby glass, neck, scarf, and wings in white and yellow stain, green foliated background. Purple cloud frame and two angels as 1a.

Iconography. Standard.

Style and Design. See 5b.

Date. Late 15th c.

4b. St. Andrew

h. 0·50 m. w. 0·58 m.

Condition. The panel is probably complete, only slight corrosion.

Colour and Technique. Purple nimbus, figure painted on white glass except for blue tunic, saltire cross in pot-metal ochre, ruby foliated background, green cloud frame, and angels as 1a above.

Iconography. Standard, saltire cross of his martyrdom.

Style and Design. See 5b.

Date. Late 15th c.

4c. Seraphim

h. 0·55 m. w. 0·48 m.

Identical with 4a.

5b. St. John Baptist

h. 0·50 m. w. 0·58 m.

Condition. The panel is incomplete, lacks the two upper angels, the paint on the white glass rather worn.

Colour and Technique. Green nimbus, figure and *Agnus Dei* painted on white glass, hem of mantle and nimbus of *Agnus Dei* in yellow stain, blue foliated background, ochre cloud frame, two angels as 1a.

Iconography. Standard.

Style and Design. All the panels in this window, except 1b,

are part of a related series, with repetition of identical cartoons for the angels and cloud frames.

Date. Late 15th c.

6b. Fragments

h. 0·34 m. w. 0·58 m.

An incomplete cherubim, white glass, late 15th c., set on fragments.

s. II   PLATE 42 (*a*)

The window contains four heads and two bust-length figures, arranged and leaded up with new backgrounds by T. Willement in 1828.

1a. Male Head

Panel: h. 0·48 m. w. 0·44 m. Head: h. 0·18 m.

Incomplete, the top of the head is missing. Painted on white glass, hair in yellow stain. The eyes are shown closed, an unusual feature.

Date. Late 15th–16th c.

1b. Female Head

Panel: h. 0·48 m. w. 0·44 m. Head: h. 0·18 m.

Incomplete, the top of the head is missing. Painted on white glass, hair in yellow stain.

Fragment of an inscription, in black-letter script: |*tus*|.

Date. Late 15th–16th c.

2a. Knight

h. 0·48 m. w. 0·44 m.

Colour and Technique. Head and hand painted on white glass, white bascinet with mail aventail in yellow stain. White cloak, yellow stain pattern, very faint, on his right shoulder the upper part of a *lion rampant azure langued gules*. Hilt of sword in yellow stain. Background diaper of fleurs-de-lis pot-metal ochre, partly restored.

Date. Late 15th–16th c.

2b. Priest ?

h. 0·48 m. w. 0·44 m.

Condition. The ruby sleeve and canopy above the head are modern, as is much of the background.

Colour and Technique. Painted on white glass, headband in yellow stain. Background diaper of fleurs-de-lis in pot-metal ochre.

Date. Late 15th–16th c.

3a. Female Head

Panel: h. 0·48 m. w. 0·44 m. Head: h. 0·23 m.

Colour and Technique. Painted on white glass, hair in yellow stain. Plain modern background.

Date. Late 15th–16th c.

3b. Male Head

h. 0·48 m. w. 0·44 m. Head: h. 0·23 m.

Colour and Technique. Painted on white glass, hair in yellow stain. The right-hand side of the hat and chest are alien insertions. Plain modern background.

Date. Late 15th–16th c.

s. IV   PLATE 42 (*b*)

1a, 1c. Lion's Head

h. 0·10 m. w. 0·14 m.

Painted on white glass, part of a larger composition, fragment of foliage background painted on same glass.

2a, 2c, 3a, 3c, 4a, 4c, 5a, 5c. Heads

h. 0·18 m. w. 0·18 m.

Each is a head from a large human figure now leaded up as roundels. Background all modern.

Colour and Technique. All painted on white glass, details of hair and beards in yellow stain.

Iconography. It has been stated that these heads are portraits of the abbots or priors of St. Bertin.[1] There is no evidence to support this, only one is tonsured, 4a, and one is probably female, 4c.

Date. Late 15th–16th c.

1b–4b. St. Peter and Donor Figure

h. 1·74 m. w. 0·58 m.

St. Peter, before him a cantor kneeling at a music lectern with a musician angel above him.

Condition. The whole arrangement is suspect, probably a clever composite by Willement. The upper part of the donor is out of all proportion to the lower part of the figure. The lead lines of St. Peter's drapery, except his left arm, suggest composite work. His nimbus is modern.

Colour and Technique. The composite nature of the panel precludes detailed comment. The purple hanging with pattern of paracletes picked out of a matt wash is noteworthy.

Date. Late 15th–16th c.

5b. Angels and Papal Tiara

h. 1·10 m. w. 0·58 m.

Placed in this window by Willement.[2]

Colour and Technique. Tiara in white glass with extensive yellow stain for the jewelled ornament and cresting. Pot-metal ochre clouds, angels in white glass, details of hair and albs in yellow stain.

Style and Design. The very large tiara is unusual. The lead lines are basically sound so there is no reason to suppose that it is a composite design.

Date. Late 15th–16th c.

s. V   PLATE 42 (*d*)

1b. 19th-c. panel with inserted female head, white and yellow stain. 15th c.

2a and 2b are English.

2a. Female Saint

h. 0·66 m. w. 0·30 m.

Crowned and nimbed, holding a sword.

Condition. Figure's left hand and arm are missing, patched with an alien fragment. Ground below feet also probably alien. The canopy and side shafts are all 19th-c.

Colour and Technique. Figure on white glass, crown and tunic in yellow stain, tunic patterned with rosettes in a trellis painted in outline. Bold line hatching on the drapery. Blue background diapered with contiguous rosettes painted in outline. Green ground at feet.

Iconography. A royal martyr but no distinctive attribute.

Style and Design. See 2b below.

Date. 15th c., second quarter(?)

2b. Female Saint

h. 0·66 m. w. 0·30 m.

Crowned and nimbed, holding a large book and a bone (?).

Condition. The area of the figure's shoulder and the upper part of the bone are 19th c. Paint on tunic very worn. Ground below feet is composite of 15th-c. tiled flooring and modern glass. Canopy and side shafts are all 19th c.

Colour and Technique. Figure painted on white glass, crown, hair, tunic, and bone in yellow stain. Drapery painting and blue background as 2a above.

Iconography. Identification uncertain, the upper part of the bone is restoration and nothing comparable has been found.

---

[1] Climenson, op. cit., description of glass 398–400.   [2] Ibid.

Style and Design. The two figures are companion pieces, very alike in drawing and drapery modelling.

Date. Second quarter 15th c.

3a. Fragments

h. 0·50 m. w. 0·30 m.

Six heads, all possibly angels, and a large head of an archangel, the latter h. 0·24 m. w. 0·20 m.

Colour and Technique. All painted on white glass, hair and decorative details in yellow stain. Background is 19th c.

Date. Late 15th c.

3b. Fragments

h. 0·50 m. w. 0·30 m.

Six heads, including two of the Christ Child, a monk, and an archangel, the last set inside out.

Colour and Technique. As 3a, the background is 19th c.

Date. Late 15th c.

A1. Fragments

h. 0·23 m. w. 0·20 m.

Head of an angel, white and yellow stain. 16th c., on a modern background.

w. I   PLATE 42 (*c*)

1a. St. John Evangelist?

h. 0·52 m. w. 0·43 m.

Colour and Technique. Head painted on white glass, hair and wide border of nimbus in yellow stain. White mantle, jewelled hem in yellow stain, purple tunic. Behind him a blue damask cloth with pot-metal ochre band at the top and plain purple above.

Iconography. Young beardless saint, appropriate for St. John Evangelist but no attribute to identify him.

Style and Design. A companion figure to 1c.

Date. Late 15th c.

1b. Eagle of St. John

h. 0·48 m. w. 0·53 m.

Condition. Restored, scroll inscribed |*S'*.| [*Jehan*].|; the name is modern. Set on a background of fragments.

Colour and Technique. Painted on white glass, border to scroll in yellow stain.

Iconography. Standard.

Date. 15th c.

1c. St. John Baptist?

h. 0·53 m. w. 0·43 m.

Colour and Technique. Head and mantle painted on white glass, nimbus and hairy tunic in yellow stain. Background as 1a but patched with alien pieces.

Iconography. The long flowing hair and hairy tunic are appropriate to St. John Baptist. The sorrowing expression of this figure suggests that originally it may have been part of a Crucifixion group.[1]

Style and Design. Companion figure to 1a.

Date. Late 15th c.

2a. Head of a Knight

d. 0·35 m.

Condition. A composite panel by Willement, the lower part of the face, nimbus, and background are 19th c.

Colour and Technique. Painted on white glass.

Date. Late 15th–16th c.

2b. Bull of St. Luke

h. 0·46 m. w. 0·53 m.

Condition. Very corroded, set on a background of fragments.

Colour and Technique. Painted on white glass, eyes and border to scroll in yellow stain.

Iconography. Standard. Scroll inscribed |*S'luc*|.

Date. 15th c.

2c. Male Head

d. 0·35 m.

Condition. A composite panel by Willement, the nimbus is 19th c.

Colour and Technique. Painted on white glass.

Date. Late 15th–16th c.

3a. The Virgin and Child

h. 0·53 m. w. 0·43 m.

Condition. Incomplete, the Virgin's face is missing.

Colour and Technique. Virgin painted on white glass, crown, hair, and jewelled hem of mantle in yellow stain. Christ's hair and cross of nimbus in yellow stain, blue tunic with white and yellow stain cuffs. Background of rays in yellow stain, purple damask above.

Date. Late 15th–16th c.

---

[1] Figures of St. John Baptist associated with Crucifixion groups are rare. Two French examples are found on a 14th-c. silver-gilt ciborium at the Musée des Antiquités, Rouen, and the Bargello Diptych, Paris, *c*. 1390. G. Ring, *Century of French Painting 1400–1500* (1949), 193, fig. 27.

3b. Lion of St. Mark

h. 0·43 m. w. 0·53 m.

Condition. Very corroded and incomplete, set on a background of fragments.

Colour and Technique. Painted on white glass, body of lion in yellow stain.

Iconography. Standard. Scroll inscribed |S'M|arc|, partly illegible because of corrosion.

Date. 15th c.

3c. God the Father

h. 0·53 m. w. 0·43 m.

Condition. Very corroded, the drapery is a composite by T. Willement.

Colour and Technique. Head painted on white glass, nimbus in yellow stain. Blue damask background.

Date. Late 15th–16th c.

4a. Cherubim

h. 0·51 m. w. 0·43 m.

Condition. Set on a background of fragments.

Colour and Technique. Painted on white glass, tiled floor alternately black and yellow stain, blue background, incomplete canopy above in white and yellow stain.

Date. Late 15th–16th c.

4b. Angel of St. Matthew

h. 0·53 m. w. 0·53 m.

Condition. Very corroded, set on a background of fragments.

Colour and Technique. Painted on white glass, hair, borders of nimbus, and scroll in yellow stain.

Iconography. Standard. Scroll inscribed |Mateus|.

Style and Design. The roundels 1b, 2b, 3b, and 4b are a single series.

Date. 15th c.

4c. Cherubim

h. 0·51 m. w. 0·43 m.

Same design as 4a, set on a background of fragments.

5a. Fragments

h. 0·68 m. w. 0·43 m.

A very decayed figure of an angel and two grotesque monkey heads, white and yellow stain.

Date. Late 15th–16th c.

5b. Canopy

h. 0·76 m. w. 0·53 m.

Condition. Incomplete, the seraphim at the top centre is an insertion.

Colour and Technique. Canopy is white and yellow stain, light-green damask background.

Date. Late 15th–16th c.

5c. Fragments

h. 0·68 m. w. 0·43 m.

An angel painted from the same cartoon, reversed, as the one in 5a, two grotesque monkey heads, that on the right blowing a trumpet, white and yellow stain.

Date. Late 15th–16th c.

A1. Fragments

h. 0·26 m. w. 0·13 m.

A grotesque monkey head, white and yellow stain. Set on fragments.

Date. Late 15th–16th c.

A2. Fragments

h. 0·48 m. w. 0·53 m.

The Holy Dove, white and yellow stain. Incomplete head of Christ.

Date. Late 15th–16th c.

A3. Fragments

h. 0·26 m. w. 0·13 m.

A grotesque monkey head, white and yellow stain. Set on fragments.

Date. Late 15th–16th c.

SOULDERN

ST. MARY

O.S. SP 524 317.

s. VI

A2. Foliage Design

Tracery light, a shield set against white foliage.

Condition. The shield *gules a pale argent* is a restorer's composite. Only a small piece of the ruby glass is genuine. The foliage of the lower right lobe has been replaced by modern white glass. White foliage set inside out.

PRINTED SOURCES
P.C. (1920), 270–2.
Pevsner (1974), 768–9.

Style and Design. Simple cabbage-like leaf form painted on white glass, probably *in situ*.

Date. Second half 14th c.

Lost Glass

The four shields of arms noted by Wood[1] and Rawlinson[2] have not survived.

SOUTH LEIGH

ST. JAMES

O.S. SP 394 091.

MS. SOURCES
London. British Library, Harleian MS. 4170, p. 49. Church notes dated 16 June 1660.
Oxford. Bodleian Library, MS. Top. Oxon. b. 75, ff. 138ᵛ, 140. Wyatt Collections 18th–19th c., *c.* 1802.

PRINTED
Parker (1846), 168.
Nelson (1913), 170.
Bouchier (1918), 96.
P.C. (1920), 272–3.
Bouchier (1932), 133.
Pevsner (1974), 770.

The church contains a small but interesting collection of fragments of fifteenth-century glass, indifferently arranged with plain pieces of modern white glass. Much of the medieval glass has been reset inside out. The present arrangement was made after 1846 when the 'fragments' were mentioned as being in the east window of the chancel.[3]

There is an incomplete head of St. James Major which, judging by the scale, was from a full-length standing figure (n. III, 2b), and may have been part of a series of the Twelve Apostles. However, an individual commemoration is not impossible as the advowson of the church was held by Reading Abbey[4] and one of the most prized relics enshrined there was the hand of St. James.[5]

A heraldic tracery-light design is of particular interest, as there are no parallels remaining in the county. It shows a shield hanging by its strap from a branch of a tree and the suggestion is made that the source of the design is to be found in thirteenth-century designs for seals.

There are two fragmentary figures of Adam digging and Eve spinning, possibly designed for tracery

---

[1] Bodl. Lib. Wood MS. B. 15, f. 77ᵛ, 1658.
[2] P.C. (1920), 270.
[3] Parker (1846), 168. No details of the glass are given.
[4] Ibid.
[5] For a comparable 13th-c. example see Stanton Harcourt.

lights (n. III, A3 and A4), which are the only extant indigenous example in the county of an Old Testament narrative scene.

Although the remaining glass is very fragmentary it should be noted that there is no coloured pot-metal glass, all the pieces are white glass and yellow stain.

n. III

1b. Fragments

h. 0·80 m. w. 0·50 m.

Condition. A composite panel, sixteen medieval fragments leaded up with plain modern and old white glass of indeterminate date.

The most complete pieces are:

Two border pieces, h. 0·11 m. w. 0·06 m. Identical design, each a crown, white and yellow stain against a plain matt ground. 15th c.

A border piece, h. 0·13 m. w. 0·06 m. A foliage design in white and yellow stain against a plain matt ground. 15th c. The three pieces were probably part of an alternating border pattern (compare North Leigh n. III, 2a-d).

Two quarries, h. 0·15 m. w. 0·11. Identical design, white and yellow stain. Quarry type 50. 15th c. Centre as type 49 one fragment of type 25.

A heraldic badge (?), h. 0·10 m. w. 0·09 m. *A double-headed eagle displayed on its breast a whirlpool for difference* UNIDENTIFIED. Painted on a single piece of white glass, stained yellow, background of cross-hatched lines. Possibly part of a repeated design, painted border at the bottom and left side. The whirlpool is four concentric circles.[1] Bouchier's suggestion that this is 'the cognisance of Richard, King of the Romans'[2] (i.e. Richard, Earl of Cornwall, King of the Romans 1256, d. 1272) is not tenable. Comparison can be made with the heraldic roundels at Ewelme and North Leigh.

2b. Composite Panel

h. 1·01 m. w. 0·50 m.

Condition. A composite panel, incorporating the remains of five figures, pieces of canopy, and decorative designs leaded up with modern plain white glass.

The more substantial pieces are:

St. James Major h. 0·19 m.

An incomplete head, from a full-length figure, facing three-quarters right. Nimbed, he wears a pilgrim's hat with a scallop badge. (For the iconography see Combe, s. IV, 3c.) Painted on white glass with stipple and line shading. First quarter 15th c.

The next three figures are alike in scale, technique, and design and probably come from a related series:

Royal Saint h. 0·15 m.

Incomplete, only the head and part of the raised right hand remain. Bearded head, nimbed and crowned, facing three-quarters left. Painted on white glass, hair, crown, and beaded border of the nimbus in yellow stain. Stippled and line shading, highlights picked out of a light matt wash. Mid 15th c.

Virgin Saint h. 0·15 m.

Incomplete, only the head and shoulders remain. Nimbed and crowned, facing three-quarters right. Adjacent to the head and painted on the same piece of glass is a foliated finial, possibly the head of a sceptre. Technique as above, the hair and crown in yellow stain. Mid 15th c.

Male Saint (St. John Evangelist?) h. 0·10 m.

Incomplete, only the upper part of the head remains. Nimbed, facing three-quarters left, the youthful beardless face is common form for St. John Evangelist. Technique as above, the beaded border of the nimbus in yellow stain. Mid 15th c.

Angel

Incomplete, bust length, facing three-quarters left. Painted on white glass, the hair and surviving wing in yellow stain. Possibly from the same series as the three heads above. Mid 15th c.

Canopy Designs

The centre cusps at the head of the light each contain a traceried arcade; the tracery designs are identical but the mouldings above are different. Each piece has a plain white outer border shaped to fit the cusp of a light. Mid 15th c.

A2. Fragments

h. 0·40 m. w. 0·17 m.

Two bird designs, see A3, but differently shaped pieces, small fragments of canopies leaded up with modern plain white glass.

A3. Heraldic Design

h. 0·60 m. w. 0·17 m.

The design when complete showed a shield suspended by

[1] For the blazon see the arms of Ralph de Gorges, Glover's Roll 192, 'Rolls of Arms of Henry III', ed. T. D. Tremlett and H. S. London, *Aspilogia* ii (1967), 152. [2] Bouchier (1918), 96.

its strap from the limb of a tree with two birds in profile perched above it.

Condition. Incomplete, the shield and lower part of the light are missing and have been replaced with fragments and modern plain white glass. The two birds at the shoulder of the light have been set inside out.

Colour and Technique. Painted on white glass. The embroidered strap, foliage of the tree, and birds in yellow stain. Background a bold pebble pattern picked out of a matt black wash.

Style and Design. The design is based on a long-established class of seal design. The earliest examples are of the later 13th c. The seal of Alianora, Countess of Leicester, d. 1264, depicts her standing beside a tree from which hangs a shield of the Montfort arms.[1] The seal used in 1270 by Alice de Lacy, widow of Edmund de Lacy, second Earl of Lincoln, has a shield of Lacy suspended by an embroidered strap from a tree of three branches.[2] This class of design on seals continues until the late 14th c.[3] It is not a common feature in glass painting, the earliest noted example being the early 14th-c. glass at Wing (Bucks.).[4] Representations in other media are also rare; a local painted example is found at South Newington, in an incomplete 15th-c. series of shields in the spandrels of the north nave arcade.[5]

It is to be noted that the two birds above the tree are each enclosed by a cusped border, which is probably their proper position in the over-all design as the pieces are shaped to the outline of the adjacent foliage and to the shoulder of the light.

Date. Mid 15th c.

Fragments:

A bird design, bird in profile facing right, cusped frame as above. The piece of glass is a different shape and its place in the over-all design is impossible to determine. Mid 15th c. Two small fragments of two others.

A fragment of a figure, a hand holding a spindle, probably from a figure of Eve spinning, a companion figure to the Adam in A4. Mid 15th c.

A4. Fragments

h. 0·60 m. w. 0·17 m.

Condition. Incomplete, fragments leaded up with modern plain white glass.

At the shoulder of the light are two bird designs, cusped frames as A3 but the top edges are shaped differently. The left one is incomplete.

Adam Digging

Incomplete. Part of the head, lower part of his tunic, feet, and fragment of the spade survive. Now set inside out.

Colour and Technique. Painted on white glass, the spade and ground at his feet in yellow stain. Background a bold pebble design picked out of a matt black wash.

Iconography. Standard late medieval type of Adam digging with a spade and Eve spinning.[6] This is the only surviving example in the county of an indigenous Old Testament narrative scene.

Style and Design. The iconographic links between the fragments in A3 and A4 are substantiated by the design details. The head and raised foot of Adam and hand and spindle of Eve are painted on the same pieces of glass as the adjacent background diapers. It is impossible to say what the original over-all design was; the plain border by Eve's spindle suggests the figures were probably in two adjacent tracery lights.

Date. Mid 15th c.

At the base of the light is a small fragment of a bird design similar to the ones above, but the shape and border suggest it comes from an apex cusp of a light. Mid 15th c. Small fragments of a nimbus, beaded border. Mid 15th c.

A5. Fragments

h. 0·40 m. w. 0·17 m.

Condition. Four fragments leaded up with modern plain white glass.

Two bird designs, identical in shape with the pair in A3 above. Mid 15th c.

Two fragments of a cable-twist border design, white and yellow stain. Mid 15th c.

n. IV

2a, 2c

Roundels: d. 0·10 m.

In the apex cusp is a roundel with a crown design, flanked in the side cusps by roundels with a star design. All painted on white glass, yellow stain on a matt black background. All set inside out. Mid 15th c.

n. VI

2a, 2b, 2c

Roundels: d. 0·10 m.

Nine identical roundels, each a star design as n. IV, 2a, 2c

---

[1] Birch, ii (1892), 6686, cast lxxx. 18.

[2] Ibid. iii (1894), 11,186. B.L. Harl. Charter 52 H. 43B.

[3] Ibid. 12,230. B.L. Harl. Charter 79 E. 8. Seal of Roger de Northwode, county of Kent, dated 1385. This is the latest example illustrated by Birch.

[4] Greening Lamborn (1949), 91, pl. 23.

[5] Only one is complete, two others are very fragmentary.

[6] Compare the 15th-c. panel at Great Malvern Priory. Rushforth (1936), 159, fig. 67. For the general iconography see *Herder* i (1968), 41–70.

above. All set inside out except for the one in the left-hand cusp of 2b. Mid 15th c.

w. I

2a, 2b. Canopy

(Measurements not obtainable.)

Two identical tops of a canopy design, white glass and yellow stain. Background design of contiguous rosettes painted in outline. 2a is set inside out. Mid 15th c.

A1. Angel?

h. 0·15 m. w. 0·15 m.

Incomplete, the head only remains, facing three-quarters right, nimbed. The paint is extremely worn. Mid 15th c.

Lost Glass

The 17th-c. antiquarian notes record a number of shields that have not survived.[1] Only one remained *c.* 1802 when it was described: 'Here in very fine painted glass among the broken bits is a shield of the arms of la Zouche of Harringworth, Argent (for gules on account of leading in so many charges) 10 bezants or 22321, a quarter charged 5 spots (ermine in trick). In Fifield church near Burford is another shield of ditto with the bezants leaded into the field gules.'[2] A drawing of the shield is added, together with a sketch of the tracery light n. III, A3 showing it as incomplete then as now.[3]

SOUTH NEWINGTON
ST. PETER AD VINCULA

O.S. SP 407 334.

MS. SOURCES

Oxford. Bodleian Library, MS. Top. Oxon. b. 75, ff. 206–7. Wyatt Collections 18th–19th c., dated 1805.

PRINTED

'S. Newington or Newington Juel'. 'N.O.A.S. (1875), 38–9.
Nelson (1913), 171.
Greening Lamborn (1949), 142–3.
Pevsner (1974), 772–3.

The glass that survives varies considerably in style, design, and technical competence. The earliest glass consists of shields of arms and geometric grisaille in s. IV. Its condition is much the same as recorded in 1805.[4] If it is *in situ* there are some stylistic differences that require explanation. The geometric grisaille at the heads of the main lights is painted with trails of oak leaves and acorns (2a and 2c), which contrasts with the very stylized trails of fruiting leaves and grapes in the lower tracery lights (B1–B3), and the flat acanthus-leaf surrounds to the shields above (D1 and D2). Hawthorn foliage occurs in the apex tracery light (F1). It is a curious mixture of styles, not to be dismissed as composite work by some restorer. The rebuilding of the south aisle has been dated *c.* 1300,[5] which is also appropriate for the glass.

The side windows of the chancel contain three early fourteenth-century roundels, each a symbol of an Evangelist. Although they are incomplete and very corroded it is evident that they were painted with meticulous attention to detail, as can be seen in the painting of the head and hand of the angel of St. Matthew (s. III, A1).

The glass in the windows of the north aisle of the nave provides a complete contrast (n. IV, n. V, and n. VI). Although the remains are slight and somewhat decayed the painting can be seen to be extremely cursory. The grotesque animals and birds are so simplified in design, and so crude in execution that they verge on the borders of caricature. The foliage designs in the tracery lights of n. VI are reduced to almost the bare outlines. This is a cheap class of design, all the remaining glass is in white and yellow stain and there is no evidence to suggest that coloured glass was used. This poverty of design also contrasts with the

[1] B.L. Harleian MS. 4170, p. 49, op. cit. P.C. (1920), 272–3.
[2] Bodl. Lib. MS. Top. Oxon. b. 75, f. 138ᵛ, op. cit.
[3] Ibid., f. 140.
[4] Bodl. Lib. MS. Top. Oxon. b. 75, ff. 206–7, op. cit.
[5] Pevsner (1974), 771.

mural paintings in the same north aisle. These are of high technical and artistic merit.[1] If the glass and mural paintings are contemporary a dating in the second quarter of the fourteenth century is probable as one of the murals depicts the beheading of Thomas, Earl of Lancaster, who was executed in 1322.[2]

n. II

A1. Bull of St. Luke

d. 0·25 m.

Only three of its legs remain. Between them is a scroll inscribed in Lombardic script:

|(EV)|ANG|(ELISTA)|LVCAS|

Condition. The glass is extremely corroded, the details obscure. Incomplete, made up with modern plain glass, all set inside out. Insertion: a small white hand, probably from s. III, A1 below.

Colour and Technique. Bull in pot-metal ochre, inscription picked out of a matt black wash on plain white glass, plain ruby background.

Iconography. Standard, the abbreviation *ANG* is not common.

Style and Design. See s. III, A1.

Date. Early 14th c.

n. III

A1. Eagle of St. John

Facing right the wings displayed and the head adossed.

Holding a scroll inscribed in Lombardic script:

|(EV)|ANG(ELISTA) IOHA|(N)NES|

Condition. Incomplete, part of the eagle's body patched with part of a green wing, probably from s. III, A1 below. The glass is extremely corroded, the details obscure.

Colour and Technique. The eagle is painted on pot-metal ochre glass, scroll as n. II, A1 above, plain ruby background.

Iconography. Standard. The abbreviation *ANG* is painted on the same glass as the beginning of the scroll.

Style and Design. See s. III, A1.

Date. Early 14th c.

s. II

A1. Fragments

d. 0·25 m.

A small lion's face in yellow stain, scraps of canopy shaftings, white and yellow stain, plain ruby and blue.

All early 14th c.

s. III

A1. Angel of St. Matthew

d. 0·25 m.

Nimbed angel, facing left.

Only a fragment of the name scroll survives in Lombardic script: |A|.

Condition. Very incomplete, only the head, one hand, and part of a scroll and wing remain. Made up with alien fragments. Extremely corroded.

Colour and Technique. Head and hands painted on white glass, smear shading, hair in matt, wings in deep green, plain ruby ground.

Iconography. Standard.

Style and Design. The three remaining symbols in these chancel windows are obviously from one series identical in size and technique. The details are obscure but the head type for the angel of St. Matthew with raised pointed eyebrows, turned-down mouth, and gesticulating long fingers has affinities with the earlier glass at Merton College Chapel, Oxford, *c.* 1289–96.

Date. Early 14th c.

n. IV

A1. Grotesque Dragon   PLATE 43 (*b*)

h. 0·26 m. w. 0·06 m.

In profile, crawling downwards to the left.

Condition. Complete, only slight corrosion. *In situ.*

Colour and Technique. Painted on white glass, dragon in yellow stain, plain background and border.

Style and Design. See A4.

Date. Second quarter 14th c.

A2. Fragments

h. 0·28 m. w. 0·17 m.

Condition. Unrelated fragments, an incomplete male head, piece of geometric grisaille, and part of a shield: *or a fess embattled sable* ADDERBURY.

Colour and Technique. Head painted on white glass, hair and beard in yellow stain. Shield in yellow stain.

Date. Second quarter 14th c. The shield was complete in 1805.[3] The Adderbury family held lands in the manor.[4]

---

[1] E. W. Tristram, *English Wall Paintings of the Fourteenth Century* (1955), 16–20, 226–9.
[2] Ibid. 228–9. For the iconography of Thomas of Lancaster see

Newton i (1961), 288–94. *Herder* viii (1976), 490–1.
[3] Bodl. Lib. MS. Top. Oxon. b. 75, op. cit.
[4] *N.O.A.S.* op. cit. Greening Lamborn (1949), 143.

A3. Fragments   PLATE 43 (d)

h. 0·28 m. w. 0·17 m.

Condition. Unrelated fragments, an incomplete male head, border piece, and geometric grisaille.

Colour and Technique, Style and Design. Head painted from the same cartoon as A2 above. Grotesque wyvern border piece in yellow stain, same cartoon as B2 and n. VI, 2a, 2b.

Date. As above.

A4. Grotesque Dragon   PLATE 43 (c)

h. 0·26 m. w. 0·06 m.

A companion piece to A1 above, but not a mirror image, slight differences in the drawing of the wings and position of the legs. *In situ.*

Colour and Technique. As A1.

Date. As above.

B1. Fragments

h. 0·26 m. w. 0·14 m.

Condition. Two fragments of white geometric grisaille and plain white glass.

Date. As above.

B2. Fragments

h. 0·26 m. w. 0·14 m.

Condition. Two grotesque wyvern border pieces in yellow stain, the same cartoon, reversed, as A3 above. Part of a crocketed arch, in yellow stain, painted on the same glass as a piece of geometric grisaille design.

Date. As above.

C1. Bird   PLATE 43 (a)

h. 0·34 m. w. 0·10 m.

Condition. Almost complete except for the apex point of the light. Only slight corrosion. *In situ.*

Colour and Technique. Painted on white glass, flat matt wash on the bird's wings and tail, oak leaf picked out of a matt wash.

Style and Design. Crude but vigorous; the connection between the bird and the oak leaf above it is not made clear. For birds in tracery lights see Fulbrook, s. II, A1, A2.

Date. As above.

C2. Fragments

h. 0·34 m. w. 0·10 m.

Condition. Originally the same design as C1 above reversed,

only the oak leaf in the top foil remains, lower foil patched with a corroded piece of white grisaille glass.

Date. As above.

n. V

A1. Grotesque Dragon

h. 0·33 m. w. 0·14 m.

Condition. Complete except for one inserted piece, the paint in the upper foil has almost completely perished. *In situ.*

Colour and Technique. Painted on white glass.

Style and Design. See A3.

Date. Second quarter 14th c.

A3. Grotesque Dragon

h. 0·33 m. w. 0·14 m.

Condition. Complete, the paint of the foliage springing from the dragon's mouth into the top foil has worn very thin. *In situ.*

Colour and Technique. Painted on white glass, the dragon is a very flat design with no modelling.

Style and Design. A1 and A3 are painted from the same cartoon. The drawing is close to the smaller dragons in n. IV, A1 and A4. Probably by the same painter.

n. VI

2a. Geometric Grisaille and Borders

h. 0·23 m. w. 0·26 m.

Condition. Incomplete, made up with modern plain white glass. The geometric grisaille is very corroded, the paint has almost completely perished, as has the lower right border piece. *In situ?*

Colour and Technique. Painted on white glass, the two upper border pieces in yellow stain.

Style and Design. See 2b.

Date. Second quarter 14th c.

2b. Geometric Grisaille and Borders

h. 0·23 m. w. 0·26 m.

Condition. Incomplete, made up with modern plain white glass. Grisaille as 2a above, the paint on the border pieces has worn very thin. *In situ?*

Colour and Technique. As 2a above, the upper right border piece in yellow stain.

Style and Design. The arrangement is probably original but some of the grisaille may be misplaced. Three border designs, all in profile, four herons, a crouched dragon, and two standing wyverns. The crouched dragon is a smaller version of n. IV, A1 above, the wyverns are identical with those in n. IV, A3 and B2 above.

Date. As above.

A1, A2, A3, A4. Foliage Designs

h. 0·30 m. w. 0·10 m.

Condition. All incomplete, made up with modern plain white glass, slight all-over corrosion. *In situ.*

Colour and Technique. Painted on white glass, the foliage is almost an outline design.

Style and Design. A simple design of leaves springing from the vertical border of each light, there is some variation in the leaf types but the work is extremely crude.

Date. As above.

B1. Shield of the Hospital of St. John

h. 0·23 m. w. 0·32 m. Shield: h. 0·15 m. w. 0·13 m.

Argent a cross formy double armed sable HOSPITAL OF ST. JOHN.

Condition. The shield is complete, slight over-all corrosion, set on a background of modern plain white glass. *In situ?*

Colour and Technique. Painted on a single piece of white glass.

Style and Design. Plain simple work, no trace of any decorative diaper work on the field.

Date. As above. The Hospital of St. John at Oxford held lands in the manor by the gift of William Scissor, tailor of Henry III.[1]

s. IV

2a. Geometric Grisaille and Borders

h. 0·35 m. w. 0·56 m.

A trellis of diamond-shaped quarries painted with strap-work, following the lines of the leads, and sprays of oak leaves and acorns springing from a vertical stem at the centre of the light. Borders left to right: *or a lion rampant sable, two fleurs-de-lis argent,* or *fretty sable on a chief sable three bezants or.*[2]

Condition. Incomplete, made up with pieces of modern plain white glass. The paint on the heraldic border pieces

has worn very thin, otherwise there is only slight over-all corrosion.

Colour and Technique. Painted on white glass except for the two heraldic border pieces in pot-metal ochre.

Style and Design. See 2c.

Date. 14th c., *c.* 1300.

2c. Geometric Grisaille and Borders

h. 0·35 m. w. 0·56 m.

Geometric grisaille as 2a above, here the border pieces are *fleurs-de-lis.*

Condition. Complete except for an alien insertion in the apex cusp.

Colour and Technique. Grisaille as 2a above, border pieces alternately white and pot-metal ochre, separated by pieces of plain ruby glass.

Style and Design. The grisaille and borders in 2a were recorded in their present position in 1805.[3] In both cases the grisaille is shaped to fit the curved shoulders of the light and would appear to be *in situ.* However, if this is the case the discrepancy in design with the grisaille in the tracery lights requires explanation.

Date. As above.

B1–B3. Shields set on Geometric Grisaille

The grisaille was a repeated single design now incomplete and disturbed, it is all catalogued under B3, below.

B1. Shield of le Cissor

h. 0·50 m. w. 0·42 m. Shield and surround: d. 0·17 m.

Argent a lion rampant sable LE CISSOR.

Condition. The shield and its surround are complete, the grisaille much disturbed, only the lower right-hand foil is substantially intact.

Colour and Technique. Shield painted on a single piece of white glass, set against a plain ruby and green roundel.

Date. 14th c. *c.* 1300. William Scissor, tailor and servant of Henry III, gave lands in Newington to the Hospital of St. John at Oxford.[4]

B2. Geometric Grisaille

h. 0·50 m. w. 0·42 m.

Condition. Much disturbed, only the lower right-hand foil is *in situ.* Originally there was probably a shield at the centre

---

[1] H. E. Salter, ed., 'A Cartulary of the Hospital of St. John the Baptist', *O.A.H.S.* ii (1914), 394. Greening Lamborn (1949), 143.
[2] The fretty coat is probably the arms of the family of St. Amand.

For heraldic charges as a class of border design see Newton i (1961), 153–7.
[3] Bodl. Lib. MS. Top. Oxon. b. 75, op. cit.   [4] See n. 1 above.

of the light, its shape was drawn in 1805 but the arms were noted as 'gone'.[1]

Date. As above.

B3. Shield of Buckland

h. 0·50 m. w. 0·42 m. Shield and surround: d. 0·17 m.

Argent an eagle displayed sable BUCKLAND.

Condition. The shield and its surround are complete but with old leaded repair. The grisaille is mostly intact except for that in the lower left foil.

Colour and Technique. Shield painted on white glass, set against a plain ruby and green roundel. Grisaille painted on white glass; at the intersection of the leads in each of the three foils of the light is an ochre triangular piece of glass painted with a flat trefoil leaf design. Plain white border.

Style and Design. Each shield was placed against identical designs of geometric grisaille consisting of three sprays of very stylized fruiting leaves radiating from the centre of the light with a coloured boss at the intersection of the leads at the centre of each foil.

Date. As above. The principal landowner in Newington at this date was John Gifford of Twyford (Bucks.). The manor had descended to him through the marriage of his grandfather Osbert Gifford with Isabel, daughter of Alan de Bocland.[2]

D1. Shield of Mohun and Geometric Grisaille

h. 0·35 m. w. 0·42 m. Shield and surround: d. 0·26 m.

Or a cross engrailed sable MOHUN.

Condition. The shield and its surround are complete, the lower foil of the grisaille is disturbed and made up with modern plain white glass.

Colour and Technique. Shield is painted on a single piece of pot-metal ochre, set on a plain ruby roundel with three blue edges. Grisaille on white glass.

Style and Design. See D2.

Date. As above. John Lord Mohun (d. 1330) married Ada, daughter of Robert de Tibetot. Her sister Harris married John Fitz Robert, Lord Clavering[3] (see D2). Neither family is known to have had any landed connection with Newington.

D2. Shield of Clavering and Geometric Grisaille

h. 0·35 m. w. 0·42 m. Shield and surround: d. 0·26 m.

Quarterly or and gules a bend sable CLAVERING.

Condition. All the coloured glass is very corroded. The lower lobe of the shield's surround and one section of grisaille replaced by plain white glass.

Colour and Technique. Shield in pot-metal ochre and ruby, the bend painted in, set on a plain green roundel with two pink lobes. Grisaille on white glass.

Style and Design. The shields and grisaille are probably *in situ* although the shields have exchanged positions since 1805.[4] The grisaille is a very simple design of flat acanthus-type leaves radiating from the shield and its surround.

Date. As above. For the Clavering family see D1.

F1. Head of Christ

h. 0·24 m. w. 0·35 m.

Condition. The face and part of the ruby nimbus have been replaced by plain white glass.

Colour and Technique. Ruby nimbus, its cross in pot-metal ochre. White ground painted with three sprays of hawthorn leaves, patterned border picked out of a matt black wash.

Date. As above.

SOUTH STOKE
ST. ANDREW

O.S. SU 599 836.

PRINTED SOURCES
Ditchfield (1903), 186.
Nelson (1913), 171.
Pevsner (1974), 773-4.

s. III

1b. Virgin and Child   PLATE 43 (*e*)

h. 0·30 m. w. 0·19 m.

The Virgin seated, frontal position, holds an apple (?) in her left hand, Christ on her left arm, his right hand raised in benediction.

Condition. The figures are set against a background of white quarries, all 19th c., a poor imitation of medieval

---

[1] Bodl. Lib. MS. Top. Oxon. b. 75, op. cit.   [2] Greening Lamborn (1949), 142.
[3] Ibid.   [4] Bodl. Lib. MS. Top. Oxon. b. 75, op. cit.

design. The original glass is very corroded. The brownish-pink glass of the faces, hands, and feet is extremely corroded, and the paint has almost completely flaked off.

Colour and Technique. Virgin: pot-metal ochre crown, blue mantle over pot-metal ochre tunic. Christ: nimbus indistinct, except for the cross, which is in pot-metal ochre, his tunic in deep-green glass. Base of throne: pot-yellow ochre, green seat with a ruby cushion. The heads, hands, and feet are probably in pink glass.

Iconography. Standard iconography stressing the Virgin's role as mother.

Style and Design. The pose of the Virgin and Christ in benediction is exactly the same as found at Dorchester, I, 4c. The drapery painting is similar but not identical. The thrones are quite different, here the bench and cushion extend beyond the base of the throne.

Date. First quarter 14th c.

STANDLAKE
ST. GILES

O.S. SP 397 036.

MS. SOURCES

London. British Library, Harleian MS. 6363, f. 73ʳ. 17th c.
Oxford. Bodleian Library:
    Wood MS. B. 15, f. 90. Notes by A. Wood dated 1653.
    MS. Top. Oxon. e. 286, f. 83ᵛ. Notes by N. Greenwood dated
      1658.
    MS. Oxf. dioc. papers c. 2207, no. 4. Restoration Report 1898.

PRINTED

'Notes of an excursion to . . . Stanlake, etc.', *N.O.A.S.* (1871), 17–18.
Bouchier (1918), 96.
P.C. (1920), 287.
Pevsner (1974), 777–8.

The repair of the fabric of the chancel in 1503 by the then rector, Dr. Richard Salter, was commemorated in an inscription in a window which depicted him kneeling before St. Osmund, Bishop of Salisbury.[1] A fragment of the inscription is all that survives of this (s. VI, 1a and 1b). Dr. Richard Salter was presented to the living of Standlake in 1473 and vacated it in 1508. He died in 1519.[2] He is also associated with the gift of a window to Newington church.

    The chancel windows had lost some of their glass by the mid seventeenth century when Wood made his notes. The few fragments that survive were collected together at the restoration of 1898 and set in a window of the south chapel.[3]

s. VI

1a, 1b. Inscription

Fragments of an inscription, in black-letter script:

    |a(n)i(m)a|ric(ard)i salter|decretoru(m) |
          |fen|rep(ar)ari fecit|anno d(omi)ni|

This is part of the inscription recorded by Wood and Greenwood. 'In the south window of the chancel is this

inscription: *Orate pro anima Magistri Ricardi Salter Decretorum doctoris quondam rectoris istius ecclesie qui istam cancellam cum hac fenestra reparari fecit Anno Domini MCCCCCIII.*

    Over the said inscription is his portraiture kneeling in a pristlie habit and out of his mouth comes this in a scrowle Sancte Osmunde ora pro nobis, therr is another picture kneeling opposite to him, but defaced.'[4]

Iconography. St. Osmund (d. 1099), consecrated Bishop of Salisbury in 1077, was buried at Old Sarum.[5] His body was

---

[1] P.C. (1920), 287.
[2] A. B. Emden, *A Biographical Register of the University of Oxford to 1500* (1947–9), 1633.
[3] Bodl. Lib. MS. Oxford dioc. papers, op. cit.
[4] P.C. (1920), 287, prints the notes from Bodl. Lib. Wood MS.

E. 1, f. 24, where the incomplete figure is omitted. The full description is given in Bodl. Lib. Wood MS. B. 15, f. 90, dated 1653, and Bodl. Lib. MS. Top. Oxon. e. 286, f. 83ᵛ, op. cit.
[5] Life printed in *Nova Legenda Angliae*, ed. C. Horstmann, ii (1901), 239–52.

translated to the new Cathedral of Salisbury in 1226. He was venerated locally as a saint from the early part of the 13th c., but was not canonized until 1456.[1] His feast was instituted in the Province of Canterbury in 1480.[2]

The known representations of St. Osmund are very few. A window of the chapel of Queen's College, Oxford, dated 1518, contains a figure much restored and added to.[3] Another figure in a window at Cirencester (Glos.), of *c.* 1523, is no longer extant.[4] A late 15th-c. mural painting in the church of St. Thomas, Salisbury, has been identified as St. Osmund, but the evidence is not conclusive.[5] The 1536 inventory of Salisbury Cathedral lists a large silver gilt image, weighing 83 ounces.[6] His relics are rare outside Salisbury: St. George's Chapel, Windsor, had a monstrance containing two of his bones, the gift of John Wygrym, canon and prebendary of St. George's and Fellow of Merton College, Oxford, d. 1468.[7]

Richard Salter's connection with Salisbury Cathedral as canon and prebendary of Netherbury in Terra, 1483–1508, explains the representation of St. Osmund at Standlake.[8]

Fragments of quarry type 35.

Date. 1503.

2a. Inscription

h. 0·04 m. w. 0·20 m.

A fragment of an inscription, in Lombardic script:

$$|RN:CU(M):FOMITE:CE|$$

Pot-metal ochre glass, 14th c. Fragments of quarry type 35.

3a. Roundel

d. 0·16 m.

Two triangular straps of foliage, interlocked, straps green and ochre glass, on a plain ruby background, 14th c.

Fragments of quarry type 35.

3b. Roundel

d. 0·16 m.

A grotesque white bird, in profile facing left, incomplete, roundel made up with alien fragments, some now broken. 14th c. Fragments of quarry type 35.

The design is virtually identical with a roundel now set in a library window at Merton College, Oxford.

4a. Roundel

d. 0·12 m.

A quatrefoil leaf design, yellow stain, plain ruby border. Complete, but with old leaded repair and very corroded. 14th c. Fragments of quarry type 35.

4b. Quarry

Fragments of quarry type 35, yellow stain on white glass, 15th c.

5a. Roundel

d. 0·16 m.

A variegated rose, painted on green glass, plain ruby border. Complete, the paint very worn. 14th–15th c. Fragments of quarry type 35.

5b. Roundel

d. 0·16 m.

The monogram *ihc̄*, border design of a continuous leafy ribbon wound around a stick. White glass, monogram and border in yellow stain, background diaper of contiguous rosettes. Complete, but with old leaded repair and somewhat corroded. Late 15th c. Fragments of quarry type 35.

6a. Inscription

A fragment, in black-letter script, incomplete at the left and top edges, |iones|; possibly Iohannes. Border design of two entwined thorn branches, painted on the same glass. White glass, inscription and border in yellow stain. Late 15th c.

All the above glass is set against a background of fragments, mostly pieces of white geometric grisaille glass, painted with trails of either maple or oak foliage, springing from a vertical stem at the centre, 14th c., also fragments of jewelled hems, white and yellow stain. 15th-c. fragments of quarry type 35 removed from the windows of the nave aisles.[9]

Lost Glass

Wood records: 'In another of the said south windows (of the chancel) is the portraiture of a bishop in his pontificalia, a Hart couchant by him, with an inscription at his feet, but defaced.'[10]

[1] A. R. Malden, 'The Canonization of St. Osmund', *Wiltshire Record Society* i (1901), xxxi, 28 seq., 167–9, 224–35.

[2] D. Wilkins, *Concilia Magnae Britanniae*, iii (1737), 612–13.

[3] Westernmost window, north side. The inscription is 17th-c. R.C.H.M. (1939), 99.

[4] W. I. Croome, 'The Stained Glass of Cirencester Parish Church', *J.B.S.M.G.P.* xiv (1964), 37.

[5] A. Hollaender, 'The Doom Painting of St. Thomas of Canterbury, Salisbury', *The Wiltshire Archaeological and Natural History Magazine*, l (1942–4), 358.

[6] W. Dodsworth, *An Historical Account of the Episcopal See and Cathedral Church of Salisbury* (1814), 229.

[7] *The Inventories of St. George's Chapel, Windsor Castle*, ed. M. F. Bond (1947), 167.

[8] J. le Neve, *Fasti Ecclesiae Anglicanae, 1300–1541* iii, Salisbury Diocese, compiled by J. M. Horn (1962), 76.

[9] 'Notes of an Excursion', op. cit. 18, records 'fragments of grisaille glass' in these windows. [10] P.C. (1920), 287.

Iconography. The figure can be identified as St. Giles, the patron saint of Standlake church, with his emblem, the hart wounded in the chase.[1] St. Giles, abbot and confessor, died *c.* 725, was the founder of the Abbey of St. Gilles, between Arles and Nîmes (France).[2] His cult was widespread throughout England in the Middle Ages, where 104 church dedications to him are recorded, ten of them in Oxfordshire.[3] Wood's description of the lost figure as 'a bishop in his pontificalia' suggests that the saint was represented either in mass vestments with a crozier, or as a mitred abbot. He is generally depicted in plain monastic robes.[4] Examples of him in mass vestments holding a crozier are found in a window at Wells Cathedral, *c.* 1325–30,[5] in a Book of Hours written and illuminated by John Lacy in 1420,[6] and in an early 16th-c. window at Sandringham, Norfolk.[7]

STANTON HARCOURT

ST. MICHAEL

O.S. SP 416 056.

MS. SOURCES

London. British Library:
    Harleian MS. 1754, ff. 49ʳ–50. Notes by W. Winchall. 17th c.
    Harleian MS. 6365, ff. 70–2 (n.d.).
Oxford. Bodleian Library:
    Rawlinson MS. B. 397. M. Hutton's Oxfordshire collections. 17th c.
    MS. Top. Oxon. e. 286, f. 81ᵛ. Notes by N. Greenwood. 1658.
    MS. Don. c. 90, pp. 635–47. Drawings by Hinton. 19th c.

PRINTED

George, Earl Harcourt, *An Account of the Church and Remains of the Manor House at Stanton Harcourt* (1808).

Parker (1846), 172–8.
Franks, A. W., *A Book of Ornamental Glazing Quarries* (1849), pl. 2.
Winston, C., *Hints on Glass Painting* i (1867), 61 cut 7, 70 note m., ii (1867), 3–4, pl. 5.
Westlake, N. J., *A History of Design in Painted Glass* i (1881–94), 95, pl. lvib.
Nelson (1913), 171.
Bouchier (1918), 96.
P.C. (1920), 279–83.
Read, H., *English Stained Glass* (1926), 42.
Bouchier (1932), 131.
Greening Lamborn (1949), 156.
Woodforde, C., *English Stained and Painted Glass* (1954), 4, pl. 3.
Goddard-Fenwick, T. J., *Stanton Harcourt. A Short History* (1962, rev. edn.).
Pevsner (1974), 778–81.

Thirteenth-Century Glass

Three lancet windows of the chancel contain some remains of geometric grisaille glass, together with a figure of St. James Major (windows s. II, s. III, and s. IV). The arrangement of the figure panel on a grisaille background was probably original. However, the grisaille design was much disturbed in the rearrangement and releading carried out in 1960. This example together with two windows at Stanton St. John are the most complete remains of this class of design in the county.

    The figure of St. James may have formed part of a series of the twelve Apostles. However, an individual commemoration would not be unusual here. The patronage of the living had been granted by Queen

---

[1] *Acta Sanctorum.* September i (Paris, 1868), 284–304; *Golden Legend,* v (1909), 91–6.

[2] P. E. Everlange, *Histoire de St. Gilles, sa vie, son abbaye et son tombeau* (1876).

[3] F. Arnold-Forster, *Studies in Church Dedications* i (1899), 50; iii. 15.

[4] Examples in English glass painting are found at: Winchester College Chapel, 19th-c. copy of original of *c.* 1387–94. J. D. Le Couteur, *Ancient Glass in Winchester* (1920), 88–9. Stamford (Lincs.). St. John's Church, *c.* 1450. Wiggenhall St. Mary Magdalene (Norfolk), 15th c. C. Woodforde, *The Norwich School of Glass Painting in the Fifteenth Century* (1950), 179. North Cadbury

(Somerset), 15th c. C. Woodforde, *Stained Glass in Somerset, 1250–1830* (1946), 61. Compton Verney (Warwicks.), early 16th c. Present whereabouts unknown, sold at the Parke-Bernet Galleries, New York, 19 March 1971, lot 46. Ladbrook (Warwicks.), late 15th c. *V.C.H. Warwickshire* vi (1951), 146. Thirsk (Yorks.), late 15th c. *The Archaeological Journal* ii (1846), 78–9. A lost window at Durham Cathedral. 'The Rites of Durham', ed. J. Fowler, *The Surtees Society* cvii (1902), 112.

[5] J. Armitage Robinson, 'The Fourteenth Century Glass at Wells', *Archaeologia* lxxxi (1931), 102, pl. xlvi, fig. 1.

[6] Oxford, St. John's College, MS. 94, f. 6ʳ.

[7] Woodforde, *Norwich School,* op. cit. 175 n. 1.

Adeliza to Reading Abbey in 1190.[1] The first important relic acquired by the Abbey in 1133 was the hand of St. James, the gift of its founder Henry I.[2]

Two oval medallions have been inserted in a window of the Harcourt aisle (s. VI, 2a and 2c). They show a bishop and a king respectively, each seated, wearing the conventional robes and with the emblems appropriate to their dignity. Neither figure has a nimbus, so they are probably not saints. The absence of emblems makes identification very tentative. The general design of a seated figure within an oval frame is allied to the design of seals. The seals of dignity of archbishops, bishops, and abbots are invariably oval in shape, but the figure is generally represented standing. A number of examples of seated figures are known, ranging in date from the twelfth to the fourteenth century.[3] The obverse of all the English royal seals of dignity has a seated figure of the king. The royal seals, however, are circular not oval in shape.[4] The glazier's design can therefore be related to the conventions of seal design. This relationship gives the figures the same characteristics of conventional, official portraits. If the panels are considered in this way then the history of the church and manor of Stanton Harcourt might provide some clues for the identification of the figures. The patronage of the living was held by the Abbey of Reading.[5] The Abbot of Reading was licensed to use episcopal insignia in 1288,[6] but this date is probably too late to be of relevance to the glass. The Harcourt family acquired the manor by the marriage in 1166 of Robert de Harcourt and Isabel, daughter of Richard de Camville, and the manor was held of the king in chief.[7] The Harcourts also held the manor of Ellenhall (Staffs.) of the Bishop of Lichfield and Coventry.[8] It is possible that the figures represent the King of England and the Bishop of Lichfield and Coventry, here honoured as feudal over-lords of the Harcourts. These oval panels may originally have been part of the glazing of the chancel, possibly set against a background of geometric grisaille. Oval figure panels set in geometric grisaille are not common, but an important example is found in the original east window of Chetwode Priory (Bucks.), of c. 1250.[9]

If these panels were part of the chancel glazing, it seems certain that the windows were either of different dates, or, if contemporary, were designed by different glaziers. There is a pronounced difference in style between the pair of figures and the St. James. The stylized facial features have nothing in common. The details of style might indicate a dating of c. 1250 for the oval panels, the St. James panel and grisaille some-what later, but probably before c. 1280.

Fifteenth-Century Glass

A window of the Harcourt aisle contains a shield of the arms of Harcourt impaling Byron, surrounded by the Garter (s. VI, 3b). Sir Robert Harcourt, K.G., married Margaret, daughter of Sir John Byron of Clayton (Lancs.). The shield must date after c. 1463 when he became a Knight of the Garter.[10] He died in 1470.[11] Greening Lamborn suggested that he built this aisle c. 1465 and that the shield is contemporary with the fabric.[12] The aisle piers are identical in section with those of the ante-chapel of Magdalen College, Oxford, dated 1475-9 and designed by William Orchard.[13] The same mason's mark is found on both.[14]

[1] W. Dugdale, *Monasticon Anglicanum*, ed. J. Caley, H. Ellis, and B. Bandonel, iv (1846), 29, citing the Cartulary, B.L. Harleian MS. 1708, f. 95b.
[2] Ibid. 29 and note q, Charter III, 41. See also 'Annales prioratus de Wigornia', ed. H. R. Luard, in *Annales Monastici* iv (1869).
[3] Alexander, Bishop of Lincoln 1123-45; Seffrid, Bishop of Chichester 1125-45; Simon, Bishop of Worcester 1125-50; Peter Wyvville, Bishop of Exeter 1280-91; Anthony Bek, Bishop of Durham 1284-1311; John Grandison, Bishop of Exeter 1327-69. Casts at the Society of Antiquaries, London.
[4] A. B. Wyon, *The Great Seals of England* (1887), *passim*.
[5] See above, n. 1.
[6] *Calendar of Papal Registers. Papal Letters* i (1893), 495.
[7] J. C. Wedgwood, 'Harcourt of Ellenhall', *William Salt Archaeological Society* (1914), 185. G. H. Farnham, 'The Harcourt Family',

Leicestershire Archaeological Society Transactions xv (1927), 105.
[8] Wedgwood, op. cit. *Cal. Inq. Post Mortem* i (1904), 411.
[9] D. Lysons and S. Lysons, *Magna Britannia* i (1806), 488, figs. 2-5. R.C.H.M. *Buckinghamshire (north)* (1912-13), 86.
[10] The exact date of his election is not known. First recorded in the minutes of the chapter in April 1463. E. H. Beltz, *Memorials of the Most Noble Order of the Garter* (1841), clxiii.
[11] Wedgwood, op. cit. 203. Farnham, op. cit. 114. Greening Lamborn (1949), 156.
[12] Greening Lamborn (1949), 156.
[13] J. H. Harvey, *English Medieval Architects* (1954), 201.
[14] R. H. C. Davies, 'Masons' Marks in Oxfordshire and the Cotswolds', *O.H.S. 84th Report* (1938), 73 n. 11, n. 20 (reference from Mr. J. H. Harvey).

J. H. Harvey attributed the design of the aisle to William Orchard c. 1470[1] but has recently revised the dating to c. 1475–80.[2]

The seventeenth-century antiquarian notes record two examples of the Harcourt–Byron arms. Winchall noted one, in the east window of the chancel, as being 'Encircled by the Garter'.[3] Unfortunately his notes contain some discrepancies and many omissions when compared with the other accounts. The notes divide into three groups:

1. Bodl. Lib. Hutton. Rawl. MS. B. 397, copied with omissions in B.L. Harl. 6365.
2. Bodl. Lib. Greenwood. MS. Top. Oxon. e. 286 and Wood MS. E. 1 both omit two shields, one of which was recorded by Hutton as being broken.
3. B.L. Winchall. Harl. MS. 1754, records shields in two windows only.

The first two groups agree in their account of the east window of the Harcourt aisle. They record five shields and a male figure in the Harcourt coat armour.

The shields depicted were:[4]

1. *Gules two bars or* HARCOURT.
2. HARCOURT *impaling argent three bends gules* BYRON.
3. *Quarterly France and England* ROYAL ARMS.
4. *Argent a chevron sable between three ravens' heads erased sable* NORREYS.
5. NORREYS *quartering bendy or and azure, a bordure gules* MERBURY.

These shields commemorate Sir Robert Harcourt, K.G., d. 1470, and his wife Margaret, daughter of Sir John Byron, and their son John, who married before 1466 Anne, daughter of Sir John Norreys of Bray (Berks.) by his first wife Alice, daughter and co-heiress of Richard Merbury.[5] Winchall's notes omit shields 2, 3, and 4, but include a shield, given in trick as *two bars impaling quarterly 1, 4 argent a castle sable* OLDCASTLE *2, 3 argent three covered cups sable* CLITHEROW. This shield may have been made up from two different shields. The impaling is inexplicable. However, the quarterly arms of Oldcastle and Clitherow refer to Eleanor the second wife of the above Sir John Norreys, d. 1466. She was the daughter of Roger Clitherow of Goldstanton, in the parish of Ash (Kent), by Mathilda, his wife, daughter and heiress of Sir John Oldcastle.[6]

Despite the discrepancies, this display of heraldry suggests that the Harcourt figure represented either Sir Robert, d. 1470, or his son John, d. 1484.[7] Wood associated the adjacent tomb of Sir Robert with this figure which he described as 'an armed man cap a pee kneeling with a book open before him, his helmet off and on his buckler are the Harcourt's arms'.[8] Winchall, however, differs in his description and identification. 'In the north[9] Chappell is a fayre Monument of Marble for Sir Robert Harcourt Knight and standard bearer to King Henry the 7th at Bosworth fielde in his Armor very compleate with his Banners hanging over his tombe and Rownde the tomb aknelinge his Almes men, in the same Chaple window himselfe kneelinge with the Banner of King Henry 7.'[10] This account is suspect as the monument described is that of Sir Robert Harcourt, d. 1470. The identification is confirmed by the fact that the figures of both him and his wife are represented wearing the insignia of the Order of the Garter.[11]

[1] Harvey, op. cit.
[2] Correspondence with the author.
[3] Harl. MS. 1754, op. cit.
[4] The identifications of the arms are not given in the MS. notes.
[5] Wedgwood, op. cit. 203–4. G. H. Farnham, op. cit. 15. See also E. Green, 'The Identification of the Eighteen Worthies Commemorated in the Heraldic Glass in the Hall Windows of Ockwells Manor House', *Archaeologia* lvi (1899), 334.
[6] Ibid. 331–2.
[7] Wedgwood, op. cit. Farnham, op. cit.
[8] P.C. (1920), 280.
[9] *Sic*, a mistake for south.

[10] Harl. MS. 1754, op. cit. No contemporary proof has been found that this Sir Robert Harcourt was the standard bearer at Bosworth. Halle's Chronicle states that Richard III 'overfrew therles standarde and slew Sir William Brandon his standarde bearer'. E. Halle, *The Union of the two noble and illustrious families York and Lancaster* (1548), f. lvii. Henry VII granted the office for life to Anthony Brown in 1486. 'Materials Illustrative of the Reign of Henry VII', ed. W. Campbell, i. 387, *Rolls Series*, 60 (1873).
[11] Engraved in R. Gough, *Sepulchral Monuments* ii, part iii (1796), 229. A. Gardner, *A Handbook of English Medieval Sculpture* (1935), fig. 480.

Although the antiquarian notes of the heraldic glass do not agree, the evidence appears to suggest that the glazing of the Harcourt aisle can be attributed to either Sir Robert, d. 1470, or his son John, d. 1484. One point favours the latter: the inclusion of two shields of Norreys, for his wife's family, suggests that the single coat of Harcourt is for John. This was not differenced and must, therefore, have been erected after his father's death in 1470. The remaining shield of Harcourt impaling Byron, if it was the one in this group, may therefore date from after 1470 and probably before John's death in 1484. This dating agrees with J. H. Harvey's later dating of the aisle fabric c. 1475–80.

s. II, s. III, s. IV   PLATE 43 (f)

A triplet of lancet windows, which formed part of a unified design and is catalogued as a single window to avoid repetition. Before 1960 the glass was distributed over the lancet windows of the chancel, the most complete section being in the westernmost lancet on the north side.[1] A complete restoration of these windows was undertaken by Mr. M. C. Farrar Bell, during 1960.[2] The decorative re-arrangement of the glass has disturbed part of the original over-all design that survived.

2b. Geometric Grisaille. St. James Major   PLATE 43(h)

Panel: h. 0·96 m. w. 0·53 m. Figure: h. 0·43 m. w. 0·26 m.

St. James full length, facing three-quarters right, holding a scroll. Plain background.

Condition. Before 1960 this glass and the geometric grisaille, now 3b, were a unified design in the westernmost lancet of the north wall. The missing portions had been made up with plain glass.[3] All the glass is corroded, the coloured glass more so than the white, although the extent of corrosion on the latter is uneven. The missing pieces of coloured glass have been made up with modern glass, stippled to tone with the original, by Mr. M. C. Farrar Bell.

Colour and Technique. St. James, ruby nimbus, brownish-pink flesh, ruby mantle over a yellow tunic, white name scroll; plain blue ground with a thin plain ochre border. All pot-metal glass, except for the yellow bosses, the foliage traced in brown paint against a groundwork of cross-hatched lines. The border has a repeated design of red roses with white stems alternating with white roses with yellow stems, set against pieces of plain blue.

Iconography. He holds a scroll, inscribed, in Lombardic script:

$$|+|[IAC]|OBVS|$$

Design: the original design of the geometric grisaille was a leaded pattern of contiguous hexagons, each enclosing an oval. At the base point of each oval is a yellow semicircular boss supporting a vertical stem with offspringing symmetrical trails of vine leaves and grapes. Similar trails occur above and below each oval within the hexagonal frame. The two contiguous half-diamond shapes, between the hexagonals, each contained three acanthus leaves radiating from a semi-circular boss at the centre. The figure panel is superimposed on the grisaille. The cusped trefoil head of the blue background of this panel does not imply a now lost architectural framing. If there had been, then the border and ground at the springing of the head would have been shaped to accommodate the capital of the side shaft (only the left-hand side is original). Similar figure panels, with a trefoil head, are found in the east window of St. Michael's, Northgate, Oxford (late 13th c.), on modern quarries.[4]

Style and Date. Winston dated this glass c. 1270–5,[5] later he revised this to c. 1290.[6] Westlake considered the geometric grisaille as old-fashioned for the later date, but also detected elements of a 'transition style' in the figure's posture and the border design.[7] Woodforde, without explanation, simply states 'grisaille and panel window, first half of the 13th century'.[8]

A late date seems more difficult to accept, particularly if the glass is coeval with the lancet windows. Westlake made comparisons with the glass at Salisbury, c. 1250–80, and Selling (Kent), c. 1298–1305.[9] The leaded geometric pattern and freer movement of the vine foliage are similar to Selling, the latter, unlike Salisbury and Stanton, omits the cross-hatched background to the foliage. At Selling the figures are set beneath a trefoil arch and small canopy, but the exclusion of this feature at Stanton does not necessarily imply an earlier dating.[10] The painting of the drapery folds of the St. James, with a thick line echoed by an adjacent thin one, is common practice of the first half of the 13th c., compare, for example, the St. Birinus panel at Dorchester, n. III, 2b. Although the details of the facial features can also be compared with work of that date, the more elongated face is closer to later 13th-c. work, for example the panels at St. Michael's, Northgate, Oxford.[11] These considerations suggest a possible dating of c. 1250–80.

---

[1] Winston, op. cit. 70.   [2] T. J. Goddard-Fenwick, op. cit. 17.
[3] Winston, op. cit. ii, pl. 5. Woodforde, op. cit., pl. 3.
[4] R.C.H.M. (1939), pl. 209.   [5] Winston, op. cit. ii. 3.
[6] This date is written on Winston's drawing of the panel, made 1844. B.L. Add. MS. 35211, vol. iii, no. 80.
[7] Westlake, op. cit. i. 95, where the date is misprinted as 1190; the mistake is corrected in the index, vol. iv.

[8] Woodforde, op. cit., caption to pl. 3.
[9] Westlake, op. cit. i. 95–8, pl. lvi, figs. b, e, f.
[10] The earliest extant English examples of figures below canopies are the prophets at Canterbury Cathedral, c. 1178. B. Rackham, *The Ancient Glass of Canterbury Cathedral* (1949), 29–43, pls. 5–8.
[11] R.C.H.M. (1939), pl. 209.

3a. Geometric Grisaille   PLATE 43 (*i*)

h. 0·76 m. w. 0·53 m.

A composite panel, as arranged in 1960, of pieces of geometric grisaille, same pattern as 2b, and a few other fragments.

Date. c. 1250–80.

3b. Geometric Grisaille   PLATE 43 (*g*)

d. 0·43 m.

Condition. Pronounced corrosion of varying intensity.

Colour and Technique. White glass, except for pot-metal blue and red bosses, foliage painted as 2b.

Style and Design. Leaded and painted design of a square, enclosing four flat serrated leaves radiating from a ruby boss at the centre, set within a circle. From the middle of the outer edge of each side of the square two symmetrical trails of vine foliage spring from a blue semicircular boss.

Date. c. 1250–80.

3c. Geometric Grisaille

h. 0·76 m. w. 0·53 m.

See 2b.

s. V

2a, 2b, 2c, 2d, 2e. Canopies   PLATE 44 (*a*)

h. 0·28 m. w. 0·42 m.

The tops of five identical canopy designs, probably *in situ*.

Condition. All incomplete, made up with alien pieces and modern glass. Restored by Mr. Farrar Bell, *c.* 1964.

Colour and Technique. The canopies and their figures in white glass with yellow stain, set against plain coloured grounds, blue alternating with purple.

Style and Design. The design shows two three-quarter length angels standing on either side of the central apex of an architectural canopy. The crocketed spires of the missing lower parts of the canopy are painted on the same pieces of glass as the angels. This design is not found elsewhere in the county.

Date. After 1463, possibly 1470–84.

A1, A10. Foliage Designs

h. 0·14 m. w. 0·10 m.

A large serrated leaf painted on white glass, the ribs of the leaf picked out in yellow stain against a plain matt black background, no border. Each painted on a single piece of glass. A10 is complete.

Date. As above.

s. VI

2a. Bishop (or Mitred Abbot)   PLATE 44 (*b*)

Oval: h. 0·46 m. w. 0·30 m.

Enthroned, in benediction holding a crozier. No nimbus.

Condition. Incomplete, the missing pieces were made up with plain white glass. Extremely corroded, so much so that the paint on the coloured glass is very obscured. Releaded and missing drapery painted by Mr. M. C. Farrar Bell.

Colour and Technique. All pot-metal glass, the white glass has a strong yellow tint. Figure: white face, hands, mitre, and amice, purple alb, green dalmatic, blue shoes, and ochre crozier. Seated on a throne: white front painted with a blind plate tracery design, ochre seat, and ruby cushion. Set against a plain blue background; border design white glass, patterned with contiguous circles, set inside a strip of plain ruby.

Iconography. Possibly represents a bishop of Coventry and Lichfield.

Style and Design. A companion figure to 2c.

Date. Mid 13th c.

2c. King   PLATE 44 (*d*)

Oval: h. 0·46 m. w. 0·30 m.

Enthroned, crowned and holding a sceptre in his left hand. No nimbus.

Condition. Very corroded, background incomplete, made up with plain white glass. Releaded 1964.

Colour and Technique. All pot-metal glass, the white glass as 2a. Figure: white face and hands, ochre sceptre and crown, purple tunic, and green shoes. Seated on a throne, white blind tracery front as 2a above, yellow top, green cushion with an ochre (?) finial on either side. Background and border as 2a above.

Iconography. Possibly represents a king of England.

Style and Design. This and 2a are companion panels: the backgrounds, borders, and blind tracery fronts of the thrones are identical. The heads of the figures are alike: long oval faces, the drawing of the features is simplified. The very round eyes with large solid pupils give the faces a solemn hieratic air; this is possibly deliberate if the affinity with seal design suggested above is accepted.

Date. Some details of the design assist in establishing a possible date. The crozier and sceptre both terminate in a foliage design with rounded trefoil leaves. The crozier's form and style of decoration are paralleled in the early 13th-c. Hyde Abbey crozier which has oak leaves and acorns[1] rather than the conventionalized foliage of 12th-c. croziers.[2] In seal design the early form of a simple curled crook persists until the second quarter of the 13th c., when the foliated crook becomes more common.[3] The long sceptre with its foliated head can be compared with the third seal of Henry III of *c.* 1263–4.[4] The blind tracery of the thrones is similar to a drawing from the circle of Matthew Paris of *c.* 1250.[5] A mid 13th-c. date, *c.* 1250–70, therefore seems feasible for the glass panels.

3b. Shield of Harcourt impaling Byron

Roundel: d. 0·32 m. Shield: h. 0·21 m. w. 0·19 m.

Gules two bars or HARCOURT *impaling argent three bends gules* BYRON *encircled by the Garter, motto, in black-letter script:* |hony|soyt|qy|mal|y|pense.

Condition. Complete, over-all corrosion, more pronounced on the coloured glass.

Colour and Technique. The coloured glass of the shield is all pot metal. The ruby ground and gold charges of the Harcourt arms are diapered with a feathery foliage design. The bends of the Byron arms are plain ruby, the field patterned with a pebble design, painted in outline. The surround is patterned with contiguous rosettes, painted in outline on yellow stain.

Date. After 1463 and possibly 1470–84.

Iconography. Greening Lamborn dated this shield *c.* 1465–70 and suggested that this is probably the earliest example of the Garter in painted glass.[6] Earlier examples are, however, known. A lost window at Old St. Pauls, adjacent to the tomb of John of Gaunt, Duke of Lancaster, included a shield of his arms encircled by the Garter.[7] The window was probably contemporary with the tomb made in 1374. Gaunt died in 1399. The earliest existing representations of a shield enclosed by a Garter are the two shields of Sir John Cornwall, Lord Fanhope, now in the nave north clerestory of Millbrook parish church (Beds.), datable *c.* 1428–*c.* 1443.[8]

4a, 4b, 4c. Decorative Design

h. 0·28 m. w. 0·42 m.

An identical design at the head of each light, probably *in situ.*

Condition. Very incomplete. Some missing parts in 4b were made up with copies by Mr. M. C. Farrar Bell after 1963.

Colour and Technique. White glass and yellow stain, trace lines in brown paint with delicate stipple and matt shading.

Style and Design. The glass is too incomplete for a reconstruction of the over-all design. Border: a trail of vine leaves and grapes. Enclosed by the border, and partly painted on the same pieces of glass, are very incomplete remains of a large foliage and fruit design, 4a and 4c. The cusps at the head of each light contain three roundels:

4a. A Star   A Crown   A Sun
4b. (Modern)   A Crown   (Modern)
4c. A Star   A Crown   A Crown

Date. Probably contemporary with the Harcourt–Byron shield (3b) after 1463, possibly 1470–84.

Not catalogued. Very small scraps of foliage design in two tracery lights.

s. VII

2a, 2b, 2c. Decorative Design

h. 0·28 m. w. 0·42 m.

Remains of a repeated decorative design, identical with window s. VI, 4a, 4b, and 4c. Modern copies in 2b by Mr. Farrar Bell, after 1963. The cusps here contain:

2a. A White Rose   A Crown   A Star
2b. (Modern)   A White Rose   (Modern)
2c. A Star   A Crown   A White Rose

Iconography. The roundels in windows s. VI and s. VII were described by Greening Lamborn as 'the flaming sun and white rose badges of Edward IV'.[9] On the seals of Edward IV the sun badge is represented as a many-rayed mullet, i.e. the edges of each ray are straight.[10] This convention is observed on the Yorkist collar of suns and roses on the tomb of Sir Robert Harcourt, K.G., d. 1470.[11] An example in glass painting occurs in the Fitz Ellis window at Waterperry, n. V, 2c, *c.* 1461–9. Only one roundel conforms to this convention, s. VI, 4a. The others, here catalogued as stars, have twelve wavy rays combined with four straight ones.[12]

Date. After 1463, probably *c.* 1470–84.

[1] W. W. Watts, *Victoria and Albert Museum. Catalogue of Pastoral Staves* (1924), 10, frontispiece.

[2] e.g. those found at St. David's. W. H. St. John Hope, 'The Episcopal Ornaments of . . . Certain Bishops of St. David's', *Archaeologia* lx (1907), 488, pl. liii.

[3] Compare the first seal of Richard Marsh, Bishop of Durham 1217–26, with those of his predecessors. C. H. Hunter Blair, 'Medieval Seals of the Bishops of Durham', *Archaeologia* lxxii (1922), pl. i. (The cast at the Society of Antiquaries shows the detail more clearly than in the reproduction.)

[4] A. B. Wyon, *The Great Seals of England* (1887), 23, pl. vii.

[5] Cambridge University Library MS. Kk. IV. 25. P. Brieger, *English Art 1216–1307* (1957), 149, pl. 50.

[6] Greening Lamborn (1949), 156.

[7] Noted by Nicholas Charles in 1605; B.L. Lansdown MS. 874, f. 115ᵛ.

[8] R. Marks, 'Some Early Representations of the Garter in Stained Glass', *Report of the Society of the Friends of St. George* v, no. 4 (1972–3), 154, pl. 13.   [9] Greening Lamborn (1949), 156.

[10] Wyon, op. cit., nos. 83, 84, and 87, pls. xiv and xv.

[11] Gough, op. cit. 229.

[12] See the remarks of H. Stanford London, *Royal Beasts* (1956), 31.

s. VIII

2a, 2b, 2c. Quarries

h. 0·28 m. w. 0·42 m.

Remains of quarry glazing, all the same design, type 23. White glass and yellow stain. 15th c., possibly *c.* 1470–84.

STANTON ST. JOHN
ST. JOHN

O.S. SP 577 094.

MS. SOURCES

Oxford. Bodleian Library:
  MS. Don. d. 90, f. 131. Drawing *c.* 1804.
  MS. Top. Oxon. b. 220, f. 19. Notes by Robinson *c.* 1810–30.
  MS. Top. Oxon. d. 92, f. 113. Notes by Revd. F. H. Woods 1882.

PRINTED

Parker (1846), 223–30.
Nelson (1913), 171–2.
Bouchier (1918), 87–8.
P.C. (1920), 283–5.
Bouchier (1932), 132.
Greening Lamborn (1949), 156–7.
Bell, H. C., *The Fabric and Furniture of the Church of St. John the Baptist. Stanton St. John* (1964 guide).
Pevsner (1974), 784–5.

The chancel windows were in a dilapidated state in 1846 with the openings partly bricked up.[1] The chancel was restored *c.* 1863–7 and the windows were arranged in their present form at that date.[2] The restoration was a very careful one, missing portions of the grisaille patterns in the three chancel windows were made up with careful copies of the original. In 1977 the glass was releaded and cleaned by the York Glaziers Trust, and the roundel, w. I, A1 is now leaded into s. IV, 1a.

Although only slight in extent the chancel windows contain the best preserved examples of geometric grisaille pattern glazing in the county. The date of the chancel has been put at *c.* 1300.[3] The stylized vine forms and hatched ground suggest that 1300 is rather late for this particular class of design.

n. IV   PLATE 45 (*a*), (*b*)

1a–4a. Geometric Grisaille

Panels: h. 0·80 m. w. 0·52 m.

An intricate leaded and painted design of circles and half-circles in a diamond-shaped trellis frame, painted with stylized trails of vine foliage and grapes.

Condition. Incomplete, over-all corrosion, much very pronounced, and some paint loss. The restored portions of *c.* 1863–7 are careful copies of the original design.

Colour and Technique. Painted on white glass, coloured glass restricted to the centres of the circles and half-circles and intersections of the trellis frame, where the bosses are either pink or ochre glass. Stylized trails of vine leaves and grapes, cross-hatched backgrounds painted in lines. Trellis frames patterned, either a painted trail of foliage or geometric design picked out of a matt black wash.

Style and Design. This and n. V below are the most complete examples of this class of design that have survived in the county. For similar designs see Stanton Harcourt, s. II–IV.

Date. 13th–14th c., *c.* 1275–1300.

1a. Two quarries. Types 30 and 33, white glass. 14th c.

3a. Modern shield of arms, the glass fragmented and splashed with paint to give it the appearance of antiquity.

n. V

1a. Fragments

h. 0·48 m. w. 0·52 m.

Small pieces of white foliage, from a geometric grisaille, leaded up with modern plain glass.

Date. 14th c. and 1863–7.

---

[1] Parker (1846), 223–30.   [2] Bodl. Lib. MS. Top. Oxon. d. 92, f. 113, op. cit.   [3] Pevsner (1974), 784–5.

2a–4a. Geometric Grisaille

Panels h. 0·48 m. w. 0·52 m.

An intricate leaded and painted design of circles super-imposed on contiguous half-circles, linked by a diamond-shaped trellis frame, painted with trails of stylized maple leaves.

Condition. As n. IV, 1a–4a.

Colour and Technique. Foliage trails painted on white glass, cross-hatched background painted in very fine outlines. Small coloured bosses at the centres of the circles in pink or ochre, trellis frame in green and ochre glass.

Style and Design. See n. IV, 1a–4a.

Date. c. 1275–1300.

2a. Modern shield of arms.

4a. Modern shield of arms, the glass fragmented and splashed with paint to give it the appearance of antiquity.

s. IV   PLATE 45 (c)

1a–4a. Quarries and Decorative Designs

h. 0·90 m. w. 0·50 m.

Condition. The glass is very corroded. Particularly deep corrosion on the reverse of the coloured glass. The paint is generally sound except that on the quarries which is very worn and faint. Restored *c.* 1863–7. Only fifteen of the quarries are genuine, the remainder good copies.

1a. Fragment of ochre drapery, very corroded.

Colour and Technique. Quarries. Types 30 and 33 on white glass, background cross-hatching painted in outline.

2a. 4a. Four identical roundels. Symmetrical trails of very stylized vine leaves and grapes radiating from a boss at the centre. Vine painted on white glass, plain background, quatrefoil bosses either plain ruby centre with foils alternately plain green and ochre, green with ruby and ochre foils, or ochre with ruby and green foils.

3a. Foliage design. At the centre a plain ruby boss with four sprays of leaves radiating from it painted on white glass, beaded border picked out of a matt wash, side pieces alternately ruby and ochre, painted with a flat trefoil leaf design.

Style and Design. It is unlikely that the present arrangement of quarries and roundels is original.

Date. 14th c., *c.* 1300.

5a. Funeral of the Virgin Mary   PLATE 44 (c)

h. 0·35 m. w. 0·35 m.

A Jew attempts to overturn the coffin carried on the shoulders of two Apostles, two censing angels above.

Condition. Incomplete, the panel made up with fragments of canopies, heraldic borders, and modern plain glass.

Colour and Technique. The pall and bier of the coffin in deep pot-yellow ochre, main figures in white tunics, strong smear shading, left angel; alb in ruby, right in green, white censers. Ground at base deep green, background plain ruby. Heraldic borders, white fleurs-de-lis and ochre castles.

Iconography. The scene has been described as the 'Assumption of the Virgin'[1] and 'figures carrying a shrine'.[2] It is more likely that the scene is the Virgin's funeral, the Jew represented twice, hanging by his hands from the coffin and falling prostrate on the ground below. The Jew's face is a caricature with flashing eyes and clenched teeth. The source is the 6th-c. text of *De Transitu Beatae Mariae*. Representations of the scene do not occur until much later. The earliest known English example is in the 12th-c. York Psalter in the Hunterian Library at Glasgow.[3] Examples are more common in the later 13th and 14th c.[4]

Style and Design. The painting is very bold and of high quality. The proportions of the Jew's arms are exaggerated, probably deliberately.

Date. 14th c., *c.* 1300.

6a. Shield of Clare   PLATE 44 (c)

Panel: h. 0·28 m. w. 0·50 m. Shield: h. 0·28 m. w. 0·28 m.

Or three chevrons gules CLARE, EARL OF GLOUCESTER.

Condition. Coloured glass is very corroded on both surfaces. Set against quarries as 1a–4a, mostly copies; on the original ones paint worn very thin.

Colour and Technique. Plain ochre and ruby glass of the shield, no decorative diapers.

Date. 14th c., *c.* 1300? There is no known connection between the Clare family and the manor. The shield was recorded by Robinson, *c.* 1804–10,[5] so it is unlikely to be a restorer's composite using old glass.

7a. Censing Angels   PLATE 44 (c)

h. 0·28 m. w. 0·21 m.

Condition. Incomplete; left, nearly all the figure missing, right; lacks hand and part; of censer chain coloured glass is

---

[1] Bouchier (1918), 87–8.
[2] Ibid. Bouchier (1932), 132. Nelson (1913), 171–2.
[3] T. S. R. Boase, *The York Psalter* (1962), 8–9.
[4] S. C. Cockerell, 'The Work of W. de Brailes', *Roxburghe Club*

(1930), 23. Sir G. F. Warner, *The Queen Mary's Psalter* (1912), pl. 292. Taymouth Hours—f. 133b. See p. 152 n. 6 above.
[5] MS. Top. Oxon. b. 220, f. 19, op. cit.

very corroded, particularly the ochre. Set against quarries as 1a–4a above, mostly copies.

Colour and Technique. Figures and censers painted on white glass, ochre wings, plain ruby backgrounds, the ruby very streaky.

Style and Design. Very linear drapery painting, no smear shading. A different artist from that of 5a.

Date. 14th c. *c.* 1300.

w. I (moved in 1977 to s. IV, 1a)

A1. Grotesque Roundel

d. 0·20 m.

A man with a sword cutting down the branches of a tree.

Condition. Complete, but cracked and coming apart in 1973.

Colour and Technique. Painted on white glass, figure and foliage white and yellow stain, against a plain matt black background. Plain green border. The black paint is extremely dark in tone.

Iconography. Probably just a humorous design rather than one of the Occupations of the Months.

Style and Design. Good-quality work. This class of design is rarely found in the county.

Date. First quarter (?) 14th c.

STONESFIELD

ST. JAMES

O.S. SP 394 171.

MS. SOURCES

Oxford. Bodleian Library, MS. Top. Gen. e. 78, f. 325. Heraldic collections by T. Willement dated 1827.

PRINTED

Willement, T., *Concise Account of Works in Stained Glass* (1840), 16.
Parker (1846), 157–8.
Bouchier (1918), 98.
P.C. (1920), 290, 293–8.
Greening Lamborn (1949), 157–60.
Pevsner (1974), 790–1.

The late-fifteenth to sixteenth-century heraldic glass now in the church appears, in part, to come from a domestic glazing scheme. Four shields (w. I, 2a–2d) relate to members of the Fettiplace family and their alliances. It is known that these shields were part of the collection of medieval glass made by Alderman W. Fletcher. His nephew Thomas Robinson employed Thomas Willement to glaze them into a south window of Begbroke church in 1827. His son the Revd. Francis Robinson removed them to Stonesfield church, where he was rector 1834–82. Willement thought that the shields had belonged to a church in the county where the family of Fettiplace was seated. However, as Greening Lamborn pointed out, it seems more likely that they are the shields noted by Wood in the windows of the Fettiplace manor house at Swinborne. The shields are all the same size, identical in outline, and very alike in the foliage patterns painted on the fields and charges. These factors suggest that, although they came from different windows in the house, the glazing was of one period.

The original provenance of the other heraldic glass in the church has not been established. It is improbable that it is indigenous to the church as the notes of Wood and Rawlinson do not record any heraldic glass there in the seventeenth and eighteenth centuries.

I

2b. Composite Panel

h. 0·63 m. w. 0·24 m.

Condition. A composite panel of a male figure, set below a canopy. Figure, paint thin and worn, head modern painted on old glass, canopy all modern, except for one piece.

Colour and Technique. Brown paint on white glass, stipple shading, details picked out in yellow stain.

Iconography. The figure points to a closed book held in his right hand, possibly a saint, but this is uncertain.

Style and Design. The figure stood in an architectural niche with an elaborate columned base. Perhaps from a tracery light, the large scale would be exceptional for the centre of a canopy design.

Date. 15th c., probably first half.

3a, 3b, 3c. Quarries

Each quarry h. 0·15 m. w. 0·12 m.

Fourteen identical quarries.

Condition. Each quarry is complete, six have old breaks with leaded repair. Corroded, paint somewhat worn.

Colour and Technique. Brown paint on white glass, leaves of foliage design in yellow stain.

Style and Design. Quarry type 22.

Date. 15th c.

3a, 3b, 3c. Crown Designs

h. 0·15 m. w. 0·12 m.

Three identical crown designs.

Condition. Each is complete, old breaks in 3a and 3c have leaded repairs, somewhat corroded, particularly 3c.

Colour and Technique. Brown paint on white glass, crowns in yellow stain, hatched line background, borders plain white and yellow stain.

Style and Design. Probably *in situ*, the shape shows that each was designed for the apex cusp of a light. The design may have been repeated in the side cusps. Similar, but not identical, crowns are found at Stanton Harcourt, s. VI, 4a–c and s. VII, 2a and 2c.

Date. Second half 15th c.

Tracery Lights

Ten roundels have been set against modern white glass in the tracery lights.

A2, A5. Roundels, Sun and Rose

d. 0·10 m.

Condition. The two suns are complete, the roses have leaded repairs. The paint is rather worn.

Colour and Technique. Brown paint on white glass and yellow stain.

Style and Design. These designs are probably to be read as the white rose and flaming sun badges of Edward IV. The large

size suggests that they were originally set in tracery lights, possibly with a decorative surround, or against quarries.

Date. Second half 15th c.

A3. Roundels, Crowns

d. 0·07 m.

Four identical crown designs.

Condition. All complete, slight corrosion.

Colour and Technique. Brown paint on white glass and yellow stain.

Style and Design. Possibly made for the cusped foil of a tracery light.

Date. Second half 15th c.

A3. Roundel, Eagle of St. John

d. 0·17 m.

Condition. Incomplete, slight corrosion, made up with modern white glass.

Colour and Technique. Brown paint on white glass, stippled shading, feathers picked out in yellow stain, herbage also in yellow stain. Background diaper of contiguous rosettes, painted in outline, with yellow centres.

Iconography. Eagle with displayed wings, holding a scroll inscribed in black-letter script:

$$|S(an)c(tu)s\ iohan(nes)|$$

Style and Design. As A4.

Date. Second half 15th c.

A4. Roundel, Lion of St. Mark

d. 0·17 m.

Condition. Complete, slight corrosion.

Colour and Technique. Brown paint on white glass, stippled shading, lion in yellow stain, herbage and background as A3.

Iconography. Winged lion, with nimbus; from its mouth runs a scroll inscribed in black-letter script:

$$|S(an)c(tu)s\ Mar(cus)|$$

Style and Design. These two roundels are the same size, the herbage and background diapers are identical. The designs are very stylized, the lion represented passant gardant as in heraldry.

Date. Second half 15th c.

s. II

2a. Shield of Dormer impaling Scriven (?)

h. 0·38 m. w. 0·26 m. Shield: h. 0·23 m. w. 0·18 m. (when complete).

Azure billety or, on a chief or a demi-lion rampant sable, on its shoulder a crescent argent for difference[1] DORMER OF THAME[2] *impaling ermine, a lion rampant sable* SCRIVEN.[3] Encircled by an elaborate chaplet.

Condition. The paint is rather worn, particularly on the chaplet. The lower parts of the shield and chaplet are missing, replaced by modern white glass. The upper clasp on the chaplet does not belong there, compare 2b below. The panel width has been reduced to fit its present position.

Colour and Technique. The colours are very thin in tone. The field of the Dormer arms is flashed blue glass, the billets abraded and stained yellow. The chief is a single piece of white glass, the demi-lion in black paint, the crescent left void, the field in yellow stain. The Scriven arms are painted on a single piece of white glass. Plain green background to the shield. Mauve chaplet, with blue bands and ornamental clasps.

Style and Design. Similar shields of Dormer, and Dormer impaling Scriven, are found at Begbroke, and at Wytham (Berks.).[4] In the latter example the chaplet is the same design as here. The Italianate Renaissance details of the chaplet denote a knowledge of continental models, but do not necessarily imply a foreign craftsman.[5]

Date. Mid 16th c. William Dormer of Thame (Oxon.) and Long Crendon (Bucks.), d. 1563, married Elizabeth Scriven.[6]

Provenance. Original provenance not known. Greening Lamborn conjectured it may have come from the house of William Dormer's brother John, who lived at Steeple Barton,[7] but there is no evidence for this. Subsequently it was in the collection of Alderman W. Fletcher, thence to his nephew Thomas Robinson, given by him to Begbroke church in 1827[8] and removed to Stonesfield by his son, the Revd. Francis Robinson, rector of Stonesfield, 1834–82.[9]

2b. Shield of The London Company of Mercers

h. 0·38 m. w. 0·26 m. Shield: h. 0·23 m. w. 0·18 m.

Gules a maiden's head and shoulders proper, crowned and crined or, rising from a band of clouds nebuly argent and azure, a bordure of clouds nebuly argent and azure THE LONDON COMPANY OF MERCERS.[10] Encircled by an elaborate chaplet.

Condition. Almost complete, the bordure, broken c. 1948, now made up with modern white glass.[11] Panel cut down at the sides to fit its present position.

Colour and Technique. Pot-metal coloured glass. Ruby field diapered with a foliage design, maiden's head painted on white glass, hair and crown in yellow stain. The band and bordure of clouds are flashed blue glass, the white portions abraded. Green chaplet with mauve bands, ornamental clasps in yellow stain on blue glass.

Style and Design. The chaplet is the same design as that of 2a, probably produced by the same workshop, but not necessarily as either a pair, or part of a related series.

Date. First half 16th c. John Dormer, d. 1584, brother of William (shield 2a), was a citizen and mercer of London.[12]

Provenance. Original provenance not known, possibly from Steeple Barton (see 2a). Later probably in the collection of Alderman W. Fletcher, but not recorded.

s. III

2a. Shield of Russell impaling Sapcotes

h. 0·38 m. w. 0·26 m. Shield: h. 0·23 m. w. 0·18 m.

Quarterly 1. *quarterly* i, iv *argent a lion rampant* (*gules*) *on a chief sable three escallops argent* RUSSELL. ii, iii (*azure*) *a tower argent* DE LA TOUR 2. (*gules*) *three herrings hauriant argent* HERRING 3. *sable a griffin segreant argent between three crosslets fitchy argent* FROXMER 4. *sable three chevrons ermine in dexter chief a crescent or for difference* WYSE *impaling quarterly* 1, 4 *sable three dovecots argent, in chief a mullet or* SAPCOTES 2, 3 *argent on a cross* (*gules*) *five mullets or* SEEMARK. Encircled by an elaborate chaplet.

---

[1] Greening Lamborn (1949), 157, blazoned the difference as 'a crescent silver enclosing another'. The charge has shading on the inside half, but is drawn as one piece. It seems more likely to be a single crescent, but compare the shield of Dormer at Begbroke. Ibid., pl. 42.

[2] Arms of Dormer of Thame as given in College of Arms MS. L10, f. 63ᵛ, no. 17, c. 1520, and Wrythe's Book of Knights n. 762, c. 1522. B.L. Add. MS. 46354.

[3] Greening Lamborn (1949), 159, notes that on the tomb of Sir John Dormer at Long Crendon (Bucks.), 1626, the field of the Scriven arms is there sprinkled with drops of blood instead of ermine spots.

[4] Greening Lamborn (1949), 108–9.

[5] Ibid. 52, suggesting that the Begbroke shield is Flemish workmanship.

[6] F. G. Lee, *The History, Description and Antiquities of the Prebendal Church of the Blessed Virgin Mary at Thame* (1883), 509–10. M. Maclagan, 'The Family of Dormer in Oxfordshire and Buckinghamshire', *Oxoniensia* xi and xii (1946–7), 98. Greening Lamborn (1949), 159.

[7] Ibid.

[8] Bodl. Lib. MS. Top. Gen. e. 78, op. cit.

[9] Greening Lamborn (1949), 158.

[10] Bouchier (1918), 98, incorrectly describes this shield as 'a queen half length'.

[11] Greening Lamborn (1949), 159, n. 1, shields referred to as mutilated, October 1948; pl. 56 shows the shield complete.

[12] Ibid. 159. Maclagan, op. cit. 98.

Condition. Complete and well preserved, except for slight paint loss on the bands of the chaplet.

Colour and Technique. The shield is painted on white glass, the gold charges in yellow stain. The proper tinctures, as given above in brackets, may have been painted in colours, now perished. Shield set on a mauve roundel, diapered with a foliage design, purple chaplet with yellow bands, clasps in yellow stain.

Style and Design. The chaplet is the same type as those in s. III, 2a and 2b, but here the detailed work is more precise and the foliage more elaborate.

Date. After 1526 and probably before 1554. John, Baron Russell 1538–9, Earl of Bedford 1549–50 (d. 1554), married, in 1526, Anne daughter of Sir Guy Sapcotes, son of Sir William Sapcotes by Anne Seemark.[1]

Provenance. Not known, possibly from the collection of Alderman W. Fletcher.

1b. Shield of Russell impaling Sapcotes

h. 0·38 m. w. 0·26 m. Shield: h. 0·23 m. w. 0·18 m.

Identical with 1a, except that here the shield is set on a blue roundel.

w. I

2a. Shield of Fettiplace

h. 0·37 m. w. 0·28 m. Shield: h. 0·27 m. w. 0·25 m.
Gules two chevrons argent, in dexter chief a crescent or FETTI-PLACE OF SWINBROOK. Pieces of a foliage design above and below the shield.

Condition. The shield is complete; painted foliage design on the field is very worn and faint.

Colour and Technique. Pot-metal coloured glass, the field of the shield is flashed ruby glass, the crescent abraded and stained yellow.

Style and Design. The strips of foliage above and below the shield may be part of its original surround.

Date. Late 15th c.–early 16th c. These are the arms of Anthony Fettiplace of Swinbrook manor house,[2] but they are not included in the shields noted there by Wood.[3]

Later in the collection of Alderman W. Fletcher, thence to his nephew Thomas Robinson, given by him to Begbroke church in 1827.[4] Removed to Stonesfield by his son, the Revd. Francis Robinson, rector of Stonesfield, 1834–82.[5]

2b. Shield of Kingston impaling Fettiplace   PLATE 9 (a)

h. 0·37 m. w. 0·28 m. Shield: h. 0·27 m. w. 0·25 m.

Sable a lion rampant queue fourchée or KINGSTON *impaling gules two chevrons argent* FETTIPLACE. Pieces of foliage above and below the shield.

Condition. The Kingston arms are incomplete, made up with modern white glass, the black paint of the field is worn with some flaking. The ruby field of the Fettiplace arms has no decorative diaper, possibly a restoration using old glass.

Colour and Technique. Pot-metal coloured glass. The Kingston arms were on a single piece of white glass, the field in black paint, the lion in yellow stain.

Date. Late 15th c.–early 16th c. Possibly the arms of John Kingston of Childrey (Berks.), d. 1514, married Susan, daughter of Richard Fettiplace.[6]

Provenance. Probably the shield recorded by Wood, then in a parlour window at Swinbrook manor house.[7] Thereafter as shield 2a.

2c. Shield of Fettiplace impaling Fabyan   PLATE 9 (b)

h. 0·37 m. w. 0·28 m. Shield: h. 0·27 m. w. 0·25 m.

FETTIPLACE *impaling ermine three fleurs-de-lis gules, a bordure engrailed gules* FABYAN. Pieces of foliage above and below the shield.

Condition. The shield is complete, the foliage design painted on the field of the Fettiplace arms and the ermine spots of the Fabyan arms are rather worn.

Colour and Technique. Pot-metal coloured glass. The ruby border of the Fabyan arms leaded as a plain piece of ruby glass, the engrailed edge done in paint on the glass of the field.

Style and Design. The foliage design on the Fettiplace arms is identical with shield 2a.

Date. Late 15th–early 16th c.

---

[1] J. H. Round, *Studies in Peerage and Family History* (1901), vi, particularly 252–3, 267. G.E.C. ii. 73–5. G. Scott Thompson, 'Some Notes on the Ancestry of John Russell, Lord Russell, First Earl of Bedford', *The Genealogists' Magazine* ix (1940), 45. Greening Lamborn (1949), 160.
[2] J. R. Dunlop, 'The Family of Fettiplace', *Miscellanea Genealogica et Heraldica*, 5th ser. ii (1916–17), 202–3. E. A. Greening Lamborn, 'On Marks of Cadency', *Notes and Queries* clxxxix (1949), 272–4. Greening Lamborn (1949), 158.

[3] P.C. (1920), 296–8.
[4] Bodl. Lib. MS. Top. Gen. e. 78, op. cit. Willement incorrectly blazons the chevrons as or.
[5] Greening Lamborn (1949), 158.
[6] Dunlop, op. cit. 185–6. J. R. Dunlop, 'Brasses Commemorative of the Fettiplace Family', *Transactions of the Monumental Brass Society* vi (1910), 101–2, where, however, the Kingston arms are incorrectly blazoned.
[7] P.C. (1920), 297. Wood's blazon omits the forked tail of the lion.

John Fettiplace of East Shefford (Berks.), d. 1464, married Joan, daughter of Edward Fabyan.[1]

Provenance. Probably the shield recorded by Wood, then in an upper room at Swinbrook manor house.[2] Thereafter as shield 2a.

2d. Shield of Harcourt impaling Limbrick

h. 0·37 m. w. 0·28 m. Shield: h. 0·27 m. w. 0·25 m.

Gules two bars or HARCOURT *impaling checky or and azure, on a bend gules three lions passant gardant or* LIMBRICK. Pieces of foliage above and below the shield.

Condition. The shield is incomplete, the foliage designs painted on the Harcourt arms and the checky pieces of the Limbrick

arms are very worn. The bend of the latter arms was broken *c.* 1943,[2] its middle portion now set upside-down, made up with modern white glass.

Colour and Technique. Pot-metal coloured glass. The bend is flashed ruby glass, the lions abraded and stained yellow.

Style and Design. The foliage design on the Harcourt arms is the same type as shields 2a and 2c above.

Date. Late 15th–early 16th c. Sir Robert Harcourt, 1466–1503/17, married Agnes, daughter of Thomas Limbrick.[4]

Provenance. Probably the shield recorded by Wood, then in a parlour window at Swinbrook manor house.[5] Thereafter as shield 2a.[6]

STRATTON AUDLEY
ST. MARY AND ST. EDBURGH

O.S. SP 608 260

MS. SOURCES

Oxford. Bodleian Library:
    MS. Top. Oxon. e. 286, ff. 136ᵛ–137. Notes by N. Greenwood, dated 1660, copied in B.L. Harleian MS. 4170, p. 26. *c.* 18th c.
    MS. Top. Oxon. b. 75, f. 167ʳ. Drawings dated 1805.

PRINTED

Bouchier (1918), 99.
P.C. (1920), 291.
Greening Lamborn (1949), 160–1.
V.C.H. vi (1959), 324–32.
Pevsner (1974), 794–5.

The east window of the north aisle of the nave has fourteenth-century glass in the tracery lights. The glass is incomplete and patched in places. The over-all design of a shield of arms set on a foliage background is probably genuine (B1 and B2). The lower range of trefoil tracery lights probably had a small shield of arms in the upper foil of each light; one remains, the arms of Segrave (A3). The outlines of two lost shields remain in lights A1 and A5. It is not certain that this arrangement is genuine. The design is repeated in the traceries of the west window of the south nave aisle.

The antiquarian notes on the armorial glass in the east window of the north aisle have been incorrectly published.[7] A correct transcript is given here, and the arms identified.[8]

'In the east window of the north Isle these armes England, viz. *three lions passant and a label of three points* (colour of label not given). *Azure three lions rampant or* FIENNES
    Sable a lion rampant argent crowned or SEGRAVE
    Ermine a chief gules MORTEYN
    Argent three (fleurs) de lis between crosses crosslet fitchy sable BEREFORD

---

[1] Dunlop, 'The Family of Fettiplace', op. cit. 184.

[2] P.C. (1920), 298.

[3] Greening Lamborn (1949), 51 n. 1, shields recorded as mutilated, October 1948; pl. 56 shows the shield complete.

[4] J. C. Wedgwood, 'Harcourt of Ellenhall', *William Salt Archaeological Society* (1914), 204. G. H. Farnham, 'The Harcourt Family', *Leicestershire Archaeological Society Transactions* xv (1927–8), 115. J. C. Wedgwood and A. D. Holt, *History of Parliament 1439–1509*.

Biographies (1936), 420–1. E. A. Greening Lamborn, 'Some Sources for the New Papworth', *Notes and Queries* cxc (1946), 269–72.

[5] P.C. (1920), 297. Wood's blazon gives only one lion on the bend.

[6] Bodl. Lib. MS. Top. Gen. e. 78, op. cit. Willement incorrectly blazons the shield as Fettiplace impaling Limbrick.

[7] P.C. (1920), 291.

[8] Wood's notes are a mixture of blazon and trick, Bodl. Lib. Wood MS. E. 1, f. 180.

Or a chevron vert INGE

Checky or and azure WARREN

The edges of this window are filled with *lions rampant or* and a *lion passant or* and *towers or*.'

The shields of Fiennes and Segrave remain in the tracery lights (B2, A3) together with the outlines of three others. Greening Lamborn[1] cited the genealogical links between the Audleys of Stratton, lords of the manor,[2] and Bereford, Segrave, and Fiennes to explain the inclusion of their arms. Similar links, however, have not been found with the other families represented. The arms of Warren can be accounted for by the tenure connection—part of the manor of Stratton was held of the Earl of Warren.[3] The families of Inge and Morteyn had no holdings in the manor, indeed the latter family had no lands in Oxfordshire.[4] The genealogical and feudal connections, so far as is known, between the families represented, do not explain this display of heraldry. The selection may reflect personal or political relationships. It might be significant that two contemporary members of the Bereford and Inge families, both with lands in Oxfordshire,[5] were important judges. Sir William de Bereford (d. 1326) was Chief Justice of the Common Bench[6] and Sir William Inge (d. 1321) was Chief Justice of the King's Bench.[7] The heraldic evidence offers, therefore, no conclusive proof as to the date of the glass. A dating in the first quarter of the fourteenth century seems the most probable.

The west window of the south aisle of the nave (s. VI) retains some fragments in the tracery lights. The incomplete foliage designs *in situ* are identical with those in the east window of the north aisle (n. III, A3). A shield of Clare, Earl of Gloucester, is inserted in one light (B3). Hugh, Lord Audley of Stratton (d. 1348) married Margaret, sister and co-heiress of Gilbert de Clare, Earl of Gloucester, in 1317. He was created Earl of Gloucester, in her right, in 1336 and assumed the arms of Clare.[8] However, this marriage does not necessarily provide dating evidence for the glass, as the Clares were overlords of the Audleys[9] and this factor could justify the display of their arms in the church.

n. III

The glass remaining in the tracery lights is very incomplete. Enough remains to reconstruct some of the over-all design. The lowest range of trefoil tracery lights each contained a foliage design of three green leaves, on a plain ruby background, radiating from a triangular blue design enclosing three ochre leaves. Each of these lights incorporates either a shield or the outline of a shield in the top foil. This arrangement may be original (A1, 3, 5). The two trefoil lights above, B1 and B2, each have a shield with a coloured circular surround set against a white foliage design on a plain ruby background. This arrangement is probably original.

The glass is all pot-metal and is very corroded.

A1. Foliage Design and Shield

h. 0·38 m. w. 0·38 m.

Condition. Very incomplete, only the lower left lobe remains. The outline of the shield survives.

Date. Early 14th c.

A2. Inserted Fragments

Plain ochre and white glass

A3. Foliage Design and Shield of Segrave

h. 0·38 m. w. 0·38 m. Shield: h. 0·13 m. w. 0·10 m.

Sable a lion rampant argent crowned (or) SEGRAVE.

Condition. Incomplete, the centre and lower left lobe of the foliage design and the shield remain.

Colour and Technique. The shield is painted in dark brown on a single piece of glass. The lion's crown, which should be gold, is in outline, no trace of any colouring.

Date. Early 14th c.

---

[1] Greening Lamborn (1949), 161.

[2] *V.C.H.* (1959), 324–32.

[3] *V.C.H.* (1959), 327. *Book of Fees*, 826. *Feudal Aids* iv. 157.

[4] Their lands were in Leics., Derbys., Notts., Staffs., and Beds., see G. A. Moriarty, 'The Morteyns of Marston and Tillsworth', *Bedfordshire Historical Record Society* ix (1923–7), 5–22. *The Genealogist*, N.S. xxxviii (1922), 194–203.

[5] The main holdings of the Berefords were at Newnham and

Brightwell Baldwin, *Cal. Inq. Post Mortem* vi, no. 748, x, nos. 249, 321. The Inge family held the manor of Great Milton, *Cal. Inq. Post Mortem* vi. 193, xii. 39. *V.C.H.* vii (1962), 123.

[6] E. Foss, *A Biographical Dictionary of the Judges of England* (1870), 84.

[7] Ibid. 366–7.

[8] Greening Lamborn (1949), 161. G.E.C. i. 347–8, v. 715.

[9] *Feudal Aids* iv. 157.

A4. Inserted Fragments

Plain ruby, green foliage, a lion's face in yellow stain.

Date. 14th c.

A5. Foliage Design and Shield

h. 0·38 m. w. 0·38 m.

Condition. Incomplete, only the lower right lobe remains. The outline of the shield remains.

Date. Early 14th c.

B1. Foliage Design and Shield

h. 0·38 m. w. 0·38 m.

Condition. Incomplete, only the outline of the shield remains with a patterned green circular surround, set against white foliage on plain ruby background, upper left lobe incomplete, patched with alien glass.

Date. Early 14th c.

B2. Foliage Design and Shield of Fiennes

h. 0·38 m. w. 0·38 m. Shield: h. 0·15 m. w. 0·15 m.
Shield: *azure three lions rampant or* FIENNES.

Condition. Apparently complete, corrosion on both surfaces.

Colour and Technique. Shield, the lions are separately leaded, plain blue field, set on a plain ruby circular surround, against white foliage on a plain ruby background, as B1.

Date. Early 14th c.

C2. Head of Christ

h. 0·38 m. w. 0·38 m.
Frontal head of Christ set against a foliage design.

Condition. The head is broken, repaired with a cement patch obscuring much of the face, left-hand lobe missing.

Colour and Technique. Head painted on white glass, ruby nimbus, cross in pot-metal ochre, foliage in green, plain white border.

Style and Design. Possibly *in situ* but the foliage here is in coloured glass, unlike the other tracery lights, so it may come from another window.

Date. Early 14th c.

─────────

[1] For remarks on this odd charge see 'Rolls of Arms, Henry III', ed. T. D. Tremlett and H. Stanford London, *Aspilogia* ii (1967), 120.

s. II

A2. Grotesque Design   PLATE 45 (*d*)

h. 0·28 m. w. 0·15 m.

Condition. Complete, old leaded repair and cracks, slight exterior corrosion. *In situ.*

Colour and Technique. Painted in brown on white glass with stippled matt and hatched line shading, details and background in yellow stain.

Design and Iconography. A frontal lion's face eating a branch of foliage that comes out behind its head. Variations on this theme are not uncommon; the design may derive from the heraldic charge: *a lion's face jessant de lis.*[1]

Date. 15th c.

s. VI

The glass remaining in the tracery lights is very incomplete and very corroded. Two traceries, B1 and B3, retain parts of a foliage design of three green leaves on a plain ruby ground, radiating from a central triangular design, identical with n. III, A1, 3, and 5 above. The shield in each of these lights may be an insertion: the ruby circular ground to the Clare shield, B3, appears to have been cut down to fit its present position. This shield was recorded in this window by Wood.[2]

A3 and B2. Each contains a fragment of a quarry type 47. White glass, the rosette in yellow stain.

B1. Foliage Design

h. 0·38 m. w. 0·38 m.

Condition. The right-hand lobe of the foliage design and the shield are missing, the outline of the latter remains.

Date. Early 14th c.

B3. Foliage Design and Shield of Clare

h. 0·38 m. w. 0·38 m. Shield: h. 0·11 m. w. 0·10 m.
Shield: *gules three chevrons or* CLARE, EARL OF GLOUCESTER.

Condition. The two lower lobes are complete, central design incomplete. Shield broken, old repairs, adjacent pieces of plain ruby may be part of its original surround.

Date. Early 14th c.

─────────

[2] Bodl. Lib. Wood MS. E. 1, f. 180; the shield is omitted in P.C. (1920), 291.

SWERFORD
ST. MARY

O.S. SP 373 312.

s. II

A1. Inserted Fragments

h. 0·20 m. w. 0·13 m.

The apex of a cusped light enclosing fragments of a cross-staff and banner, probably the top of a canopy. Painted on white glass, yellow stain.

Date. Mid 14th c.

Fragment of a foliage design. Flat leaf enclosed by a plain white border. 14th c.

A2. Fragments of Foliage Design

h. 0·20 m. w. 0·13 m.

An arabesque of trefoil leaves radiating from a circular boss, cusped quatrefoil at the centre. Painted on white glass, foliage in yellow stain against a matt black background. 14th c.

A3. Fragments of Foliage Design

h. 0·20 m. w. 0·13 m.

As A2, except that here the leaves are more pointed, and there are the remains of a broad cusped border enclosing the foliage. From a tracery light. 14th c.

PRINTED SOURCES
Pevsner (1974), 798.

A4. Quarry

h. 0·20 m. w. 0·13 m.

A single quarry, type 23. Painted on white glass, foliage in yellow stain set against plain glass. 14th c.

s. III, s. IV

s. III. Tracery lights A1 to A6. s. IV. Tracery Lights A1 to A3 and A5

h. 0·23 m. w. 0·30 m.

Quarries.

Each tracery light contains an inserted quarry, all type 45, set against small fragments of similar quarries.

Condition. The quarries in s. III, A4 and A6 had fallen out at some date prior to 1962, and could not be found at that date.

Date. 14th c.

Lost Glass

Rawlinson notes that 'in the South window of the Chauncell is a figure of St. Paul and another person holding in his hand an Agnus Dei, and a person mitred with his crozier in his right hand'.[1] The second figure was probably St. John Baptist. No trace of these figures remains.

SWINBROOK
ST. MARY

O.S. SP 279 122.
PRINTED SOURCES
'Notes of an excursion to Shipton-under-Wychwood, Swinbrook, Asthall, and Burford', *N.O.A.S. Report* (1870), 10–11.
Nelson (1913), 172.
Bouchier (1918), 98.
P.C. (1920), 295.
Bouchier (1932), 132.
Greening Lamborn (1949), 161.
Pevsner (1974), 800–1.

The tracery lights of the east window of the chancel formerly contained fragments of fifteenth-century glass and part of a mid sixteenth-century shield of the quarterly arms of Brydges.[2] The glass in the four

---

[1] P.C. (1920), 293.   [2] For the lost armorial glass see P.C. (1920), 295, and Greening Lamborn (1949), 161.

middle lights was blown out by a land-mine on 26 September 1940. The shattered pieces have been re-assembled and set in the east window of the south aisle of the nave.

The most noteworthy feature of the collection is six large bust-length figures of angels. They are identical in style and show some repetition in design. Unfortunately there is no evidence to relate them to the over-all composition and iconographic programme of a window or series of windows. It is possible that originally they held shields of arms, but this cannot be proved. They are unlike any other glass in the county.

I

B2. Composite Panel

h. 0·60 m. w. 0·30 m.

A medley of fragments: two figures of angels, now bust length, one very incomplete and set sideways; two pieces of canopy work, and a chequered floor design.

Condition. The present arrangement probably dates from 1863, when the window was repaired.[1] The panel was unharmed by the bomb explosion in 1940. There is only slight corrosion on both surfaces.

Colour and Technique. The more complete figure is executed in brown paint on white glass, fine stipple shading and slight smear shading, the cross diadem worn on the head, and the tips of the feathered wings are in yellow stain.

Iconography. The original context in which the angels appeared is not known. Bouchier's observation 'that above their foreheads are tongues of fire in the shape of a golden trefoil'[2] is a misinterpretation of the cross diadems worn by the angels.

Style and Design. The big eyes and over-large nose give the angel's face an individual character, but the effect is some-what coarse. The more complete angel is essentially from the same cartoon, in reverse, as the figure in s. III, 4b below. There are slight differences in detail between the two, in the drawing of the eyes, finial of the cross diadem, and border of the nimbus.

Date. Second half 15th c.

B7. Composite Panel

h. 0·60 m. w. 0·30 m.

A medley of fragments: an angel, now bust length, part of an inscription, gold rays, and foliage, the latter, in the lower cusp, may be *in situ*.

Condition. As B2.

Colour and Technique. Angel as B2, the remainder is all white glass and yellow stain.

Iconography. A fragment of an inscription, in black-letter script:

| *mere han*|........|

Style and Design. The angel and two other angels, now s. III, 2a, 4a are all from the same cartoon with only very slight differences in detail.

Date. Second half 15th c.

s. III   PLATE 45 (*e*)

The fragments now in this window came from the tracery lights of w. I. The most important pieces are the four figures of angels, identical in style and technique with the two remaining in window I, B2 and B7. The detailed descriptions have not, therefore, been repeated. The fragments are all painted on white glass, with brown stipple shading and yellow stain. The corrosion varies in intensity, some pieces have very slight corrosion, others are virtually opaque.

1a, 1b, 3a, 3b. Inscription

'These fragments of old glass formerly filled the upper tier of the east window. A German land-mine, with parachute attached, was dropped in a field between the church and the river at 9.20 in the evening of 26 September 1940. The explosion shattered the windows, displaced roof tiles, and shook down plaster throughout the church . . . in memory of William Grenville Boyd, Vicar 1938–41, who collected and began arranging this old glass.'

The inscription is slightly misleading; the fragments filled six of the eight tracery lights of the east window.[3] Their former positions are noted below.

2a. Composite Panel

h. 0·48 m. w. 0·46 m.

Fragments including an angel from B4, a hand holding a book from B5, and pieces of architectural design from B6 of window I.

Condition. The bust-length angel was shattered in the explosion. The pieces have been stuck edge to edge and

---

[1] *N.O.A.S. Report*, op. cit., p. 10.   [2] Bouchier (1918), 98.   [3] Photographs N.M.R.

plated on both sides. The wings are now incomplete at the top.

Iconography. The fragment of a large hand, holding a closed book, probably belonged to a figure of a saint. The letter '*s*', painted on part of an architectural base, is probably the final letter of a name.

Style and Design. The angel is drawn from the same cartoon as I, B7.

Date. Second half 15th c.

2b. Composite Panel

h. 0·48 m. w. 0·46 m.

Fragments including an angel and a piece of canopy with an inscription, both from B6.

Condition. The bust-length angel shattered and repaired as 2a above; the wings are now very incomplete.

Iconography. Part of an inscription, in black-letter script:

|.sitis|

painted on the same glass as a piece of canopy work.

Date. Second half 15th c.

4a. Composite Panel

h. 0·34 m. w. 0·46 m.

Fragments, including an angel from B5, pieces of foliage design from either B3 or B6, and scraps of canopy work.

Condition. The angel shattered and repaired as 2a above, the wings are intact.

Style and Design. The angel is drawn from the same cartoon as 2a above and I, B7 above. The large pieces of foliage were in the cusps of the tracery lights of window I and may have been *in situ*.

Date. Second half 15th c.

4b. Composite Panel

h. 0·34 m. w. 0·46 m.

Fragments including an angel from B3, pieces of foliage design from either B3 or B6, and scraps of canopy.

Condition. The angel is in the same condition as before 1940, except for slight loss of the upper left wing.

Style and Design. The angel is drawn from the same cartoon in reverse as I, B2. Foliage as 4a.

Date. Second half 15th c.

TADMARTON
ST. NICHOLAS

O.S. SP 393 378.

PRINTED SOURCES
Ditchfield (1903), 186.

Nelson (1913), 172.
Pevsner (1974), 803–4.

n. II

B1. Head of Christ

h. 0·28 m. w. 0·38 m.

Condition. Virtually complete, and probably *in situ*. Patched with a small piece of 16th–17th-c. foliage design with a modern plain glass border.

Colour and Technique. The head, neck, and nimbus of Christ are painted on a single piece of white glass. The cross of the nimbus in yellow stain. Set against a plain ruby ground. The features and hair of the head are modelled with a flat matt paint, white highlights of the hair and raised eyebrows picked out of the matt.

Iconography and Style. Other examples of the head of Christ in the apex of a tracery light are to be found at Sandford

St. Martin and Toot Baldon. The drawing of the features with the mouth and arched eyebrows is extremely close to that in Merton College Chapel, Oxford. The design of the halo with elaborated border, the cross itself with the splayed ends, and the patterning of the nimbus between the arms of the cross are unusual.

Date. First quarter 14th c.

s. III

A1. Tracery Light. Floral Design

h. 0·20 m. w. 0·10 m.

A single piece of white glass painted with a rosette in a plain border.

Condition. Decayed on both surfaces with a small piece

missing which has not been replaced. This was probably a complete tracery light cut down to fit its present position.

Colour and Technique. Painted on white glass, rosette in yellow stain with a plain white border.

Style and Design. Similar to quarry type 47.

Date. 15th c.

TOOT BALDON
ST. LAWRENCE

O.S. SP 569 003.

s. IV

B1. Head of Christ

h. 0·20 m. w. 0·26 m.

Condition. All the glass is very decayed on both surfaces.

Colour and Technique. The head of Christ is painted on a single piece of white glass, the hair, beard, and cross of the nimbus in yellow stain set against a plain blue background. Border, repeated pattern of rosettes in yellow stain picked

PRINTED SOURCES
Pevsner (1974), 818–19.

out of matt black paint. Strong smear shading on the hair and beard of Christ. The yellow stain in this panel has a very strong tone, almost orange.

Iconography and Style. The glass is probably *in situ*. Comparable examples of an apex tracery light of the head of Christ are to be found, for example, at Tadmarton and Sandford St. Martin.

Date. Excessive decay makes precise dating difficult to determine. Probably the second half of the 14th c.

WARBOROUGH
ST. LAWRENCE

O.S. SP 599 937.

MS. SOURCES
Oxford. Bodleian Library, MS. Top. Oxon. b. 220, f. 254. Church notes by J. E. Robinson, *c.* 1808.

n. II

1b. Geometric Grisaille

h. 0·42 m. w. 0·49 m.

Condition. Twelve quarries, fragment of a larger design. Slight corrosion, old leaded repairs.

Colour and Technique. Painted on white glass.

Style and Design. Original design of quarries painted with a vertical stem at the centre of the light, with offspringing trails of oak leaves. The painted border of one of the quarries

PRINTED SOURCES
Franks, A. W., *A Book of Ornamental Glazing Quarries* (1849), pl. 87.
Nelson (1913), 173.
Bouchier (1918), 88.
Bouchier (1932), 88.
Pevsner (1974), 821.

is slightly curved, suggesting that the original design incorporated a geometric design and a trellis of quarries.

Date. 14th c.

3a. Roundels

In the cusps of the light are three fragmentary roundels, each originally painted with a rose. See 3b.

3b. Quarry and Roundels

h. 0·28 m. w. 0·49 m.

Quarry: h. 0·14 m. w. 0·11 m.

Design of *Ihs* (*Ihesus*) inscribed on a circle set on rays.

Condition. All roundels incomplete, slight corrosion.

Colour and Technique. White glass, rays in yellow stain.[1] Crude 15th-c. work.

Style and Design. Similar designs inscribed *Ihc* and *Maria* occur at Marston, I, 4a. One quarry, type 44.

Date. Second half 15th c.

Roundels: d. 0·14 m.

Rose design: a large white rose with a central floret.

Star design: twelve wavy rays.

Condition. See above.

Colour and Technique. Rose: painted on white glass, floret in yellow stain, fine stippled and hatched line shading. Star: white and yellow stain, stippled and line shading.

Iconography. It would be unwise to regard these designs as representing the white rose and sun badge of the House of York.[2]

Style and Design. The roundels are probably *in situ*. Compare similar roundels at Stanton Harcourt s. VI, 4a, 4c, and s. VII, 2a–c.

Date. Second half 15th c.

Lost Glass

Robinson noted that 'By the fragments that remain the windows seem to have had much painted glass in them, the East window only has a perfect figure viz. a Bishop in his Pontifical Habits, part of another figure near it.'[3] No trace of these now remains.

WATERPERRY

ST. MARY

O.S. SP 629 063.

MS. SOURCES

Oxford Bodleian Library:
  MS. Top. Oxon. e. 286, ff. 128ᵛ–130. Notes by N. Greenwood dated 1660.
  MS. Top. Oxon. b. 75, f. 192. Notes dated 1803.
  MS. Top. Oxon. b. 220, f. 105. Notes *c.* 1808.

PRINTED
Parker (1846), 248–53.
Visitations (1871), 104–6.
Nelson (1913), 172.
Bouchier (1918), 88–9.
P.C. (1920), 317–20.
Bouchier (1932), 132.
Greening Lamborn (1949), 162–4.
V.C.H. v (1957), 296–307.
Pevsner (1974), 827–8.

The surviving glass, although very incomplete and indifferently restored, belonged to a series of at least seven windows, ranging in date from the thirteenth to the sixteenth centuries.

The earliest glass, probably *c.* 1250–75, is the geometric grisaille designs in three lancet windows of the chancel (n. II, n. III, and n. IV). Although very decayed and incomplete, this and the related glass at Stanton Harcourt and Stanton St. John are the most complete examples of this class of design remaining in the county.

The fourteenth-century window in the nave (n. VI) presents some problems. The two outer main lights each contain a donor figure set against a trellis of white quarries, painted with trails of oak leaves and acorns. The quarries are much disturbed and misplaced but the general arrangement of the figures on a simple quarry ground is probably original. The donors, a man and a woman, both wear secular dress; there is no evidence or record of such, to establish their identity and date. It is possible that they commemorate members of either the Beaufeu or Fitz Ellis family, tenants of the manor.[4] The original over-all design of

---

[1] Illustrated in Franks, op. cit., pl. 87.   [2] See Stanton Harcourt s. VI.
[3] Bodl. Lib. MS. Top. Oxon. b. 220, f. 254.   [4] *V.C.H.* v (1957), 296–8.

the main lights of this window is uncertain. Before the nineteenth-century restoration the donor panels were set at the head of their respective lights and the remainder was plain quarry glazing.[1] The donors are represented kneeling in prayer; originally they may have been accompanied by either a votive figure or another donor, possibly set beneath larger figures of saints. The large tracery light contains a Christ in Majesty and a fragmentary figure, all much disturbed and incomplete.

A small mid fourteenth-century fragment of a knight of the Fitz Ellis family is now incorporated with the fifteenth century glass in the Fitz Ellis window (n. V).

This later Fitz Ellis window is also the simple class of design of figures against a background of quarries. In this case each quarry is painted with an identical foliage pattern, a bold and striking design which is not found elsewhere in the county. The main lights contain three donor figures: Robert Fitz Ellis, his wife Margaret, and a small girl. His identity is established by his tabard of arms and the initials R.F. in the tracery lights. A dating of after 1461 is suggested by the Yorkist collar of suns and white roses, with a pendent white hart badge of Richard II, which he wears. Fitz Ellis was dead before 1469 when his widow Margaret died, leaving as heiress their granddaughter Sibyl, then aged six.[2] A dating of *c.* 1461–9 therefore seems probable. A more precise dating might be possible if the identity of the child could be established. Greening Lamborn described her as Margery, daughter of Robert and Margaret Fitz Ellis.[3] If this identification is correct an early dating in the period is indicated as she was married before 1463 when her daughter Sibyl was born. However, the small size of the figure and particularly the simple headband and loose hair suggest that a very young girl is represented here. Margery predeceased her parents, so it is possible that the child represents the granddaughter and heiress Sibyl, born in 1463. If this is correct, a dating of *c.* 1468–9 is necessary, the window perhaps being commissioned by Margaret Fitz Ellis after her husband's death.

The latest window in the series is a memorial to Walter Curson and his family, erected after his death in 1527 (s. IV). An inscription records the date of his death and the reroofing of the church at his expense. He made provision for the latter in his will, dated 24 November 1526.[4] This window is an interesting example of the paradox of much late medieval glass painting—technical excellence combined with stereotyped repetitive design. The figures are competently drawn and painted but the effect is dull and lifeless. The technical expertise is particularly evident on the heraldic shields and tabard of the Curson arms where the small charges are skilfully abraded.

The Curson donor figures are placed either side of an incomplete figure of the Virgin and Child. The background of quarries is a modern restoration, added after 1846. There is no evidence to suggest that the quarry design is copied from a medieval one. Other examples of this design in nineteenth-century glass are known.[5]

At the head of this window are two made-up shields of the arms of Montagu; their date is uncertain but they are probably fifteenth-century. John Fitz Ellis granted the manor of Oakley to Thomas Chaucer in 1413, and it has been suggested that these arms may refer to Thomas Montagu, Earl of Salisbury, husband of Chaucer's daughter Alice.[6] One shield of Montagu was recorded in this window in association with two other shields of the arms of Bryan and Pipard respectively.[7] Guy, Lord Bryan (d. 1390), married Elizabeth, daughter of William Montagu, first Earl of Salisbury.[8] No connection is known between these two families and that of Pipard, and the identity of the bearer of the Pipard arms has not been established.

I

A2. Fragments

h. 0·50 m. w. 0·46 m.

Three large white roses, possibly the Yorkist badge,[9] 15th c. Fragments of grisaille, 13th c., and borders, 14th c. The lower half of a small figure, white and yellow stain, 14th c.

[1] See the engraving in Parker (1846), 250.
[2] *V.C.H.* v (1957), 298, citing *Cal. Inq. Post Mortem* iv. 348. C. 140/511/22.
[3] Greening Lamborn (1949), 162.
[4] Will quoted by J. Baron in Parker (1846), 263.
[5] e.g. Sheringham (Norfolk) (information from Mr. Dennis King).
[6] Greening Lamborn (1949), 164.
[7] *Or three piles in point azure* BRYAN; *party per saltire argent and azure* PIPARD. Greenwood MS., op. cit. P.C. (1920), 319.
[8] G.E.C. ii. 361.
[9] See n. V, 2c.

A3. Fragments

h. 0·50 m. w. 0·46 m.

Nine border pieces, each a white oak leaf, stem in yellow stain, 14th c. Small fragments of canopy work and foliage diapers, 14th c.

B2. Fragments

h. 0·42 m. w. 0·42 m.

Mostly post-medieval fragments, except for the head of a youth, facing three-quarters right, white glass, hair in yellow stain, smear shading, mid 14th c.

n. II

1a. Modern Quarries, imitation 14th-c. design

2a. Geometric Grisaille

h. 0·81 m. w. 0·20 m.

Condition. Substantially complete, but corroded on the exterior.

Colour and Technique. Painted in black on white glass, except for the threequarter medallions which are in pot-metal ochre glass.

Style and Design. A complicated geometric design of ovals and vine foliage; three contiguous ovals, linked together by medallions; running up the centre of the ovals is a vertical stem with offspringing symmetrical trails of stylized vine leaves, painted in outline on a cross-hatched ground. A similar, but not identical, design occurs at Stanton Harcourt (s. II, s. III, and s. IV).

Date. Second half 13th c.

n. III

1a. Modern Quarries, imitation 14th-c. design

2a. Geometric Grisaille

h. 0·46 m. w. 0·20 m.

Condition. Old leaded repairs, the glass is extremely corroded.

Colour and Technique. Painted in black on white glass except for the green rosette at the centre of each section.

Style and Design. A repeated pattern of contiguous squares, at the centre of each a small green rosette roundel with four offspringing sprays of very stylized vine leaves and grapes. The foliage is painted in outline on a cross-hatched ground.

Date. Second half 13th c.

n. IV

1a. Modern Quarries, imitation 14th-c. design

2a. Geometric Grisaille

h. 0·71 m. w. 0·20 m.

Condition. Badly repaired, the left-hand side of the panel cut down at some time; exterior corrosion, but not excessive.

Colour and Technique. Painted in black on white glass, except for the green rosette at the centre of each section.

Style and Design. Repeated pattern of contiguous squares, at the centre of each a small green rosette roundel with four offspringing cinquefoil leaves, the latter painted in outline on a cross-hatched ground. A similar design, but combined with vine foliage in a large circle, occurs at Stanton Harcourt (s. III, 3b).

Date. 13th c.

n. V

1a, b, c, and 2b

Modern white quarries; their foliage design copies the original 15th-c. ones in 2a and 2c below.

2a. Margaret Fitz Ellis and a Child   PLATES 10 (*a*), 46 (*a*)

h. 0·51 m. w. 0·33 m.

Margaret Fitz Ellis with either her daughter Margery or granddaughter Sibyl, kneeling in prayer, facing right.

Condition. Incomplete and disarranged, the missing pieces on the hem of Margaret Fitz Ellis's robe made up with alien pieces of medieval glass; part of the quarry background is a modern restoration. The white glass is well preserved, the coloured glass very corroded.

Colour and Technique. Painted in brown on white glass, except for the purple dresses. Margaret Fitz Ellis wears a purple dress with a broad white collar, over a white underdress, and a white butterfly head-dress. The net enclosing her hair is patterned with a trellis enclosing fleurs-de-lis; where the veil of the head-dress covers part of the hair-net the latter is painted on the reverse of the glass. Her gold waist belt, elaborate necklace with its pendant cross, and her finger-rings are all picked out in yellow stain. The child wears an identical dress, her hair loose, bound by a jewelled fillet. Her hair, hair net, fillet, necklace, with its pendant *IHC* medallion, and finger-rings are all picked out in yellow stain. The architectural base and tiled floor are painted on white glass, patterns picked out in yellow stain. Background of white quarries, repeated foliage design, type 52, the leaves in yellow stain.

Style and Design. The arrangement of figures, architectural base, tiled floor, and background of quarries is probably original although much disturbed. The child's head and her belt are each painted on the same glass as the adjacent quarry.

Date. Between 1461 and 1469.

2c. Robert Fitz Ellis   PLATES 10 (*b*), 46 (*b*)

h. 0·51 m. w. 0·33 m.

Robert Fitz Ellis, kneeling in prayer facing left. Arms on the sleeve of his tabard: *argent a bend between six fleurs-de-lis* FITZ ELLIS.[1] The same arms repeated on his tabard, now incomplete.

Condition. Incomplete; the upper part of the figure, pommel of sword, and feet remain, the missing parts made up with alien fragments of 13th and 14th-c. glass including a small fragment of a knight of the Fitz Ellis family wearing a coat of plates and shinbalds over mail chausses and a long gown bearing the arms of Fitz Ellis. Architectural base and tiled floor are both incomplete, the quarry background partly restored.

Colour and Technique. No coloured glass, the figure painted in brown on white glass, his tabard patterned with circles picked out of a very light wash of brown paint. The heraldic charges on the sleeve and body of his tabard are painted in outline, omitting their proper tincture: gules.[2] The pendant badge of his livery collar in yellow stain. The architectural base and tiled floor painted on white glass, the patterns picked out in yellow stain. Quarry background as 2a.

Style and Design. A companion figure to 2a. The architectural base is simpler in design and the tiled floor has a different pattern, but the quarry background is identical. The hilt of the sword at his waist overlaps the adjacent quarry and both are painted on the same piece of glass.

Iconography. It has been stated that the centre light of this window originally contained a figure of the Virgin Mary.[3] However, the evidence cited[4] has no reference to such a figure and no other record of its existence has been traced.

Date. He wears plate armour, a tabard of his arms, and around his neck the Yorkist livery collar of white roses alternating with suns,[5] with a pendant of the white hart badge of Richard II.[6] This suggests a dating after the accession of Edward IV in 1461 and probably before 1469, when Margaret, widow of Robert Fitz Ellis, died.

Insertion. Adjacent to the feet of Fitz Ellis is a fragment of a mid 14th-c. figure of a knight as described above.

A1. Roundel

h. 0·15 m. w. 0·17 m. Roundel: d. 0·09 m.

A roundel bearing a capital letter R for Robert, set against a foliage background, white and yellow stain, *c.* 1461–9. The upper lobe of the light is alien.

A2. Shield of Fitz Ellis impaling Fawkener

h. 0·68 m. w. 0·53 m. Shield: h. 0·37 m. w. 0·38 m.

Argent a bend gules between six fleurs-de-lis gules FITZ ELLIS *impaling sable a mullet argent between three falcons argent beaks legs and bells or* FAWKENER.

Robert Fitz Ellis (d. before 1469) of Waterperry and Oakley, married Margaret (d. 1469), daughter of William Fawkener of Kingsclere.[7]

Condition. The bend of the Fitz Ellis arms is modern, the field made up with alien white glass. The charges of the Fawkener arms were originally painted on the same glass as the field, now repaired with leading. The arrangement is composite, made up from two shields of different sizes.[8] Background of modern white quarries, copying the 15th-c. design as 2a, c.

Date. c. 1461–9.

A3. Roundel

h. 0·15 m. w. 0·17 m. Roundel: d. 0·09 m.

A roundel bearing a capital letter F for Fitz Ellis. A companion to A1 above, identical foliage background, white and yellow stain, 1461–9. The upper lobe of the light is alien.

n. VI

1a, b, c, 2b. Modern Quarries, imitation 14th-c. design

2a. Donor   PLATE 46 (*c*)

h. 0·86 m. w. 0·33 m. Figure: h. 0·25 m.

---

[1] Greening Lamborn (1949), 162, describes this sleeve as 'a small shield on his shoulder'. The shape is slightly misleading but the position of the bend in relation to the fleurs-de-lis suggests a sleeve covering the upper arm. The lower edge of the far side sleeve is also visible below his hands.

[2] Greening Lamborn (1949), 162, conjectured that possibly some semi-permanent red was used here. This is unlikely.

[3] Parker (1846), 251.

[4] Bodl. Lib. Wood MS. E. 1, ff. 224–6, published in P.C. (1920), 319.

[5] H. Ellis, 'Enumeration and Explanation of the Devices formerly borne as Badges of Cognizance by the House of York', *Archaeologia*

xvii (1814), 226–7. J. R. Planché, 'On the Badges of the House of York', *British Archaeological Association Journal* xx (1864), 8–33, particularly 29. H. Stanford London, *Royal Beasts* (1956), 30–1.

[6] Greening Lamborn misleadingly describes this as 'a pendant bearing a hart couched'. The hart is correctly depicted collared and chained; see J. H. Harvey, 'The Wilton Diptych—a Re-examination', *Archaeologia* xcviii (1961), 7–8, pl. 11.

[7] Greening Lamborn (1949), 162–4.

[8] The 1574 Visitation records a shield of Fitz Ellis impaling Fawkener, *Visitations* (1871), 104. The other antiquarian sources record these arms as separate shields.

A lady kneeling in prayer, facing right.

Condition. The figure is complete, slight exterior corrosion, background of quarries disarranged.

Colour and Technique. The figure's head and hands painted in brown on white glass, the hair cauls in very light yellow stain, gown and kirtle in green glass. Background trellis of white quarries painted with trails of oak leaves and acorns, the latter in yellow stain.

Style and Design. The arrangement of figure and quarry background may be original. The style is rather plain, no matt wash modelling. The drapery contours are painted in bold lines with thin lines for the minor folds.

Date. Early 14th c.

2c. Donor   PLATE 46 (*d*)

h. 0·86 m. w. 0·33 m. Figure: h. 0·25 m.

A layman, kneeling in prayer, facing right.

Condition. The figure is complete, slight exterior corrosion, more pronounced on the ochre glass. Quarry background incomplete and disarranged.

Colour and Technique. The figure's head and hands are brown on pink glass. His gown is of two colours, divided vertically, pot-metal blue and deep ochre, white fur lining and hood, blue tunic and ochre shoes. Quarry background as 2a.

Iconography. A companion figure to 2a. Originally this figure may have been in the centre light with a votive figure at 2c.

Style and Design. As 2a, except that here a very light matt wash is used to model the drapery.

Date. Early 14th c.

A1, A3

Inserted fragments of 14th-c. glass.

A2. Christ in Majesty   PLATE 10 (*c*)

d. 0·42 m.

Christ seated in benediction, holding a book, a man kneeling in prayer beside him.

Condition. Incomplete, the missing pieces made up with alien medieval glass. Christ's mantle is disarranged, the throne incomplete. Only the head and hands of the smaller figure survive. It is impossible to say if the general arrangement of figures and background is original.

Colour and Technique. Christ's head, hands, and feet painted in brown on white glass, pot-metal yellow mantle, and blue tunic; the small figure's head and hands on pink glass.

Style and Design. As 2a and 2c.

Date. Early 14th c.

s. IV

1a, b, c. Inscription

In black-letter script. Mr. M. C. Farrar Bell has restored missing and illegible letters from Wood's transcript:

Pray: | [ye for] | the soul|e of Walter | Cursson: and | Isabeil|: his wife | whose | goodys as | [well]| the | roofe of th|[is ch]urche | and the: | roof | [fe] | of this | the lordye | Ile and the | coveri|ng of lee|de of | all the same | [as] | also | this wynd|[ow] | were made | wh|ose bodies r|est yn the: | augustyne: | freers | churche yn | Oxf|orde: whiche || Walter died the | VII day of: | A|pryle yn: the | yere of || our lord | god | M.CCCCC|XX|VII^ti on || whos: soules | god: have: | [Mercy].|

Date. c. 1527.

2a. Shield of Curson   PLATE 46 (*e*)

Shield: h. 0·26 m. w. 0·20 m.

Quarterly 1 *argent on a bend sable three parrots or* CURSON 2, *argent on a fess gules three hinds heads couped argent* CURSON 3, *paly argent and sable, on a chevron gules a crosslet or* CURSON 4, *party per chevron sable and gules three peewits heads erased argent, on the fess point a mullet gules.*

Condition. Complete, old breaks leaded, some loss of paint particularly in the third and fourth quarters. Cleaned and restored by Mr. M. C. Farrar Bell.

Colour and Technique. The fields of the first and second and base of the fourth quarters are diapered with a feathery foliage design. The or charges are in yellow stain. The fess, chevron, and base field of the second, third, and fourth quarters respectively are leaded in, the charges abraded.

Date. c. 1527.

Set against a background of modern quarries.

2b. Shield Curson impaling Saunders   PLATE 46 (*f*)

h. 0·26 m. w. 0·20 m.

CURSON *quarterly impaling party per chevron sable and argent, three elephants' heads erased counter coloured* SAUNDERS. Walter Curson (d. 1527) married Isabel, daughter of Edward Saunders of Harington (Northants.).[1]

---

[1] L. G. H. Hornton-Smith, 'A Curson-cum-Saunders Marriage', *Notes and Queries*, 187, no. 11 (1944), 222–5.

Condition. Complete, old breaks leaded, the paint of the Curson coat much worn.[1]

Colour and Technique. The Curson arms as 2a, the argent field of the Saunders coat diapered with a feathery foliage design, the tusks of the two upper elephants in yellow stain.

Date. c. 1527.

Background of modern quarries.

2c. Shield of Saunders

h. 0·26 m. w. 0·20 m.

Arms of SAUNDERS as 2b.

Condition. Complete, old breaks leaded.

Colour and Technique. As 2b.

Date. c. 1527.

Background of modern quarries.

3a. Walter Curson and his Sons   PLATE 47 (*a*)

h. 0·36 m. w. 0·43 m.

Walter Curson, behind him his eldest son Richard and his seven other sons, all kneeling in prayer.

Condition. Fairly complete, except for the tiled floor which is partly set inside out, old breaks leaded, the paint somewhat worn in parts, slight exterior corrosion.

Colour and Technique. Curson in white plate armour with a heraldic tabard of the quarterly arms of Curson, as 2a. The eldest son has a blue sleeved gown over a white shirt. The other sons have identical blue gowns with arm slits, the first two with blue and white shirts respectively. Painted in brown with stippled matt shading of varying intensity, the highlights scratched out by needlepoint, slight use of yellow stain on hair.

Style and Design. The technical excellence of the abraded heraldic charges and the fluidly modelled draperies is not matched by the rather wooden faces; the younger sons, in particular, despite their varied hair styles, are stereotyped and lifeless.

Date. c. 1527.

Background of modern quarries.

3b. The Virgin and Child

h. 0·36 m. w. 0·43 m.

Condition. Incomplete, the Virgin's head and feet are lacking, her mantle made up with alien glass.

Colour and Technique. The Virgin has a purple mantle, lined ermine, over a white tunic powdered with the repeated monogram *MAR*, the letters interlaced, for Maria, in yellow stain. Christ's hair and the apple (?) held by the Virgin in yellow stain. Painted in brown stippled matt shading, the highlights scratched out by needlepoint.

Iconography. Greening Lamborn described this figure as 'a saint probably the B.V.M.'.[2] The Maria monograms support this identification and it is proved by the very slight traces of the cross on the child's nimbus. The Virgin probably holds an apple, but this is incomplete.

Style and Design. Although incomplete the scale and details of drawing, particularly Christ's head, suggest this is a companion to the Curson panels.

Date. c. 1527.

Background of modern quarries.

3c. Isabel Curson and her Daughters   PLATE 47 (*b*)

h. 0·36 m. w. 0·43 m.

Isabel Curson, her six daughters behind her, all kneeling in prayer.

Condition. Incomplete, Isabel's head and that of the extreme right-hand daughter were particularly bad 19th-c. restorations. Mr. M. C. Farrar Bell has recently replaced these with carefully copied replicas of the surviving daughters.

Colour and Technique. She wears a heraldic mantle of the arms of Saunders, as 2b above, over a purple dress with a yellow-stain gold belt, separately leaded. The daughters' costumes are identical: pedimental white head-dress, a blue dress with a green belt, done in yellow stain on the blue glass of the dress, white undersleeves and partlet at the neck. Painted in brown, stippled matt shading, the highlights scratched out by needlepoint.

Style and Design. As 3a; the heads of the daughters vary only in the different patterned edges of their head-dress.

Date. c. 1527.

Background of modern quarries.

4a. Fragments

A piece of white glass painted with a rose trail, with a cusped border; small pieces of patterned diaper and crocketed shafts; all 14th c.

4b. Fragments

Small pieces of 14th and 15th-c. glass.

Two made-up shields *argent a fess of three fusils gules* MONTAGU. 15th c. (?).

4c. Fragments

Part of a canopy set on a ruby ground, pieces of white glass painted with oak trails. 14th c.

---

[1] Greening Lamborn (1949), 163, doubted the authenticity of the fess in the second quarter of the Curson coat. Although much worn it appears to be genuine.   [2] Greening Lamborn (1949), 163.

w. I

2b. Fragments

h. 1·37 m. w. 0·61 m.

Over one hundred fragments leaded together in a medley panel. The fragments are mostly scraps of canopy work, in white and yellow stain, all 15th c.

An incomplete figure of a Cherubim or Seraphim, its nimbed head probably alien to the body, white and yellow stain, 15th c.

A large white sun, possibly the Yorkist sun badge (as n. V, 2c).

A fragment of an inscription, in black-letter script: |rgarete|, possibly 'Margarete' for Margaret Fitz Ellis (see n. V).

A4. Small Fragments

Lost Glass

The 1574 Visitation records two shields, now lost, which were in one window: *per pale gules and sable an eagle displayed argent legged and beaked or* (UNIDENTIFIED), and *sable a fess dancetty argent* (SCHAMFER).[1] The later antiquarian notes of Wood and Greenwood add three shields of the arms of Fitz Ellis, Peytevyn, and Pipard then in the east window of the south chapel.[2] The display of the Schamfer and Peytevyn arms has not been accounted for.

WATERSTOCK
ST. LEONARD

O.S. SP 635 056.

MS. SOURCES

London. British Library, Lansdown MS. 874, ff. 137ʳ–137ᵛ. Notes collected by N. Charles *c.* 1610.
Oxford. Bodleian Library:
  MS. Top. Oxon. e. 286, ff. 117ᵛ–118ᵛ. Notes by N. Greenwood dated 1660.
  MS. Top. Oxon. b. 75, f. 194. Wyatt Collections 18th to 19th-c., copy of notes by D. P. Powell *c.* 1805.
  MS. Top. Oxon. b. 220, f. 136ᵛ. Notes *c.* 1808.

PRINTED

Visitations (1871), 42.
Macnamara, F., *Memorials of the Danvers Family* (1895).
Nelson (1913), 172.
Bouchier (1918), 89–90.
P.C. (1920), 321–4.
'Some Oxfordshire Wills', ed. J. Weaver and A. Beardwood, *O.R.S.* 39 (1958), 75.
Pevsner (1974), 828–9.

The sixteenth to seventeenth-century antiquarian accounts record a considerable amount of medieval glass in eight windows of the church. Some losses occurred after the 1574 visitation as the inscriptions given in the later accounts are less complete. In 1660 Greenwood noted that the shield of Bishop Waynflete was 'broke out'.[3] Wood also noted that three shields then in the windows of the chancel were originally 'in a window of the north aisle of the church, as I shall anon tell you'.[4] The later history of the windows has not been recorded; it is possible that much of the glass was removed *c.* 1791, when the church, with the exception of the north aisle of the nave and west tower, was rebuilt by Sir William Ashhurst.[5] Powell, *c.* 1805, noted 'only one bit of painted glass remaining . . . a small figure of a Bishop. All the painted glass is vanished and no one here knows anything about it.'[6]

There is some evidence to show that the medieval church was rebuilt during the late fifteenth to early sixteenth centuries, mostly through the benefactions of the lord of the manor, Sir Thomas Danvers, and his family. The north aisle contained one window commemorating him and his two wives, with an inscription stating that they built the church in 1480.

It is known, however, that the rebuilding went on after that date. The will of Sir Thomas (dated 1 November 1501 and proved 26 September 1502) states, 'I will that Ile in Waterstok churche be finnyshed in as goodly hast as it may be and covered with leede. A newe chauncell (to) be made in Waterstok churche according as I have begonne and as my wif knowith my mynde.'[7]

[1] Visitations (1871), 104–6.
[2] Bodl. Lib. MSS. Wood E. 1, f. 224, Rawl. B. 400 b, f. 259, P.C. (1920), 318–20.
[3] Greenwood, op. cit., f. 118ᵛ.
[4] P.C. (1920), 322.
[5] Bodl. Lib. MS. Top. Oxon. b. 220, op. cit., f. 136ᵛ.
[6] Bodl. Lib. MS. Top. Oxon. b. 75, op. cit., f. 194.
[7] Macnamara, op. cit. 168. O.R.S., op. cit. 75.

There are only slight remains of medieval glass. An incomplete fourteenth-century figure of an arch-bishop was presumably retained in the later rebuilding. Of the later glass only two incomplete panels from a north window survive. These depict the figures of John Brown, rector of the church 1469–1500, and his father Thomas. The small scale of the church might suggest that the north-aisle windows were probably all about the same date as the Danvers window, 1480.

n. III

7a. Donor John Brown　　　　　　　PLATE 9 (c)

h. 0·30 m. w. 0·46 m.

John Brown kneeling in prayer facing right.

Condition. A composite panel, the figure is almost complete, lacking the hands and feet; the shoulder cape and green cuff are alien insertions. Pieces of chequered floor pattern set inside out. Slight external corrosion, but badly cracked with old *in situ* repair. The other glass is post-medieval.

Colour and Technique. He wears a plain blue gown, or pelisse, with short sleeves, shoulder cape, both edged white, pink surplice, and plain white hood. Head painted on white glass, matt wash for the hair. The trace line painting is very fine, with stippled modelling. The coloured glass has a very thin, diluted tone.

Iconography. His hair is tonsured, and originally he was represented kneeling before a prayer-desk.

Style and Design. See 7c.

Date. After 1469 and probably before 1500.

7b. Archbishop

h. 0·3 m. w. 0·46 m.

Frontal, in benediction, mass vestments with archiepiscopal pall and cross staff.

Condition. A composite panel, an archbishop, now half-length and lacking the mitre, set against fragments of canopy shafting and ruby foliage diaper. The figure is cracked, the leading insecure; extensive corrosion of the coloured glass, particularly on the face.

Colour and Technique. The figure's head and amice are painted on a single piece of pale pink glass, chasuble in pot-metal ochre, the pall painted on the same glass, the crosslets fitchy scratched out of the paint, green alb, white gloves and cross staff. Trace lines in dark brown paint with slight smear shading.

Iconography. Probably a devotional image of a saint, the nimbus now missing. The church is dedicated to St. Leonard and this is a possible identification; however, it is unusual to find him represented as an archbishop.[1] The figure has

been wrongly identified as George Neville, Archbishop of York, 1464–76.[2]

Style and Design. There is some affinity in style with the glass at Merton College Chapel, Oxford, of *c.* 1289–96. Compare, for example, the rather triangular face, with broad brow and long thin hands with articulate fingers, with the figures of the Archangel Gabriel and St. Nicholas at Merton College, Oxford.[3] The style is not identical: the eyes are rounder, the mouth less turned down at the corners. These details are more akin to the figure of St. Lawrence, at Dorchester (I, 3d), probably 1320–30.

Date. 14th c. (second quarter?).

7c. Donor Thomas Brown　　　　　　PLATE 9 (d)

h. 0·30 m. w. 0·46 m.

Thomas Brown kneeling at a prayer-desk, holding a rosary, facing left.

Condition. A composite panel, a complete donor figure kneeling at a prayer-desk, fragments of a chequered floor pattern. Slight external corrosion, cracked with old *in situ* repair. The remainder is post-medieval.

Colour and Technique. Figure has a blue gown with a green belt, undershirt, at neck, in yellow stain, a light pink scarf over his left shoulder. Head in white glass, matt wash for the hair; the prayer-desk is in white and very pale yellow stain. The hands, holding a rosary, are painted on the same piece of glass as the prayer-desk. The tone of the blue glass differs, the upper part of the gown is much deeper, the whole appears to be all of a piece rather than composite. Technique as 7a.

Style and Design. The two figures 7a and 7c are identical in style, particularly in the delicate stippling of the draperies, and the drawing of the eyes with the pupils in solid black. The faces are highly individual, there is a distinct portrait quality about them.

Iconography and Date. These figures have been incorrectly described as 'kneeling ecclesiastics'[4] and as 'monks in blue'.[5] A precise identification can be made from Wood's description:

'In the north window of the church
Two pictures, one Clergyman another a layic, all in Blew kneeling before two desks, over them are the pictures of

---

[1] For the iconography of St. Leonard see Drayton St. Leonard.
[2] Bouchier (1918), 89–90.
[3] R.C.H.M. (1939), pls. 145, 146.
[4] Nelson (1913), 172.　　　　[5] Bouchier (1918), 89–90.

saints with their names under them, viz Ignatius, Sancta Maria, Swithinus under all this inscription Orate pro animabus magistri Johannis Browne quondam Rectoris istius ecclesie et Thome Brown et ... llic ... uxoris eius parentum eius qui me fieri fecit.'[1]

The inscription suggests that originally there was a third donor figure, the mother of John Brown and wife of Thomas.

John Brown, rector, was presented to the living of Waterstock in July 1469 and died before March 1499.[2] The window was probably made within this period. If the north aisle windows were all of the same date then a closer dating of c. 1480 is suggested by the evidence of the lost Danvers window.

St. Swithun was Bishop of Winchester 852–62. The centre of his cult was at Winchester, where his body was enshrined.[3] The earliest known representation of him is found in the Benedictional of St. Ethelwold, of c. 971–84.[4] Fifty-eight medieval church dedications to him are known.[5] Extant representations of him are rare, both in glass painting and manuscript illumination. In glass painting the only undisputed examples are two at Winchester, one in the College chapel (a copy of the late 14th-c. original), the other in the Cathedral, early 16th c.[6] The 15th-c. figures at Trinity College, Oxford,[7] and Wiggenhall St. Mary Magdalene, Norfolk,[8] cannot be identified with certainty.

St. Ignatius, Bishop of Antioch, was martyred at Rome c. 110.[9] It has been stated that during the Middle Ages he was disregarded in England.[10] This is not quite correct. His martyrdom is entered in the Anglo-Saxon Chronicle, under the year A.D. 110.[11] There is liturgical evidence for his cult in England. His feast is commemorated in Benedictine[12] and Carmelite[13] calendars. St. Albans Abbey[14] and Reading Abbey[15] both had relics of the saint in the 12th c. At Christchurch, Canterbury, the inventory of relics of 1315–16

includes portions of the saint's dust and bones.[16] Extant representations of the saint are rare in English art, only three other examples have been found. A lost figure of c. 1380–6 is recorded from a window at New College, Oxford.[17] The Book of Hours of the hermit John Lacy, dated 1420, contains a memoria with an illustration of the saint, flanked by two lions.[18] At Sandringham (Norfolk) in a tracery light of an early 16th-c. window[19] the saint is shown, vested as a bishop, holding a red heart[20] in reference to the legend that after his death his body was opened and they 'drew out his heart and cut it open, and they found within the name of Jesus written with fair letters of gold'.[21]

The later representations may have been prompted by his devotion to the name of Jesus. In the later Middle Ages this was an extremely popular devotion, not only in England[22] but throughout Europe.[23]

Lost Windows of the Nave

The 1574 Visitation and Wood's notes have both been published, but with inaccuracies and omissions. The following account is collated from the original MSS. together with the unpublished collections of Charles and Greenwood. It is of particular interest in that it records the patronage of the Danvers family over a period of some twenty years.

North window, north aisle of the nave.

1. *Quarterly* 1, 4 *argent on a bend gules three martlets vert* DANVERS 2, 3 *ermine on a bend gules three chevrons or* BRULEY.

2. *Quarterly* 1, 4 DANVERS 2, 3 BRULEY *impaling party per fess.* 1 *ermine on a canton gules an owl argent collared or* FOWLER 2 *argent two bars gules, on a chief or a lion passant azure* ENGLEFIELD.

[1] P.C. (1920), 323, where *rectoris istius* is incorrectly given as *rectoris ipsius* and the incomplete name is omitted.

[2] White Kennett, *Parochial Antiquities* ii (1818), 414. A. B. Emden, *A Biographical Register of the University of Oxford to A.D. 1500*, i (1957), 284.

[3] *Golden Legend* iv, 53–5. J. D. Le Couteur and D. M. Carter, 'Notes on the Shrine of St. Swithun formerly in Winchester Cathedral', *Antiquaries Journal* iv (1924), 360–9.

[4] G. F. Warner, *The Benedictional of St. Ethelwold, Bishop of Winchester* (1910), xxviii, f. 97ᵛ. F. Wormald, *The Benedictional of St. Ethelwold* (1959), 12.

[5] F. Bond, *Dedications and Patron Saints of English Churches* (1914), 329.

[6] J. D. Le Couteur, *Ancient Glass in Winchester* (1920), 37–8, 97.

[7] R.C.H.M. (1939), 112, pl. 186. The inscription is a modern restoration.

[8] Nelson (1913), 155, as St. Swithun, but C. Woodforde, *The Norwich School of Glass Painting in the Fifteenth Century* (1950), 165, gives the inscription as 'hun or bun'.

[9] *Golden Legend* iii, 16–19.

[10] R. L. P. Milburn, *Saints and their Emblems in English Art* (1949), 130.

[11] *The Anglo-Saxon Chronicle*, ed. D. Whitelock with D. C. Douglas and S. I. Tucker (1961), 8.

[12] At the abbeys of Abingdon (Berks.), St. Albans (Herts.), Croyland (Lincs.), and Dunster Priory (Somerset). 'English Benedictine Calendars after 1100', ed. F. Wormald, *Henry Bradshaw Society* lxvii (1939), 20, 35, 118, 151.

[13] F. Wormald, 'An Early Carmelite Liturgical Calendar from England', *Bulletin of the Institute of Historical Research* xxxix (1966), 117.

[14] The gift of Gaufridus, abbot 1119–46. 'Gesta Abbatum Monasterii Sancti Albani', i. 94, ed. H. T. Riley, *Rolls Series* xxviii. 1 (1867).

[15] Relicts List. *De sancto Ignatio.* B.L. Egerton MS. 3031, f. 7ᵛ.

[16] J. Wickham Legg and W. St. John Hope, *Inventories of Christchurch, Canterbury* (1902), 87, 92.

[17] Woodforde (1951), 18, 72.

[18] Oxford, St. John's College MS. 94, f. 16.

[19] C. Woodforde, *Norwich School*, op. cit. 171 n. 1. The figure is not described.

[20] M. Drake and W. Drake, *Saints and their Emblems* (1916), 63, incorrectly describe the heart as a fiery globe.

[21] *Golden Legend* iv, 19.

[22] The official liturgy contained no special feast of the Holy Name, but the Jesus Mass was in general the Mass Nominis Jesu. F. Procter and C. Wordsworth, *Breviarium ad usum insignis Ecclesiae Sarum*, Fasc. ii (1879), 548–54.

[23] P. R. Biasiotto, *History of the Devotion to the Holy Name* (1943).

3. *Quarterly* 1, 4 DANVERS 2, 3 BRULEY *impaling quarterly* 1, 4 DANVERS 2, 3 BRULEY *over all an escutcheon of pretence, gules a fess azure between four dexter hands couped argent* QUARTERMAIN.

4. *Quarterly* 1, 4 DANVERS 2, 3 BRULEY *impaling quarterly* 1, 4 *quarterly or and gules* SAY 2, 3 *azure three lions rampant or* FIENNES, Lord Say and Sele.

Motto, *Thank God.*

Incomplete inscriptions below the shields: . . . *Orate pro animabus . . . filiae Jacobi Finys . . . qui istam ecclesiam fecerunt anno graciae* MCCCCLXXX.

Above the shields figures of a man and two women in prayer, above them the figures of St. Barbara, the Trinity, and St. Ann, inscribed: *Sancta Barbara, Sancta Trinitas, Sancta Anna.*

The shields and figures commemorated Sir Thomas Danvers, *c.* 1422–1502, and his two wives. He was the eldest son of John Danvers by his second wife Joan, daughter of John Bruley.[1] Sir Thomas married firstly a daughter (christian name unknown) of James Fiennes, Lord Say and Sele. His second wife was Sibyl, daughter of Sir William Fowler, of Rycote (Oxon.), d. *c.* 1468–9, by his wife Cecilia, daughter and coheiress of Nicholas Englefield.[2]

West Window, north aisle of the nave.

1. BRULEY *impaling* QUARTERMAIN.
Figure of a man in armour. Inscription: *Orate pro animabus Thome Danvers armigeri filii Johannis Danvers ac heredis Domine Johannis Bruly uxor sua.*[3]

2. DANVERS *impaling* BRULEY.
Figure of a man in armour.

3. *Azure a cross engrailed between four choughs*[4]*/martlets*[5] *sable, over all an escutcheon* (incomplete)[6] MAUNTELL *impaling* BRULEY.

4. *Quarterly* 1, 4 DANVERS 2, 3 *Party per pale,* i BRULEY ii QUARTERMAIN.

Inscription: *Orate pro animabus Johannis Danvers armigeri et Domine Johanne Mauntell uxoris sue, filie et heredis Johannis Bruly et Matildae Quatermanys uxoris sue quondam patronorum istius ecclesie.*

John Bruley of Waterstock married Maud, daughter of

Thomas Quartermain of Weston (Oxon.).[7] Their daughter Joan married John Danvers, d. *c.* 1448.[8] She afterwards married Sir Walter Mauntell, d. *c.* 1490.[9] Sir Thomas Danvers, d. 1502, was her son by her first marriage.

In the north window of the church.

Window given by John Brown, rector, and his father, Thomas Brown. See n. III, 7a, 7c.

In the tower[10] window (unspecified).

1. QUARTERMAIN.
2. BRULEY.

Inscription: *Orate pro . . . haweria*[11] *Bruly . . . domine Johanne uxoris Johannis Danvers.*

Both Wood and Greenwood record these shields and inscription. The window commemorated Joan, wife of John Danvers, d. *c.* 1448; the other person named has not been identified.

In a south window.

1. *Quarterly* 1, 4 (argent) *on a bend* (gules three martlets vert) *in sinister canton a mullet sable charged with a plate*[12] DANVERS 2, 3 BRULEY *impaling argent* (or azure)[13] *a fess between six martlets sable* PURY?

Inscription: . . . *Willelmi Danvers . . . filie et heredis . . . armigeri.* The 1574 Visitation translates the inscription as 'Wyllm Danvers and Anne daughter and heir of John Pury Esqr'.[14]

2. *Quarterly* 1, 4 DANVERS 2, 3 BRULEY *impaling azure on a cross argent five mullets or* VERNEY.

Inscription: *Orate pro animabus Henrici Danvers et Beatricis uxoris sue filie Radulphi Verney militis.*

3. *Argent a chevron between three tree trunks eradicated and couped at the top sable* BREKNOKE[15] *impaling quarterly* 1, 4 *azure two bars gemelles*[16] *and a chief or* SIFREWAST 2, 3 *lozengy argent and gules.*

Inscription: *Orate pro anima Margarete Brecknock . . . ille uxoris sue . . . ac Brecknock fil et hered.*

The first shield and inscription commemorated Sir William Danvers, 1430–1504, the second son of John Danvers by his second wife Joan Bruley. He married Anne, daughter and heir of John Pury of Chamberhouse, Thatcham (Berks.).[17]

---

[1] Macnamara, op. cit. 95–7, 202.

[2] Ibid. 155–6, 171–3.

[3] Visitations (1871), 42. Only the first part is recorded in the later accounts.

[4] Greenwood, op. cit., f. 117ᵛ.

[5] Visitations (1871), 42. P.C. (1920), 323.

[6] Only Greenwood, op. cit., records the escutcheon.

[7] Macnamara, op. cit. 214.

[8] Ibid. 95–7, 202.

[9] Ibid. 101, 226.

[10] P.C. (1920), 323, incorrectly prints this as 'lower'.

[11] Ibid., incorrectly printed as 'manerii'.

[12] Wood MS. E. 1, f. 254ᵛ, and Greenwood, op. cit., f. 117ᵛ, both record this shield as incomplete. P.C. (1920), 323, gives an incorrect transcript.

[13] Visitations (1871), 43, and Greenwood, op. cit., as argent, P.C. (1920), 323, as azure.

[14] Visitations (1871), 43.

[15] Blazon as recorded by Wood and Greenwood, but see the trick in B.L. Harleian MS. 6163, f. 27b. J. Foster, *Two Tudor Books of Arms* (n.d.), 170.

[16] P.C. (1920), 323.

[17] Macnamara, op. cit. 174–5.

She died 1530–1 and both were buried at Thatcham.[1] The arms above the inscription were incomplete when recorded and were also probably composite as the arms of Pury were *argent on a fess sable between three martlets sable three mullets pierced argent*.[2]

The second shield commemorates the marriage of Sir William's brother Henry Danvers, citizen of London and mercer. He married Beatrice, daughter of Sir Ralph Verney of Middle Clayton (Bucks.). Henry Danvers was dead before 1503.[3]

The blood relationships of the families represented by the third shield to the Danvers have not been fully established. Sibyl, second wife of Sir Thomas Danvers (d. 1502) was formerly married to Robert Brenock.[4] Her will, proved in 1511, makes provision for prayers for 'myn husbande souls Thomas Danvers and Robert Breaknoke' and for the souls of her father and mother and for the souls of David Breknoke, Margaret, and John.[5] Margaret the wife of David Breknoke was one of the daughters and heirs of John Sifrewast.[6]

In another south window.

1. DANVERS *impaling* BRULEY.

Inscription: *Orate pro animabus Johannis Danvers armigeri et .... et domine Johanne Bruly uxorum suarum ac ... Richardi Danvers de Prescote et Johannis .... Wald.... de Stafford.*[7]

2. *Quarterly* 1 FOWLER 2 *vairy argent and azure* GERNON 3. ENGLEFIELD 4 *argent three wolves heads erased gules a bordure azure semy of castles or* FITZLOWE.

Inscription: *... Willelmi Fowler Armigeri et Cecilie uxoris eius ....*

3. *Quarterly* 1, 4 FOWLER 2, 3 ENGLEFIELD *impaling quarterly* 1, 4 DANVERS 2, 3 BRULEY.

Sir William Fowler of Rycote (d. 1468–9) married Cecilia daughter and coheiress of Nicholas Englefield.[8] Their son and daughter both married into the Danvers family. The son Sir Richard Fowler (d. 1477) married Joan, daughter of

John Danvers by his second wife Joan Bruley.[9] Sir Thomas Danvers (d. 1502), son of the said John Danvers, married secondly Sibyl Fowler, sister of Sir Richard.[10] Richard Danvers of Prestcote (d. 1489) was the half-brother of Sir Thomas and Joan, being the son of John Danvers by his first wife Alice, daughter of William Verney.[11]

In another south window.

1. SEE OF YORK *impaling quarterly* 1, 4 *quarterly* i, iv MONTAGUE ii, iii MORTIMER 2, 3 NEVILLE *with a label gobony argent and azure* GEORGE NEVILLE, Archbishop of York.

Above the shield a figure described as a bishop[12] or a cardinal.[13] Another bishop, praying, over his head the inscription *Collegium Marie*,[14] and below him the WAYNFLETE arms.[15]

Inscription: *Orate pro animabus Georgii Neville quondam Archiepiscopi Eboracensis ac Willelmi Waynflete Wyntoniensis episcopi et Thome Danvers et sray.geri eorum pnictis.*[16] Greenwood read the last words as '*stroygeri eorum pnietis*'.[17] The original form is probably indicated by the translation given by Nicholas Charles, ending 'and Thomas Danvers their servant'.[18]

George Neville was elected Archbishop of York in 1465 and died in 1476.[19] William Waynflete was Bishop of Winchester from 1447 until his death in 1486.[20] Sir Thomas Danvers (d. 1502) was closely connected with the affairs of Magdalen College, Oxford, founded by Waynflete in 1474.[21] He also made provision in his will for prayers to be said 'for the soule of My Lorde Waynflete and myne' at Winchester.[22] No personal connection between Archbishop Neville and Sir Thomas Danvers is known. The link may derive from their involvement in the affairs of the University of Oxford. Neville was Chancellor of the University, 1453–7, and again 1461–72.[23] He was particularly interested in the revival of Greek studies there.[24] In addition he was also the protector of the Paston family.[25] The correspondence between John

---

[1] Macnamara, op. cit. 178, 182.

[2] E. Green, 'The Identification of the Eighteen Worthies commemorated in the Heraldic Glass in the Hall Windows of Ockwells Manor House in the Parish of Bray, in Berkshire', *Archaeologia* lvi (1899), 335. The same arms impaled by Danvers quartering Bruley were found on the brass, now lost, of Sir William Danvers and his wife at Thatcham (Berks.).

[3] Macnamara, op. cit. 190–1.

[4] Ibid. 156.

[5] Ibid. 173.

[6] Ibid. 167.

[7] Both Greenwood, op. cit., f. 118ᵛ, and the Wood MS. E. 1, f. 255, record the inscription thus. The last three words are omitted in P.C. (1920), 323. Macnamara, op. cit. 166, incorrectly transcribes the last word as Rufford.

[8] Ibid. 170–1. W. F. Carter, 'Gresley and Gernon', *Genealogist*, N.S. xxxv (1919), 176–7. A. H. Lloyd, 'Two Monumental Brasses in the Chapel of Christ's College', *Cambridge Antiquarian Society Proceedings* xxxiii (1931–2), 72.

[9] Macnamara, op. cit. 171.

[10] Ibid. 155–6, 171–3.

[11] Ibid. 116–26.

[12] P.C. (1920), 324.

[13] Greenwood, op. cit., f. 184ᵛ.

[14] Ibid. Only Greenwood records the inscription.

[15] Ibid., noted as 'under him his arms broke out'.

[16] The incomplete portions as recorded in Wood's MS. were omitted as illegible in P.C. (1920), 324. Macnamara, op. cit. 166, read the final word as 'p nichs'.

[17] Greenwood, op. cit., f. 118ᵛ.

[18] Charles, op. cit., f. 137ᵛ.

[19] J. le Neve, *Fasti Ecclesiae Anglicanae 1300–1541*, compiled by B. Jones, vi (1963), 5.

[20] Ibid. iv (1963), 46.

[21] Macnamara, op. cit. 160–3.

[22] Ibid. 168.

[23] Emden, op. cit. 1347.

[24] J. Tait, 'Letters of John Tiptoft, Earl of Worcester, and Archbishop Neville to the University of Oxford', *English Historical Review*, xxxv (1920), 570–1, 572–4. R. Weiss, *Humanism in England during the Fifteenth Century* (2nd edn., 1957), 141–8.

[25] *The Paston Letters*, ed. J. Gairdner (1872–5), particularly ii. 324–5, 346; iii. 3, 33.

Paston and Thomas Danvers shows their mutual interest in classical Latin texts and their friendship with various members of the University[1] including Thomas Chippenham, Chancellor of Archbishop Neville 1460–3.[2]

In another south window.

1. *Argent a fess between three beehives or* FRAY *impaling* DANVERS.

Inscription: *Johannis Fray militis et Agnetis uxoris eius . . . et Joane Danvers . . . et Margarete Beynham et Elizabethe Waldegrave et Katherine Stafford.*[3]

2. *Quarterly* 1, 4 DANVERS 2, 3 BRULEY *impaling argent a fess sable between three martlets sable for* PURY. Inscription noted by Wood: 'From the inscription I find that it was set up for William Danvers and Anne his wife, daughter and heir of William Pury, esqr. This William Pury was afterwards a knight and lived at Chabhouse in Berkshire.'[4]

3. *Argent a bend between six fleurs-de-lis gules* FITZ ELLIS Inscription: *brules wyffe fitzellis*,[5] *Fitz ellis wife of Bruley.*[6]

The incomplete inscription below the first shield commemorated Agnes, daughter of John Danvers (d. *c.* 1448),

her second husband Sir John Fray (d. 1461), and three of their four daughters, Elizabeth who married Thomas Waldegrave, Margaret, wife of John Lynham, and Katherine, wife of Humphrey Stafford.[7] The Joan Danvers also mentioned is the second wife of the above John Danvers, stepmother to Agnes. Agnes died in 1478 and was buried near her second husband in the church of St. Bartholomew-the-Less in Smithfield, London.[8] The second shield and inscription relate to her half-brother Sir William Danvers (d. 1504) who married Anne, daughter and heiress of John Pury of Chamberhouse, Thatcham (Berks.). The shield of Fitz Ellis and its inscription refer to a forebear of Joan Bruley, second wife of John Danvers, included in the inscription below the first shield, but the alliance has not been traced.[9]

The shields and inscriptions as recorded contain some inaccuracies, probably being incomplete or corroded. The arms of Fray were *ermine a fess sable between three fig-frays or.*[10] The Pury arms were *argent on a fess sable between three martlets sable, three mullets pierced argent.* The surname Beynham in the first inscription was either a composite or a misreading of 'Leynham.'

WESTWELL

ST. MARY

O.S. SP 223 101.
PRINTED SOURCES
Ditchfield (1903), 186.

Nelson (1913), 172.
P.C. (1920), 335–6.
Pevsner (1974), 834–5.

The few remaining fragments appear to be all of the same date and may come from a window dated by an inscription to the years 1522–3. It is possible that this window originally contained a large Crucifixion, extended over three lights, with kneeling donor figures and inscription at the base of each light.

s. IV

1b. Inscription

h. 0·05 m. w. 0·39 m.

Fragments of an inscription, right to left.

|*Orate pro bono statu Roberti*|*lockene: T*|*ome treker*|*Henrici grelly*|

Condition. The fragments, with one exception, are all set upside-down.

Date. When complete the inscription was recorded as:

'In a south window

Orate pro bono statu Roberti Lockene, Thome Treker, Henrici Grelle et Isabella uxoris ejus, Roberi Menschune qui hanc fenestram vitreari ordinaverunt anno regni Henrici VIII XIIII°.'[11]

[1] *Paston Letters*, ed. cit. ii. 296–8.
[2] Ibid. See also Emden, op. cit. i. 417–18.
[3] Only the 1574 Visitation, Visitations (1871), 43, records the last name.
[4] P.C. (1920), 324.
[5] Visitations (1871), 43.
[6] P.C. (1920), 324.
[7] Macnamara, op. cit. 143–54.
[8] Ibid. 150.
[9] Ibid. 167 and 202–4.
[10] London College of Arms MS. L. 1, p. 246, shield 3; MS. L. 2, p. 201, shield 2.
[11] P.C. (1920), 335–6, where Lockene is transcribed as Lockerne. 'Lockene' is as given in Wood's MS. Bodl. Lib. Wood MS. E. 1, f. 12ᵛ.

The fourteenth regnal year of Henry VIII was from 22 April 1522 to 21 April 1523.

2b. Donors

h. 0·3 m. w. 0·27 m.

Two women and three youths, kneeling in prayer.

Condition. Incomplete at each side, the glass is extensively corroded, with old breaks, the leading weak.

Colour and Technique. Left-hand woman has a light-purple dress, the other woman's dress and the youths' gowns in deep pot-metal blue. The five heads are painted on a single piece of white glass, hair of the youths in yellow stain. Prayer-desks in deep-orange yellow stain. Stipple shading, and matt washes of paint with the highlights scratched out in fine needlepoint work.

Style and Design. A companion panel to the Crucifixion 3b.

Iconography and Date. Standard representation of donors praying before prayer-desks. The gabled head-dresses of the women are indicative of a late 15th–early 16th-c. date. It is probable, but not certain, that the panel and dated inscription of 1522–3 were part of the same window. If so, the more prominent woman probably represents Isabella, wife of Henry Grelle, the only woman named in the inscription.

3b. The Crucifixion

h. 0·62 m. w. 0·39 m.

Condition. Incomplete, fragments of a large composition. The head and chest, part of one arm, and the lower legs of Christ on the cross, and the heads of the Virgin Mary and St. John Evangelist are all that remain, leaded with pieces of herbage, patterned floor diaper, ruby drapery, and part of an inscription, black-letter script, |omi|. The glass is extensively corroded, the leading weak.

Colour and Technique. The figures are painted on white glass, details of Christ's crown of thorns and cross, the hair and nimbus of St. John are in yellow stain. Stipple shading and matt washes of paint with the highlights scratched out in fine needlepoint.

Iconography. The extant portions are all conventional iconography.

Style and Design. Despite the considerable difference in scale the painting is close to the donors (2b), particularly in the large round eyes and pursed lips. The style is hard, rather lifeless. The nimbs of the Virgin and St. John are tilted at an angle, as if in perspective, giving a rather incongruous effect. There is some similarity to the Curson donor figures at Waterperry (s. IV, 3a and 3c) of *c.* 1527. The resemblance is not close enough to suggest that it was produced by the same workshop.

Date. Probably 1522–3.

WHEATFIELD
ST. ANDREW

O.S. SP 688 993.

PRINTED SOURCES

P.C. (1920), 336.

Greening Lamborn (1949), 165–6.
V.C.H. viii (1964), 272.
Pevsner (1974), 836–7.

The church was rebuilt in the first half of the eighteenth century, and the surviving fourteenth-century glass was replaced in the windows of the chancel. A complete tracery light contains a shield of the arms of Whitfield. This family held lands in the manor from the eleventh century until the late fourteenth century. In 1390, after the death of Katherine, widow of Sir John de Whitfield (d. *c.* 1361), the inheritance passed to Edmund Stretley, son of Hugh Stretley by Joan, daughter and coheiress of Sir John de Whitfield.[1]

s. II

1b. Shield of Whitfield

h. 0·41 m. w. 0·33 m. Shield: h. 0·22 m. w. 0·18 m.

Argent on a bend sable three owls or WHITFIELD.

Condition. A complete sexfoil tracery light, set inside out on a ground of white 18th-c. quarries.

Colour and Technique. Pot-metal glass. The field of the shield diapered with a design of oak leaves and acorns. The charges on the bend are picked out of a wash of dark-brown

---

[1] The pedigree given by G. A. Moriarty, 'The Stretley Family', *Records of Buckinghamshire* xiii (1934–40), 392–3 (and used by Greening Lamborn), is very inaccurate; see *V.C.H.* viii (1964), 266.

paint. Plain ruby surround with radiating sprays of foliage, in the three main foils this is in white glass, separately leaded, in the smaller foils painted in outline on the ruby.

These arms are not found in any roll of arms. They occur, however, on the seal of Sir William de Whitfield used by Edmund Stretley in 1399.[1]

Date. Early 14th c.

n. IV

1a. Fragments

h. 0·36 m. w. 0·36 m.

Part of a large canopy and the head of a saint. The glass is extremely corroded, virtually opaque, the details indistinct. Early 14th c.

Lost Glass

The antiquarian notes record the Whitfield arms and two shields now lost: *argent on a bend sable five bezants, a label of five points azure* CURSON? and *argent a bend between six fleurs-de-lis gules* FITZ ELLIS. There is no evidence to establish the date of the lost glass.

WIGGINGTON
ST. GILES

O.S. SP 391 333.

PRINTED SOURCES
Price, F. D., *The Church of St. Giles, Wiggington* (1965).
Pevsner (1974), 841–2.

n. II

A1. Foliage Design

h. 0·18 m. w. 0·18 m.

Condition. Complete and *in situ*, with only slight decay on both sides. The lower lobe is slightly damaged at the edge.

Colour and Technique. At the centre a small yellow-stain rosette encircled by a white stem with four offspringing stems of white foliage, touched yellow stain, against a plain matt background, and plain white border. The design is painted on a single piece of glass, set directly into the stone, without the use of leads.

Style and Design. Similar sprays of foliage radiating from a quatrefoil enclosed by the stem at the centre are found at Charlton-on-Otmoor and Swerford.

Date. The tight foliage trails, and small leaves are indicative of a date in the second quarter of the 14th c.

B1. Foliage Design

h. 0·32 m. w. 0·15 m.

Condition. Incomplete. Only the lower lobe *in situ*. Patched with pieces of similar foliage design.

Colour and Technique. Lower lobe, the large leaf is of yellow stain on white glass, against a matt black background in a plain white border. The other foliage is the same technique.

Date. Second half of the 14th c.

n. III

A1. Foliage Design

h. 0·38 m. w. 0·34 m.

A thick stem springing from the base of the lower lobe of the light, with offspringing sprays of tight foliage spreading up into the lobes of the upper foil.

Condition. Complete. The lower half is slightly decayed, and the remainder is very worn, much of the paint has been lost. *In situ?*

Colour and Technique. Painted on white glass against a matt black background, with slight touches of yellow stain. The plain white border is painted on the same glass as the foliage.

Style and Design. Similar sprays of foliage springing from the base of the light form the background to the shields at Asthall (n. IV, A2, A3, B2).

Date. Second quarter 14th c.

s. IV

A2. Grotesque Dragon

h. 0·21 m. w. 0·11 m.

A dragon in profile, facing left, with a long neck. The head is turned back to bite its own neck.

[1] G. A. Moriarty, op. cit.　　[2] P.C. (1920), 336.

Condition. Slight decay. The whole panel is set inside out. The lower half of the body is cracked. Originally set in light A3 of this window.

Colour and Technique. Painted on white glass against a matt black background, with slight, possibly accidental, touches of yellow stain. The drawing is of exceedingly high quality.

Style and Design. Grotesque figures occupying a complete tracery light are rare. Compare the much inferior traceries at South Newington, n. IV, A1, A4. Other important examples are to be found in the windows at Dronfield (Derbys.)[1] and in the collegiate church at Astley (Warwicks.).[2]

Date. As above.

A4. Foliage Design

h. 0·08 m. w. 0·05 m.

Foliage design *in situ*, with a spray of leaves painted on a single piece of glass.

Condition. Complete. Little decay.

Colour and Technique. Painted on white glass, the foliage in yellow stain against a matt black background within a plain white border.

Style and Design. The same type of foliage as n. II, A1.

Date. As above.

C1. Lion's Face

h. 0·10 m. w. 0·08 m.

Condition. Complete. Slight traces of decay.

Colour and Technique. Painted on a single piece of white glass with yellow stain touches against a plain matt black background, in a plain white border. Set directly into the masonry without any leading. Probably *in situ*, but the head has been set upside down.

Style and Design. Frontal lion's faces used as a decorative design are a not uncommon feature in 14th and 15th-c. glass painting. There are 15th-c. examples at Stratton Audley (s. II, A2) and North Leigh (n. II, C1–4, n. III, C1–4, n. IV, C1–4).

Date. As above.

WOLVERCOTE
ST. PETER

O.S. SP 489 096.

PRINTED SOURCES
R.C.H.M. (1939), 155.
Pevsner (1974), 851.

s. II

3a, 3b. Geometric Grisaille and Borders

h. 0·31 m. w. 0·46 m.

Condition. The white glass is all very well preserved with little trace of decay. Green glass very decayed.

Colour and Technique. Grisaille in white glass, offspringing trails of oak leaves painted in black outline with slight modelling, inset bosses in blue. Border leaves alternately pot yellow and white set against plain pieces of ruby glass.

Style and Design. The geometric grisaille at the heads of the main lights is incomplete, and the over-all original design cannot be established. In part it seems to have consisted of large contiguous quatrefoils with a coloured blue inset where the foils overlapped. The design is made up of a geometric framework in lead and painted line with a vertical stem at the centre of the light, with offspringing trails of oak leaves and acorns. Border design: a green serpentine stem with offspringing leaves.

This glass is said to have come from Merton College, Oxford, but there is no documentary proof of this.

Date. 14th c.

A1. Fragments of geometric grisaille and border work, as 3a and 3b.

---

[1] Newton ii (1961), 1–2.   [2] Ibid. i. 72, iii. 829–31.

WOODSTOCK

CHAPEL OF ST. MARY MAGDALENE

GLASS NOW IN THE BODLEIAN LIBRARY, OXFORD

MS. SOURCE
Oxford. Bodleian Library, MS. Top. Oxon. c. 16, ff. 118, 122.

PRINTED
Froude, J. A., *History of England*, iii (1870), 50–2.
Marshall, E., *Early History of Woodstock Manor* (1873), 334–6.
O.A.H.S. Proceedings N.S. iv, no. xxix (1883), 133–4.

Macray, W. D., *Annals of the Bodleian Library* (2nd edn., 1890), 38.
Nelson (1913), 165.
Bouchier (1918), 30.
Knowles, J., 'On Two Panels of Glass from the Bodleian Library representing Scenes from the History of St. Thomas Becket', *Bodleian Library Record* v (1926), 100–4.
Bouchier (1932), 126.
Spokes (1973), 24–5, nn. 21–2.

It is known that the chapel at Woodstock had a Becket window and that one of the scenes represented was the Penance of Henry II.[1] The chapel was renovated in the late 18th c., when the two extant panels were probably acquired by Alderman William Fletcher and were given by him to the Bodleian Library, Oxford in 1797.[2]

Glass removed from Woodstock

Oxford. Bodleian Library

West Window, Selden End, Window LVIII, Spokes Serial No. 242.

1b. St. Thomas Becket Received at Soissons by Louis VII   FRONTISPIECE, PLATE 48 (*a*), (*b*), (*c*)

h. 0·67 m. w. 0·61 m.

St. Thomas Becket is represented left of centre, kneeling before King Louis VII of France who stands facing him and raises the saint by his arms. Four attendants and the archbishop's cross-bearer stand behind the saint on the left, five courtiers behind Louis VII on the right. The figures are set against a rich landscape background.

Condition. Incomplete, two of the heads are old insertions. The lower edge of the panel had been made up with 18th–19th-c. glass. Cleaned and releaded by D. King in 1964 when the later insertions were replaced with fragments of medieval glass.

Colour and Technique. The hands and faces are painted on white glass, details of hair and ornament picked out in yellow stain. Becket has a deep blue travelling armaluca, deep blue tippet with white fur trim and collar, white undershirt. Louis VII has a light murrey tunic, mantle of the same colour lined with ermine, and ermine tippet. Becket's cross-

bearer has a deep ruby armaluca with white fur trim and tippet. The draperies of the other attendants on the left are incomplete and disturbed. The courtier behind Louis VII has a long light blue robe, with white fur trim, belted at the waist, white undershirt, and pale pink hat. The two other courtiers have similar robes in ruby and light blue respectively. Stippled and line modelling, highlights on the faces picked out of a thin matt wash, most of the flowers in pale pink glass separately leaded, centre tree has brown trunk and deep pink foliage.

Iconography. Before the 1964 restoration the panel contained an inserted late 18th-c. inscription identifying the scene as 'W^m king of Scotland, with his Barons, abbots etc. paying Homage to Hy 2d in York Cathedral Anno 1175'. The impossibility of this identification was pointed out by Knowles, who suggested that the subject represented is 'doubtless St. Thomas Becket in exile being kindly received by the King of France'.[3] In 1164 the self-exiled archbishop was received at Soissons by Louis VII, King of France.[4] This identification of the scene was accepted by Borenius but he knew of no other English representation of the event.[5] A recently identified English 15th-c. alabaster table at the Musée des Antiquités, Rouen, doubtless represents the same scene. The composition is extremely close to the Oxford panel.[6]

Style and Design. See panel 1c.

Date. Third quarter 15th c.

---

[1] Froude, op. cit. 50–2, citing a document of 1537. MS. State Paper Office, 2nd series, xiv.
[2] Macray, *Annals*, op. cit. 38. Marshall, op. cit. 334–5. For Alderman Fletcher's collection of glass see Yarnton.   [3] Knowles, op. cit. 101.
[4] 'Vita S. Thomae auctore Herberto de Bosham', ed. J. Robertson,

Rolls Series lxvii, vol. ii (1877), 338–9.
[5] T. Borenius, *St. Thomas in Art* (1932), 44.
[6] P. A. Newton, 'Some New Material for the Study of the Iconography of St. Thomas Becket', in *Thomas Becket. Actes Du Colloque International De Sédières, 19–24 Août, 1973* (1975), 256, pl. x. 2.

1c. The Penance of Henry II, King of England, before the Shrine of Thomas Becket PLATE 11, 48 (d)

h. 0·67 m. w. 0·61 m.

Henry II is represented kneeling on the right, naked except for crown and pair of drawers. He venerates the martyr's shrine, upper left. Facing the king are three monks with scourges, the centre monk beats the king's arms with his scourge. Behind the king are three laymen.

Condition. Virtually complete but cut down somewhat at the vertical sides. The present borders of 15th-c. glass were added at the 1964 restoration, replacing a miscellaneous collection of 15th-c. fragments.

Colour and Technique. Heads and flesh painted on white glass, yellow stain for hair and crown. The monks have deep purple habits. Henry II has white drawers and kneels on a deep murrey cushion with a green tasselled edging. Secular figure, possibly the civic sword-bearer, upper right, has a deep blue robe with light pink trim and a white undershirt. Shrine of the saint in yellow stain. Tiled floor and carpet before the shrine in matt wash and trace lines. Stippled matt and line modelling, highlights on faces and body of Henry II picked out of a plain matt wash.

Iconography. The solemn penance of Henry II took place on 12 July 1174 before the tomb of the martyr in Canterbury Cathedral: 'Rogabat itaque ad pedes omnium prostratus et corpus suum flagris exponens, injurias martyris in se vindicare, et pro se orari.'[1] The scene is not often found represented.[2] The earliest example is 13th c., a very fragmentary wall-painting in the crypt of Canterbury Cathedral.[3]

Style and Design. The two panels are evidently part of a series produced by a single workshop. The proportions of the figures and the drawing of the facial details are identical. It is distinguished work, unusual in its colour range, deep purple, murrey, light pinks, and vivid greens, and technique, the leaded-in flowers of the plants in 1b, for example. The

characterization of the faces, particularly Louis VII in 1b and Henry II in 1c, is particularly fine and has been commented upon by Knowles.[4] The incomplete panel of a miracle of St. Frideswide at Kidlington (w. I, 1c) can be attributed to the same workshop.

Date. Third quarter 15th c. The poll-cut hair style with the hair shaved in a straight line above the ears was fashionable c. 1415–75. The style possibly originated at the court of Henry IV.[5] The drawing of the facial features, particularly the accentuation of the upper eyelid, prominent pupils, firm mouth, and stylized drawing of the ears, is similar to the Fitz Ellis figure at Waterperry, 1461–9 (n. V, 2c).

Lost Glass

The antiquarian notes record two shields of arms in the windows:[6]

Gules three catherine wheels or (ROET FOR CHAUCER) *impaling argent a chief gules over all a lion rampant queue fourchée or* (BURGHERSH)

Barry nebuly of six argent and gules, on a bend sable three bezants (GOLOFRE)

Per pale argent and gules a bend counterchanged (CHAUCER) *impaling* (BURGHERSH).

Also recorded are a crest, *a unicorn's head couped argent issuing out of a coronet or* 'very old in glass', and an incomplete shield associated with an inscription: *Quarterly per fess indented, in the first quarter a lion passant* (CROFT?) *impaling* (blank). 'Written over it, *Thomas Croft ob*(*it*) *MCCCCXXX-VIII Elizabeth his wyffe ob*(*it*) *MCCCCLXXX* (sic).'

The Chaucer arms commemorated Thomas Chaucer (d. 1434) and his wife, Maud Burghersh (d. 1436). In 1411 Johanna, Queen of England, granted Thomas Chaucer a lease of the manors of Woodstock, (Church) Hanborough, Wootton, and Stonesfield.[7] The shields were probably of later date, and the donors Croft have not been traced.

---

[1] 'Vita Passio et Miracula S. Thomae Cantuarensis archiepiscopi auctore Willelmo Cantuariensi' (written before 1189), ed. J. Robertson, *Rolls Series* lxvii, vol. i (1875), 488.

[2] Borenius, *St. Thomas in Art* (1932), 44. Also 'Addenda to the Iconography of St. Thomas of Canterbury', *Archaeloogia*, lxxxi op. cit. 25, pl. xxi, fig. 1, and 'Some Further Aspects of the Iconography of St. Thomas of Canterbury', *Archaeologia*, lxxxiii (1933), 180, pl. l, fig. 2. A 14th-c. glass panel at Checkley (Staffs.) has been incorrectly identified as showing the Penance of Henry II, see Newton, op. cit. 256. The subject of a 14th/15th-c. Pilgrim's badge, also claimed as showing Henry II's penance, is somewhat doubtful; London Museum A 26, 156, the *London Museum Medieval Catalogue* (1968 edition), 258.

[3] W. Urry, 'Some Notes on the Resting Places of St. Thomas Becket at Canterbury', in *Thomas Becket. Actes Du Colloque*, op. cit. 198–9.

[4] Knowles, op. cit. 103–4.

[5] Compare the hair style on the effigy of Richard II, 1394, with that of Henry IV, 1410–20. The style of the latter is similar to that found on the effigies of Richard Beauchamp, Earl of Warwick, 1449–50, and Robert, Lord Hungerford, c. 1460. L. Stone, *Sculpture in Britain. The Middle Ages* (1955), pls. 151, 155A, 164, and 171.

[6] *Visitations* (1871), 53; P.C. (1920).

[7] H. Napier, *Historical Notices of Swyncombe and Ewelme* (1858), 28.

WROXTON ABBEY

GLASS NOW IN PHILADELPHIA MUSEUM OF ART PENNSYLVANIA, U.S.A.

O.S. SP. 417 415.

PRINTED SOURCES

Eden, F. S., *The Collection of Heraldic Stained Glass at Ronaele Manor, Elkins Park, Pennsylvania* (1927), 12, 20, 22, pls. 11, 12.

Eden, F. S., 'Heraldic Glass at Ronaele Manor', *The Connoisseur* (July 1930), 30–1, fig. iv.
V.C.H. ix (1969), 172.
Pevsner (1974), 862–3.

The two panels from Wroxton Abbey were acquired, during the 1920s, by Mr. and Mrs. Fitzeugene Dixon and were part of their collection at Ronaele Manor. In 1952 they were given by Mrs. Widener Dixon to the Philadelphia Museum of Art.[1]

The present house at Wroxton was built in the second decade of the seventeenth century by Sir William Pope, later Earl of Downe, who died in 1631.[2] It has been conjectured that these panels were transferred from the older building,[3] about which nothing is known. The Augustinian priory was dissolved in 1536 and a clause in the first lease of the site, in the same year, directed that most of the buildings should be destroyed.[4] A reversion of the lease was obtained by Sir Thomas Pope in 1537,[5] and the panels may have been commissioned by him. Some of the heraldic glass formerly at Wroxton was bought from other houses by the Norths; Francis North, Lord Keeper, d. 1685, married a sister of the last Earl of Downe.[6]

1. Shield of England for Henry VIII   PLATE 50 (*a*)

Panel: h. 0·87 m. w. 0·35 m. Shield: h. 0·3 m. w. 0·20 m.

Quarterly 1, 4 azure three fleurs-de-lis or FRANCE 2, 3 *gules three lions passant gardant in pale or* ENGLAND. for Henry VIII.

Encircled by an elaborate chaplet with an imperial crown above.

Condition. Complete and well preserved, some slight paint loss on the lions in the second and third quarters. Old breaks have leaded repairs, particularly on the crown. Set against modern white glass.

Colour and Technique. The colours are pot-metal glass. Shield: the fleurs-de-lis are leaded inserts, blue ground diapered with a foliage design; the lions abraded and stained yellow. Chaplet: green foliage with blue bands. Side clasps mauve, upper and lower ones green. Crown: yellow stain on white glass.

Style and Design. As below.

Date. Probably 1537–47.

2. Shield of England, Heir Apparent   PLATE 50 (*b*)

Panel: h. 0·86 m. w. 0·35 m. Shield: h. 0·3 m. w. 0·20 m.

Quarterly 1, 4 azure three fleurs-de-lis or FRANCE 2, 3 *gules three lions passant gardant in pale or, over all a label of three points argent* ENGLAND, HEIR APPARENT for Edward Tudor. Encircled by an elaborate chaplet, an imperial crown above.

Condition. Complete and well preserved, slight paint loss on the lions in the second and third quarters of the shield. Old breaks in the upper half of the shield and the chaplet have leaded repairs. Set against modern white glass.

Colour and Technique. Colours identical to the royal arms above. Shield, in the first quarter the label is on the same piece of glass as the upper right fleur-de-lis, in the second quarter it is abraded ruby flash. Chaplet, purple; ruby bands, clasps, mauve.

Style and Design. Both panels are extremely fine examples of de-luxe quality glass painting. The detailed work is meticulous, without being mechanical; although the two chaplets are identical in design there are slight variations in details of the features of the figures. Cruder versions of the side clasps from chaplets are found at Holton,[7] Yarnton,[8] Trinity College, Oxford,[9] and Chilton (Bucks.).[10] A very debased version of the design is also found in a window at Iffley Rectory. The leaf ornament, putti, and heads are

---

[1] Information from Mr. D. DuBon, Curator of Medieval and Renaissance Decorative Arts, Philadelphia Museum of Art.
[2] *V.C.H.* ix (1969), 172.   [3] Eden, *Collection,* op. cit. 20.
[4] *V.C.H.* ix (1969), 172.   [5] Ibid. 176.   [6] Ibid. 172.

[7] Holton, w. I, A1.   [8] Yarnton, n. IV, 6a, 6c.
[9] South window of the Old Library.
[10] Unpublished photograph C.I 754/50(9). I am grateful to Dr. R. Marks for this information.

derived from Italian Renaissance art. The earliest examples of this influence in English painting occur in humanistic book decoration, c. 1500.[1] It is known that Henry VIII employed Italian artists, and by the second quarter of the century this type of detail, particularly for architectural and ornamental decoration, is a common feature in paintings,[2] manuscripts,[3] and stained-glass design.[4]

A particular detail of the Wroxton chaplets, the profile male head thrust through an oculus, rather than contained within a circular frame, can be linked, in type, with goldsmith's work[5] and sculpture.[6]

Eden attributed the Wroxton panels to Galyon Hone, who succeeded as king's glazier to Henry VIII in 1517.[7] There is, no documentary evidence for this attribution.

Date. The royal arms, with a label for the heir apparent, give limitations of date, either 1486–1509, or 1537–47. Prince Arthur, eldest son of Henry VII, was born 1486 and died 1502. His brother Henry was created Prince of Wales in 1503 and succeeded to the throne in 1509. His only surviving son Edward was born in 1537 and succeeded in 1547. The later dating is more consistent with the style and design.

YARNTON
ST. BARTHOLOMEW

O.S. SP 477 127.

MS. SOURCES

Oxford. Bodleian Library:
MS. Top. Oxon. e. 286, f. 84[r]. Church Notes of N. Greenwood (1685).
MS. Top. Oxon. b. 220, ff. 35, 41–3[r]. Church Notes and drawings (c. 1804–40) attributed in part to J. E. Robinson.
MS. D.A. Par. Yarnton d. 1, ff. 9[v]–27. Correspondence of Alderman Fletcher (early 19th c.) together with a copy of F. S. Eden's report on the condition of the windows prior to the restoration of 1912.
MS. Don. c. 90, f. 188[v]. 19th-c. drawing.
MS. Top. Oxon. c. 313, f. 164[v]. Drawing by H. Hurst (c. 1908).

PRINTED

Gough, H., *Heraldic Notices of Yarnton Church* (1844).
Parker (1846), 104–7.
Thomas, V., *Yarnton Church* (1850).
Guidebook, *Some Account of Yarnton Church and Parish* (n.d., printed 1856?).
Stapleton, B., 'Three Oxfordshire Parishes', *O.H.S.* xxiv (1893), 239–49.
Nelson (1913), 172–3.
P.C. (1920), 361–5.
Bouchier (1932), 132–3.
Woodforde, C., 'Some English Medieval Glazing Quarries Painted with Birds', *Journal of the British Archaeological Association*, 3rd. ser., ix (1944), 1–11.
Pevsner (1974), 864–7.

The medieval glass at Yarnton presents many problems. Only four panels are part of the original glazing and *in situ* (n. IV, A1–A4). The remainder came from the collection of Alderman Fletcher, who presented it to the church in 1813.[8] Unfortunately no records of the collection have survived, and nothing is known of the original provenance of these pieces. It cannot be assumed that they were only collected locally as some of the roundels are Continental in origin (n. IV, 1a–c, 3a).

The reglazing of the windows commenced in 1815, when the glazing of the two south aisle windows over the door was undertaken.[9] In 1816 the fourteenth-century head and inscription (s. II) were acquired for insertion in a window.[10]

[1] E. Croft-Murray, *Decorative Painting in England, 1537–1837*, i (1962), 17 n. 1.
[2] The panels in the Oxenbridge chantry, St. George's, Windsor, dated 1522, can be contrasted with the grotesque panels, probably painted by Toto del Nunziata and Bartholomeo Penni, after 1543, probably for Nonsuch Palace, now at Loseley Park, Surrey. Ibid. 175 and pl. 27; 18, 165, and pls. 17–20 respectively.
[3] E. Auerbach, *Tudor Artists* (1954); particularly 42, 69, pls. 10c 22a, 22b.
[4] King's College, Cambridge, 1515–31, being the most important example. H. Wayment, *The Windows of King's College Chapel*

Cambridge. *C.V.M.A. Great Britain*, Supplementary vol. i (1972).
[5] For example, Holbein's design for Jane Seymour's Cup. P. Ganz, *Les Dessins de Hans Holbein le Jeune* v (1939), nos. 207–8.
[6] Provost's stall, King's College, Cambridge, 1533–6. R.C.H.M., *City of Cambridge*, pt. i (1959), pl. 189.
[7] Eden, *Collection*, op. cit. Eden, 'Heraldic Glass', op. cit. 30.
[8] Painted table recording benefactors, in the north aisle of the church.
[9] Fletcher correspondence. Bodl. Lib. MS. D.A. Par. Yarnton d. 1. ff. 9[v]–27.
[10] Ibid., f. 29.

At a later date in the nineteenth century some of the glass was removed. The undated guide printed by Baxter, *c.* 1856, records Fletcher's benefaction and comments, 'some of the pieces are remarkably fine and, being scriptural, very proper; some have been removed being on subjects legendary'.[1] A small amount of restoration, making good missing pieces, was done by F. S. Eden in 1912.[2] The west window of the vestry (s. VIII) was rearranged and releaded in 1972 by D. King of Norwich.

I

1a. An Angel

h. 0·57 m. w. 0·25 m.

Condition. A composite figure made up from two figures of angels facing in different directions; the head is modern.

Colour and Technique. Painted in brown on white glass, stippled matt shading, details picked out in yellow stain.

Date. c. 1450–80.

1b. Roundel

d. 0·19 m.

Monogram, *I.H.S.* (*Jesus Hominum Salvator*), brown paint, stippled matt and yellow stain on white glass. At the base of the light, fragments of inscriptions in black-letter script:

|*M(aria) Mag(dalena)*| *mira·*|

The paint of the second piece has scaled off.

Date. Late 15th c.

1c. The Virgin Mary PLATE 12 (*a*)

h. 0·51 m. w. 0·26 m.

The Virgin crowned and nimbed, facing three-quarters left.

Condition. Incomplete, and partly composite. The lower part of the figure and most of the background are missing.

Colour and Technique. Purple mantle powdered with large gold *M*s, lined ermine, ruby tunic powdered with white and gold sun's rays, head painted in brown with stippled shading, hair and crown in yellow stain. The large *M*s on the mantle are in yellow stain and matt, individually leaded. The sun's rays on the tunic are abraded on the flashed ruby and stained yellow.

Iconography. Crowned, the head inclined forward, the hands raised, appropriate to a Virgin enthroned with Christ.

Date. Late 15th to early 16th c.

2a. Cherubim

h. 0·58 m. w. 0·25 m.

Cherubim, six wings, wearing a neck scarf, and standing on a wheel.

Condition. Good, slight exterior corrosion, originally a tracery light.

Colour and Technique. White glass, stippled matt shading, hair and feathers in yellow stain, ruby ground, diapered seaweed foliage design.

Iconography. The wheel is properly associated with cherubim only (Ezekiel 10) but wheels are given to the seraphim and other angels in the later medieval period. Figures of cherubim in the tracery lights of a window are not uncommon; the most extensive series in the country is at Combe.

Style and Design. Close in style to the cherubim in the east window of Merton College Chapel, Oxford, and those at St. Michael's, North Gate, Oxford.

Date. 1400–30.

2b. Apostle, St. Thomas?

h. 0·79 m. w. 0·27 m.

Nimbed, full length, facing three-quarters right, holding a spear.

Condition. Incomplete, the original background and surround, except for part of the tiled floor at his feet, are missing. Slight corrosion on both surfaces. The spear point and the left shoulder drapery are Eden's restorations; the date, 1912, is inscribed on the glass.

Colour and Technique. All painted on white glass, plain mantle with patterned hem in yellow stain, tunic patterned with repeated design of three rosettes in a very deep yellow stain, white head, nimbus and spear in yellow stain. The painting is extremely delicate with very fine stipple shading.

Iconography. Parker identified this figure as St. Bartholomew, the patron of the church, as it was then associated with an inscription, *Scūs Bartholomeus*.[3] However, the saint holds a spear, the emblem of St. Thomas,[4] not the small flaying knife of St. Bartholomew. Although the point of the spear is modern, the tasselled collar at its base suggests that the restoration is correct.

Date and Style. There is some similarity to the rather more elaborate figures of Apostles at All Souls College, Oxford, of *c.* 1441–7.[5]

---

[1] Guidebook, op. cit. 6. [2] See p. 219 n. 9 above.

[3] Parker (1846), 104–7.

[4] M. R. James, *The Apocryphal New Testament* (1924), 371–3.

[5] Hutchinson (1949), pls. v and vii.

2c. Cherubim

h. 0·58 m. w. 0·25 m.

Condition. A composite figure made up from two similar figures of cherubim, slight differences in the drawing of the feathers, one figure identical with 2a. Originally in tracery lights.

Colour and Technique. As in 2a, except that here the seaweed foliage ground is ruby.

Iconography. As 2a.

Style and Design. As 2a.

Date. 1400–30.

3a, 3c, 4b. Canopy Fragments

h. 0·34 m. w. 0·23 m.

A bust-length, frontal angel standing behind a parapet, possibly from the centre section of a large canopy design.

Condition. Good, slight surface corrosion.

Colour and Technique. White glass, stipple shading, details of hair, wings, and drapery in yellow stain.

Style and Design. 3a and 3c are identical in design. 4b has a slightly different form of turret in front of the angel, but is otherwise identical with the other two. The quatrefoil patterns on the parapet are the same as a fragment at Little Faringdon s. IV, 1b, but there only the head and shoulders of the angel are represented.

Date. c. 1400–30.

n. II   PLATE 49 (*a*)

A lancet window containing eight quarries painted with birds, and three other pieces, all set on a background of modern plain white quarries. The bird quarries are all the same size. h. 0·14 m. w. 0·10 m.

Iconography of Bird Quarries

The eight quarries, one incomplete, are each painted with a design of a bird accompanied by a scroll, with an inscription in English. This class of design is found throughout the country, although there are no other examples in Oxfordshire. Woodforde considered that 'judging from the examples now remaining, birds were first painted upon English glazing quarries during the last years of the fourteenth century'.[1] A mid-14th-c. example is found at Whitwell, Rutland.[2] It was not unusual to show birds holding inscribed scrolls in their beaks. The idea of showing birds uttering sentiments and engaged in occupations proper to human beings doubtless stems from the long-established literary conventions of debates between birds,[3] and dialogues between a human and a bird.[4] The earliest examples of vernacular inscriptions in English art are found on the 13th c. Great Seal of Evesham Abbey.[5] Examples of birds holding inscriptions in manuscript painting are rare. In a Book of Hours of after 1322, now in the Walters Art Gallery, Baltimore, U.S.A., the fable of Barlaam and Josaphat is combined with a Tree of Vices, with birds holding exclamatory scrolls, and texts in Anglo-French referring to the Vices depicted.[6] A copy of Michael de Massa's treatise on the Passion of Christ, dated 1404, has two examples of birds with scrolls; here the texts are in English and Latin.[7] In English glass painting all the extant examples with inscriptions in English date from the late 15th to early 16th c.[8]

Style and Date of the Yarnton Bird Quarries

The quarries divide into two distinct groups. The first group, numbers 2a, 7a, and 7b, is far superior in invention, design, and execution. The second group, numbers 3a, 3b, 4a, 5a, and 5b, is, by comparison, badly drawn in a very summary way, with little attention to detail. The epigraphy of the scrolls of each group is quite distinct.

It is extremely difficult to date these quarries without external evidence. The first group, being finer in execution, might be assumed to be earlier than the second group, but this is by no means certain. A dating of late 15th c. and early 16th c., respectively, seems probable.

1a. A Memento Mori fragment

2a. Bird Quarry

A bird with a key hanging from a cord around its body, a drinking-vessel in its raised claw.

Scroll inscribed: |who blamyþ þis ale|

Condition. Some pitting on the exterior and slight paint loss.

Colour and Technique. Painted in brown on white glass, stippled shading. Slight touches of yellow stain. Very precisely drawn.

Iconography, Style and Design. See above.

Date. c. 1485–1500?

---

[1] Woodforde, op. cit. 1.

[2] Newton iii (1961), 514.

[3] e.g. the 12th–13th c. *The Owl and the Nightingale*, ed. E. G. Stanley (1960), and the late 13th c. 'The Thrush and the Nightingale', ed. B. Dickins, and R. M. Wilson, *Early Middle English Texts* (1951), 70–6.

[4] e.g. 'The Clerk and the Nightingale', ed. R. H. Robbins, *Secular Lyrics of thr XIVth Century and XVth Century* (1960).

[5] Birch i (1887), no. 3113.

[6] U.S.A. Baltimore, Walters Art Gallery MS. W. 105, f. 9ᵛ.

[7] Bodl. Lib. MS. Bodley 785, f. 9ᵛ.

[8] Figures of birds with their names written in English, either on scrolls, or above them, do not strictly belong to the class of design discussed here. For such examples see the Sherborne Missal, datable 1396–1407. J. A. Herbert, *The Sherborne Missal* (Roxburghe Club, 1920), frontispiece.

3a. Bird Quarry

A bird, perhaps a thrush, holding a scroll inscribed in black-letter script:

|: and: make: god: thy: frende: |

Colour and Technique. Painted in brown on white glass, stippled shading, very deep orange-coloured yellow stain. The drawing is rather crude, and the stain carelessly applied.

Iconography, Style and Design. See above.

Date. c. 1500–30?

3b. Bird Quarry

A bird, perhaps a thrush, holding a scroll inscribed:

|at: thy: last: ende|

Colour and Technique. As 3a.

Iconography, Style and Design. See above.

Date. c. 1500–30?

4a. Bird Quarry

Condition. Incomplete, the scroll is missing.

Colour and Technique. As 3a.

Iconography, Style and Design. See above.

Date. c. 1500–30?

5a. Bird Quarry

A bird, perhaps a thrush, holding a scroll inscribed in black-letter script:

|make: the: pour: to: pray: well·|

Condition. The quarry was badly fired, the paint has gone very thin, particularly on the inscription.

Colour and Technique. As 3a.

Iconography, Style and Design. See above.

Date. c. 1500–30.

5b. Bird Quarry

A bird, perhaps a thrush, holding a scroll inscribed in black-letter script:

|: be: styll: or: ellis: say: wele: |

Condition. Badly fired, the paint, like 5a, has gone very thin, particularly on the inscription.

Colour and Technique. As 3a.

Iconography, Style and Design. See above.

Date. c. 1500–30?

6a. Leaf Design

h. 0·14 m. w. 0·10 m.

A quatrefoil leaf design.

Condition. Complete, slight corrosion only.

Colour and Technique. White glass, stippled shading, the leaves are counterchanged white and yellow stain.

Style and Design. Possibly intended for a tracery light, the design and execution are extremely crude.

Date. 1500–30?

7a. Bird Quarry

An owl holding a bell, a scroll inscribed:

|Ye schal praye for þe fox.|

Condition. As 2a.

Colour and Technique. As 2a.

Iconography. Woodforde refers to the ancient custom of ringing a bell and exhorting a condemned prisoner on the night before his execution, and also on the way to execution. On the evidence of the inscription he suggests that this quarry was one of a set, showing the execution of the fox, based on the Roman de Renard, or one of the related texts.[1] The execution scene was not uncommon in English art.[2] However, the inscription in association with the bell is perhaps more appropriate to the funeral of Renard.[3]

Style and Design. See above.

Date. c. 1485–1500?

7b. Bird Quarry

A bird wearing a head-dress composed of a wimple surmounted by a sheaf of corn, and holding a scroll inscribed in black-letter script:

|greete richlyng greete|

(woe, rich fool, woe).

Condition. Slight pitting on the exterior.

Colour and Technique. As 2a.

Iconography. The curious head-dress in association with the text might be intended as a comment on the evils of extravagant dress. Such comments occur in sermon literature of the later Middle Ages.[4]

Style and Design. See above.

---

[1] Woodforde, op. cit. 8–9.

[2] K. Varty, *Reynard the Fox, A Study of the Fox in Medieval English Art* (1967), ch. 8.

[3] See F. McCullock, 'The Funeral of Renart the Fox', *The Journal of the Walters Art Gallery* xxv–xxvi (1962–3), 9–12, with illustrations from Walters MS. 102, a Psalter and Hours, English, *c.* 1300.

[4] G. R. Owst, *Preaching in Medieval England* (1926), 170–1, and G. R. Owst, *Literature and the Pulpit in Medieval England* (2nd revised edn. 1961), 321 n. 5.

9a. Head of a Cleric? or an Angel?

h. 0·10 m. w. 0·06 m.

Head facing three-quarters right, wears an amice.

Condition. A fragment of a large figure, slight corrosion only.

Colour and Technique. Painted on white glass, stippled matt shading.

Style and Design. The painting and drawing are competent, slightly stereotyped rendering of the hair.

Date. Mid 15th c.

n. IV

1a. Roundel. The Virgin and Child   PLATE 50 (c)

d. 0·19 m.

The Virgin crowned and nimbed, seated on a grassy bank and offering an apple to the Christ Child on her right knee.

Condition. Good, three old breaks repaired with leading, a small piece of the left foreground is missing.

Colour and Technique. White glass, stippled matt shading, the highlights scratched out in very fine needlepoint. The Virgin's nimbus, crown, and tunic, Christ's nimbus, and the herbage in yellow stain.

Iconography. The Virgin offers the Child an apple, the 'Gaudia Paradisi' lost through the Fall of Man, but regained through Mary, 'the New Eve'.[1]

Style and Design. English or Netherlandish, later 15th c.? The flecked background is very uncommon.

1b. Roundel. Abimelech Restoring Sarah to Abraham

PLATE 50 (d)

d. 0·29 m.

In the background God appears to the sleeping Abimelech, the latter appears again, left foreground, clasping the hand of Abraham. Sarah stands on the right.

Condition. Poor, broken into nine pieces, plated on both sides, the pieces now loose inside the plating.

Colour and Technique. White glass, stipple shading, and yellow stain.

Iconography. Not previously identified; the text illustrated is Genesis 20: 4–18.

Style and Design. Extremely distinguished piece of painting, perhaps to be associated with Antwerp and the Circle of Diric Vellert. Flemish.

Date. Probably second quarter of 16th c.

1c. Roundel. Archbishop Saint

d. 0·19 m.

An archbishop nimbed, mitred, with cross pall and cross-staff, holding a book.

Condition. Good, two old breaks repaired with leading. The top of the mitre and nimbus and adjacent head of the cross staff are modern.

Colour and Technique. White glass, stipple shading, restricted use of yellow stain.

Iconography. No particular attribute.

Style and Design. The sophisticated drawing of the figure contrasts strongly with the perfunctory treatment of the trees on either side. Flemish (?).

Date. Early 16th c.

3a. Roundel. The Prodigal Turned Away from the Brothel

d. 0·29 m.

A woman left, with raised staff, rejects the Prodigal. Five women are in a room behind left.

Condition. Complete, very well preserved.

Colour and Technique. White glass with stippled matt shading, highlights scratched out with fine needlepoint, and yellow stain, double staining on the chequered paving stones.

Iconography. Text, Luke 15: 11–32.

Style and Design. Roundels of the parable of the Prodigal Son are a common feature of Netherlandish and Flemish glass painting of the 16th c. The product of various workshops, they vary considerably in style and date.[2]

Date. First quarter of 16th c.

3b. Royal Badge: Feathers and Crown

h. 0·23 m. w. 0·19 m.

Three feathers, encircled by a crown, motto *ICH DIN* (roman letters).

Condition. Incomplete, the original border missing.

Colour and Technique. White glass, stipple shading, slight touches of yellow stain.

Iconography. The earliest example of this form of the badge is said to be a piece of glass, supposed to have come

---

[1] See C. de Tolnay, *Le Maître de Flemalle et les frères Van Eyck* (1938), 33 and 5, note 7. For the symbolism of fruit see also H. Friedmann, 'The Symbolism of Crivelli's Madonna and Child Enthroned', *Gazette des Beaux Arts*, ser. 6, xxxii (1947), 65 ff. esp. 70.

[2] B. Rackham, *A Guide to the Collections of Stained Glass* (1936), 109.

from Reynolds Place, Horton Kirby (Kent), where it is associated with the letters EP for Prince Edward, afterwards Edward VI (born 1537, succeeded 1547).[1] However, the same badge is sometimes found on the royal charters of Henry VIII.[2] It appears that during this period the badge of ostrich feathers first came to be considered to belong exclusively to the sovereign's eldest son.[3]

Date. c. 1525–1540 (?). The particular letter forms of the motto are found on seals of the first quarter of the 16th c.[4]

4a. Quarry. Badge of Henry VIII

h. 0·14 m. w. 0·10 m.

Badge: a Tudor rose, surmounted by a crown and the letters H.R.

Colour and Technique. White glass, stipple shading, the rose stem and inner rose, the crown, and letters all in deep-orange yellow stain.

Date. 1509–30. See 4c.

4c. Quarry. Badge of Catherine of Aragon

Original size h. 0·14 m. w. 0·10 m., now slightly cut down.

Badge: a Tudor rose superimposed on a bunch of arrows and surmounted by a crown.

Colour and Technique. As 4a.

Iconography and Date. The two quarries, 4a and 4c, are companion pieces, the drawing of the crown is identical. Greening Lamborn described them as 'a crowned rose, the badge of the Dukedom of York, with the letters HR for Henry VIII, a white rose on a bunch of arrows gold, surmounted by a royal crown, a badge used by Prince Arthur'.[5] This is misleading. The bunch of arrows is a badge of Aragon, here combined with the Tudor rose for Catherine of Aragon.[6] Catherine married Arthur, Prince of Wales, in 1501; he died the following year. In 1509 she married Henry VIII who divorced her in 1530. A joint commemoration after this date is most unlikely. The bunch of arrows badge, without the rose, occurs on the frieze of Prince Arthur's Chantry at Worcester.[7] Henry VIII, at a banquet given in the first year of his reign, wore a garment 'powdered with castles and sheafs of arrows (the badge of his queen Katherine) of fine dokett gold'.[8]

6a and 6c. Decorative Clasps

h. 0·22 m. w. 0·19 m.

Two identical designs: the heads of two men each thrust through an oculus, decorative clasps from the bases of two chaplets each of which surrounded a shield.

Condition. 6a is incomplete at its base, 6b is complete, both have old leaded repairs, little corrosion.

Colour and Technique. Painted on white glass, with stippled and matt shading and yellow stain. The yellow stain varies in intensity of tone.

Style and Design. Identical clasps at Holton (w. I, A1) and Trinity College, Oxford.[9] It is a somewhat crude version of the design attributed to Galyon Hone as formerly found at Wroxton Abbey.[10]

Date. Mid 16th c.

6b. Ornament

h. 0·22 m. w. 0·17 m.

Two naked putti kneeling either side of a decorated column.

Condition. A complete piece, little corrosion.

Colour and Technique, Style and Design. Same technique as 6a and 6c. The shape of the glass suggests that it is an upper clasp of a heraldic wreath, and possibly belongs with 6a and 6c.

Date. Mid 16th c.

Tracery Lights

Four of the six tracery lights retain a related series of figures, A1–A4. These are probably *in situ*,[11] with the exception of A2, probably displaced from A6, and now set inside out. The figures are St. Nicholas and St. Thomas Becket, with two donors, both Cistercian monks. The original contents of the two remaining lights are not known. Figures of donors in tracery lights are rare; earlier examples are found at Christ Church, Oxford (*c.* 1300–7), and, contemporary with Yarnton, at Horley (n. IV, B1 and n. V, B1), and the west window of Merton College Chapel.

A1. Donor Monk

h. 0·40 m. w. 0·15 m.

A monk kneeling in prayer facing three-quarters right.

---

[1] N. H. Nicholas, 'Observations on the origin and history of the Badge and Mottoes of Edward, Prince of Wales', *Archaeologia* xxxi (1846), 370–1. Glass then in the possession of A. Way.

[2] Shrewsbury (Salop) Public Library. *Lilleshall Muniments*, Deed 16294, dated 24 December 1539.   [3] Nicholas, op. cit. 370.

[4] The forms H and I occur on the seals of the Merchant Taylors' Company, London, dated 1502, and the Golden Bulla of Henry VIII, dated 1527. C. Kingsford, 'The Epigraphy of Medieval English Seals', *Archaeologia* lxxix (1929), 169, 178.

[5] Greening Lamborn (1949), 170.

[6] T. Willement, *Regal Heraldry* (1821), 67–8.

[7] Engraved in F. Sandford, *Genealogical History of the Kings of England* (1677), 446–7.

[8] E. Halle, *Chronicle: The Union of the Noble and Illustrate Famelies of Lancastre and Yorke* (Grafton edn., 1550), f. vii, reprinted Ellis (1809).

[9] South window of the Old Library.

[10] Now Philadelphia, Museum of Art, U.S.A., see Wroxton, where the sources of the style are more fully discussed.

[11] First recorded in the drawings of Robinson, dated 1804, i.e. before Fletcher's benefaction. Bodl. Lib. MS. Top. Oxon. b. 220, op. cit. Robinson's identification of the figures in A3 and A4 as Nicholas and Thomas, both abbots of Eynsham, is untenable.

Condition. Panel complete, but extensive corrosion on both surfaces, the coloured glass almost completely opaque.

Colour and Technique. Figure in white glass, with very fine stippled shading, ruby background diapered with a seaweed foliage design, tiled floor in matt and yellow stain.

Iconography. See A2.

Style and Design. The Yarnton figures are of extremely high quality, very precise design with a delicate use of very thin stipple shading. This excellence, however, is obscured by the excessive corrosion of the glass, particularly of the pot-metal coloured backgrounds. No further examples of this workshop have been found.

Date. c. 1400–20.

A2. Donor Monk

h. 0·40 m. w. 0·15 m.

A monk kneeling in prayer, originally facing three-quarters right.

Condition. As A1 above. Here the whole panel is set inside out.

Colour and Technique. As A1.

Iconography. The identities of the two figures, A1 and A2, are unknown. They both wear white habits. Mrs. Stapleton wrongly described them as 'two monks, one in a black habit, the other in white', and cited the identification by Dr. Thomas of the first figure as William de Cudlington, the first vicar of Yarnton (1235–52).[1] There is no authority for this fanciful speculation. The white habits suggest that these figures represent two members of the Cistercian Abbey of Rewley. The Manor of Yarnton was granted to the Abbey in 1294 but the presentation to the vicarage was retained by Eynsham Abbey.[2]

Style and Design. See A1 above.

Date. c. 1400–20.

A3. St. Nicholas

h. 0·40 m. w. 0·15 m.

Full length, facing three-quarters right in benediction. Label at base of light inscribed:

|nicolaus|

in black-letter script.

Condition. Incomplete, the lower part of the figure below the knees is missing, excessive corrosion, particularly on the coloured background.

Colour and Technique. Figure in white glass, stippled shading, details of the vestments, the amice, mitre, and the vexillum,

around the crozier, all picked out in yellow stain. Ruby background diapered with a seaweed foliage design.

Iconography. St. Nicholas, Bishop of Myra. Nimbed, he wears full episcopal vestments, but does not have any of his usual attributes.

Style and Design. See A1 above.

Date. c. 1400–20.

A4. St. Thomas Becket

h. 0·40 m. w. 0·15 m.

Full length, facing three-quarters left in benediction.

Label at base of light inscribed:

|Thomas|

in black-letter script.

Condition. Complete. Excessive corrosion, the background colour completely opaque, as is the inscription.

Colour and Technique. As A3.

Iconography. St. Thomas Becket, Archbishop of Canterbury. Canonized in 1173. Nimbed, he wears full archiepiscopal vestments and carries a cross staff, but is without any emblem of his martyrdom.

Style and Design. See A1 above.

Date. c. 1400–20.

A5. Composite Panel

h. 0·40 m. w. 0·15 m.

Unrelated fragments: head of a crozier, piece of corroded blue, head of the Apostle St. Jude, nimbus inscribed:

|S(an)c(tu)s Judas|[3]

in black-letter script.

A6. Composite Panel

h. 0·40 m. w. 0·15 m.

Unrelated fragments, plain corroded glass, pieces of canopy, head of the Apostle St. James Major, nimbus inscribed:

|Jacob(us) Maior|[4]

set inside out.

The heads of SS. Jude and James Major are identical in size, technique, and style. They probably formed part of a series of the twelve Apostles; their size suggests that they were tracery lights. The practice of painting the saint's name on the nimbus, although common in Continental glass painting generally, is rarely found in English glass painting. The only other example in the county is the closely related

---

[1] Stapleton (1893), op. cit. 240.
[2] Stapleton, op. cit. 208–11, 219–20; *V.C.H.* ii (1907), 82.

[3] Stapleton, op. cit., 240, misread this as '*Sca Julias* (?)'.
[4] Ibid. Noted as illegible and not transcribed.

head of Joseph, doubtless of the same workshop, now in the Bodleian Library, Oxford.[1]

Date. Probably *c.* 1480–1500.

n. V

The medieval glass is set on a groundwork of modern plain quarries and patterned quarries. All the latter are probably clever imitations of medieval design made by F. S. Eden at the 1912 restoration.

1a. Fragment of Inscription

In black-letter script:

|q gaude forte|, alternatively |q gaude sorte|.

2a. St. Christopher   PLATE 49 (*b*)

h. 0·51 m. w. 0·21 m.

St. Christopher, full length, facing three-quarters left, bearing the Christ Child on his shoulders. Inscription on the base:

|S(an)c(tu)s|(Christo)for|(us)

in black-letter script.

Condition. General condition very good, little corrosion. Missing pieces made up in 1912, dated on the glass, also alien pieces at the head of the panel.

Colour and Technique. White glass, stippled matt shading, details of hair and patterns picked out in yellow stain. The arrangement of figures, architectural base, and groundwork of quarries (type 14) is genuine as part of the saint's legs and the adjacent quarries are painted on the same glass.

Iconography. Standard late medieval type, the saint fording the river, grasping his staff with both hands. Christ seated on his shoulder. His staff is a plain branch, conforming to the Golden Legend,[2] and not to the earlier German text where the staff flowers in mid stream.[3]

Style and Design. See 2b.

Date. Second quarter 15th c.

2b. The Virgin Suckling the Child Christ

h. 0·51 m. w. 0·21 m.

The Virgin, crowned and nimbed, seated on a throne, suckling the nude Christ Child seated on her right knee.

Condition. General condition is good, but the paint has worn thin and there is some exterior corrosion. The panel is partly composite, the architectural bases are made up from two different designs. Missing pieces made up in 1912, dated on the glass.

Colour and Technique. White glass, stippled matt shading, details picked out in yellow stain. The foliage design on the Virgin's mantle is painted on the exterior surface of the glass. Groundwork of quarries, identical with 2a above.

Iconography. Perhaps the earliest example of the Virgin holding a completely nude child was the lost Madonna, of *c.* 1250, on the screen of Strasbourg Cathedral, although the practice does not seem to have become general until the first half of the 14th c.[4] Even though the first extant representation of the Virgin suckling the child is said to be a painting of the 2nd c. in the catacomb of Priscilla,[5] the subject is rarely found before the mid 13th c. The earliest examples of the Virgin suckling the nude child are found in MS. paintings of the Metz area, combined with the theme of the Madonna of Humility.[6]

Style and Design. Panels 2a and 2b are doubtless companion pieces painted by the same artist; the drawing and stippled shading are very detailed and delicate. It is highly sophisticated work, not really comparable to anything else in the county. It has some affinity with the later work associated with Thomas of Oxford, for example, the Virgin and Child at Merton College, Oxford, but has an individuality of its own. The architectural bases, patterned floor with diagonal projections are of a type that can be paralleled elsewhere, for example, the north window of Haddon Hall Chapel (Derbys.), datable 1429,[7] the windows of the Old Library at All Souls College, Oxford, of *c.* 1441–7,[8] and the Apostles' Creed window at Drayton Beauchamp (Bucks.), mid 15th c.[9]

Date. Second quarter 15th c.

4a. Saint

h. 0·41 m. w. 0·13 m.

Nimbed head of a youth facing three-quarters left.

Condition. The head only remains, pronounced exterior corrosion.

---

[1] Duke Humfrey, north side, south-west window in study. Spokes (1973), 20, serial no. 192.

[2] *Golden Legend* iv (1911), 112 ff.

[3] A. Schönbach, in *Zeitschrift für Deutsches Alterthum* xvii (1874), 85 ff. *Herder* v (1973), 496–508.

[4] M. Meiss, *French Painting in the time of Jean de Berry, The late fourteenth century and patronage of the Duke* i (1967), 126–7.

[5] L. Reau, *Iconographie de l'art chrétien* ii (1957), 296–7.

[6] Meiss (1967), op. cit. 127. See also *The Year 1200*, Exhibition Catalogue, The Metropolitan Museum, New York (1970), no. 40.

[7] Newton ii (1961), 40.

[8] Hutchinson (1949), pls. xix–xxxi. Although these panels were extensively restored and added to in the 19th-c. restoration by Clayton & Bell, the design and much of the glass are original.

[9] M. Caviness, 'Fifteenth Century Stained Glass from the Chapel of Hampton Court, Herefordshire: The Apostles' Creed and Other Subjects', *The Walpole Society* xlii (1968–70), pl. 41a.

Colour and Technique. White glass, stippled matt shading, the hair and jewelled edge of the nimbus in yellow stain.

Iconography. Identity unknown; the youthful beardless head type would be appropriate to a St. John the Evangelist.

Style and Design. The elaborate jewelled edge to the nimbus is similar to examples at All Souls College, Oxford, of 1441–2,[1] although the execution of the Yarnton head is less sophisticated.

Date. c. 1450–75?

4b. Angel

h. 0·13 m. w. 0·13 m.

A crowned angel facing three-quarters left.

Condition. Good, incomplete, the head, shoulders, and hands only remain.

Colour and Technique. White glass, stippled shading, the hair and wings in yellow stain.

Iconography. Possibly part of a series of the Nine Orders of Angels; Dominions and Principalities are generally crowned.

Style and Design. The detailed painting of the hair contrasts with the simplified blocked outline of the drapery which is more akin to woodcut designs.

Date. c. 1480–1500?

n. VI

1b. Donor

h. 0·35 m. w. 0·22 m.

A priest kneeling in prayer facing right.

Condition. The arrangement of the figure, pieces of geometric grisaille, and arch is a restorer's composite. The figure's robes are very corroded, the head is intact but the paint is completely worn off, trace lines visible in a raking side light.

Colour and Technique. Figure has a blue pot-metal mantle and light purple tunic, face and hands on white glass. Geometric grisaille in white glass, no yellow stain.

Iconography. The figure appears to be tonsured.

Date, Style and Design. c. 1300? It is too corroded and incomplete to date precisely.

2a. Composite Figure

h. 0·51 m. w. 0·21 m.

Condition. The panel shows a full-length nimbed figure facing three-quarters right. However, it is a composite made up from at least four different figures, all 15th c.

Colour and Technique. Nimbed head, painted on white glass, stippled and matt shading, hair in yellow stain.

Iconography. Probably an angel.

Style and Design. The angel's head is identical with the reused angel's head now in the Crucifixion panel of Merton College Chapel.[2] The painting on the Yarnton head, however, is somewhat coarser in execution.

Date. 1400–30.

2b. St. John the Baptist   PLATE 12 (*b*)

h. 0·68 m. w. 0·24 m.

St. John the Baptist, full length, facing three-quarters right, holding the *Agnus Dei* in his left hand.

Condition. The white glass is well preserved, the ruby background is modern. The architectural surround is actually made up from parts of five or six original canopies, probably recut for the present arrangement.

Colour and Technique. Modern ruby background diapered with a seaweed foliage design, remainder in white glass, stippled matt shading, details in yellow stain.

Iconography. The saint points to the *Agnus Dei*, standing on a book with a cross-banner, held in his veiled left hand (John 1: 29). The tunic of a complete camel skin, instead of the camel hair mentioned in the Gospel (Mark 1: 6), is found from the mid 14th c. onwards.[3]

Style and Design. The pose of the figure and the cut lines of the glass are close to a tracery light at Haddenham (Bucks.).[4] The styles are quite distinct, both figures probably derive from a standard design.

Date. Mid 15th c.

2c. St. Thomas Apostle

h. 0·35 m. w. 0·15 m.

St. Thomas nimbed, full length, facing three-quarters left, holding a T-square.

Condition. Virtually complete, the upper and lower edges of the panel are alien insertions. Little decay.

Colour and Technique. White glass, stippled shading, strong yellow stain on mantle and beard, plain blue curtain with yellow stain cresting behind the saint.

Iconography. He holds a T-square in allusion to the legend that he built a palace in India for the King Gundaphorus.[5]

---

[1] Hutchinson (1949), pls. vi and xi.
[2] R.C.H.M. (1939), pl. 147.
[3] Rushforth (1936), 235, gives thirteen English examples, 14th–16th c., without attempting a complete list.
[4] Unpublished photograph, C.I.
[5] Acts of Thomas. M. R. James, *The Apocryphal New Testament* (1924), 371–3.

Style and Design. The style is rather crude, the curious side columns with their bulbous bases appear to be a rather rustic interpretation of Renaissance details.

Date. c. 1530?

3a. Composite Roundel

d. 0·17 m., with border 0·255 m.

Two incomplete figures leaded up with miscellaneous fragments of 14th- and 15th-c. glass.

A deacon holding an open book, facing three-quarters right.

Condition. Incomplete, only the upper half of the figure remains, glass is well preserved, only slight decay.

Colour and Technique. Painted on white glass with stippled and matt shading, the hair and fringe of the dalmatic in yellow stain.

Iconography. Probably part of a large composition. Subject uncertain, possibly a Mass scene.

Style and Design. Very uneven in design, the careful painting on the face and hair contrasts with the bold pattern of the dalmatic where there is little attempt to relate the drapery to the underlying form.

Date. Second half 15th c.

A naked man in prayer, facing left

Condition. Incomplete, only the upper half of the figure remains. Pronounced corrosion on both surfaces.

Colour and Technique. Painted on white glass, hair in yellow stain, modelling disfigured by the corrosion.

Iconography. Probably a resurrected figure from a Last Judgement scene.

Style and Design. A rather simplified style, but the corrosion prevents detailed comment.

Date. Second half (?), 14th c.

3b. Fragment of a white finial, very corroded. 14th c.

3c. Roundel. St. Chad

d. 0·18 m.

St. Chad, full length, frontal, in episcopal vestments, holding a crozier and standing in a landscape.

Inscription. |[S]|cedd|. The S is modern.

Condition. The upper part of the figure is modern, the genuine parts are very corroded.

Colour and Technique. White glass, stippled matt shading, slight yellow stain.

Iconography. St. Chad, Bishop of York 644–69, Bishop of Mercia 669, d. 674, was buried at Lichfield (Staffs.). The saint wears episcopal vestments and holds a crozier and a small branch of a tree; the latter is modern, and was probably derived from a misreading of an early 15th-c. MS. illustration.[1] Figures of St. Chad are rare.[2] Rushforth's conclusion that in the later Middle Ages St. Chad was little known outside the diocese of Lichfield is perhaps incorrect.[3] He has an office with nine lections in the Sarum Breviary,[4] and his feast was instituted in the province of Canterbury in 1397.[5] A representation of him, and three scenes from his life, in a window in York Minster,[6] probably reflect the personal devotion of the donor, Robert Wolvedon, canon and treasurer, 1426–32, rather than a local cult.[7] His legendary association with King Wulfhere,[8] reputed builder of Peterborough Abbey, was formerly depicted in the cloister windows at Peterborough, mid 15th c.[9]

Style and Design. Good quality work, the absence of the head makes comparisons very difficult. The square form of the E and rounded ∂ can be paralleled with letter forms on seals of the late 15th, early 16th c.[10]

Date. Early 16th c.

4b. Canopy Fragment

h. 0·25 m. w. 0·22 m.

A bust-length frontal angel, head inclined three-quarters right, standing behind a parapet, possibly from the centre section of a large canopy.

Condition. Good, slight surface corrosion.

Colour and Technique. White glass, stipple shading, hair and wings in yellow stain.

Style and Design. Similar in type to the angels in I, 3a, 3c,

---

[1] R. H. Warner, *Life and Legends of St. Chad* (1871), 142, citing Bodleian Library, MS. Tanner 17, f. 28. The 'branch' is actually the fringed hem of the dalmatic.

[2] Nelson (1913), 72, records only one example at Norbury (Derbys.), 15th c. There is a late 15th-c. figure at Ladbrook, *V.C.H. Warwicks.* vi (1951), 146. The saint was twice represented in the windows of Battlefield (Salop) now lost, but probably *c.* 1434–5 (B.L. Add. MS. 21236, ff. 342, 347). A lost window at St. Chad's, Lichfield, contained scenes from his life (B.L. MS. Egerton 3510, p. 192).

[3] Rushforth (1936), 139.

[4] F. Procter and C. Wordsworth, *Breviarium Sarum* iii (1886), 193–204.

[5] Wilkins, *Concilia Magnae Britanniae* iii (1737), 234–5.

[6] Benson, *Stained Glass of York* (1911), 95–6.

[7] Wolvedon was also Dean of Lichfield. Thomas of Chesterfield, 'Historia de Successione episcoporum Conventrensium et Lichfieldensium', in H. Wharton, *Anglia Sacra* (1691), i. 452.

[8] 'Vita SS Wifadi et Ruffini', in *Acta Sanctorum*, 24 July (xxiv), 570.

[9] T. Gunton, *History of the Church of Peterborough* (1685), 51, 103.

[10] C. Kingsford, 'Epigraphy of English Medieval Seals', *Archaeologia* lxxix (1929), 167–8.

and 4b, but probably not the same series, as there are differences in architectural details and patterned drapery.

Date. 1400–30.

A2, A3, A4, A5. Quarries and Head of Christ

h. 0·14 m. w. 0·11 m.

Four identical quarry designs, type 29, painted on white glass, leaves and plain border in yellow stain. Two identical quarries, stylized pomegranate design, A3, A4: painted on white glass, strong yellow stain on the leaves and fruit. Crude, mechanical work.

Date. 16th c.

A5. Head of Christ?

h. 0·18 m. w. 0·14 m.

Frontal head and shoulders, incomplete, probably cut down to fit its present position, slight decay. Set inside out.

Colour and Technique. Painted on white glass, stippled and matt shading, hair and beard, pattern on robe, and jewelled clasp all in yellow stain.

Style and Design. The painting is extremely sophisticated, very soft modelling, with detailed drawing of the features. The style is extremely close to the head of God the Father in the apex tracery light of a chancel window at Maids Moreton (Bucks.), n. III, A1, and another head, also of God the Father, formerly in the apex tracery light of a window in the north aisle of the nave at St. Michael's North Gate, Oxford.[1] The three heads are so close that they should be considered as the product of a single workshop, if not an individual artist.

Iconography. The connection with the glass at Maids Moreton and St. Michael's North Gate, Oxford, suggests that the Yarnton figure is to be identified as Christ, and was probably an apex tracery light of a window. The head type, ermine collar of the mantle, and jewelled clasp are appropriate for a figure of Christ.

Date. 1400–30.

s. II

1b. Head of a Prophet?

h. 0·16 m. w. 0·08 m.

Bearded head facing three-quarters left; above the head, a scroll, inscribed in Lombardic capitals:

|MATER: DEI: MISERERE MEI|

Condition. Head from a larger figure, very corroded.

Colour and Technique. Head painted on pink glass, smear and matt shading.

Iconography. The head and scroll do not necessarily belong together, the bidding inscription on the scroll is appropriate to a donor figure kneeling before the Blessed Virgin Mary. The bearded head is too large in scale for such a donor figure.

Style and Design. The head is very like one at Christ Church, Oxford.

Date. First quarter 14th c.

N.B. It is proposed to place this glass in one of the windows of the south aisle at a future restoration.

s. VI

A composite window of fragments of medieval glass set against modern plain white glass. The glass is so fragmentary and jumbled that a detailed description would not serve much purpose. The more complete pieces are as follows:

1a. Composite Figure

h. 0·11 m. w. 0·11 m.

Head of a youth facing right, attached to the torso of a deacon in a fringed dalmatic. White glass, stippled shading, and yellow stain.

2a. Cherubim

h. 0·56 m. w. 0·35 m.

Composite figure, the head and torso are one piece, the remainder made up from other figures. All 15th c.

4a. Roundel

d. 0·07 m.

Flat ivy-leaf design, pot-metal ochre. 14th c.

s. VII

A composite window as s. VI. The more complete pieces are as follows.

1a. Male Figure

h. 0·10 m. w. 0·11 m.

Head and shoulders, hands raised before chest, naked, possibly from a Last Judgement. Painted on white glass, stippled shading, hair in yellow stain. Second half of 15th c.

---

[1] This panel was almost completely ruined by fire in 1953, and is known only from photographs.

2a. Cherubim

h. 0·37 m. w. 0·34 m.

A composite figure made up from at least two different figures. The bold peacock feathers of the wings should be noted. The head is close to that in s. VI, 2a; both have very long thin faces. Painted on white glass, stippled shading and yellow stain. 15th c.

3a. Male Head

h. 0·90 m. w. 0·80 m.

The head of a man, facing three-quarters left, a fragment of a full-length figure, slight corrosion. Painted on white glass, stippled shading. The drawing of the features is very like the two Becket panels from Woodstock Old Chapel, now in the Bodleian Library; see Woodstock.

Date. 15th c.

Adjacent to the head are fragments of drapery and two raised hands, the latter set inside out.

4a. Roundel

Foliage design of three ivy leaves. Pot-metal ochre glass, well preserved. 14th c.

s. VIII

The glass was releaded in 1972 by D. King of Norwich.

2b. Composite Figure

h. 0·24 m. w. 0·10 m.

An angel's head, painted on white glass, the hair in yellow stain, close in style and design to the angel's head in window n. VI, 2a. 15th c., *c.* 1400–30.

Figure of a bishop, full length, facing three-quarters left, in benediction, holding a crozier, probably a saint; the head is missing. Painted on white glass. 15th c.

4a, 4c. Tracery Lights

h. 0·24 m. w. 0·24 m.

Four leaves radiating from a central boss, each leaf is in a cusped frame within a plain border.

Condition. Incomplete, the roundels at the centre are missing.

Colour and Technique. Leaves painted on white glass against a matt black background, cusped frames in yellow stain. Plain white border. The painting is rather mechanical.

Date. 15th c.

4b. Composite Panel

h. 0·38 m. w. 0·14 m.

Incomplete head of a male saint, bearded, facing three-quarters left, painted on white glass, stippled shading. Late 15th c.

A raised hand, fragment of a canopy, and part of a tracery design. All 15th c.

5b. Canopy Design

h. 0·38 m. w. 0·42 m.

Condition. A composite assembly of pieces of canopy design.

Colour and Technique. Painted on white glass, stippled and matt shading, details picked out in yellow stain.

Date. First half 15th c.

6d. Composite Panel

h. 0·38 m. w. 0·38 m.

A centre portion of a canopy design, similar to the composite pieces in n. VI, 2b. 15th c.

Three roundels, identical design: a Tudor rose painted on white glass, the centre in yellow stain. 15th c.

A1, A6. Quarries

h. 0·14 m. w. 0·11 m. (original measurement).

Condition. Four identical quarries cut down to fit into their present position.

Quarry design as n. VI, A2–A5.

Date. 16th c.

INDEX

The places catalogued and their page numbers in the volume are listed in bold type. Proper names are in capital letters, and the subject-matter of the glass is in italics. Where there have been boundary alterations, the new county designations appear after the old following the place name.

John, 41, 42
William, 41
STONARD, *see* STONOR
Stonesfield, 9, **190–4** 217
STONOR, arms of, 107
   Alice, 107
   Thomas, 107
   Sibyl, 107
Stonyhurst College, 139
STRANGE, arms of, 126, 133, 134
   Isabel, 127
   Roger, Lord le, 127
STRANGBOU, J., 117 n. 5
Strasbourg Cathedral, screen at, 226
Stratton Audley, 3, 126, **194–6,** 215
STREET, G. E., 108
STRETLEY, Edmund, 213, 214
   Hugh, 213
   Joan, 213
Stukely Priory (Oxon.), 29
   seal of, 29 n. 2
style, general discussion of, 11–18
SUTTON, arms of, 50
    Eleanora, 96
    Oliver, Bishop of Lincoln, 77
Sutton-cum-Buckingham (Lincs.), 114
Swacliffe (Oxon.), wall-painting at, 43
Swerford, 197, 214
Swinborne (Oxon.), 190
Swinbrook, 193, 194, **197–9**
Swithin, St., 209
SYDENHAM, arms of, 98
symbols of the Evangelists, see *Evangelist symbols*
SYMMONDS, R., 138, 141, 141 n. 11, 149, 153
Syon cope, 30 n. 7

Tadmarton, 9, 12, 57, 137, **199–200**
Tamworth (Staffs.), 1
techniques, general discussion of, 6–7
Templars, 49
Teva, Abbey of Santa Maria, sculpture at, 73 n. 3
Thame (Oxon.), 192
THAME, Philip de, Prior of the Order of St. John of Jerusalem, 49 n. 7
Thatcham (Berks.), 210, 211, 211 n. 2, 212
THEOPHANO, Empress, 67
Thirsk (Yorks.), glass at, 89 n. 7, 182 n. 4
THOMAS, Abbot of Eynsham, 224 n. 11
   Earl of Lancaster, arms of, 85; 176, 176 n. 2
   of Oxford, glazier, 14, 15, 20, 21, 53, 57, 74, 89, 115, 226
   and Sons, 109
   V., 225
Thomas, St., 8, 9, 15, 30, 32, 74, 75, 96, 97, 220, 227
Thomas Becket, St., 10, 13, 15, 17, 35, 36, 128, 129, 152, 216, 217, 224, 225, 230
Thornham Parva (Suffolk), retable, 152
TIBETOT, Ada de, 179
   Robert de, 179
TIPTOFT, arms of, 164
TIWE, Radulphus de, 78, 79, 80

Tobit, 34
Toledo, 43
Tong (Salop.), glass at, 52
TONY, arms of, 86
Toot Baldon, 9, 137, 199, **200**
TOUR, de la, arms of, 192
Tree of Jesse, 4, 5, 8, 11, 12, 14, 78, 83, 84, 128, 129, 136
Tree of Knowledge, 117
Tree of Vices, 221
TREKER, Thomas, 212
TRIELOC, *see* TRILLOCK
TRILLOCK, arms of, 135
   Anne, 135
   Lawrence, 135
TRILLOWE, Elizabeth, 159
   Sir John, 159
Trinity, 7, 8, 9, 33, 34, 81, 117, 130, 132, 154, 155, 156, 156 n. 3, 210
TRUSSELL, arms of, 97
TUDOR, badge, 76, 122, 123, 224
TYES, arms of, 85
   Henry, Lord, 85
TYNNY, Thomas, Prior of Cogges, 70

Ulcombe (Kent), wall-painting at, 101 n. 2
URBAN VI, Pope, 32
Upper Heyford (Oxon.), 143

VALOIGNES, Joan de, 70
VAVASOUR, arms of, 163
Velabro, San Giorgio, 166
VELLERT, Diric, 223
VERDON, arms of, 134
   Isabel de, 108
   Sir Theobald de, 108
VERDUN, arms of, 116
VERE, arms of, 86
   Sir Hugh de, 86
   Robert de, Earl of Oxford, 86
VERNEY, arms of, 210
   Alice, 211
   Beatrice, 211
   Sir Ralph, 33, 210, 211
   William, 211
Verona, 152
Virgin Annunciate, see *Mary, annunciation to*
Virgin Mary, see *Mary*

WACE, arms of, 102
   Elena, 102
   William, 102
WAKE, arms of, 87
   John, Lord, 87
WALDEGRAVE, Elizabeth, 211
   Thomas, 211
WALTER, Hubert, Archbishop of Canterbury, 36
WALTON, arms of, 99, 100
Warborough, 4, **200–1**
WARREN, arms of, 195
WARRENNE, arms of, 82, 97, 140, 142

PLATES

PLATE 1

(a) BECKLEY. I, A1. Coronation of the Virgin

(b) BECKLEY. I, A2. The Assumption of the Virgin

(c) BECKLEY. n. II, A1. St. Edmund

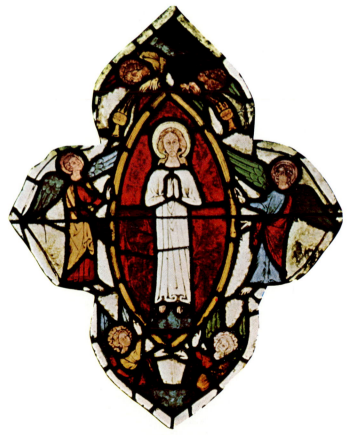

(d) BECKLEY. s. II, A1. The Assumption of the Virgin

PLATE 2

(*a*) BRIGHTWELL BALDWIN. n. IV, 1a. The weighing of a soul

(*b*) BRIGHTWELL BALDWIN. n. IV, 2a. St. Peter

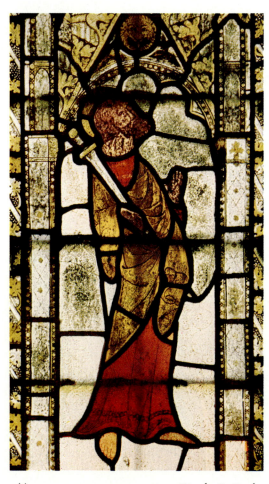

(*c*) BRIGHTWELL BALDWIN. n. IV, 2b. St. Paul

PLATE 3

(a) CHINNOR. S. II, 2b. St. Alban (detail)

(b) DORCHESTER. I, 5b. Resurrection of
a king (detail)

(c) DORCHESTER. I, 3b. St. Michael (detail)

PLATE 4

(*a*) DORCHESTER. I, 3e. St. Birinus preaching (detail)

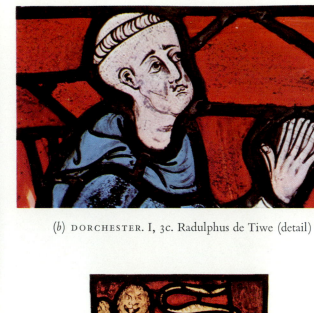

(*b*) DORCHESTER. I, 3c. Radulphus de Tiwe (detail)

(*c*) DORCHESTER. n. IX, 1a. Shield of England

(*d*) GREAT MILTON. n. V, A2. Death of Lazarus

(*e*) GREAT MILTON. n. V, A3. Lazarus begging

PLATE 5

GREAT ROLLRIGHT. Now in Oxford, Bodleian Library. Sacrament of Marriage

(*a*) HARDWICK. w. I, 1b. Christ on the Cross

(*b*) HARDWICK. w. I, 1b. The Virgin Mary (detail)

(*c*) HARDWICK. w. I, 1b. St. John (detail)

PLATE 7

(*a*) HEYTHROP. S. II, 1a. John Ashfield (detail)

(*b*) HORLEY. n. IV, B1. Henry Rumworth

(*c*) HORLEY. n. V, B1 Robert Gilbert

PLATE 8

KIDLINGTON. I, IC. A miracle of St. Frideswide

PLATE 9

(a) STONESFIELD. w. I, 2b. Arms of Kingston
impaling Fettiplace

(b) STONESFIELD. w. I, 2c. Arms of Fettiplace
impaling Fabyan

(c) WATERSTOCK. n. III, 7a. John Brown

(d) WATERSTOCK. n. III, 7c. Thomas Brown

PLATE 10

(a) WATERPERRY. n. V, 2a. Margaret Fitz Ellis

(b) WATERPERRY. n. V, 2c. Robert Fitz Ellis

(c) WATERPERRY. n. VI, A2. Christ in Majesty

PLATE 11

WOODSTOCK. Now in Oxford, Bodleian Library. The Penance of Henry II

PLATE 12

(a) YARNTON. I, IC. The Virgin Mary

(b) YARNTON. n. VI, 2b. St. John Baptist

KEY TO RESTORATION DIAGRAMS

Post–Medieval Glass   Re-used Medieval Glass

PLATE 13

ADDERBURY. Now in Bodleian Library. A knight

PLATE 14

(*a*) ASTHALL. n. IV, 2b. Christ on the Cross

(*b*) ASTHALL. n. IV, 2b. Restoration diagram

(*c*) ASTHALL. n. IV, 2c. St. John Evangelist

(*d, e, f, g*) ASTON ROWANT. n. IX, A2–5. Fragments

PLATE 15

(a) BECKLEY. I, A1. The Coronation of the Virgin

(b) BECKLEY. I, A1. Restoration diagram

(c) BECKLEY. n. II, A1. St. Edmund

(d) BECKLEY. n. II, A1. Restoration diagram

PLATE 16

(a) BECKLEY. I, A2. The Assumption of the Virgin

(b) BECKLEY. I, A2. Restoration diagram

(c) BECKLEY. S. II, A1. The Assumption of the Virgin

(d) BECKLEY. S. II, A1. Restoration diagram

PLATE 17

(a) The De Lisle Hours of the Virgin

(b) BECKLEY. n. V, 1a. St. James Major and St. Christopher

(c) BEGBROKE. s. II, 1a. St. Frideswide

(e) BEGBROKE. s. V, 2b. Joseph meeting his father Jacob

(d) BEGBROKE. s. II, 3a. God the Father

PLATE 18

(b) BIX. n. V, 2a. The Miracle at Cana

(a) BIX. n. IV, 2a. Joseph meeting his father Jacob

PLATE 19

(a) BRIGHTWELL BALDWIN. n. III, 2a. St. Paul Apostle.
2b. The Virgin Annunciate

(b) BRIGHTWELL BALDWIN. n. III, 2a, 2b. Restoration
diagram

(c) BRIGHTWELL BALDWIN. s. V, 3a. The Archangel
Gabriel

(d) BRIGHTWELL BALDWIN. s. VII, A2. The Virgin
Annunciate

PLATE 20

(a) BRIGHTWELL BALDWIN. n. IV, A3. Hart couchant

(b) BRIGHTWELL BALDWIN. n. IV, A4. Lion statant

(c) BURFORD. w. I. Composite panels

PLATE 21

(a) CASSINGTON. n. II, 1c. Joseph taking leave of his father Jacob

(b) CASSINGTON. s. III, 2a. Head of Christ.
1a. A deacon saint

(d) CHALGROVE. n. V, 1a, 1c.
Heads of two angels

(c) CASSINGTON. n. III. St. Paul

PLATE 22

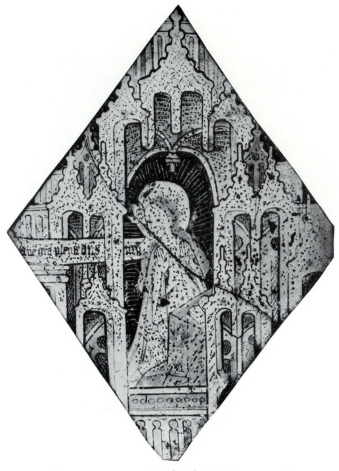

(a) CHASTLETON. n. II, 1b. The Virgin Annunciate

(b) CHINNOR. n. II. Restoration diagram

(c) CHINNOR. n. II, 2a. A bishop

(d) CHINNOR. n. II, 2b. An archbishop

PLATE 23

(b) CHINNOR. S. II, A2. Clothing the naked

(a) CHINNOR. S. II. Restoration diagram

(c) CHINNOR. S. II, 2a. St. Lawrence

(d) CHINNOR. S. II, 2b. St. Alban

PLATE 24

(*a*) CHINNOR. n. V, A1. Censing angels. A2. Christ in Judgement

(*b*) COGGES. n. II. Tracery lights pre-restoration

(*c*) COGGES. n. II. Tracery lights in 1965

PLATE 25

(*a*) COGGES. n. II. Restoration diagram

(*b*) COMBE. S. IV, 3C. St. James Major

(*c*) COMBE. S. IV, 3C. Restoration diagram

PLATE 26

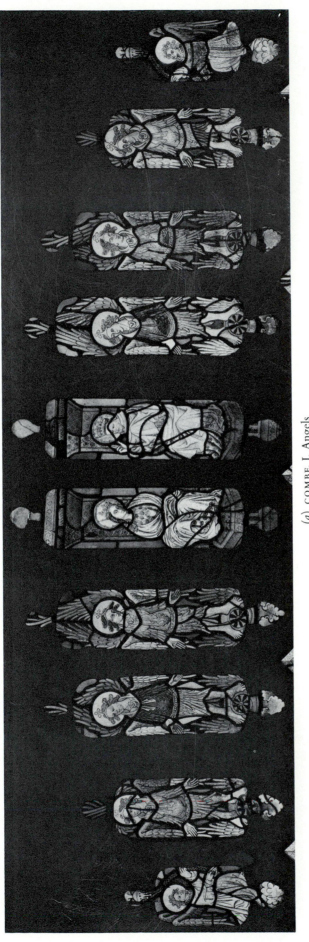

(a) COMBE. I. Angels

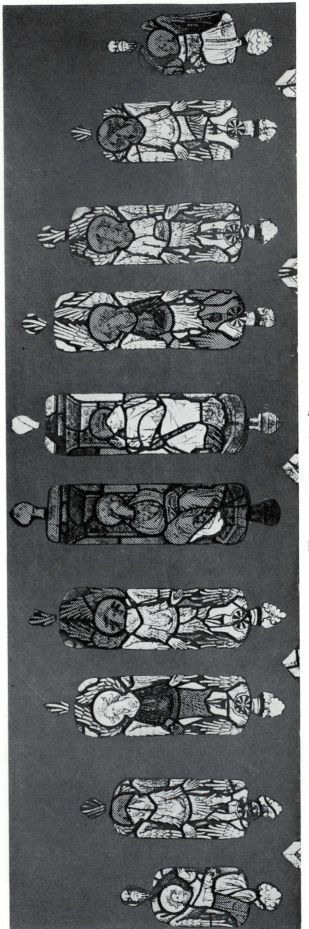

(b) COMBE. I. Restoration diagram

PLATE 27

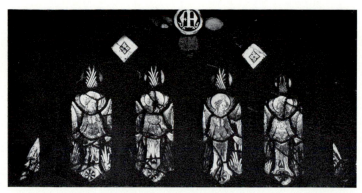

(*a*) COMBE. n. III. Angels

(*b*) COMBE. n. III. Restoration diagram

(*c*) COMBE. n. IV. Angels

(*d*) COMBE. n. IV. Restoration diagram

(*e*) COMBE. n. V. Angels

(*f*) COMBE. n. V. Restoration diagram

(*g*) COMBE. s. V. Angels

(*h*) COMBE. s. V. Restoration diagram

PLATE 28

(*a*) CROPREDY. n. V, 2b. Head of a virgin saint

(*b*) DORCHESTER. I, 3a. The Annunciation

(*c*) DORCHESTER. I, 3a. Restoration diagram

PLATE 29

(*a*) DORCHESTER. I, 3e. St. Birinus preaching

(*b*) DORCHESTER. n. II, 1c. Head of a youth

(*c*) DORCHESTER. I, 3a. Head of a king

(*d*) DORCHESTER. I, 3b. St. Michael

(*e*) DORCHESTER. I, 3b. Dragon

PLATE 30

(a) DORCHESTER. I, 5b. Head of a queen, The resurrection of a king

(b) DORCHESTER. I, 4g. Emblem of the Trinity

(c) DORCHESTER. I, 5e. Head of a queen, The resurrection of a bishop

(d) DORCHESTER. I, 3d. St. Lawrence

(e) DORCHESTER. I, 4b. Roundels and fragments

(f) DORCHESTER. I, 3f. A bishop

(g) DORCHESTER. I, 4c. The Virgin and Child

(h) DORCHESTER. Chancel sedilia 1c. A pope

(i) DORCHESTER. I, 4f. Christ in Majesty

PLATE 31

(a) DORCHESTER. n. III, 2b. St. Birinus receiving
a cross-staff

(b) DORCHESTER. n. III, 2b. Restoration diagram

(c) DORCHESTER. Chancel sedilia 1a. A Mass scene

(d) DORCHESTER. Chancel sedilia 1b. An archbishop

(e) DORCHESTER. Lost glass, drawing by John Carter

PLATE 32

(a) DRAYTON ST. LEONARD. n. II, 1a. St. Leonard

(b) EYNSHAM. s. IX, 2a. St. Thomas

(c) EYNSHAM. s. IX, 4a. A crane

(d) EWELME. s. II, 4d. Heads of St. Paul and St. Peter

PLATE 33

(a) GREAT MILTON. n. V, A2. The death of Lazarus,
restoration diagram

(b) GREAT MILTON. n. V, A3. Lazarus begging,
restoration diagram

(c) GREAT ROLLRIGHT. Now in Bodleian Library.
The sacrament of marriage

(d) GREAT ROLLRIGHT. The sacrament of marriage, 18th c. drawing

PLATE 34

(a) HAMPTON POYLE. n. II, A1. The lion of St. Mark

(b) HAMPTON POYLE. n. II, A2. The angel of St. Matthew

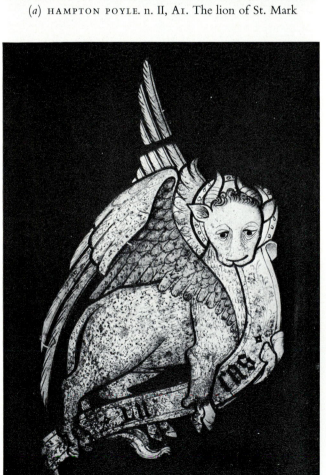

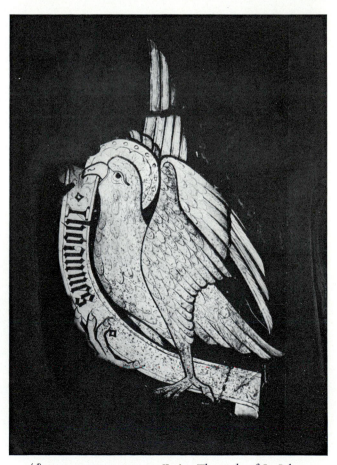

(c) HAMPTON POYLE. n. II, A3. The bull of St. Luke

(d) HAMPTON POYLE. n. II, A4. The eagle of St. John

PLATE 35

(*a*) HEYTHROP. I, A3. St. Mark

(*b*) HEYTHROP. I, A4. St. Luke

(*c*) HEYTHROP. S. II, 1a. Sir John Ashfield

(*d*) HEYTHROP S II, 1c Lady Eleanor Ashfield

PLATE 36

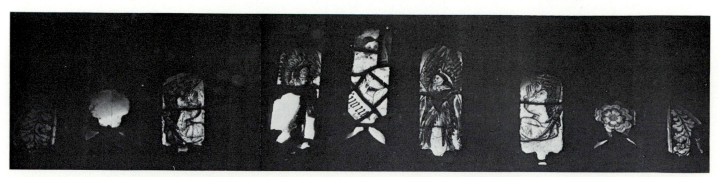

(*a*) IFFLEY. n. V, A3–7. Fragments, kneeling angels and archangels

(*b*) HORSPATH. n. III, 2b. A virgin saint

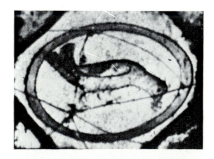

(*c*) IFFLEY. s. V, A4–5. Bird quarries

(*d*) KELMSCOTT. I, 2b. St. George

PLATE 37

KIDLINGTON. I

PLATE 38

(a) MARSH BALDON. I, 2b. St. Anne and the
Virgin

(b) LITTLE FARINGDON. S. IV, 2b.
Vine foliage

(c) New York, Metropolitan Museum.
Vine foliage

(d) MAPLEDURHAM. I, 2a.
St. Stephen

(e) MAPLEDURHAM. I, 2b. St. Sitha

(f) MARSTON. n. III, 1b.
Geometric grisaille

(g) MINSTER LOVELL.
I, A3. Isaac

(h) MINSTER LOVELL
I, A8. The Prophet Daniel

(i) MINSTER LOVELL. S. V, A3.
St. Cosmas or Damian

PLATE 39

(a) NEWINGTON. n. II. Restoration diagram

(b) NEWINGTON. n. II, 2a. The Assumption of the Virgin

(c) NEWINGTON. n. II, 2b. The Trinity

(d) NEWINGTON. n. II, 1b. Donor figure

(e) NEWINGTON. s. VI, 2a. The Annunciation

PLATE 40

(a) NORTH LEIGH. n. III, 2a. A stag

(c) SANDFORD ST. MARTIN. s. IV, A2. Christ in
Majesty

(b) NORTH LEIGH. n. II, 2a. Canopy

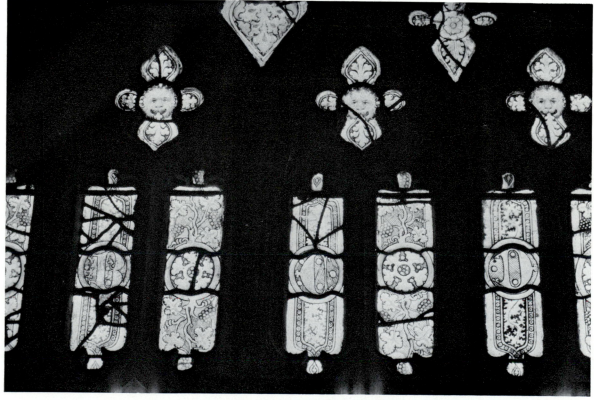

(d) NORTH LEIGH. n. IV. Tracery lights

PLATE 41

(*a*) SHIPLAKE. I

(*b*) SHIPLAKE. I, 1a. St. Anthony Abbot

(*c*) SHIPLAKE. I, 2a. St. Barbara

PLATE 42

(*a*) SHIPLAKE. S. II

(*b*) SHIPLAKE. S. IV

(*c*) SHIPLAKE. W. I

(*d*) SHIPLAKE. S. V

PLATE 43

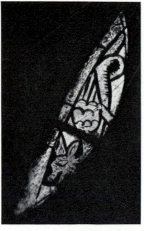

(a) SOUTH NEWINGTON.
n. IV, C1. A bird

(b) SOUTH NEWINGTON.
n. IV, A1. Grotesque dragon

(c) SOUTH NEWINGTON.
n. IV, A4.
Grotesque dragon

(d) SOUTH NEWINGTON. n. IV,
A3. Fragments

(g) STANTON HARCOURT. s. II, 3b.
Geometric grisaille

(e) SOUTH STOKE. s. III, 1b. The Virgin
and Child

(h) STANTON HARCOURT. s. II, 2b.
St. James

(f) STANTON HARCOURT. s. II.
Pre-restoration

(i) STANTON HARCOURT. s. II, 3a.
Geometric grisaille

PLATE 44

(*a*) STANTON HARCOURT. s. V. Canopy designs

(*b*) STANTON HARCOURT. s. VI, 2a. A bishop

(*d*) STANTON HARCOURT. s. VI, 2c. A king

(*c*) STANTON ST. JOHN. s. IV, 5a. The funeral of the Virgin. 6a. Shield of Clare. 7a. Censing angels

PLATE 45

(a) STANTON ST. JOHN.
n. IV. Geometric grisaille

(b) STANTON ST. JOHN.
n. IV. Restoration diagram

(c) STANTON ST. JOHN. s. IV

(d) STRATTON AUDLEY. s. II, A2. Face of
a lion

(e) SWINBROOK. s. III. Fragments

PLATE 46

(a) WATERPERRY. n. V, 2a. Margaret Fitz Ellis

(b) WATERPERRY. n. V, 2c. Robert Fitz Ellis

(c) WATERPERRY. n. VI, 2a. Donor figure

(d) WATERPERRY. n. VI, 2c. Donor figure

(e) WATERPERRY. s. IV, 2a. Shield
of Curson

(f) WATERPERRY. s. IV, 2b. Shield of
Curson impaling Saunders

PLATE 47

(a) WATERPERRY. S. IV, 3a. Walter Curson

(b) WATERPERRY. S. IV, 3c. Isabel Curson

PLATE 48

(*a*) WOODSTOCK. Now in Bodleian Library.
Head of Louis VII

(*b*) WOODSTOCK. Now in Bodleian Library.
Becket's cross-bearer

(*c*) WOODSTOCK. Now in Bodleian Library. Two courtiers

(*d*) WOODSTOCK. Now in Bodleian Library. Henry II

PLATE 49

(b) YARNTON. n. V, 2a. St. Christopher

(a) YARNTON. n. II. Bird quarries

PLATE 50

(a) WROXTON ABBEY. Now in Philadelphia Museum of Art. Royal arms of England for Henry VIII

(b) WROXTON ABBEY. Now in Philadelphia Museum of Art. Royal Arms of England for the heir apparent

(c) YARNTON. n. IV, 1a. The Virgin and Child

(d) YARNTON. n. IV, 1b. Abimelech restoring Sarah to Abraham

CORPUS VITREARUM MEDII AEVI

Published under the auspices of the Comité International d'Histoire de l'Art
and the patronage of the Union Academique Internationale
by the International Committee of the C.V.M.A.

LOUIS GRODECKI, *President*

STATE OF PUBLICATIONS AS IN THE SUMMER 1979

AUSTRIA 5 volumes.

Published

I Die mittelalterlichen Glasgemälde in Wien, EVA FRODL-KRAFT, Vienna 1962

II 1 Die mittelalterlichen Glasgemälde in Niederösterreich, Albrechtsberg-Klosterneuburg, EVA FRODL-KRAFT, Vienna 1972

III 1 Die mittelalterlichen Glasgemälde in der Steiermark, Graz und Straßengel, ERNST BACHER. Vienna 1978

In preparation

II 2 Die mittelalterlichen Glasgemälde in Niederösterreich, Krenstetten-Zwettl, EVA FRODL-KRAFT

III 2 Die mittelalterlichen Glasgemälde in der Steiermark, Admont-Vorau, ERNST BACHER

Published by the Institut für österreichische Kunstforschung des Bundesdenkmalamtes; Verlag H. Böhlaus Nachf., Vienna/Cologne/Graz.

BELGIUM 5 volumes

Published

I Les vitraux médiévaux conservés en Belgique, 1200–1500, JEAN HELBIG, Brussels 1961

II Les vitraux de la première moitié du XVIe siècle conservés en Belgique, Province d'Anvers et Flandres, JEAN HELBIG, Brussels 1968

III Les vitraux de la première moitié du XVIe siècle conservés en Belgique, Brabant et Limbourg JEAN HELBIG and YVETTE VANDEN BEMDEN, Ledeberg/Ghent 1974

In preparation

IV Les vitraux de la première moitié du XVIe siècle conservés en Belgique, Province de Liège, Luxembourg et Namur, JEAN HELBIG and YVETTE VANDEN BEMDEN

V Les vitraux de la première moitié du XVIe siècle conservés en Belgique, Hainaut

Published by the Ministère de l'Éducation Nationale et de la Culture, Brussels.

CZECHOSLOVAKIA

Published

Mittelalterliche Glasmalerei in der Tschechoslowakei, FRANTIŠEK MATOUŠ, Prague 1975

Published by the Czechoslovak Academy of Sciences, Prague; Verlag Academia, Prague/H. Böhlaus Nachf., Vienna/Cologne/Graz.

FRANCE 30 volumes

Published

I 1 Les vitraux de Notre-Dame et de la Sainte-Chapelle de Paris, by MARCEL AUBERT, LOUIS GRODECKI, JEAN LAFOND, and JEAN VERRIER, Paris 1959

IV 2 Les vitraux de l'église Saint-Ouen de Rouen, tome I, JEAN LAFOND with the assistance of FRANÇOISE PERROT and PAUL POPESCO, Paris 1970
Série annexe: Les vitraux de Saint-Denis, volume I, Histoire et restitution, LOUIS GRODECKI, Paris 1976
Récensement général des vitraux de France, vol. I: Paris, région parisienne, Picardie et Nord-Pas-de-Calais, under the direction of LOUIS GRODECKI, FRANÇOISE PERROT, and JEAN TARALON, Paris 1978

In preparation

I 2 Les vitraux de Paris. Collections publiques et monuments, FRANÇOISE PERROT

IV 2 Les vitraux de l'église Saint-Ouen de Rouen, tome II, JEAN LAFOND

VI Les vitraux du département de la Moselle, MARIE-LOUISE HAUCK

VII 1 Les vitraux de la Cathédrale de Strasbourg, VICTOR BEYER and CHRISTINE WILD-BLOCK

Published by the Caisse Nationale des Monuments Historique Centre National de la Recherche Scientifique, Paris.

GERMANY

WEST GERMANY 15 volumes

Published

I 1 Die Glasmalereien in Schwaben von 1200–1350, HANS WENTZEL, Berlin 1958 (out of print)

II 1 Die mittelalterlichen Glasmalereien in Baden und der Pfalz (ohne Freiburg i. Br.) RÜDIGER BECKSMANN, Berlin 1979

IV 1 Die mittelalterlichen Glasmalereien des Kölner Domes, HERBERT RODE, Berlin 1974

In preparation

I 2 Die Glasmalereien in Schwaben von 1350–1520 (ohne Ulm), HANS WENTZEL and FERDINAND WERNER (publication in 1980)

I 3 Die mittelalterlichen Glasmalereien im Ulmer Münster, HANS WENTZEL and FERDINAND WERNER

II 2 Die mittelalterlichen Glasmalereien in Freiburg i. Br. RÜDIGER BECKSMANN (publication in 1981)

VII, 1 Die mittelalterlichen Glasmalereien in Niedersachsen, ULF-DIETRICH KORN

XII Die mittelalterlichen Glasmalereien in Augsburg und Bayerisch-Schwaben, RÜDIGER BECKSMANN

XIII 1 Die mittelalterlichen Glasmalereien im Regensburger Dom ELISABETH SCHÜRER-VON-WITTZLEBEN

Published by the Akademie der Wissenschaften und der Literatur, Mainz, and the Deutschen Verein für Kunstwissenschaft, Berlin; Deutscher Verlag für Kunstwissenschaft, Berlin.

EAST GERMANY 6 volumes

Published

I 1 Die mittelalterliche Glasmalerei in den Ordenskirche und im Angermuseum zu Erfurt, ERHARD DRACHENBERG, KARL-JOACHIM MAERCKER, CHRISTA SCHMIDT, Berlin 1976

In preparation

I 2 Die mittelalterliche Glasmalerei im Erfurter Dom, Text- und Tafelteil ERHARD DRACHENBERG

II Die mittelalterliche Glasmalerei in Mühlhausen, CHRISTA RICHTER

V Die mittelalterliche Glasmalerei in Stendal, KARL-JOACHIM MAERCKER

Published by the Institut für Denkmalpflege, Berlin; Akademie-Verlag, Berlin.

GREAT BRITAIN 30 volumes

Supplementary Volume I. The Windows of King's College Chapel, Cambridge, HILARY WAYMENT, London 1972

In preparation

II The Medieval Stained Glass of Canterbury Cathedral, MADELINE HARRISON CAVINESS

III City of Oxford, JILL KERR and PETER NEWTON

Published by The British Academy, London; Oxford University Press, London.

HOLLAND

In preparation

Die Glasmalereien in der Kirche St. Johann zu Gouda, C. COEBERGH-SURIE

ITALY 5 volumes

Published

I Le vetrate dell 'Umbria, GIUSEPPE MARCHINI, Rome 1973

In preparation

II Le vetrate del Duomo di Firenze, GIUSEPPE MARCHINI with the assistance of GEZA VON HABSBURG

IV Le vetrate del Duomo di Milano, CATERINA GILLI-PIRINA

Published by MARIO SALMI; De Luca Editore, Rome.

POLAND 1 volume

In preparation

Les vitraux de Cracovie et de Thorn, LECH KALINOWSKI

PORTUGAL 1 volume

In preparation by CARLOS VITORINO DA SILVA BARROS

SCANDANAVIA 1 volume

Published

Die mittelalterlichen Glasmalereien Skandinaviens, AARON ANDERSSON, SIGRID CHRISTIE, CARL A. NORDMAN and AAGE ROUSSEL, Stockholm 1964.

SPAIN 6 volumes

Published

I Las vidrieras de la catedral de Sevilla, VÍCTOR NIETO ALCAIDE, Madrid 1969

II Las vidrieras de la catedral de Granada, VÍCTOR NIETO ALCAIDE with the assistance of CARLOS MUÑOZ de PABLOS, Granada 1973

In preparation

III Las vidrieras de la catedral de León, VÍCTOR NIETO ALCAIDE and EFRÉN GARCÍA FERNÁNDEZ

IV Las vidrieras de Castilla la Vieja, VÍCTOR NIEOT ALCAIDE with the assistance of CARLOS MUÑOZ DE PABLOS

SWITZERLAND 5 volumes

Published

I Die Glasmalereien der Schweiz vom 12. bis zum Beginn des 14. Jahrhunderts, ELLEN J. BEER, Basle 1956

III Die Glasmalereien der Schweiz aus dem 14. und 15. Jahrhundert, ohne Königsfelden und Berner Münsterchor, ELLEN J. BEER, Basle 1965

Published by Hans R. Hahnloser; Birkhäuser Verlag, Basle.

U.S.A. AND CANADA

In preparation

I 1 The Stained Glass in the Metropolitan Museum and in the Cloisters at New York, JANE HAYWARD